Revealing the Inner Worlds of Young Children

REVEALING THE INNER WORLDS OF YOUNG CHILDREN

THE MACARTHUR STORY STEM BATTERY AND PARENT-CHILD NARRATIVES

Edited by
Robert N. Emde
Dennis P. Wolf
David Oppenheim

2003

OXFORD
UNIVERSITY PRESS

Oxford New York
Auckland Bangkok Buenos Aires Cape Town Chennai
Dar es Salaam Delhi Hong Kong Istanbul Karachi Kolkata
Kuala Lumpur Madrid Melbourne Mexico City Mumbai Nairobi
Sao Paulo Shanghai Taipei Tokyo Toronto

Copyright © 2003 by Oxford University Press, Inc.

Published by Oxford University Press, Inc.
198 Madison Avenue, New York, New York 10016

www.oup.com

Oxford is a registered trademark of Oxford University Press

All rights reserved. No part of this publication may be reproduced,
stored in a retrieval system, or transmitted, in any form or by any means,
electronic, mechanical, photocopying, recording, or otherwise,
without the prior permission of Oxford University Press.

Library of Congress Cataloging-in-Publication Data
Revealing the inner worlds of young children : using the MacArthur story
stem battery and parent-child narratives / edited by Robert N. Emde,
Dennis P. Wolf, and David Oppenheim.
p. cm.
Includes bibliographical references and index.
ISBN-13 978-0-19-515404-7
1. Storytelling ability in children. 2. Cognition in children.
3. Children—Language. I. Emde, Robert N. II. Wolf, Dennis P.
III. Oppenheim, David.
BF723.S74 A37 2003
155.4'13—dc21 2002015930 Rev.

9 8 7 6 5 4 3

Printed in the United States of America
on acid-free paper

Dedication

We dedicate this volume to our treasured colleague Elizabeth A. Bates. Although she was not a member of our collaborative group on narratives, her encouragement, innovations, and leadership in the MacArthur Network on Early Childhood Transitions has inspired us in many ways.

Acknowledgments

The work presented in this book was supported by the John D. and Catherine T. MacArthur Foundation and its Research Network on Early Childhood Transitions. We also wish to acknowledge the help of the many investigators of that network as well as the assistance of Shirley Speller, Chara Kurtz, and Cynthia Uhlhorn, who helped with the text, editorial guidance, and communications among authors. Most important, we are grateful to the wonderful children and their families who participated in our studies.

Contents

Contributors

Nazan Aksan, Department of Psychology, University of Iowa, Iowa City, IA.

Eva Appelman, Department of Psycholgy, Bar Ilan University, Ramat Gan, Israel.

Ora Aviezer, Oranim Teachers' College and Center for the Study of Child Development, University of Haifa, Haifa, Israel.

†Miriam Ben-Aaron, Department of Psychology, University of Haifa, Haifa, Israel.

Inge Bretherton, Department of Human Development and Family Studies, University of Wisconsin-Madison, Madison, WI.

Carla Croft, Department of Child and Adolescent Psychiatry, Institute of Psychiatry, King's College London, London, UK.

Robert B. Clyman, Child Maltreatment and Family Health, Departments of Pediatrics and Psychiatry, Kempe Children's Center, University of Colorado Health Sciences Center, Denver, CO.

Robert N. Emde, Department of Psychiatry, University of Colorado Health Sciences Center, Denver, CO.

Yohanan Eshel, Department of Psychology, University of Haifa, Haifa, Israel.

Ayelet Etzion-Carasso, Center for the Study of Child Development, University of Haifa, Haifa , Israel.

Nicolas Favez, Department of Psychology, University of Fribourg, Fribourg, Switzerland.

Peter Fonagy, Sub-Department of Clinical Health Psychology, University College London, London, UK.

Christine Gertsch, Ruelle des Galeries, Hermance, Switzerland.

Hill Goldsmith, Department of Psychology, University of Wisconsin-Madison, Madison, WI.

Zipi Haimovich, Center for the Study of Child Development, University of Haifa, Haifa, Israel.

Kaye Henderson, Sub-Department of Clinical Health Psychology, University College London, London, UK.

Saul Hillman, Anna Freud Centre, Hampstead, London, UK.

Jill Hodges, Anna Freud Centre, Hampstead, London, UK.

Dannie Johnson, University of California at Berkeley, Berkeley, CA.

Kim Kelsay, Department of Psychiatry, University of Colorado Health Sciences Center, Denver, CO.

Vered Kipnis, Department of Psychology, University of Haifa, Haifa, Israel.

Kai von Klitzing, Department of Child and Adolescent Psychiatry, University of Basel, Basel, Switzerland.

Nina Koren-Karie, School of Social Work and Center for the Study of Child Development, University of Haifa, Haifa, Israel.

Rivka Landau, Department of Behavioral Sciences, Ben-Gurion University of the Negev, Beer-Sheva, Israel.

Linda Mantz-Simmons, ChildSafe, Ft. Collins, CO.

David Oppenheim, Center for the Study of Child Development and Department of Psychology, University of Haifa, Haifa, Israel.

JoAnn L. Robinson, Department of Psychiatry, University of Colorado Health Sciences Center, Denver, CO.

Howard Steele, Department of Psychology, Graduate Faculty of Political and Social Science, New School for Social Research, New York, NY.

Miriam Steele, Anna Freud Centre, Hampstead, London, UK.

Daniel Stern, Faculte de Psychologie, University of Geneva, Chêne-Bourg, Switzerland.

Susan L. Warren, George Washington University, Washington, DC.

Dennie Palmer Wolf, Opportunity and Accountability, Annenberg Institute for School Reform, Brown University, Providence, RI.

Matthew Woolgar, Department of Psychology, University of Reading, Reading, UK.

Susan Yabsley, The Hincks-Dellcrest Centre, Toronto, Ontario, Canada.

Revealing the Inner Worlds of Young Children

ROBERT N. EMDE

1

Early Narratives: A Window to the Child's Inner World

Narrative organizes the stream of life's experience. Clinicians, in acknowledging this fact, have described successful psychotherapy as a process wherein one makes a coherent narrative for one's life. Putting together large chunks of memories into a storied whole that makes sense can promote health. But more immediate, everyday experience is also organized in narrative form. We make sense of everyday events for ourselves in relation to others in a way that takes on a story form and is connected to our feelings. In other words, we pull together what is emotionally meaningful to us. We are then able to tell others about our experience, engage their interest, share meanings, and, in so doing, enlarge or "co-construct" new meanings. Affective meaning making in narratives, both for ourselves and for sharing with others, is a vital human endeavor. It is thus a momentous development when a child acquires the capacity for narrative at around three years of age.

This book reports the work of a research consortium that has assembled a new tool for eliciting a narrative that can reveal vivid aspects of a young child's inner world. The tool consists of a systematic group of story beginnings, enacted in play, and referred to as "the MacArthur Story Stem Battery (MSSB)."[1] What is exciting to us is that most preschool children enthusiastically complete these story stems and, in so doing, they allow us access to their representational worlds, to what they understand, and to their inner feelings. They provide us with compelling examples of how they construct unique emotional meanings in their playful completions. The MSSB builds upon a rich tradition of play therapy (Winnicott, 1971; Slade & Wolf, 1994) and, to some extent, upon the use of projective techniques for young children such as the CAT (Bellak & Bellak, 1949; see also Wolf in chapter 2 of this volume). A common goal of this tradition is to understand the child's inner world. The MSSB is structured, moreover, to yield information that can be evaluated psychometrically. The narrative completion responses it elicits are scored with multiple dimensions in coding schemes that allow for a high degree of interrater reliability and, as indicated by chapters in this volume, convergent and discriminative validity can be assessed. Thus, the prospect is that psychologists, using this tool, can use opportunities for exploring significant individual differences among young children in areas of importance. Clinicians can gain information directly from children, using a research-based assessment for exploring the child's concerns and suffering at this age. Thus, systematic information from the child can supplement developmental information that was previously restricted to the domain of parental reports.

The purpose of this chapter is threefold. First, it will introduce examples of story stem completions and link them to the ways we think about narratives. Second, it will provide a background for narratives in terms of our current knowledge about emotions and their development. Third, it will indicate the topics of subsequent chapters.

Story Stem Responses and Thinking About Narratives

Many of the narratives discussed in this book are in the form of responses to story beginnings, or "stems," that portray a dramatic circumstance. The stem is enacted by an engaging examiner (E) who sets the scene for the child (C) with small dolls who are introduced as Mom, Dad, and two children with the same gender names as the child. The following responses are to a story stem about lost keys portraying a parental argument, a situation that is often upsetting to children. This stem is presented after the child has warmed up by completing other stories and is familiar with our play narrative settings. The story begins with the mother saying angrily to the father doll, "You lost my keys!" The father doll then curtly answers, "I did not!" To which the mother replies, "Yes you did, you always do." In a neutral voice, the examiner then asks the child to "show me and tell me what happens now." Here are three different story completions in dialogue with the examiner.

Completion A, from a 4-year-old girl:

C: (*sighs*) No fighting! No fighting guys!

E: Who says that?

C: Susan (*indicates the child doll*).

E: Susan says no fighting guys.[2]

C: She said, who lost her keys? . . . I know where they are.

E: I know where they are.

C: They're in my room.

E: So what does she do?

C: Um, she goes . . . take Mom . . . in my room. (*She enacts going to a room with doll.*) See, the keys are right here . . . wow!

Completion B, from a 3½-year-old boy:

C: . . . She runs away! (*moves the mother doll off the table, and adds with a gruff voice*) and never will be his mom!

E: And never will be his mom . . . mmm.

C: Well, I won't be your dad! (*states this also in a gruff voice and moves the father doll away*)

E: I won't be your dad.

C: (*Also voiced gruffly*) But the kid won't be her kid either! . . . She don't have any kids.

E: She don't have any kids. Who doesn't? Mom?

C: (*Indicates that this is the case*) No!

E: Anything else happen in this story?

C: Yeah they, they come back. Dad gives . . . when the boys are sleeping . . . Dad gives the keys to Mom. And then . . . now . . . now they're happy! . . . Thanks.

E: Thanks? Who says that?

C: Mom.

Completion C, from a 5-year-old boy:

C: I lost them, says Michael (*indicates the child doll*).

E: Oh, so Michael says I lost them.

C: I hid 'em under the couch.

E: He says I hid them under the couch.

C: Mom grabs right under and gets 'em (*moves mother doll around the table*). . . . She spanks him (*mother doll hits the child doll*). And he goes to his room.

E: Oh.

C: It's here.

E: He goes to his room.

C: The end.

E: And that's the end?

C: Yeah, it was a really short story.

E: Yeah. How does Michael feel in his room?

C: Sad.

E: Oh, sad? . . . How come?

C: Cause whenever I get spanked I feel bad.

C: It hurts really bad.

E: Mmhm.

In completion A, the girl has the child doll announce that there is to be no fighting and she takes the mom doll to a room where she finds the keys. In completion B, the boy has the mom doll say angrily that she won't be a mom as she leaves; this is followed by the dad doll and then the child doll angrily saying similar things. The story is then concluded when the dad gives the keys to the mom and the mom says thanks. In completion C, the 5-year-old boy enacts the child doll hiding the keys under the couch, confessing this act, being spanked, and then being sent to his room, where he feels sad. As the reader can see, the responses of individual children are quite different and suggest insights about their inner worlds. Exploring the meaning of such responses to a variety of stems, as well as other forms of early childhood narrative, is what this book is about. Before going further, however, it seems appropriate to explain our thinking about these responses as narratives.

Narratives have increasingly become a focus of interest in the human developmental sciences. Jerome Bruner (1986) has dubbed the study of narratives the "new paradigm for psychology," devoted to "verisimilitude" or a sense of realness as a criterion for usefulness, in contrast to earlier experimental paradigms that lacked such relevance. Richard Shweder (1991), from the perspective of anthropology, agrees with the need for a focus on narrative, placing accounts of experience centrally in an expanding discipline that explores shared meaning in terms of what is valued by developing peoples in a particular place and time. Narratives have also become a focus of interest for a broad range of humanists for whom narrative activity is seen to organize and connect what is coherent in history, literature, and ethics (see the *Journal of Narrative and Life History* and the links to the vast writings on literary criticism, for example, Culler, 1997). Our interest in early childhood narratives was more specific. We began with the assumption that narratives exemplify a vital process of meaning making in everyday life and that we could tap into this process by using children's spontaneous interest in play and stories.

There are multiple ways of thinking about the everyday narratives of the preschooler. Specific narratives can have three aspects or "levels": representations, plot, and discourse. Narratives communicate *mental representations* of experience, as well as the role of self and others in that experience. Narratives also have organized plots or points; typically a plot involves a problem or tension followed by some kind of resolution (Labov & Waletsky, 1967; Bruner, 1986). Finally, narratives are spoken *discourse,* located in a specific conversation with another person. The preschooler usually tells the narrative to one or two others—for example, a mother, a father, or other children—who are involved in "co-constructing" meaning with the child as they collaborate in play or storytelling. In our story stem technique researchers play this collaborative role.

Narratives can also be thought about from a number of different perspectives. Perhaps the most prominent perspective used in this book involves *emotional tone.* The plot of a narrative is sometimes understood as beginning with a dramatic tension that rises to an emotional "high point," and then is addressed and resolved such that order is restored in the world of the story (McCabe & Peterson, 1991).

The story stem technique uses this common pattern in a joint narrative. The examiner engages the child with an interesting story beginning, by enacting a scenario with dolls, until the narrative reaches a "high point." At that moment the child is requested to "show me and tell me what happens now." The child has to provide a "resolution" in play and in words, and this requires using the feelings aroused to inform what happens next. In other words, the child makes emotional meaning out of an unresolved situation. The following response of a 5-year-old boy is to another illustrative story stem. The examiner first portrays a situation where a dog has been lost, asks the child to tell what happened, and then adds a scene when the dog re-appears safe and sound.

C: He ran away.

E: Who ran away?

C: Barney. And then . . . he is really sad.

E: Who is sad?

C: Michael (*points to child doll*).

E: So Michael's really sad.

C: Yeah.

E: Uh-uh.

C: He is . . . extremely sad . . . (like) when my cat ran away.

E: Oh I bet.

C: We found him after a couple of days.

E: Uh-uh.

C: And that's the end of the story.

E: Okay, so does anything else happen here?

C: No.

E: Oh look who's back! (*Barney doll is brought back by E and placed on the table with the other dolls.)*

C: (*Moves the Barney doll close to the child doll and portrays hugging and kissing.*)

E: So they're kissing each other?

C: Barney is happy.

C: He wants to go in the house.

E: Okay.

C: Cause he's been really hot. (*Moves Barney and child doll closer to Mom doll, presumably in the house.*)

E: Uh-uh. He's been hot outside?

C: Yeah.

E: Ah.

C: Barney's back, Mom! Hi (*makes kissing noises; moves Barney and child doll close to Dad doll and makes more kissing noises*). . . . Man . . . Barney is a nice dog.

The stem sets up an unhappy and problematic situation in which the dog is lost. C then portrays the child doll, Michael, as being sad. C then brings in his own life experience when he lost his cat who was then found after a couple of days. Interestingly, C cannot get back into the story frame after this recollection about the cat, and he either cannot resolve the story himself or implies that the story is resolved since it was in his own experience. In response to a prompt by E in the second part of the stem, however, C does provide the framing for a resolution, portraying a set of joyous reunions with expressions of affection and sympathy for the dog. C's response illustrates the emotional contours and shapes of meaning that a child can provide after a story stem. Indeed C makes emotional meaning not only at the level of plot or theme for his completions but also at the level of representations (mother, dad, child, and dog, as well as self). Moreover, at the level of discourse, C colors the way he relays his story to E, who then helps in a co-construction (i.e., through the follow-up probe with a return of Barney).

C's response also illustrates another perspective relevant for the preschooler's narrative, namely, *attachment* (Bowlby, 1969, 1973, 1980). The story stems of the book involve family members in doll-play scenarios, and these allow the child to express representations of attachment figures in relation to one's self. As chapter 3 documents, the possibility of assessing aspects of attachment based on children's representations of their inner worlds provided one of the strongest motivations for consortium members to create a story stem battery. Accordingly, a number of stems were designed that present separations followed by reunions in the tradition of other attachment investigations (Bretherton & Waters, 1985). In the lost dog illustration, C portrays appropriate sadness after a separation and also later portrays family members in affectionate reunions. All of these features suggest that C has a working model of secure attachment. Another story begins when the parents leave for the weekend and the child remains with a grandmother. In an illustration of a response to that stem, a 4-year-old girl portrays a lot of kissing goodbye to Mom and Dad. After they have gone, she portrays the child doll as laughing with Grandma as they play a game of hide-and-seek. The response to the follow-up stem that represents the reunion episode, like the reunion example with Barney, also protrays a happy meeting that illustrates the child's secure representational model:

E: Okay, you know what? Mom and Dad come back (*enacts the return of mom and dad with the dolls*).

C: (*Laughs*)

E: What does she say when she sees Mommy and Daddy?

C: (*Enacts the child doll kissing Mom and Dad.*)

E: She kisses Mommy? She kisses Daddy, huh?

C: (*Enacts next the mom doll kissing Grandma.*)

E: And the Mom kisses the grandma.

C: (*Laughs.*) She's gonna go home.

E: She's gonna go home. Bye.

C: Bye!

E: See you later.

C: Okay (*enacts grandmother driving away, with others waving*).

Another perspective that fuels our interests concerns *conflict.* Bruner, in his treatises (1986, 1990), borrows from the dramatic literary perspective of Burke (1945), in which a narrative structure consists of five parts: setting, characters, goals, action, and means. What motivates the narrative work, however, is an imbalance: trouble or conflict in the story world. Consequently, the stems used in the MSSB also build to an imbalance or problem in which the child has an opportunity to deal with a form of conflict, often involving figures that represent family members. The "lost keys" stem begins with a conflict between parents. Other stems begin with conflicts involving siblings, peers, and a child doll. Some stems are explicitly conceptualized as dilemmas.

This leads us to review a *moral* perspective on narratives. To a greater or lesser extent, all stories reflect values, and their co-construction provides an opportunity for family members and caregivers to inculcate values, standards, and ways of behaving. From the child's point of view, narratives necessarily involve a moral stance, as the child chooses a particular view of events and their possibilities. The stems that draw the most attention to the moral nature of daily life are those in which the child is presented with a dilemma in which the child character must choose between two conflicting demands represented by important figures in a child's life, such as parents, siblings, or friends.[3]

The following responses are to a moral dilemma in which the child doll's younger sibling wants to join him while he is playing ball with a friend. The child agrees but the friend refuses, saying, "If you let your little sister [or brother] play, I won't be your friend anymore!" If the subject responds by refusing to include his sibling, the examiner makes the sibling doll plead, "But I am your little sister!" If the subject responds by describing the child playing with his sister but not with his friend, the examiner makes the friend doll angrily say, "Well, I won't be your friend anymore. I'm leaving!" Here are three very different responses to this dilemma from children who are 40 months old.

The first is from a girl who continues playing with her sister, saying that her friend is not "a best friend anymore." She doesn't deal with the other side of the dilemma, maintaining the friendship with the peer.

C: Um she . . . she not played.

E: She's not playing?

C: Just her and and me.

E: Just her and you? How come she's not playing?

C: Because she doesn't wanna cuz she's not a best friend anymore.

E: She's not her best friend anymore? How come she's not her best friend anymore?

C: . . . I don't know.

E: So just Susan and Jane are playing? Two sisters? Okay.

Next is another girl who provides a complex series of responses to the same stem, influenced by the subsequent probes from the examiner. She puts the ball away, then changes her mind, getting the ball and playing with herself. Finally, she gets another favorite toy (a bear) for the little sister so the protagonist doll can play ball with her friend.

C: I won't be your friend anymore.

E: So show me and tell me what happens now.

C: I put um this ball away.

E: I'll put the ball away, Susan says. How come she's putting the ball away?

C: Because someone can play with it.

E: But Susan I want to play with you. . . . Susan, I'm your little sister. I want to play with you.

C: No, you can't.

E: You can't. So what's going to happen now?

C: Um yes you could come play with us with the ball.

E: You could play with us with the ball.

C: Come on, I'll get the ball. . . . There we go.

E: If you let your little sister play, I won't be your friend.

C: Huh, I'll be her friend.

E: Yeah but I won't be your friend.

C: Hum I'm going to play with . . . I'm going to play with myself.

E: Oh so she's going to play with herself.

C: Can I play with you? No um this little sister can't play with us. Oh you can find some other toys um. Bear xxx play with with your favorite toy. Go get it. Where's bear?

E: What?

C: The bear for this little girl.

E: We can pretend like she's playing with a bear.

C: Yeah.

E: Okay, so she's going to play with a bear?

C: Uh-uh.

The third moral dilemma response is one that provided us with quite a surprise early in our work, as we began to set up our story stems with a set of small wooden dolls. The boy makes his choice from the alternatives provided by the dilemma, but when confronted with the probe, his facial expressions (as later studied in our videotape) indicate how much he struggles with the dilemma.[4] His final response is remarkably creative and taught us something surprising about the setting we had constructed.

C: Oh I won't be your friend either.

And then he walks away.
And they play ball.

E: But I thought Bob says, "But I wanna play with you, George. I'm your little brother!"

C: (*The videotape shows that C's facial expression changes and he appears sad. He then looks uncertain, and a bit strained, as he pauses looking at the doll. After several seconds, his face relaxes. He then looks up at E as if resolved.*) Well you can't. (*C has look of satisfaction, holding the younger brother doll.*) He has the stripes like him. (*C holds up the friend doll for E to see.*) He has stripes. (*C holds up the protagonist doll for E to see.*) So they're buddies. But not him because he doesn't have stripes (*indicating the younger brother doll*). Only they can play ball (*indicating the protagonist and the friend doll*).

The stripes referred to by the child are the suspenders (looking like "stripes") that were painted on the two dolls engaged in playing ball . These same stripes did not appear on the younger brother doll who is excluded in the story. In other words, the child resolves the moral dilemma by a form of classification: according to the "stripes," two dolls belong and a third does not. This resolution illustrates how early an apparently cognitive process like classification is informed by non-cognitive issues. Beginning at a young age, emotions and a variety of goals seem likely to be influential in classifying experience. The resolution also illustrates another point about narratives. They are creative. Narratives allow for alternative possible actions and imaginative possibilities (Bruner, 1986; Emde, Kubicek, & Oppenheim, 1997). This point is given a new emphasis by Bruner in his latest book (Bruner, 2002) wherein he demonstrates that narratives provide an invitation to problem finding as much if not more than problem solving. In the story stems approach we invite the child to elaborate, explore, and create possible problems from his or her inner world, and tell them to an interviewer. In variants of this approach, highlighted in the book's second part, we invite the child to explore possible problems with the mother or some other familiar person.

The Role of Emotions and Their Early Development

Emotions and their regulation are central to our perspectives on early childhood narratives—so much so that we use the phrase "emotional meaning making" to describe what happens in the process of completing or generating a story. We designed the stems to present initial emotionally charged events that young children might typically encounter. Their responses can be viewed in terms of their emotional tone and the extent to which they help young children regulate the emotions stirred by the story stem. Thus, even though children's responses to stems are not always "reports" of actual experiences (see extended discussion of Clyman in chapter 11), children's emotion narratives give us ways to understand the likely course of human behavior in the face of strong feelings. Such information might otherwise be implicit or altogether hidden.[5]

This brings us to a further consideration of emotions. Our view of emotions has changed as a result of recent decades of developmental research. Whereas behavioral scientists once regarded emotions as reactive, intermittent, and disruptive states, they are now regarded as active, ongoing, and adaptive processes (see reviews in Emde, 1998, 1999). Emotions during early development, as well as later, have two central adaptive functions that help define the meaning of experience: *motivation* and *communication.* Because emotions are central in our view of narratives as emotional meaning making, and because their adaptive functions in infancy and toddlerhood provide a basis for narratives in the preschooler, these functions are worth reviewing.

First, let us review the motivational functions of emotions. A recent summary, integrating the science of early development, prepared by a panel of national experts in the United States, highlighted the motivational function of emotions at birth. It concluded that the infant is "born wired for feelings and ready to learn" (Shonkoff & Phillips, 2000).[6] Indeed, recent developmental research indicates that not only is the infant biologically prepared for feelings at birth but colorations of feelings such as curiosity and pleasure guide exploration of the world and learning. At a more basic level, ethologists have long known that emotions motivate an infant to approach or withdraw from a situation, to maintain or terminate incoming stimulation. After birth, the infant monitors experience according to what is pleasurable or not, and what the infant does is guided by this monitoring. Piaget (1952) referred to a tendency of "cognitive assimilation" as "a basic fact of life." Following Piaget, we think of this tendency as a seeking out of the new in order to make it familiar, a process also guided by emotions. The infant, in emotional monitoring, increasingly takes remembered experience into account. Seeing, hearing, smelling, touching, and moving with Mom in a pleasurable state carries forward in memory to the next time when this occurs and adds to an expectation of security and delight. Infant emotions not only fuel individual behavior; they are also motivational from the perspective of others. Emotional expressions of infants, as they may be linked to physiological need states, can motivate actions by caregivers. This is particularly so for expressions of distress that may indicate being hungry, wet, cold, or in pain. But it is equally true for expressions of contentment and alert pleasure. When a baby is delighted, the expression of that pleasure draws caregivers into continuing pleasurable interaction.

The linkage to physiological need states points to the second adaptive function of emotions, namely, communication. From earliest infancy, crying communicates a clear and peremptory message to caregivers to "change something!" Social smiling, on the other hand, communicates something different. Beginning around two months of age, smiling communicates a message of "keep it up, I like what you are doing." Over time and with development, infant emotions communicate intentions to others, in addition to need states. The rises and falls of emotions, and the importance of their contours in early infant social exchanges, have been studied by Stern (1985) and others (Tronick, 1988, 1989; Papousek & Papousek, 1979; Papousek, Jurgens, & Papousek, 1992; Sroufe, 1995), who indicate their centrality for communication with the caregiver and for the enlivening of experience that contributes to relationship building.

Emotional signals thus become an intrinsic aspect of the child's social functioning and social development. Others observe, respond, and participate in emotionally meaningful social exchanges with the infant and young child. The communication of pleasure, interest, surprise, or particular forms of distress—all become linked to intentions as well as states of being and guide exchanges with others who care.

Throughout life, emotions continue to guide behavior via their motivational and communicative functions. Subjectively, we know that emotions contribute to ongoing background experiences, giving us a sense of continuity about ourselves, as well as to more salient episodic experiences, giving more immediate experiences a sense of meaning (see reviews in Bucci 1997; Damasio, 1994; Campos, Campos, & Barrett, 1989; LaDoux, 1996; Emde, 1999). Today's researchers also know that emotions, whether from the point of view of motivation or communication, are dynamic systems that have two core dimensions—hedonic tone (pleasure/unpleasure) and arousal (low intensity/high intensity)—and that these dimensions vary over time, with dynamic rises and falls. Although emotions usually operate in a regulatory zone of dynamic and adaptive functioning with respect to arousal and hedonic tone, they can also become dysregulated. For instance, when young children experience fear, distress, or overexcitement, their emotions may flood them and leave them unable to focus or communicate in an articulate way. Along these lines, the MSSB contains a range of story beginnings that vary in qualities and intensities. Responses to the content of these story beginnings give us clues to the child's capacity to regulate emotions and engage others in helping to return to a more manageable state. During the MSSB procedure, the child is expected to provide on-line imaginative responses in the presence of a relative stranger. In this way, responses may provide information about two aspects of the child's emotional world—1) the current capacity to experience and regulate emotions and 2) the willingness and ability to engage others in the process of regulation.

This brings us to what is shared in emotional meaning making. This capacity has its origins in a series of developmental shifts that occur well before the 3-year-old begins to express narratives (Emde, 1988). Since emotional sharing forms a basis for narratives, it seems appropriate to portray the early development of this capacity.

Early on, emotional exchanges are in one sense shared and in another sense private. The infant, prior to 7–9 months, monitors experience emotionally and accumulates such emotionally toned experiences, but does not intentionally seek out such experiences with others. A major developmental shift then occurs. The infant now begins to seek out emotional signals from significant others when confronted by states of uncertainty in order to resolve the uncertainty and regulate behavior accordingly, a process we and others have referred to as social referencing (Feinman & Lewis, 1983; Klinnert, Campos, Sorce, Emde, & Svejda, 1983; Emde, 1992; Feinman, 1992). Thus, the infant, when confronted by an unfamiliar moving toy, an approaching stranger, or other situations of uncertainty that we have designed experimentally, will look to its mother in order to resolve a state of uncertainty. If the mother's emotional expression is one of interest or pleasure, the infant is likely to approach or explore, whereas if her expression is one of fear, wariness, or anger, the infant is likely to stay put or withdraw. Social referencing is a form of emotional signaling that is lifelong, but begins at this age when a host of other related features of shared meaning also become prominent. These include the onset of back-and-forth and peek-a-boo games with others, wherein the infant now expresses pleasure in anticipation of surprise and reappearance, and takes delight in minor variations of the game as introduced by self or other. Such games indicate some remarkable features in the development of shared meaning. The infant now has a shared sense not only of the current context (for example, I recognize this game, I know my part in it) but, additionally, a shared sense of the past (I have experienced this before with her, I know the rules and I felt pleasure and surprise) and of the future (I anticipate what will happen with delight).

As Piaget (1952) pointed out, in this shift in development, the infant comes to appreciate that means can be separated from ends in that intentionality can go beyond immediate action. Out of sight is not entirely out of mind: the infant can now follow a moving object that becomes hidden under a cloth and can retrieve it, or can remove a barrier to get a desired object. Thus, the infant can now begin shared referencing behaviors in looking, in using early sounds and words, and, somewhat later, pointing to another (Bruner, 1983). Referencing behaviors become a major aspect of communication development for nearly the next year. The infant typically begins to express single meaningful words around 10 months of age, and the so-called one-word phase typically lasts about 10 months. What does this have to do with shared emotional meaning making? During this prolonged phase of language development, the infant is not only accumulating single words in a lexicon but is also applying these single words to different contexts. In other words, the infant is engaging in referential activities. Such activities often demand that the infant and a communicative partner jointly focus on specific third events or objects that provide meaning for a particular word. Thus, the meaning of "up" voiced by a familiar adult in a pleasurably excited way and with upstretched arms may convey one message but a different one when this word is voiced in a hurried way when buttoning the child's coat to go outside. Such exchanges are inherently social, and messages are informed not only by reference but by emotions such as interest, surprise, joy, sadness, disgust, fear, anger, and boredom, in addition to affection and more complex socially linked emotions. Social referencing becomes more subtle and complex. The shared meaning of emotional expressions of mother and father, for example, vary in different contexts and at different shades of intensity according to situation. And new, more complex emotions, linked to situations, develop.

During the 2nd year, the toddler comes to experience and express the more complex emotions of pleasure in accomplishments acknowledged by others (e.g., puffed up pride) as well as rudiments of shame in circumstances wherein actions are chastised by others (Lewis & Brooks-Gunn, 1979). Toward the end of the 2nd year, the child comes to experience the emotion of empathy in situations where the distress of another is encountered. Not only is resonant distress experienced by the child in these situations but inclinations to help or soothe may also be experienced that lead to prosocial behaviors (Zahn-Waxler, Radke-

Yarrow, & King, 1979; Zahn-Waxler, Radke-Yarrow, Wagner, & Chapman, 1992; Zahn-Waxler, Robinson, & Emde, 1992).

Another developmental shift toward the end of the second year brings with it a new sense of self in relation to another. Self-reflective awareness soon shows itself in the child's use of pronouns such as "I" and "mine"(Lewis & Brooks-Gunn, 1979; Kagan, 1981). Additionally, multiword speech begins along with the onset of the child's acquisition of grammar. Rules about the sequences of words in relation to their meanings become automatic knowledge, and soon propositional speech becomes possible. As Bates and her colleagues have put it, there is a shift from "reference to predication" (Bates, Thal, & Janowsky, 1992). Again, such acquisitions are connected with new domains of emotional meaning. Experienced emotions, originating from oneself or from another, are understood to have a variety of consequences and form an important background for communications involving speech.

Another aspect of early emotional development deserves special emphasis, namely, that such development takes place within caregiving *relationships*. Experiences within such relationships are crucial for guiding emotional development and form a basis for the preschooler's different qualities of narrative themes and expectations. Let me review some of what we have learned about the relationship context in infancy and toddlerhood. During the first 2 years, emotional development is enabled by consistent caregiver interactions. Another way of putting this is that the child's experiences of emotional exchanges, with time, become internalized and become part of what is expected and practiced. Varying qualities of emotion such as interest, joy, surprise—as well as anger, fear, and sadness—become connected to expectations, goals, actions, and their consequences. Such connections build through repeated circumstances that occur with significant others in the child's daily life, beginning during the 1st year. Similarly, more complex qualities of emotion that involve the child's intentions (e.g., pride, empathic tendencies, shame, and the forerunners of guilt) usually begin during the 2nd year and also develop in specific circumstances with others. Emotionally meaningful experiences of interactions with others become internalized and form representations that, because of their links to adaptive variations, have been the subject of recent clinical theorists, perhaps most prominently those working in the tradition of attachment theory (see chapter 3 for more discussion of this point in relation to our story stem narratives). John Bowlby's concept of "internal working models of attachment" is a form of representation that results from emotionally meaningful repeated experiences with caregivers and links affective memories and expectations of self in relation to attachment figures. Internal working models of attachment develop during infancy, according to this theory, and provide varying degrees of security for the young child after the 1st year (Bowlby, 1969, 1973, 1980). Daniel Stern's (1985) concept of "representations of interactions that become generalized" (RIGs) presents a similar idea. Theorized to guide infant expectations and behavior, they increasingly influence ways of sharing and adaptation. Other theorists have pointed to both clinical and experimental evidence indicating that early experiences with emotionally available caregivers and everyday routines are important for adaptation (Tronick, 1989; Sorce & Emde, 1981; Emde, Korfmacher, & Kubicek, 2000).

Several psychoanalytic theorists have emphasized that affective representations of self in relation to others arise in early experiences within caregiving relationships where they are linked to need states and that such affective representations continue to be important for later adaptation (Bion, 1962; Erikson, 1959; Fairbairn, 1963; Guntrip, 1971; Klein, 1967; Sander, 1980; Spitz, 1959; Winnicott, 1965). Otto Kernberg (1976, 1990) has proposed that such affect-linked representations are motivational—and make better theoretical sense than the more abstract and traditional psychoanalytic notions of drive. Basic units of integrated motives are formed from experiences in infancy, and these involve affectively arousing representations of self and other. For Kernberg, peak affective states of experienced pleasure or unpleasure with the caregiver, when internalized, motivate corresponding wishes either to repeat or to avoid similar affective experiences. More recent psychoanalytic concepts linking self in relation to others and affect in early development are provided by Peter Fonagy and Mary Target (1997). Their concept of "reflective functioning" is connected to observational assessments and refers to the ability to appreciate others' mental states (i.e., feelings, beliefs, and intentions) as well as one's own.

A current way of thinking about the units of representation, especially when they are incorporated in the narratives of preschoolers, is in terms of schemas and scripts (Nelson, 1995). Drawing on recent knowledge from the cognitive and neurosciences, Bucci (1997) has proposed a cogent developmental theory in which emotion schemas begin to develop in nonverbal form and later incorporate linguistic components. Emotion schemas are prototypic representations of the self in relation to others that are built through repetitions of emotionally meaningful episodes. Prototypic representations of episodes, incorporated in memory, then become in effect "working models" of what is likely to happen when one has a desire or a need. In such situations, they provide expectations of what other people are likely to do and how one is likely to feel. With increasing developmental complexity, different schemas become linked with different emotion categories and different relationship situations.

This chapter opened with a definition of psychotherapy as a process whereby individuals are helped to make emotionally coherent narratives of their lives. Not surprisingly, narratives in psychotherapy have become a focus of research. Emotion-based schemas of self in relation to others have been studied as representational units in psychotherapy narratives. Most prominently, units of narrative conflict known as core conflictual relationship themes (or CCRTs) and their variants have been central in psychodynamic psychotherapy process research (for a review see Luborsky & Luborsky, 1993). A CCRT consists of a wish of the self, the expected response of the other, and the represented emotional response of the self to the other's response. A review of psychotherapy narrative research is beyond the scope of this book, but the reader might imagine that a correspondence might be found between our early childhood story stem narratives and the coding emotion-based core relationship themes and conflicts. An exploratory research study by Luborsky and colleagues found a correspondence that seemed meaningful. A collection of our story stem responses in preschoolers could be coded meaningfully using modified CCRT criteria and with evidence of individual longitudinal consistency from ages 3 to 5 years (Luborsky et al., 1996).

The examples of story stem responses presented so far indicate intriguing individual differences. Even though the completions of the child involve play narratives, and our method correspondingly takes account of non-verbal as well as verbal behavior (see chapters 3 and 4), it is hoped that the reader can sense the richness of different responses from our textual presentations. Responses of preschoolers involve emotional meaning making, reflect early relationship experiences, and indicate the child's representations of attachment figures and of emotional conflict. This chapter's background for narratives in terms of current emotion theory and of our knowledge of emotional development in the first 2 years, an early period when communication is mostly an emotional matter, and discussion of shifts as a way of reviewing early development provides a prologue to the developmental shift that brings with it a narrative capacity. Typically, this begins toward the end of the child's 3rd year and continues during the 4th year. The preschooler narratives of this book are based on these beginnings. And, as the reader will see, they go much further. The next chapter describes more about the development of narratives.

The Chapters of the Book

Some readers may appreciate a forecasting of the topics and chapters of the book. Others may wish to skip the following section and proceed directly to chapters of interest.

The first part of the book sets the stage by providing an introduction and theoretical framework. Following this chapter, Wolf's deepens the framework outlined here by emphasizing what is distinctive about the approach that informs the MSSB and examining the features of narratives that make them so prominent and so useful to the process of emotional meaning making. Narratives help organize emotional experience through joint acts of evaluation. Such evaluative acts are present in the early protonarratives of infants with their caregivers, and the development of such acts is vividly described, leading up to the period from 3–6 years of age when elicited narratives from the MSSB provide poignant examples of more sophisticated narrative strategies. In discussing the role of narratives in emotional meaning making, Wolf describes narratives as live performances that are jointly constructed, likely to change over time, and portray aspects of experience (as contrasted with historically accurate accounts). Thus, narratives can be seen both in terms of content (from the child) and interactive process (from the child with other). Wolf goes on to discuss how emerging language abilities and developing social understandings jointly contribute to narrative development. The child comes to know that others have intentions and mental states, and increasingly the child has experiences that are separate from caregivers and comes to understand that she has to *create, rather than assume,* a shared bank of affective experiences. Examples of these points are provided from the spontaneous play and talk of children at different ages as well as from responses using the MSSB.

The second part of the book presents the MSSB, its characteristics, and some coding procedures. The chapters are intended not only to provide the technical details for administration and coding but also to indicate how the MSSB is used to gain access to the young child's inner world. This section also lays out a systematic basis for using the stems in a way that gives a framework for its scientific use and validation.

Chapter 3, by Inge Bretherton and David Oppenheim, provides a compelling background for the use of story stem narratives (SSNs) with young children. It includes a review of the relevant history of psychoanalytic play therapy, as well as recent research in attachment, early moral development, event representations, and early language development. The original MSSB is described, and practical advice is given for its administration. This is followed by a useful overview of coding approaches, along with early sources of validity for the battery's application in preschool children.

Chapter 4, by JoAnn L. Robinson and Linda Mantz-Simmons, describes an initial coding system for the MSSB that has become widely used as a "core" for many investigators who use the battery to assess the emotional world of preschool children. The coding identifies categories of content (i.e., themes created by the child) and features of performance (i.e., the manner in which the stories are delivered by the child). Performance features of emotional expression and narrative coherence are given special attention. The adaptations of the coding system for samples in a variety of cultures and settings are discussed, and practical points are offered on the training of coders.

Susan L. Warren's chapter presents an additional coding system that complements the core coding system developed by Robinson and Mantz-Simmons described in the previous chapter. In describing how she used the MSSB to document variations in response that may be related to internalizing disorders, Warren demonstrates how the stems can be adapted as evaluative tools for a variety of purposes. Warren illustrates how new stems can be introduced into the battery in order to elicit particular emotions. She also demonstrates that it is possible to score variations in emotional regulation, emotional coherence, and themes with this modified set of stems. Information on reliability and validity using the additional coding system is presented, along with recommendations for its use.

In chapter 6, Kai von Klitzing, Kimberly Kelsay, and Robert N. Emde provide additional psychometric information that results from the first-ever analysis of a large collection of narratives. The MSSB described in chapter 3 and the coding system described in chapter 4 were applied to 654 5-year-old children engaged in a twin study. In addition to examining the overall factor structure of responses (separately carried out for content themes, performance features, and parental representations), the authors also provide information about individual story stems and their expectable elicited responses. Particularly useful are the analyses that suggest eight story stems elicit meaningful information instead of the full battery of 14. This information can provide other investigators with a basis for making decisions about selecting story stems or creating new ones.

The third part of the book presents studies of emotional meaning making in preschoolers' narratives, using the MSSB and emphasizing significant individual differences among children.

Nazan Aksan and H. H. Goldsmith explore the relationships of temperament and guilt representations in 5-year-olds in chapter 7. The representations are elicited using two story stems that involve transgressions. Children's responses are coded for themes of confession, punishment, and repair (indicating active engagement) as well as withdrawal (indicating avoidance of responsibility). Findings offer the exciting possibility that individual differences in temperament (or emotionality) contribute differentially to the child's representations of guilt at this age. Assessment of 114 children with varying temperaments indicates that children with higher internalizing components of temperament told stories with more confession themes and fewer withdrawal themes. Just as important, none of the assessed temperament characteristics was associated with punishment or repair themes.

In chapter 8, David Oppenheim deals with how children address and resolve the human problems described in story stem narratives. A detailed consideration of a 40-month-old girl's response to a stem that presents a moral dilemma illustrates the complexity of an emotional resolution as well as the child's collaboration with the examiner in developing a resolution. An analysis of 48 children studied at 4.5 and 5.5 years reveals that low emotion resolutions are associated with parental reports of child emotional and behavioral problems and also with parental reports regarding their own emotional distress. Additionally, emotional resolution ratings increase with age and demonstrate a moderate continuity of individual differences.

Chapter 9, by Miriam Steele, Howard Steele, Matthew Woolgar, Susan Yabsley, Peter Fonagy, Dannie Johnson, and Carla Croft, links evaluations of narratives across generations, by examining the emotion narratives of parents expecting their first child and those elicited some 5 years later from their 5-year-old children. These results extend the findings of the London longitudinal study of intergenerational patterns of attachment. The authors build on the conceptual overlap between the Adult Attachment Interview (AAI) and the responses of children to the MSSB. Expectations were that mothers whose AAIs were characterized by coherence, autonomy, and evidence of security would have children who at age 5 would demonstrate similar narrative qualities. The study used a subset of 11 story stems taken from the MSSB and the coding system developed by Robinson and Mantz-Simmons (chapter 4) in examining the responses of 86 children. From intensive psychometric analyses, three aggregates of themes emerged: limit setting, prosocial, and antisocial. Cross-generational continuities were found. Children's use of limit setting themes were significantly more likely if their mothers' attachment interviews had been scored as secure-autonomous. This linkage held even when the researchers controlled for language level. Not surprisingly, girls received higher prosocial scores on narratives than boys, but this effect was concentrated in children of insecure mothers.

Chapter 10, by Eva Appelman and Dennis P. Wolf, describes a core process in shared meaning making: "emotional apprenticeship," the patterns of interactions adult caregivers use to help children develop their capacities for regulating and communicating emotional experience. In emotional apprenticeships, caregivers offer guidance using very explicit and subtly implicit strategies. These strategies operate in both face-to-face interactions (e.g., whether the child will engage with the story stems) and in story interactions (e.g., whether the child will take on or avoid a conflict or dilemma presented in a story stem). To illustrate this process with enough detail, the authors present what happens when an inhibited 3-year-old girl experiences anxiety when asked to complete the story stems of the MSSB. The analysis depicts how the child, supported by her father and mother, is able to tolerate the demands of such an ambiguous and revealing performance. In order to explore the possible consequences of successful emotional apprenticeships, the authors analyze how the same child, at 5, is able to negotiate and respond to the demands of story stems. The portrayal and its analysis offer an initial, but compelling, view of how a young child may learn the strategies for regulating highly charged emotional experiences and the means for engaging others in supporting her efforts.

The fourth part of the book reviews clinically relevant studies using the MSSB and its modifications in children at risk.

Robert B. Clyman, in chapter 11, addresses a key question in the story stem responses of maltreated children. When such children portray children and parents in their stories, to what extent do they *represent* actual experiences and to what extent do they use stories to *regulate* their emotions or explore new possibilities? Evidence from previous studies involving the play of maltreated children supports both features. The chapter reports a study of 5-year-old maltreated children and an appropriate comparison group of non-maltreated 5-year-olds that explores this issue. A number of findings emerged. In line with a representational hypothesis, maltreated children portrayed less prosocial behavior, more disobedience, and more sexual behavior than did non-maltreated children. In line with an emotion regulation hypothesis, maltreated children portrayed fewer children in distress. In a thoughtful discussion, Clyman reviews what is known about play enactments following trauma, illustrating how both representation and regulation play a role. The author also discusses the difficulty of distinguishing moral from cognitive representations—those based on the knowledge that behaviors are permissible versus those based on the knowledge of how their parents actually treated them. Overall, a problem in interpreting children's narrative portrayals is that while narratives often communicate emotion-laden propositions, it is much more difficult to infer the attitudes toward the propositions (e.g., avoidance, wishes, or beliefs). These points suggest future directions for the coding and analysis of children's story stem narratives and, in particular, for coding the responses of children who have suffered maltreatment.

Chapter 12, by Susan L. Warren, discusses the usefulness of SSNs for understanding the representations of young children at risk for disorder and those already identified with disorder. The recent empirical literature in this area is reviewed under the headings of (1) troubled parent-child relationships, (2) child maltreatment, (3) externalizing child behavior problems, (4) internalizing behavior problems and anxiety, and (5) low competence/self-esteem. Following this review, the author offers valuable impressions about the use of SSNs in clinical populations and speculates about their future use in clinical assessment and practice.

In chapter 13, Jill Hodges, Miriam Steele, Saul Hillman, and Kaye Henderson present the usefulness of responses to story stem narratives (eight from the MSSB and five new ones) in assessing young children in London who may have experienced maltreatment. Responses are viewed as portraying basic scripts for human relationships, or following the thinking of Daniel Stern, as portraying representations of expectable interactions with others that are generalized. In addition to examining responses as realistic representations of past experience, the authors examine the defenses evident in play narratives, as well as the way in which children can represent alternative possibilities or wishes in their play. After providing some compelling individual examples, the authors present preliminary findings from a comparison between the narratives of previously maltreated children and those who were not maltreated. The representational models of the maltreated children appear to contain fewer realistic or pleasurable portrayals of domestic life, more portrayals of unresponsive caregivers, more frequent situations in which distress receives no response, and characters who make incoherent or unreasoned shifts between "bad" and "good" during the course of a narrative.

The fifth part of the book presents studies wherein relationships and co-constructed narratives are the contexts for meaning making.

Christine Gertsch Bettens, Nicolas Favez, and Daniel N. Stern, in chapter 14, investigate the transformation of the child's lived experience into a narrated experience. In this pioneering study, the authors examined the extent to which the mother's knowledge of an event lived by the preschool child influenced a later narrative co-construction. The event consisted of a carefully designed 11-episode scenario that was emotionally loaded in which the child actively participated. Immediately following the event, and also 2 weeks afterward, the child told the story of the event to his or her mother. One half of the mothers of this study viewed the original event from behind a one-way mirror, and the other half of the mothers did not view the event. Mothers who had viewed the event did assist the child in achieving greater narrative accuracy, but, contrary to expectations, they did not engage in more co-construction; instead, mothers used the event to expand the child's knowledge in a tutorial fashion. Fascinating details of the co-constructed narratives in relation to the child's original experience are discussed, including the role of the child's affective and coping responses.

Nicolas Favez, in a second chapter contributed from the Stern laboratory, reports a detailed discourse analysis of the child-mother co-construction episodes described in the previous chapter. Functionally meaningful patterns of affect regulation are shown to exist in the preschoolers' co-constructions with their mothers. These patterns are similar to child-mother patterns of interaction that have been described at earlier ages. Moreover, a functional regulatory pattern is apparent when the child and mother address the affective core of the story (i.e., its "high point"). In contrast, a dysfunctional regulatory pattern may hinder the child's retelling of the experienced event.

Chapter 16, by R. Landau, Y. Eshel, V. Kipnis and M. Ben-Aaron, a study in an Israeli kibbutz, systematically compares the co-constructions of narratives by 3-year-olds with two different adults who are important in their lives—their mothers and their caregivers (metaplot). Each child engaged in two narrative co-construction tasks, separately, with each adult: to construct a story with a dollhouse and a doll family and to construct a story from a standard picture book without a text. Detailed analyses revealed that both mothers and metaplot participated in the child's experiences and interests, with evidence of intersubjective sharing. There were important differences, however. Metaplots were more often task-oriented than were mothers in the co-constructions, and mothers were more often expressing their own interests and wishes in addition to those of their child. The authors discuss these differing patterns of interactions in terms of the different functional roles involved in these caring relationships.

In chapter 17, Nina Koren-Karie, David Oppenheim, Zipi Haimovich, and Ayelet Etzion-Carasso, drawing on attachment theory, suggest that emotionally matched dialogues, in narrative co-constructions between parents and their children, contribute to establishing and maintaining a psychological secure base. This study explores such connections by assessing dialogues between mothers and their 7-year-olds who were engaged in a task of remembering an event when the child felt each of four different emotions—happy, sad, mad, and scared. The task then included the joint construction of a story about each of these events. A typology is presented with reliably coded transcripts of stories between emotionally matched and emotionally unmatched dyads. When the members of the dyad are emotionally matched, their co-construction dialogues are characterized by partners being task-oriented, engaged, and cooperative. Emotionally unmatched dyads produce three subtypes of co-construction dialogues. Some are exaggerated, overreactive, and overwhelming. Others are flat and uninvolved. Still other dialogues are inconsistent.

In the last chapter, Ora Aviezer's remarkable naturalistic study provides vivid documentation of narrative co-constructions among peers at the very dawn of narrative competence. Three conversation groups of 3-year-olds, living in an Israeli kibbutz, were recorded unobtrusively as the children were put to bed for their afternoon naps. Children in each of the groups became involved in joint constructions with one or two other children. Some of the constructions referred to occurrences in the "Here and Now," but most referred to events in the "There and Then" including imaginary play, fantasy, and internal experiences such as feelings. Typically, the thematic content of the narratives reflected recollections of personal experiences, as well as attempts to make sense of knowledge about behavioral scripts removed from the "Here and Now" and of emotional dilemmas. The fascinating examples of this chapter are supplemented by discussion of how narratives co-constructed by young peers help them make sense of the world in which they live including their interpersonal interactions. The importance of shared meaning while preserving different perspectives is also highlighted.

NOTES

1. The research consortium is an outgrowth of the John D. and Catherine T. MacArthur Research Network on Early Childhood Transitions. The core battery of the MSSB is described in chapter 3 and is used, with specified modifications, throughout the book. The research consortium encourages others to add story stems to the battery and modify it, as appropriate, to local circumstances

2. The illustrations of story stem completions are taken from transcripts prepared from recordings. Interpretations and coding are usually done from videotapes that indicate behavior as well as verbal responses. As indicated later in the book, we have found it important for the examiner to repeat responses of the child on occasion in order to confirm and encourage the child as well as to help with the coding. Some of these repeats are eliminated from the examples in this chapter.

3. A report describing the responses to three moral dilemma stems in a longitudinal study at 3, 4, and 5 years is available in Oppenheim et al., 1997. At age 3, a small minority of healthy children acknowledge the dilemmas in their initial responses, and somewhat less than half evidence acknowledgment after the probe. The examples above were from children who were age 40 months.

4. The actions and words of this 3-year-old were shown as part of an address to the Society for Research in Child Development to illustrate early emotion-based classification abilities (Emde, 1994).

5. I am grateful to Dennis Wolf for suggesting this point.

6. This report was prepared by the National Research Council and the Institute of Medicine of the National Academy of Sciences for the purpose of guiding science policy and public thinking.

REFERENCES

Barrett, K. C., & Campos, J. J. (1987). Perspectives on emotional development II: A functionalist approach to emotions. In J. D. Osofsky (Ed.), *Handbook of infant development* (2nd ed. pp. 555–578). New York: Wiley.

Bates, E. (1992). Language development. *Current Opinion in Neurobiology, 2,* 180–185. (Special Issue on Cognitive Neuroscience.)

Bates, E., Thal, D., & Janowsky, J. (1992). Early language development and its neural correlates. In I. Rapin and S. Seagalowitz (Eds.), *Handbook of neuropsychology: Vol. 7: Child neuropsychology* (pp. 69–110). Amsterdam: Elsevier.

Bion, W. R (1962). *Learning from experience.* New York: Basic Books.

Bowlby, J. (1969). *Attachment and loss: Vol. 1. Attachment.* New York: Basic Books.

Bowlby, J. (1973). *Attachment and loss: Vol. 2. Separation, anxiety and anger.* New York: Basic Books.

Bowlby, J. (1980). *Attachment and loss: Vol. 3. Loss, sadness and depression.* New York: Basic Books.

Bretherton, I., & Waters, E. (Eds.) (1985). Growing points in attachment theory and research. *Monographs of the Society for Research in Child Development, 50*(1–2), Serial No. 209).

Bruner, J. S. (1983). *Child's talk: Learning to use language.* New York: Norton.

Bruner, J. S. (1986) *Actual minds, possible worlds.* Cambridge, MA: Harvard University Press.

Bruner, J. S. (1990) *Acts of meaning.* Cambridge, MA: Harvard University Press.

Bruner, J. S. (2002). *Making stories: Law, literature, life.* New York: Farrar, Straus and Giroux.

Bucci, W. (1997). *Psychoanalysis and cognitive science: A multiple code theory.* New York: Guilford Press.

Burke, K. (1945). *The grammar of motives.* New York: Prentice-Hall.

Campos, J. J., Campos, R. G., & Barrett, K. C. (1989). Emergent themes in the study of emotional development and emotion regulation. *Developmental Psychology, 25*(3), 394–402.

Culler, J. D. (1997). *Literary theory: A very short introduction.* New York: Oxford University Press.

Damasio, A. R. (1994). *Descartes' error.* New York: Avon Books.

Emde, R. N. (1980). Emotional availability: A reciprocal reward system for infants and parents with implications for prevention of psychosocial disorders. In P. M. Taylor (Ed.), *Parent-infant relationships* (pp. 87–115). Orlando, FL: Grune & Stratton.

Emde, R. N. (1992). Social referencing research: Uncertainty, self, and the search for meaning. In S. Feinman (Ed.), *Social referencing and the social construction of reality in infancy* (pp. 79–94). New York: Plenum Press.

Emde, R. N. (1994). Individuality, context, and the search for meaning (Presidential address). *Child Development, 65*(3), 719–737.

Emde, R. N. (1999). Moving ahead: Integrating influences of affective processes for development and for psychoanalysis. *International Journal of Psycho-Analysis, 80*(2), 317–339.

Emde, R. N., Korfmacher, J., & Kubicek, L. F. (2000). Toward a theory of early relationship-based intervention. In J. D. Osofsky & H. E. Fitzgerald (Eds.), *WAIMH Handbook of infant mental health. Vol. 2. Early intervention, evaluation, and assessment* (pp. 3–32). New York: Wiley.

Emde, R. N., Kubicek, L., & Oppenheim, D. (1997). Imaginative reality observed during early language development. *International Journal of Psycho-Analysis, 78*(1), 115–133.

Emde, R. N., Robinson, J., & Corley, R. (1998). Early emotional development: Integrative perspectives from longitudinal study. In D. M. Hann, L. C. Huffman, I. I. Lederhendler, & D. Meinecke (Eds.), *Advancing research on developmental plasticity. Integrating the behavioral science and neuroscience of mental health* (pp. 125–133). Washington, DC: National Institute of Mental Health, National Institutes of Health.

Erikson, E. H. (1959). Identity and the life cycle. *Psychological Issues, 1*(1). New York: International Universities Press, pp. 50–100.

Fairbairn, W. D. (1963). Synopsis of an object-relations theory of the personality. *International Journal of Psycho-Analysis, 4,* 224–225.

Feinman, S. (Ed.). (1992). *Social referencing and the social construction of reality in infancy.* New York: Plenum Press.

Feinman, S., & Lewis, M. (1983). Social referencing at ten months: A second-order effect on infants" responses to strangers. *Child Development, 54*(4), 878–887.

Fonagy, P., & Target, M. (1997). Attachment and reflective function: Their role in self-organization, *Development and Psychopathology, 9,* 679–700.

Guntrip, H. (1971). *Psychoanalytic theory, therapy, and the self.* New York: Norton.

Kagan, J. (1981). *The second year: The emergence of self-awareness.* Cambridge, MA: Harvard University Press.

Kernberg, O. F. (1976). *Object relations theory and clinical psychoanalysis.* New York: Jason Aronson.

Kernberg, O. F. (1990). New perspectives in psychoanalytic theory. In R. Pluchik & H. Kellerman (Eds.), *Emotion: Theory, research, and experience* (pp. 115–131). New York: Academic Press.

Klein, G. S. (1967). Peremptory ideation: Structure and force in motivated ideas. In R. R. Holt (Ed.), *Psychological Issues, 5(2–3)*, Monograph 18/19. New York: International United Press.

Klinnert, M. D., Campos, J. J., Sorce, F. J., Emde, R. N., & Svejda, M. J. (1983). Social referencing: Emotional expressions as behavior regulators. In R. Plutchik & H. Kellerman (Eds.), *Emotion: Theory, research and experience: Vol. 2* (pp. 57–86). New York: Academic Press.

Labov, W., & Waletsky, J. (1967). Narrative analysis: Oral versions of personal experience. In J. Helms (Ed.), *Essays on the verbal and visual arts.* Seattle, WA: University of Washington Press.

Lazarus, R. W. (1991). *Emotion and adaptation.* New York: Oxford University Press.

Lewis, M., & Brooks-Gunn, J. (1979). Toward a theory of social cognition: The development of self. In I. Uzgiris (Ed.), *New directions in child development: Social interaction and communication during infancy* (pp. 23–33). San Francisco: Jossey-Bass.

Luborsky, L., & Luborsky, E. (1993). The era of measures and transference: The CCRT and other measures. *Journal of the American Psychoanalytic Association, 39* (suppl), 329–351.

Luborsky, L., Luborsky, E. B., Diguer, L., Schmidt, K., Dengler, D., Schaffler, P., Faude, J., Morris, M., Buchsbaum, H., & Emde, R. (1996). Extending the core relationship theme into early childhood. In G. Noam & K. Fisher (Eds.), *Development and vulnerability in close relationships* (pp. 287–308). New York: Erlbaum.

Main, M. (1993). Discourse, prediction, and recent studies in attachment: Implications for psychoanalysis. In T. Shapiro & R. N. Emde (Eds.), *Research in psychoanalysis: Process, development, outcome* (pp. 209–244). Madison, CT: International Universities Press.

McCabe, A., & Peterson, C. (Eds.). (1991). *Developing narrative structure.* Hillsdale, NJ: Erlbaum.

Nelson, C. A. (1995). The ontogeny of human memory: A cognitive neuroscience perspective. *Developmental Psychology, 31*, 723–738.

Oppenheim, D., Emde, R. N., Hasson, M., & Warren, S. (1997). Preschoolers face moral dilemmas: A longitudinal study of acknowledging and resolving internal conflict. *International Journal of Psycho-Analysis, 78*, 943–957.

Papousek, H., Jürgens, U., & Papousek, M. (Eds.). (1992). *Nonverbal vocal communication. Comparative & developmental approaches.* Cambridge: Cambridge University Press.

Papousek, H., & Papousek, M. (1979). Early ontogeny of human social interaction: Its biological roots and social dimensions. In K. Foppa, W. Lepenies, & D. Ploog (Eds.), *Human ethology: Claims and limits of a new discipline* (pp. 456–489). Cambridge: Cambridge University Press.

Piaget, J. (1952). *The origins of intelligence in children* (2nd ed.). New York: International Universities Press.

Sander, L. (1980). *Polarity, paradox and the organizing process in development.* Presentation at First World Conference on Infant Psychiatry, Cascais, Portugal.

Shonkoff, J., & Phillips, D. (2000). *From neurons to neighborhoods.* Washington, DC: National Academy Press.

Shweder, R. A. (1990). Cultural psychology: What is it? In J. W. Stigler, R. A. Shweder, & G. Herdt (Eds.), *Cultural psychology: Essays on comparative human development* (pp. 1–43). Cambridge: Cambridge University Press.

Shweder R. A. (1991). *Thinking through cultures: Expeditions in cultural psychology.* Cambridge: Cambridge University Press.

Slade, A., & Wolf, D.P. (1994). *Children at play: Clinical and developmental approaches to meaning and representation.* New York: Oxford University Press

Sorce, J. F., & Emde, R. N. (1981). Mother's presence is not enough: The effect of emotional availability on infant exploration. *Developmental Psychology, 17*(6), 737–745.

Sorce, J. F., Emde, R. N., Campos, J., & Klinnert, M. D. (1985). Maternal emotional signaling: Its effect on the visual cliff behavior of 1-year-olds. *Developmental Psychology, 21*(1), 195–200.

Spitz, R. A. (1959). *A genetic field theory of ego formation.* New York: International Universities Press.

Sroufe, L. A. (1995). *Emotional development: The organization of emotional life in the early years.* Cambridge: Cambridge University Press.

Stern, D. (1985). *The interpersonal world of the infant.* New York: Basic Books.

Tronick, E. Z. (1998). Dyadically expanded states of consciousness and the process of therapeutic change. *Infant Mental Health Journal, 19*(3), 290–299.

Tronick, E. Z. (1989). Emotions and emotional communication in infancy. *American Psychologist, 44,* 112–126.

Tronick, E. Z., & Cohn, J. F. (1989). Infant-mother face-to-face interaction: Age and gender differences in coordination and the occurrence of miscoordination. *Child Development, 60,* 85–92.

Winnicott, D. (1965). *Ego distortion in terms of true and false self. The maturational processes and the facilitating environment.* New York: International Universities Press.

Winnicott, D. O. (1971). *Playing and reality.* New York: Basic Books.

Zahn-Waxler, C., Radke-Yarrow, M., & King, R. A. (1979). Child rearing and children's prosocial initiations toward victims of distress. *Child Development, 50,* 319–330.

Zahn-Waxler, C., Radke-Yarrow, M., Wagner, E., & Chapman, M. (1992). Development of concern for others. *Developmental Psychology, 28,* 126–136.

Zahn-Waxler, C., Robinson, J., & Emde, R. N. (1992). The development of empathy in twins. *Developmental Psychology, 28,* 1038–1047.

DENNIS PALMER WOLF

2

Making Meaning From Emotional Experience in Early Narratives

We depend on narrative. It is the raw material of family history and our own sense of evolving personal identity. Narrative is also the centerpiece of counseling and therapy as well as the core of depositions and testimony. Narratives break through the surface of conversation, as regularly as breathing. But why? Drawing on literary models, many writers suggest that when we narrate, we turn blind chronology into stories in which we articulate heroes, villains, problems, and possible resolutions. Further, since stories focus on goals and attempts, they articulate our chances for agency and for authorship (e.g., taking hold of how our lives unfold and are told) (Bruner, 1986, 1990; Shaefer, 1992). Other writers argue that, rather than first and foremost a personal expression, storytelling is how we connect our life to other lives. It is how we create a pool of common knowledge, how we make the internal flow of subjective experience into interpersonal negotiation or understanding. (Not only did my sister have her baby on Saturday, but, when I heard her voice, I felt some jealousy.) We borrow legends and images from our families and communities as storylines on which build personal histories. In addition, our cultural identities are defined by the larger historical narratives we borrow or reject (Passerini, 1992; Polanyi, 1989; Portelli, 1997). (The discovery of the "New World" is the destruction of an older world for Native Americans. The "Crusades" rank as one of many incursions of Infidels for many Muslim historians.) In the introductory chapter of this volume, Emde proposes that in personal narratives, private experience meets public forms of communication. In particular, he argues that personal narratives provide young children and their caregivers with the means to regulate, understand, and communicate their affective experiences in ways that help them and those close to them negotiate the emotional challenges of early childhood (e.g., separation, rivalry, and a variety of family conflicts).

This chapter builds on Emde's double premises. First, narratives are shared forms of making sense of experiences that challenge the ordinary and require understanding. Second, such exchanges are vital for affective well-being and growth. The central argument of this chapter is that the meaning-making process depends on joint acts of evaluation (Bamberg & Damrad-Frye, 1991). When a speaker evaluates experience, she highlights the information that will allow her listener (and herself) to understand how her world was affected by the event(s) she narrates. She does so by foregrounding some events and dropping others into the background. Evaluative strategies emerge first as performance qualities (e.g., volume, gesture, pointing) and only later in more explicit linguistic structures such as verb tense, metaphors, story problems, formal plots, and genres. Though important as signals, these linguistic strategies are only a means to two larger outcomes: the commitment to use narrative as a form of understanding and the will to join others in making sense of lived experience. A speaker may announce import, but a listener remains silent or responds by confirming or challenging. Thus, even though the chapter details the emergence of particular linguistic forms, they are like islands that indicate much larger formations.

Evaluation is the human capacity to select, emphasize, and communicate the shape and weight of affective experience. The central tenet of this chapter is that narratives help to organize and interpret our lives because they are, first and foremost, occasions for evaluation. Evaluation is present from the earliest proto-narratives of infancy and only eventually takes the elegant form of story problems or plots. Between the ages of 3 and 6, children develop an explicit repertoire of evaluative strategies that range from simple performance dimensions (e.g., speaking louder and faster) to extremely sophisticated uses of genre. These strategies are not the sum of evaluation, only markers of wider process for exchanging meaning. Evaluation is essentially a dance demanding the attention and contribution of both narrator and listeners in real time. An example illustrates how pervasive—and important—the process of evaluation is to understanding what happens. A 16-month-old girl narrates a Sunday outing with her recently divorced father:

Narrative Example 1

(Mo = Mother, C = Child)

Mo: So what did you do with Daddy?

C: Cookie.

Mo: You had a cookie. And then what?

C: More, more cookie. (She looks over to her mother with glee.)

Mo: (pausing) . . . Lucky girl.

If we boiled this exchange down to a series of events ("I ate one cookie. I ate more cookies."), we would miss both what was meant and what was heard. When the child repeats the word "more," saying it emphatically each time as she looks gleefully at her mother, she is not only delivering the fact that she ate multiple cookies but also *evaluating* her experience, making her sense of indulgence and exception clear. The word is also an action. With it, she asks about the contrast between her outing and her daily experience. As a result, her mother may hear something like "I ate cookies, like never before." Her mother's reply is remarkable. She confirms her daughter's experience and acknowledges what the event means to her. She pauses and then says "Lucky girl," with a mixture of sadness and irony that may be the tone of an "everyday" parent who cannot afford to be so extravagant. But her remark is also more than commentary. She uses her evaluation to cap the narrative. She doesn't go on to ask "What kind?" or "Before breakfast?" She leaves the cookie banquet to stand as a singular event, unconnected to other portions of her child's history. She never says, "Like when we made cookies with Gram." Where the two evaluations meet is in their sense that mother and child are inventing themselves as a new family.

The exchange is brief; nevertheless, it helps to underscore key points about the process of making meaning. First, evaluation is fundamental. Only if we are instructed to hold back (as in court testimony) do we refrain from weighing and shaping events. Second, the evaluations speakers produce in making meaning are polysemic: like a crystal, the utterance, "More, more cookies" throws off multiple possible meanings. It signals the delight and excitement the child experiences in her father's presence. It is also signals that she grasps the contrast between the usual course of events and the indulgent breakfast she just had. As her mother hears it, the short narrative signals that she could be facing contrasts between an extravagant father and a "regular" mother or between a cherished child and a single woman. Finally, the girl and her mother are making meaning jointly. The account of eating cookies is not a message that the child formulates and sends off to her mother who opens and absorbs the meaning as sent. In many respects, the longer-term effect of the story could well be "delight" + "pause."

The first section of this chapter sketches an interpretive, as compared to a historical, view of narrative. The second section describes children's development of a range of language-based evaluative strategies and the kinds of narrative interactions they enable during the early childhood years. A third section explicitly examines the social process of co-constructing an evaluated narrative. In each section, examples from the MacArthur Story Stem Battery, as well as from spontaneous play and talk, are used as illustrations. The broad similarities evident in children's evaluative behaviors across the two types of narrative performances suggest that the MacArthur Story Stem Battery provides a tool for sampling how young narrators and their partners make sense of affective experience through language. This discussion of narrative evaluation is explicitly linked to other chapters in the volume in order to illustrate how pervasive the processes and consequences of evaluation are. The point is not that all the authors in this volume endorse the role of evaluation in making sense of affective experience. Rather, their work informs the work presented here.

An Evolving View of Narrative: From Event to Experience

For centuries, narrative was valued chiefly as a means of saving the past by turning personal memory into history. As the historian Herodotus wrote: "The account of the researches of Herodotus of Halicarnassus is here set down so that the memory of the past may not be lost; of the astonishing achievements both of the Greeks and of the foreigners; and more particularly, of the way in which they came into conflict" (Lang, 1984, p. 3). But this memorial, or documentary, conception of narrative has undergone seismic shifts in the last century, as we have come to value narratives less as objective records of events and more as the expression of experience: how an individual makes meaning from the stream of events (internal and external) that constitute being alive. As the 19th century became the 20th, there was a strong interest in internal experience, including not only feelings but also memories, thoughts, religious states, and imagination. Once viewed as too phantasmagoric for study, phenomena like the self and belief were on the table as topics for science, not just philosophy. Psychoanalysts began to influence the medical conception of illness, arguing that physical disorders such as hysteria and paralysis often had roots in mental states (Freud, 1955). In a less well known, but parallel manner, lawyers, with the help of psychologists and sociologists, began to formulate legal defenses around internal states, pleading that their clients experienced "brainstorms" (later known as temporary insanity) that totally changed the way they regarded violent acts such as murder (Perry, 1987). These were the underpinnings of a radically different view of human activity. In this view, feelings are not irrational and disorganizing (Nussbaum, 2002). Instead, affective experience was not a set of private tremors that came and went, distorting the "real" nature of experience. The mind (not the brain) was the fly-wheel for understanding: Thus, imagination, and the moral sense, not only facts and sensory data, informed human actions and the sense a person made of events. Second, mindfulness was not the province of philosophers or elders. It could exist apart from years of experience or access to education. In fact, young children engaged in it all the time.

Nowhere is this interest in internal experience more vivid than in fiction. Omniscient narrators relating observable events gave way to circumscribed narrators who were "unreliable," as they could share only what they experienced, not what "actually" happened. Not only were these narrators trapped in their own perspective; they were fickle. The human mind was forever re-evaluating experience in the light of new realizations. In *What Maisie Knew*, Henry James recounts the story of a young child "at an age when all stories are true and all conceptions are stories. The actual was the absolute, the present alone was vivid" (1912, p. 11). However, as Maisie "grows sharper," she comes to understand that she has meanings for events that she had once stored dimly in memory. James writes:

> By the time she had grown sharper . . . she found in her a collection of images and echoes to which meanings were attachable—images and echoes kept for her in the childish dusk, the dim closet, the high drawer, like games she wasn't yet big enough

> to play. The great strain meanwhile was that of carrying by the right end the things her father said about her mother. . . . A wonderful assortment of objects of this kind she was to discover there later, all tumbled up too with the things, shuffled into the same receptacle, that her mother had said about her father. (11–12)

James had two points. Narratives matter, not because they nail down the past, but because they keep the past unstable, capable of soaking up new meanings as understanding shifts.

Like James, Freud and his colleagues argued for the central role that evaluation played in making sense of affective experience. Personal narratives of all kinds (stories, dreams, and jokes) were fundamentally evaluative, but often split into two. Working in strait-laced, upper-middle-class Vienna, he argued that the most powerful forms of evaluation were driven underground. When his patients told personal narratives, he heard the acceptable surface story (the manifest content) that dealt largely with "what happened" in the sense of observable, polite events. But underneath that account, he sensed a much more fully affective and personal evaluation of the emotional significance of events (the latent content), which told the story of conflicting impulses and desires. Part of the "talking cure" was to rejoin the plot (the manifest content) with the affective evaluation (the latent content).

Standing half behind a door, Freud (1955) observed an 18-month-old boy who was closely attached to his mother:

> Occasionally, however, this well-behaved child evinced the troublesome habit of flinging into the corner of the room or under the bed all the little things that he could lay his hands on, so that to gather up his toys was often no light task. He accompanied this by an expression of interest and gratification, emitting a loud, long drawn out, "O-o-o-o—oh," which in the judgement of his mother (one that coincided with my own) was not an interjection but meant "go away" (fort), I saw this was a game and that the child used all his toys only to play "being gone" (fort sein) with them. One day I made an observation that confirmed my view. The child had a wooden reel with a piece of string wound round it. It never occurred to him, for example, to drag this after him on the floor and so play horse and cart with it, but he kept throwing it with considerable skill, held by the string, over the side of his little draped cot, so that the reel disappeared into it, then said his significant "O-o-o-oh" and drew the reel by the string out of the cot again, greeting its reappearance with a joyful "Da" (there). This was therefore the complete game generally observed by onlookers, and the one untiringly repeated by the child as a game for its own sake, although the greater pleasure unquestionably belonged to the second act. . . . This interpretation was fully established by a further observation. One day when the mother had been out for some hours she was greeted on her return by the information "Baby o-o-o-oh," which at first remained unintelligible. It soon proved that during his long lonely hours he had found a method of bringing about his own disappearance. He had discovered his reflection in the long mirror that nearly reached to the ground and had then crouched down in front of it, so that the reflection was "fort." (15–16)

Like any other person in the room, Freud saw the acceptable play narrative in which a boy threw and then reeled in a spindle. However, he argued that the observable actions of throwing and retrieving were acceptable physical metaphors for the boy's sense of loss, his struggle to gain agency, and his eventual triumph over the passivity imposed on him.[1]

Contemporary linguists and oral historians have carried these points about the evaluative nature of narrative a step further. They argue that a narrator has three basic tasks. The first is to supply enough information for listeners to be able to make good inferences. (Is this narrative occurring on a farm or in the big bad city? If it is happening at 12:00, is that high noon or midnight?) The second task is to provide enough structure and chronology so that a listener can accrue and make sense of information as he listens. The third is to evaluate or assign prominence to events and themes connecting them so that a listener can build an understanding of the narrated experience that parallels what the narrator intends to convey. (Was the trip to the amusement park unfamiliar, arousing, or terrifying?) The process of assigning prominence occurs at multiple levels of performance. Physically, a narrator can point or pound the table to underscore a point. A child might make a play figure jump up and down or supply noises that capture the intensity of events. Phonologically, a teller can pronounce a word in a distinctive way, or lower his voice, or change her tone when presenting highly salient information. Syntactically, a speaker can use unusual constructions such as negations or metaphors. At the discourse level, a teller can repeat, incrementally embellish key events, or establish ties with earlier events ("So, like I said, she can't be left alone—ever again") (Polyani, 1989). In developmental studies of oral narratives, researchers have demonstrated that children as young as 3 distribute the strength and density of their evaluations to establish themes as well as the point of their narrative (McCabe & Peterson, 1991). In addition, additional research suggests that both the number and type of children's evaluative strategies expand with age (Haslett, 1986; Peterson & McCabe, 1983). More specifically, there are predictable patterns to this expansion. Three-year-olds use comparisons (e.g., "like at home," "just like the one I got," etc.). Four-year-olds add on emotional evaluations ("I didn't want to go there, I was scared," or "He was so happy he jumped"). By the age of 5, children also use size, amount, and quantity markers (e.g., "She ate the *whole* box of cookies," "He ran *so fast* a car couldn't get him") (Umiker-Sebeok, 1979).

Contemporary oral historians have also argued for the centrality of evaluation. They agree that informants regularly evaluate their experiences, embellishing or even totally reshaping what "really happened" (Passerini, 1992; Portelli, 1997). They argue that informants' "errors" actually evaluate the current meaning of past events. Repressions, displacements in time, along with changes in the names and places, are clues to what matters to individuals and communities. These errors are actually clues to how people see the world, regardless of what the facts are. When Italian workers associate the death of a comrade with major labor riots (rather than the actual scuffle over joining NATO), they are claiming his death as one more loss in the long struggle of labor against management and certifying their own identities as socialists and patriots (Portelli, 1997). When a Kentucky miner recalls the labor strikes and violence of the 1940s and 1950s, he draws on the story lines that currently serve many miners and their families:

struggle against oppression, dogged determination, or David and Goliath. Just as much as faithful evaluative moves, these omissions and changes point to what matters.

Drawing across these diverse bodies of work, one may perceive narratives as interpretations rather than historical records of events. But far from useless, narratives index what matters to a speaker and his listeners. During any given narrative performance, a narrator and her listeners select, emphasize, communicate, and negotiate the shape and weight of personal experience. Where evaluation is missing, narrators lose the thread and listeners begin to think of other things.

The Development of Evaluative Language in Narratives

Like oral narratives, children's play can be dismissed as "just fooling around." But contemporary developmental and clinical scientists emphasize the adaptive features of play narratives (Emde, 1992a; Lowe, 1975; Harris, 1999; Winnicott, 1971). In this view, the years between two and six are a period of rapidly evolving symbolic activity (Bretherton, 1984, 1993; Wolf, 1984). Freud emphasized that early childhood play took place in the adaptive service of mastery. In his observations, the mastery concerned the boy's distress over separation from his mother wherein he enacted a repeated disappearance and return. The boy's games that Freud described also provide an example of symbolic activity in microdevelopment (Freud, 1955). In the first round of the game, he flung small objects into the corner, accenting the importance of this action with a long drawn out "O-o-o-oh," (a mix of sound effect and word that Freud believed to be a primitive version of the German "fort"). In this way, he combined word and gesture into a complex communication (Bates, 1985). In the second round of his game, the boy constructed a more deliberate scenario in which he represented both the disappearance and reappearance of the reel, marking the importance of the later event with a single word utterance: a loud "Da" ("There"). In the third game, the boy became an active agent who recognized his own image appearing and disappearing in front of the mirror. He pulled his recently returned mother to see what he invented, explaining "Baby o-o-o-oh," using a two-word proposition to highlight the pleasure of his own agency.

This evolution continues on a large scale throughout early childhood, fueled by conceptual development (Wolf, Rygh, & Altshuler, 1984) coupled with language acquisition. The child's growing investment in making meaning also sparks rapidly developing investment by family members and friends who are often drawn into discussions and interpretations that can make them, as adults and caregivers, stop, think, and be amazed by their children's investment in understanding experience. In order to review major elements in the course of early narrative development, the following section uses a particularly provocative stem from the MacArthur Story Stem Battery to outline how particular forms of language development change types of narrative interactions and understandings.

Early Meaning: Sequences, Shared Reference, and Implied Narratives

Infants possess some of the fundamental building blocks for understanding narratives of human experience. One of these fundamentals is an ability to grasp the usual or typical order of events. For instance, once habituated to a particular order, babies register surprise when that order is changed (Mandler, 1984; Shank & Abelson, 1977). Infants are also skilled turn-takers capable of matching the intensity and type of their movements and vocalizations to that of a partner (Appelman & Wolf, chapter 10; Stern, 1985). In such interactions, both participants focus intently on the other, just as they must do in intimate exchanges of experience throughout their lives. However, their interactions change sharply once they can focus joint attention on a third element: a picture in a book or a figure moving across the street outside their window. An early form of this intersubjectivity is social referencing beginning in the latter part of the infant's 1st year (Emde, 1992b). Another is successful pointing (Bruner, 1986). The sophistication of this implicit narrative system shows when child and partner play a game drawn from their shared history whether it be a conventional exchange like peek-a-boo or one of their own invention. As Bruner notes, infants are delighted by "jokes" about changes in the order of events or the assigned roles (Bruner, 1986). At that moment, a child and his partner are both playing with a new pattern *and* their memory of how the game typically unfolds. Such games are elemental forms of narrative attunement, where a teller need say very little, because his partner shares his history and his will to make maximum sense of even small or implicit clues in order to stay with him.

These early forms of implicit joint reference become explicit with the onset of one-word utterances. At that juncture, children can convey a range of meanings by combining word and context, thus learning another lesson in intersubjectivity. Thus, a single word, "key," can be understood, in context and with a specific listener, to refer to an object (or things like it), an action (going for a ride), or a person (someone whom the child associates with keys).

Narrative Example 2: Child Age 18 Months

(Mo: = Mother, C: = Child)

(Several months earlier, the child's uncle visited and had to remove the seats to hunt for a lost key.)

C: (Points, while looking out the window at an old Volkswagen bus.) Key.

Mo: Yeah, like Uncle Mark's van. He lost his keys.

C: (Emphatically) No Mark. Key.

Mo: Key?

C: Key . . . Going (Walks toward the front door.)

The child and his mother use language, objects, and gesture to create two competing narratives, one about an uncle, one about a trip. They have created an elemental story-world, as they alternately focus on the here and now *and* events that unfolded in another time and place. But in this new narrative world, the caregiver is no longer the sole arbiter of meaning. The *child* expresses a meaning of her own and redirects the narrative from a recollection to a plan, saying, "No, Mark. *Key.*" When her mother is puzzled, she clarifies: "Going." Her language and intention make her an author: a narrator with the right to safeguard her *own* meaning.

Evaluation in Propositional Language

During the 2nd year, children's command of symbolic activity grows exponentially. At the heart of this explosion is a set of new understandings about how reference works and how smaller units can be combined into larger meanings (Slade & Wolf, 1994; Wolf, 1982). At this age, children can grasp the relationship between words, pictures, and models and their referents in the physical world. They can also create the kind of transformations involved in turning a reel and a spindle into "a mother who comes and goes" (Bretherton, 1984; Freud, 1955; Wolf, 1984). But a landmark change occurs when children begin speaking in multiword utterances and pretending sequences of events. In that process, they move from reference ("Up") to predication ("[I] want up" or "pick Lilly up") (Bates, 1985, Emde, chapter 1). Two-word speech implies a developing grammar, a conventional and articulate system for making precise meanings (Bruner, 1990) communicable to others. But, at least as important as the rules of syntax is the organization of experience into fundamental semantic categories: agent, action, object, instrument, means, and so on (Halliday, 1975). To get some sense of the significance of this development, think about Freud's young boy who punctuated his early games with single-word utterances like "Da" and "Oooohhhhh." Once he understood and used the categories of agent–action ("*baby . . . ooohh*"), he could claim he (the agent) appeared and disappeared (acted autonomously). Using these same semantic categories, a child can portray a range of shifting relationships (e.g., "Mommy leave baby" or "Baby leave Mommy"; "Mommy sad?" or "Daddy mad?") (Dunn, 1988, 1993).

Evaluation in Early Forms of Discourse

Propositions can also be combined into longer stretches of connected language, or discourse. As children produce multi-utterance narratives, they create sequences of events that carry new possibilities for evaluation and meaning. With multiple utterances, children can formulate narratives that cover a series of events. Even the simplest of these chains of specific events creates possibilities for more complex meanings than previously available. A sequence of propositions all featuring the same agent ("Mommy," "she," "her") defines a character who persists over time and accrues a history across activities. Agents begin to have personal histories (Wolf, 1982). For example, here is a short play narrative from a 2-year-old about losing and finding.[2] While the story is sparse, it is clear that the two characters are independent agents with individual histories.

Narrative Example 3: Child Age 2

(Mo = Mother, C = Child)

C: They going. (Puts a child and a mother figure in the back of a toy truck.)

C: Rmmmmmm (Pushes car and figures around and around the legs of a chair. The child figure falls out.)

C: Oh-oh.

C as Baby: Waaa Waaa.

C: Mommy looking. (Jumps the Mo figure out of the truck and makes her hop around.)

C as Mo: Baby, baby (somewhat annoyed).

C: Find him. (Makes Mo figure hunt in multiple locations.)

C as Mo: Got you. Bad baby. Bad, bad.

C: (Tosses child figure in the back of the truck. Drives it along again.)

Extended propositional speech opens up a second possibility: the development of recurrent motifs or themes. Across the propositions, the mother figure is consistently the agent who speaks her mind; whereas the baby is an object, lost and restored like an errant suitcase. The mother is annoyed, when we might expect intimacy, even blaming (rather than comforting) the baby for falling off the back of a fast-moving truck. If these same patterns occurred in many of this child's parent-child narratives, and especially if they persisted over time, an observer might see a characterization of mother-child relationships as responsible, but gruff.

Between 2 and 3, young children acquire an initial set of discourse abilities that allow them—with the help of their narrative partners—to tell more articulate narratives. Among the most significant acquisitions is the onset of distinctive narrative voices that permit the child to present multiple perspectives on the central events in the narrative. First, the child distinguishes between non-narrative and narrative voices. The non-narrative voice includes that of the child and her partner(s) when they speak about the immediate, "real" world. In addition, children distinguish between multiple narrative voices: (1) the narrator who provides the overvoice and (2) character voices (e.g., mother, father, Mary, etc.). Children may also use the voice of a stage-manager who shepherds the narrative through with comments like: "Pretend she didn't say that," or "I didn't say it, the cat did").

Narrative Example 4: The "Lost Keys" Stem, Child Age 3:6

(EXP = Experimenter, C = Child who is responding to the story stem, MO = Mother figure, FA = Father figure, MA = Child figure in the story, NAR = Narrator/over voice)

(The mom and dad figures are at the table facing each other, with the child figure alone and off to the side.)

EXP as Narrator: Tells the story stem of two parents arguing about who lost the keys. She turns to the child and says, "Show me and tell me what happens next."

C as FA: You lost my keys. (Brings FA figure to a position right in front of the MO figure. Moves him up and down as she speaks for him.)

C as MO: No, I don't. You lost my keys. (Moves the MO figure up and down as she speaks for her. Looks up at EXP as if she is done.)

EXP: So, the dad and the mom say, "You lost my keys." Then what happens? Can you show me and tell me. . .

C as NAR: He's looking. (C moves father figure around the play space.) She's looking. (Moves the mother figure around.) And the girl's looking, too. (Moves the girl figure around.)

C as NAR: Look, look, look.

EXP: Everybody is looking. Who says, "look, look, look"?

C as C: Me.

EXP: Okay. What happens now?

C as NAR: They... he's tired. (Lays the father figure down.) The mom, too. (Lays the mother figure by the father.) Her, too. (Lays the girl beside the mother figure.) So they went to bed. (Appears to be finished.)

EXP: They all got tired and went to bed. But what happened to the keys?

C: Pauses. Looks at the figures. Pauses again.

C as NAR: She found them. (Indicates MA, the girl figure.)

C as MA: (Makes the girl figure stand up and move about as if looking.) Mommy, Daddy, I got the keys. Here. (Girl figure offers imaginary keys to the parent figures.)

EXP: The girl found them and gave them to Mom and Dad. What did Mom and Dad do?

C: They went to sleep again. (Lays all three figures down, side by side.)

EXP: Is that the end?

C: (Nods.)

EXP: Thanks for telling me that story.

Neither the immediate story problem of lost keys nor the wider psychological challenge of resolving family conflict compels the child's attention. In fact, she has to be strongly prompted to address and resolve the story problem. Yet she can move smoothly across three characters and two worlds: the here and now world of exchanges about the prop, questions about who spoke, and the fictional world of the story. Within the fictional world of the story, the child distinguishes the voices (literally, but also conceptually) so that there is a clear line of talk for each "intelligence" or character perspective. The child also uses her control of different narrative voices to create the girl as the main character. She is the only figure who speaks directly ("Mommy, Daddy, I got the keys. Here."). This creates the possibility of narratives told from the point of view of particular agents who, nevertheless, can also be described by an external narrator.

Narrative Systems as Sources of Evaluation: Webs of Meaning

Between 3 and 5 years of age, children gain command over a range of internal-to-narrative systems that permit them to create webs of meanings. Two internal systems, one semantic and one syntactic, illustrate this point. By the age of 3, many children have the internal state vocabulary (e.g., happy, scared, sad, etc.) with which to describe a specific state or a simple transformation in that state (e.g., "They found the keys, so everybody's happy.").

A year or so later, children possess clusters of related internal state terms (e.g., "get mad," "be really angry") as well as associated emotionally valenced vocabulary (e.g., "slammed," "push," "shout," etc.). Using these semantic tools, a 4-year-old can portray, not just mention, an affective state. ("The dad was *so angry*, he *sent* the girl *to her room.* "*No* coming out!" he said and he *slammed* the door."). The father's anger is amplified by states, action, and dialogue. In addition, many children acquire (or are read) the background knowledge and specific vocabulary to create distinct story worlds (e.g., a calm domestic world of predictable everyday events as contrasted with a fantasy world where characters fly off the table and houses catch on fire). Children can attribute a consistent emotional tone to episodes or an entire narrative. They can also create the contrasts between safe and dangerous or violent and tender story worlds.

These semantic tools are complemented by syntactic ones, including the coordinated use of tense and other temporal markers ("later," "after that," "the next day," etc.) (Bamberg, 1984, 1985, 1997). As young as 2:6, the majority of children command several simple tenses (i.e., present, past, and future). They can modulate those tenses by using modal markers such as "should," "could," or "might have"). These modal markers signal the status of particular actions (e.g., whether they are certain, durative, conditional, or imagined). Five-year-olds add compound tenses (e.g., "She had been thinking," "Pretend they didn't know it when they were coming") All combined, these constructions provide the tools for establishing tightly knit temporal relations throughout a story. By 5, children can link events as sequential, causal, consequential, or parallel occurrences using terms such as "because," "since," "so," "while," "when") (Peterson & McCabe, 1985). As a result, children replace simple chains of events with a network of occurrences in which background and foreground events are linked and events can be set in relation to numerous other occurrences in the narrative (e.g., "When she wasn't looking, he took all cookies because he wanted to eat them later").

Children's acquisition of causal and explanatory connectors makes it possible to express how events are informed and motivated by internal states such as knowledge or affect (e.g., "He looked all over, *because* he thought he heard the Mom put them (the keys) there"; "The mom was mad *so* she yelled at the dad"; or "She took the keys *because* she wanted them"). Consequently, children can follow out the long-term implications of an early occurring event, or end a story by referring back to the events that initiated the action, action occurring early in a narrative (see Narrative Example 5 in which the girl character borrows the keys, an action that sets the stage for the father's anger, the child's self-defense, and the mother's negotiating).

Genres as a Source of Meaning

Extensive research describes children's gradual acquisition of formal story structure (Bamberg, 1997; Haslett, 1986; Peterson & McCabe, 1983; Stein, in press). Stories provide children and their listeners with a culturally valued and explicit form for communicating important sequences of events. For example, here is a 5-year-old "Lost Keys" stem to compare with the example at 3:6.

Narrative Example 5 "Lost Keys" Stem, Child Age 5

(EXP = Experimenter, C = The child who is responding to the story stem, MO = The mother figure, FA = The father figure, MA = Mary, the child figure in the story, NAR = The child speaking as the narrator)
(The italics indicate how both the child and the experimenter use canonical story form to address experiential and psychological issues that the characters face in restoring the keys and mending the rift between the parents.)

EXP: Tells the story stem in which a mother and father argue with each other about who lost the car keys. "Show me and tell me what happens now." *(Experimenter has introduced the setting and the basic conflicts that C's story is to resolve.)*

C as MA: I just borrowed them (be)cause I wanted to open the door to get . . . to get my toys. (*An initial attempt to resolve the problem of the lost keys through explanation.)*

EXP: Oh, Mary said she borrowed them because she wanted to open the door to get her toys. Then what happened?

C as MO: Okay. (*The problem of the lost keys appears resolved.)*

C as NAR: And now she says

C as MA: Here're your keys, Mom. *(Another attempt to resolve the central issue, this time by physically returning the keys.)*

EXP: Mom said okay and Mary said, "Here are your keys."

C as NAR: And that's the end. *(This indicates that spontaneously this child would attend only to the issue of physical loss.)*

EXP: What happened to Mom and Dad's arguing? *(Experimenter probes for resolving the psychological conflict.)*

C as NAR: They said *they were sorry.* (*A prompted response phrased in terms of a psychological resolution.)*

EXP: They said they were sorry about arguing. Do you wanna show that? *(Pushing for a more substantial playing out of the conflict resolution.)*

C as FA: I'm sorry. (She taps Dad up and down a little as she talks.) (*Prompted physical enactment of the resolution.)*

C as MO: You didn't know that she (points to Mary figure) had them. *(A fuller psychological resolution that takes in both the girl's and the father's perspectives.)*

C as FA: She shouldn't take them. *(Conflict resurfaces.)*

C as MO: She needed to get her toys. *(Another attempt at resolution by adding in the child's innocent motives.)*

C: as FA: It makes me mad. (C hops the father figure in place emphatically as he speaks.) *(Conflict resurfaces.)*

C as MO: She just borrowed them. We have them safe now. *(A double resolution of the loss of the keys and the parental conflict.)*

C as NAR: Now it's the end. (*This suggests that the conflicts are resolved at least to the level that the child wants to engage with them.)*

EXP: Okay, great. (*The experimenter now accepts the child's response, as it satisfies not only the stem, but the experimenter's own sense of story structure, particularly with respect to resolving conflicts that are psychological.*)

This is a story, but not in terms of large-scale actions: no forests burn, no mountains crumble. It works as a story because it plays out how negotiated human understanding is.

Genre is also important because it allows narrators to *withhold* meaning. Here, for instance, is a 4-year-old who is uncomfortable telling the "Lost Keys" narrative. Even during the stem, she tells the experimenter "No, they (the parents) didn't fight." However, she struggles to balance her obligation to respond. The result is a meager script. She speeds through a response, never once taking on either the lost keys or the conflict between the mother and father.

Narrative Example 6: Child Age 4

(EXP = Experimenter, C = The child who is responding to the story stem, MO = The mother figure, FA = The father figure, MA = The child figure in the story)
(The mom and dad figures are at the table facing each other, with the child figure alone and off to the side.)

EXP: Tells the story stem in which a mother and father argue with each other about who lost the car keys.

C as C: No, they didn't fight.

EXP: Show me and tell me what happens next.

C as NAR: The dad looked. The mom looked. The girl looked. Then they got tired. They ate dinner. They went to bed. The end.

Young narrators develop a repertoire of conventional narrative forms. Thus, a 5-year-old can relate an experience in the form of an account, a script, a dramatization, a story, etc. This is a choice about a particular "container" for meaning. It may also be a choice about openness. In a script, a narrator describes a predictable sequence of events. He has little obligation to say anything about the motivations, feelings, or human consequences. On the other hand, when a narrator offers a script in place of a personal narrative, he communicates restraint and privacy. Listeners hear a bare and meager account when they expected evaluation and perspective. The message is "Not now," "Not for you," or "Not from me."

Narrative Frames as Meaning Making

However, in examining young children's narratives of affective experience, it may be more useful to think in terms of types of *affective frames* for narrative—the ways children use their repertoire of evaluative skills to portray the meaning of affective experience. Children use frames in highly flexible ways and frequently move between these frames as part of communicating different types of affective worlds. In addition, a child's response to a story stem can incorporate several distinct narrative frames, with the shifts highlighting different affective experiences, different degrees of distance or involvement, and different approaches to representing meaning (e.g., as direct actions, images, dialogue, or narrated events; Tulchensky, 1995).

To illustrate the nature and consequences of these shifts, the following presents a 5-year-old girl responding to the story stem we refer to as "child exclusion by parents." The story beginning is one in which a mother and father exclude a child from their intimacy, sending the child character off to care for her younger sister. During the course of this stem, the girl uses a suite of different narrative frames to represent the character's (or her own) affective experience (Drucker, 1994).

Narrative Example 7: The "Privacy Stem," Child Age 5

(EXP = Experimenter, C = The child who is responding to the story stem, MO = The mother figure, FA = The father figure, MA = The child figure in the story)

EXP: Performs the stem in which a mother excludes an older child (Mary) from her own intimate interaction with the father. The mom and dad figures are sitting on a couch, Mary is standing next to them, and Jane is standing in the corner of the table next to a toy box.

Predictable human action frame.

EXP as MO speaking to Mary: Could you bring Jane up to her room and shut the door?

C: (Slides Mary slowly over to the toy box and then to Jane and then to Mom.)

C as C: (Mimes closing a door.)

C as MO: Is the door shut?

C: (Nods her head.)

EXP: Mom gives dad a big kiss. (Makes kissing sounds as she touches mom's face to dad's face.)

EXP: How does Mary feel in her room?

C as NAR: She wants her mommy.

C as MA: (Slowly slides Mary toward mom and the couch.)

C as NAR: She wants her mother.

EXP: How does she feel?

C: (unintelligible)

EXP: She is angry with someone?

Metaphorical frame: Shift to different narrative frame that is more performed and carried by an image in which touching conveys longing.

C as NAR: Then she goes downstairs and she lies down behind the couch.

C: (Lays Mary down behind the couch.)

EXP: Who is she . . . tell me.

C as NAR: She lies down behind the couch.

C as NAR: And then she touches Mommy's hair and then she runs into her room.

C as MA: (Makes Mary run to the opposite end of the table, by the toy box.)

C as NAR: She touches Mommy's hair and runs into her room and locks the door behind her.

EXP: She locks the door behind her.

Shift back to the frame of a predictable human action, following Experimenter's intervention.

C as C: Yeah.

EXP: Who is she angry at?

C as C: (Taps Dad's head.)

C as C: And Mom.

EXP: So she touches Mom's hair and she runs to her room.

EXP: How come she's angry?

C as NAR: Because she wants to be with them.

EXP: She wants to be with them.

EXP: What do you think happens next?

Shift back to metaphoric frame.

C as NAR: She goes to her sister's room and touches her hair. (She touches Mary to Jane's head.)

C as NAR: And runs away. (She makes Mary run to a spot in the middle of the table.)

EXP: She goes to her sister's room and touches Jane's hair and runs away?

C as NAR: And then she touches her daddy's hair. (She touches Mary to dad's head.) And goes into her room.

C as NAR: (Makes Mary run back to her spot in the middle of the table.)

EXP: And then she touches her daddy's hair and goes to her room?

C as C: Yeah.

EXP: What happens at the very end?

C as NAR: They're all mad at her (be)cause they found out. (Holds up Mary.)

EXP: They're all mad at Mary 'cause they found out what?

C as C: That she was doing that.

EXP: That she was doing that? Do you wanna show that they're all mad at Mary?

Shift to enacted narrative frame (perhaps due to the experimenter's intrusion or because the child has already done considerable affective "work").

C as NAR: (Takes mom and dad off the couch and jumbles mom, dad, and Mary around in her hands.)

EXP: What's happening?

C as NAR: They're fighting.

EXP: They're fighting.

C as NAR: They're all fighting together. (She takes Jane and jumbles all four figures around in her hands.)

EXP: They're all fighting together?

C as NAR: (Continues to jumble the four figures around in her hands.)

EXP: Okay.

C as NAR: (Drops the four figures onto the table.)

EXP: So what happens at the very end?

C as NAR: Um that's the end.

Shift out of enacted narrative frame to present moment interaction.

EXP: It's the end?

C as C: (Nods.)

EXP: A great job! The end.

In the first portion of her performance, the child portrays a probable sequence of human actions (e.g., being asked to leave, going to her room, and closing the door). However, by the middle section of the narrative, she presents the child's isolation using a metaphoric frame, portraying the character's experience of isolation and longing through a powerful repeating gesture: reaching out to touch the hair of each family member and then running away. In the final portion of the narrative, the child shifts abruptly to an entirely action-based, less modulated enactment of the characters fighting. (Possibly this is a result of the experimenter breaking in on her narrative about touching and insisting that she depict the anger between the several characters.) In essence, each shift provides a different frame for interpreting human actions and reactions. If the child had jumbled the family figures together in the early frame featuring predictable human actions, the jumbling actions might have signaled disruption; here, following the experimenter's added requests, the jumbling may well signal "Enough."

Table 2.1 summarizes (but does not exhaust) the different types of affective narrative frames that appear in the MSSB corpus. Unlike formal genres, these frames combine medium (e.g., action or speech), formal features (e.g., plots or images) and degrees of evaluation (meager scripts vs. fully evaluated stories). These frames establish an affective context for communicating and interpreting narrative content. Individual children or groups of children facing particular affective demands may develop their own range of frames (see Appelman & Wolf, chapter 10). In terms of sharing affective experience, a shy child's personal story may be the equivalent of a more outgoing child's highly evaluated dramatic play.

Young children make similar use of narrative frames in their spontaneous narratives. What follows is a pair of excerpts from two narratives told by a 6-year-old girl about the birth of her younger brother. Each excerpt covers the same episode: the girl's first encounter with her baby brother. The two genres afford her the chance to highlight different aspects of her affective experience. The play version emphasizes action and dialogue, re-creating the events on-line with a sense of immediacy. In her spoken narrative, the child highlights explanation and reflection. At the same time, within each rendition, she uses different narrative frames to portray aspects of that particular version of the event.

TABLE 2.1: Examples of Affective Narrative Frames

(In the examples that follow, the narrator communicates emotional experience by portraying)

Situation narratives The current status of a child's interaction or relationship either to a narrative partner or to having been asked to tell/play out a narrative. While appearing to comply, children may tell skeletal or wild narratives that refer chiefly to their desire to escape or evade the request to finish a particular narrative or to go on to new scripts. The skeletal narratives lack any commitment or expressiveness. The "wild" narratives often feature drastic or silly events. These events often build to a crescendo that makes it "impossible" for the story to go on. Thus, situation narratives refer to a child's discomfort, boredom, or fatigue, not the events likely to follow the stem.

Personal experience The time and space of lived experience, portraying temporally organized events, evaluated in numerous ways in order to make a larger point about personal experience. Characters act and speak in plausible ways. Events may contain highly detailed elements. Frequently, these narratives occur in the past tense (especially if spoken); characters tend to be given specific names and to be given direct discourse (dialogue) or reported speech. These types of narrative often portray the child's willingness to make a connection to her own remembered experience.

Script or feasible human narrative The highly characteristic routines and stereotyped action of generalized characters (often referred to as the mother, the father, etc.) who play predictable roles in human events. These narratives may be told in the historical present (e.g., comes, says, goes) or in the simple past (came, said, went). There is very little evaluation; the child concentrates on actions and dialogue. In these narratives (or portions of narratives), the child portrays what he or she thinks is a typical or possible course of events.

Dramatic narratives The interactions between two or more characters in the form of a dialogue. The dialogue is often short, present tense, particularly among familiars. Sections of this kind of narrative often portray the most basic relationships between actors: intimacy or distance, nurturance or disinterest, collaboration or conflict.

Emotion state narrative The experience of being in a distinct, (often extreme) emotional state. In these narratives, children use bold expressive actions (e.g., flying, rocking, crashing, floating) to demonstrate how a character feels. The actions are often repetitive and accompanied by a sing-song narration or chant rather than discursive language. These narratives often portray characters caught up in a particular emotion state (e.g., anger expressed through crashing, affection denoted by rocking or gliding two figures together, aggression depicted by jumbling all the character figures together).

Idealized narrative The way that events ought to go if all humans were good, all events fair, and children's wishes were attended to. In many respects, these narratives are often very similar to personal narratives. However, the emotional valence in these narratives is very positive and children figures are central. They are often models of good behavior, or in the right. Child characters are respected and granted their wishes.

Metaphoric narrative The core affective states at the heart of a narrative by creating an image, an evocative gesture, or a figure of speech that dominates the narrative. For instance, the child character is scolded and sent off to her room as punishment. To portray her shame, the child narrator hides the girl from family members, placing her inside her toy box, pulling down the lid. The rest of the narrative is about family members seeking her, but her never answering. Typically these images are not explained, but their presentation is so apt they "speak" for themselves.

Narrative Example 8: Excerpt from the Symbolic Play Birth Story, Child Age 6

In earlier portions of play M enacted her mother going into contractions, her father taking her to spend the night at a friend's family, her father rushing her mother to the hospital, and the baby being born. At this juncture, he introduces her to her new brother (table 2.2).

Later in the same afternoon, M retells the birth narrative to a family friend who asks her about it. This time, M offers a very different portrayal of the event. Her narrative is entirely spoken, and she consistently uses the occasion to explore the affective theme of becoming a big sister, drawing on her linguistic resources at all levels: word choice, sentence structure, and discourse patterns. The narrative has a long introductory section (which is not reproduced here) in which the child describes going to a family friend's house for the night and how her father called early in the morning to tell her that she had a new baby brother.

Narrative Example 9: Excerpt from a Personal Experience Narrative, Child Age 6

(Narrative comments = regular type, Elements emphasizing herself as a competent older sister = **bold**.)

When the nurse brought him

And I **ran over** to him,

And I **pushed** myself up,

TABLE 2.2: Symbolic Birth Play Story

Actions	Language
	Predictable domestic narrative
M. walks up to Mo.	Ch: Where is the baby?
	Mo: He is so tiny he is hard to see. But you can hold him because you are his sister.
Fa picks up the baby and brings it to M.	Fa: You sit here in this big chair (M. brings over a small plastic container).
Mo places M. and baby figures together in the barrel.	Fa: If you are very, very careful you can hold him and rock him so he doesn't cry like a baby.
M. sings and turns the barrel in big circles on the floor.	M: Rocky, rocky the baby, The baby brother, the baby who is a brother, rocky baby.
Fa faces M.	You can stay here all, all morning you don't have to go to school because you are the sister now.
M. figure jumps up and down excitedly.	"Yeah, yeah, no school." "Time for the big sister."
	Real world interaction frame
M. speaks in her own voice in an aside to the nearby adults.	M.: I really did have to go to school, but pretend.
	Enactment frame
M. rocks the container very slightly, then faster, and faster.	Rocky, rocky, rocky, the baby, the brother, the brother baby.
M. dances the tub around with the figures in it, humming.	

Fa = Father, M. = Child, Mo = Mother.

Cause I was
Cause I
And I pushed myself up so that I could see him.
Cause I
So that I could see **Mikey, my new baby brother**
Because I was not tall enough to see
to see without standing on tiptoe
"Oh Mikey." (dialogue)
"He's gorgeous." (dialogue)
And I sat down in the chair
And **telled my brother** that
He was **fast asleep** for a little while
I talked with mommy
I went, while I talked with mommy
And daddy telephoned his parents
He had telephoned me first
Because it was more important . . . for me to know
Because he was MY (vocal emphasis) **brother**
I felt proud to be a big sister
Soon my father's parents came
And . . . and **I got** my parents, my mother and father
my grandmother and grandfather to hold him
To hold Mikey
Even though my grandfather didn't want to
I convinced him to do it
I convinced him that he should do it (repair)
I convinced him that he ought to do it (repair)
When he saw me holding little Mikey

This portion of her spoken narrative contrasts with her enacted account of the "same" events. M uses her considerable hold on the linguistic features of extended discourse to develop her theme of being the older child (the bold text). This past-tense reflection permits M to build an idealized account in which she "stars" as the older sister with all events radiating from her.

The Social Exchange of Narrative Meanings

The danger of describing the development of narrative strategies for evaluation is that the process takes on a highly individualistic and linguistic emphasis. But a narrative is a highly social, rather than private, undertaking. Considerable work in clinical and developmental psychology demonstrates how intensely social, rather than private, emotions and emotional communication can be, even in earliest infancy (Emde, chapter 1). Building on this work, we suggest, first, that children's interactions with specific narrative partners provide important information about that dyad's skill and style in creating shared meaning. This variation provides clues to that child's concept of specific relationships. Conversely, play narratives provide insight into adults' conceptions of their role in helping young children to examine and understand the invisible, but powerful, world of emotions, motivations, and consequences. Signals have to be read and interpreted to have meaning (Fivush, 1994; Hudson, 1990). As an example, here is a section of a play session between a 3-year-old boy and his father annotated to indicate the meaning-bearing narrative signals that the father, in the role of a narrative partner, must notice and interpret.

Narrative Example 10: "Lost Keys" Stem, Experimenter and Child Age 3

(Roman type = The language and action of the story, Italics = A narrative feature influencing the shared process of making meaning)

(The mom and dad figures are on the table facing each other, with two child figures alone and off to the side. The experimenter tells the "Lost Keys" narrative and then says, "Show me and tell me what happens next.")

Change of narrative world: Leave here-and-now world, interpret content as part of the fictional story-world.

C as FA: You lost my keys. (Brings FA figure to a position right in front of the MO figure. Moves him up and down as she speaks for him.)

Character voice: Child speaking as the father. Information should be attributed to him.
Evaluation: Emphatic stress, volume, and gestures.

C as MO: No, I don't. You lost *my* keys. (Moves the MO figure up and down as she speaks for her.)

Character voice: Child speaking as the mother. Information should be attributed not to narrator but to her.
Evaluation: Action with emphatic stress, volume, and gestures.

C as C: (Looks up at EXP as if she is done.)

Change of narrative world: Child is now communicating in the frame of the current interaction.

EXP: So, the Dad and the mom say, "You lost my keys." Then what happens? Can you show me and tell me…?

Adjust/Correct: Child may have thought her job was to mimic the argument.
Support additional child's narrative performance without suggesting content.

C as NAR: He's looking. (C moves father figure around the play space.)
She's looking. (Moves the mother figure around.)
And the girl's looking, too. (Moves the girl figure around.)
Change of narrative world: Child is back to speaking in the story world.

Character voice: Child is speaking as narrator, providing "overview" of action.
Evaluation: The repetition of "looking" underscores how central this action is.

C as NARR: Look, look, look.

Continuation of the voice: Child speaks as narrator.
Evaluation/Emphasis: Repetition.
This repetition may be character speech or an indication of the duration of searching,

EXP: Everybody is looking.
Who says, "look, look, look?"

Change of narrative world: This question refers to the real world.
Clarify nature of comment without directing the narrative.

C as C: Me.

Character voice: Child speaking as the child in the real world. The utterance is not intended to contribute information to the narrative.

EXP: Okay. What happens now?

C as NAR: They . . . he's tired.

Character voice: The child is speaking as the narrator.
Repair: The final version (i.e., "he's tired") is the only addition to the narrative.

. . . .(Lays the father figure down.)

. . . . .The mom, too. (Lays the mother figure by the father.)
Her, too. (Lays the girl beside the mother figure.)

. . . . .So they went to bed.

Genre: The child may be rehearsing the script for a typical day that ends with going to bed.
This may be this child's spontaneously available type of resolution (i.e., the day ends).
Extend/Prompt to see if she can address the problem. But do not lead child.

EXP: They all got tired and went to bed. But what happened to the keys?

C: (Pauses. Looks at the figures. Pauses again.)

C as NAR: She found them. (Indicates MA, the girl figure.)

C as MA: (Makes the girl figure stand up and move about as if looking.) Mommy, Daddy, I got the keys. Here. (Girl figure offers imaginary keys to the parent figures.)

In this example, the pair exposes a basic disposition to collaborate with one another on creating coherent narrative content (Bretherton, 1990; Bretherton & Oppenheim, chapter 3). Nevertheless, the MSSB is a deliberately constrained set of circumstances in which to look at the co-construction of meaning. To what extent do structured story-stem interactions model what happens between more intimate narrative partners, when the stories are spontaneous, rather than elicited (Polyani, 1989)? In the following sample of spontaneous play, a 4-year-old boy and his father construct a play narrative together. Their interactions illustrate how intimate narrative partners use both narrative choices and narrative signals in order to be together and to discuss a serious behavioral issue: the boy's difficulties with impulse control (Miller & Sperry, 1987, 1988). This has become a prominent issue as he now attends group care for much of the day. When their joint narrative begins, the father is preparing supper and his son is playing with blocks and small figures across the kitchen floor.

Narrative Example 11: A Father and Son, Age 4, Negotiate Frustration and Anger

(Roman type = story actions, Italics = narrative signals that father must understand and respond to)

J: (Is playing on the kitchen floor with an array of blocks, small figures, and models. He attempts to build a stairway from small cube blocks, like one he saw someone else build. He gets very angry and scatters the blocks with a bag of marbles. He sees his father turn to watch what is going on.)

J: (speaking to his father) I can't do it, I don't know how.

Father has to hear this comment as a real world remark, not as a play world comment. J is speaking about his own frustration with his skills. This matters since this is exactly the kind of situation in which he quickly slides into acting out.

Play narrative

(J returns to building and relocates the bag of marbles. Taking several out, he jokes at trying to stack them up. He does this three times, each time getting more exaggerated and his near-anger turns to humor. He hams up his surprise when the marbles tumble and roll away each time.)

Father must see this as progress and certify it, without drawing too much attention. He can make good use of this return to the bracketed world of play.

J: These stairs are too hard to make.

Father must hear the evaluation (i.e., the emphatic "too hard") and realize that J is close to slipping back into frustration.

J: (Rebuilds a stack of blocks and makes a little doll figure hop up to the top of the stack of blocks. He makes that figure call down to another figure to join him.)

Father must notice J is back into a play world and that J is now projecting the actions onto small figures, not getting personally involved.

Father also has to realize that these actions count as events in the story, even though they are not explicitly narrated. There is a "safe" projected narrative shaping up. It might provide a venue for playing out and discussing anger and control, if handled well.

J (as Figure 1): Hey, come on up here.

J is no longer speaking for himself. It is the small figure speaking.

(J makes the second figure struggle up, as there is only a stack with no toe-holds. The stack topples. Luckily J counts this as a story event, rather than a real-world accident for which he is responsible.)

J: (picks up Figure 2). You dummy, that didn't work. You make dumb stairs.

There is now a second character in the story.

This may be a projected version of the troublesome frustration that appeared earlier.

J (for Figure 1): Hey, no dummies here.

The first character is the voice of regulation. He speaks for not fueling the fires with insults.

(This is a key moment for intervention.)

(J's father is across the kitchen, setting the table. He holds up a fork as if it were a character.)

Father decides to join in at this point.

F (for fork): Yeah, he's right, nobody's a dumb guy. Help him do it. Put one block, then two blocks, then three blocks up.

Father latches to J's play, continuing and extending it. In a way, he is recognizing J as the person who put a stop to insulting behavior. He joins in directly, as a character, using the fork to offer building strategies, without explicitly turning into an instructor.

(J builds successively higher stacks of blocks, pushing them together until they abut, then sits back on his haunches, smiling.)

The use of the play world has been successful for both emotional regulation and cognitive scaffolding. J is delighted.

J: (calling out in the direction of his father): Hey, fork.

Father has to recognize that he is being invited into the story world as a character. He is being invited in by the small figures.

F: (goes back to the kitchen table and gets the original fork off the table and waggles it aloft, as if cheering and jumping up and down.)

F certifies J's persistence and control without ever suggesting that it might have been otherwise.

J and his father silently agree to telling a problem-resolution narrative. One character tries to build stairs. His efforts yield a sheer cliff instead. A second character tries to scale those steps and gets hurt. While enacting this story, both narrators are addressing J's own issues with quick frustration and equally quick anger. But they "discuss" this issue safely within the bracketed world of play. In the play, J triumphs over his "short fuse" by sticking to his building project, despite its difficulty. He, together with his father, examines the consequences of flaring up and calling other people names. His father joins in, in the role of a talking fork, to offer directions, support, and acknowledgment. He follows his son so closely that he is careful to use this same fork when he cheers at the end of the episode. Through mutual narrative attunement, the boy and his father enact their way toward what could be an emerging understanding that a person can feel intense anger, but regulate its expression. Although this is a relatively simple narrative, it clearly demonstrates the narrative choices and signals that allow the father to follow the son and the son to follow the father (Reese & Fivush, 1993).

This process of making and understanding emotionally important points is one of the ways in which young children and their caregivers expand their earlier, largely physical, attunement to one another's internal lives. The humorous intimacy that J experiences with his father makes it possible for him to "rewrite" his own most recent personal history as a "bad boy." In his marble and blocks play, J renarrates the story of what happens when he is frustrated. On this occasion he doesn't erupt in anger and throw objects. He jokes about using impossible materials (marbles) that no one could master. His father, in the guise of wise fork, keeps him company, roots for him, and applauds his victory over the anger that has been dogging him. J's father tracks the evaluative cues his son offers and creates a finely tuned model for what it must be like for J to teeter on the edge of anger.

It is not enough to narrate in order to make sense of affective experience. The narrative has to be heard—whether it is certified or challenged—in order to have meaning. As Shaefer writes,

> We are forever telling stories about ourselves. In telling these self-stories to *others* we may, for most purposes, be said to be performing straightforward narrative actions in saying that we also tell them to *ourselves*. However we are enclosing one story within another. This is the story that there is a self to tell something to, someone else serving as audience who is one self or one's self. When the stories we tell others about ourselves concern these other selves of ours, when we say for example "I am not master of myself," we are again enclosing one story with another. On this view, the self is a telling. From time to time and from person to person this telling varies in the degree to which it is unified, stable, and acceptable to informed observers as reliable and valid. (1992, p. 31)

Conclusion

Human beings, once they are not starving, hunt for purpose. One of those purposes (and pleasures) is making the flow of events into a life history that contains more than birthdays or official public events like kindergarten, first communion, or graduation. We all have raw materials—unruly banquets of cookies, a father playing the talking fork, or the first time we saw a younger brother. In order to hold on to these events and share them with others, we have to evaluate what happened, giving our experience the shape and weight that permit others to listen and understand why this moment in the kitchen or that moment in the hospital room mattered then and now.

The capacity to make meaning using narrative activity matures rapidly between the ages of 3 and 6. In that short period, young children's concepts of people as independent agents, or as having minds (with thoughts, wishes, feelings, and knowledge) evolve rapidly. Children's language also grows articulate. Children who have had basic life opportunities can choose words, syntax, and discourse structures that signal to an attentive listener how it feels to be in a particular situation: whether it is real or framed as a story. The language is not the same as the internal experience: words can inflate or underplay. However, the resulting narrative exchanges permit children to examine and organize their experience and they offer conversational partners the chance to hear and respond, to negotiate and extend.

NOTES

1. A more extensive discussion of Freud's observations of the boy, now known to be his grandson, and their relations to Freud's theory of the development of play can be found in Emde (1991, 1995).

2. This child is younger than the subjects in the MSSB narratives. The narrative was chosen for its theme of losing and finding from another corpus of longitudinal narrative data. Cf. Wolf, Moreton, & Camp (1994).

REFERENCES

Bamberg, M. (Ed.). (1984). Oral versions of personal experience: Three decades of narrative. Hillsdale, NJ: *Journal of narrative and life history* (entire volume). Hillsdale, NJ: Lawrence Erlbaum.

Bamberg, M. (1985). The acquisition of narrative: Learning to use language. *New Babylon Studies in the Social Sciences, 49.*

Bamberg, M. (1997). *Narrative development: Six approaches.* Hillsdale, NJ: Lawrence Erlbaum.

Bamberg, M., & Damrad-Frye, R. (1991). On the ability to provide evaluative comments: Further explorations of children's narrative competencies. *Journal of Child Language, 18,* 689–710.

Bates, E. (1985). *Language and context.* New York: Academic Press.

Bretherton, I. (1984). Representing the social world in symbolic play: Reality and fantasy. In I. Bretherton (Ed.), *Symbolic play* (pp. 1–39). New York: Academic Press.

Bretherton, I. (1990). Open communication and internal working models: Their role in attachment relationships. In R. Thompson (Ed.), *Socioemotional development. Nebraska symposium on motivation, 36* (pp. 57–113). Lincoln: University of Nebraska Press.

Bretherton, I. (1993). From dialogue to internal working models: The co-construction of self in relationships. In C. A. Nelson (Ed.), *Memory and affect in development, Minnesota symposia for child development, 26* (pp. 237–263). Hillsdale, NJ: Lawrence Erlbaum.

Bruner, J. S. (1986). *Actual minds, possible worlds.* Cambridge, MA: Harvard University Press.

Bruner, J. S. (1990). *Acts of meaning.* Cambridge, MA: Harvard University Press.

Drucker, J. (1994). The role of symbolization in the treatment of children. In A. Slade & D. P. Wolf (Eds.), *Children at play* (pp. 62–80). New York: Oxford University Press.

Dunn, J. (1988). *The beginnings of social understanding.* Cambridge, MA: Harvard University Press.

Dunn, J. (1993). *Young children's close relationships.* Newbury Park, CA: Sage.

Emde, R. N. (1991). Positive emotions for psychoanalytic theory: Surprises from infancy research and new directions. *Journal of the American Psychoanalytic Association, 39*(Suppl), 5–44.

Emde, R. N. (1992a). Individual meaning and increasing complexity; contributions of Sigmund Freud and Rene Spitz to developmental psychology. *Developmental Psychology, 28*(3), 347–359.

Emde, R. N. (1992b). Social referencing research: Uncertainty, self, and the search for meaning. In S. Feinman (Ed.), *Social referencing and the social construction of reality in infancy* (pp. 79–94). New York: Plenum Press.

Emde, R. N. (1995). Fantasy and beyond: A current developmental perspective on Freud's "Creative Writers and Daydreaming." *Monograph Series of the International Journal of Psycho-Analysis* (pp. 133–163). New Haven, CT: Yale University Press.

Fivush, R. (1994). Constructing narrative, emotion, and self in parent-child conversations about the past. In U. Neisser (Ed.), *The remembering self: Construction and accuracy in the self-narrative* (pp. 136–157). New York: Cambridge University Press.

Freud, S. (1955). *Beyond the pleasure principal. Standard Edition.* London: Hogarth Press (Imprint of Chatus and Windum).

Halliday, M. A. K. (1975). Learning how to mean: A sociolinguistic exploration in the development of language. London: Edward Arnold.

Harris, P. L. (1999). Individual differences in understanding emotion: The role of attachment status and psychological discourse. *Attachment and Human Development, 1,* 307–324.

Hasslet, B. (1986). A developmental analysis of children's event narratives. In D. G. Willis & A. Donahue (Eds.), *Contemporary issues in language and discourse processes* (pp. 87–109). Hillsdale, NJ: Lawrence Erlbaum.

Hudson, J. A. (1990). The emergence of autobiographic memory in mother-child conversation. In R. Fivush & J. A. Hudson (Eds.), *Knowing and remembering in young children* (pp. 166–196). Cambridge: Cambridge University Press.

James, H. (1912). *What Maisie knew.* New York: Charles Scribner & Sons.

Lang, M.R. (1984). *Herodotean narrative and discourse.* Cambridge, MA: Harvard University Press

Lowe, M. (1975). Trends in the development of representational play in infants from one to three years: An observational study. *Journal of Child Psychology and Psychiatry, 16,* 33–47.

Mandler, J. (1984). *Stories, scripts and scenes: Aspects of schema theory.* Hillsdale, NJ: Lawrence Erlbaum.

McCabe, A., & Peterson, C. (1991). Getting the story: A longitudinal study of parental styles in eliciting narratives and developing narrative skill. In A. McCabe & C. Peterson, (Eds.), *Developing narrative structure* (pp. 217–253). Hillsdale, NJ: Lawrence Erlbaum.

Miller, P., & Sperry, L. (1987). The socialization of anger and aggression. *Merrill-Palmer Quarterly, 33.*

Miller, P., & Sperry, L. (1988). Early talk about the past: The origins of conversational stories about personal experience. *Journal of Child Language, 15,* 293–315.

Nussbaum, M. (2002). *Upheavals of thought.* Princeton, NJ: Princeton University Press.

Passerini, L. (1992). Oral history in Italy after the Second World War: From populism to subjectivity. *International Journal of Oral History, 9*(2), 114–124.

Perry, H. S. (1987). *Psychiatrist of America: The life of Harry Stack Sullivan.* Cambridge, MA: Belknap Press.

Peterson, C., & McCabe, A. (1983). *Developmental psycholinguistics: Three ways of looking at a child's narrative.* New York: Plenum.

Peterson, C., & McCabe, A. (1985). A naturalistic study of the production of causal connectives by children. *Journal of Child Language, 12,* 145–159.

Polanyi, L. (1989). *Telling the American story.* Cambridge, MA: MIT Press.

Portelli, A. (1997). *The battle of Valle Guilia.* Madison: University of Wisconsin Press.

Reese, E., & Fivush, R. (1993). Parental styles of talking about the past. *Developmental Psychology, 29,* 596–606.

Shaefer, R. (1992). *Narration and dialogue in psychoanalysis.* New York: Basic Books.

Shank, R., & Abelson, R. (1977). *Scripts, plans, goals and understanding.* Hillsdale, NJ: Lawrence Erlbaum Associates.

Slade, A., & Wolf, D. (Eds.). (1994). *Children at play: Clinical and developmental approaches to meaning and representation.* New York: Oxford University Press.

Stein, N. (In press). *Memory of everyday and emotional events.* Hillsdale, NJ: Lawrence Erlbaum.

Stern, D. (1985). *The interpersonal world of the infant.* New York: Basic Books.

Tulchensky, D. (1995). *Young children's representations of affect.* Doctoral dissertation, Boston University.

Umiker-Sebeok, D. J. (1979). Preschool children's intraconversational narratives. *Journal of Child Language, 6,* 91–119.

Winnicott, D. W. (1971). *Playing and reality.* London: Routledge.

Wolf, D. (1982). Understanding others: A longitudinal case study of the concept of independent agency. In G. Forman (Ed.), *Action and thought: From sensorimotor schemes to symbol use* . New York: Academic Press.

Wolf, D., Moreton, J., & Camp, L. (1994). Children's acquisition of different kinds of narrative discourse: Genres and lines of talk. In J. Sokolow & C. E. Snow (Eds.), *Handbook of research in CHILDES* (pp. 286–320). Hillsdale: NJ: Lawrence Erlbaum.

Wolf, D. P., Rygh, J., & Altshuler, J. (1984). Agency and experience: Actions and states in play narratives. In I. Bretherton, (Ed.), *Symbolic play* (pp. 195–214). New York: Academic Press.

INGE BRETHERTON
DAVID OPPENHEIM

3

The MacArthur Story Stem Battery: Development, Administration, Reliability, Validity, and Reflections About Meaning

In the mid-1980s several members of the MacArthur Research Network on Early Childhood Transitions discovered a common interest in using storytelling procedures to explore young children's inner worlds. In a sense, they were building on the clinical writings of pioneers in psychoanalytic play therapy, such as A. Freud (1946), Waelder (1933), Winnicott (1958), and Erikson (1950), all of whom believed that young children's play revealed much about their psychic conflicts and their efforts to master or adapt to those conflicts. However, renewed impetus for the use of play narratives also came from a plethora of emerging findings about young children's social, emotional, and moral understanding, and the development of symbolic play, memory talk, story schemas, and scripts. These showed that preschoolers' narrative capacity and understanding of themselves and others was considerably more complex than had been assumed. Further inspiration for using storytelling methods as a window into young children's inner worlds came from an attachment study that revealed links between the quality of parent-child attachment relationships and children's narratives about a set of attachment-related pictures.

The first part of this chapter describes three pioneering studies by members of the MacArthur Network in which story beginnings (or stems), enacted with small family figures, were used to elicit play narratives from preschool children. The issues probed by these story completion tasks centered on attachment and moral conflict. However, despite the family resemblance with play therapy techniques, neither the supporting materials nor the story stems were designed to elicit the equivalent of free associations. Rather, the child was invited to address a standard set of hypothetical story problems, based on or similar to situations that he or she was likely to have encountered in everyday life.

During the second phase of the MacArthur Research Network on Early Childhood Transitions, members of the Narrative Work Group, led by Robert Emde and Dennis Wolf, decided to build on the findings from these three initial studies by creating a more comprehensive battery of story stems that reflected group members' wider interests in emotional, social, moral, and narrative development. This battery was to be incorporated into a number of longitudinal studies conducted by network members. In the second part of this chapter we describe the development of the resulting MacArthur Story Stem Battery (MSSB), followed by directions for its administration. We also discuss various approaches to coding children's responses. In the third part, we summarize empirical evidence for the developmental stability, contextual stability, and external validity of the MSSB. In the concluding section, we reflect briefly on the sense in which the themes, presentation, and organization of young children's responses to the MSSB can be said to provide a window into their thoughts and feelings about moral issues and social relationships.

Precursors of the MacArthur Story Stem Battery

In the course of pilot-testing their newly developed Attachment Story Completion Task (ASCT), Bretherton and Ridgeway learned that Buchsbaum and Emde were planning to use a similar narrative technique to tap preschoolers' internalization of moral rules and prohibitions. This led the two teams to join forces, coordinate their training methods, and administer an overlapping set of story stems to two samples of 3-year-olds (Bretherton, Biringen, Ridgeway, Maslin, & Sherman, 1989; Bretherton, Ridgeway, & Cassidy, 1990; Buchsbaum & Emde, 1990; Emde & Buchsbaum, 1990). Independently, Oppenheim, who joined the MacArthur Network later, had developed a set of separation and distress stories to assess the attachment-exploration balance in preschoolers (published in Oppenheim, 1997). Inspired by his previous clinical work with children and by attachment research, he also used a combination of enactment and narration in his story task. These three studies provided the basic framework for the development of the MSSB.

The Attachment Story Completion Task

The creation of the ASCT (Bretherton & Ridgeway, 1990) was prompted by Main, Kaplan, and Cassidy's (1985; see also Kaplan, 1987) longitudinal attachment study, but was also influenced by current research on symbolic play, event representation, and story schemas.

Related Attachment Research Main et al. had used a new version of the Separation Anxiety Test (SAT) developed by Klagsbrun and Bowlby (1976). This version of the SAT consisted of six drawings depicting severe and mild parent-child separation scenes. An interviewer provided a standard description of each picture and then asked how the child in the picture was feeling and what he or she was going to do next. Main et al. (1985) reported that 6-year-olds who produced constructive solutions in response to the separation scenarios and were able to talk about the separations with emotional openness were highly likely to have been classified as securely attached when observed in the Strange Situation (Ainsworth, Blehar, Waters, & Wall, 1978) with their mothers in infancy. The mothers of these children were able to talk coherently and openly about their own childhood attachments in response to the Adult Attachment Interview (George, Kaplan, & Main, 1985).

Based on Main et al.'s findings, slightly revised versions of the SAT, with a standard set of photographs, were used in studies with 4-year-olds (e.g., Slough & Greenberg, 1990; Shouldice & Stevenson-Hinde, 1992). These corroborated some of Main et al.'s (1985) earlier results. In addition, Cho (1994) found that children with secure SAT evaluations were judged by their mothers to be more positively responsive and less detached/distancing. Together, these studies supported the assumption that narrative responses to a semi-projective task reveal important aspects of a child's actual relationships experiences.

Reasoning that a task requiring purely verbal responses, even if supported by pictures, might be too difficult for younger preschoolers, Bretherton and Ridgeway (1990) devised a series of attachment-related story stems that were acted out with small family figures and props. Grounded in attachment theory, their story stems represented a greater variety of attachment scenarios than the SAT, including situations in which a child protagonist experienced mishaps, fear, or pain, as well as separation from and reunion with parents.

Related Research on Symbolic Play, Event Representations, and Stories In structuring the story stems and pilot-testing methods of administration, Bretherton and Ridgeway drew on available research about language acquisition, cognitive and socioemotional development, and symbolic play. Some studies of early symbolic play had demonstrated that even 18-month-old toddlers are able to enact brief pretend sequences of everyday routines (for reviews, see Bretherton, 1984; Fein, 1981). In the course of the 3rd year, as Wolf, Rygh, and Altshuler (1984) had demonstrated, 2-year-olds already begin to create simple stories with replicas of human figures and animals. Through intensive, weekly observations of the spontaneous and elicited "replica play" of nine children from 1 to 7 years old, Wolf et al. identified five increasingly complex levels of this play: (1) acting toward the figure or replica as if it were alive, (2) making it act toward and interact with other figures, (3) ascribing feelings and sensations to it, (4) endowing it with simple moral judgments, and finally (5) imbuing it with cognitions. By 2.6 years, all nine children in the Wolf et al. study had mastered the first four levels, and by 4 years all had attained the fifth level. In creating their stories, the children combined manipulation, speaking, facial expressions, and gesturing. They talked both for or through the figures, or acted as narrators by describing what the figures were doing.

In related studies, Nelson and Gruendel (1981) had shown that, by 3 years of age, children can correctly answer simple questions about "what happens when" concerning routines such as lunch at the daycare center or a birthday party. Older children added more details, but even 3-year-olds described causally related events in the appropriate order.

In designing the ASCT, Bretherton and Ridgeway were also influenced by Mandler's theorizing and research on story schemas or story grammars (for a review, see Mandler, 1983). According to Mandler, properly constructed stories contain (1) a beginning section that provides the necessary background or setting, (2) a complication or problem the protagonist faces, (3) the protagonist's attempt to solve the problem, and (4) the success or failure of the attempt (see also Stein & Glenn, 1979). The story may end with a moral. Mandler noted that both children and adults find it easier to retell stories when they follow this structure. Moreover, children or adults reinstitute the expected or canonical order on retelling a slightly scrambled story even when they are asked to retain the scrambled order (Mandler & DeForest, 1979). Along the same lines, Poulsen, Kintsch, Kintsch, and Premack (1979) reported that 4-year-olds appeared to use a story schema when asked to interpret a series of pictures conveying a reasonably complex sequence of events.

Influenced by the story grammar findings, Bretherton and Ridgeway made sure that protagonists and props were spatially laid out and moved in a manner that facilitated the children's understanding of the setting and story issue as simultaneously narrated by the interviewer. Through the invitation, "Show me and tell me what happens next," the child interviewee was then given the task of attempting a problem resolution and perhaps enacting an outcome.

The ASCT included five story stems, each focusing on a specific attachment theme (mishap, fear, pain, separation, and reunion). Clarifying prompts were to be used when the participating child was speaking for a nonspecified protagonist and when a character's action was ambiguous. If the child did not address the central issue posed by the story, or denied it, he or she was prompted with the question: "What did they do about . . . ?" The wording of this "issue" prompt was prescribed for each of the story stems so as not to suggest a specific solution.

Transcripts of the videotaped sessions included both enactments and verbatim narratives. They were evaluated for story coherence versus disjointedness, constructive versus bizarre/chaotic resolutions, and avoidance of the story issue, loosely following prior evaluations of the SAT by Kaplan (1987; see also Main et al., 1985). The separate assessments were combined into a 4-point security rating, ranging from 1 (very insecure) to 4 (very secure).

Results Children whose stories received higher security ratings were also judged as more secure based on an observed separation-reunion with their mothers at the same age, Waters and Deane's (1985) attachment Q-sort at 25 months, and the Strange Situation (Ainsworth et al., 1978) with their mothers at 18 months (Bretherton, Ridgeway, & Cassidy 1990). An insight-sensitivity scale applied to transcripts of the Parent Attachment Interview (Bretherton & Ridgeway, 1986), administered to mothers at 25 months, as well as maternal reports of family adaptability/cohesion and marital satisfaction filled out at 37 months, was also correlated with the story-based security scale (Bretherton et al., 1989). In addition, there were correlations with mother-rated child temperament and a vocabulary inventory, assessed at 25 months. In a later re-analysis evaluating the story completions in terms of their resemblance to an ideal "secure script," Waters, Rodrigues, and Ridgeway (1998) discovered significant correlations between responses to the ASCT at 3 and 4.5 years. They also reported that secure scripts rankings at 4.5 years were predicted by earlier attachment measures.

Story Assessments of Moral and Prosocial Development

Emde and Buchsbaum (who had previously used a play-therapy assessment of empathy) developed a series of analogous story stems, but with a focus on moral internalization that grew out of Emde's work on early moral emotions and children's responses to and negotiations about rules and prohibitions (e.g., Emde, Biringen, Clyman, & Oppenheim, 1991; Emde, Johnson, & Easterbrooks, 1988). Their story stems centered on moral transgression, prosocial behavior, conflict resolution, and empathy with peers.

Particularly noteworthy was Emde's creation of a moral dilemma (he called it the "Heinz dilemma" for 3-year-olds, after Kohlberg's study of moral judgment, 1971). In Emde's version, a child protagonist faced the quandary of whether and how to obey a maternal command that interfered with providing help to a hurt sibling. Buchsbaum and Emde were particularly intrigued by the child interviewees' guilt expressions as they enacted the child protagonist's transgressions against the maternal prohibition not to touch anything on the bathroom shelf in the mother figure's absence. Given his psychoanalytic background, Emde was also interested in exploring representations of oedipal feelings (see Emde, 1990). This led him to design an exclusion story stem during which the parents send the child to play in a separate room while they remain together. Buchsbaum and Emde (1990) published a detailed account of responses to the moral story stems by a group of 26 3-year-olds, reporting that most of the participating children were able to articulate coherent stories about moral rules, reciprocity, empathy, and internalized prohibitions. In a second report, they used the same data to relate children's responses to the story stems to their conception of the self (Emde & Buchsbaum, 1990).

Attachment Doll-Play Interview

Oppenheim became interested in play narratives as a window into preschool children's inner worlds through clinical work at the University of Haifa, Israel, but was also influenced by Main et al.'s (1985) attachment study using the SAT.

Oppenheim's story completion task (developed at the University of Utah in the late 1980s) presented children with a variety of parent-child separation-reunions as well as other distress scenarios. After enacting each separation and again after each reunion, child interviewees were asked to explain what the protagonist child might do in the situation and how he or she felt. Children whose responses received higher ratings of emotional openness, constructive resolutions, and quality of mother-child interactions presented in response to the story stems were also given higher ratings for self-esteem by their teachers and were observed to engage in more exploration of the classroom environment during their first 2 days at preschool (see Oppenheim, 1997).

Development of the MacArthur Story Stem Battery

Content of the MacArthur Story Stem Battery

The Narrative Work Group, chaired by Emde and Wolf and formed during the second phase of the MacArthur Research Network on Early Childhood Transitions, reflected a wide variety of interests: language and narrative development (Dennie Wolf and Judy Reilly), role understanding (Kurt Fisher and Malcolm Watson), moral development and family conflict (Robert Emde and Helen Buchsbaum), and attachment and family relationships (Inge Bretherton, David Oppenheim, and JoAnn Robinson). The group also included researchers interested in the narratives of maltreated and chronically ill children (Rob Clyman and Betsy Rubin), as well as children with behavior problems (Carolyn Zahn-Waxler). Katherine Nelson and Robin Fivush occasionally served as consultants.

The group felt sufficiently encouraged by the findings from the three precursor studies already reviewed to undertake the development of a more comprehensive battery of story stems. These were to reflect several types of family relations (parent-child, marital and peer conflict, parent-child attachment, the oedipal and other triads), moral rules (do's and don'ts), moral emotions (guilt, shame, and empathy), and competence (pride). Several story stems were directly taken over or adapted from the Bretherton-Ridgeway, Buchsbaum-Emde, and Oppenheim batteries; Bretherton (assisted by Charlynn Prentiss and Arlene Lundquist) developed several additional dilemmas with input from the MacArthur Narrative Group. The whole battery (Bretherton, Oppenheim, Buchsbaum, Emde, and the MacArthur Narrative Group, 1990) was pilot-tested by Inge Bretherton and colleagues at the University of Wisconsin and by David Oppenheim, who had joined Robert Emde at the University of Colorado Health Sciences Center. Brief descriptions of the stems and their underlying themes are presented in table 3.1. The full text of the original battery can be found in the appendix of this book.

Whereas each story stem was created with a particular theme or dilemma in mind, the open-ended nature of the task meant that children could coherently address many of the stems in more than one way. For example, in the Spilled Juice story, some child interviewees treated the spill as an accident requiring the pouring of more juice, whereas others saw it as the result of carelessness or naughtiness that required some form of discipline. Similarly, the story stem in which a child climbs a high rock at the park was resolved as a mastery story by some children who made the character proudly stand on top of the rock and proclaim "I did it," whereas others resolved it as a distress-comfort story by making the child fall off the rock, followed by parental care. One interviewee who took the mastery approach remarked that this was "a lesson story" (a parent or sibling

Table 3.1. Summary of the MacArthur Story Stems

Story stem	Brief description	Participants	Issues
1. Spilled Juice	One of the children accidentally spills the pitcher of juice at the dinner table	Two siblings, mother, father	Parent as attachment or authority figure in response to transgression; repairing "damage"
2. Lost Dog	Part I: When going outside to play, a child discovers the family dog is gone. Part II: The dog returns.	Child, mother, father, dog (in part II)	Concern for/sadness about a lost animal, joyful, angry, or avoidant reunion response
3. Mom's Headache	The mother has a headache, turns off the TV, and asks the child to be quiet. A friend comes over and asks to watch an exciting TV show (if the child says no, the friend asks again).	Mother, child, child's friend	Empathy with mother's headache/compliance with mother's request vs. compliance with friend's request, selfish pleasure; resistance to temptation
4. Gift for Mom or Dad	The child who has made a beautiful drawing at his or her preschool shows it to the parents on coming home. The interviewer asks whether the child will give the picture to mom or dad.	Child, mother, father	Does the child favor the same sex or opposite sex parent? How does child deal with triadic conflict?
5. Three's a Crowd	A child is playing with his or her friend. The child's sibling wants to play too, but the friend threatens: "I won't be your friend" anymore if the child does not exclude the younger sibling.	Two siblings, friend, parents	Loyalty to friend versus loyalty to sibling; conflict resolution by children or parental intervention
6. Hot Gravy	A child is warned by the mother not to touch the pot of gravy on the stove, but becomes impatient, touches the pot, and gets burned.	Two siblings, mother, father	Noncompliance with maternal request and parent as authority/attachment figure
7. Parental Quarrel	The mother accuses the father of having lost her keys, and argument ensues.	Mother, father, and one child	Child response to parental conflict
8. Stealing Candy	A child ask the mother for candy at the store, but she refuses. The child takes a candybar while the mother is not looking and is discovered by the cashier.	Mother, child, storekeeper	Getting caught during a transgression, owning up to a misdeed

continued

TABLE 3.1. *Continued*

Story stem	Brief description	Participants	Issues
9. Departure	The parents go on an overnight trip while the grandmother babysits.	Mother, father, two siblings, grandmother	Separation anxiety
10. Reunion	The parents return from their trip.	Mother, father, two siblings, grandmother	Reunion quality
11. Bathroom Shelf	Part I: The mother announces that she must return something to the neighbors and asks the children, who are playing, not to touch anything on the bathroom shelf. While the mother is gone, one of the children requires a bandaid from the bathroom shelf. Part II: In the second part of this story, the mother returns.	Mother, two siblings	Compliance with maternal request versus empathy with sibling
12. Climbing a Rock at the Park	At the park, the child tells the parents that she or he will climb to the top of the very high rock. The mother warns the child to be careful.	Two siblings, mother, father	Child mastery (accident, parental comforting)
13. Child Exclusion by Parents	Mother and father are sitting on the family couch, talking. They tell the child they would like to spend some time alone and ask the child to play in his/her room. After the child has left (if necessary with assistance from the interviewer), the parents kiss.	Mother, father, one child	Child's response to being excluded from the parental dyad (compliance with parents' request)
14. The Cookie Jar	One of the siblings takes a cookie from the jar in the kitchen and is reminded by the other sibling that the parents said not to take cookies. The first sibling then asks "please don't tell mom or dad about it." At this point, the parents enter.	Two siblings, mother, father	Honesty or compliance with rule versus loyalty to sibling (or empathy with sibling who might get punished otherwise, tattling)

shows the protagonist how to climb the rock successfully next time). The "Mom's Headache" dilemma also gave rise to dual interpretations. Some children viewed the mother's request for quiet as a request for obedience (or occasion for punishment if the request was not heeded), whereas other interviewees invented solutions suggesting the child protagonist's empathy for the mother. We will return to this issue when discussing the diverse coding procedures used to analyze the story completions.

Directions for Administering the MacArthur Story Stem Battery

Rapport It is vital that the interviewer establish good rapport with the child interviewee through playful interaction before engaging him or her in the story completion task. For shy children, this will take longer than for sociable children. When the child is brought to a university playroom by a parent or when the task is administered at home, rapport is best established in the presence of the parent, though the parent normally leaves before the story completion task begins. If the task is administered in a separate room at the child's preschool or daycare center, making friends with the child in the classroom, or participating in classroom activities for a while, is highly advisable. Proper training of the interviewer(s) is crucial. We strongly recommend that researchers new to this procedure consult others who have already used the task and that only skilled interviewers with experience in interacting with young children be asked to administer it.

Materials Originally we used "realistic, bendable" doll families. Such dolls can be obtained through toy stores or school supply firms. In pilot-testing the MSSB and during some of the subsequent studies, "Duplo" figures were used, while in a more recent study Bretherton employed a small bear family. For older preschoolers and school-age children, "Playmobil" figures are appropriate. The precise appearance of the family figures is less important than that they are realistic enough to suggest their identity: mother, father, grandmother, older and younger siblings (two boys or two girls, depending on the gender of the child who is interviewed), additional children to serve as friends, and a family dog. It is important that the figures can stand up and that they match the child's racial background if human figures are used.

The "scenery" props should be easy to handle and should suggest the intended setting without being overly elaborate. For example, in the story in which a child accidentally spills juice at the dinner table, we no longer ask the child to set the table with miniature dishes and silverware (as we did in its first implementation) but to use only a pitcher. Likewise, the family car used in the departure-reunion story should not be a vehicle with shiny, turning wheels that may attract undue fascination. A small box with painted wheels is sufficient, though it is important that the whole family can fit inside it. A piece of green felt is appropriate to suggest the lawn in the park, but provision of miniature trees or swings would be distracting. For the rock (a required prop), we chose a sponge cut into the shape of a rock. A piece of stone might have been more realistic but could have represented a safety hazard.

It is also important to follow the layout of the props and positioning/orientation of the figures recommended in the manual. In addition to making it easier for the child to follow the story line, this facilitates interpretation of a child's responses. For example, in the Lost Dog story, the returning dog should be placed at a distance from the child figure, so that the child interviewee can enact unambiguous proximity seeking by the dog to the child figure and vice versa.

Warm-Up The task is administered at a child-sized table, with the child and tester sitting opposite, at right angles, or beside one another. To begin the task, the interviewer introduces and names the family members one by one and then checks that the child can recall the identity of each figure. The props for the warm-up story (a small table and birthday cake) are then placed on the table, followed by acting out the warm-up story stem. This first story stem is not considered part of the battery proper but is meant to provide an opportunity to convey to the child what is expected of him or her. We chose a birthday story as introduction because most children 3 and older are able to describe a birthday sequence (Nelson & Gruendel, 1981). After setting up and narrating the birthday stem, the interviewer invites the child to "show me and tell me what happens next." If the child does not initially respond by spontaneously acting out a birthday scenario or responds only minimally, the interviewer should model verbal descriptions of what the story characters are doing (e.g., "they are eating cake") and character speech (e.g., making the child protagonist say: "That cake tastes yummy."). However, no such modeling should occur during the task proper.

The interviewer should have memorized and practiced the story scripts sufficiently well to be able to present them with expressiveness and without having to refer to a "crib-sheet" more than occasionally. The MSSB task was not designed as a test-like procedure during which the interviewer asks questions and the child provides brief answers. To create the appropriate atmosphere for the task, the interviewer should convey interest in the child's stories by tone, gesture, and the provision of psychological "space." We have noticed that the narrative frame established in the first few moments is likely to influence the rest of the task. A patient, attentive, and even curious stance by the interviewer is most likely to encourage the child to become engaged.

After the child has completed or has actively participated in completing the birthday story (i.e., has made the figures move, has talked for or about them), the interviewer requests that the child set the figures back in their original position at the side of the table, saying: "Can you get them ready for the next story?" For each of the subsequent story stems, the interviewer first creates the setting by bringing out the relevant props and placing them in accordance with the spatial layout suggested in the MSSB manual while describing the scene. The interviewer then enacts the remainder of the stem in accordance with the script, always followed by the invitation: "Show me and tell me what happens next."

Interviewer Reactions to the Child's Story Completions Close attention should be paid to how the interviewer reacts to the child's story completions. Although we gave approving feedback during earlier studies, we now refrain from comments such as "That was a great story" because interviewers will find it difficult to use such remarks after a child creates a very violent or disjointed story, and such comments may direct children to certain topics or themes. It is especially important to retain a nonjudgmental stance when the child enacts highly negative or chaotic stories that end with catastrophes. We have observed that untrained interviewers sometimes respond to such stories with unhelpful comments such as "No, they wouldn't do that!"

An alternative approach is to reinforce the storytelling act rather than the story. For example, comments such as "I can see you are really working hard on this story" can be useful following both negative and positive stories. In some cases, particularly in studies of children from clinical or high-risk populations, additional reinforcers have been employed. For example, some researchers have found stickers useful in encouraging cooperation (note, however, that there are no studies showing how these forms of encouragement influence story completions).

Prompts Some children intervene in the presentation of one or more story stems (see vignette in chapter 8, for example). If this occurs, the interviewer can tactfully say, "I'll tell the beginning and you get to finish it." Prompts during the child's response are required if a child moves the family figures in ways that are ambiguous. For example, when a child moves two figures against each other and it is unclear if hitting or hugging is meant, the interviewer may ask, "What are they doing?" Similarly, if the child speaks for an unidentified protagonist, the interviewer can ask, "Who said that?" If the child replies, "I did," the interviewer can say, "Who in the story said that?" The "who" prompt is also helpful if the child interviewee uses pronouns such as "he went to sleep" without designating an actor or acting out the event. Occasionally, a child may ask for an additional prop or a prop used in a previous story. If this occurs, the interviewer can say, "Just pretend." If the child insists, the interviewer might say, "You'll get to play with it after we finish the stories." The prompt "anything else?" can be used if the child's initial response is very brief.

Each story stem has one prompt that should be used if the child fails to address the main story issue. The reason for this prompt is twofold. Several attachment studies have shown that consistent avoidance of the central story issue may be related to insecure-avoidant mother-child attachment (e.g., Kaplan, 1987). This avoidance can take a number of different forms, ranging from "I don't know" to denying that the problematic event happened, commenting on the physical properties of the props instead of enacting a meaningful resolution, or ignoring the stem and creating an unrelated story completion. Using the issue prompts twice (if necessary) allows the interviewer to ascertain the extent to which a child is unwilling to address the story problem. Alternatively, if the child actually produces an appropriate resolution after prompting, we have greater certainty that she or he has grasped the main point of the story. The difference between spontaneous and prompted completions can be taken into account during coding.

Repeating the Child's Utterances It is often useful to repeat what children, especially young children, say during the narratives. Doing so not only conveys to them that they are heard but also helps transcribers understand narratives spoken in a quiet or unclear voice. Most young children accept these repetitions and respond to them favorably. However, with some older or very articulate children, using this technique can be awkward and may even become an interruption. These children are also typically quite clear in their narration, rendering repetitions unnecessary.

Ending a Story Many children, especially children 4 and older, will end stories themselves by saying "all done" or "the end." If the child does not do so, the interviewer must judge when it is time to move on to the next story stem. Several criteria may be used to facilitate this decision. For example, if the enactment becomes perseverative, the interviewer can ask, "Is this the end?" If the child has resolved the issue and begins to enact a lengthy unrelated tale, the interviewer can ask, "How does this story end?" This question is successful most of the time, though one creative child replied to this question, "This story never ends." To lead into the next story stem, the interviewer may say, "Now I have an idea for a different story" or "Are you ready for something different now?"

There are different ways of making the figures move "off stage" when they are not needed for the next story. The interviewer may say, "The grandma is going home now" or "For this story, Jane is going to her friend's house." Alternatively, the interviewer may just remove the figure, saying, "The grandma isn't in this story," and place the figure in the box where the props are kept, usually on the floor beside the interviewer's seat.

Wind-Down After all of the stories have been presented, the interviewer invites the child to have the family engage in a fun activity. At this point, the child interviewee is told that he or she can play with any figure or prop he or she wants. The purpose of the "wind-down" story is to provide a pleasant and relaxed ending for the session during which no other specific demands are made of the child.

Standardization and Variation The MSSB was not developed as a standardized test. Although we have written a set of standard instructions, the usefulness of the battery is not, in our view, based on literal adherence to a set of strict rules, but rather on following the battery's spirit or underlying aim of facilitating storytelling.

Some researchers have omitted a few of the stems, others have developed additional stems tailored to their particular aims, or they have "mixed and matched" stems from the original Bretherton and Ridgeway or Buchsbaum and Emde studies with those of the MSSB or story stems developed by other members of the MacArthur Narrative Group (e.g., Zahn-Waxler et al., 1994). We strongly recommend, however, that if additional stems are created for particular purposes, they should be pilot-tested carefully, both in terms of the script and the spatial layout presented during the enactment.

If changes in procedure are made, they should be implemented consistently and described carefully. Ultimately, the validity of a task of this nature depends on (1) how well the story scripts are constructed, (2) how well the task is administered, (3) what analysis procedures are used, and (4) what its external correlates turn out to be.

Coding Approaches

Before considering evidence for the external validity of the MSSB, we briefly describe the approaches researchers have used to evaluate children's performances in response to the task. When relevant, we include findings from the precursor studies.

Approaches to coding have emphasized four domains: (1) story content or themes, (2) theme organization or coherence, (3) emotional expression, and (4) interaction with the interviewer (see Page, 2001, for a review). A few studies have used more global assessments.

All of these approaches do not assess success or failure, but rather evaluate how the child interviewee chose to interpret and finish the story. For this reason, stories with a moral focus are not only examined in terms of whether the moral issue presented in the stem was meaningfully addressed or resolved. Rather, if the child enacted attachment themes during moral stories or moral themes during attachment stories, this can also enter into the overall assessment.

Inventories of Content Themes and Face Validity Both Buchsbaum and Emde (1990) and Bretherton, Prentiss, and Ridgeway (1990) created inventories of children's responses to their respective sets of stems, detailing agents, recipients, and their specific enacted or narrated actions. The fact that most of the 36- or 37-month-olds participating in these two precursor studies were able to produce relevant and comprehensible resolutions to the story stems provided preliminary evidence for the face validity of the story completion procedure. However, we regard 36 months as the lower age boundary for the MSSB.

Theme-Based Coding Systems JoAnn Robinson and colleagues, in consultation with the MacArthur Narrative Group, were charged with designing a coding system specifically tailored to the MSSB. After viewing a number of MSSB videotapes, they created a list of common themes related to the issues probed by the various stems (moral rules, prosocial behavior, empathy, exclusion, attachment, parental nurturance and nonnurturance, and conflict/aggression; see Robinson, Mantz-Simmons, & Macfie, 1992, and discussion in chapter 4 here). All themes, except those concerning parental nurturance, were coded without regard to agent and recipient, thus yielding an overall score for the specific theme whether the behavior was directed by the mother figure toward a child, a child toward the mother, or two children against each other. Each theme was tallied no more than once per story. Theme codes were then added across the story set, yielding a maximum score of 12 for each theme. Page and Bretherton (1993) developed a related coding manual for MSSB and ASCT stories that focused primarily on dyadic and family interaction themes derived from attachment theory (mother-child, father-child, child-child, and mother-father interactions). In this coding manual, the absolute frequency of themes across story stems is retained. A system by Hodges, Hillman, and Steele (2002) contains similar theme codes but with a greater emphasis on clinical evaluations (see appendix of chapter 13).

Process Coding Given the important role of story coherence in prior attachment studies based on narrative approaches (e.g., Main et al., 1985; Bretherton Ridgeway, & Cassidy, 1990; Cassidy, 1988), Robinson et al. also developed a narrative coherence rating for the MSSB. In addition, because the child's rapport with the interviewer might affect the content of his or her story completions, they devised scales to assess aspects of the child's social interchanges with the interviewer. Finally, in response to group members' interest in emotion regulation, the Robinson team developed scales to assess children's emotional expressions of joy, anger, concern, sadness, and anxiety. The emotion scale was further developed and elaborated by Warren, Oppenhein, and Emde (1996, see chapter 5).

The coding system by Hodges, Hillman, and Steele (2002) cited previously also proposed a number of process ratings, such as premature foreclosure, or no closure, changing motivational constrainst (avoidance), and sudden unmotivated plot shifts from constructive to destructive and vice versa. Another coding system that focused primarily on narrative process was created by a group of clinicians based in England (Jonathan Hill at the University of Liverpool and Peter Fonagy at University College London) and the United States (Daniel Hoover at the Menninger Clinic) who worked in consultation with Robert Emde and JoAnn Robinson. Their scales (Hill, Hoover, & Taliaferro, 1999) have undergone extensive reliability testing and include coherence and avoidance, as well as affect regulation, escalation of aggression, and danger situations, as well as events without agents. Narrative style is evaluated in terms of elaboration, embellishment, and sudden shifts in the narrative. The team also developed several performance scales designed to capture the child's transactions with the interviewer, including attention, oppositional behavior, and controlling behavior (see chapter 9).

Comparison of the Robinson et al. Coding System with Other Approaches. In one of the initial MSSB studies with 45 upper-middle-class preschoolers from two-parent families, Bretherton, Winn, Page, Macfie, and Walsh (1993) compared the Robinson et al. system with a more clinically based coding system devised primarily by Page and a second theme-based system devised primarily by Winn. Winn's system differed from Robinson et al.'s in that themes were tallied separately for each protagonist and counted in terms of absolute frequency across stories.

Comparisons among the resulting codes yielded correlations in the .6 to .7 range when related domains were compared. For example, theme-based story scores of parental nurturance assessed with the Robinson system were not only highly correlated with Page's clinical rating of parental nurturance but also with Winn's frequency score of mother and father nurturance themes.

Perhaps more interesting, children who told disorganized stories (rated according to Page's clinical system) received significantly higher scores for all negative themes, including anger, punishment, aggression, verbal conflict, self-blame, and dishonesty, whether assessed with the Robinson et al. or Winn systems. Disorganization ratings were also correlated with interviewees' facial expressions of distress and concern, assessed with the Robinson et al. emotion scale. In contrast, story presentations rated as more avoidant (based on Page's clinical assessment) were negatively correlated with almost all positive theme scores, whether they were tallied once per story or in terms of absolute frequency across stories. In contrast, narrative coherence from the Robinson et al. system was positively correlated with all prosocial and other positive themes, whether assessed with the Robinson or Winn systems. Finally, Robinson's narrative coherence ratings were significantly correlated with Page's clinical assessment of positive family interaction. These analyses reveal that interpersonal themes, theme organization, coherence, manner of responding, emotional expressivity, and rapport with the interviewer turn out to be closely intertwined in children's story completions, issues to which we will return later.

Global Assessments In a precursor study based on attachment theory, Bretherton, Ridgeway, & Cassidy (1990) developed a security rating scale for children's responses to story stems. This approach has been used to code children's responses to the MSSB in a more recent study by Heller (2000). Security scores were created by averaging scales for narrative coherence, constructiveness of resolutions (including positive relationship themes), and relationship with the interviewer. Another elaborate system for deriving security scores from ASCT responses (validated against the Strange Situation and the AAI) was developed by Gloger-Tippelt, Gomille, Koenig, and Vetter (2002). Yet a further system for the evaluation of attachment stories from the ASCT and MSSB was the development of a 65-item Q-sort. Theoretically based mega-items from this Q-sort predicted maternal AAI classifications (Miljkovitch, Pierrehumbert, Bretherton, & Halfon, 2002).

We suggest that the choice of coding method be governed by the specific aims of each particular study, as well as the age of the child participants and the size of the sample. Significant results have been obtained with all of the coding systems described, but narrative coherence seems to be a particularly telling indicator of the child's adjustment, as are highly aggressive or chaotic themes or representations. In terms of evaluating the quality of resolutions and coherence, it may be particularly useful to develop codes for the evaluation of separate story stems (see chapter 8).

Consistency, Developmental, and Validity Issues

Cross-Contextual Consistency To our knowledge, only two studies have compared story completions assessed at home and in the laboratory. Buchsbaum and Emde (1990), using a precursor of the MSSB, administered 4 story stems in the child's home and 11 stems at a university playroom. Of the 4 stories presented at home, 3 were repeated at the university. For the repeated stories, children tended to choose the same actors to complete the stems, but postresolution enactments were not identical (i.e., the same protagonist might clean up the spilled juice; subsequent family interaction might be different). Buchsbaum and Emde reasoned that complete correspondence should not be expected and might actually index stereotypic rather than creative responding.

Oppenheim, Emde, and Wamboldt (1996) approached the issue of cross-situational consistency by developing alternate forms of two MSSB narratives (Spilled Juice and Exclusion). These alternate stems were administered during a home visit 1 or 2 weeks after a laboratory observation during which the entire MSSB had been administered. The consistency issue was examined, not by asking whether children told similar stories in different settings, but rather by examining cross-context correlations of narrative coherence and of prosocial, aggressive, and discipline themes assessed with Robinson et al.'s coding system. Relationships were significant, but very modest, ranging from .23 to .31, as might be expected based on the small number of story-stems obtained at home (two). Further investigations of test-retest stability are required, and such efforts have to be based on developing alternate versions of the entire battery of story stems to rule out the possibility that children remember the stems and their completions from the previous session. In our experience, such remembering is possible even when the assessments are a year apart, and some children have explicitly told us they remember the stories.

Developmental Changes Bretherton, Prentiss, and Ridgeway (1990) compared responses by 25 children at 3 and 4.5 years of age, using one of the MSSB precursors. They reported that the content of the resolutions presented by the 4.5-year-olds was not strikingly different from that of 3-year olds (e.g., at both ages the child protagonist who spilled the juice might be punished, or the spill cleaned up and more juice poured). Rather, older children's narratives/enactments were more complex in role portrayals (more frequent inclusion of the father figure, quasi-parental behavior by the older toward the younger child, more father-mother interactions not involving the child figures, and use of grandmother figure as a substitute parent rather than playmate) and the enactment of more and longer conversations among the protagonists. In addition, older children more often ended their stories with some form of family togetherness (eating, sleeping, or going on a trip together). In their reanalysis of transcripts from the Bretherton, Ridgeway, & Cassidy study, Waters et al. (1998) documented that the number of idea units used increased significantly from 3 to 4.5 years of age.

For the complete MSSB, Oppenheim, Emde, and Warren (1997) reported two developmental findings concerning content themes. In their examination of mother representations at child age 4.5 and 5.5 years, they noted an increase in positive and disciplinary representations with a concomitant decrease in negative representations. This corroborated Bretherton et al.'s (1993) MSSB cross-sectional findings with 3-, 4-, and 5-year-olds that had also reported an age increase in positive themes.

In another study, Oppenheim, Emde, Hasson, and Warren (1997) examined the development of preschoolers' capacity to acknowledge moral dilemmas. Analyses were based on the three MSSB narratives in which the child figures are placed in a moral quandary whose resolution requires holding both sides of the dilemma in mind simultaneously (Bathroom Shelf, Mom's Headache, and Three's a Crowd). In Bathroom Shelf, this involves attending to the maternal prohibition not to touch anything on the bathroom shelf in the mother's absence and to the sibling's need for a band-aid, located on that very shelf. Oppenheim et al. noted a steady increase from 3.5 to 4.5 years, and again from 4.5 and 5.5 years, in the percentage of child interviewees who acknowledged both sides or horns of the dilemma (e.g., 32%, 53%, and 85% for the three ages, respectively, with regard to the Bathroom Shelf story stem). The same pattern held for all three dilemmas, although preschoolers appeared to find some dilemmas more difficult to resolve than others. The study also showed that the standard issue prompt, given to children who did not spontaneously acknowledge both horns of the dilemma, enabled a significantly higher number of children to do so.

Given these findings, we concur with Oppenheim and Waters (1995), who recommend that researchers using story completion tasks during the preschool years pay closer attention to developmental changes in storytelling and perspective-taking skills. Developments in understanding psychological causality, role-taking, and false beliefs, they note, can affect the structure, complexity, and content of the stories children produce in response to MSSB and similar story stems. To mention just one example from Bretherton's unpublished data, 3-year-olds presented with the ASCT Monster in the Bedroom story stem tend to have a parent figure dispose of the monster, whereas 4.5-year-olds often make the parent figure explain to the child protagonist that the supposed monster is "only a blanket" or "not real." Both resolutions are coherent and depict parental reassurance and protection of the child, but the performances of the 4.5-year-olds indicates an understanding that the story protagonist can have false beliefs, an emerging ability recently investigated in "theory of mind" studies (Wimmer & Perner, 1983). Given that the cognitive complexity and coherence of story completions increase with age, and that a number of studies have included mixed age groups, we need careful developmental MSSB analyses. Many of the original story stems seem to remain fruitful elicitors of interesting narratives (Granot, & Mayseless, 2001), though some researchers have invented new stems specifically designed for older children (e.g., the New MSSB; Warren, Emde, & Sroufe, 2000).

Longitudinal Stability Waters et al. (1998) reported significant though moderate longitudinal correlations between assessments at 3 and 4.5 years with a precursor of the MSSB. For the complete MSSB, Oppenheim, Emde, and Warren (1997) found moderate correlations between aggregate scores of positive, negative, and disciplinary mother-child themes. In a second study, Oppenheim, Nir, Warren, and Emde (1997) obtained moderate longitudinal correlations between ratings for narrative coherence, investment in performance, and relationship with the interviewer ratings, as well as prosocial and aggressive themes, based on the Robinson et al. coding system (see also chapter 8).

Gender In their cross-sectional MSSB study of 3-, 4-, and 5-year-olds, Bretherton et al. (1993) noted that girls enacted significantly more prosocial and conflict resolution themes, whereas boys incorporated more aggressive themes into their story completions. In their longitudinal MSSB study, Oppenheim, Nir, et al. (1997) also found that girls enacted more prosocial and fewer aggressive themes than boys, but only at the age of 4.5 years. At 5.5 years, these differences had disappeared. Oppenheim et al. additionally reported that girls received higher ratings for relatedness to the interviewer (based on the Robinson et al. coding system) at both ages. Von Klitzing, Kelsay, Emde, Robinson, and Schmitz reported more aggressive themes for boys than girls, but only girls' aggressive themes predicted concurrent preschool behavior problems. In a recent study of children from divorced families, Page and Bretherton (2000) also noted that girls and boys differed in terms of story themes (girls depicted less aggression and more prosocial themes). In addition, they found that representations of father-nurturance by boys and girls had different external correlates, predicting positive outcomes for boys and negative outcomes for girls. Similarly, Steele, Woolgar, Yabsley, Fonagy, Johnson, and Croft (chapter 9) discovered interaction effects when boys' and girls' prosocial MSSB themes were compared with maternal responses to the Adult Attachment Interview (AAI; George et al., 1985). Boys whose mothers received insecure AAI classifications had low prosocial scores, whereas girls with mothers classified as insecure had high prosocial scores. Boys and girls with intermediate scores had mothers whose AAI was classified as secure-autonomous. These findings highlight the need for more attention to gender differences and interaction effects in analyses of story completions in relation to external correlates.

Language Competence Whether or not story completions are correlated with language assessments may turn on how story completions are coded. The security scores devised for Bretherton, Ridgeway, & Cassidy's (1990) original ASCT study of 3-year-olds were moderately correlated with vocabulary size at 25 months. However, the scriptedness coding applied to the same data by Waters et al. (1998) was not correlated with verbal ability. In their MSSB study, Bretherton et al. (1993) found that a verbal comprehension test was moderately related to children's positive theme scores but controlling for language did not affect the correlations with other measures. Oppenheim, Emde, and Wamboldt (1996) and Oppenheim, Emde, Hasson, and Warren (1997) also discovered some evidence for links between MSSB scores and linguistic competence and therefore controlled for language competence in regression analyses. Receptive vocabulary was associated with narrative coherence and discipline themes at 3.5 years, whereas expressive vocabulary was moderately related to narrative coherence at 4.5 and 5.5 years. At 5.5 years, expressive vocabulary was also correlated with positive representations and aggressive theme aggregates (negative correlation in the latter case).

Temperament Bretherton et al. (1993) found that child temperament rated by mother and father, using the Colorado Temperament Inventory (Rowe & Plomin, 1977), showed significant correlations with MSSB responses. Theme scores for empathy, affection, exclusion, guilt/reparation, conflict resolution, dishonesty, aggression, and conflict escalation (Robinson et al. coding system) were negatively related to maternal and paternal shyness ratings of the child. The Robinson et al. ratings for responsiveness to the examiner were also negatively correlated with shyness, whereas concern and distress expressions were positively correlated with shyness. Only sporadic correlations were noted with other CCTI scales. For example, temperament ratings for activity level were correlated with aggressive and accident themes. (See chapter 7, by Aksan and Goldsmith, for further data on the connections between child temperament and narrative responses to story stems.)

Variations and Adaptations of the MSSB and Related Batteries As already noted, some studies using the MSSB have added or removed particular story stems, although the precise substitutions and subtractions are not always clearly indicated. For example, Oppenheim, Nir, et al. (1997) omitted two of the stems from the full MSSB. Toth, Cicchetti, Macfie, Manghan, and VanMeenen (2000) used the ASCT with maltreated children at two ages but coded it with the Robinson et al. MSSB coding system. They report a decrease in moral themes in maltreated children from 3 to 5 years old, whereas the reverse was found for matched nonmaltreated children. Steele and colleagues (see chapter 9, this volume), who selected only three of the MSSB story stems, report that theme codes were meaningfully related to the AAI scales. In short, the MSSB and precursors yield correlations with other assessments of interpersonal relatedness and adjustment, even when only a subset of the story stems is used.

Yet other investigators have added their own special purpose stems to the MSSB or ASCT-MSSB combinations. For example, Vandell created two day-care-related stems as an addition to the ASCT that were administered to a subset of the children participating in the National Child Care Study (see San Juan, Bretherton, & Vandell, 2002). The authors report correlations with observed maternal sensitivity. Bretherton and Page (1993) adapted a combination of ASCT and MSSB story stems for use with children of divorce by portraying mother and father as living in two different houses, symbolized by pieces of felt. They documented significant associations of story themes with preschool social competence (Page & Bretherton, 2001). Grych, Wachsmuth-Schaefer, and Klockow (2002) created a set of family conflict stems adapted from the MSSB, and found correlations between children's conflict stories and assessments of actual parental discord. Poehlmann and Huennekens (2003) adapted the ASCT for children of incarcerated mothers, administering a slightly adapted version of the story stems twice. In one version, the caregiving parent figure represented the child's current foster mother (aunt, grandmother, nonrelated foster mother), and in the second version the caregiving figure was specifically said to be the child's own mother. Poehlmann and Huennekens reported that children's story completions differed significantly, depending on which figure was used as caregiver. Hodges, Steele, Hillmann, and Henderson (chapter 13) compared MSSB story completions with additional story stems (the Little Pig Stems; Hodges, Hillman, & Steele, 2002). They found both story sets useful in the clinical assessment of maltreated children. Finally, Guenter, Di Gallo, and Stohrer (2000) created a parallel set of 10 story stems, designed to provide an alternative to the MSSB. When administered to 8- to 12-year-olds, the results in terms of external correlated were equivalent (Aurnhammer & Koch, 2001).

Finally, the successful use of the MSSB and ASCT have encouraged others to devise additional narrative techniques. For example, Murray, Woolgar, Briers, and Hipwell (1999) asked the child to use a doll's house to enact a "mean story" and a "nice story" about the mother and father figures. Green, Stanley, Smith, and Goldwyn (2000) devised an emotional induction technique to ensure that the child interviewee was engaged in the protagonist's distress before inviting the child to complete the story stem.

We welcome such variations and adaptations of the story completion procedure, but we recommend that new stories be carefully pilot-tested in terms of the script and the spatial placement of figures and props. We also recommend that the story scripts, whether based on the MSSB manual or additional story stems, be carefully followed if comparability with other studies is desired. In addition, we encourage researchers to report the specific stories they have included, excluded, adapted, or added.

Tasks for the Future: Reflections on Meaning

As our review and other chapters in this volume show, a fairly extensive and rapidly growing body of evidence now links the content and organization of young children's story completions about family relationships and moral issues to other aspects of their social development, especially their relationships with parents and peers. However, we still have much to learn about the more specific ways in which children's responses to the MSSB and related story tasks can be said to reflect their inner life (for discussions, see Bretherton, 1993; Emde & Spicer, 2000; Oppenheim & Waters, 1995).

Closer examination of the story transcripts themselves has already proved revealing (e.g., Buchsbaum, Toth, Clyman, Cicchetti, & Emde, 1993; Bretherton, Munholland, & Page, 1999; Herman & Bretherton, 2001; Page & Bretherton, 2002, in press). Analyses show that children draw on a variety of sources when they engage in emotional meaning making through storytelling. That the stems evoke autobiographical memories is evident from comments that many children intersperse in their narratives, such as "My mommy does that when I fall down," after enacting a story in which a hurt child is comforted by the mother figure. Other story completions suggest that children are defensively distancing themselves from the story problem (by refusing to become engaged in the story, or by denying or ignoring that the problematic event occurred), and yet others are very obviously not literal replays of experienced interactions of self with parents, siblings, or peers but may represent hoped-for events (e.g., the reunification of divorced parents) or feared scenarios (e.g., the child figure is eaten by a monster). Finally, some superficially bizarre or catastrophic representations (e.g., family members being violently tossed about by tornadoes, objects crushing a protagonist, vehicles spinning out of control) may represent metaphoric depictions of emotions aroused by the story problems, though without clinical probing this is difficult to show unambiguously. These and related matters are discussed in some detail in chapter 11for children who have suffered maltreatment.

Further insights into the meaning of children's story completions may also come from studies that combine several different narrative techniques. For example, Oppenheim, Nir, et al. (1997) compared children's resolutions of MacArthur story stems with co-constructed mother and child play narratives, and Heller (2000) contrasted MSSB responses and mother-child talk about remembered events based on Fivush (1993).

Finally, the sense in which story completions index children's actual attachment and peer relationships also needs further clarification. Despite significant correlations with child adjustment and security of attachment reviewed, the stories children produce in response to the MSSB and related tasks cannot be interpreted as direct portrayals of experienced relationships. Rather, as Oppenheim and Waters (1995) suggested, individual differences in children's growing ability to share, co-construct, and resolve narratives about emotionally laden personal topics with others may be mediated by emotionally open styles of communication learned in the family (see also Bretherton, 1990, 1993). In the MSSB and related tasks, the co-constructive aspect may be less obvious than in other studies that have examined more active dyadic narrative co-constructions by children and parents (Oppenheim, Nir, et al., 1997; Etzion-Carasso & Oppenheim, 2000; also see chapter 18). Nevertheless the interviewer's engaged attention and encouragement of the child through prompts makes the MSSB, too, a co-constructive task.

Some children have free access to their representations and can therefore create and co-create spontaneous, coherent, and constructive resolutions for the emotionally charged problems posed by the story stems. These children tend to have experienced open and supportive communication patterns with parents and to engage in prosocial behavior with peers. Other children have a propensity to narrate and enact bizarre, destructive, incoherent story completions or, alternatively, to respond to emotionally charged story stems with avoidance. These children tend to have had a history of emotional communication difficulties with parents and problems in relating to peers. The content of children's stories may be inspired by and drawn from many sources. While it does not reflect literal reality, it reflects children's affective reality through the coherent organization of themes, constructiveness of resolutions, and ability to collaborate with the interviewer with emotional openness.

In conclusion, findings obtained with the MSSB and related instruments have begun to provide many insights into the creative processes of young children's meaning making through stories. In addition, they have revealed linkages with communication patterns in actual relationships. We hope that the MSSB and its variants will continue to be helpful resources for developmental psychologists and child clinicians in their future explorations of both topics.

REFERENCES

Ainsworth, M. D. S., Blehar, M. C., Waters, E., & Wall, S. (1978). *Patterns of attachment: A psychological study of the strange situation.* Hillsdale, NJ: Erlbaum.

Aurnhammer, M. C., & Koch, I. N. (2001). *"Da wollte der Barney mal alleine spazierengehen" Untersuchung der Spielnarrative 8–12 jaehriger Schueler und Schuelerinnen mit einer deutschen Fassgung der MacArthur Story Stem Battery.* Thesis, University of Tuebingen, Germany.

Bretherton, I. (1984). Representing the social world in symbolic play: Reality and fantasy. In I. Bretherton (Ed.), *Symbolic play: The development of social understanding* (pp. 3–41). New York: Academic Press.

Bretherton, I. (1990). Open communication and internal working models: Their role in attachment relationships. In R. Thompson (Ed.), *Nebraska Symposium on Motivation, vol. 36: Socioemotional development* (pp. 57–113). Lincoln, NE: University of Nebraska Press.

Bretherton, I. (1993). From dialogue to internal working models: The co-construction of self in relationships. In C. A. Nelson (Ed.), *Memory and affect in development, Minnesota symposia for child development* (vol. 26, pp. 237–263). Hillsdale, NJ: Lawrence Erlbaum.

Bretherton, I., Biringen, Z., Ridgeway, D., Maslin, C., & Sherman, M. (1989). Attachment: The parental perspective. *Infant Mental Health Journal, 10,* 203–221.

Bretherton, I., Munholland, K. A., & Page, T. (1999). *"He lives with them now": Divorce-related themes in preschoolers' family story completions.* Paper presented at the biennial meeting of the Society for Research in Child Development, Albuquerque, NM.

Bretherton, I., Oppenheim, D., Buchsbaum, H., Emde, R. N., & the MacArthur Narrative Group. (1990). *The MacArthur Story Stem Battery (MSSB).* Unpublished manual, University of Wisconsin-Madison.

Bretherton, I., & Page, T. (1993). *The expanded attachment story completion task adapted for children of divorce.* Unpublished manuscript, University of Wisconsin-Madison.

Bretherton, I., Prentiss, C., & Ridgeway, D. (1990). Children's representations of family relationships in a story completion task at 37 and 54 months. In I. Bretherton & M. Watson (Eds.), *New directions in child development:* Vol. 48. *Children's perspectives on the family* (pp. 85–105). San Francisco: Jossey-Bass.

Bretherton, I., & Ridgeway, D. (1986). *The parent attachment interview.* Unpublished manuscript, University of Wisconsin-Madison.

Bretherton, I., & Ridgeway, D. (1990). Story completion task to assess children's internal working models of child and parent in the attachment relationship. In M. Greenberg, D. Cicchetti, & E. M. Cummings (Eds.), *Attachment in the preschool years* (pp. 300–305). Chicago, IL: University of Chicago Press.

Bretherton, I., Ridgeway, D., & Cassidy, J. (1990). Assessing internal working models of the attachment relationship. In M. T. Greenberg, D. Cicchetti, & E. M. Cummings (Eds.), *Attachment in the preschool years: Theory, research, and intervention* (pp. 273–308). Chicago: University of Chicago Press.

Bretherton, I., Winn, L., Page, T., Macfie, J., & Walsh, R. (1993, March). *Concordance of preschoolers' family stories with parental reports of family climate, family stress and child temperament.* Paper presented at the biennial meeting of the Society for Research on Child Development, New Orleans, LA.

Buchsbaum, H., & Emde, R. N. (1990). Play narratives in 36-month-old children: Early moral development and family relationships. *Psychoanalytic Study of the Child, 40,* 129–155.

Buchsbaum, H. K., Toth, S. L., Clyman, R. B., Cicchetti, D., & Emde, R. N. (1993). The use of a narrative story stem technique with maltreated children: Implications for theory and practice. *Development and Psychopathology, 4,* 603–625.

Cassidy, J. (1988). Child-mother attachment and the self in six-year-olds. *Child Development, 59,* 121–134.

Cho, E. (1994). *Mothers' authoritative and authoritarian parenting: Attitudes related to preschoolers' attachment representations and teacher-rated social competence.* Doctoral dissertation, University of Wisconsin-Madison.

Easterbrooks, M. A., & Emde, R. N. (1987). Marital and parent-child relationships: The role of affect in the family system. In R. A. Hinde & J. Stevenson-Hinde (Eds.), *Relations between relationships within families* (pp. 83–103). Oxford: Oxford University Press.

Emde, R. N. (1990). Toward a new research-based theory of the Oedipus complex. In K. Wakai & K. Miyake (Eds.), *Research and clinical center for child development.* Annual Report 1988–1989, 12, 151–159, Sapporo, Japan: Hokkaido University.

Emde, R. N., Biringen, Z., Clyman, R. B., & Oppenheim, D. (1991). The moral self of infancy: Affective core and procedural knowledge. *Developmental Review, 11,* 251–270.

Emde, R. N., & Buchsbaum, H. K. (1990). "Didn't you hear my mommy?": Autonomy with connectedness in moral self emergence. In D. Cicchetti & M. Beeghly (Eds.), *Development of the self through the transition: Infancy through childhood* (pp. 35–60). Chicago: University of Chicago Press.

Emde, R. N., Johnson, W. F., & Easterbrooks, M. A. (1988). The do's and don'ts of early moral development: Psychoanalytic tradition and current research. In J. Kagan & S. Lamb (Eds.), *The emergence of morality in young children* (pp. 245–277). Chicago: University of Chicago Press.

Emde, R. N., & Spicer, P. (2000). Experience in the midst of variation: New horizons for development and psychopathology, *Development and Psychopathology, 12,* 313–331.

Erikson, E. H. (1950). *Childhood and society.* New York: Norton.

Etzion-Carasso, A., & Oppenheim, D. (2000). Open mother-pre-schooler communication: Relations with early secure attachment. *Attachment and Human Development, 2,* 362–385.

Fein, G. G. (1981). Pretend play in childhood: An integrative review. *Child Development, 52,* 1095–1118.

Fein, G. G. (1989). Mind, meaning, and affect: Proposals for a theory of pretense. *Developmental Review, 9,* 345–363.

Fivush, R. (1993). Emotional content of parent-child conversation about the past. In C. A. Nelson (Ed.), *Minnesota symposia in child psychology,* Vol. 26, *Memory and affect* (pp. 39–77). Hillsdale, NJ: Lawrence Erlbaum.

Freud, A. (1946). *The psycho-analytical treatment of children.* London: Imago.

George, C., Kaplan, N., & Main, M. (1985). *The Berkeley Adult Attachment Interview.* Unpublished manuscript, University of California at Berkeley.

Gloger-Tippelt, G., Gomille, B., Koenig, L., & Vetter, J. (2002). Attachment representations in 6-year-olds: Related longitudinally to the quality of attachment in infancy and mothers' attachment representations. *Attachment and Human Development, 4,* 318–339.

Granot, D., & Mayseless, O. (2001). Attachment security and adjustment to school in middle childhood. *International Journal of Behavioral Development, 25,* 530–541.

Green, J., Stanley, C., Smith, V., & Goldwyn, R. (2000). A new method of evaluating attachment representations in young school-age children: The Manchester Attachment Story Task. *Attachment and Human Development, 2,* 48–70.

Grych, J. H., Wachsmuth-Schaefer, T., & Klockow, L. (2002). Interparental aggression and young children's representations of family relationships. *Journal of Family Relationships, 16*, 259–272.

Guenter, M., Di Gallo, A., & Stohrer, I. (2000). *Tuebingen-Basel Narrativ Kodierungs-Manual.* Unpublished manuscript, University of Tuebingen, Germany.

Heller, C. (2000). *Attachment and social competence in preschool children.* Master's thesis, auburn University, AL.

Herman, P., & Bretherton, I. (2001). "He was the best Daddy": Postdivorce preschoolers' representations of loss and family life. In A. Goncu & E. Klein (Ed.), *Children in play, story, and school* (pp. 177–203). New York: Guilford.

Hill, J., Hoover, D., & Taliaferro, G. (1999). *Process scales for the MacArthur Story Stem Battery.* Unpublished scoring manual, Menninger Clinic, Topeka, Kansas.

Hodges, J., Hillman, S., & Steele, M. (2002). *Little pig narrative stems: A coding manual.* Unpublished manual, Anna Greud Centre, London, UK.

Kaplan, N. (1987). *Individual differences in children's thoughts about separation.* Unpublished doctoral dissertation, University of California at Berkeley.

Klagsbrun, M., & Bowlby, J. (1976). Responses to separation from parents: A clinical test for young children. *British Journal of Projective Psychology, 21*, 7–21.

Klein, M. (1932). *The psycho-analysis of children.* London: Hogarth.

Klitzing, K. von, Kelsay, K., Emde, R. N., Robinson, J., & Schmitz, S. (2000). Gender-specific characteristics of 5-year-olds' play narratives and associations with behavior ratings. *Journal of the American Academy of Child and Adolescent Psychiatry, 39*, 1017–1023.

Kohlberg, L. (1971). From is to ought: How to commit the natural fallacy and get away with it in the study of moral development. In T. Mischel (Ed.), *Cognitive development and epistemology* (pp. 151–235). New York: Academic Press.

Main, M., Kaplan, N., & Cassidy, J. (1985). Security in infancy, childhood, and adulthood: A move to the level of representation. In I. Bretherton & E. Waters (Eds.), *Growing points of attachment theory and research. Monographs of the Society for Research in Child Development, 50*(1–2), Serial No. 209, 66–104.

Mandler, J. M. (1983). Representation. In J. H. Flavell & E. M. Markman (Eds.), *Handbook of child psychology, Vol. 3: Cognitive development* (pp. 420–494). New York: Wiley.

Mandler, J. M., & DeForest, M. (1979). Is there more than one way to recall a story? *Child Development, 50*, 886–889.

Miljkovitch, R., Pierrehumbert, B., Bretherton, I., & Halfon, O. (2002). *Intergenerational transmission of attachment representations.* Paper submitted for publication.

Murray, L., Woolgar, M., Briers, S., & Hipwell, A. (1999). Children's social representations in dolls' house play and theory of mind tasks, and their relation to family adversity and child disturbance. *Social Development, 8*, 179–200.

Nelson, K. (1986) *Event knowledge: Structure and function in development.* Hillsdale, NJ: Lawrence Erlbaum.

Nelson, K., & Gruendel, J. (1981). Generalized event representations: Basic building blocks of cognitive development. In M. E. Lamb & A. L. Brown (Eds.), *Advances in developmental psychology* (vol. 1, pp. 131–158). Hillsdale, NJ: Lawrence Erlbaum.

Oppenheim, D. (1997). The attachment doll play interview for preschoolers. *International Journal of Behavioral Development, 20*, 681–697.

Oppenheim, D., Emde, R. N., Hasson, M., & Warren, S. (1997). Preschoolers face moral dilemmas: A longitudinal study of acknowledging and resolving internal conflict. *International Journal of Psychoanalysis, 78*, 943–957.

Oppenheim, D., Emde, R. N., & Wamboldt, F. S. (1996). Associations between 3-year-olds' narrative co-constructions with mothers and fathers and their story completions about affective themes. *Early Development and Parenting, 5*, 159–160.

Oppenheim, D., Emde, R. N., & Warren, S. (1997). Children's narrative representation of mothers: Their developments and associations with child and mother adaptation. *Child Development, 68*, 127–138.

Oppenheim, D., Nir, A., Warren, S., & Emde, R. N. (1997). Emotion regulation in mother-child narrative co-construction: Associations with children's narrative and adaptation. *Developmental Psychology, 33*, 284–294.

Oppenheim, D., Koren-Karie, N., & Sagi, A. (in press). Mothers' empathic understanding of their preschoolers' internal experience: Relations with early attachment. *International Journal of Behavioral Development.*

Oppenheim, D., & Waters, H. S. (1995). Narrative processes and attachment representations: Issues of development and assessment. In E. Waters, B. E. Vaughn, G. Posada, & K. Kondo-Ikemura (Eds.). *Caregiving, cultural and cognitive perspectives on secure base behavior and working models. Monographs of the Society for Research in Child Development, 60* (2–3), Serial No. 244, 197–233.

Page, T. (2001). The social meaning of children's narratives: A review of the attachment-based narrative story stem technique. *Child and Adolescent Social Work Journal, 18*, 171–187.

Page, T., & Bretherton, I. (1993). *Manual for coding the expanded story completion task adapted for children of divorce.* Unpublished manuscript, University of Wisconsin-Madison.

Page, T., & Bretherton, I. (2001). Mother- and father-child attachment themes as represented in the story completions of preschoolers in postdivorce families: Linkages with teacher ratings of social competence. *Attachment and Human Development, 3*, 1–29.

Page, T., & Bretherton, I. (2002). Representations of attachment to father in the narratives of preschool girls in post-divorce families: Implications for family relationships and social development. *Child and Adolescent Social Work Journal, 20*, 99–122.

Page, T., & Bretherton, I. (in press). Gender differences in stories of violence and caring by preschool children post-divorce families. *Child and Adolescent Social Work Journal.*

Poehlmann, J., & Huennekens, B. (2003). *Narrative representations of attachment relationships in children of incarcerated mothers.* Poster session presented at the biennial meeting of the Society for Research in Child Development, Tampa, FL.

Poulsen, D., Kintsch, E., Kintsch, W., & Premack, D. (1979). Comparison of young and older children's comprehension of out-of-order picture stories. *Journal of Experimental Child Psychology, 28*, 379–286.

Robinson, J., Mantz-Simmons, L., Macfie, J., & the MacArthur Narrative Working Group. (1992). *The narrative coding manual.* Unpublished manuscript, University of Colorado, Boulder.

Rowe, D. C., & Plomin, R. (1977). Temperament in early childhood. *Journal of Personality Assessment, 41*, 151–156.

San Juan, R., Bretherton, I., & Vandell, D. (2002). *Three-year-olds' representations of mother-child attachment within the child-care context.* Unpublished manuscript, University of Wisconsin-Madison.

Shouldice, A. E., & Stevenson-Hinde, J. (1992). Coping with security distress: The separation anxiety test and attachment classification at 4.5 years. *Journal of Child Psychology and Psychiatry, 33*(2), 331–348.

Slough, N., & Greenberg, M. (1990). 5-year-olds' representations of separation from parents: Responses from the perspective of self and other. In I. Bretherton & M. Watson (Eds.), *New directions for child development: Children's perspectives on the family*, 48 (pp. 67–84). San Francisco: Jossey-Bass.

Solomon, J., & George, C. (1999). The measurement of attachment security in infancy and childhood. In J. Cassidy & P. R. Shaver (Eds.), *Handbook of attachment: Theory, research, and clinical applications* (pp. 287–316). New York: Guilford.

Stein, N. L., & Glenn, C. G. (1979). An analysis of story comprehension in elementary school children. In R. O. Freedle (Ed.), *New directions in processing* (vol. 2, pp. 53–120). Norwood, NJ: Ablex.

Toth, S. L., Cicchetti, D., Macfie, J., Maughan, A., & VanMeenen, K. (2000). Narrative representations of caregiver and self in maltreated preschoolers. *Attachment and Human Development, 2*, 271–305.

Waelder, R. (1933). The psychoanalytic theory of play. *Psychoanalytic Quarterly, 2*, 208–224.

Warren, S. L., Emde, R. N., & Sroufe, L. A. (2000). Internal representations: Predicting anxiety from children's play narratives. *Journal of the American Academy of Child and Adolescent Psychiatry, 39*, 100–107.

Warren, S. L., Oppenheim, D., & Emde, R. N. (1996). Can emotion and themes in children's play predict behavior problems? *Journal of the American Academy of Child and Adolescent Psychiatry, 34*, 1331–1337.

Waters, E., & Deane, K. E. (1985). Defining and assessing individual differences in attachment relationships: Q-methodology and the organization of behavior in infancy and early childhood. In I. Bretherton & E. Waters (Eds.), *Growing points of attachment theory and research. Monographs of the Society for Research in Child Development, 50*, Serial No. 209 (1–2), 41–65.

Waters, H. S., Rodrigues, L. M., & Ridgeway, D. (1998). Cognitive underpinnings of narrative attachment assessment. *Journal of Experimental Child Psychology. 71*, 211–234.

Wimmer, H., & Perner, J. (1983). Beliefs about beliefs: Representation and constraining function of wring beliefs in young children's understanding of deception. *Cognition, 13*, 103–128.

Winnicott, D. W. (1958). *Collected papers: Through paediatrics to psycho-analysis.* New York: Basic Books.

Wolf, D. P., Rygh, J., & Altshuler, J. (1984). Agency and experience: Actions and states in play narratives. In. I Bretherton (Ed.), *Symbolic play: The development of social understanding* (pp. 195–217). Orlando: FL: Academic Press.

Zahn-Waxler, C., Cole, P. M., Richardson, D. T., Friedman, R. J., Michel, M. K., & Belouad, F. (1994). Social problem solving in disruptive preschool children: Reactions to hypothetical situations of conflict and distress. *Merrill-Palmer Quarterly, 40*, 98–119.

JOANN L. ROBINSON
LINDA MANTZ-SIMMONS

4

The MacArthur Narrative Coding System: One Approach to Highlighting Affective Meaning Making in the MacArthur Story Stem Battery

The investigator who wishes to capture the child's response continuities across stories faces a potential dilemma. Should coders watch responses to multiple story stems before applying a rating; or should they focus attention on story stem responses one at a time? The former approach would capture the pattern of story responses as a whole, potentially one dimension at a time, whereas the latter would lead to strong interrater reliability and greater breadth of coverage of response dimensions. Because the MacArthur Narrative Coding System (MNCS) was developed first to be applied to story responses of 700 young twins in the MacArthur Longitudinal Twin Study (MALTS), the authors opted for high reliability and breadth of coverage, using the latter approach, and created a scoring system that would "survey the territory," detailing thematic content and performance features for each narrative.

In this chapter, we discuss the MNCS from numerous perspectives. We give a brief history of its development, followed by an overview of the structure of the coding system. Following a discussion of the goals of the scoring system, we briefly discuss the importance of adapting the scoring system to specific populations and offer an example of our attempt to do that in a recently completed study of African American children. We then address specific issues concerning administration of the story stems as they affect the coder's ability to reliably and accurately score them. This leads, naturally, to a discussion of reliability and training issues for coders. In the last section of the chapter, we take up the issue of construct development and measures, where we return to capturing meaning making and summarizing the child's responses to the stories.

Overview

In the context of the MacArthur Narrative Working Group, the first author (Robinson), working with two research assistants, Linda Mantz-Simmons and Jenny Macfie, summarized the many discussions of the MacArthur collaborators into a core or basic scoring system (the MacArthur Narrative Scoring System; Robinson, Mantz-Simmons, Macfie, & the MacArthur Narrative Working Group, 1992). This system was intended to serve a mapping or survey function for scoring each of the child's story stem responses.

Two broad domains of response were identified: the content or themes the child created and the performance features or the manner in which the story responses were delivered. In other words, each story response was summarized in terms of the presence or absence of themes and performance features. Many themes had been identified by the MacArthur Narrative Working Group in their discussions and were based on the prior experience of participants as reviewed in chapter 3. Additional themes emerged from the narrative responses of the 3-year-old twins who were the initial focus in developing the scoring system. Continuing work with the scoring system led to the inclusion of still other themes that captured important relationship/moral content of older children's narratives (for example, teasing, dishonesty). A limitation of thematic coding in this system is that each theme can be endorsed only once per story, thus eliminating information about children who represent multiple instances of a theme within a story.

Content themes are organized within five domains as follows:

Interpersonal Conflict
- Competition
- Rivalry/Jealousy
- Exclusion Other
- Active Refusal of Empathy/Helping
- Verbal Conflict

Empathic Relations
- Sharing
- Empathy/Helping
- Affiliation
- Affection

Dysregulated Aggression
- Aggression
- Escalation of Conflict
- Personal Injury
- Atypical Responses
- Sexualized Aggression

Moral Themes
- Conflict Resolution
- Compliance

Non-compliance
Shame
Blame
Teasing/Taunting
Dishonesty
Punishment/Discipline
Reparation/Guilt
Politeness

Avoidant Strategies
Self Exclusion
Repetition
Denial
Refusing Empathy Passively
Family Disruption
Sudden Sleep Onset
Sensorimotor/Mechanical Preoccupation

Ten areas of performance were highlighted:

1. intensity of specific affects portrayed in the children's narrative responses,
2. presence of controlling behaviors by the child (for example, insisting that other dolls be made available, interrupting the examiner during the story beginning),
3. repetitions indicative of perseveration (for example, of a story fragment from prior story response or repetition of the story stem),
4. degree of child's investment in performance, including degree of dramatization and narration, manipulation of dolls/props,
5. inclusion of parental characters in the story response,
6. child responsiveness and involvement with the examiner during the narrative,
7. use of a direct versus indirect performance style,
8. ignoring or contradicting the story conflict in the construction of the story response,
9. demonstrated understanding of the conflict presented in the stem, and
10. level of coherence of the narrative response.

Two performance features deserve specific discussion here: specific affects and narrative coherence. The rating of the intensity of children's specific affects encompasses both facial and vocal cues and spontaneous as well as dramatized affect. Our initial attempts to capture affect tried to preserve differences between affects expressed by characters in the story versus the child. However, this proved almost impossible to differentiate reliably. Young children's stories are so dynamic and the boundary between self and character representations so fluid that the distinction appeared arbitrary. The scope of affects that are rated is limited to those that commonly occur in the MSSB (joy, anger, distress, sadness, anxiety, and concern). Each is rated on a 4-point scale (from 0 = not present to 3 = high intensity). Tone of voice and facial cues are described for each affect. Less common affects, such as disgust and contempt, are not included in the scoring system but might be noteworthy in a specific clinical context or in story responses of older children.

The second feature, narrative coherence, has been an important indicator of adult as well as child functioning (Fiese & Sameroff, 1999). The telling of a narrative requires the teller to maintain a thrust or plot of the story across several actions, demonstrating planfulness as well as verbal ability. Though elaboration of a story enriches its interest, it may also detract from its coherence if the teller is not moderately skilled in sequencing events. Not surprisingly, the young child's narrative coherence is affected by verbal and cognitive abilities and in several published studies has been significantly correlated with measures of verbal intelligence (e.g., Oppenheim, Nir, Emde, & Warren, 1997). The rating of narrative coherence in the MNCS considers several issues. First, the coder must ask whether the child's response addresses the conflict inherent in the story stem. The lowest ratings (0–5) are applied to story responses that fail to address or resolve the conflict or that resolve the conflict indirectly, for example, by changing the constraints of the story. Although some of these stories may be coherent, they are not well adapted to the particular story stem or they avoid the central conflict in the story. The upper ratings on the scale (6–10) are applied to responses that do address/resolve the central conflict but vary in the degree of elaboration and presence of incoherence. The highest score is given to story responses that are embellished, that provide a resolution to the central conflict, and that have no incoherence. The 10 points on the scale do not necessarily imply a single dimension, and empirical work with the scale has produced different results. Whereas von Klitzing found that in the MALTS, two scales could be identified, others have found that a unitary scale is meaningfully related to other constructs. Chapter 6 addresses this issue in some depth.

In summary, the intent of this system was to retain broad coverage to create a survey level of scoring. More refined systems might target specific dimensions of behavior for in-depth analysis after the initial, broad scoring was applied. For example, after identifying those narratives that utilize parent characters in the survey level of coding, one might apply a second, in-depth scoring of parental representations only to those narratives where parents were represented. However, coders in several studies have made a single scoring pass through the narratives, and the supplemental scoring systems have been applied simultaneously with the MNCS. For most studies that have used the MNCS, specific aspects have been elaborated to address areas of special concern to the investigators (for example, elaborating specific types of aggressive behavior) or of special relevance to specific ethnic and cultural groups. One strong example of this is the inclusion of the Coding of Parental Representations in Narratives (developed by Oppenheim, Emde, & Warren, 1997) into the main body of the MNCS manual.

Adaptation of Scoring System to Fit Sample

Culture-specific and sample-specific adaptations are important to consider in applying the MNCS to any sample. Both the MSSB and the MNCS were developed in the context of studies of white, middle-class children. Since then, investigators have applied these narrative tools to many nonmainstream samples in the United

States as well as to a number of different linguistic cultures in Europe and Asia (see Robinson & Corbitt-Price, 2000, for a review). In the case of the MSSB, investigators have altered situations to fit analogous circumstances in their culture (for example, British colleagues have translated the Monster in the Dark story into a story about a burglar in the dark). In this way, they ensure that the examiner and child are able to share meaning within their culture about the events. Similarly, the coding system also needs to be carefully considered to ensure that culturally appropriate meaning making is captured by the coder. New definitions may need to be written in light of cultural expectations and common meanings given to events.

In our recent work with a large, urban African American sample, we faced issues pertaining to the different meaning of several child and parental behaviors (Robinson, Herot, Haynes, & Mantz-Simmons, 2000). Our approach was to conduct key informant discussions with African American colleagues, to search the literature for relevant discussions, and to make modifications in concert with these sources. We modified definitions of aggression to include several categories of behavior that highlighted differences in the meaning of specific behaviors: (1) playful aggression (including verbal dueling and tussling of children), (2) hurtful aggression (hitting, kicking, thumping, and banging of dolls to indicate fighting), (3) dysregulated aggression (out-of-control fighting or unprovoked aggressive acts), and (4) child assault on an adult (a generally forbidden act, indicative of disrespect). Similarly, physical and nonverbal expressions of parental discipline practices were found to differ from those in middle-class families where, for example, "whoopings" were a common and culturally accepted method (see also Jenkins & Bell, 1997). A new category boundary for parental representations (disciplinary vs. negative) was therefore implemented in this study to accommodate greater harshness in parental use of punishments within the disciplinary category than is commonly accepted in white, middle-class culture (Deater-Deckard, Dodge, Bates, & Pettit, 1996).

The Impact of Narrative Administration on Scoring

Two crucial factors in administration influence the creation of the child's narrative and need to be taken into account in scoring: conduct of the examiner and provision of a comfortable setting conducive to storytelling.

The Examiner

The examiner plays a crucial role in the story stem narrative assessment. Two qualities in the examiner are particularly important for the scoring of the narratives. The examiner must demonstrate a degree of playfulness and an ability to actively engage with a young child through all phases of the narrative administration. This helps to ensure that the child will remain interested and involved throughout the narrative battery and will enhance affective meaning making through their relationship. If there are extreme variations in these qualities between examiners within a given study, children with equal storytelling ability may receive very different scores because the examiners are creating different opportunities for expression. For example, a child who is not adequately and appropriately engaged by the examiner will typically produce shortened and sometimes less coherent story stem responses or he may appear more anxious and tentative in his responses.

Equally important is the examiner's ability to set and enforce boundaries when needed. The young child needs a clear statement and modeling of the expectations for engaging in this task early on. The examiner must therefore begin the storytelling process by using simple descriptive language that establishes roles: "Now, we're going to tell stories together. I will begin each story and then ask you to finish it." The examiner co-creates the "Birthday Story," an uncoded warm-up story. By modeling actions with the dolls and portraying a range of emotions and expressive vocalizations, the examiner suggests the acceptability of open expression of thoughts and feelings to the child.

This warm-up story serves several purposes for the examiner and the child. For the child, the Birthday Story is an opportunity to understand the intent of the task. For the examiner, the Birthday Story is, first, an opportunity to evaluate the child's linguistic and play skills with the goal of providing structure and support as needed.

The second opportunity for the examiner in the Birthday Story is to create boundaries for engaging in the task. These boundaries include establishing limits on the amount of poorly controlled action that is acceptable and limits on the length of the story response. The former is particularly important for scoring because the young child may become quite dysregulated by the portrayal of conflict and will be relieved when limits are placed on the acting out of distress. Placing limits on the length of story responses is also crucial for the scoring process; children who are allowed to meander in their story line will appear less competent than children who are encouraged to finish a narrative thread once it has achieved elaboration and a natural endpoint. The converse of limiting the length is encouraging story elaboration; this is particularly important for children who are reluctant to narrate a story response.

The coder relies on the examiner to sufficiently engage the child within these boundaries to elicit responses that reflect the child's ability. This permits the coder to count on the variation observed as reflecting the child and not the vagaries of the examiner. The data are less reliable and the coder more frustrated when the examiner has not made clear the child's intentions throughout the stories. For example, if the child says, "He got punished," the coder is not given sufficient information to record which character administered the punishment and what type of punishment it was. Vague statements such as this should be clarified at the time of administration by the examiner asking the child to clarify who punished whom and the type of punishment.

Setting

Published reports using the MSSB indicate that it has been administered in office-based settings (for example, at a university play room or in a clinic setting), in a preschool setting, and in children's homes. Some studies, such as the

Denver Narrative Study (e.g., Oppenheim, Nir, et al., 1997; Warren, Oppenheim, & Emde, 1996) and the MacArthur Longitudinal Twin Study (e.g., Zahn-Waxler, Schmitz, Fulker, Robinson, & Emde, 1996), administered story stems in both home- and office-based settings. Each setting has advantages in terms of its ambiance. Office settings permit greater control over extraneous events and distractions. Familiar home or preschool settings encourage greater relaxation and, potentially, greater freedom of expression, for the child. However, distraction and interference may seriously compromise the examiner's ability to assess the child in the home, whereas inhibition in a novel setting may constrain the child's freedom of expression. A balance must be struck between feasibility and preference of the investigator/clinician.

Availability of recording equipment may play an important role in the choice of setting because the child's performance must be videotaped, with a clearly audible sound track. Examiners can enhance audibility by encouraging siblings to play somewhere else for a time or repeating each segment of a quiet child's narrative. This echoing of the child's spoken narrative is especially important in cases when the child has a tendency to look down or away from the camera while talking, or when the child has a very soft voice, or there is excessive background noise. This echoing of the child's responses, if done in a nonintrusive manner, also conveys appreciation of the child's performance by the examiner. Special attention needs to be paid to the position of the audio equipment in relation to the child and examiner. When possible, it is preferable to have the microphone and camera placed at the approximate height of the child and close enough to the testing area that background noise is kept to a minimum and the coder is able to see the child's face and the testing area.

Training and Reliability of Coders

The second author of this chapter has been involved in training several teams of researchers in Europe and North America. Her experience suggests that working with smaller training groups of 4–12 people facilitates the types of in-depth discussions necessary to clarify scoring issues. Initial training occurs over the course of 3 full days. Each day is allotted to one or more of the various sections of the coding system. The 1st day typically presents content themes; the 2nd day, performance codes; and the 3rd day, narrative coherence and the relationship-with-the-examiner codes. Training begins with a review of the overall layout of the coding manual in relation to the coding sheet to be used. It is recommended that the group meet as a whole to discuss how the specific codes are interpreted. They observe videotaped examples of the codes across story stems and across several different children with different narrative styles. Breakout groups then convene to practice coding from pre-selected tapes of children's narrative responses. The group again meets as a whole to compare coding and to discuss discrepancies. This format is repeated throughout the 3 days. Following this, each trainee must independently code 15–20 children's narratives in order to attain reliability. Once reliability is established, it should be checked frequently in order to guard against drift in coding. This may be done by having another trained coder periodically double-code selected tapes and then compare and discuss any discrepancies.

Creating Higher-Order Measures From Codes

One way of summarizing the child's responses to the MSSB as a whole has been to follow a general aggregation strategy of summing information across all stories. This approach enhances the reliability of measures because each dimension has multiple observation points that inform it (up to 14 data points if the entire MSSB is administered). However, it ignores broader concerns about the timing or context of themes and performance features (for example, whether the child introduces aggression during stories about loss and injury or during stories that deal explicitly with conflict).

Another approach has been to combine similar themes to create more robust or reliable constructs (for example, using an average of three codes that indicate the presence of interpersonal conflict: physical aggression, verbal conflict, and personal injury).

Factor analyses that include both thematic content and performance features have also been employed to create higher-order constructs; for example, Peter Fonagy and colleagues have identified two contrasting constructs, open-direct response style versus negative-closed response style (Peter Fonagy, personal communication, 1999). However, story-specific approaches that delimit the context in which themes are portrayed also have merit. For example, story stems can be grouped into moral stems (such as Band-Aid, Cookie Jar, Candy Store, Spilled Juice) and relationship stems (such as Lost Dog, Three's a Crowd, Lost Keys, Exclusion, Separation, Reunion). Thematic content and performance features can then be aggregated within these groupings to illuminate the significance of specific issues that are most relevant to a specific narrative context, for example, the degree of reparation represented in the moral stems.

Two principal aggregates have been reported in the literature: an atypical aggression aggregate and a positive affiliation aggregate (Warren, Oppenheim, & Emde, 1996; Oppenheim, Emde, & Warren, 1997; Toth, Cicchetti, Macfie, Rogosh, & Maughan, 2000; von Klitzing, Kelsay, Emde, Robinson, & Schmitz, 2000). The atypical aggression aggregate is generally composed of themes pertaining to assault and injury (aggression, verbal conflict, atypical negative). Reported internal consistency has been high, with Cronbach's alpha ranging from .69 to .87. Not surprisingly, this measure is more consistently elevated in boys than in girls (chapter 6; Warren et al., 1996; Zahn-Waxler et al., 1994; Zahn-Waxler, Schmitz, et al., 1996). This measure also has been reported to correlate significantly with children's externalizing behavior problems reported by parents in several samples (e.g., Warren et al., 1996; Zahn-Waxler, Schmitz, et al., 1996) and, when combined with high levels of incoherence, was particularly predictive of these outcomes (von Klitzing et al., 2000). Similarly in these published reports, dysregulated aggression correlated significantly with teachers' reports of externalizing problems. In addition, in the study of urban African American children reported in Robinson et al. (2000), dysregulated aggression correlated with two other aspects of teacher-reported classroom adjustment, low frustration tolerance and low task persistence, in addition to disruptive, acting-out behavior problems. These correlations were low and ranged from .18 to .25 in this very large sample of 598 children.

A positive affiliation composite has been created by aggregating several prosocial themes including affection, affiliation, and empathy/helping (e.g., Zahn-Waxler, Friedman, Cole, Mizuta, & Hiruma, 1996). Reported internal consistency has also been high, with alphas ranging from .71 to .79. Positive/affiliative themes are generally more common among girls (see Oppenheim, Nir, et al., 1997).

New Applications and Directions

Recently the first author has applied the story stem method and the MNCS in a randomized control study of David Olds's nurse home visitation intervention model. This study, as described in Robinson et al. (2000) seeks to determine whether the mother-focused intervention conducted during the children's prenatal months and for 2 years postnatally affected the children's representations in response to the story stem conflicts. A particular emphasis was placed on the reduction of dysregulated aggressive themes as well as on an increase in representations of internalized controls (e.g., punishment and discipline themes) and of greater reliance on adults to help solve conflicts in the theoretical model to explain the program's influence on the prevention of antisocial behavior (Olds et al., 1998). Results from this study supported the theoretical model. Children whose mother had had a nurse visitor represented parent figures as warm and nurturant more frequently than their control counterparts. In addition, among children born to women with fewer psychological resources (less sense of mastery, lower IQ, and greater mental health problems), positive impacts were seen in significantly fewer dysregulated aggressive themes, fewer incoherent stories, and greater reliance on adults to address conflicts (Olds et al., 2002).

A similar study is also beginning with a large subgroup of children participating in the national study of Early Head Start, which began in 1996. Children from six Early Head Start program sites (and their randomly assigned comparison groups, approximately 800 children) will be assessed with a subset of narratives from the MSSB prior to entering kindergarten. Early Head Start is not a single program model but includes both home-based and center-based interventions with very low-income women and their children from birth to 3 years of age. Each of the participating programs (in Denver, Colorado; Seattle, Washington; New York City, New York; Los Angeles, California; and rural Arkansas) has had an emphasis on the importance of relationships with parents and other caregivers that has led each of the investigative groups to consider this zone of children's emotional development of high importance as an outcome.

With new incentives for psychotherapies to demonstrate their effectiveness, the MSSB and MNCS may prove to be invaluable tools for clinicians. Applying this method of meaning making in our assessments of young children may allow them to share their strengths as well as their suffering so that we may better meet their needs for support and guidance.

REFERENCES

Deater-Deckard, K., Dodge, K. A., Bates, J. E., & Pettit, G. S. (1996). Physical discipline among African-American and European-American mothers: Links to children's externalizing behaviors. *Developmental Psychology, 32,* 1065–1072.

Fiese, B. H., & Samaroff, A. J. (1999). The family narrative consortium: A multidimensional approach to narratives. In B. H. Fiese, A. J. Sameroff, H. D. Grotevant, F. S. Wamboldt, S. Dickstein, & D. L. Fravel (Eds.), *The stories that families tell: Narrative coherence, narrative interaction, and relationship beliefs* (pp. 1–36). *Monographs of the Society for Research in Child Development, 64* (Serial No. 257).

Jenkins, E. J., & Bell, C. C. (1997). Exposure and response to community violence among children and adolescents. In J. Osofsky (Ed.), *Children in a violent society* (pp. 9–31). New York: Guilford Press.

Olds, D., Kitzman, H., Cole, R., Robinson, J., Henderson, C., Sidora, K., Luckey, D., Henderson, C. R., Hanks, C., Bondy, J., & Holmberg, J. (2002). Enduring effects of nurse home visiting on maternal life-course and child development: Results of a randomized trial. Unpublished manuscript.

Olds, D., Pettitt, L., Robinson, J., Eckenrode, J., Kitzman, H., Cole, R., & Powers, J. (1998). Reducing risks for antisocial behavior with a program of prenatal and early childhood home visitation. *Journal of Community Psychology, 26,* 65–84.

Oppenheim, D., Emde, R. N., & Warren, S. L. (1997). Children's narrative representations of mothers: Their development and associations with child and mother adaptation. *Child Development, 68,* 127–138.

Oppenheim, D., Nir, A., Emde, R. N., & Warren, S. L. (1997). Emotion regulation in mother-child narrative co-construction: Associations with children's narratives and adaptation. *Developmental Psychology, 33,* 284–294.

Robinson, J. L., & Corbitt-Price, J. (2000). *The use of story stems in the assessment of risks for psychopathology in young children.* Unpublished manuscript, University of Colorado Health Sciences Center, Denver.

Robinson, J., Herot, C., Haynes, P., & Mantz-Simmons, L. (2000). Children's story stem responses: A measure of program impact on developmental risks associated with dysfunctional parenting. *Child Abuse and Neglect, 24,* 99–110.

Robinson, J., Mantz-Simmons, L., Macfie, J., & the MacArthur Narrative Working Group. (1992). *The MacArthur Narrative Coding System.* Unpublished document, University of Colorado Health Sciences Center, Denver.

Toth, S. L., Cicchetti, D., Macfie, J., Rogosch, F. A., & Maughan, A. (2000). Narrative representations of moral-affiliative and conflictual themes and behavioral problems in maltreated preschoolers. *Journal of Clinical Child Psychology, 29,* 307–318.

von Klitzing, K., Kelsay, K., Emde, R. N., Robinson, J., & Schmitz, S. (2000). Gender specific characteristics of five-year-old's play narratives and associations with behavior ratings. *Journal of the American Academy of Child and Adolescent Psychiatry, 39,* 1017–1023.

Warren, S. L., Oppenheim, D., & Emde, R. N. (1996). Can emotions and themes in children's play predict behavior problems? *Journal of the American Academy of Child and Adolescent Psychiatry, 34,* 1331–1337.

Zahn-Waxler, C., Cole, P. M., Richardson, D. T., Friedman, R. J., Michel, M. K., & Belouad, F. (1994). Social problem solving in disruptive preschool children: Reactions to hypothetical situations of conflict and distress. *Merrill Palmer Quarterly, 40,* 98–119.

Zahn-Waxler, C., Friedman, R. J., Cole, P. M., Mizuta, I., & Hiruma, N. (1996). Japanese and United States preschool children's responses to conflict and distress. *Child Development, 67,* 2462–2477.

Zahn-Waxler, C., Schmitz, S., Fulker, D., Robinson, J., & Emde, R. N. (1996). Behavior problems in 5-year-old monozygotic and dizygotic twins: Genetic and environmental influences, patterns of regulation, and internalization of control. *Development and Psychopathology, 8,* 103–122.

SUSAN L. WARREN

5

Narrative Emotion Coding System (NEC)

This chapter describes the Narrative Emotion Coding System (NEC) (Warren, Mantz-Simmons, & Emde, 1993), developed to provide additional codes for examining a child's internal worldview and to aid clinical assessment. The coding system investigates several areas not included in the MacArthur Narrative Coding System (Robinson, Mantz-Simmons, Macfie, and the MacArthur Narrative Working Group, 1992, see chapter 4) and can thus be used as a supplement to that system. Additional emotional areas assessed in the NEC include sudden shifts in the emotional tone of the stories and incongruent affect (potentially indicating difficulties coping with certain emotions), as well as the child's description of emotions experienced and several new themes (e.g., danger, loss). We also added two codes that captured the child's negotiation of the beginning of the stem response and its ending: a coding of the child's initial response to the story stems (potentially providing information about the child's initial response to certain types of situations) and coding the manner in which the child ends the stories (potentially providing information about the child's expectations concerning the resolution of situations). Finally, we added a coding of the child's representations of the child dolls in the story stems (potentially providing information about the children's views of themselves). A central reason for developing the NEC was to obtain information useful for clinical assessment. Because we wished to focus on emotion regulation, anxiety, and responses related to internalizing disorders, we developed several new emotion story stems (Warren, Emde, & Oppenheim, 1993). The new stems describe fear-inducing and anxiety-provoking situations as well as situations that may provoke feelings of anger, conflict, and loss (see table 5.1).

Table 5.1 New Stories

Stories Involving Anxiety-provoking Situations

Scary Dog (Fear of dogs)

The family is in the park and the child kicks a ball farther and farther away from the family. Suddenly, a scary dog appears and barks loudly, and the child expresses fear.

Monster in the Dark (Fear of monsters and the dark)

It's nighttime and the family is downstairs while the child plays upstairs in the bedroom. Suddenly the lights go out and the child hears a sound, which the child thinks is a monster.

New Neighborhood (Social fears)

The family has moved to a new neighborhood and the child is invited to a party at the neighbors but doesn't know any of the nine children at the party.

Song (Performance fears)

The child starts to sing a song in front of an audience but can't remember the song.

Stories Involving Anger and Conflict

Fight with Friend (Conflict with a peer)

The child is playing with a ball and the friend comes over and grabs the ball, hurting the child's hand.

Favorite Chair (Conflict with a sibling)

The child is sitting in his or her favorite chair and the sibling pushes the child off the chair because the sibling wants to sit there. In the struggle, the child's foot is hurt.

Story Involving Loss

Canceled Visit

The child has been looking forward all day to visiting with a friend but Mom tells the child that he or she can't go.

Most of the NEC codes are designed to be used with any story including responses to the new story stems and those of the original MacArthur Story Stem Battery (Bretherton et al., 1990). Some codes, however, are designed to provide information about specific stories. For example, codes pertaining to parental responses to the monster were developed for the Monster in the Dark story. In addition, codes pertaining to the child's fearfulness/anxiety related to performance and meeting strangers were developed for the Song and New Neighborhood stories, respectively.

Advantages of the NEC coding system are that it provides information that can be particularly useful in the identification of children with internalizing and anxiety symptoms. It also can be used to examine feelings of vulnerability and anxiety in children with externalizing disorders. Themes of danger, grandiose representations of the child doll as a superhero, and belief in monsters may identify a child with externalizing problems who feels quite vulnerable and anxious. The NEC can link themes identified in the MacArthur narrative coding system (Robinson et al., 1992) with specific time points of the narratives. Thus, the NEC may provide information about the child's initial response to situations, expectations about outcomes of difficult scenarios and about the handling of specific challenging emotional themes.

Details for each code are described in the following section. For clarity, the listed codes are grouped into the following categories: (1) narrative style and negotiating the task, (2) initial and final responses, (3) emotional regulation and coherence, (4) emotional themes and knowledge, (5) representations of self and others, and (6) codes for specific stories. After the description of each code is a brief discussion of reliability and validity, as well as additional suggestions for use of the coding system and future research.

Description of Codes

Narrative Style and Negotiating the Task

These codes describe specific overt behaviors displayed by the child during the procedure and the child's approach toward narrating the story.

Startle This code describes the degree to which a child startles (demonstrating a slight lean, freeze, or jump) when confronted with a frightening situation. The code can be used with any story but appears most useful for describing the child's behavior in response to the Scary Dog story stem in which a dog is introduced suddenly with a loud barking sound.

Difficulty Telling the Narratives This code is used when children say they don't know what happens next in the story or cannot seem to tell a narrative.

Storytelling Technique This code is utilized to describe the manner in which the children tell the stories (e.g., with words only, with actions only, or with both words and actions). It differs from direct versus indirect performance style and investment in performance (coded in the MacArthur Narrative coding system; Robinson et al., 1992) in that this code does not try to determine the clarity of meaning of the story but focuses on the style of presentation, does not try to quantify degree of involvement but focuses on the type of involvement.

Initial and Final Responses

These codes capture the child's negotiation of the beginning of the stem response and the manner in which the child ends the stories.

Initial Response This code is meant to identify the child's initial response to the problem presented by the story stem. The initial response directly follows the presentation of the narrative. Though the code examines themes in some cases, the code differs from the other theme codes in that it is tied to a particular time point of the narrative. The rationale for the development of this code was that children may have certain tendencies in their responses to certain situations, such as avoiding conflict or seeking parental help in anxiety-provoking situations. Possible responses for this code include aggression/destruction/injury, denial of the story stem, avoidance of conflict or of a fearful situation, help seeking (child gets help from the parents), help arrives (parents come to help), child resolution (child resolves the situation him- or herself), self/blame to relieve conflict, fear/ anxiety, positive content, and angry or negative content. Not seeking parental help as an initial response was used as part of the aggregate to predict anxiety (see Warren, Emde, & Sroufe, 2000). Negative responses to separation (such as refusing to separate when a separation was expected) were also used as part of the aggregate to predict anxiety (see Warren et al., 2000). In terms of the analyses conducted for this chapter, consistent with the linkages previously found between aggression, personal injury, and atypical negative response themes and externalizing behavior problems (Warren, Oppenheim, & Emde, 1996), aggression/destruction/injury as an initial response was significantly correlated with maternal and paternal reports of externalizing symptoms (see reliability and validity section and table 5.2).

Final Content This code describes how the child ends the stories (e.g., positive, neutral, negative, fearful, angry, aggression/destruction/injury). Like initial response, this code differs from the other theme codes because it describes a particular time during the narratives. The rationale behind this code was that children who ended stories negatively and not positively could have negative expectations about the outcome of situations. Ending stories in a negative manner and not in a positive manner was used as part of the aggregate used to predict anxiety (see Warren et al., 2000). Moreover, in the analyses conducted for this chapter, negative final content significantly correlated with maternal reports of internalizing and externalizing symptoms. Consistent with previous findings linking aggressive themes to externalizing behavior problems (Warren et al., 1996), in the analyses conducted for this chapter, aggressive final content significantly correlated with maternal and teacher reports of externalizing symptoms, and paternal reports of internalizing and externalizing symptoms (see reliability and validity section and table 5.2).

Final Affect This code categorizes the final affect displayed in each narrative.

Ending Transformation Because prompts are used after the conclusion of some of the stories, some children would obtain a positive final content response code, even though the children had ended their stories negatively, because they would respond positively to the prompt. Thus, this code was developed to identify children with negative endings who were not identified by the final content code. In the initial version of the coding system, this code was also used for children who shifted their endings suddenly when no prompt was given. In a later version of the coding system, a new code was developed that identified which children had shifted their endings in response to a prompt and which had shifted their endings spontaneously. Consistent with previous research linking aggres-

Table 5.2. Correlations Between Some of the Individual Codes from the Narrative Emotion Coding System and the Child Behavior Checklist (CBCL) and Teacher Report Form (TRF)

	Mom Int.	Dad Int.	Teacher Int.	Mom Ext.	Dad Ext.	Teacher Ext.
Initial content (aggression)	.24	.27	.08	.32*	.33*	.23
Final content (not positive)	.36**	.14	.09	.41**	.12	.19
Final content (aggression)	.14	.44**	.17	.57**	.54**	.37**
Ending transformation (aggression)	.05	.18	.17	.42**	.38**	.28′
Emotional incoherence (aggression)	-.14	.03	.34*	.41**	.37*	.59**
Child representations (not competent)	.01	.27	.04	.36**	.34*	.15
Child representations (grandiose)	.17	.41**	.06	.39**	.45**	.06
Danger themes	.06	.22	.04	.41**	.35*	.06
Destruction of objects	.21	.25	-.04	.34*	.32*	.15
Oral themes	.14	.25	.12	.38**	.33*	.39**
Existence of the Monster	-.04	-.03	.22	.21	.23	.35*

Mom Int. = Mom's report of internalizing symptoms with the CBCL Teacher Ext. = Teacher's report of externalizing symptoms with the TRF.

$^{*}p < .05$.

$^{**}p < .01$.

sive themes with externalizing behavior problems (Warren et al., 1996), in the analyses conducted for this chapter, ending transformations from an aggressive theme significantly correlated with maternal and paternal reports of externalizing symptoms (see reliability and validity section and table 5.2).

Emotional Regulation and Coherence

These codes assess the ease and clarity with which the child handles challenging emotional themes.

Emotional Incoherence This scale refers to sudden and unexplained shifts in the emotional themes of a story, which occur at any time (not just at the end of the story). For example, if a child is fighting with another child and then suddenly becomes friends with that child (without a clear explanation), that would be considered emotional incoherence because there is no clear, coherent resolution of the emotional theme. In the first version of the coding system, only emotional themes that shifted from negative to positive themes were coded. In a later version of the coding system, a code was added to describe emotionally incoherent shifts from a positive emotion to a negative emotion, as these seemed to occur in children who had been maltreated (J. Macfie, personal communication, 1995). A code was also developed to capture incoherent shifts from a neutral to a negative emotion. Consistent with previous research linking aggressive themes with externalizing behavior problems, in the analyses conducted for this chapter, emotional incoherent shifts from aggressive to positive themes significantly correlated with maternal and paternal reports of externalizing symptoms and teacher reports of internalizing and externalizing symptoms (see reliability and validity section and table 5.2).

Emotional Shift This code describes the particulars of shifts in emotional themes that are coherent or understandable (e.g., a shift from fear to anger).

Seemingly Incongruent Affect in Response to a Negative Situation This code is scored as present when the child smiles or laughs while he or she is witnessing a frightening or negative situation (in the story stem) or while he or she is describing or portraying a negative scene (e.g., fighting, presentation of scary dog or monster, loss of the family dog, wrongdoing, punishment).

Reaction to Blocked Goals/Desires This code describes the child's response when faced with a situation in the story in which he or she cannot satisfy desires easily or immediately. Possible responses include accepting the limitation, arguing, or doing what the child wants despite parental prohibition.

Emotional Themes and Knowledge

These codes allow for the coding of additional themes, some of which relate specifically to fears and loss. In addition, one of the codes rates the child's responses when asked directly about emotions.

Danger Themes Children receive a danger theme code when they continue a danger theme (e.g., make the dog continue to growl in Scary Dog), worsen the danger theme (e.g., make the dog become a monster), or create a new danger theme. The increased danger often leads to injury or aggression. Thus, danger themes were predicted to relate to externalizing symptoms. In fact, danger themes did significantly correlate with maternal and paternal reports of externalizing symptoms (see reliability and validity section and table 5.2).

Disappointment/Loss Theme This code is used to score themes of loss (e.g., the child gets a box of candy but then loses it).

Destruction of Objects This code is used when objects in the story are destroyed (e.g., the dog eats the ball). As would be expected because of linkages between aggressive and injury themes and externalizing behavior problems (Warren et al., 1996), destruction of objects significantly correlated with maternal and paternal reports of externalizing symptoms (see reliability and validity section and table 5.2).

Oral Themes This code is meant to capture themes of "orality" or neediness as described by early psychoanalysts. It is coded when the child seems preoccupied with eating in the narratives. The rationale behind this code was that children who felt deprived might take the opportunity to remedy this situation in the stories. This conceptualization is similar to that applied to the actions of a child who portrays the child doll as a superhero when feeling vulnerable. The view is that the child is attempting to overcome a perceived lack. Our group hypothesized that oral themes would significantly relate to behavior problems because children who were focusing more on perceived deprivations might have difficulty attending to developmentally appropriate activities and learning developmentally appropriate behaviors. In the analyses conducted for this chapter, oral themes did significantly correlate with maternal, paternal, and teacher reports of externalizing symptoms (see reliability and validity section and table 5.2).

Knowledge of Emotions This code is used when the children are asked how a particular character felt in a given situation. Such a probe is a routine part of the Exclusion story and can also be used after other stories that elicit strong emotions. The specific emotion discussed (e.g., happiness, fear, anger, sadness) is coded. Reporting positive emotions after the separation story (when in many cases the child has refused to separate) was used as part of the aggregate to predict anxiety (see Warren et al., 2000).

Representations of Self and Others

These codes describe the manner in which the child portrays the child doll and parent doll perspectives in the stories. Such portrayals presumably relate to representations of self and others.

Child Representations This code describes how the child depicts the children in the stories (e.g., as competently handling difficult situations, as assuming the parental role or responsibilities, or as acting in a grandiose manner like a superhero). The rationale behind this code was that the child might portray the child doll as acting like himself. If a child felt competent to handle most situations, the child might tend to represent the child doll as acting competently. If the child felt he or she needed to assume some parental roles or responsibilities, the child might represent the child doll as assuming the parental role or responsibilities. If a child felt vulnerable and felt that aggressive or superhuman qualities were needed to overcome difficult situations, the child might have the child doll act like a superhero. Representing the child doll as not competent and having the child doll assume the parental role or responsibilities was included as part of the aggregate used to predict anxiety (see Warren et al., 2000). In terms of the analyses conducted for this chapter, representing the child doll as not competent significantly correlated with maternal and paternal reports of externalizing symptoms. Grandiose representations of the child doll's behavior significantly correlated with paternal reports of internalizing symptoms and maternal and paternal reports of externalizing symptoms (see reliability and validity section and table 5.2).

Parents as People This code is used when the child seems to understand the feelings of the parents and portrays their perspective.

Codes for Specific Stories

These codes are to be used only with specific stories, as they describe specific response content.

Existence of the Monster This code applies only to the Monster in the Dark story and determines whether the child portrays an actual monster in the story. Portraying the monster as real significantly correlated with teacher reports of externalizing symptoms (see reliability and validity section and table 5.2).

Parental View of the Monster This code describes how the parents respond to the monster (as real or imaginary).

Singing the Song This code describes the child's response to the Song story (e.g., whether the child doll remembers the song or not and whether the child gets help).

Audience Response Rating This code is used only in the Song story and describes whether the audience likes the presentation of the song.

New Neighborhood This code describes whether the child doll approaches the new peers in the New Neighborhood story.

Peer Response Rating Scale This code describes whether peers respond well to the main child doll. It was developed for the New Neighborhood story.

Reliability and Validity

One article is currently published using NEC (Warren et al., 2000). For the purposes of this chapter, additional analyses were conducted with the same sample to demonstrate specific features of the coding system and to provide contrasting information with the MacArthur Narrative coding system. Both sets of analyses use data obtained from a previously reported longitudinal study of 51 children (26 girls and 25 boys) who were recruited from a volunteer, nonclinical population (Oppenheim, Emde, Hasson, & Warren, 1997; Oppenheim, Emde, & Warren, 1997; Oppenheim, Nir, Warren, & Emde, 1997; Warren et al., 1996, 2000). Most of the parents who participated were Caucasian (94%) and of higher socioeconomic status (70% level I or II according to Hollingshead & Redlich, 1958). Children completed narratives at 3, 4, 5, and 6 years of age. All 12 stories from the MacArthur Story Stem Battery (Bretherton et al., 1990) were administered at ages 3, 4, and 5. Four additional stories from the New MacArthur Emotion Story Stem Battery (Warren et al., 1993) were added at age 5 (Scary Dog, Monster in the Dark, Fight with Friend, Canceled Visit). (New Neighborhood, Song, and Favorite Chair were added to the battery for 6-year-olds, replacing Spilled Juice and Cookie.) In terms of assessing validity, both parents completed the Child Behavior Checklist at all ages (CBCL; Achenbach, 1991a), teachers completed the Teacher Report Form (TRF; Achenbach, 1991b) when children were 5 and 6 years of age, and portions of the anxiety disorders section of the Diagnostic Interview for Children (DISC Version 2.3 based on DSMIII-R; Shaffer et al., 1996) were administered to the mothers when the children were 6 years of age. Coding for the 5-year sample only was included in the following analyses.

Reliability

Interrater reliability for the codes is listed in table 5.3. Figures are based on coding of 44 narratives in 10 children at 5 years of age and provide information on interrater reliability for each specific code. Interrater reliability figures are high for initial response, final content, reaction to blocked goals/desires, disappointment/loss themes, knowledge of emotions, child representations, and the codes pertaining to the monster story. Reliability is lower for startle, storytelling technique, ending transformation, emotional incoherence, seemingly incongruent affect in response to a negative situation, and destruction of objects.

Validity

Information concerning validity comes from two sources: (1) analyses previously conducted for predicting internalizing and anxiety symptoms at 6 years of age (Warren et al., 2000) and (2) analyses conducted for this chapter examining concurrent linkages with the CBCL and TRF, focusing particularly on externalizing symptoms.

In terms of the first source, Warren et al. (2000) created an aggregate of narrative codes measured in 5-year-old children, which they hypothesized would relate to internalizing and anxiety symptoms when the children were 6 years of age. Because of associations between attachment and anxiety disorders (Warren, Huston, Egeland, & Sroufe, 1997), construction of the aggregate was based upon research examining attachment and narratives (see chapter 12). The aggregate was constructed by taking the mean of the individual scores for each code across all 16 stories (except for the codes that referred only to the separation stories, in which case, means were taken across the stories involving separation

Table 5.3. Interrater Reliabilities for the Narrative Emotion Coding System (using Cohen's kappa)

Startle	.59
Difficulty Telling the Narratives[a]	
Storytelling Technique	.62
Initial Response	.86
Final Content	.75
Ending Transformation	.55
Emotional Incoherence	.53
Seemingly Incongruent Affect in Response to a Negative Situation	.56
Reaction to Blocked Goals/Desires	.83
Danger Themes	.64
Disappointment/Loss Themes	.76
Destruction of Objects	.48
Child Representations	.82
Knowledge of Emotions	.88
Existence of the Monster	1.00
Parental View of the Monster	.82

[a]None of the children displayed difficulty telling the narratives in the narratives coded for interrater reliability.

only). The ratings were then converted to *z* scores and an aggregate was made by taking a mean of the *z* scores. Specific codes included in the aggregate were (1) *initial response* not involving seeking parental help; (2) *initial response* being negative in the stories for separation, which generally meant that the child doll did not separate from the parent dolls when this was directed by the story; (3) *final content* negative for all stories; (4) *final content* not positive for all stories; (5) *knowledge of emotions* for the separation stories with the child saying that he or she felt happy after forced separations in the separation stories, even while that same child might refuse to separate; (6) *child representations* not portraying the child doll as competent; and (7) *child representations* having the child doll assume the parental role. This aggregate of seven codes significantly predicted combined mother, father, and teacher reports of internalizing and anxiety symptoms when the children were 5 and 6 years of age. The aggregate of seven codes also significantly predicted maternal reports of separation anxiety, overanxious, and social phobia/avoidant disorder symptoms obtained from a diagnostic interview (DISC) when the children were 6 years of age (Warren et al., 2000).

In terms of the second source of validity information for NEC, analyses were conducted for this chapter examining linkages between externalizing behavior problems and several NEC codes. Such an exploration could provide interesting information related to how NEC could be used to complement and augment the MacArthur Narrative Coding system (Robinson et al., 1992). Previous work with the MacArthur Narrative Coding system (Robinson et al., 1992) had shown that emotional distress and combined themes of aggression, personal injury, and atypical negative response predicted externalizing behavior problems (Warren et al., 1996). However, it was not possible with that coding system to examine aggressive themes linked with specific time points of the story (such as at the beginning and end of the story) as could be done with NEC. In addition, NEC offered the possibility of examining the child's response to the aggressive themes (with the *emotional incoherence* code) and additional codes that could indicate feelings of vulnerability in children with externalizing behavior symptoms.

Thus, for purposes of these analyses, it was predicted that NEC codes involving aggression would significantly correlate with externalizing behavior problems. Relevant NEC codes include (1) aggressive *initial response*; (2) aggressive *final content*; (3) aggressive *ending transformation* (captures aggressive conclusions to stories that may be coded positive because of additional prompts); (4) aggressive *emotional incoherence* or sudden, unexplained shifts when dealing with aggressive themes from the aggressive to neutral or positive themes (perhaps indicating a lack of comfort with these aggressive themes); and (5) increased *destruction of objects*. As table 5.2 indicates, all of these codes were found to correlate significantly with behavior problems. The highest and most consistent correlations were found for aggressive final content and aggressive emotional incoherence. These results support the findings obtained with the MacArthur Narrative Coding system (Robinson et al., 1992; Warren et al., 1996). In addition, they provide interesting additional information because it seems that children with higher levels of externalizing symptoms not only show aggressive themes but also tend to have difficulty resolving those themes in a clear manner.

In still other analyses, children with higher levels of externalizing symptoms were predicted to create less positive endings to their stories (*final content* not positive), indicating that they expected negative outcomes to situations. Such children were also expected to show less competent child doll coping behaviors (i.e., noncompetent *child representations*) because they would tend to use more aggressive behaviors than competent behaviors. These predictions and findings were similar to those for children who had higher levels of internalizing and anxious symptoms (Warren et al., 2000) because children with any type of behavior problems would be expected to demonstrate difficulties with positive and competent behaviors.

Additional codes were examined to explore potential feelings of vulnerability in children with higher levels of externalizing behavior symptoms. The codes selected were chosen because they commonly accompanied aggressive themes in the stories. Because danger themes were so often associated with aggressive and personal injury themes, it was hypothesized that children with higher levels of externalizing behavior problems would also create more danger themes (indicating that they perhaps become aggressive because of perceived danger). Because grandiose child representations and monster themes often involved aggression, it was also anticipated that children with higher levels of externalizing problems would display more grandiose child representations (perhaps indicating feelings of vulnerability) and would portray the monster as real (perhaps indicating more difficulty with fears and more immaturity since 5-year-old children are attempting to actively overcome a belief in monsters). It was also hypothesized that such children would produce more oral themes (perhaps indicating increased neediness). There was some support for all of these hypotheses.

Though aggregating the codes is recommended, correlations for these individual codes with the internalizing and externalizing subscales of the Child Behavior Checklist and Teacher Report Form are presented in table 5.3 to provide more information about the individual codes for potential users of the system.

Recommendations for Use of the System and Directions for Future Research

The NEC can be used by those who wish to study emotional regulation, temperament, attachment, and psychopathology. The focus on emotional coherence, emotional shifts, affect, and initial responses to stories that trigger specific emotions makes the system useful for researchers of emotional regulation. Codes such as startle, incongruent affect, and storytelling technique and the codes focused on the child's discomfort in new situations may be useful for the study of temperament. Examination of initial and final responses to the separation stories, as well as child representations and other codes, as described in Warren et al. (2000), may be useful in research concerning attachment and anxiety. Several codes appear to relate to psychopathological processes. This coding system appears to be useful for those wishing to study anxiety and internalizing disorders (Warren et al., 2000) and appears to link with aspects of externalizing disorders as well.

In terms of implementation, several stories that are anticipated to produce the desired information (e.g., several anxiety-provoking stories) should be used. Then, codes should be averaged across the stories and grouped for optimal results. Codes will need to be recoded prior to analyses to obtain the specific information desired. For example, if the aim is to determine whether children have initial difficulties with separation, it will be important to create a variable for the initial content code that identifies children who resist the separation. To create an aggregate, it is useful to take the *z* score of the different codes to be combined and then take the mean of the resulting *z* scores.

Advantages of the system include its ability to focus on linkages related to internalizing and anxiety symptoms, to delineate themes at specific narrative time points, and to code child representations. However, additional research is needed to replicate findings and to further explore the meaning of children's narratives. These analyses were all conducted with one small sample of low-risk nonclinical children. Additional research is therefore needed to replicate findings with different samples and in more diverse populations.

In a similar vein, work is needed to determine whether certain types of narrative responses actually reflect the hypothesized dimensions. For example, researchers could examine whether inappropriate child doll representations are related to low self-esteem measured by child reports or observed behaviors. Researchers could also examine whether children who don't allow the child doll to separate from the parents in the stories will actually not easily separate from their parents in daily life. New stories and codes can be added to enhance explorations. At this point, one can conclude that the NEC indicates considerable promise in linking story stem responses to a greater understanding of the child's emotions and inner world.

NOTE

This research was supported by funds from the John D. and Catherine T. MacArthur Foundation Network on Early Childhood Transitions, NIMH postdoctoral research training grants MH15442 and IF32MH10712, and NIMH Scientist Development Award for Clinicians 1K08MH01532. I gratefully acknowledge the help and support of Dr. Robert N. Emde.

REFERENCES

Achenbach, T. M. (1991a). *Manual for the Child Behavior Checklist/4–18 and 1991 Profile.* Burlington: University of Vermont Department of Psychiatry.

Achenbach, T. M. (1991b). *Manual for the Teacher's Report Form and 1991 Profile.* Burlington: University of Vermont Department of Psychiatry.

Bretherton, I., Oppenheim, D., Prentiss, C., Buchsbaum, H., Emde, R., Lundquist, A., Ridgeway, D., Watson, M., Wolf, D., Rubin, B., & Clyman, R. (1990). *The MacArthur Story Stem Battery.* Unpublished manuscript.

Hollingshead, A. B., & Redlich, F. C. (1958). *Two-factor Index of social position.* New York: Wiley.

Oppenheim, D., Emde, R. N., Hasson, M., & Warren, S. L. (1997). Preschoolers face moral dilemmas: A longitudinal study of acknowledging and resolving internal conflict. *International Journal of Psychoanalysis, 78,* 943–957.

Oppenheim, D., Emde, R. N., & Warren, S. L. (1997). Children's narrative representations of mothers: Their development and associations with child and mother adaptation. *Child Development, 68,* 127–138.

Oppenheim, D., Nir, A., Warren, S. L., & Emde, R. N. (1997). Emotion regulation in mother-child narrative co-construction: Associations with children's narratives and adaptation. *Developmental Psychology, 33,* 284–294.

Robinson, J., Mantz-Simmons, L., Macfie, J., and the MacArthur Narrative Working Group. (1992). *The MacArthur narrative coding manual.* Unpublished manuscript.

Shaffer, D., Fisher, P., Dulcan, M. K., Davies, M., Piacentini, J., Schwab-Stone, M. E., et al. (1996). The NIMH Diagnostic Interview Schedule for Children Version 2.3 (DISC-2.3): Description, acceptability, prevalence rates, and performance in the MECA study. *Journal of the American Academy of Child and Adolescent Psychiatry, 35,* 865–877.

Warren, S. L., Emde, R. N., & Oppenheim, D. (1993). *New MacArthur emotion story stems.* Unpublished manuscript.

Warren, S. L., Emde, R. N., & Oppenheim, D. (1996). Can emotions and themes in children's play predict behavior problems? *Journal of the American Academy of Child and Adolescent Psychiatry, 35,* 1331–1337.

Warren, S. L., Emde, R. N., & Sroufe, L. A. (2000). Internal representations: Predicting anxiety from children's play narratives. *Journal of the American Academy of Child and Adolescent Psychiatry, 39,* 100–107.

Warren, S. L., Huston, L., Egeland, B., & Sroufe, L. A. (1997). Child and adolescent anxiety disorders and early attachment. *Journal of the American Academy of Child and Adolescent Psychiatry, 36,* 637–644.

KAI VON KLITZING
KIM KELSAY
ROBERT N. EMDE

6

The Structure of 5-Year-Old Children's Play Narratives Within the MacArthur Story Stem Methodology

This chapter presents new psychometric information about the MacArthur Story Stem Battery (MSSB; Bretherton, Oppenheim, Buchsbaum, Emde, & the MacArthur Narrative Group, 1990) and the MacArthur Narrative Coding System (MNCS; Robinson, Mantz-Simmons, Macfie, and the MacArthur Narrative Working Group, 1996) that emerges from the analysis of the narratives of 654 5-year-old nonclinical children within the MacArthur Longitudinal Twin Study (MALTS; Emde et al., 1992; Plomin et al., 1993).

Assessment of Narratives in Different Research Settings

As discussed earlier in the book, the MSSB is a new research technique that provides a window into the representational world of children, their understanding of family relationships, and their views of themselves. Achieving narrative competence is a major characteristic of the developmental transition from 3 to 4 years of age. This competence enables preschoolers to represent past experience and future expectations and talk about them to others coherently. Achieving narrative competence indicates a significant developmental step toward the child's ability to understand and regulate his or her own emotional life. Moreover, telling stories and enacting them through play is an often used tool in psychotherapeutic settings, providing the clinician with insight into the subjective world of children and their conscious and unconscious conflicts. The MSSB elicits children's play narratives in a standardized way so that they may be coded systematically. In so doing, it holds the promise of bridging the gap between clinically useful diagnostic procedures and highly standardized procedures of research settings.

The MSSB can be applied in a variety of research settings with different aims. In longitudinal studies on early development, play narratives can be compared with children's observable behavior and with child-caregiver interactions. Using play narratives, one can add the window into the child's representations to the window of interactions and behavior. In clinical research settings, learning more about the subjective world of children may tell us more about therapeutic approaches and psychotherapy indications. Finally, the MSSB may become a useful research tool in the study of process and outcome of child psychotherapy because it provides us with an "off line" possibility (in contrast to the "on line" view within the therapeutic setting) to assess changes in the inner world of children over time.

How one codes children's play narratives depends on the questions researchers are interested in. Several coding systems have emerged recently from different contexts in which the narratives are used. For example, Warren, Oppenheim, and Emde (1996), with an interest in understanding internalizing problems, have developed a coding scheme that focuses on children's emotionality and self-representations. Hill and collaborators, with an interest in externalizing problems, have developed a coding scheme that focuses on the quality of narratives and their coherence in a dynamic, sequential way (Hill, J., personal communication, 1997). Von Klitzing and collaborators, with an interest in triadic functioning, have developed a coding scheme that focuses on the inner triadic representations of the child (available on request from the first author). The MNCS is one of the earlier coding systems, and other coding systems often incorporate elements from it. In addition, this coding scheme has been used in several publications and has allowed for comparisons between studies.

There is a need for more psychometric information regarding the MNCS. Among these are (1) the need for data reduction by forming meaningful aggregates out of a great number of coding items; (2) the need for descriptive data about children's narratives within different samples, including information about sex differences; and (3) the need for knowledge about the specific features of each story. Concerning the latter need, different stories were designed to elicit different themes. Investigators need to know if this is true, and if so, what themes do each of the stories elicit and which stories elicit similar themes. For example, investigators might tailor the stories administered to address a particular question, and studies with a longitudinal design might avoid recall bias by using different stories that elicit similar themes.

An Overview of the MNCS and Coding Aggregates Used in Initial Studies

The MNCS assesses three areas: *content themes* (e.g., aggressive themes, themes of empathy and help, exclusion), *parental representations* (positive, negative, and disciplinary-controlling roles of the parents), and *performance* of the narrative (e.g., shown and told emotions, narrative style and quality, narrative coherence and relatedness to the examiner). Content themes and parental representations are coded in categories (presence vs. absence of a theme), whereas different aspects of performance are coded on scales with defined scale points.

The need for creating meaningful aggregates out of the large number of single coding categories that sometimes represent infrequent events has been taken into account in initial studies. Oppenheim, Emde, and Warren (1997) found distinct patterns of positive, negative, and disciplinary parental representations, with "positive" comprising codes of protective, caregiving, affectionate, helpful, and forgiving parental behavior and "negative" comprising codes of abusive and bizarre parental behavior. Oppenheim et al. found parental representations to be correlated with behavioral problems as assessed by parental questionnaires, such as the Child Behavior Checklist (CBCL/4–18; Achenbach, 1991). In the newest version of the MNCS, these factors are included as coding categories and replace the original more differentiated items. Warren et al. (1996) used a clinically derived aggregate "aggressive/destructive themes" comprising codes of aggression, atypical negative responses, and personal injury. They found this aggregate correlated with the externalizing scores of the CBCL administered to teachers and parents. Oppenheim, Nir, Warren, and Emde (1997) used this aggregate as well as a "prosocial" aggregate consisting of empathy/helping, reparation/guilt, affiliation, affection, and interpersonal conflict resolution and found correlations between each of these aggregates and emotional coherence of a mother-child co-constructed narrative. Steele et al. (1997) described, as the result of their factor analysis, four aggregated scores for "limit setting" (including codes of shame toward another, exclusion of another, verbal punishment, and discipline by mother), "prosocial" content (codes of affection, positive mother, (–) physical aggression), "antisocial" content (codes of physical aggression, physical punishment, (–) guilt/reparation), and "naughtiness" (codes of shame toward another and dishonesty). The authors found meaningful correlations between these aggregates and attachment classifications within the parents measured by the Adult Attachment Interview, and in parent-child interactions as measured by the Strange Situation Procedure. All the mentioned ways of aggregating variables came out of studies of nonclinical samples; Toth, Cicchetti, Macfie, and Emde (1997) applied the MSSB to a maltreated sample of preschoolers. They formed aggregates termed "positive self-representation" composed of content theme codes of empathy/helping, compliance, affection, and affiliation and "negative self-representation" composed of content theme codes of aggression, noncompliance, and shame. Maltreated children showed significantly more "negative self-representations" than did children of a comparison group from the same socioeconomic class who were not maltreated.

Due to the relatively small sample sizes, these cited studies were able to include only a few items of the MNCS into their final aggregates, and in some studies (e.g., Steele et al., 1997) infrequently used codes, such as atypical negative response, were excluded from analysis even though they are potentially relevant clinically. Steele et al. also identified another problem: the meaning of an item may change according to the story. For example, a code of compliance in the stories called Exclusion and Headache may represent a prosocial action indicating empathy and respect toward the parents. In contrast, a code of compliance in Bathroom Shelf represents an obedient and not empathic way of solving a moral dilemma. If a mean for this coding category is computed typically across the whole set of stories per subject, misleading results may appear.

Another limitation of most of these aggregates is that, with the exception of aggregates from Toth et al. (1997), they include only content themes and parental representations and do not include results of the performance scales. This strategy is contrary to our impression that emotions children show during the narrative procedure, the quality and coherence of a story, and the child's responsivity to the examiner may sometimes provide valuable clinical information regarding children's emotional and behavioral disturbances, just as much as what is revealed by content themes.

The analysis of narratives in the MALTS sample allowed for a unique opportunity to provide information that can address these needs and questions. For example, we attempted to identify and remove codes that might have different meaning in different stories from our factor analysis of variables that represent item scores aggregated over all stories (it would only make sense to use the results of these items in every story separately). We also chose to exclude content theme codes that occur almost exclusively in one story, such as interpersonal conflict resolution, which in this sample occurs primarily in Three's a Crowd. Finally, we chose to include performance codes in our analysis.

Sample and Procedures

The MALTS encompasses more than 400 same-sex twin pairs assessed at least eight times prior to age 4, and then once a year until age 7. An overview of the rationale, sample, and measures of the MALTS can be found in Emde et al. (1992) and Reznick, Corley, and Robinson (1997). Briefly, the sample in this report consists of 421 same-sex twin pairs recruited from birth reports from the Colorado Department of Health. The sex distribution was approximately equal, and the ethnic distribution was 92% European-American, 4% Hispanic-American, 0.3% Asian-American, and 3.7% American Indian and mixed ethnicity. Families consisted almost exclusively of two parents, the mean age of parents was 30 years, and the mean education was 14.3 years. The mean birth weight of twins was 2,574 grams.

The MSSB narratives were administered during a home visit when the children were 5 years old. Fifteen stories were administered to 654 children. Because of limited funding, the complete set of 15 stories was coded for only 25% (n = 166) of the sample. The coding of the remaining children (n = 488) was restricted to eight stories that were chosen based on amount of content themes as well as the variety of conflicts and moral dilemmas elicited. The eight "core" stories were Spilled Juice, Looking for Barney, Gift Giving, Three's a Crowd, Lost Keys, Bathroom Shelf, Exclusion, and Cookie Dilemma. The remaining seven stories that were coded in the smaller portion of the sample were Mom's Headache, Hot

Gravy, Stealing the Candy Bar, Departure, Reunion, Outing to the Park, and Family Fun.[1]

Narrative Coherence: Transformations in Use of the Code

The "Narrative Coherence" code is one of the most interesting items within the performance area. It provides 11 defined categories describing the way children deal with the conflicts in the story stems as well as the quality and the coherence of narrative. Oppenheim, Nir, et al. (1997) found a correlation between narrative coherence (using this scale) in children's narratives and emotional coherence in child-mother co-constructed narratives. However, we identified two potential problems with the narrative coherence scale. First, the 11 points appear to describe categories and not points on an ordinal or metric scale. Second, the categories listed describe two different aspects of the narratives. One aspect describes how the conflict of the story stem is addressed in the narrative and how much embellishment is used to tell the story, whereas the other aspect describes the degree of coherence in the narrative. An example demonstrates this problem. A rating of 8 on the narrative coherence code describes a higher amount of embellishment used for telling a narrative compared to a rating of 7. In terms of coherence, however, it is the opposite: a rating of 7 describes more coherence within the narrative than a rating of 8 does. In response to this problem, we pulled these two aspects apart by transforming narrative coherence into two new scales: "Embellishment/Addressing the Conflict" and "Coherence." This transformation is shown in table 6.1

A further exploration, including a theoretical rationale for using two scales instead of one, may be helpful. Children might employ each of these differently in defending against emotions. For example, a child may avoid emotions by telling a story with low "Embellishment/Addressing the Conflict" (hypothetically showing rigidity of defense), whereas another child may be overwhelmed by emotions

TABLE 6.1: Transformation of the Category "Narrative Coherence"

Scale point	Description	Categories of "Narrative Coherence"
New scale: Embellishment/Addressing the Conflict		
1	No response	0
2	Fragments	1
3	Strategy of avoiding conflict	2, 3, 4, 5
4	Addressing and solving conflict without embellishment	6, 7
5	Addressing and solving conflict with embellishment	8, 9, 10
New scale: Coherence		
1	Completely incoherent	1
2	No clear story line, some incoherence	2, 3, 4
3	Story line with some incoherence	6, 8
4	Coherent story	5, 7, 9, 10

and have a high amount of "Incoherence" (hypothetically showing weakness of defense). In the first case, a child might limit spontaneity in order to avoid conflict. In the second, a child might not succeed in avoiding the conflict and connected fears, and his or her ability to tell a coherent story is weakened. Two scales may help discriminate between these two hypothesized defensive styles.

Factor Structure

Principal components analyses with varimax rotation of the MacArthur Narrative Coding system items were performed in two steps: (1) the items of each coding category (content themes, parental representations, performance) were entered separately, and (2) the resulting factors from step one that met criteria of Cronbach's alpha >.3 were used to compute overall aggregates. The criteria to include coding items in step 1 were frequency across all stories (item used in more than 5% of the stories), distribution between stories (used in more than one story), and for content themes, consistency (apparently similar meaning in all stories). The following coding items met these criteria and were included: Aggression, Escalation of Conflict, Atypical Negative Responses, Exclusion Self, Exclusion Other, Punishment Physical and Verbal, Reparation/Guilt, Affiliation, Empathy/Help, Affection, Tattling, Dishonesty, Positive Representation Mother and Father, Negative Representation Mother and Father, Discipline/Control Mother and Father, Anger, Distress, Concern, Anxiety, Joy, Sadness, Direct versus Indirect Performance Style, Investment in Performance, Embellishment/Addressing the Conflict, Coherence, and Responsivity with Examiner. Table 6.2 displays the results of principal components analyses using these items for the three separate areas of content themes, parental representations, and performance. The table shows the aggregates of items in each coding area that tended to occur together as reflected by high loadings on a particular component.

The mean alpha of all 12 factors is .50, ranging from .71 to .10. We excluded factors with alpha less than .3 from further analysis.

Factor Analysis

Content Themes

The "Aggressive Themes" aggregate is very similar to the aggregate used by Warren et al. (1996), except that it includes the more prevalent item "Escalation of Conflict" instead of "Personal Injury," which is mainly used in Outing to the Park. Like Steele et al. (1997), we also found " Limit Setting" to be the heading of an important group of themes. Our analysis found two separate factors, one involving more moderate and external ways of disciplinary actions (Exclusion Other, Punishment Verbal) and one with more harsh and internal ways of limit setting (Punishment Physical, Exclusion Self, Reparation/Guilt, and Affiliation). One may be astonished that "Affiliation" is included in harsh limit setting. This

TABLE 6.2: Step One Factor Analysis: Aggregates of Items Found in Different Coding Areas

Content Themes	Parental Representations	Performance
Aggressive Themes (2.72) Aggression, Escalation, Negative Atypical Response	*Positive Parental Representations* (1.72) positive mother, positive father	*Angry Involvement* (3.08)Anger, Distress, Concern, Investment in Performance, Embellishment
Limit Setting Themes (2.01) Exclusion Other, Punishment Verbal	*Negative Parental Representations* (1.54) Negative Mother, Negative Father	*Quality of Story/Open Relatedness* (1.58) Direct Performance Style, Responsivity with Examiner, Coherence, Embellishment, –Anxiety
Guilt Themes (1.46) Punishment Physical, Exclusion Self, Reparation/Guilt, Affiliation	*Disciplinary Parental Representation* (1.15) Disciplinary Mother, Disciplinary Father	*Anxious Relatedness* (1.17) Joy, Responsivity with Examiner, +Anxiety
Affection Themes (1.10) Empathy/Help, Affection		*Sadness, Coherence* (1.16)
Dishonesty Themes (1.01) Tattling, Dishonesty		
Explained variance: 59.3 %	Explained variance: 73.4%	Explained variance: 63.6 %

Note. Eigenvalues in parenthesis.

is probably due to the fact that many acts of affiliation (e.g., in Three's a Crowd) are performed between two characters in order to exclude a third character. In these instances, affiliation may not be prosocial. In future revisions of the MNCS, it might be useful to distinguish between the prosocial aspect and the excluding aspect of affiliation. For further analysis, we chose to aggregate the two distinct factors to a comprehensive "Limit Setting" factor, which comprises Punishment Verbal and Physical, Exclusion Self and Other, Reparation/Guilt, and Affiliation (alpha = .60).

Parental Representations

The analysis of the "Parental Representation" items showed that representations of fathers and mothers are associated probably because in the MSSB stems include only the mother or mother and father in the same roles (exceptions are Gift Giving and Lost Keys). Thus, it may be necessary to create new stories that involve the parental figures in a more dynamic and distinguishable manner to elicit triadic narratives.

Performance Codes

We found four factors in the performance part of the coding system. The first ("Angry Involvement") describes an aggregate of negative emotions (Anger, Concern, Distress), as well as investment in performance and embellishment. Children who score high on this factor are invested in telling embellished stories that contain or display anger and distress. In contrast, children who score high on the second factor ("Quality of Story/Open Relatedness") tell more coherent stories in a relaxed (not anxious) way and are very related to the examiner. The third factor includes "Responsivity with Examiner" but differs from the second factor by including Anxiety and not including markers of a well-told narrative (Coherence, Embellishment, and Direct Performance Style). "Joy" is mainly defined by the child's smiling. A low rating (1) of joy was more frequent than a higher rating (2). Our impression is that a slight smile often may suggest embarrassment, or it may indicate the child's need to be assured by the examiner. Thus, joy may frequently covary with anxiety. The last performance factor implies that the infrequent expression of sadness is associated with a coherent way of telling the story. The factors "Dishonesty Themes" and "Sadness/Coherence" showed a very low level of internal consistency (alpha = .24 and .10) and were therefore excluded from further analysis.

Combined Analysis

The first factor analysis, already described, was carried out separately for each of the three areas of the coding system (content themes, parental representations, and performance style). A second factor analysis was then carried out using the factors derived from the first analysis. Again, a principal components analysis was performed and lead to four overall factors. The factor loadings for the varimax rotation appear in table 6.3.

Four factors resulted, which, upon inspection, we labeled as (1) "Anger and Discipline," (2) "Positive Themes and Positive Representations," (3) "Negative Themes and Negative Representations," and (4) "Quality of Story and Relatedness." The aggregates based on these factors are presented in table 6.4, along with the coding items that compose them. Interrater reliability according to these aggregates was calculated from 202 stories coded by two independent raters using intraclass correlations. Reliability for the four overall factors ranged from .75 to .92.

TABLE 6.3. Step Two Factor Analysis: Factor Loadings of the Story Stem Aggregates From Step 1

	Factor 1	Factor 2	Factor 3	Factor 4
Aggressive Themes			.88	
Limit Setting Themes (comprehensive)	.84			
Affection Themes		.80		
Positive Parental Representation		.81		
Negative Parental Representation			.84	
Disciplinary Parental Representation	.88			
Angry Involvement	.49			
Quality of Story/Openness				.76
Anxious Relatedness				.90

Like Steele et al. (1997), we found distinct factors describing positive and negative themes characterizing the content of the narratives. These kinds of aggregates were to be expected because positive or negative actions performed by parent characters are coded under content themes as well as under parental representations. In the described factor solution, the shown or told Anger, Distress, and Concern negative affects are associated with the limit-setting themes of Exclusion, Punishment, and Reparation/Guilt. This may be due to the nonclinical sample in which children may regulate the presented anger and distress by concluding their narratives with limit-setting themes. Conversely, it is possible that themes of discipline and punishment lead to affects of anger and distress within the child or the represented characters. In any case, children scoring high on this scale tend to show a high investment in performance and to tell embellished narratives that address the conflict.

The fourth factor found in our analysis is within the domain of performance and aggregates the two subfactors "Quality of Story/Open Relatedness" and "Anxious Relatedness." As Anxiety is used with a negative sign in the one subfactor and with a positive sign in the other subfactor, it becomes neutralized by aggregating the two subfactors. Therefore, it is no longer part of the overall aggregate Quality of Story, Relatedness with Examiner. This scale describes how children represent the narratives and comprises the coherence, directness, and

TABLE 6.4: Overall Aggregated Scores and Their Internal Consistency

Anger and Discipline	Positive Themes and Positive Representations	Negative Themes and Negative Representations	Quality of Story and Relatedness
Exclusion Self + Other	Empathy/Help	Aggression	Direct Performance
+	+	+	+
Punishment Verbal	Affection	Escalation	Responsivity with
+ Physical	+	+	Examiner
+	Positive Mother	Negative Atypical Responses	+
Reparation/Guilt	+	+	Coherence
+	Positive Father	Negative Mother	+
Affiliation		+	Embellishment
+		Negative Father	+
Disciplinary Mother			Joy
and Father			
+			
Anger + Distress			
+ Concern			
+			
Investment in			
Performance			
+			
Embellishment			
alpha = .75	alpha = . 62	alpha = .72	alpha = .61
r = .91	r = .83	r = .80	r = .91

Internal consistency (alpha = Cronbach's alpha).
Inter-rater reliability (r = intraclass correlation).

embellishment of the told story as well as the amount of joy shown and the child's relatedness to the examiner.

We performed our factor analysis in two steps for several reasons.[2] The first is theoretical. We wanted a system of aggregates that could be used on several levels. Aggregates from the first level were content themes, parental representations, and performance codes with each category entered separately into a factor analysis for that category. This may provide more valid information in some settings or samples, whereas in others the larger factors from the two-step analysis may be more useful. For example, in predicting clinical problems in children, it may be that the relatively small aggregate of Aggressive Themes provides us with more valid or specific information on the child's representational organization than the broader aggregate of Negative Themes and Negative Representations, which includes some redundant information (e.g., one narrative event coded twice as theme *and* as parental representation). Indeed, our analysis shows that factors derived from content themes are distributed differently than factors derived from performance codes.

Distribution of Themes and Performance Characteristics in Different Stories

To get information on characteristics of different stories and the differences between stories, we computed the means of theme and performance codings for every story. These descriptive figures provide information about the themes and performance styles each story typically pulls for. Figures 6.1–6.8 show the mean scores of content theme aggregates, parental representation aggregates, and performance aggregates in the eight core stories (Looking for Barney, Gift Giving, Lost Keys, Three's a Crowd, Bathroom Shelf, Exclusion, Spilled Juice, and Cookie Dilemma). Additionally, the graphs show the mean number of themes (Total *N* of Themes) coded in each story and the mean of Compliance and Noncompliance scores, which are not included in any of the aggregates. The mean scores are based on the evaluation of 654 5-year-old children of the sample described. For the purpose of comparability, the scores are *z* transformed so that zero indicates the average of a score across all eight stories, positive scores indicate above average, and negative scores indicate below average. In contrast to the other aggregates, the performance aggregates are not independent from each other because some of the codes are used in more than one aggregate.

The stories Bathroom Shelf and Three's a Crowd apparently elicit the largest numbers of content themes (about half of a standard deviation above the mean), whereas Looking for Barney and Gift Giving elicit the lowest numbers of content themes (nearly half of a standard deviation below the mean). The latter two stories show scorings of affection high above the mean (Looking for Barney half of a standard deviation and Gift Giving one standard deivation).

Looking for Barney, Gift Giving, and Spilled Juice are story stems that apparently elicit from children of this age narratives with some similar patterns. In Looking for Barney and Spilled Juice, the highest numbers of Positive Parental

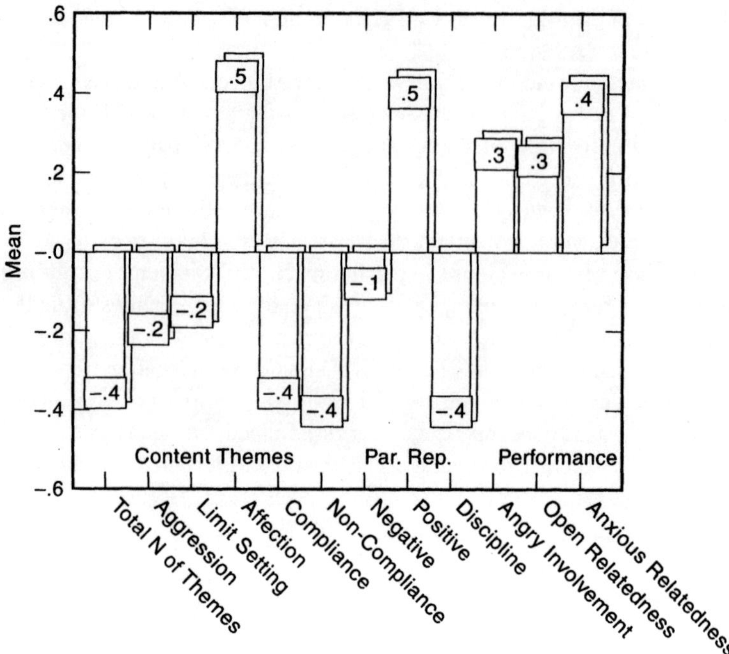

FIGURE 6.1. Mean scores in Looking for Barney

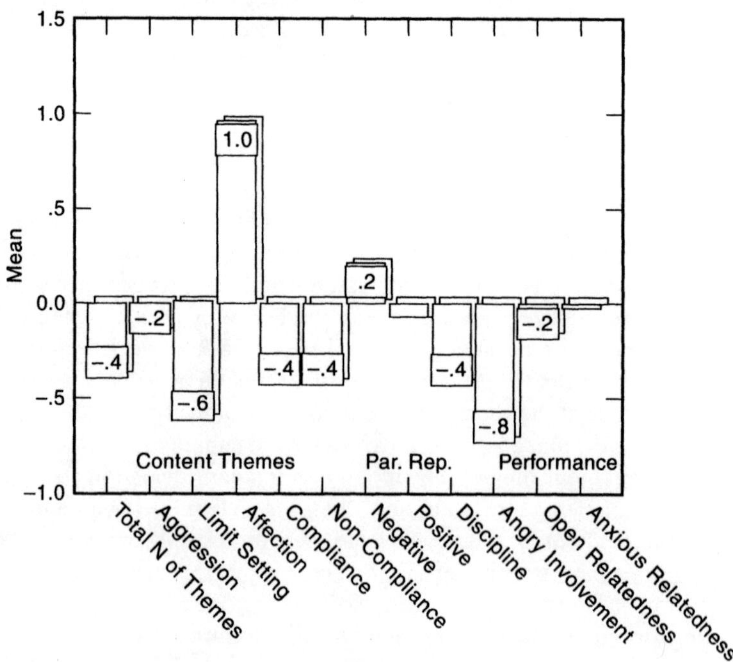

FIGURE 6.2. Mean scores in Gift Giving

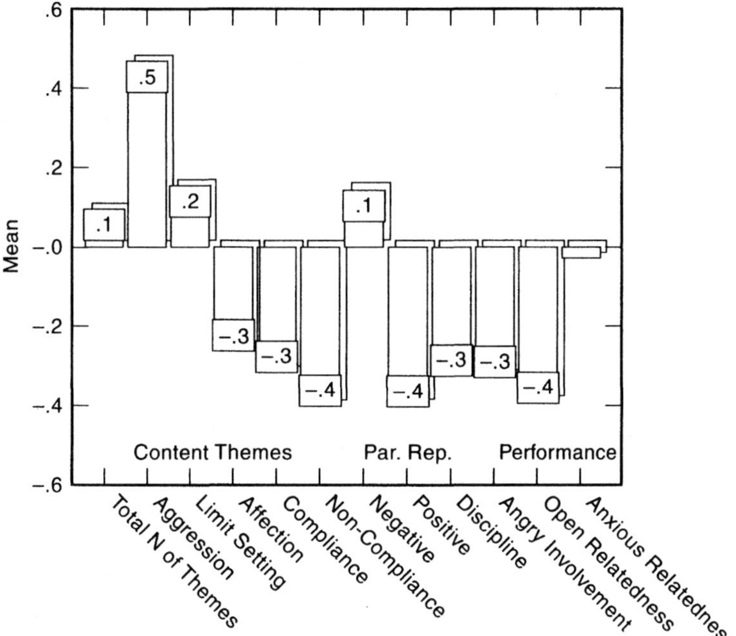

FIGURE 6.3. Mean scores in Lost Keys

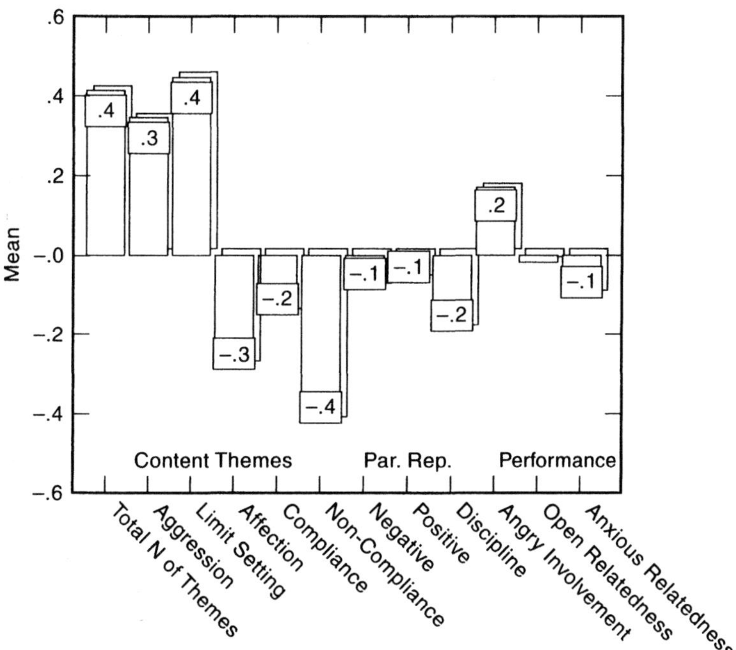

FIGURE 6.4. Mean *z* scores in Three's a Crowd

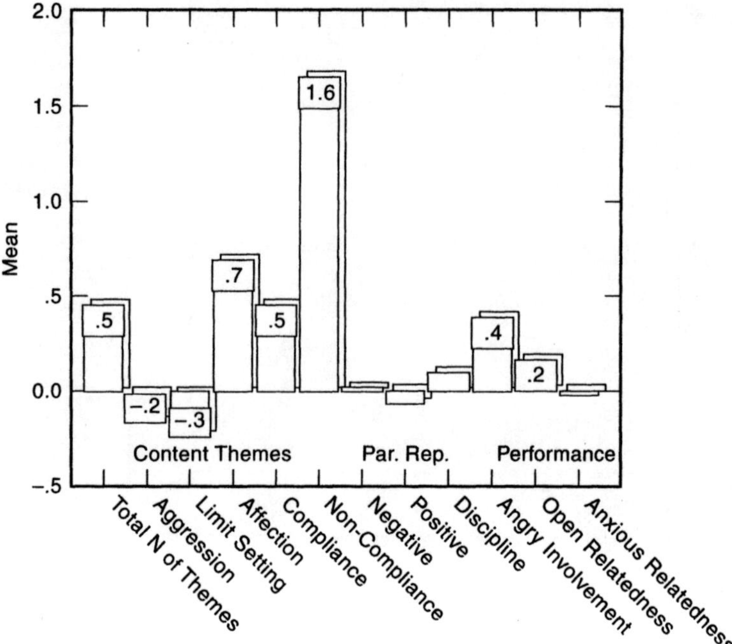

FIGURE 6.5. Mean *z* scores in Bathroom Shelf

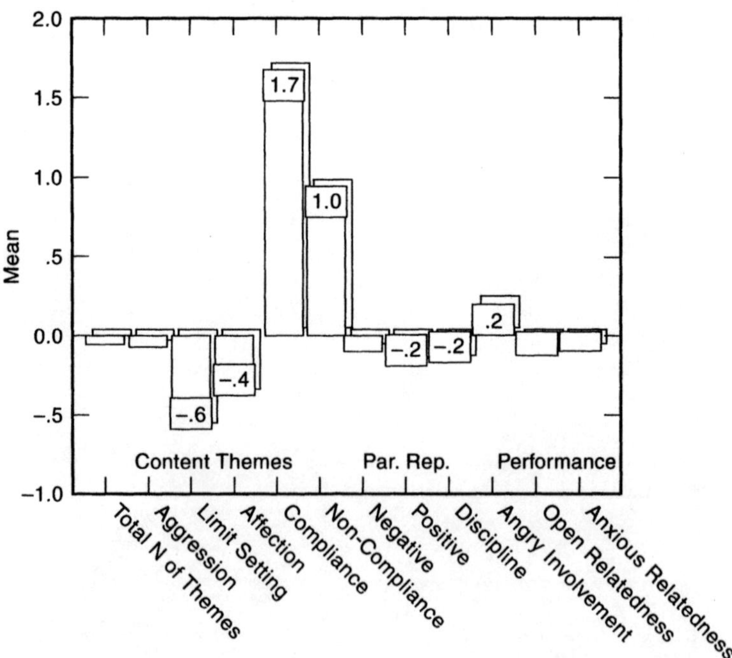

FIGURE 6.6. Mean *z* scores in Exclusion

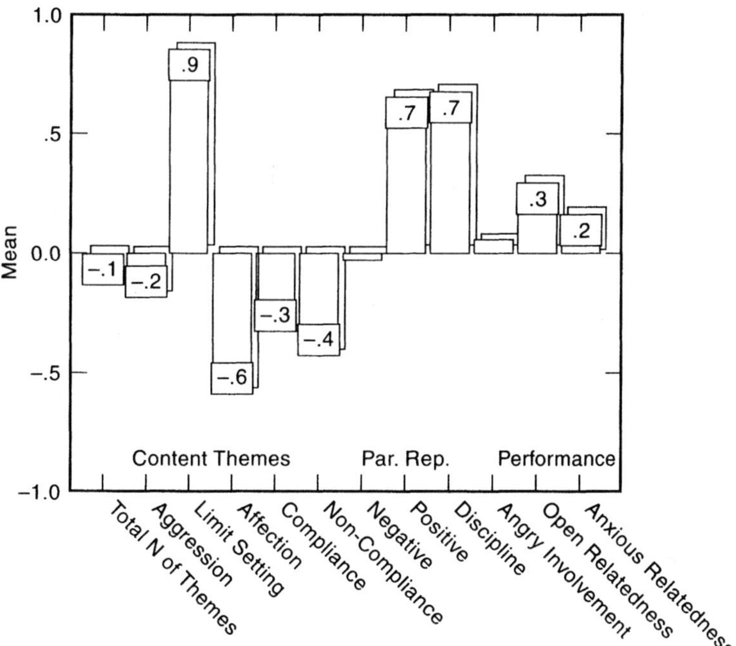

FIGURE 6.7. Mean *z* scores in Spilled Juice

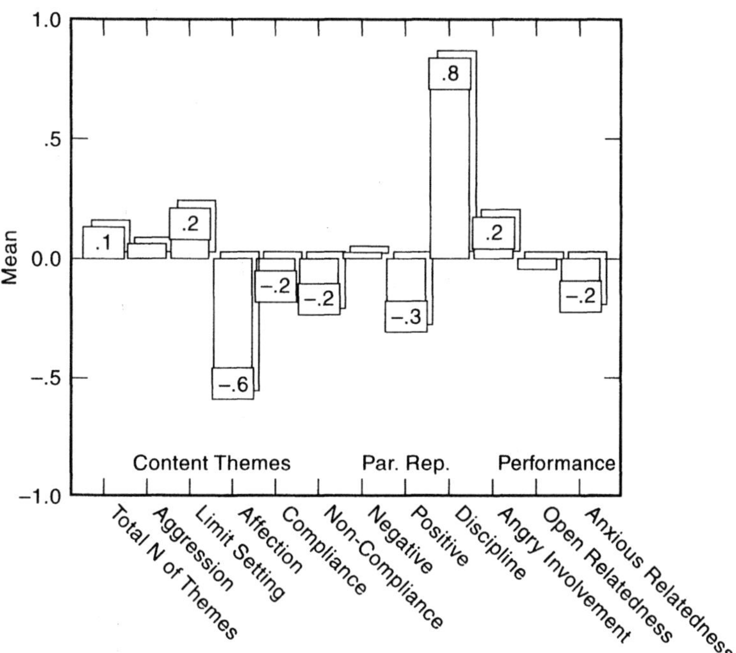

FIGURE 6.8. Mean *z* scores in Cookie Dilemma

Representations can be found (Spilled Juice has also a high number of Disciplinary Parental Representations). That this is not the case in Gift Giving may be an artifact of the coding rules of this study, according to which a decision was made not to code positive parental reactions to the child's gift because they were so common. The stories with the highest number of Positive Parental Representations also have an above average number of Affection Themes (Looking for Barney and Gift Giving) and Limit-Setting Themes (Spilled Juice). Summarizing these patterns, one can characterize these three stories by their elicitation of the most positive themes and representations. It may not be by chance that these three story stems were used as the first three of the battery. They are different in terms of the performance results, Looking for Barney eliciting a large number of positive and negative emotional and relational reactions, Gift Giving eliciting a below average number of these performance scorings, and Spilled Juice lying between these two according to performance aggregates. The Cookie Dilemma story stem elicits, like Spilled Juice, a large number of Limit-Setting Themes and Disciplinary Parental Representations. In contrast to Spilled Juice, it elicits fewer Affection Themes and less Open Relatedness.

Bathroom Shelf and Exclusion are the two story stems that elicit narratives dominated by Compliance/Noncompliance themes. In Bathroom Shelf noncompliance scores exceed the compliance scores, showing that most of the children in our sample tended to disregard the parental rule in order to provide help for the injured sibling. In Exclusion the pattern is the reverse. More children are compliant than noncompliant to the parents' request to leave them alone. This supports the impression that high compliance scores indicate different qualities of representations in these two stories, perhaps showing a strict rule-boundedness in the Bathroom Shelf story, on the one hand, and a mature way of respecting parental intimacy in the Exclusion Story, on the other hand. The above average number of "Angry Involvement" indicates that both stories expose most of the children to emotionally difficult conflicts.

Lost Keys and Three's a Crowd elicit the highest number of Aggressive Themes. That in Three's a Crowd the number of Limit-Setting Themes even exceeds the number of Aggressive Themes may be in part an artifact, because whenever Exclusion is coded in this story, it is likely to indicate an aggressive solution of the conflict between the three children characters (one is excluded so that the other two may have fun with each other) rather than a true limit-setting parental measure ("time out") as in the other stories. Interestingly, in Three's a Crowd these Aggressive Themes are combined with an above average amount of "Angry Involvement" (negative emotions, investment in performance), whereas in Lost Keys all performance scores are below average, indicating that the narratives elicited by this story stem usually are characterized by less expressed emotional involvement.

The mean z scores of the seven noncore stories appear in appendix 6.1. These data are based on the evaluation of stories from 167 children. Mom's Headache elicits mostly compliance/noncompliance themes and can be compared with Exclusion and Bathroom Shelf. Hot Gravy is similar to Spilled Juice with respect to the large number of Affection and Limit-Setting Themes. Stealing the

Candy Bar is similar to Cookie Dilemma with respect to the large number of Limit-Setting Themes and Disciplinary Parental Representations. The other four story stems (Departure, Reunion, Outing to the Park, and Family Fun) elicit narratives with low scores in all coding domains.

Intercorrelations Between Stories

Table 6.5 and appendices tables 6.2–6.4 show the intercorrelations of the overall factor aggregates (see table 6.4) among the eight stories. In other words, they give information about the likelihood that a child who scores high on a certain measure in one story will score high on the same measure in an other story.

Appendix 6.2 shows the cross-correlation table of the overall factor aggregate "Positive Themes and Positive Representations" among the eight stories. The correlations are all very low, ranging from .02 to .23. This is probably due to the low variance of the positive scores in most of the stories.

The interstory correlations of the scores that involve performance data seem to be higher than those that measure exclusively themes and representations. Appendix 6.3 and appendix 6.4 show the cross-correlation tables of the overall factor aggregates "Anger and Discipline" and "Quality of Story and Relatedness." The correlations are higher, ranging from .33 to .53 in the former and from .28 to .55 in the latter factor aggregate. The cross-correlation table of the factor aggregate "Quality of Story and Relatedness," which exclusively aggregates performance codes, shows a slight decrease of correlations between the two first stories and the following stories according to the order these stories were presented to the child. That tendency could be caused by the sequence of administration or by the fact that the stories with a lower level of conflict are presented first and the stories with a higher level of conflict are presented later.

TABLE 6.5. Correlations (Pearson) Between Stories: Factor Negative Themes and Representation

	Spilled Juice	Looking for Barney	Gift Giving	Three's a Crowd	Lost Keys	Bathroom Shelf	Exclusion	Cookie Dilemma
Spilled Juice	1.000	.301	.324	.199	.204	.076	.181	.180
Looking For Barney		1.000	.324	.208	.165	.120	.297	.092
Gift Giving			1.000	.262	.324	.176	.306	.120
Three's a Crowd				1.000	.357	.141	.304	.311
Lost Keys					1.000	.265	.344	.326
Bathroom Shelf						1.000	.413	.254
Exclusion							1.000	.301
Cookie Dilemma								1.000

Listwise $N = 479$.

The cross-correlations of the scores on the factor aggregate "Negative Themes and Representations" between the eight stories are shown in Table 6.5. Because these correlations differ highly from each other (range: .08 to .41), they will be discussed in more detail to detect patterns that differentiate between stories.

There are moderate correlations (range: .30 to .32) between the stories Spilled Juice, Looking for Barney, and Gift Giving. As we have already seen, these three stories can be summarized as a group of positive stories with little conflict.

Gift Giving correlates similarly with Lost Keys (.33) and Exclusion (.31). It could be hypothesized that in these three stories the child is confronted with the parental couple (although in different circumstances) and that this common topic leads to the interstory correlations with respect to the aggregate Negative Themes and Representations. Three's a Crowd as a story exposing its characters to a triadic conflict joins this group, mainly correlating with Lost Keys (.36) and Exclusion (.30), as does Cookie Dilemma (correlating . 31 with Three's a Crowd, .33 with Lost Keys, and .30 with Exclusion).

The highest correlation links Bathroom Shelf and Exclusion. The common theme of these two stories is a dilemma between the necessity of compliance toward the parental rules on the one side and empathy with the injured sibling (Bathroom Shelf) or the wish to be close to the parents (Exclusion) on the other side. This similarity of conflict may cause the high between-story correlation with respect to the aggregate Negative Themes and Representations.

All the described patterns are based on the interpretation of descriptive data. To find patterns based on a statistical model of common factors explaining covariances of scores between different stories, we performed a principal component analysis with varimax rotation using the aggregate Negative Themes and Representations in different stories as eight different variables. Table 6.6 shows the two-factor solution of this procedure.

Factor 1 is a compound of the stories Three's a Crowd, Lost Keys, Bathroom Shelf, Exclusion, and Cookie Dilemma (alpha = .68), which can be summarized under the heading Conflict Stories. Factor 2 is a compound of the stories Spilled Juice, Looking for Barney, and Gift Giving (alpha = .52), which can be summarized as Positive Event Stories. One could argue that spilling juice is not a positive event, but it elicits positive reactions as reparation and limit setting.

Discussion and Future Research

The analysis of more than 5,000 play narratives elicited by eight MSSB story stems showed differences and similarities between the content themes and performance characteristics these story stems elicit. The differences confirm that different stories can elicit different themes and representations and that a battery of story stems will more likely capture the richness of the child's inner world.

On the other hand, the analyses of the distributions of themes and performance characteristics and the intercorrelations between the narratives elicited by the different story stems reveal patterns of story groups with common characteristics.

TABLE 6.6. Principal Component Analysis With the Variables "Negative Themes and Representations" in Different Stories; Varimax Rotated Factor Loadings

	Factor 1 Conflict stories	Factor 2 Positive theme stories
Spilled Juice		.72
Looking for Barney		.73
Gift Giving		.69
Three's a Crowd	.51	
Lost Keys	.63	
Bathroom Shelf	.69	
Exclusion	.67	
Cookie Dilemma	.69	

These patterns can provide criteria for the creation of new story stems that could help build groups of similar stories. Out of these groups, batteries can be designed for repeated application of the instrument within longitudinal studies without repeatedly using the same stories, which the children usually remember.

Two dimensions cut across stories in terms of their themes and performance dimension. The first dimension has to do with conflict. One can differentiate between stories with low conflict, which usually pull for positive content themes, and stories with high conflict, which usually pull for negative content themes. The low conflict group of positive theme stories includes Spilled Juice, Looking for Barney, and Gift Giving. The high conflict group includes Lost Keys, Three's a Crowd, Bathroom Shelf, Exclusion, and Cookie Dilemma.

A second dimension concerns the extent to which stories elicit high performance ratings and a high number of content themes. Interestingly, subdivisions across this dimension yield nearly the same groups: a group of story stems that mainly pull for performance characteristics and a group of story stems that mainly pull for content themes. The "performance-oriented" story stems include Looking for Barney and Spilled Juice but not Gift Giving. The story stems that elicit more content themes include Lost Keys, Three's a Crowd, Bathroom Shelf, Exclusion, Cookie Dilemma, and Gift Giving.

Within these story stems that elicit more content themes, the following typical theme groups and conflict configurations can be described:

1. Compliance versus nonompliance: Bathroom Shelf, Exclusion;
2. Moral dilemma: Bathroom Shelf, Cookie Dilemma, Three's a Crowd;
3. Triadic themes: Gift Giving, Exclusion, Lost Keys, Three's a Crowd.

Why do story stems that do not contain emotional highly loaded conflict situations (like Looking for Barney) elicit more expressed and told emotions and therefore lead to higher performance codes than story stems that contain emotionally very difficult situations and conflicts (like Lost Keys)? One possibility is that a struggle between parents may elicit more anxiety within the child than the running away of a dog. Thus, evoked anxiety and fear may increase the child's defense and therefore decrease a readiness for showing emotional involvement and display. In other words, rising anxiety may lead to an overregulation of emotions and to avoidance. This hypothesis is supported by the fact that Looking for Barney, a story that seems associated with low internal anxiety, elicits the highest amount of emotional involvement of all the applied story stems. Such a consideration may be a typical pattern in a nonclinical sample of children from mainly middle-class families. It is an open question whether children of a clinical sample may react differently. In a clinical sample, the story stems with a high load of frightening conflicts may lead to emotional dysregulation, which could lead to an increase of (mostly negative) performance characteristics and a decrease of identifiable and coherent content themes in the told narratives. Further research is necessary to examine this hypothesis.

Another result of our analysis is that the two stories with the lowest total numbers of content themes, namely, Looking for Barney and Gift Giving, show scorings of positive themes of affection that are high above the mean. This suggests a limitation of the MSSB and MNCS. Story stems and coding scores in the current battery appeared to generate an overrepresentation of negative content themes and an underrepresentation of positive content themes (this is not so of parental representations, however, where positive representations predominate in our sample). The limitations of a low number of positive themes may also contribute to the very low intercorrelations of scores on the positive overall factor aggregate between stories. Considering this limitation, we face an important procedural question. How can one better detect positive aspects of children's representational worlds in their narratives? Earlier trials of the team developing the MNCS found that presenting positive story stems without problems was not productive. Children seemed uninterested and some seemed bored. A similar conclusion might be reached as we consider the results of our noncore stories, namely, the Family Fun story, with most scores much below the mean scores of all stories (see appendix 6.1). It would appear that most children told short and limited stories in response to this story stem. This result probably is consistent with what Jerome Bruner (1990, p. 49) describes as a central function of a narrative, namely, that it deals with "a deviation from a canonical cultural pattern." In other words, if the story stem does not bring up any "trouble" (if there is no imbalance between the actors, the goals, or other elements of the story stem), there is no reason for telling a narrative. In contrast, story stems that confront the child with some, but not too overwhelming, trouble, like a lost dog, spilled juice, or a hurt hand, give the child an opportunity to include positive themes of reunion or affection into the narrative, as can be seen in Looking for Barney, Spilled Juice, Gift Giving, and Hot Gravy.

This leads us to more thoughts about future research. First, there is a need for more stories that elicit positive themes. Second, in further revisions of the coding system, further work should be done to improve the positive codes in the MNCS. As we reported in our results, the prosocial part of "affiliation" seems to get lost because this code is often used when two characters affiliate in order to exclude a third character. Therefore, in our factor solution, affiliation was included into the Limit-Setting Aggregates and not into the Positive Themes and Representations aggregate. This code could be further specified so that it is limited to the prosocial situations and does not include situations in which characters exclude others.

This is the first time such a large collection of narratives has been analyzed. We were able to derive factors using a two-step factor analysis; to look at the distribution of these factors, total themes, and compliance across stories; and to look for stories that can be grouped together based on common characteristics. The low-risk nature of this sample may mean that it would not be appropriate to generalize this factor structure to clinical or high-risk populations.

We confined our analysis to the MSSB to provide needed descriptive data of this measure. Although other groups have examined external validity and found correlations with other measures (Steele et al., 1997; Oppenheim, Emde, & Warren, 1997; Warren et al., 1996), our analysis does not address this issue. The MacArthur Longitudinal Twin Study does include many other measures across several ages, and in future work, we are interested in looking at validity across a range of functions, including social functioning within the family, behavioral observations by research assistants, and reports by parents and teachers. Gender differences were not included in these analyses, but they will be included in the future, and there is every reason to believe they will provide an important context for assessing external validity (first results in von Klitzing, Kelsay, Emde, Robinson, & Schmitz, 2000).

Finally as the discussion implies, our analysis of a core battery of stories was undertaken to increase our understanding of the findings from this technique, and we hope this additional knowledge will encourage other groups to generate new stories based on their interests, rather than restrict this technique to the previously generated stories. Longitudinal studies requiring repeated measures in the same children will need new stories, for children are likely to remember the stories, and analysis of our battery does not reveal stories that are similar enough to be used interchangeably across time.

APPENDIX 6.1. Mean *z* Scores in 7 "Non-Core" Stories (Based on Narratives From 167 Children)

	Mom's Headache	Hot Gravy	Stealing the Candy Bar	Departure	Reunion	Outing to the Park	Family Fun
Total N of themes	.14	.41	.20	–.43	–.59	–.31	–.72
Aggression	–.18	–.07	.12	.11	–.13	–.23	–.27
Limit Setting	–.35	.65	.59	–.28	–.40	–.43	–.33
Affection	–.30	.76	–.48	–.28	–.10	.16	–.44
Compliance	1.93	–.30	–.17	–.23	–.30	–.30	–.30
Non-compliance	1.45	–.33	–.18	–.35	–.35	–.31	–.33
Negative Parental Representation	–.14	.04	–.06	–.11	–.05	–.11	.05
Positive Parental Representation	–.42	.80	–.38	–.38	–.12	.23	–.37
Disciplinary Parental Representation	–.07	.33	.40	–.51	–.39	–.26	–.37
Angry Involvment	.11	.15	.09	.07	–.12	.13	–.30
Open Relatedness	.05	.05	–.11	.06	.02	.08	.13
Anxious Relatedness	.16	.05	–.07	–.05	–.08	–.08	–.23

APPENDIX 6.2. Correlations Between Stories: Factor Positive Themes and Positive Representations

	Spilled Juice	Looking for Barney	Gift Giving	Three's a Crowd	Lost Keys	Bathroom Shelf	Exclusion	Cookie Dilemma
Spilled Juice[a]	1.000	.148	.132	.183	.090	.100	.047	.227
Looking For Barney		1.000	.068	.131	.099	.156	.114	.072
Gift Giving			1.000	.086	.063	.127	.049	.053
Three's a Crowd				1.000	.232	.024	.153	.163
Lost Keys					1.000	.081	.179	.107
Bathroom Shelf						1.000	.083	.083
Exclusion							1.000	.081
Cookie Dilemma								1.000

[a]Listwise $N = 479$.

APPENDIX 6.3. Correlations Between Stories: Factor Anger and Discipline

	Spilled Juice	Looking for Barney	Gift Giving	Three's a Crowd	Lost Keys	Bathroom Shelf	Exclusion	Cookie Dilemma
Spilled Juice[a]	1.000	.478	.339	.400	.390	.364	.325	.341
Looking For Barney		1.000	.405	.503	.447	.403	.350	.347
Gift Giving			1.000	.372	.378	.339	.339	.336
Three's a Crowd				1.000	.529	.469	.409	.430
Lost Keys					1.000	.486	.404	.517
Bathroom Shelf						1.000	.469	.451
Exclusion							1.000	.482
Cookie Dilemma								1.000

[a]Listwise $N = 476$.

APPENDIX 6.4. Correlations Between Stories: Factor Quality of Story and Relatedness

	Spilled Juice	Looking for Barney	Gift Giving	Three's a Crowd	Lost Keys	Bathroom Shelf	Exclusion	Cookie Dilemma
Spilled Juice[a]	1.000	.550	.419	.502	.476	.416	.366	.356
Looking For Barney		1.000	.378	.448	.431	.335	.371	.280
Gift Giving			1.000	.429	.350	.379	.408	.348
Three's a Crowd				1.000	.475	.458	.432	.402
Lost Keys					1.000	.439	.415	.352
Bathroom Shelf						1.000	.479	.392
Exclusion							1.000	.404
Cookie Dilemma								1.000

[a]Listwise $N = 452$.

NOTES

The work discussed in this chapter was funded through the John D. and Catherine T. MacArthur Foundation's Network on Early Childhood Transitions.

1. Analyses were also performed on the seven additional narratives for the 166 children where these data were available; the analyses will be presented later.

2. We performed a one-step principal component analysis with all original items included on the same level to see if the results are similar to those of the two-step procedure. The results again showed four factors describing compounds of limit setting themes, aggressive themes, and positive themes as well as a factor describing the quality of the narrative. In contrast to the "two-step solution," in the "one-step solution" the negative affects of anger and distress were linked to negative themes and negative parental representations to form a factor "Anger and Aggression" (Aggression + Escalation + Negative Atypical Response + Negative Father + Negative Mother + Anger + Distress – Coherence). The scale formed by aggregating these items describes a combination of negative themes, parental representations, and negative affects that are performed in an incoherent way. This aggregate may form an important scale for clinical samples of children with externalizing behavioral problems, whereas in our nonclinical sample it reaches a lower level of consistency (alpha = .64) than the "Anger and Discipline" scale (alpha = .75).

REFERENCES

Achenbach, T. M. (1991). *Manual for the child behavior checklist 4–18 and 1991 profile.* Burlington, VT: University of Vermont Department of Psychiatry.

Bretherton, I., Oppenheim, D., Buchsbaum, H., Emde, R. N., and the MacArthur Narrative Group. (1990). *The MacArthur Story Stem Battery (MSSB).* Unpublished manual, University of Wisconsin–Madison.

Bruner, J. (1990). *Acts of meaning.* Cambridge, MA: Harvard University Press.

Emde, R. N., Plomin, R., Robinson, J., Corley, R., DeFries, J., Fulker, D. W., Reznick, J. S., Campos, J., & Kagan, J. (1992). Temperament, emotion, and cognition at fourteen months: The MacArthur Longitudinal Twin Study. *Child Development, 63,* 1437–1455.

Oppenheim, D., Emde, R., & Warren, S. (1997). Children's narrative representations of mothers: Their development and association with child and mother adaptation. *Child Development, 68,* 127–138.

Oppenheim, D., Nir, A., Warren, S., & Emde, R. N. (1997). Emotion regulation in mother-child narrative co-construction: Associations with children's narratives and adaption. *Developmental Psychology, 33,* 284–294.

Plomin, R., Kagan, J., Emde, R. N., Reznick, J. S., Braungart, J. M., Robinson, J., Campos, J., Zahn-Waxler, C., Corley, R., Fulker, D. W., & DeFries, J. C. (1993). Genetic change and continuity from fourteen to twenty months: The MacArthur Longitudinal Twin Study. *Child Development, 64,* 1354–1376.

Reznick, J. S., Corley, R., & Robinson, J. (1997). A longitudinal twin study of intelligence in the second year. *Monographs of the Society for Research in Child Development, Serial No. 249, 62,* 1.

Robinson, J., Mantz-Simmons, L., Macfie, J., & the MacArthur Narrative Working Group. (1996). *MacArthur narrative coding manual.* Unpublished manuscript.

Steele, H., Steele, M., Woolgar, M., Yabsley, S., Croft, C., Johnson, D., & Fonagy, P. (1997). *The MacArthur Story Stem Battery and attachment in longitudinal perspective.* Poster session presented at the 1997 conference of the Society for Research in Child Development.

Toth, S. L., Cicchetti, D., Macfie, J., & Emde, R .N. (1997). Representations of self and other in the narratives of neglected, physically abused, and sexually abused preschoolers. *Development and Psychopathology, 9,* 781–796.

Von Klitzing, K., Kelsay, K., Emde, R., Robinson, J., & Schmitz, S. (2000). Gender specific characteristics of five-year-olds' narratives and associations with behavior ratings. *Journal of the American Academy of Child and Adolescent Psychiatry, 39,* 1017–1023.

Warren, S., Oppenheim, D., & Emde, R. (1996). Can emotions and themes in children's play predict behavior problems? *Journal of the American Academy of Child and Adolescent Psychiatry, 35,* 1331–1337.

NAZAN AKSAN
H. H. GOLDSMITH

7

Temperament and Guilt Representations in Children's Narratives

Children's narratives are a rich, flexible, and complex instrument for understanding social, emotional, and moral development, as other chapters in this book well illustrate. In this chapter, we examine the concurrent and predictive interrelations between guilt representations in narratives and temperament.

A Perspective on the Content of Narratives

Affective narrative paradigms take advantage of children's growing representational abilities to tap into their understanding of emotionally charged situations. Affective narratives are especially welcome for the study of emotional processes, such as guilt or pride, that purportedly depend on complex appraisal processes such as a growing sense of self-other distinction (Lewis, 1993; Lewis, Sullivan, Stanger, & Weiss, 1989; Lewis, Alessandri, & Sullivan, 1992). Children's narrative continuations have been interpreted with varying emphases, however. Some researchers view the content of children's story completions as reflecting affective moral orientation (Buchsbaum & Emde, 1990; Kochanska, 1991), whereas a complementary perspective holds that such content reflects cognitions relevant to social conflict and emotions such as guilt and empathy (Hay, Zahn-Waxler, Cummings, & Iaonotti, 1992; Mize & Ladd, 1988; Oppenheim & Waters, 1995; Zahn-Waxler et al., 1994; Zahn-Waxler, Kochanska, Krupnick, & McKnew, 1990). The cognitive approach to narrative paradigms has shown that children at risk for behavior disorders view emotionally charged situations differently than do typically developing controls (Zahn-Waxler et al., 1990, 1994). For example, children of depressed mothers represent guilt, empathy, and their associated eliciting circumstances differently than children of nondepressed mothers (Zahn-Waxler et al., 1990). In addition to providing a unique window into children's understanding of emotionally charged situations, these narrative paradigms provide a different methodology from the observational and maternal report assessments so common in studies of children's socioemotional development. Too many studies in this broad domain incorporate maternal input for both predictor (e.g., temperament) and criterion (e.g., some aspect of social development). Hypothetical dilemma paradigms introduce the child as a distinct respondent and thus help minimize the shared method variance due to maternal influence in multiple measures.

Much of the early research on children's narratives has emphasized the presence or absence of prosocial and aggressive resolutions across these stories, in addition to children's ongoing affective reactions during story completion (see Buchsbaum & Emde, 1990; Kochanska, 1991; Zahn-Waxler et al., 1994, as well as other chapters in this book). We believe, however, that it is important to also consider a dimensional approach in characterizing the content of children's verbal productions along the dominant theme for each story.

The MacArthur narratives, as presented in this book, present children with story stems that call for the resolution of social conflicts such as dealing with the aggressive behavior of a peer (bike story), parental request for privacy (couch story), resolving a conflict between helping an injured friend and noncompliance with a parental rule (band-aid story), compliance with a parental request (nap story), and emotional responses following compliance with a parental request (clean-up story). Completions to each story stem can often be characterized as involving one or two dominant content themes. For example, the bike story elicits aggression-related themes, the nap story elicits compliance, the clean-up story elicits pride, the band-aid story elicits prosocial content, and the couch story elicits both compliance and exclusion-related elaboration. In this chapter, we address narratives that yield guilt-relevant themes.

Guilt in Children's Narrative Completions

The study of complex emotions such as guilt is important to different avenues of developmental research. Guilt and empathy are viewed as the central affective components in the development of a "moral sense of self" (Emde & Buchsbaum, 1990; Emde, Biringen, Clyman, & Oppenheim, 1991; Emde, Johnson, & Easterbrooks, 1987; Hoffman, 1976; Kochanska, 1993, 1995). Emergence of guilt is also an important milestone for those who study the development of self-conscious emotions (Lewis, 1993; Lewis et al., 1989; Lewis et al., 1992). For example, differences in behavioral markers and eliciting circumstances of guilt, as opposed to embarrassment and shame, are issues of interest to research on emotional development in the 2nd year of life (Barrett, Zahn-Waxler, & Cole, 1993; Ferguson, Stegge, & Damhuis, 1991). A central question for both domains of inquiry is the relation between individual differences in primary emotionality and later emerging emotion systems, such as guilt (Averill, 1992; Lutz & White, 1986).

Individual differences in early emotionality predict children's moral development, social competence and adaptation, and aspects of childhood behavioral problems (Bates, 1989; Cole & Zahn-Waxler, 1992; Emde & Buchsbaum, 1990; Kochanska, 1991, 1993, 1995; Coplan, Rubin, Fox, & Calkins, 1994; Zahn-Waxler et al., 1990, 1994). The evidence supporting this claim falls under the rubric of temperament research. Most research on prediction, however, has been restricted to either of two temperament dimensions: difficult temperament (Bates, 1989) or behavioral inhibition (Coplan et al., 1994; Kagan, Reznick, & Gibbons, 1989; Kochanska, 1991). In this chapter, we examine multiple dimensions of temperament, both concurrently and longitudinally, to investigate their relation to one aspect of socioemotional development, narrative guilt representations.

Two story stems involving stealing were used to probe preschoolers' cognitive representations relevant to feelings of guilt or remorse. In the first story, the target child ate the friend's candy during his or her short absence, and in the second story the target child picked an item from a shelf during grocery shopping without telling his or her mother, and they left the grocery story without paying for it. We adopted a dimensional approach in characterizing five-year-olds' productions in these story stems. Prior research using story completions as a measure of children's affective/moral orientation has made global characterizations of children's verbal production involving guilt (Kochanska, 1991). This literature suggests several distinct indicators of guilt in children's narrative. For example, admission of guilt (confession), attempts to make amends (repair), and consequences for misbehavior (punishment) have been used as indicators of guilt. However, these indicators of guilt have generally not been examined as separate dimensions of guilt in children's narrative. We adopted a dimensional approach in characterizing the degree of confession, repair, punishment, and avoidance of responsibility (referred to as withdrawal) evident in children's productions as separate indicators of guilt in the narrative.

Goals and Hypotheses of the Study

The first goal of our study was to examine the organizations of these indicators in children's spontaneous productions. It seems reasonable that the degree of coherence among these indicators should reflect the representational organization of guilt. We believe that both confession and repair themes can be conceptualized along a gradient of willingness to confront implications of guilt-inducing situations. For example, confession themes reflect active engagement because the protagonist admits wrongdoing, and repair themes reflect an other-oriented, active role in taking responsibility to make amends. Punishment themes may also indicate some degree of active engagement; however, they are more self-oriented than confession or, especially, repair themes. Given that confession, repair, and punishment all reflect active engagement, we expected that their intercorrelations should be moderate and positive. On the other hand, withdrawal that reflects avoidance of engagement or responsibility should be moderately and negatively correlated with confession, repair, and punishment elements.

Our second goal was to conduct exploratory analyses examining the interrelations between individual differences in *multiple* temperamental characteristics and components of guilt representations in the narrative. We view much of the behavior that falls under the temperament rubric as essentially emotional, in agreement with many theorists (Allport, 1937; Averill, 1992; Goldsmith & Campos, 1982, 1986; Campos, Barrett, Lamb, Goldsmith, & Sternberg, 1983; Goldsmith, 1993; Malatesta, 1990; Rothbart, 1989). Because our foremost goal was to explore the nature of the relations between emotionality and guilt representations, we assessed children's temperamental characteristics using a set of questionnaires that emphasize distinct dimensions of emotionality, in particular Rothbart's Children's Behavior Questionnaire (CBQ; Rothbart & Ahadi, 1994; Rothbart, Ahadi, & Hershey, 1994) and Goldsmith's Toddler Behavior Assessment Questionnaire (TBAQ; Goldsmith, 1996).

The literature on internalized behavior or moral development has emphasized the importance of certain temperamental traits. For example, fearful and shy children who are exposed to non-power-assertive discipline strategies tend to show a higher degree of internalization in their narrative continuations as well as behavior (Kochanska, 1991, 1995). This literature suggests that children who are high in temperamentally based internalizing and low in such externalizing tendencies generally internalize the socialization message (Dientsbier, 1984; Kochanska, DeVet, Goldman, Murray, & Putnam, 1994; Lepper, 1981). An advantage of the CBQ is that it captures behavioral modulatory aspects of temperament, such as inhibitory control and impulsivity also linked to young children's internalized behavior or conscience (Kochanksa, Murray, & Coy, 1997). Thus, we used the CBQ to assess clusters of emotional and behavioral reactions related to temperamentally based internalizing and externalizing tendencies. Dimensions of shyness, fearfulness, and sadness were components of internalizing tendencies, and dimensions such as anger and activity level were components of externalizing tendencies. In addition to internalizing and externalizing tendencies, we also examined positive affectivity and control propensities as temperamental differences.

Although we used the existing body of findings on temperament and moral development as a guide in our predictions, we adopted an exploratory approach in examining these interrelations. Because we currently do not fully understand which elements in children's verbal productions parallel their real-life behavioral and affective reactions, the interrelations between temperament and children's narrative continuations need not parallel the predictions and findings in the literature concerning interrelations between actual internalized behavior and temperament. Children's verbal productions likely reflect children's representations of guilt-inducing situations, which might differ from their actual behavioral reactions. However, the literature on moral development is largely silent on the links between the representation of affectively charged situations and temperamental predispositions. Thus, we made only general predictions about the relationship between toddler and preschool age temperament and guilt representations.

Because confession and repair themes indicate an active role in taking responsibility, these elements are likely associated positively with internalizing tendencies and negatively with externalizing tendencies. In contrast, withdrawal themes, which indicate active avoidance, are likely negatively associated with internalizing and positively with externalizing tendencies. The temperamental correlates of punishment themes are harder to predict. Although inhibited children may contemplate punishment themes as they engage in the narrative tasks, they will not likely produce these themes because of the threatening prospect of consequences for misbehavior implied by punishment themes. Similarly, it is difficult to predict the direction or the presence of interrelations between control tendencies and individual narrative guilt components. The literature is silent regarding any possible associations of positive affect propensities and guilt.

With a sample of toddlers, we assessed angry and fearful arousal along with positive affectivity, interest, and activity levels using Goldsmith's TBAQ (1996). Dimensions of angry arousal and activity level are relevant to externalizing tendencies at toddler age. On the other hand, fearful arousal is the only dimension relevant to internalizing tendencies at this age. Thus, we expected that proneness to angry arousal as well as activity level at toddler age would correlate negatively with confession and repair themes but positively with withdrawal themes. Similarly, given the strong predictions in the literature on the role of inhibition (Kochanska, 1991), we expected that children who had been highly fearful toddlers would tend to produce confession and repair themes.

In summary, this study was motivated by questions about individual differences in primary emotionality and narrative guilt representations in a longitudinal framework. Because our understanding of the relationships between representations of affectively charged situations and actual behavior is incomplete, our analyses are primarily exploratory.

Method

Sample

A total of 114 five-year-olds (59 girls) participated in the study. Children came primarily from middle-class families of Caucasian origin. Thirty-five mothers were recruited through community flyers/ads. The remaining 78 mothers had participated in an earlier study of temperament when their children were toddlers and they were originally recruited from published birth records. In this group of 78 mothers, 33 had participated when their children were 12 months of age and the remaining 45 when their children were 18 months of age.

Assessment: Overview

Mothers completed temperament questionnaires before coming to the laboratory. After a warm-up period, the mother moved into an adjoining control room while the interviewer engaged the child in the narrative stories. The administration of the narratives was similar to that described in other chapters here.

Assessment: Maternal Report of Temperament

Mothers completed the CBQ at the time of the narrative visit. The 195-item version of the CBQ yields 16 scales tapping individual differences in the expression of primary emotions in addition to attentional and behavioral regulatory processes such as inhibitory control and impulsivity. The items are rated on a 7-point Likert scale. We derived four composite scores from the 16 scales. The composites were derived on the basis of both scale intercorrelations and relative emphasis in the internalization literature as a dimension relevant to children's moral development. The internalizing tendency score was an average of the Shyness, Fear, Sadness, and Perceptual Sensitivity scales. This score reflects the propensity for anxious arousal and withdrawal in social and nonsocial contexts, coupled with a sensitivity to minor flaws in objects (Kagan, 1981), a dimension implicated in affective reactions during mishap paradigms (Kochanska, Casey, & Fukumoto, 1995). The average correlation among these four components of the CBQ was significant, $r(101) = .22, p < .05$. The externalizing score, an average of CBQ High Pleasure, Impulsivity, Anger, and Activity Level scales, reflects the propensity to be outgoing, energetic, bold, and undercontrolled. The average correlation among these four component scales also provides empirical validation for the composite, $r(101) = .40, p < .01$. The control tendency score, an average of the Inhibitory Control and Low Pleasure scales, reflects the propensity to delay gratification as well as take pleasure from low intensity stimulation. The correlation between these two component scales was $r(101) = .50$, $p < .001$. The degree of independence among these three composite variables is shown in the Results section.

The 33 mothers who were first contacted when their children were 12 months old completed the Infant Behavior Questionnaire (IBQ; Rothbart, 1981), and the 45 mothers who were first contacted when their children were 18 months of age completed the TBAQ (Goldsmith, 1996). These similarly constructed temperament questionnaires have content overlap; they both emphasize individual differences in emotionality and show good internal consistency and discriminant validity (Goldsmith & Rothbart, 1991). Both questionnaires are rated on a 7-point Likert scale. The following scale descriptions and exemplary items illustrate the extent of the overlap between comparable IBQ and TBAQ scales.

Activity Level (IBQ and TBAQ) Both of these scales index the degree of gross motor activity and locomotor activity in age-appropriate contexts. An example from the IBQ is the following, "During feeding, how often did the baby lie or sit quietly?" An item from the TBAQ is the following, "How often did your child climb over the furniture?"

Distress to Novelty (IBQ) and Social Fear (TBAQ) These scales both index the degree of distress/inhibition or latency to approach novel situations and persons in age-appropriate contexts. An example from the IBQ is this question, "When introduced to a strange person how often did the baby hang back from the stranger?" An item from the TBAQ is this question, "When first visiting a baby-sitting co-op, day care center, or church nursery, how often did your child feel at ease within 10 minutes?" As reflected in their names, the TBAQ scale has more social (shyness) content.

Distress to Limitations (IBQ) and Anger Proneness (TBAQ) These scales both index the degree of distress to limiting situations such as being prevented from playing with a desired object or being confined. This is a sample question: "During feeding how often did the baby fuss, cry when given food she disliked?" An item from the TBAQ is this question, "When your child was given something to eat s/he did not like, how often did s/he push the plate away?"

Duration of Orienting (IBQ) and Interest (TBAQ) Both scales tap the degree of extended visual or extended vocalization related to various objects in the absence of any sudden changes in stimulation, typically during solitary play. This question is an example from the IBQ: "After sleeping how often did the baby vocalize for a period of 5 minutes or longer?" This question is from the TBAQ: "How often did your child play alone with his/her favorite toy for 30 minutes or longer?"

Smiling and Laughter (IBQ) and Pleasure (TBAQ) Both scales index the extent of positive affect expressed in smiling and laughter across a variety of nonthreatening situations. This is an example from the IBQ: "When being dressed or undressed how often did the baby smile or laugh?" And this is a question from the TBAQ: "When in the bath tub, how often did your child babble or talk happily?"

Deriving Common Toddler Temperament Scores Given this conceptual similarity in both the descriptions and the item content of the scales just described, we derived predicted TBAQ scores for the 34 mothers who had completed the IBQ. This transformation involved solving for the predicted standardized TBAQ score for each scale from the corresponding IBQ scale score, after adjusting for differences between the TBAQ and CBQ in scale means and standard deviations. Of course, this procedure required an independent derivation or "calibration" sample of mothers who completed both the IBQ and TBAQ on one occasion. Such a calibration sample was reported by Goldsmith (1996), and we used these data. Thus, five predicted TBAQ scores were obtained for the 34 children with IBQ scores. For the rest of the analyses, we used the standardized scores on the toddler temperament measures.

Assessment: Guilt Themes in the Narrative

The story stems were as follows. In the candy story, the target child (doll) and a friend were each given a piece of candy. The target child ate the friend's candy during a short absence and was later confronted by the friend. The shoplifting story involved the target child and the mother at a supermarket. The target child took something from a shelf and told no one until after the mother had checked out. Then the stolen item was pointed out.

Scoring For both of the stories, the same coding system was used. The scoring of the responses assesses the prominence of guilt themes produced for each story. Four components—confession, punishment, repair, and withdrawal—reflected the guilt in the narrative continuations. As indicated earlier, confession themes pertained to admission of guilt, withdrawal themes to avoidance of responsibility, punishment themes to negative consequences, and repair themes to attempts to makes amends. Each of these components was coded on a 5-point scale. Coders reached 90% reliability for each of the following categories. In the examples that follow, "Jimmy" refers to the protagonist and "Billy" refers to the victim.

Code 1. No indication of confession/withdrawal/punishment, or repair themes. For the majority of the cases, this code reflects either silence or absence of the relevant component in verbal productions.

Code 2. Ambiguous indications of the relevant component. For example, a "2" for confession themes might include the child depicting a confession on behalf of the nontarget character; statements such as "Billy said 'sorry' to Jimmy." In the case of punishment themes, Billy might suffer mild negative consequences for having lost his candy.

Code 3. Child indicates partial punishment/confession/withdrawal/repair, without an explicit acknowledgment of guilt. For instance, the victim might have his stolen candy replaced, but without clear evidence that the protagonist intended a repair.

Code 4. The relevant component is indicated early in the narrative, but is incomplete, or the component is fully expressed, but only after the interviewer's probe. For example, after the interviewer says, "Did Jimmy say anything to Billy?" the child says, "Sorry."

Code 5. The relevant component is fully expressed early in the narrative continuation and is sometimes extended or elaborate.

To assess the convergent validity of these four components as indicators of children's guilt in the narrative, we asked a subsample of mothers to complete Rothbart's Guilt/Shame scale, a social behavior scale used in conjunction with the CBQ (Rothbart et al., 1994). Most of the items in the Guilt/Shame scale concern affective discomfort following wrongdoing and willingness to admit misbehavior. Given this item content, confession and withdrawal elements ought to be intercorrelated with maternal ratings of guilt. The intercorrelations confirmed that children's narrative confession was positively correlated, $r(44) = .25$, $p < .05$, whereas withdrawal themes, which indicate avoidance of responsibility, were negatively correlated with maternal reports of a tendency to feel guilty upon wrongdoing, $r(44) = -.26$, $p < .05$. These correlations from disparate methods support the validity of the confession and withdrawal content measures that we scored from children's verbal productions.

Results

Overview

Following the summary statistics for temperament dimensions and narrative guilt variables, we first present the relations between guilt components and concurrent maternal ratings of temperament. Then, we present the relations between guilt components and toddler age maternal ratings of temperament. Standardized scores are used for temperament and guilt measures for all of the analyses.

Descriptive Statistics

Table 7.1 presents the summary statistics for the narrative guilt components and the age 5 and toddler age temperament ratings. Three separate multivariate analyses of variance with gender as the between-subject factor (using Wilks's lambda criterion) on narrative guilt measures and preschool and toddler age temperament ratings revealed no significant gender differences, $F(4, 105) < 1$; $F(4, 97) = 1.55$, ns; $F(3,60) = 1.36$, ns; respectively.

Correlations Among Guilt Components

Our correlational analysis relevant to the coherence and the organization of narrative guilt representations appear in the upper portion of table 7.2. Confes-

TABLE 7.1. Means and Standard Deviations of Narrative Guilt Components and Temperament Scores.

	Means	Standard Deviations
Narrative guilt components[a]		
Confession	2.83	1.28
Withdrawal	1.98	1.29
Punishment	2.46	1.37
Reparation	1.84	.92
Temperament at preschool age (CBQ)[b]		
Internalizing tendencies	4.20	.54
Externalizing tendencies	4.76	.61
Control	5.09	.62
Positive affect	5.51	.56
Temperament at toddler age (TBAQ)[c]		
Activity level	4.18	.56
Anger	3.64	.49
Fearfulness	3.60	.56
Interest	3.31	.50
Pleasure	5.12	.70

[a]N = 108.
[b]N = 102.
[c]N = 64.

sion themes were moderately and positively associated with punishment and repair themes, indicating only modest contingencies among these themes. In other words, components indicating an active involvement on the part of the protagonist were positively associated with each other. In contrast, negative associations were found between withdrawal and confession themes and between withdrawal and punishment themes. The magnitude and the direction of these correlations suggested that these components capture different aspects of children's representations of guilt.

Zero-Order Temperament by Guilt Component Correlations

The exploratory correlational analyses among concurrent maternal ratings of temperamentally based internalizing and externalizing tendencies and the narrative guilt components also appear in table 7.2. Internalizing tendencies were positively associated with confession themes and negatively associated with withdrawal tendencies. The sadness and perceptual sensitivity component scales were largely responsible for the association between confession and internalizing tendencies. The zero-order correlations were $r(97) = .24$, $p < .05$, for confession with sadness and $r(97) = .21$, $p < .05$, for confession with perceptual sensitivity. The zero-order correlations between withdrawal themes and the following component scales of the internalizing tendencies carried the significant negative association: $r(97) = -.23$, $p < .05$, with sadness; $r(97) = -.25$, $p < .05$, with fearfulness; and $r(97) = -.21$, $p <. 05$, with perceptual sensitivity. The correlations in table 7.2 also show that control tendencies and propensity to express positive affect were largely unrelated to narrative guilt components, except for a significant negative correlation between control scores and withdrawal tendencies. The scatter plots of guilt components and concurrent temperament ratings revealed no nonlinear trends.

Associations Within the Temperament Domain

Table 7.2 also presents the associations among age 5 temperamental characteristics. As expected, temperamentally based externalizing scores were negatively associated with internalizing tendencies. Furthermore, the control scores were negatively associated with externalizing but positively associated with internalizing tendencies. Although positive affect was not associated with internalizing, it was positively associated with externalizing scores. These correlations suggested that the temperament scales capture moderately independent dimensions.

Guilt Components and Toddler Temperament Scores

Next, we examined the predictive relations from toddler age temperament to narrative guilt components, using correlations among the temperament and individual narrative guilt components. The correlational analyses showed that toddler activity level scale was the only significant predictor of confession, $r(59) = -.29$, $p < .05$. The dearth of significant correlations between narrative guilt

TABLE 7.2. Correlations Between and Within Narrative Guilt Components and Temperament

	Narrative guilt components				Temperament		
	Confession	Withdrawal	Punishment	Reparation	Externalizing tendencies	Internalizing tendencies	Control
Withdrawal[a]	−.39**						
Punishment[a]	.19*	−.22*					
Reparation[a]	.28**	.02	.12				
Externalizing tendencies[a,b]	−.16	.16	−.06	.04			
Internalizing tendencies[a,b]	.20*	−.26**	.01	−.13	−.40**		
Control[a,b]	.11	−.24*	.07	−.01	−.47**	.31**	
Positive affect[a,b]	.10	.04	.05	.07	.38**	.11	.30**

[a]Correlations between temperament dimensions and narrative guilt components are based on 97 degrees of freedom.
[b]Interrelation within temperament dimensions are based on 101 degrees of freedom.
*$p < .05$.
**$p < .01$.

components and toddler age temperament suggests that the significant association between activity level and confession may be a chance finding. However, these correlational analyses emphasize only linear relations between toddler age temperament and narrative guilt components. In fact, an examination of the scatter plots suggested several quadratic relations between narrative components and toddler age temperament. We conducted regression analyses to examine if these quadratic trends were statistically significant. In these regression analyses, the four guilt components served as dependent variables in a series of regressions wherein toddler age temperamental characteristics served as predictors. Because the sample sizes in these longitudinal analyses were small, each of the five temperamental characteristics was considered as a predictor one at a time. We now turn to the results of these regression analyses.

Table 7.3 presents the model F, the betas for the linear and quadratic effect, as well as the percentage of variance accounted for in each of the regressions. The direction of betas for the quadratic effects is informative for our understanding of the nature of the relationships. A significant quadratic effect indicates that the direction of the relationship between the predictor and the criterion changes at different points in the domain or range of the scores for the predictor. In all of our scatter plots, the direction of the relationship changed around the mean (i.e., zero) for each predictor. Thus, when the beta for the quadratic effect is positive (a U-shaped function) and when the predictor takes on values less than zero, there is a negative relationship between the predictor and the criterion. When the beta is still positive but the predictor takes on values greater than zero, there is a positive relationship between the predictor and the criterion. Conversely, when the beta for the quadratic effect is negative (an inverted U-shaped function) and the predictor takes on values less than zero, there is a positive relationship between the predictor and the criterion. With a negative beta and when the predictor takes on values greater than zero, there is a negative relationship between the predictor and the criterion.

As shown in table 7.3, there were two instances when the value of the beta for the quadratic effect was negative. We obtained negative betas in predicting confession scores using fearfulness and interest scores at toddler age. The regression model of fearfulness on confession was marginally significant, $F = 2.48$, $p < .10$, whereas the regression of interest on confession was significant at the conventional alpha level. The scatter plots indicated that children who ranged from average to low in fearfulness and interest as toddlers tended to produce more confession themes in their narratives, but children who ranged from average to high in fearfulness and interest as toddlers tended to produce fewer confession themes in their narratives. When both fearfulness and interest were entered as predictors, this quadratic effect remained significant, as did the overall model, $F(4, 55) = 2.65$, $p < .05$; however, the quadratic effect of fearfulness was no longer significant. This can be attributed to some combination of low power or dependence between fearfulness and interest scores at toddler age, $r(58) = .22$, $p < .05$.

Similar quadratic effects of toddler age interest and fearfulness were also found for withdrawal themes in the narratives. In this case, however, the betas associated with the quadratic effect were positive. Given the moderate negative rela-

TABLE 7.3. Linear and Nonlinear Relationships Between Toddler Age Temperament and Narrative Guilt Components

Dependent variables	Toddler age predictors	Beta (linear)	Beta (quadratic)	R-square	Model F
Confession	Activity	–.29	—	.08	5.27*
	Anger	—	—	—	ns
	Fear	.16	–.24	.06	2.48*
	Interest	.03	–.35	.12	3.82*
	Pleasure	—	—	—	ns
Withdrawal	Activity	—	—	—	ns
	Anger	—	—	—	ns
	Fear	.10	.39	.17	5.94**
	Interest	.02	.41	.17	5.83**
	Pleasure	—	—	—	ns
Punishment	Activity	—	—	—	ns
	Anger	—	—	—	ns
	Fear	—	—	—	ns
	Interest	—	—	—	ns
	Pleasure	–.17	.29	.11	3.52*

*$p < .10$.
**$p < .05$.
***$p < .01$.

tionship between withdrawal and confession themes presented in table 7.2, it is unsurprising that both interest and fearfulness predicted withdrawal themes but in a direction opposite from that for confession. Furthermore, the quadratic effects of both fearfulness and interest contributed uniquely to the prediction of withdrawal when they were entered simultaneously, $F(4, 55) = 5.59, p < .001$, and the R^2 for their combined effects was .29. The scatter plots indicated that children who ranged from average to low in fearfulness and interest as toddlers tended to produce less withdrawal content in their narratives, but children who ranged from average to high in fearfulness and interest as toddlers tended to produce more withdrawal themes in their narratives.

There were other qualitative differences in the toddler age predictors of confession and withdrawal themes. For example, as shown in table 7.3, activity level did not predict the extent of withdrawal at all, but it was linearly associated with confession themes. Furthermore, when we controlled for the strongest concurrent temperamental predictor of confession and withdrawal themes (i.e., internalizing tendencies), the influence of the toddler age interest and fearfulness on withdrawal remained significant, $F(5, 49) = 6.61, p < .001$, with total $R^2 = .41$, each predictor adding 10% to 12% to this total. On the other hand, when we controlled for internalizing tendencies in predicting the extent of confession, toddler age interest and fearfulness dimensions did not contribute any additional significant variance. Toddler activity level continued to be a significant predictor after controlling for concurrent internalizing tendencies, $F(2, 52) = 6.25, p < .01, R^2 = .19$.

The scatter plots also indicated a quadratic effect of toddler age pleasure or positive affectivity on punishment themes. However, none of the toddler age temperamental characteristics helped predict the extent of repair in children's narratives.

Discussion

This study offers initial evidence of concurrent and predictive interrelations between *multiple* temperamental characteristics and representations of guilt in affective narratives. Both the concurrent and predictive relationships were complex, but especially the predictive relationships were complex and nonlinear in some cases. Our findings thus caution us against simplistic views of the relations between these two domains.

Our results indicate that individual narrative components are distinct dimensions of children's guilt representations. Furthermore, the pattern of intercorrelations suggests that components indicating active engagement (confession, repair, punishment) on the part of the protagonist are positively associated with each other, but negatively associated with the withdrawal element that indicates avoidance of responsibility.

As a sample of the complexity of our findings, internalizing components of temperament were associated with more confession themes but fewer withdrawal themes. On the other hand, none of the age 5 temperamental characteristics was associated with punishment or repair themes. Apparently, only some of the dimensions that characterize children's construals of guilt-inducing situations are associated with individual differences in emotionality. The lack of any associations between repair and punishment narrative elements and concurrent temperament suggests other origins, such as salient social learning history.

In fact, findings from a recent study of guilt in school-age children suggest that maternal rearing styles have a direct influence, whereas toddler age inhibition has an indirect influence, on 8- to 10-year-old children's repair themes (Kochanska, 1991). The interaction of toddler age inhibition or fearfulness with maternal rearing styles was a significant predictor of repair themes in that study. Thus, temperamental inhibition had an indirect, moderating influence on children's affective/moral orientation rather than a direct influence. Moreover, there may be developmental differences in school-age and preschool-age children's representations of guilt-relevant situations. The general lack of associations between temperament and repair themes both concurrently and longitudinally suggests that confession and withdrawal themes may be more salient elements of preschoolers' representations relative to repair themes. This salience of confession and withdrawal may be a reflection of parents' focus on admission of misbehavior and feelings of guilt/remorse upon wrongdoing at this age. In contrast, for school-age children who are embedded in a rich network of peer relations, repair—the most appropriate prosocial behavior—is likely to be a salient dimension of situations that involve wrongdoing.

The exploratory longitudinal analyses revealed several nonlinear associations between toddler age temperament and narrative guilt components. Interest, fearfulness, and pleasure were not linearly associated with any of the guilt components in the narratives, but the quadratic effects of these dimensions remained reliable and powerful when we controlled for the influence of concurrent temperament, especially in withdrawal themes in the narratives. These significant quadratic effects suggest, for example, that both fearful and fearless toddlers tended to depict strong avoidance themes and weak or nonexistent confession themes in their narratives. In contrast, children average in fearfulness and interest tended to depict a higher degree of confession and lower degree of withdrawal themes.

In attempting to explain the surprising associations between early temperamental interest scores and avoidance of responsibility indicated by withdrawal themes in the narrative, we examined the correlations between IBQ interest scores and the individual CBQ scales—administered later—that constituted the broad internalizing and externalizing scores. These examinations revealed marginal quadratic effects of toddler age interest on the Impulsivity and High Pleasure scales of the CBQ, both of which were constituents of the externalizing score. That is, preschoolers who were rated as average to high in interest as toddlers tended become impulsive, energetic, and bold in the expression of positive affect. Of course, they also tended to depict the protagonist as likely to avoid responsibility.

The quadratic effect of toddler age fearfulness on withdrawal showed that children who were low in fearfulness as toddlers tended to depict avoidance of responsibility. This finding is generally consistent with the moral development literature, in that security of attachment is a more important factor in the development of internalized behavior for fearless and bold children (Kochanska, 1995). On the other hand, children high in fearfulness also tended to depict avoidance of responsibility. If we view children's productions in these narratives as reflecting their affective/moral orientation, this is an unexpected finding in the context of the predictions of the socialization literature. Prior research on moral development suggests that when fearful children are exposed to non-power-assertive socialization strategies, they are more likely to internalize the socialization message. In attempting to explain our finding, we note that fearful children probably have a low baseline probability to misbehave. Thus, we speculate that these fearful children find the situations (e.g., stealing) depicted in the story stems novel and threatening. Thus, they do not identify with the story's protagonist, and their narrative completions are dominated by avoidance themes.

Some Implications

Although these findings, especially the longitudinal ones, require replication, they suggest an intrinsic ambiguity in the meaning of children's productions. If the findings are real, then we need to understand why very different children produce similar narrative content after guilt-relevant story stems but in real life tend to behave very differently from one another. These findings also alert us to the possibility that children with certain temperamental characteristics may not identify sufficiently with the protagonist, if the protagonist's behavior seems novel, strange, or threatening. In both the shoplifting and the candy stories, the protagonist engages in willful behaviors that well-internalized children may not engage in at all.

The ambiguity in our findings concerning interrelations between temperament and guilt representations also raises the issue of how children's actual behaviors map onto their narrative productions. The joint use of these paradigms with observational mishap paradigms (Barrett et al., 1993) would elucidate how indicators of guilt in narrative productions components map onto children's actual behavioral reactions. In such research, it might be important to use confession, repair, and avoidance measures instead of a global guilt characterization.

NOTE

This research was supported by grants from NIMH (MH41200 and MH50560) and a small grant from the MacArthur Foundation. Amy Davis, Catherine Harman, Pamela Unfried, and Stephan Ahadi helped collect and analyze some of the data. We also appreciate a crucial suggestion from Carolyn Zahn-Waxler and advice from the Affective Processes subgroup of the MacArthur Foundation's Network on Early Childhood Transitions.
We can be reached by e-mail (*nsaksan@students.wisc.edu* or *hhgoldsm@facstaff.wisc.edu*).

REFERENCES

Allport, G. W. (1937). *Personality: A psychological interpretation.* New York: Holt.

Averill, J. (1992). Structural bases of emotional behavior: A metatheoretical analysis. In M. S. Clark (Ed.), *Emotion* (pp. 1–24). Newbury Park, CA: Sage.

Barrett, K. C., Zahn-Waxler, C., & Cole, P. M. (1993). Avoiders vs. amenders: Implications for the investigation of guilt and shame during toddlerhood? *Cognition and Emotion, 7,* 481–505.

Bates, J. (1989). Applications of temperament concepts. In G. A. Kohnstamm, J. A. Bates, & M. K. Rothbart (Eds.), *Temperament in childhood* (pp. 321–356). New York: Wiley.

Bretherton, I., Ridgeway, D., & Cassidy, J. (1990). Assessing internal working models of the attachment relationship. In M. T. Greenberg, D. Cicchetti, & M. E. Cummings (Eds.), *Attachment in the preschool years* (pp. 273–308). Chicago: University of Chicago Press.

Buchsbaum, H. K., & Emde, R. N. (1990). Play narratives in thirty-six-month-old children: Early moral development and family relationships. *Psychoanalytic Study of the Child, 40,* 129–155.

Campos, J. J., Barrett, K. C., Lamb, M. E., Goldsmith, H. H., & Sternberg, C. (1983). Socioemotional development. In M. M. Haith & J. J. Campos (Eds.), *Infancy and developmental psychobiology* (Vol. 2). In P. H. Mussen (Series Ed.), *Handbook of child psychology* (4th ed., pp. 783–915). New York: Wiley.

Cole, P. M., & Zahn-Waxler, C. (1992). Emotion dysregulation in disruptive behavior disorders. In D. Cicchetti & S. L. Toth (Eds.), *Rochester Symposium on Developmental Psychopathology, Vol. 4. Developmental perspectives on depression* (pp. 173–209). Rochester: University of Rochester Press.

Coplan, R. J., Rubin, K. H., Fox, N. A., & Calkins, S. (1994). Being alone, playing alone, and acting alone: Distinguishing among reticence and passive and active solitude in young children. *Child Development, 65,* 129–137.

Dientsbier, R. A. (1984). The role of emotion in moral socialization. In C. Izard, J. Kagan, & R. B. Zajonc (Eds.), *Emotions, cognitions and behavior* (pp. 484–513). New York: Cambridge University Press.

Emde, R N., Biringen, Z., Clyman, R. B., & Oppenheim, D. (1991). The moral self of infancy: Affective core and procedural knowledge. *Developmental Review, 11,* 251–270.

Emde, R. N., & Buchsbaum, H. K. (1990). "Didn't you hear my mommy?" Autonomy with connectedness in moral self-emergence. In D. Cicchetti & M. Beeghly (Eds.), *Development of the self through the transition* (pp. 35–60). Chicago: University of Chicago Press.

Emde, R. N., Johnson, W. F., & Easterbrooks, A. (1987). The do's and don'ts of early moral development: Psychoanalytic tradition and current research. In J. Kagan & S. Lamb (Eds.), *The emergence of morality in young children* (pp. 245–276). Chicago: University of Chicago Press.

Ferguson, S., Stegge, H., & Damhuis, I. (1991). Children's understanding of guilt and shame. *Child Development, 62,* 827–839.

Goldsmith, H. H. (1993). Temperament: Variability in developing emotion systems. In M. Lewis & J. M. Haviland (Eds.), *Handbook of emotions* (pp. 353–364). New York: Guilford.

Goldsmith, H. H. (1996). Studying temperament via construction of the Toddler Behavior Assessment Questionnaire. *Child Development, 67,* 218–235.

Goldsmith, H. H., & Campos, J. J. (1982). Toward a theory of infant temperament. In R. N. Emde & R. J. Harmon (Eds.), *The development of attachment and affiliative systems* (pp. 161–193). New York: Plenum.

Goldsmith, H. H., & Campos, J. J. (1986). Fundamental issues in the study of early temperament: The Denver Twin Temperament Study. In M. E. Lamb, A. L. Brown, & B. Rogoff (Eds.), *Advances in developmental psychology* (vol. 4, pp. 231–283). Hillsdale, NJ: Lawrence Erlbaum.

Goldsmith, H. H., & Rothbart, M. K. (1991). Contemporary instruments for assessing early temperament by questionnaire and in the laboratory. In A. Angleitner & J. Strelau (Eds.), *Explorations in temperament: International perspectives on theory and measurement* (pp. 249–272). New York: Plenum.

Hay, D. F., Zahn-Waxler, C., Cummings, E. M., & Iaonotti, R. J. (1992). Young children's views about conflict with peers: A comparison of the daughters and sons of depressed and well women. *Journal of Child Psychology and Psychiatry, 33,* 669–683.

Hoffman, M. (1976). Empathy, role-taking guilt and the development of altruistic motives. In T. Likona (Ed.), *Moral development: Current theory and research* (pp. 124–143). New York: Holt, Rinehart, & Winston.

Kagan, J. (1981). *The second year: The emergence of self-awareness.* Cambridge, MA: Harvard University Press.

Kagan, J., Reznick, J. S., & Gibbons, J. (1989). Inhibited and uninhibited types of children. *Child Development, 60,* 838–845.

Kochanska, G. (1991). Socialization and temperament in the development of guilt and conscience. *Child Development, 62,* 1379–1392.

Kochanska, G. (1993). Toward a synthesis of parental socialization and child temperament in early development of conscience. *Child Development, 64,* 325–347.

Kochanska, G. (1995). Children's temperament, mothers' discipline, and security of attachment: Multiple pathways to emerging internalization. *Child Development, 66,* 597–616.

Kochanska, G., Casey, R. J., & Fukumoto, A. (1995). Toddlers' sensitivity to standard violations. *Child Development, 66,* 643–656.

Kochanska, G., De Vet, K., Goldman, M., Murray, K., & Putnam, S. (1994). Maternal reports of conscience development and temperament in young children. *Child Development, 65,* 852–868.

Kochanska, G., Murray, K., & Coy, K. C. (1997). Inhibitory control as a contributor to conscience in childhood: From toddler to early school age. *Child Development, 68,* 263–277.

Lamb, M. E., Thompson, R., Gardner, W., & Charnov, E. L. (1985). Predictive validity of strange situation classification. In M. E. Lamb, R. Thompson, W. Gardner, & E. L. Charnov (Eds.), *Infant-mother attachment: The origins and developmental significance of individual differences in strange situation behavior* (pp. 139–169). New York: Lawrence Erlbaum.

Lepper, M. R. (1981). The intrinsic and extrinsic motivation in children: Detrimental effects of superfluous social controls. In W. A. Collins (Ed.), *Minnesota symposia on child psychology* (vol. 14, pp. 155–214). Minneapolis: University of Minnesota Press.

Lewis, M. (1993). Self-conscious emotions: Embarassment, pride, shame and guilt. In M. Lewis & M. Haviland (Eds.), *Handbook of emotions* (pp. 353–364). New York: Guilford.

Lewis, M., Alessandri, S., & Sullivan, M. (1992). Differences in shame and pride as a function of children's gender and task difficulty. *Child Development, 63,* 630–638.

Lewis, M., Sullivan, M., Stanger, C., & Weiss, M. (1989). Self development and self-conscious emotions. *Child Development, 60,* 146–156.

Lutz, C., & White, G. M. (1986). The anthropology of emotions. *Annual Review of Anthropology, 15,* 405–436.

Malatesta, C. Z. (1990). The role of emotions in the development and organization of personality. In R. A. Thompson (Ed.), *Nebraska symposium on motivation: Vol. 36. Socioemotional development* (pp. 1–56). Lincoln: University of Nebraska Press.

Mize, J., & Ladd, G. W. (1988). Predicting preschoolers' peer behavior and status from their interpersonal strategies: A comparison of verbal and enactive responses to hypothetical dilemmas. *Developmental Psychology, 24,* 782–788.

Oppenheim, D., & Waters, H. S. (1995). Narrative processes and attachment representations: Issues of development and assessment. In E. Waters, B. Vaughn, G. Posada, & K. Kondo-Ikemura (Eds.), *Monographs of the Society for Research in Child Development, Vol. 60, Constructs, cultures, and caregiving: New growing points in attachment theory and research* (pp. 197–215). Oxford: Blackwell.

Rothbart, M. K. (1981). Measurement of temperament in infancy. *Child Development, 52,* 569–578.

Rothbart, M. K. (1989). Temperament and development. In G. A. Kohnstamm, J. E. Bates, & M. K. Rothbart (Eds.), *Temperament in childhood* (pp. 187–247). New York: Wiley.

Rothbart, M. K., & Ahadi, S. A. (1994). Temperament and the development of personality. *Journal of Abnormal Psychology, 103,* 55–66.

Rothbart, M. K., Ahadi, S. A., & Hershey, K. L. (1994). Temperament and social behavior in childhood. *Merrill-Palmer Quarterly, 40,* 21–39.

Zahn-Waxler, C., Cole, P., Richardson, D. T., Friedman, R. J., Michel, M., & Beloud, F. (1994). Social problem-solving in disruptive preschool children: Reactions to hypothetical situations of conflict and distress. *Merrill-Palmer Quarterly, 40,* 98–119.

Zahn-Waxler, C., Kochanska, G., Krupnick, J., & McKnew, D. (1990). Development of guilt and empathy in children of depressed and nondepressed mothers. *Developmental Psychology, 26,* 51–59.

DAVID OPPENHEIM

8

Children's Emotional Resolution of MSSB Narratives: Relations With Child Behavior Problems and Parental Psychological Distress

The MacArthur Story Stem Battery (MSSB; Bretherton, Oppenheim, Buchsbaum, Emde, & the MacArthur Narrative Group, 1990) includes a series of story beginnings (or stems) describing a range of emotionally evocative, realistic family scenes portrayed using dolls and props that children are asked to complete in action and narration. One of the incentives behind the development of the MSSB involved developing a systematic approach for the study of young children's emotional worlds. This incentive was sparked by a long clinical tradition demonstrating that play narratives provide a useful and compelling avenue for learning about the inner world of the child (e.g., Erikson, 1950; Winnicott, 1971; Axline, 1947; Freud, 1946). Purportedly, children's emotional worlds, including central emotion and relational themes, representations and conflicts, as well as defenses and coping mechanisms, are revealed in their play narrations. Studies using the MSSB have supported this conjecture. For example, children's struggles with moral dilemmas (Buchsbaum & Emde, 1990; Oppenheim, Emde, Hasson, & Warren, 1997), experience of abuse (Buchsbaum, Toth, Clyman, Cicchetti, & Emde, 1993), and emotion dysregulation (Robinson, Herot, Haynes, & Mantz-Simmons, 2000) have all been examined with the MSSB.

Many using the MSSB ask an additional question, however. Beyond learning about the inner world of the child—a worthy goal in its own right—investigators have asked whether it is possible to link the MSSB with measures "outside" the world of narrative (Bretherton & Oppenheim, chapter 3, this book). One reason for examining the links between MSSB narratives and children's "real-world" functioning is to evaluate whether the MSSB can effectively assess young children with whom traditional self-report measures have not been found useful. A related incentive involved providing a "voice" for young children, rather than relying only on adults to report about children's emotional life (e.g., Warren, Oppenheim, & Emde, 1996). Finally, an additional incentive involved generating hypotheses involving the *causal role* of children's internal representations and emotional processes in their behavioral and emotional functioning and mental health (Bretherton & Munholand, 1999; Main, Kaplan, & Cassidy, 1985; Steele et al., chapter 9, this book).

Thus, several related incentives have led researchers to examine links between children's narratives and important domains outside the world of narratives, and a small but growing literature is encouraging. Studies have linked MSSB narratives to maltreatment (Toth, Cicchetti, Macfie, & Emde, 1997; Macfie et al., 1999), children's behavior problems (Oppenheim, Emde, & Warren, 1997), and symptoms (Warren, Emde, & Sroufe, 2001). This chapter adds to this growing literature by focusing on the degree of *emotional resolution* preschoolers achieve in responding to the story stems and by linking such resolution to children's behavioral and emotional problems and parents' psychological distress. An additional developmental focus of the study addressed continuity and change in emotion resolution during the preschool years, between the ages of 4.5 and 5.5 years. This focus is important due to the significant developments in children's emotional organization during the time span; it provides the necessary developmental context for investigating the links between emotion resolution and child and family adjustment. We now expand on the issue of children's emotion resolution of narratives and illustrate with a vignette.

General discussions of narratives have suggested that conflicts, dilemmas, problems, and points of tension are at the core of narratives, as are the resolutions that follow (Labov & Waletzky, 1967). This is true of the MSSB narratives as well. As mentioned, the MSSB presents children with story stems portrayed using dolls and props. The story stems present the child with a problem or dilemma designed to be emotionally evocative, complex, and often negatively charged. Furthermore, they invite the child to complete the narrative after the examiner has stopped at the "high point," where the narrative tension is maximal. The child is then requested to show and say what happens next. This request carries an implicit message to the child to resolve the tension portrayed by the narrative and involves openly addressing the emotional themes in the stems and integrating them into a meaningful and organized narrative that leads toward a resolution. Thus, children's emotional resolution of conflicts and problems is at the core of the story-stem approach.

When resolution of story stems is discussed, it is possible to look both at the *stories* children produce and at the child as story*teller*. One can examine the story completions and ask to what extent they represent a resolution of the issues raised in the stem. In addition, it is possible to focus not only on the extent to which the child's *narrative* moves toward a resolution but also on whether the *child*, as storyteller, appears emotionally resolved after addressing the core conflict or difficulty in the story stem. Thus, we want to examine not only the endpoint of the story, when the child has completed narrating, but also the process that leads the child toward the endpoint. We also want to take into account the moment-by-moment shifts in the child's affective engagement with the task as she struggles with the issue presented in the story stem and draws on emotional, cognitive, linguistic, and interpersonal resources to lead toward closure. An example of a 40-month-old girl completing a story stem illustrates this process.

The child in this vignette participated in a study of emotion narratives (Oppenheim, Emde, & Wamboldt, 1996), and the vignette is taken from the Bathroom Shelf story stem. In this stem the child is placed in a dilemma between a maternal prohibition and the distress of a sibling (Buchsbaum & Emde, 1990). Following the presentation of the story stem, the child completes the story. The text in italics describes the conversation between child (C) and examiner (E) during the presentation of the story stem.

Story Stem
Examiner (E) introduces a bathroom shelf prop.

E: This is the bathroom shelf where Mommy keeps all the Band-aids. Susan and Jane are playing. Mom comes in.

E (as mother): Children, I need to go next door to the neighbors to return some things but I will be right back. Don't touch anything on the bathroom shelf. OK?

C: Um um um I'm gonna keep 'em from it. (*Child shows mild stutter and displays a tense, worried expression*).

E: OK, you can put them right here *(points to table)* and keep them from it.

C: I can just put them in the bed to play a little bit.

E: OK.

C: (*turning to examiner*) But don't make them touch the bathroom shelf! (*emphatically, worried*).

E: OK, I won't make them touch the bathroom shelf.

E: But I'll tell you the story, what happens.

E: Susan and Jane are playing.

(The examiner needs dolls to enact the story, but child is clutching the dolls, not wanting to hand the dolls over to the examiner.)

E: Let me show you how they play.

C: But they can't.... I'm gonna keep 'em from it!

E: Ok, you're gonna keep 'em from it.

(Child hands dolls to E.)

E (as Jane): Ow, I cut my finger, I need a Band-aid!

E (as Susan): "OK.... Oh no—but Mom said not to touch anything on the bathroom shelf!

E (as Jane): But my finger is bleeding!

E: Show me and tell me what happens now.

Story Completion

C: Now now the mom is all done talking to the neighbors.

E: She's all done talking to the neighbors?

C: And and and.

E: Here she is (*E brings mother doll*).

C: And and along she comes.

E: And then what happens?

C (as mother): Did you guys touch anything on the bathroom shelf?

E: And what do they say?

C: No.

E: (*repeats*) No.

C: Um um um but she said my finger is bleeding (*pointing to "Jane"*).

E: My finger is bleeding.

C (as mother): Um then I then I'll get a Band-aid.

ts ts ts (*sounds of putting the Band-aid on*) there you go (*said in a comforting tone*).

E: There you go.

C (as mother): Now now don't do anything else (*said in a directive, disciplinary tone*).

E: Don't do anything else.

C (as mother): Now I'm going in the in the kitchen.

(Child accidentally knocks the bathroom shelf prop.)

Oops I bonked I knocked all the Band-aids over (*Child smiles*).

now she (*pointing to "Susan"*) has a finger bleed.

E: She has a finger bleed . . . so what happens?

C: She calls Mommy.

E: Uh-huh show me.

C (as mother): Um now do you have a finger bleed?

E: Uhuh.

C (as mother): Okay ts ts ts (*sounds of putting Band-aid on*) there you go now don't do anything else you two! *(said in a directive tone)*

E: Don't do anything else.

C (as mother): Well I am now I'm gonna be in the other room.

(short pause, then C brings mother from "other room".)

C (as mother): I'm I'm back!

E: I'm back.

C (as mother): Um um now my finger is bleeding.

E: Now your finger is bleeding.

C (as mother): So I'll get one with my other hand.

E: Oh Mom Mom has a . . . uh-oh, I see. Mommy's finger is bleeding.

C (as mother): Now *I'm* (*said emphatically*) not gonna do anything else (*smiling*).

E: Okay.

C: That is funny (*smiles, relaxed*).

E: Yeah.

C: That they all keep on getting finger bleeds.

E: That's right.

(Child appears calm and relaxed and waits for the next story-stem.)

This excerpt demonstrates the moment-by-moment shifts in the child's affective state as she is trying to regulate her worry and tension, dealing with what for her appears to be a troubling, perhaps frightening situation, and gradually and creatively bringing it to resolution.

The excerpt begins with the examiner's presentation of the parental rule ("Don't touch anything on the bathroom shelf"). The child, perhaps based on previous story stems in the MSSB in which children transgress (e.g., spilling juice), becomes quite distressed, interrupts the presentation of the story stem and says she will "keep them from it" (i.e., from taking the Band-aid). This is said even before any transgression is presented (in fact, the Bathroom Shelf story stem does not include a transgression—the children are not portrayed as taking Band-aids from the prohibited shelf). In other words, for this child, the presentation of a rule appears to bring up the *possibility* of transgression, even the thought of which makes her quite distressed. Her solution is not a resolution of the central dilemma. Instead, she avoids the dilemma by putting the girls to bed, where they can cause no harm. Then she warns the examiner not to "make them touch the bathroom shelf." As the transcript and the videotape show, the child becomes increasingly worried. She is not reassured by the examiner's promise that he will not "make them touch the bathroom shelf," and she clutches the dolls, not handing them over to the examiner. Only when the examiner says that "she can keep them from it" is the child willing to hand the dolls over. Thus, it is very clear that the dilemma presented by the story stem is very real for this child, evoking tension that she needs to resolve.

As soon as the child is handed the dolls, she narrates that the mother returns and reaffirms the rule, hinting at the possibility that a transgression had happened ("Did you guys touch anything on the bathroom shelf?"). After she takes care of the finger bleed, the child's tension is visibly reduced. Her representation of parental authority ("Now don't do anything else") and her assumption of an active role seem to reassure her. At this point she could have stopped because the narrative has been completed. The main problem has been resolved, order has been restored, and the troubles have been addressed. But it appears that, for this young child, the story is not over yet. The distress that she experienced cannot, perhaps, be resolved so quickly. So the child creates another finger bleed, this time for the other sister. In the creative world of play-narratives the child now becomes the master of events. This time *she* will create the problem, rather than being presented with a problem over which she has little control. *She* will decide what happens, and *she* will be able to resolve the problem. So the sister gets a finger bleed, and, again, the mother takes care of the finger bleed and voices a mild disciplinary statement ("Now don't do anything else"). Again, the story could have ended here, but, for this child, the story is apparently not over yet. The child adds a new, creative, humorous twist. This time the mother, perhaps seen by the child as the all powerful agent of rules, authority, and "moral" behavior, is the one who gets a finger bleed. Perhaps the child is "getting back" at mother. Perhaps she is showing that mother is not only an omnipotent authority figure but also a person who, like the children, can get hurt and can be taken care of. Through narrative, the child can create possibilities that help her regulate her emotions and return to a calmer, emotionally positive state. The child now describes, only half seriously, mother disciplining herself. Now she can even say, with a relaxed smile, and only a few moments after experiencing considerable distress, "that is funny, they all keep on getting finger bleeds!" The threatening, frightening, and anxiety-producing situation has been transformed and resolved through creative, imaginative, narrative construction.

To what extent are the processes illustrated in this vignette meaningfully related to children's socioemotional functioning? This question provided the context for our first hypothesis, which was that higher emotional resolution of the narratives would be associated with fewer behavior/emotion problems. Empirically, this hypothesis was backed by previous work that showed associations between MSSB narratives and children's behavior problems (Warren et al., 1996). Theoretically, it was guided by the assumption that the MacArthur story stems present an emotional challenge to the child. The stems in the MSSB describe complex, conflictual events within the context of close family relations. Completing a story stem and resolving it emotionally involve addressing the issues raised in the stem, negotiating these issues, and resolving the conflict, dilemma, or problem. Difficulties in emotional resolution can be expressed in various ways, such as avoiding emotionally charged issues, escalating negative themes, and failing to keep both positive and negative aspects in mind at the same time. Thus, emotional resolution of story stems involves many of the skills required for competent and well-regulated "real-life" socioemotional functioning (Cole, Michel, & O'Donnell-Teti, 1994; Denham, 1998; Sroufe, 1995), and therefore links with children's behavioral and emotional problems were expected.

The second hypothesis was that children who were better able to emotionally resolve the MSSB narratives would have parents who experience less psychological distress. These links were based on the idea that story completions reflect not only the child's emotional functioning but also the wider family emotional climate, perhaps because of the negative impact of parental psychological distress on the child's emotional organization, or because in disorganized or unstable settings there is less time and care taken to narrativize experience or use language to make sense of difficult events.

Two additional hypotheses involve developmental continuity and change of children's emotional resolution between the study's two age points: 4.5 and 5.5 years. This age bracket was selected because by age 4.5 years imaginative play and narrative are fluent, so that the shape of narratives was thought to less likely reflect straightforward difficulty in performing the task, as it may be with younger children. The study's third hypothesis was that the level of emotional resolution children exhibit would increase with age. This increase may be the result of young children's increased exposure to more structured and task-oriented school-like activities that are likely to promote development in narrative skill during this age span. In addition, considerable development in children's emotion regulation and capacity to deal with difficult and complex emotions takes place during these years (Denham, 1998; Fischer & Ayoub, 1994; Sroufe, 1995).

Age-related increases do not preclude continuity in individual differences, however. Thus, the study's fourth hypothesis was that individual differences in children's emotional resolution would show a moderate degree of continuity. This hypothesis was based on the assumption that emotional resolution reflects children's relatively stable ways of dealing with emotional conflicts and difficulties. This relative stability is thought to be maintained due to individual differences in children's temperaments as well as the relative stability of parent-child relationship patterns, at least in low-stress, middle class samples (Denham, 1998; Sameroff & Emde, 1989). This hypothesis was also based on previous research that documented continuity in children's narrative themes and coherence (Oppenheim et al., 1997).

Method

Participants

Forty-eight children and their parents participated in this study at the ages of 4.5 and 5.5 years. Families were part of a longitudinal study regarding the development of children's emotion narratives and were primarily European-American and middle class (for complete details, see Oppenheim et al., 1996, 1997). All families included two parents and were intact at the time of recruitment.

Procedure

Both of the study's time points involved observations of children's completions of MSSB story stems, assessments of children's vocabulary, and questionnaires completed independently by both parents.

Measures

MacArthur Story Stem Battery (MSSB) (Bretherton et al., 1990) The MSSB was used to elicit children's narratives (see chapter 3 for details regarding the MSSB). At child age 4.5, eight of the MSSB stems were used (Birthday, Spilled Juice, Looking for Barney, Mom's Headache, Hot Gravy, Steeling the Candy Bar, Separation/Reunion, Bathroom Shelf). These stories were selected because they appeared to be most productive, yielding narratives that were easier to code reliably. At child age of 5.5, two stories were added to the battery to increase the number of stories tapping fear and anxiety (see Warren et al., 1996, and chapter 5, this book), and they were used in this study as well (Scary Dog, Monster).

Coding Emotional Resolution from MSSB Narratives A 4-point scale, ranging from 1 (unresolved) to 4 (resolved) was used to assess children's emotional resolution as reflected in the story completions. Summary descriptions of the scale's extremes are provided for illustration. Children received a score of 1 under several different circumstances, if they (1) completely avoided the main issue of the story stem, (2) referred to the issue but could not bring it to resolution, (3) could not bring the story to an end even when asked "how does the story end," (4) became incoherent or behaviorally disorganized. Children received a score of 4 if they addressed the story problem, issue, or dilemma in a complete, emotionally engaged way and brought it to resolution. In coding emotional resolution, emphasis was placed both on the process of telling the story and on the completion of the story. Special weight was given to the completion, however. Thus, even if the story involves emotional themes indicating difficulties in resolving the conflict presented in the story stem or the child exhibits markers of emotional difficulties while constructing the story, it may be rated as resolved or partially resolved (3 or 4) if the child is successful in bringing the story to a resolution (this excludes cliche endings such as "they lived happily ever after"). The coding manual for emotional resolution included stem-specific criteria for the themes that constitute the central issue, conflict, or dilemma in each of the stems to facilitate the decision of coders regarding the extent to which the central themes of the stems have been addressed. Twenty percent of the stories were coded by two raters blind to any other information about the children. Mean interrater reliability was $r = .88$. Differences between raters were conferenced and resulting consensus scores were used for analyses.

Exploratory principal component analyses on the emotional resolution scores of each of the stories conducted separately on the age 4.5 and 5.5 data revealed only one factor. Based on this, and to generate a more reliable score, we aggregated emotional resolution scores across stories. The emotional resolution aggregate revealed good internal consistency (alpha = .82 at the age of 4.5; alpha = .86 at the age of 5.5).

Expressive One-Word Picture Vocabulary Test (EOWPVT) Children's level of expressive one-word vocabulary was assessed using the EOWPVT (Gardner, 1990) during the age 4.5 and age 5.5 laboratory observations, and standardized scores were computed based on the norms provided by the test's authors.

The following questionnaires were completed by each parent separately at children's ages 4.5 and 5.5 years.

Child Behavior Checklist (CBCL) Parents completed the CBCL/4–18 (Achenbach, 1991) to assess the level of children's behavioral and emotional problems. The CBCL is a widely used measure that includes 113 items describing a range of behavioral and emotional problems rated by mothers or teachers as not true (0), somewhat or sometimes true (1), and very true or often true (2). Overall internalizing and externalizing behavior problems scores were generated according to instructions provided by Achenbach (1991).

Brief Symptom Inventory (BSI) The BSI (Derogatis & Spencer, 1982) is a well-accepted measure of adult psychological symptoms and was used to assess parents' psychological distress. The BSI includes a list of 53 symptoms (e.g., How much were you distressed in the past 7 days by nervousness or shakiness inside?) that respondents rate on a 5-point scale ranging from 0 (not at all) to 4 (extremely). The BSI yields an overall psychological distress measure that is generated by summing scores across all items.

Results

Preliminary Analyses

Gender Differences Gender differences on the study's variables were examined using two-tailed t tests. Only a few variables showed gender differences. Girls' narratives were rated as more emotionally resolved ($M = 2.78$, $SD = .61$) than boys' narratives ($M = 2.58$, $SD = .82$; $t = 2.93$, $p = .005$) but only when children were 4.5 years old. In addition, mothers reported boys as having more externalizing behavior problems at both time points (age 4.5: $M_{boys} = 10.71$, $SD = 7.98$, $M_{girls} = 6.43$, $SD = 6.03$; $t = 2.01$, $p = .05$; age 5.5: $M_{boys} = 12.19$, $SD = 8.75$, $M_{girls} = 7.22$, $SD = 7.03$; $t = 2.05$, $p = .05$).

Vocabulary Associations between the emotional resolution aggregate and children's concurrent vocabulary assessments revealed a marginally significant correlation at age 4.5 ($r = .24$, $p = .058$) and a significant correlation at age 5.5 ($r = .27$, $p = .03$).

Agreement between Mothers and Fathers Mothers and fathers showed agreement when reporting on their children's behavior problems. Particularly high was agreement on externalizing behavior problems (rs equaling .70 and .73 at ages 4.5 and 5.5, respectively), but significant correlations were also found between maternal and paternal reports on children's internalizing behavior problems (rs equaling .39 and .31 at ages 4.5 and 5.5, respectively).

Developmental Continuity in Parental Report Measures The parental report measures showed considerable continuity between the study's two time points (rs = .70 and .90 for maternal CBCL internalizing and externalizing scores, respectively; rs = .70 and .88 for paternal CBCL internalizing and externalizing scores, respectively; rs = .84 and .62 for maternal and paternal BSI scores, respectively; all ps < .001).

Associations Between Emotional Resolution and Children's and Parents' Emotional/Behavioral Difficulties

We move now to analyses involving the study's first and second individual differences hypotheses involving links between emotion resolution of children's MSSB narratives and children's CBCL scores and parents' BSI scores. Overall, emotion resolution was associated with the concurrent parental report measures but more so at age 5.5 than 4.5 (analyses were also conducted separately for boys and girls, and a very similar pattern of associations emerged. Therefore, results are reported for the entire sample). At the age of 4.5, emotional resolution was associated with fewer externalizing behavior problems as reported by both mothers ($r = -.30$, $p = .02$) and fathers ($r = -.30$, $p = .02$). No associations were found with internalizing behavior problems or with the BSI. At the age of 5.5, emotional resolution was also associated with fewer externalizing behavior problems as reported by both mothers ($r = -.59$, $p < .001$) and fathers ($r = -.53$, $p < .001$). In addition, emotional resolution was associated with fewer internalizing behavior problems, but only as reported by fathers ($r = -.39$, $p = .004$). Emotion resolution was also associated with both maternal ($r = -.25$, $p = .048$) and paternal ($r = -.27$, $p = .04$) lower emotional distress scores.

Do BSI scores account for variance in children's narratives beyond the variance accounted for by the CBCL? This question was important in order to evaluate whether variability in emotional resolution reflects not only children's behavior problems, which are conceptually and empirically proximal to emotion resolution, but also parental psychological distress, which is conceptually and empirically more distal. To examine this question, we conducted linear regression analyses with emotion resolution as the dependent variable. Child vocabulary was entered as the first block, CBCL internalizing and externalizing scores as reported by both parents were entered as the second block, and BSI scores as reported by both parents were entered as the last block. The regression analyses were conducted separately for age 4.5 and 5.5 measures. The analysis at age 4.5 did not yield a significant regression model, but a significant model was obtained for age 5.5, $F = 3.29$, $p = .009$. The child vocabulary score entered first did not account for a significant amount of the variance, $F_{change} = 2.96$, $p = .09$. Children's CBCL scores (internalizing and externalizing) were entered next and accounted for a significant amount of the variance, $F_{change} = 4.69$, $p < .004$, following which the BSI scores (of mothers and fathers) did not account for additional variance, $F_{change} < 1$, ns.

These analyses indicated that parental emotional distress, as indexed by the BSI, did not account for variance in children's emotion resolution scores beyond the variance accounted by the CBCL scores. This finding does not mean, however, that parental emotional distress is insignificant when children's emotion resolution of MSSB narratives is concerned. As described earlier, bivariate analyses showed that both mothers' and fathers' BSI scores were associated with emotion resolution, at least at the child age of 5.5. To further understand these associations, we conducted an additional analysis that combined the emotional distress scores of both parents. This analysis, conducted from a "risk factor" perspective, asked whether having one parent who experiences relatively high psychological distress is related to low emotion resolution of child narratives or whether the negative impact occurs only when both parents experience relatively high distress. Parental BSI scores were split at the median to form high and low distress scores for each parent, and three groups were formed. Ten children had parents who both experienced low distress; 15 children had one parent who experienced high distress and one experiencing low distress; and 13 children had parents who both experienced high distress (numbers do not add up to the total n of 48 because of missing data). A planned comparison revealed that the children with two parents experiencing high distress had significantly lower emotion resolution scores ($M = 2.38$, $SD = .73$) than both children who had one parent who experienced high distress ($M = 2.82$, $SD = .87$) and children whose parents experienced low distress ($M = 2.92$, $SD = .65$; $t = 1.92$, $p < .05$). The latter two groups did not differ from one another.

Developmental Continuity and Change in Emotional Resolution

We turn now to the study's second goal, which was to examine continuity and change in children's emotional resolution of MSSB narratives. Both change and continuity were revealed in children's emotional resolution scores. Children's scores increased between the ages of 4.5 ($M= 2.40$, $SD = .56$) and 5.5 ($M = 2.66$, $SD = .72$; $t= 2.43$, $p = .019$). In addition, individual differences showed moderate continuity between the two age points ($r = .44$, $p < .002$). We next asked whether this association could simply be explained by individual differences in children's vocabulary. To examine this, we computed a partial correlation between emotion resolution scores at age 4.5 and 5.5, controlling for children's vocabulary scores at 4.5 and 5.5 years. The correlation remained essentially the same ($r = .43$, $p = .003$), suggesting that the continuity was not due to stability of individual differences in vocabulary.

Our final developmental question asked whether within-child age-related changes (i.e., increases or decreases) in emotional resolution are associated in the expected direction with changes in children's behavior problems and parents' psychological distress. In other words, although at the group level emotional resolution scores showed relative stability over time as well the expected age-related increase, these group-level trends do not imply that all subjects conformed to this pattern. For example, it is possible that some subjects showed a decrease in emotional resolution with age, and the question posed was whether such a decrease is associated with an increase in behavior problems and parental psychological distress. To explore this issue, we first computed change scores of children's emotional resolution, CBCL (total score, combining internalizing and externalizing problems), and parents' BSI scores by subtracting age 4.5 scores from age 5.5 scores. Next, correlations were computed between the change score of emotion resolution and the change scores of the BSI and CBCL. We expected significant negative correlations, because these would indicate that increases (i.e., improvements) in emotion resolution were associated with decreases (i.e., improvements) in parental and child behavioral and emotional difficulties. Results showed that children whose emotion resolution scores improved showed decreases in CBCL scores, whereas children whose emotion resolution scores decreased showed increases in behavior problems. This pattern was found based on both maternal ($r = -.27, p = .039$) and paternal ($r = -.24, p = .05$) CBCL scores. No significant associations were found between the emotion resolution change scores and the BSI change scores.

Discussion

Children's emotional resolution of MSSB narratives emerged from this study as meaningfully related to their behavioral and emotional functioning and their parents' psychological distress. Low emotional resolution was associated with parental reports of emotional and behavioral problems. In addition, low emotional resolution was also associated with parental reports regarding their own emotional distress, particularly when *both* parents reported relatively high distress. As expected, emotional resolution ratings increased with age and also showed moderate continuity of individual differences. Embedded in these overall, group-level continuity findings were interesting patterns of individual children's developmental pathways. Children whose emotion resolution increased with age showed improvements in their emotion and behavior problems, and those whose emotion resolution scores decreased with age showed a worsening of their emotional and behavioral problems.

The study's first and second hypotheses involved links between emotion resolution and children's behavior/emotion problems as well as their parents' psychological distress. These hypotheses received support particularly from the data of 5.5-year-olds. At the age of 4.5 years, children's emotion resolution ratings were associated only with parental reports of children's externalizing behavior problems, but at 5.5 years associations included, in addition to externalizing behavior problems, children's internalizing behavior problems (at least as reported by fathers), as well as both parents' reports regarding their own psychological distress. The findings thus cohere with previous work using the MSSB linking story completions to children's behavior problems (e.g., Oppenheim et al., 1997) and indicate that the way children address and resolve conflictual and emotionally charged story stems reflects not only the world of narrative construction but also their behavioral and emotional functioning, as well as their parents' experiences of distress.

How can we explain the difference between the age 4.5 and age 5.5 patterns of findings? Given the stability of the parental report measures, it seems less likely that they can explain the difference. It is possible that because story stems were added at the age of 5.5 years, the reliability of the emotional resolution measure improved. Another possibility is that the added experience of the older children in the study in school-like activities improved their capacity to meaningfully participate in a story completion task. In other words, story completions may mean something different at 4.5 versus 5.5 years. It appears that, at the age of 5.5 years, children's story completions are more clearly a reflection of their and their parents emotional functioning and well-being. It is possible that at the age of 4.5 other factors also influence children's story completions. For example, at the age of 4.5, the narrative skills required for completion of the story stems may be less developed in some children. Or the social and behavioral skills required to participate in a testing session with an unfamiliar adult may be less mature at the younger age. These factors might shape children's story completions and weaken the links between such completions and children's "real-life" behavioral and emotional functioning (Oppenheim & Waters, 1995).

The latter interpretation has an important implication. As mentioned earlier, researchers (and clinicians) often use story completion approaches for assessing children's emotional regulation or internal representations, operating under the assumption that variability in story completions reflects such "deeper" constructs rather than more method- and context-related factors related to the task of completing a story. Although previous research (e.g., Warren et al., 1996), as well as (to some extent) these findings indicate that this assumption has some validity even with younger preschoolers, there is also a risk of misinterpreting the stories of such children. The main risk involves attributing variability in narratives to emotional processes rather than to the immaturity of the skills required to participate in the story stem procedure.

We move next to discussion of the links between parental psychological distress and children's emotional resolution. These analyses were based on seeing children's story completions as reflecting not only their own functioning but also the broader family emotional context (Fiese et al., 1999), here assessed through parental reports regarding their psychological distress. As mentioned, children's emotional resolution at 5.5 was negatively related to both parents' reports regarding their psychological distress. Thus, children's story completions appear to be sensitive to parental distress. Perhaps parental distress results in less competent parenting behavior, including less time spent in coherent, sustained language exchanges involving coherent narrativization of emotional experiences. Another possibility is that parental distress influences the child's emotion regulation, which in turn affects the child's story completions. Of course, other family-level factors may influence both parents' and children's emotional well-being. Further research is needed, and our findings regarding the links between both mothers' and fathers' distress and children's story completions suggest that such research would benefit from including both parents.

What are the joint influences of the psychological distress of mothers and fathers on children's emotional resolution? We addressed this question with a risk/protective factor approach. Results showed that children whose mother and father both reported relatively high distress were at highest "risk" in the sense that their emotional resolution ratings were significantly lower than those of children with only one parent experiencing high distress or no parent experiencing high distress. In fact, the emotional resolutions of children having one parent with high distress were no different than those having no parent report distress. These results should be evaluated with the following caveats in mind. First, they are based on post-hoc exploration of the data. Second, the designation of "high distress" is relative (i.e., based on a median split) and does not reflect clinical levels of distress. Finally, analyses of risk and protective factors usually have well-established indices of psychopathology as an outcome, but that is not the case here. Nonetheless, this analysis is instructive, because it shows that emotion resolution of the story stems is sensitive not only to the child's problems but also to wider family factors, namely, parental emotional distress. In addition, family contexts in which both parents experience distress may be particularly stressful for children. Based on what we know regarding the impact of parental psychological distress on children (e.g., Seifer & Dickstein, 2000), these results are not surprising, but the evidence that the negative impact may also be evident in children's narratives, reflecting their emotional meaning making, adds another important dimension.

The study's second goal was to examine continuity and change in children's emotional resolution between ages 4.5 and 5.5 years. As expected, a moderate level of continuity in emotional resolution emerged, indicating that the scale assessing resolution taps relatively stable individual differences. The study's analyses indicated that the continuity found does not seem to be explained by continuity in children's vocabulary, but it is not possible to conclude from this study what accounts for this continuity. Continuity could be due to intrapersonal individual differences in children's temperament, emotion regulation, or representations, stability in children's relationships and family context, and the use of the same assessment at both time points. Here, too, more research is needed.

Along with the continuity findings there was evidence for developmental change. As expected, children's emotional resolution increased with age. As in many developmental studies, it is not possible to tease apart developmental effects (i.e., a "real" increase in children's emotional resolution) from testing effects (i.e., the effects of repeated assessments using the same procedure). Furthermore, it appears that the group-level age-related increase and moderate continuity, though both statistically significant, concealed a more complex picture. When the data were examined from the perspective of within-child change, the analyses revealed that, although for the group as a whole there was an increase of emotion resolution scores with age, for some children there was an increase with age, whereas for some there was a decrease. Furthermore, these divergent pathways seemed to be meaningful and theoretically coherent, at least in terms of convergence with parental reports of behavior problems. Children whose emotion resolution scores increased were reported by both parents to show a decrease in behavior problems, whereas children whose emotion resolution scores decreased were reported by both parents to show an increase in behavior problems. The importance of these findings is in showing coherent links between parental reports of changes in children's "externally" observed behavior problems and ratings of emotion resolution reflecting children's "internal" world.

Taken together, the developmental analyses of emotion resolution provide additional support for the use of the MSSB as a measure of the young child's emotional experience. The stability of individual differences and the age-related increase indicate that the measure taps relatively stable individual differences but is also sensitive to age-related developments. The within-child change analyses are significant because they suggest that change over time in emotional resolution, whether positive or negative, is associated with independently obtained maternal and paternal reports regarding corresponding changes in children's emotion and behavior problems.

As always, when new measures are introduced, replication of the findings is important. Also, many questions are left unanswered regarding the mechanisms responsible for the associations found. Nonetheless, the findings are promising because they suggest that children's emotional resolution of story stems may parallel the way they resolve (or have difficulties resolving) the many emotional challenges inherent in their daily lives.

NOTE

Part of this study was completed while I was a postdoctoral fellow in the John D. and Catherine T. MacArthur Foundation Network for Early Childhood Transitions, Robert M. Emde, Chair. I would also like to thank Susan Warren for her help in data collection and Rakefet Milika for her help in coding the data.

REFERENCES

Achenbach, T. M. (1991). *Manual for the Child Behavior Checklist/4–18 and 1991 profile.* Burlington: University of Vermont, Department of Psychiatry.

Axline, V. M. (1947). *Play therapy.* New York: Ballantine.

Bretherton, I., & Munholland, K. A. (1999). Internal working models in attachment relationships: A construct revisited. In J. Cassidy & P. Shaver (Eds.), *Handbook of attachment: Theory, research, and clinical applications* (pp. 89–114). New York: Guilford.

Bretherton, I., Oppenheim, D., Buchsbaum, H., Emde, R. N., & the MacArthur Narrative Group. (1990). *The MacArthur Story Stem Battery (MSSB).* Unpublished manual, University of Wisconsin-Madison.

Buchsbaum, H., & Emde, R. N. (1990). Play narratives in 36-month-old children: Early moral development and family relationships. *Psychoanalytic Study of the Child, 40,* 129–155.

Buchsbaum, H. K., Toth, S. L., Clyman, R. B., Cicchetti, D., & Emde, R. N. (1993). The use of a narrative story stem technique with maltreated children: Implications for theory and practice. *Development and Psychopathology, 4,* 603–625.

Cole, P. M., Michel, M. K., & O'Donnell-Teti, L. (1994). The development of emotion regulation and dysregulation: A clinical perspective. *Monographs of the Society for Research in Child Development, 59*(2–3), 73–100.

Denham, S. (1998). *Emotional development in young children.* New York: Guilford.

Derogatis, L., & Spencer, P. M. (1982). *The Brief Symptom Inventory (BSI): Administration, scoring & procedures manual-I.* Baltimore: Johns Hopkins University School of Medicine.

Erikson, E. H. (1950). *Childhood and society.* New York: Norton.

Fiese, B., Sameroff, A. J., Grotevant, H., Wamboldt, F. S., Dickstein, S., & Lewis-Fravel, D. (1999). The stories that families tell: Narrative coherence, narrative interaction, and relationship beliefs. *Monographs of the Society for Research in Child Development, 64*(2, Serial No. 257).

Fischer, K. W., & Ayoub, C. (1994). Affective splitting and dissociation in normal and maltreated children: Developmental pathways for self in relationships. In D. Cicchetti & S. L. Toth (Eds.), *Rochester Symposium on Developmental Psychopathology, Vol. 5. Disorders and dysfunctions of the self* (pp. 149–222). Rochester, NY: University of Rochester Press.

Freud, A. (1946). *The psycho-analytical treatment of children.* London: Imago.

Gardner, M. D. (1990). *Expressive One-Word Picture Vocabulary Test (revised).* Novato, CA: Academic Therapy.

Labov, W., & Waletzky, J. (1967). Narrative analysis: Oral versions of personal experience. In J. Helm (Ed.), *Essays in the verbal and visual arts* (pp. 12–44). Seattle: University of Washington Press.

Macfie, J., Toth, S. L., Rogosch, F. A., Robinson, J., Emde, R. N., & Cicchetti, D. (1999). Effects of maltreatment on preschoolers' narrative representations of responses to relieve distress and role reversal. *Developmental Psychology, 35,* 460–465.

Main, M., Kaplan, N., & Cassidy, J. (1985). Security in infancy, childhood, and adulthood: A move to the level of representation. In I. Bretherton & E. Waters (Eds.), *Growing points of attachment theory and research. Monographs of the Society for Research in Child Development, 50*(1–2), Serial No. 209, 66–104.

Oppenheim, D., Emde, R. N., Hasson, M., & Warren, S. (1997). Preschoolers face moral dilemmas: A longitudinal study of acknowledging and resolving internal conflict. *International Journal of Psychoanalysis, 78,* 943–957.

Oppenheim, D., Emde, R. N., & Wamboldt, F. S. (1996). Associations between 3-year-olds' narrative co-constructions with mothers and fathers and their story-completions about affective themes. *Early Development and Parenting, 5,* 149–160.

Oppenheim, D., Emde, R. N., & Warren, S. (1997). Children's narrative representation of mothers: Their developments and associations with child and mother adaptation. *Child Development, 68,* 127–138.

Oppenheim, D., & Waters, H. S. (1995). Narrative processes and attachment representations: Issues of development and assessment. In E. Waters, B. E. Vaughn, G. Posada, & K. Kondo-Ikemura (Eds), *Caregiving, cultural and cognitive perspectives on secure base behavior and working models. Monographs of the Society for Research in Child Development, 60*(2–3), Serial No. 244, 197–233.

Robinson, J., Herot, C., Haynes, P., & Mantz-Simmons, L. (2000). Children's story stem responses: A measure of program impact on developmental risks associated with dysfunctional parenting. *Child Abuse and Neglect, 24*(1), 99–110.

Sameroff, A., & Emde, R. N. (1989). *Relationship disturbances in early infancy.* New York: Basic.

Seifer, R., & Dickstein, S. (2000). Parental mental illness and infant development. In C. H. Zeahan (Ed.), *Handbook of infant mental health* (pp. 145–160). New York: Guilford.

Sroufe, L. A. (1995). *Emotional development: The organization of emotional life in the early years.* Cambridge: Cambridge University Press.

Toth, S. L., Cicchetti, D., Macfie, J., & Emde, R. N. (1997). Representations of self and other in the narratives of neglected, physically abused, and sexually abused preschoolers. *Development and Psychopathology, 9,* 781–796.

Warren, S., Emde, R. N., & Sroufe, L. A. (2001). Internal representations: Predicting anxiety from children's play narratives. *Journal of the American Academy of Child and Adolescent Psychiatry, 39,* 100–107.

Warren, S., Oppenheim, D., & Emde, R. N. (1996). Can emotions and themes in children's play predict behavior problems? *Journal of the American Academy of Child and Adolescent Psychiatry, 34,* 1331–1337.

Winnicott, D. (1971). *Playing and reality.* London: Tavistock.

Zahn-Waxler, C., Cole, P. M., Richardson, D. T., Friedman, R. J., Michel, M. K., & Belouad, F. (1994). Social problem solving in disruptive preschool children: Reactions to hypothetical situations of conflict and distress. *Merrill-Palmer Quarterly, 40,* 98–119.

MIRIAM STEELE
HOWARD STEELE
MATTHEW WOOLGAR
SUSAN YABSLEY
PETER FONAGY
DANNIE JOHNSON
CARLA CROFT

9

An Attachment Perspective on Children's Emotion Narratives: Links Across Generations

Attachment teaches us ends, not means—and thus imposes on us our parents' dreams.

M. Minsky, *The Society of Mind*

What has belonged to the lowest [i.e., earliest] part of mental life of each of us is changed, through the formation of the ideal, into what is highest in the human mind by our scale of values. . . . When we were little we knew these higher natures [i.e., our experience of our parents], we admired them and feared them; and later we took them into ourselves.

Sigmund Freud, "Ego and the Id"

This chapter reports on a study that investigated the possibility of links across generations in the emotion narratives provided by parents expecting their first child and those elicited from their 5-year-old children. We describe the rationale for this hypothesized link across generations, before introducing the data from an ongoing longitudinal study of intergenerational patterns of attachment (Steele, Steele, & Fonagy, 1996).

In a highly accessible 1985 compendium of thoughts and readings on "the society of mind," the acclaimed cognitive scientist Minsky advances the idea that learning from attachment figures involves the acquisition of goals or ideals themselves, not merely the acquisition of tools or methods to reach a given goal. Such a viewpoint is consistent with the range of psychoanalytic and developmental theory that assumes children internalize, identify with, or appropriate their parents' beliefs and behaviors (e.g., Freud, 1923/1961; Hoffman, 1983). Attachment theory may offer a uniquely empirical account of this cross-generational phenomenon, as there are well-validated research methods for activating the attachment behavioral system in infants (e.g., Ainsworth, Blehar, Waters, & Wall, 1978; Spangler & Grossman, 1993; Sroufe & Waters, 1977) and adults (Bakerman-

Kranenburg & van Ijzendoorn, 1993; Dozier & Kobak, 1993; Main, Kaplan, & Cassidy, 1985). Further, as amply documented (see van Ijzendoorn's 1995 meta-analysis), there is a highly significant degree of overlap between behavioral assessments of attachment security in preverbal infants (i.e., Strange Situation) and narrative-based assessments of attachment and caregiving processes in adults (i.e., Adult Attachment Interview [AAI]). Moreover, the attachments infants form to their fathers appear to develop independently from those they form with their mothers, and each of these infant-parent relationships is predicted by the attachment narratives their parents tell (Steele, Steele, & Fonagy, 1996). Thus, attachment learning is arguably a relationship-specific process, or a reflection of nonshared enviornmental influences, a view supported by twin studies of attachment patterns in preschoolers (e.g., O'Connor & Croft, 2001).

Despite powerful specific associations between parents' attachment interviews and infants' attachments to their parents (van Ijzendoorn, 1995), and evidence that mothers' attachment interviews are associated with caregiving characteristics in infancy (Haft & Slade, 1989) and early childhood (Crowell & Feldman, 1988), important questions remain concerning the extent to which children themselves have internalized this attachment learning in ways that go beyond infancy. For example, we do not yet know if individual differences in young children's own verbally elaborated perceptions of their parents and of family life in general are related to parents' attachment interviews. This chapter presents longitudinal data comparing parents' attachment narratives, collected when they were expecting their first child, to their children's emotion narratives at age 5.

The current widespread resurgence of interest in doll-play techniques for accessing the thoughts and feelings of young children invites consideration of the extent to which children's narratives reflect what they have learned from attachment figures (see Bretherton & Oppenheim, chapter 3, this book; Oppenheim & Waters, 1995; Woolgar, 1999, for reviews). Indeed, previous reports suggest that the organization and coherence of children's narratives offered in response to challenging queries and prompts does indeed reflect their current attachment security to their mothers (e.g., Bretherton, Ridgeway, & Cassidy, 1990; Cassidy, 1988; Oppenheim, 1997). This chapter follows this line of inquiry by addressing whether relationship themes produced by 5-year-olds in doll play overlap with relationship themes produced by their parents in independently administered attachment interviews more than 5 years previously, before the children were born.

In our approach to this chapter, we assume that children's responses to emotionally challenging story beginnings will reflect their habitual strategies for dealing with attachment-related distress, acquired initially during infancy through interactions with caregivers (Bretherton et al., 1990), and consolidated or perhaps modified through conversation and interpersonal negotiation with caregivers and others in the preschool years (e.g., Dunn, 1988). The extant data support two quite distinct claims. First, it may be that children's enacted emotion narratives reflect the powerful long-term influence of early (preverbal) attachment experiences. Second, children's narratives may reflect the diverse ways that early and ongoing relationship experiences are reworked via language and the striving for meaning, between and within people. There can be little doubt that linguistic development makes possible, or at least greatly enhances, the capacity to narrate and redescribe one's experiences. In other words, children's narratives may reflect the underlying nature of the attachment relations they have constructed with their caregivers or that children have acquired a style of using language or "narrativizing" experience characteristic of, and likely to create or perpetuate, certain patterns of attachment relationships. The hypotheses explored in this study, though pertinent to both claims, are particularly relevant to the investigation of the former claim: that children's narratives reflect the continuation or perpetuation of early attachment relations with parents. This chapter focuses not on the immedate proximal influence of parent-child conversation on children's narratives but on the distal influence of parents' expressed thoughts and feelings concerning their attachment history, assessed via the Adult Attachment Interview when the parents were expecting their first child (Steele, Steele, & Fonagy, 1996).

A considerable amount of face validity comes with the idea of a possible overlap between the AAI (George, Kaplan, & Main, 1985) and the MacArthur Story Stem Battery (see Bretherton & Oppenheim, chapter 3, this book). In both interview techniques, the respondent's audio-recorded narrative is the focus of close scrutiny by trained raters. Both tasks demand that the listener consider what he or she might do (or have done) when faced with emotionally challenging situations that are part of everyday childhood experience, including emotional upset, physical hurt, separation from parents, parental discipline, and rejection/exclusion. Further, in both tasks specific prompts invite the respondents to express how they think a parent ought to behave in response to a child's misdemeanors. And, finally, both instruments tax the speakers' capacity for providing an emotionally balanced and coherent story that may be seen to represent a resolution to the frequently occurring dilemmas in family life. In the case of the AAI, at the end of a long day of coding, each interview transcription is assigned to one of four categories: (1) insecure-dismissing; (2) insecure-preoccupied; (3) autonomous-secure; (4) unresolved with respect to past loss or trauma (see Hesse, 1999, for a full overview of AAI scoring and extant results).

In sum, this study observed children's depiction of parent-child relations in the story completions they provided and then compared these to qualities of their parents' attachment narratives provided five years earlier. We expected that parents, particularly mothers, whose AAIs were typified by coherence, autonomy, and a valuing of attachment (i.e., indications of adult attachment security) would have children who at age 5 would demonstrate similar narrative qualities. Specifically, we expected from such children an organized expression of negative and positive elements to story dilemmas, together with a hopeful resolution that included presentation of a "stronger" and "wiser" attachment figure. Where parents' attachment narratives were strikingly lacking in coherence and correspondingly insecure (either dismissing or preoccupied or unresolved), we anticipated elevated levels of reference to attachment figures who were neither stronger nor wiser (i.e., weak or ineffectual or rejecting) and corresponding depictions of confused, sad, or angry/aggressive children.

In the literature on parenting, optimal child development results from parental behavior high in warmth and control (the authoritative stance), as initially suggested by Baumrind (1967). These parental characteristics have also been identified as central to the healthy child's perception of parenting (Bretherton, Golby, & Cho, 1997; Oppenheim, Emde, & Warren, 1997). Thus, if a parent showed evidence of an autonomous-secure state of mind in response to the AAI during the initial pregnancy assessments, then we anticipated their child would present narratives with strong indications of authoritative parenting.

In general, then, this chapter considers the attachment-driven hypothesis that story completion narratives provided by 5-year-olds will overlap significantly with the narratives provided by their parents in the context of the AAI. We further expected these cross-generational associations in attachment narratives to obtain, even after controlling for children's levels of verbal skills. Additionally, we consider whether the gender of the parent matters in these links across generations in narratives. Because children's narratives are emotion narratives about family relationships, a domain of experience traditionally regarded as intrinsically more familiar to girls and women (e.g., Gilligan, 1982), we wondered whether maternal narratives would be more influential than paternal ones.

Correspondingly, the results reported also include tests for the possible influence of children's gender on the stories they provide. Drawing on the literature on gender differences (e.g., Maccoby, 1988; Zahn-Waxler, in press; Zahn-Waxler, Cole, & Barret, 1991), we anticipated that aggressive themes might be more pronounced in boys' stories, whereas prosocial themes might be more pronounced in girls' stories (see also Bretherton & Oppenheim, chapter 3, this book). Beyond these anticipated gender differences, we planned to test for possible interactions between attachment patterns of parents and gender of child on the observed content of children's stories. Interestingly, Turner (1991, 1993) showed that aggression was a marked behavioral characteristic not of boys in general but of boys with an insecure attachment to their mothers.

In summary, this chapter explores two main hypotheses concerning influences on children's narratives, one concerning parental attachment, the other concerning gender differences and their possible moderation by maternal attachment. First, will parental attachment security, particularly maternal security, predict children's emotion narratives typified by the depiction of authoritative parenting? Second, if expected gender differences appear (i.e., boys' stories being more aggressive), will this difference lessen in children if mothers' attachment status was secure?

Method

The data referred to in this chapter stem from an ongoing prospective longitudinal study of attachment patterns (known as the London Parent-Child Project and initially begun by Miriam Steele (1990) and Howard Steele (1991), and which has led to a number of published reports (e.g., Fonagy et al., 1991; Steele & Steele, 1994; Steele, Steele, & Fonagy, 1996; Steele, Steele, Croft, & Fonagy, 1999;

Woolgar, Steele, Steele, Yabsley, & Fonagy, 2001). The co-authors in this chapter were all instrumental in the follow-up work on which this chapter is based. The first phase of the London Parent-Child Project was launched in 1987 when 100 pregnant woman were recruited for the study, described as "a study aimed at better understanding how one's own experience of childhood influences the parenting of the next generation." Recruitment took place during prenatal classes at the Obstetrics and Gynaecology Department of University College Hospital during the autumn and winter of 1987. Selection criteria included primiparous status, current cohabitation with the father of the child, fluency in the English language, and age above 20 years. Expectant parents who volunteered were, on average, in their early 30s. About 50% of those who were told about the study agreed to participate. The resulting sample was largely white, middle class, and 70% university-educated. The couples seemed jointly devoted to becoming parents and shared an interest in participating in research on relationships. In their last trimester of pregnancy, the AAI was administered to the expectant mothers and their partners.

Slightly more than 5 years after the pregnancy assessment, the families were invited to a lab visit where the focus children were administered a measure of expressive language ability, as well as 11 selected story stems from the MacArthur Story Stem Battery (Bretherton et al., 1990), identified in our pilot work as evocative for 5-year-old British children.

Participants in the Five-Year Follow-Up

Eighty-six of the original hundred families agreed to participate and provided data referred to in this chapter. The mean age of the children (40 girls and 46 boys) was 61 months (range: 59 to 65 months). The stems were administered as part of a testing procedure that took between 1½ to 2 hours in the absence of the parents. The main reason for attrition from earlier phases of the project was families moving far outside the greater London area, or moving without us being able to trace them. The 5-year sample was demographically similar to the original sample, and the composition of the 5-year sample in attachment terms, either of parents or children, was highly representative of the original group. Approximately 10% of the 86 families were separated or divorced (less than the national average), and in each of these cases the parents had shared-custody arrangements. Thus, a strong commitment to parenting continued to characterize the largely middle-class, educated sample who participated in the 5-year follow-up.

Measures

The Adult Attachment Interview The interview administered to all parents closely followed the schedule outlined by George, Kaplan, and Main (1985). The AAI is structured entirely around the topic of attachment, principally the individual's relationship to his mother and father (or to alternative caregivers) during childhood. Subjects are asked to describe their relationship with their parents during childhood and to provide specific memories to support global evaluations. The interviewer asks directly about childhood experiences of rejection, being upset, ill, and hurt, as well as about loss, abuse, and separations. In addition, the subjects are asked to offer explanations for parental behaviors and to describe the current relationship with their parents and the influence they consider their childhood experiences have had on their adult personality. Ultimate classification of the interview into the secure or one of the insecure groups depends largely on how the narrative satisfies four criteria of coherence: (1) a good fit between memories and evaluations concerning attachment, (2) a succinct yet complete picture, (3) the provision of relevant details, and (4) clarity and orderliness (Main & Goldwyn, in press). The basic classification system assigns interviews to one of three groups, two insecure (dismissing or preoccupied) and one deemed autonomous-secure. An insecure-dismissing narrative is brief but incomplete, marked by a lack of fit between memories and evaluations, often punctuated or sustained by an unrealistically positive evaluation of parents or self. An insecure-preoccupied narrative is neither succinct nor complete and contains many irrelevant details, together with much passive (weak, nonspecific) speech or high anger toward one or both parents. By contrast, the autonomous-secure narrative robustly fulfills all or most of the criteria of coherence, *whether or not* the speaker was well cared for during childhood. In other words, a narrative that refers to neglecting, rejecting, or even abusive experiences during childhood may be judged autonomous-secure if these malevolent relationship patterns are clearly relegated to the past, with the narrative conveying understanding and acceptance of how these have influenced the individual's development.

A further important consideration when rating and classifying attachment interviews concerns past loss and trauma. When there is clear evidence of a significant loss or trauma (physical or sexual abuse), the rater or judge follows a number of specified guidelines (Main & Goldwyn, in press) for assessing the extent to which the past trauma is resolved. In sum, this comes down to determining the extent to which the overwhelmingly negative experiences are identified as such and spoken about in a way to indicate that they belong to the past, without lapses in the speaker's monitoring of reason or discourse when discussing the past loss or trauma (after Main & Goldwyn, in press). For example, where loss has occurred, it is important for the speaker to demonstrate full awareness of the permanence of this loss. And, where abuse has occurred in speakers' childhood experiences, it is important for speakers to at once acknowledge the abuse and also show that they understand they are not responsible for the maltreatment. Important clues as to the extent of resolution in the speaker's mind follow from careful study of the narrative for a logical and temporally sequenced account of the trauma that is neither too brief, suggesting an attempt to minimize the significance of the trauma, nor too detailed, suggesting ongoing absorption.

All interviews were independently rated by the first, second, and sixth author. Consistently high levels of interrater reliability were obtained and have been previously described in detail (see Fonagy, Steele, & Steele, 1991; Steele, Steele, & Fonagy, 1996).

We provide details on the distribution of mothers' interviews, not the fathers, as the latter did not have significant effects on children's narratives. Possible reasons for this are taken up in the discussion. Of the 86 maternal interviews available for the 5-year sample, 20 were dismissing, 11 were preoccupied, 48 were autonomous-secure, and 7 were unresolved with respect to past loss. These seven unresolved interviews from the mothers were also assigned to their best-fitting three-way classifications, one to the dismissing group, three to the preoccupied group, and three to the autonomous-secure group. Placing unresolved interviews into their alternate secure or insecure classifications, we obtained a two-way split of 35 insecure and 51 secure interviews. This binary approach to the interviews was favored because of the small numbers of preoccupied and unresolved interviews and because we had no specific expectations concerning type of maternal insecurity. Also, the binary coding of interviews enhanced our power to detect predicted interactions of attachment interview groups and child gender.

Children's Emotion Narratives A subset of 11 story stems, taken directly from the MacArthur Story Stem Battery (after Bretherton et al., 1990), were selected to assess the children's responses across a range of socioemotional dilemmas. All the stems consisted of a brief narrative introduced by the experimenter and ending with a dilemma or a problem. The stem was staged by the experimenter moving Duplo dolls and props through the relevant actions and speaking in character. The experimenter then invited the child to "show me and tell me what happens next." Each stem contained the elements of an age-appropriate dilemma in the context of everyday socioemotional situations.

The 11 story stems employed were Spilled Juice, Mother's Headache, Three's a Crowd, Burned Hand, Lost Keys, Sweet Shop, Separation, Reunion, Bathroom Shelf, Exclusion, and Biscuit Tin (see Bretherton & Oppenheim, chapter 3, this book for details on content and procedure with regard to administering these stems). The 11 story stems took about 45 minutes to complete. The children's responses were videotaped from behind a one-way mirror and their narratives transcribed verbatim from audiotape, for subsequent coding.

Reliability and Data Reduction of Story Stem Coding Content themes were coded according to the MacArthur Narrative Coding Manual (Robinson, Mantz-Simmons, Macfie, and the MacArthur Narrative Working Group, 1995; see also Robinson & Mantz-Simmons, chapter 4, this book) with three minor modifications. First, categories such as aggression and punishment that coded several types of behavior were broken down into their components (e.g., recoded into verbal aggression and physical aggression, or into verbal punishment, physical punishment, and unspecified punishments). Second, categories that distinguished between self and other (e.g., exclusion, blame, and shame) were also recoded into separate items specifying the agent. Third, the reparation/guilt theme consisted of instances of both practical reparation (e.g., cleaning up juice or putting the biscuit back) and empathic reparation (e.g., apologizing or describing a character as feeling sorry), and, for this study, these were coded separately. Representations of parental positiveness, negativeness, and disciplining were also coded, but in common with other researchers, because the mother characters were used in the setup of all the story stems, whereas the father characters were used only in a subset of these, only the maternal codes were considered for analysis (after Oppenheim, Emde, & Warren, 1997).

All story stem completions (946 narratives) were double coded by raters trained by Linda Mantz-Simmons, a co-author of the manual. Eighteen items from the original set of 34 were reliably rated with kappa > .60 (median kappa = .74; range: .62 to .84). The 16 items that were not reliably rated were very rarely seen (median frequency = 0.8%, range: 0.1 to 3.0), and the kappa statistic does not give a fair measure of the extent of interrater agreement when events are either rare or very frequent. However, the low themes found for some of the codes were not surprising, given the manual was designed to address a wide range of research issues across all the MSSB stems, and not just the subset in this study. Of the reliably coded items, 10 (physical punishment, verbal punishment, other exclusion, shame, affection, positive maternal representations, maternal disciplining representations, dishonesty, guilt/reparation, and physical aggression) showed at least moderate consistency when aggregated across the 11 stems (median alpha = .55; range: .44 to .66).

Next, the 10 reliably rated and consistently used items were aggregated to form a smaller number of themes characterizing the children's narratives. A principal components analysis was used to guide the aggregation of the items, and a three-component solution was suggested from the Scree test, which helps identify substantial and nonoverlapping dimensions or factors. Loading positively on the first factor were the four nonphysical disciplining techniques, with physical punishment loading negatively, accounting for 24% of the variance. We computed an aggregate scale based on this factor and termed it limit-setting. Loading positively on the second factor were affection and the positive maternal representation scales, with a notable negative loading on this second factor for physical aggression, suggesting a prosocial cluster of items accounting for 18% of the variance. Loading positively on the third factor, accounting for 13% of the variance, were the scales for physical aggression and physical punishment, and a negative correlation with the guilt variable, indicating an antisocial aggregate. The dishonesty item did not have high loadings on any of the three components and was therefore dropped from further consideration. We were left with three well-discriminated aggregate scales, each having high levels of internal consistency: (1) limit-setting; (2) prosocial; and (3) antisocial, as depicted in table 9.1 and table 9.2. Table 9.2 displays the intracorrelations of the scales for the full sample and for boys and girls separately.

Table 9.2 reveals that the profile of response to the story-completion task varied somewhat depending on the child's gender. Specifically, the correlations among scales highlight that when boys score highly for their use of antisocial themes, they score lowly on prosocial themes ($r = -.61$, $p < .001$, two-tailed), an association that leads to a significant correlation for the full sample but is not nearly so marked for girls. Girls are singled out by the significant positive correlation between their use of limit-setting themes with antisocial (i.e., physical punishment) themes ($r = .41$, $p < .01$, two-tailed), a strategy not in boys' responses.

TABLE 9.1 Descriptive Statistics for the Emotion Narrative Scales

	Limit setting	Prosocial	Antisocial
Mean	8.68	1.26	1.88
Standard deviations	5.13	3.20	2.78
Alpha	.79	.70	.69
Variance accounted for	24%	18%	13%

The observation of these gender-specific patterns mandated attention to the issue of gender in the results.

Children's Language Ability The Bus Story (Renfrew, 1991) is a measure commonly used by speech and language therapists in Britain to assess general language development for children between 3 and 8. The test involves listening to a short story about a naughty red bus, told with the aid of a picture book, and the child is then asked to retell the story as the experimenter turns the pages of the book. A composite score is derived by summing dimensions rating the quality of information, the average sentence length, and the number of subordinate clauses.

Results

Results are organized into three sections. First, we consider how child characteristics (language skills and gender) may be seen to influence their narratives. Second, the results focus on our principal hypothesis, that is, the extent to which classification (insecure vs. secure) of mothers' attachment narratives may be seen to influence children's narratives. Third, we report on the consideration of possible interactions between attachment and gender influences on children's narratives.

Children's Language Skills and Gender as Influences in Their Narratives

This first section of results explored possible associations between child characteristics (language skills and gender) and the aggregate narrative scores obtained from story completions. Nonsignificant correlations were observed when children's verbal skills, as indexed by the Bus Story test, were compared with the narrative prosocial score ($r = .04$), as well as with the antisocial score ($r = .04$).

TABLE 9.2 Intracorrelations of the Aggregate Scales for Full Sample, Boys and Girls

	Prosocial	Antisocial
Limit setting	$-.06_F$, $.05_B$, $-.20_G$	$.17_F$, $.04_B$, $.41_G^*$
Prosocial		$-.53_F^*$, $-.61_B^*$, $-.30_G$

Note: F = full sample, n = 86; B = boys, n = 45; G=girls, n = 41.
$^*p < .01$, two-tailed.

However, children's verbal skills were positively and significantly correlated with the narrative score for limit setting themes ($r = .22, p < .05$, two-tailed, $n = 86$). Following from this, we decided that in subsequent analyses involving the limit-setting score, children's verbal skills would be entered as a covariate. We next looked at children's narrative scores grouped by their gender, and these results are shown in table 9.3.

Table 9.3 reveals highly significant gender differences for children's scores on the prosocial and antisocial dimensions, with girls and boys appearing to conform to gender-stereotypic patterns of response; girls score markedly higher than boys on the prosocial dimension, and boys score dramatically higher than girls on the antisocial dimension. Table 9.3 also shows that girls and boys were not differentiated in terms of their scores on the limit-setting dimension.

Attachment Predictors of Children's Emotion Narratives

To consider the central question of whether mothers' attachment narratives predicted children's emotion narratives, we first grouped children's narrative scores according to insecure versus secure groups of mothers' attachment interviews. These results are shown in table 9.4.

Table 9.4 reveals that children's use of limit-setting themes was significantly more likely if their mothers' attachment interviews had been scored autonmous-secure ($p < .01$, two-tailed). Table 9.4 also reveals similarity in 5-year-olds' story completions in terms of the presence of either prosocial or antisocial themes. These appear in similar proportions across maternal attachment groups. We next computed a partial correlation comparing the bivariate measure of maternal security of attachment with children's limit-setting aggregate score, controlling for the effect of the Bus Story test. Results revealed little or no effect of children's verbal skills, zero-order correlation = .28, $p = .009$, two-tailed; partial correlation = .27, $p = .012$. Thus, the observed overlap between children's verbal skills and emotion narrative limit-setting scores appears to be largely independent of the cross-generational link between maternal security in the AAI and children's elevated reliance on limit-setting themes in their narratives.

TABLE 9.3 Means (and Standard Deviations) for Children's Narrative Scores Grouped by Gender of Children

	Girls ($n = 41$)	Boys ($n = 45$)	t-value (df 1, 84)	Significance (two-tailed)
Limit-setting score	8.6 (4.4)	8.8 (5.8)	0.2	N. S.
Prosocial score	2.2 (3.1)	0.4 (3.0)	2.8	$p < .01$
Antisocial score	0.7 (2.3)	3.0 (2.7)	4.2	$p < .0001$

TABLE 9.4 Means (and Standard Deviations) for Children's Narrative Scores Grouped by Security of Mothers' Attachment Interviews

	Mothers' interviews			
Children's narrative scores	Insecure (n = 35)	Secure (n = 51)	t-value (1, 84)	Signifiance (two-tailed)
Limit setting	7.0 (4.1)	9.9 (5.5)	2.7	$p < .01$
Prosocial	1.3 (3.2)	1.2 (3.2)	0.1	N. S.
Antisocial	2.1 (3.0)	1.8 (2.7)	0.5	N. S.

Gender by Attachment Effects on Children's Narratives

To explore our hypothesis that observed gender differences in children's narratives may be moderated by the attachment status of mothers, we checked for possible interactions between the two fixed factors of child gender and maternal security, in ANOVA models considering main effects and the attachment by gender interaction, on the dependent variables of the three reliable themes from the children's emotion narratives. Of the three bivariate analysis of variance (ANOVA) models generated, only one suggested a significant attachment by gender interaction. This pertained to children's use of prosocial themes in their story completions, where we observed an interaction between gender and maternal interview status.

Though overall girls received signficantly higher scores than boys on the prosocial score, this effect varied signficantly depending on the gender of the child and the AAI (insecure vs. secure) status of mothers. In the relevant analyses, there was an expected main effect of gender, $F(1, 82)$ 9.7, $p < .005$, observed power = .87; and, additionally, there was an interaction between gender of child and AAI of mother, $F(1, 82)$ 3.9, $p < .05$, observed power = .50. R^2 for the overall model was .13. When mothers' interviews were judged insecure (either dimissing or preoccupied or unresolved), children's prosocial scores varied greatly (boys $n = 17$, $M = -.46$; girls $n = 18$, $M = 2.90$). By contrast, when mothers' interviews were judged autonomous-secure, the difference in boys' ($n = 28$, $M = .87$) and girls' ($n = 23$, $M = 1.58$) prosocial scores was reduced to less than a quarter of the magnitude of difference observed when mothers' interviews were insecure. Thus, children of insecure mothers appear to conform to the gender stereotypic patterns, whereas children of secure mothers appear much less restricted by these biological/cultural expectations and correspondingly more alike.

Discussion

Discussion unfolds in three parts, addressing first the significant finding that maternal and child narratives overlap significantly, despite the many years intervening between these assessments. Second, we address the observed gender differences and association to children's verbal skills. And, finally, we address the interaction of attachment and gender effects.

These results point to strong evidence of a link between a free-autonomous state of mind concerning attachment in a pregnant woman and the observed capacity of her child 5 years later to produce an emotion narrative that contains thematic references to a maternal caregiving figure setting limits in the context of providing guidance or discipline. Mothers' free and autonomous states of mind were assessed via the well-established narrative technique known as the Adult Attachment Interview (George et al., 1985). This narrative technique has been shown to have powerful predictive associations to infant-parent attachment (e.g., van Ijzendoorn, 1995) and to maternal caregiving behavior (Crowell & Feldman, 1988; Haft & Slade, 1989). Recently, maternal AAI responses, collected more or less concurrently with children's responses to attachment story-completion tasks, reveal significant overlaps between these measures (Gloger-Tippelt, Gomille, Kooenig, & Vetter, 2002; Goldwyn, Stanley, Smith, & Green, 2000).Yet this is the first report demonstrating that maternal attachment interviews collected during pregnancy identified as coherent and secure predict a central organizing feature of 5-year-olds' narratives, that is, the extent to which they resolve social and emotional dilemmas by referencing an authoritative parent (after Baumrind, 1967). Where maternal interviews were observed to be insecure, either dismissing or preoccupied regarding attachment, their children were much less likely to depict their mothers (in story stem doll-play responses) as possessing this authoritative characteristic long recognized as an attribute of effective parenting.

Interestingly, it appears that the concept of parental authority was systematically reviewed from an attachment perspective for the first time only recently (see Bretherton, Golby, & Cho, 1997). Attachment researchers have paid more attention to the early infant-mother relationship than to older children and their parents in the relatively distinct literatrure on child rearing and socialization (see Richters & Waters, 1992). The pathways of these related lines of inquiry are overlapping more as the children in longitudinal attachment studies have matured, and the socialization literature has looked backward to the early familial and representational origins of children's value systems. Most important, perhaps, attachment and socialization researchers are currently using similar methods, with the MacArthur Story Stem Battery a notable case in point (Bretherton et al., 1990; Kochanska, Padavich, & Koenig, 1996).

As Bretherton et al. (1997) point out, Bowlby (1973) himself noted that aspects of the parenting style described as *authoritative* in the socialization literature (e.g., Baumrind 1967, 1971) are compatible with the sensitive, accepting, and cooperative parenting behaviors held as optimal in attachment theory and research. Authoritative parents resembled responsive attachment figures in paying attention to their children's needs and point of view and tended to use persuasion, negotiation, and reasoning to engage their children's cooperation. In addition, authoritative parents were firm and self-confident and did not allow themselves to be coerced by their children. As Bretherton et al. (1997) put it, authoritative parents are leaders, not dictators. These results confirm and extend this line of thinking in showing that children's narratives depicting mothers with authoritative characteristics likely came from children whose mothers provided (some 5 years previously) an attachment interview deemed autonomous-secure, organized, balanced, and coherent.

If we take a further look at the construct of *limit setting* in a context of social and emotional arousal and uncertainty, as is created by the presentation to children of the MacArthur Story Stem Battery, its association to attachment security may become more clear. The wider psychoanalytic literature from which attachment theory arose may provide some clues. For example, limit setting has much to do with normal development conceived in terms of ego skills including frustration tolerance, delay of gratification, and impulse control (A. Freud, 1965). Further, the normative development of these affect-regulatory and cognitive skills may depend on the bedrock provided by a consistent and caring adult (normally mother), who provides the growing child with a background sense of safety (Sandler, 1960). Interestingly, the title of Joseph Sandler's (1987) collection of published essays dating from this early article through the mid-1980s bears the title "from safety to superego," suggesting that moral development depends on a sufficient amount of early attachment experiences that enhance an ongoing sense of safety. The child's psychological and social development is not well served by a parent who has difficulty providing warmth and affection, to be sure, but neither is it well served by the parent who has difficulty setting limits.

Warranting further discussion, in our view, are possible reasons for limit-setting themes in children's narratives to be associated with maternal coherence and security in the context of the AAI. For the reader familiar with listening to or reading adult attachment interviews, this association may not be so surprising, as an almost defining characteristic of the autonomous-secure interview is a flexible adherence to limits. The narrative is unlikely to be judged either too long or too short, but rather often conveys the feeling of being an emotionally and cognitively balanced response to the speaker's unique range of experiences with caregivers during childhood, credibly presented. By contrast, dismissing interviews typically reflect a controlled habit of mind involving cognitive adherence to self-imposed limits on the expression of feelings, not infrequently punctuated by bursts of cool derogation concerning disliked attachment figures. Also in contrast to the relaxed feel of the autonomous-secure interview is the preoccupied interview, which may express a pronounced difficulty with setting limits on feelings concerning attachment, with the consequence that ongoing anger, and sometimes fear, concerning childhood experiences is often thematic.

Some thought must be given to fathers and the previous observation that consideration of the fathers' attachment interviews did not yield any significant associations to the children's narratives. To the extent that the cross-generational link observed between mothers' and children's narratives is, in all likelihood, mediated by the quantity and quality of mother-child conversation concerning everyday dilemmas and worries,[1] it is probable that fathers and their preschool children in this middle-class British sample lacked opportunity for conversations of this kind. Indeed, the most well-known work demonstrating a link between parent-child conversation and children's emerging understanding of mind and emotion was, not surprisingly, based on observations of *mothers* and their children (Dunn, 1988). There are compelling statistical and conceptual reasons for thinking that mothers not only spend more time with their young children but are also intrinsically better suited to promoting an understanding of emotion and the corresponding emergence of a moral, prosocial self (e.g., Gilligan, 1982).

Thinking about parent gender leads naturally to the observed findings concerning child gender. Boys' narratives were scored higher than girls' stories for evidence of aggressive themes, and girls' stories were scored higher than boys' stories for prosocial themes. These pronounced and very significant differences concur with a number of previous reports (see Bretherton & Oppenheim, chapter 3, this book). As the intracorrelations among aggregate scores assigned to children's narratives revealed, when girls did display aggressive or physically punitive themes, there was a signficant likelihood that this would appear in the context of co-occurring limit-setting themes—evidence of a self-regulating force not present to the same extent in boys' responses. It is appropriate to recall, at this point, that the differences we are commenting on concern variations in the way boys and girls *tell stories* about family life and social relations, not about how they *actually behave* in interpersonal settings. And it should be emphasized that the aggression observed in the stories obtained from this sample primarily involved mild physical punishment (e.g., a parent smacking a child). Of a very different order is the high frequency of responses reliably coded for extreme aggression (beating and killing) observed in narratives obtained from clinical, especially maltreated, samples (see Hodges, Steele, Hillman, & Henderson, chapter 13, this book; Hodges, Steele, Hillman, Henderson, & Neil, 2000; Steele et al., 1999).

The observation that girls showed vastly more evidence of prosocial themes in their narratives than did boys also deserves comment. In some respects, this is hardly surprising given the repeated finding that mothers talk more about emotions, particularly negative emotions and interpersonal strategies for their resolution, to their daughters than to their sons (e.g., Reese & Fivush, 1993). In addition, there is the traditional folk psychology understanding of girls being made from sugar, spice, and all things nice. Thus, if not also a predispositon arising from their biological make-up, then certainly in the wide set of cultural expectations operating from birth across the life span, girls and then women are assumed to be caregivers. The gender by attachment interactions observed in this study highlight one of the likely social psychological origins of girls' high, and boys' low, prosocial awareness. This concerns mothers who lack autonomy and security in their thinking and feeling about attachment. By contrast, mothers who showed a coherent and organized capacity for valuing attachment, typical of the secure-autonomous stance in the AAI, had children—boys and girls alike—whose proscocial scores on the narrative task were in the moderate range. In other words, maternal attachment security was shown to minimize gender differences in children's emotion narratives. To our minds, this finding highlights fresh implications of the words "autonomous-secure." In addition to autonomy from one's family of origin, in the context of valuing attachment relationships in the present, we would add autonomy from unnecessarily restrictive cultural expectations. In other words, the imagination of a boy is likely to be just as prosocial as that of a girl, provided he has benefitted from having a mother capable of providing a coherent and secure attachment narrative.

In conclusion, the cross-generational results presented in this chapter offer new evidence of the construct validity of the MacArthur Story Stem Battery as a measure of social and emotional development, broadly, and attachment processes more specifically. Children's attachment learning from their mothers, as Minsky (1985) and Freud (1923) speculated, is something powerful that extends beyond infancy and deep into the imagination.

NOTES

The research on which this chapter is based was supported by a project research grant (R000233684) from the Economic and Social Research Council (ESRC) in the UK, a project grant from the Kohler Stiftung (Germany), and a grant from the MacArthur Network node chaired by Robert Emde on the Transition from Infancy to Early Childhood. Postgraduate fellowships to research students working on the study have been received from the ESRC, the Medical Research Council (MRC, UK), the British Council, the Social Sciences and Humanities Research Council (SSHRC, Canada), and the Overseas Studentship Awards (ORS) in the UK. At the beginnings of the work reported here, John Bowlby and George Moran provided invaluable encouragement. Particular thanks are owed to the families participating in the research who are consistently generous with their time and interest. Correspondence should be addressed to Miriam or Howard Steele, Sub-Department of Clinical Health Psychology, University College, London, 1–19 Torrington Place, London WC1E 7JD <h.steele@ucl.ac.uk>.

1. As infant-mother Strange Situation data are available for this sample, we have been able to statistically explore this probability (Steele, Steele, Woolgar, Yabsley, Fonagy, & Croft, in preparation). That is, we have addressed the question of whether the influence of maternal AAIs on children's narratives is mediated by an influence of the infant-mother attachment on the children's later narratives. If such were the case, then an early experience "innoculation" effect from the 1st year could be suggested by the results presented in this chapter. In fact, we have observed some mediation, alongside independent influences from both mothers' AAIs and from the 1-year Strange Situation assessments, suggesting early and later maternal influences. In other words, the infant carries something forward from her 1st year attachment to mother, but mother does also adapt to the new challenges of the toddler and preschool period in ways representing continuity or discontinuity from infancy. These results are relevant to the question of intergenerational (AAI to Strange Situation) mismatches in attachment. To summarize the most favorable implications of these mediational analyses, consider, for example, some mothers with secure pregnancy AAIs who later presented with anxiously attached infants. Our data points to evidence of them "rebounding" after, or perhaps in response to, the vocabulary spurt at the end of the 2nd year, with the consequence of a subsequent child narrative that resembles a child who had "always" been secure. On the other hand, for some babies who were securely attached to their mothers at 1 year, despite their mothers presenting with an insecure AAI during pregnancy, there is the likelihood that they may have evolved into preschoolers who have carried forward this hard-won security, perhaps maintained by a positive shift in the maternal state of mind concerning attachment occasioned by the transition to parenthood.

REFERENCES

Ainsworth, M. D. S., Blehar, M. C., Waters, E., & Wall, S. (1978). Patterns of attachment: A psychological study of the strange situation. Hillsdale, NJ: Lawrence Erlbaum.

Bakerman-Kranenburg, M. J., & van Ijzendoorn, M. H. (1993). A psychometric study of the Adult Attachment Interview: Reliability and discriminant validity. *Developmental Psychology, 29*, 870–879.

Baumrind, D. (1967). Child care practices anteceding three patterns of preschool behaviour. *Genetic Psychology Monographs, 75*, 43–88.

Baumrind, D. (1971). Current patterns of parental authority. *Developmental Psychology Monographs, 4*, 1–103.

Bowlby, J. (1973). *Attachment and loss. Vol. 2: Separation.* New York: Basic Books.

Bretherton, I., Golby, B., & Cho, E. (1997). Attachment and the transmission of values. In J. Grusec & L. Kucszynski (Eds.), *Handbook series: Parenting and children's internalization of values.* New York: Wiley.

Bretherton, I., Oppenheim, D., Buchsbaum, H., Emde, R. N., & the MacArthur Narrative Working Group. (1990). *MacArthur Story Stem Battery.* Unpublished manual.

Bretherton, I., Prentiss, C., & Ridgeway, D. (1990). Family relationships as represented in a story completion task at thirty seven and fifty four months of age. In I. Bretherton & M. W. Watson (Eds.), *Children's perspectives on the family* (vol. 48, pp. 85–106). San Francisco: Jossey-Bass.

Bretherton, I., Ridgeway, D., & Cassidy, J. (1990). Assessing internal working models of the attachment relationship. In M. T. Greenberg, D. Cicchetti, & E. M. Cummings (Eds.), *Attachment in the preschool years: Theory, research, and intervention* (pp. 273–308). Chicago: University of Chicago Press.

Buchsbaum, H. K., & Emde, R. N. (1990). Play narratives in 36-month-old children: Early moral development and family relationships. *Psychoanalytic Study of the Child, 45*, 129–155.

Buchsbaum, H. K., Toth, S. L., Clyman, R. B., Cicchetti, D., & Emde, R. N. (1992). The use of a narrative story stem technique with maltreated children: Implications for theory and practice. *Development and Psychopathology, 4*, 489–493.

Cassidy, J. (1988). Child-mother attachment and the self in six-year-olds. *Child Development, 59*, 121–134.

Cicchetti, D., Ed. (1989). *Rochester Symposium on Developmental Psychopathology. The emergence of a discipline.* Hillsdale, NJ: Lawrence Erlbaum.

Crowell, J. A., & Feldman, S. S. (1988). Mothers' internal models of relationships and children's behavioural and developmental status: A study of mother-child interaction. *Child Development, 59*, 1273–1285.

Dozier, M., & Kobak, R. (1992). Psychophysiology in attachment interviews: Converging evidence for deactivating strategies. *Child Development, 63*, 1473–1480.

Dunn, J. (1988). *The beginnings of social understanding.* Cambridge: Polity.

Emde, R. N., Biringen, Z., Clyman, R. B., & Oppenheim, D. (1991). The moral self of infancy: Affective core and procedural knowledge. *Developmental Review, 11*, 251–270.

Emde, R. N., & Buchsbaum, H. K. (1990). "Didn't you hear my mommy?" Autonomy with connectedness in moral self emergence. In D. Cicchetti & M. Beeghly (Eds.), *The self in transition: Infancy to childhood* (pp. 35–60). Chicago: University of Chicago Press.

Emde, R. N., Johnson, W. F., & Easterbrooks, M. A. (1988). The do's and don'ts of early moral development: Psychoanalytic tradition and current research. In J. Kagan &

S. Lamb (Eds.), *The emergence of morality in young children* (pp. 245–277). Chicago: University of Chicago Press.

Fonagy, P., Steele, H., & Steele, M. (1991). Maternal representations of attachment during pregnancy predict the organization of infant-mother attachment at one year of age. *Child Development, 62,* 891–905.

Freud, A. (1965). *Normality and pathology in childhood.* Harmondsworth: Penguin Books.

Freud, S. (1961). Ego and the id. In J. Strachey (Ed. & Trans.), *The standard edition of the complete psychological works of Sigmund Freud* (Vol. 19, pp. 3–66). London: Hogarth. (Original work published 1923)

George, C., Kaplan, N., & Main, M. (1985). *The Adult Attachment Interview.* Berkeley: Department of Psychology, University of California.

Gilligan, C. (1982). *In a different voice: Psychological theory and women's development.* Cambridge, MA: Harvard University Press.

Gloger-Tippelt, G., Gomille, B., Kooenig, L., & Vetter, J. (2002). Attachment representations in 6-year olds: Related longitudinally to the quality of attachment in infancy and mother's attachment representations. *Attachment & Human Development, 4,* 318–399.

Goldwyn, R., Stanley, C., Smith, V., & Green, J. (2000). The Manchester Child Attachment Story Task: Relationship with parental AAI, SAT, and child behaviour. *Attachment & Human Development, 2,* 71–84.

Haft, W., & Slade, A. (1989). Affect attunement and adult attachment: A pilot study. *Infant Mental Health Journal, 10,* 157–172.

Hesse, E. (1999). The adult attachment interview: Historical and current perspectives. In J. Cassidy & P. R. Shaver (Eds.), *Handbook of attachment* (pp. 395–433). New York: Guilford Press.

Hinde, R., & Stevenson-Hinde, J. S. (1987). Implications of a relationship approach for the study of gender differences. *Infant Mental Health Journal, 8,* 221–236.

Hodges, J., Steele, M., Hillman, S., Henderson, K., & Neil, M. (2000). Effects of abuse on attachment representations: Narrative assessments of abused children. *Journal of Child Psychotherapy, 26,* 433–455.

Hoffman, M. (1983). Affective and cognitive processes in moral internalization. In E. Higgins, D. Ruble, & W. Hartup (Eds.), *Social cognition and social development: A sociocultural perspective* (pp. 236–274). New York: Cambridge University Press.

Kochanska, G., Padavich, D. L., & Koenig, A. L. (1996). Children's narratives about hypothetical moral dilemmas and objective measures of their conscience: mutual relations and socialization antecedents. *Child Development, 67,* 1420–1436.

Maccoby, E. E. (1988). Gender as a social category. *Developmental Psychology, 24,* 755–765.

Main, M., & Goldwyn, R. (in press). Adult attachment rating and classification systems. In M. Main (Ed.), *A typology of human attachment organization assessed in discourse, drawings and interviews* (working title). New York: Cambridge University Press.

Main, M., Kaplan, N., & Cassidy, J. (1985). Security in infancy, childhood and adulthood: A move to the level of representation. In I. Bretherton & E. Waters (Eds.), *Growing points in attachment theory and research, Monographs of the Society for Research in Child Development, 50,* Serial No. 209 (pp. 66–104).

Minsky, M. (1985). *The society of mind.* New York: Simon & Schuster.

O'Connor, T. G., & Croft, C. M. (2001). A twin study of attachment in pre-school children. *Child Development, 75,* 1501–1511.

Oppenheim, D. (1997). The attachment doll play interview for preschoolers. *International Journal of Behavioral Development, 20,* 681–697.

Oppenheim, D., Emde, R. N., Hasson, M., & Warren, S. (1997). Preschoolers face moral dilemmas: A longitudinal study of acknowledging and resolving internal conflict. *International Journal of Psychoanalysis, 78,* 943–957.

Oppenheim, D., Emde, R. N., & Warren, S. (1997). Children's narrative representations of mothers: Their development and associations with child and mother adaptation. *Child Development, 68,* 127–138.

Oppenheim, D., & Waters, H. S. (1995). Narrative processes and attachment representations: Issues of development and assessment. In E. Waters, B. E. Vaughn, G. Posada, & K. Kondo-Ikemura (Eds.), *Caregiving, cultural and cognitive perspectives on secure base behavior and working models. Monographs of the Society for Research in Child Development, 60* (2–3, Serial No. 244), pp. 197–233.

Reese, E., & Fivush, R. (1993). Parental styles of talking about the past. *Developmental Psychology, 29,* 596–606.

Renfrew, C. E. (1991). *The Bus Story: A test of narrative speech.* Oxford, UK: Winslow Press.

Richters, J. E., & Waters, E. (1992). Attachment and socialization: The positive side of social influence. In M. Lewis & S. Feinman (Eds.), *Social influences and behavior* (pp. 185–214). New York: Plenum.

Robinson, J., Mantz-Simmons, L., Macfie, J., & the MacArthur Narrative Working Group. (1995). *MacArthur narrative coding manual.* Unpublished manuscript.

Sandler, J. (1960). The background of safety. In J. Sandler (1987) *From safety to superego: Selected papers by Joseph Sandler* (pp. 1–8). London: Karnac.

Sandler, J. (1987). *From safety to superego.* London: Karnac Books.

Spangler, G., & Grossman, K. (1993). Biobehavioural organisation in securely and insecurely attached infants. *Child Development, 64,* 1439–1450.

Sroufe, L. A., & Waters, E. (1977). Attachment as an organizational construct. *Child Development, 48,* 1184–1199.

Steele, H. (1991). *Adult personality characteristics and family functioning: The development and validation of an interview-based technique.* Unpublished doctoral dissertation. University of London.

Steele, H., & Steele, M. (1994). Intergenerational patterns of attachment. In K. Bartholomew & D. Perlman (Eds.), *Attachment processes during adulthood.* Volume 5 of *Advances in personal relationships series* (pp. 93–120). London: Jessica Kingsley.

Steele, H., Steele, M., Croft, C., & Fonagy, P. (1999). Infant-mother attachment at one-year predicts children's understanding of mixed emotions at six years. *Social Development, 8,* 161–178.

Steele, H., Steele, M., & Fonagy, P. (1996). Associations among attachment classifications of mothers, fathers and their infants: Evidence for a relationship-specific perspective. *Child Development, 67,* 541–555.

Steele, M. (1990). *Intergenerational patterns of attachment.* Unpublished doctoral dissertation. University of London.

Steele, M., Hodges, J., Kaniuk, J., Henderson, K., Hillman, S., & Bennett, P. (1999). The use of story stem narratives in assessing the inner world of the child: Implications for adoptive placements. In *Assessment, preparation and support: Implications from research* (pp. 19–29). London: BAAF Publications.

Steele, M., Steele, H., Woolgar, M., Yabsley, S., Fonagy, P., & Croft, C. (in preparation). A mediational analysis of early attachment influences upon preschoolers' reliance on authoritative themes in doll play.

Turner, P. J. (1991). Relations between attachment, gender, and behaviour with peers in preschool. *Child Development, 62,* 1475–1488.

Turner, P. J. (1993) Attachment to mother and behaviour with adults in preschool. *British Journal of Developmental Psychology, 11,* 75–89.

Van Ijzendoorn, M. J. (1995). Adult attachment representations, parental responsiveness and infant attachment: A meta-analysis on the predictive validity of the Adult Attachment Interview. *Psychological Bulletin, 117,* 387–403.

Woolgar, M. J. (1999). Projective doll play methodologies. *Child Psychology and Psychiatry Review, 4,* 126–134.

Woolgar, M., Steele, H., Steele, M., Yabsley, S., & Fonagy, P. (2001). Children's play narrative responses to hypothetical dilemmas and their awareness of moral emotions. *British Journal of Developmental Psychology, 19,* 115–128.

Zahn-Waxler, C. (in press). The early development of empathy, guilt and internalization of responsibility: Implications for gender differences in internalizing and externalizing problems. In R. J. Davidson (Ed.), *Anxiety, depression, and emotion.* Oxford: Oxford University Press.

Zahn-Waxler, C., Cole, P. M., & Barret, K. C. (1991). Guilt and empathy: Sex differences and implications for the development of depression. In J. Garber & K. A. Dodge (Eds.), *The development of emotion regulation and dysregulation* (pp. 243–272). Cambridge: Cambridge University Press.

EVA APPELMAN
DENNIS PALMER WOLF

10

Emotional Apprenticeships: The Development of Affect Regulation During the Preschool Years

There is a place where time stands still. Raindrops hang motionless in air. Pendulums of clocks float midswing. Dogs raise their muzzles in silent howls. Pedestrians are frozen on the dusty streets, their legs cocked as if held by strings. The aromas of dates, mangoes, coriander, cumin are suspended in space.

As the traveler approaches this place from any direction, he moves more and more slowly. His heartbeats grow farther apart, his breathing slackens, his temperature drops, his thoughts diminish, until he reaches dead center and stops. For this is the center of time. From this place, time travels outward in concentric circles—at rest at the center, slowly picking up speed at greater diameters.

Who would make pilgrimage to the center of time? Parents with children, and lovers.

Alan Lightman, *Einstein's Dreams*

Say the word "apprentice" and what comes to mind is a cluster of young boys "learning the ropes" of an art or a trade: novices painting the folds of a cloak that the master just sketched, or young tailors learning to make a suit by rolling out bolts of fabric and watching as a more experienced hand places the pattern (Chaiklin & Lave, 1993). Recently, developmental psychologists have borrowed this image in order to challenge predominant views of learning in which acquiring understanding is conceived as an act of individual insight and learning or as the transfer of preexisting information. When viewed as an apprenticeship, learning becomes a sociocultural activity. First, the concept of apprenticeship is a powerful antidote to a view of learning as a solo enterprise: Rodin's statue of the self-absorbed "Thinker." In an apprenticeship model, learning is, first and foremost, a social activity. Not only does it occur between individuals; it also is an exchange that often partakes of long-running human enterprises such as a craft or a social role. Second, in the course of apprenticeships there are no "miniaturized" tasks designed only for novices (e.g., the spelling tests, book reports, or flash cards characteristic of elementary classrooms). In an apprenticeship, learners witness and practice both the explicit declarative knowledge and the subtle procedural knowledge *of an entire mature practice.* Thus, a young tailor learns not only the names of fabrics and weaves but also how to hold silk taut in order to cut it or how to lay out patterns economically. Finally, the idea of apprenticeship portrays learning as an intimate and iterative human process. It is intimate because the teacher must engage in careful observation of the learner and exhibit a keen sense for exactly which small increment of the larger performance a particular learner can take on next. If the learner succeeds, the pair moves on to a new "zone of proximal development" just beyond where they were a moment, an hour, or a week earlier (Vygotsky, 1978). It is this quality of mutual and incremental calibration that gradually allows an apprentice to achieve master status (Bruner, 1981; Rogoff, 1990).

To date, the model of apprenticeship has been applied chiefly to cognitive and social tasks that have clear and observable routines (e.g., weaving, learning to play peek-a-boo, etc.). But learning to tailor or paint is also an emotional process. When the cloth is cut poorly, a public rebuke may ring out across the room. A painter has to pass on a deep love for the work, as much as drafting skill. This raises the question of what we might learn about emotional development if we looked at it as a process of apprenticeship characterized by similar intuitive understandings, mutuality, and joint movement toward new levels of performance. This chapter uses a case study of parent-child narrative play to explore what the concept of emotional apprenticeship can add to our understanding of emotional growth and narrative play as an important setting for that growth. We examine a single episode of emotional apprenticeship: what happens as one family triad (an inhibited girl, along with her father and mother) confront the child's anxiety when she is asked to engage in playing out emotionally charged situations (e.g., the conflicts and dilemmas represented by the story stem narratives examined in this book). The chapter presents a close analysis of how one set of parents (and especially the father) engages their daughter in an apprenticeship that helps her to tolerate the often overwhelming feelings she experiences while engaged in narrating story stems, when faced with new situations, particularly those that contain negative emotions.

Narrative as Site for Emotional Apprenticeship

Narratives have long been used to explore how people construe their outside and inner worlds and the links between them (Freud, 1926; Polanyi, 1985; Wolf & Hicks, 1989). Narratives involve both organization of events across time and the means to make those events public at any later time (Labov, 1972; Polanyi, 1985). As such, the ability to narrate provides a powerful medium for the continued development of affect-regulation and modulation of emotions that link the inner world and the expressed narration (Malatesta, 1985; Beebe & Jaffe, 1992;

Kestenberg, 1985). As clinicians have long argued, narratives provide both children and their caregivers one means to present what would otherwise remain private: their internal emotional lives (Stern, 1994, 1995; Wolf, 1990). But narrative as a strategy for emotion regulation goes beyond immediate presentation. As Stern (1985) has suggested, a child's narrative may indicate his or her ability to give initial meaning to a recent, but disturbing situation or to regulate the difficult emotions that the memory of a past event continues to ignite, long after the original event. There is yet another way in which narratives may serve to regulate emotion. A narrative is a signal of significance. A narrative not only attracts attention; it brings others into a situation from the perspective of the teller (see Wolf, chapter 2, this book).

The development of narrative skill starts as soon as infants and caregivers develop routines that can be anticipated or, if interrupted, can cause surprise. Single words may point to past events ("Daddy" pointing to last summer's barbecue). During the third year of life, narrative interaction between child and caregiver "takes off" as a means of sharing meaning (Nelson, 1989). Child-caregiver dyads can represent a sustained effort to regulate emotions and give meaning to experience, coupling both verbal and nonverbal dimensions.

The Process of Emotional Apprenticeship

Examination of the communication routines developed between children and their caregivers throughout infancy reveals that many pairs engage in a joint, but tacit, process, often referred to as attunement, in which the partners learn to read and respond to the other's current state. This continuous process yields a growing understanding of the expectations, capacities, and cues of the partner (Stern, 1983). Emotional apprenticeship builds on this attunement process, yet helps the child and his or her caregiver to learn how to regulate newly emerging, and often increasingly complex and sustained, forms of affective experience. During the process of emotional apprenticeship, the dyad communicates in ways that converge between the adult's and the child's realities and cross the barriers that usually set apart the adult's from the child's world.

Apprenticeship takes place in the "zone of proximal development" (Vygotsky, 1978), where the child is not quite able to manage an emotional challenge independently. Exactly as in cognitive exchanges, emotional apprenticeships are characterized by deliberate scaffolding in which the strategies modeled by the caregiver gradually become the child's approaches for dealing with fear, distress, or anger, or conversely experiencing and expressing delight, exhibiting curiosity, or developing the will to communicate about complex emotional experiences. Thus, emotional apprenticeship occurs when a sensitive caregiver helps the child to tolerate a complex range of emotions, including many negative ones. The adult's support (that is, emotional scaffolding) brings an enhanced level of affect regulation that is beyond the child's self-regulatory capacities. As a child's inner state is regulated with help, the child achieves a better self-regulated affective inner state. This new state in turn makes a new level of mutual regulation possible. Thus, there is a gradual and continuous change upward in the "zone of proximal development" as the apprentice's experience progresses. This cyclical nature of emotional apprenticeship is compatible with Beebe et al.'s (Beebe & Lachmann, 1994, 1998; Beebe, Lachmann, & Jaffe, 1997) transformational model.

Where emotional apprenticeship unfolds successfully, young children and their caregivers *both* gradually learn how to address especially challenging emotional experiences. During emotional apprenticeship, the partners address the same issue or theme over a sustained period of time (e.g., balancing the child's fears of darkness, sleep, and loneliness with the parent's need to put the child to bed or the shared process of learning to bear the feelings of separation and loss occasioned by day-care.) In this process, partners continue to use enacted (bodily and vocal) and procedural strategies for achieving mutual regulation (Cohen & Squire, 1980; Winnicott, 1953). However, newer strategies for communication (e.g., language, play, and other symbolic forms) and emerging forms of cognition (e.g., self-awareness, memory, etc.) make the process of mutual signaling and responding more complex (for instance, learning to tolerate and even enjoy the presence of a new sibling).

In sum, emotional apprenticeship processes have much in common with the nonconscious mutual regulations that infant researchers such as Emde (1993) and Stern (1993) have described. The focus of emotional apprenticeship is on *stretching* the capacity for tolerating and addressing emotional challenges. (It is important to note that it is not just the child's capacities that are affected; caregivers may also shift or enlarge their emotional repertoire.) Other symbolic processes, such as explicit invitations, requests, questions, and references to the process itself, are also part of the apprenticeship.

The Role of Shared Narratives in Emotional Apprenticeship

This chapter argues, like other chapters in this book, that the exchange of narratives is an especially powerful forum for the communication, modulation of affect, and emotional apprenticeship. As mentioned, in the process of telling his or her story, a teller uses language, coupled with performance, to transform an inner world of private experience into a public and shared account (Polanyi, 1985; Wolf & Hicks, 1989). Co-construction of narratives is one way to create shared interpretations of experience and affect (Oppenheim, Nir, Warren, & Emde, 1997). But storytelling is more than the information or interpretations exchanged. Hence, there is a second, and much more present-tense, manner in which narrative may play a role in affective development. Narratives engage both teller and listener in a mutual process of offering and responding. Thus, a growing body of research indicates that joint narrations, whether in words or in play, often reflect the current quality of the relationship between young children and their caregivers (Oppenheim et al., 1997; Slade, 1987). Thus, stories reflect whether and how dyads raise or ignore highly charged topics, and in their process of storytelling, partners also demonstrate their capacity to express and respond to affect in real time. Thus, questions of the expression and regulation of affect are at the heart of stories.

In particular, play narratives of the kind demanded by the MacArthur story stems provide an excellent setting for examining both the emotional content and the negotiations between caregivers and their young children (Bretherton & Oppenheim, chapter 3, this book; Bretherton, Prentiss, & Ridgeway, 1990). The stems focus on highly charged situations such as loss, competition, separation, and reunion. At the same time, the "as if," or bounded, nature of play permits both children and adults to explore or "try on" a wide range of emotions and actions (e.g., making people fly, cars talk, etc.). Moreover, the invented aspect of the play demands explicit self-expression and choice (e.g., "No, I don't want the mother to be in this one," "I want to be the brother," etc.). In this kind of play, improvisation is the rule: on the spur of the moment, a player has to generate actions, gestures, and vocalizations quickly, almost without thought. If the play is interactive, the child's moves have to respond instantly to those of the other player, requiring close interaction.

Genuine and co-constructed narratives afford an exceptional setting for emotional apprenticeships to develop. The child offers a narrative that points to an event or issue. The caregiver hears the *child's* story, no matter how fragmentary. The caregiver handles that narrative respectfully, even gently, "stretching" it just enough to extend meaning, without colonizing or fracturing it. When successful, this process of mutual regulation in turn *creates* an enlarged account of "what happened," and expanded strategies for sharing experience. These, in turn, become tools for new forms of self-regulation. This co-construction of emotional narratives enables the child to acquire and internalize patterns of negotiation between a "moment" in the outside world and the internal experience that the "moment" stirs up (Oppenheim, Emde, & Wamboldt 1996; Oppenheim et al., 1997). The more sensitively involved a caregiver is, the more coherent the narratives are. Slade (1987), for example, found that secure children can make effective use of an active caregiver and that the resulting dyads play longer and in more complex ways. Similarly, research on fantasy play reveals that securely attached preschool children exhibit more elaborate and robust play that is protected by the dyad's ability to repair mismatched dialogues (Rosenberg, 1984). In addition, despite developmental changes in narratives across different ages, several studies have shown associations between the quality of early caregiver-child communications and the child's later independent narratives (Main, 1993; McCabe & Peterson, 1991; Hudson, 1990; Fivush, 1991; Oppenheim et al., 1997).

Factors Influencing the Development of Emotional Apprenticeship

In general, the variability found among pairs engaged in emotional apprenticeship might be attributed in part to differences in self-regulatory capacities that result from imbalances between self and mutual regulation (Beebe & Lachmann, 1998). The study of the temperamental trait of inhibition/uninhibition (Kagan,

1994a, 1994b; Kagan, Reznick, & Gibbons, 1989; Kagan, Reznick, & Snidman, 1988; Kagan & Snidman, 1991) might be instrumental in this context. It reveals that temperament per se is not a stable, constant characteristic, intrinsic to the individual, but a predisposition to exhibit certain behaviors under specific conditions. Fear, timidity, avoidance of conflict, and long latency to talk are typical characteristics exhibited by inhibited children in unfamiliar situations. The difficulty in self-organizing and self-regulating vis-à-vis environmental stimuli constricts the opportunity for balanced self- and mutual regulation so that the behavior is too inhibited/uninhibited. Specifically, the inhibited individual tends to withdraw and rely chiefly on self-regulatory processes, without the expansion made possible by mutual regulation. It takes observant and supportive caregivers to create the kind of buffering, but developmentally demanding, partnerships in which very inhibited children can achieve new levels of affect regulation (Nachmias, Gunnar, Mangelsdorf, & Parritz, 1996).

The Story Stem Narratives of Susan

What follows is an examination of the co-constructed play narratives of an extremely inhibited child, Susan. For inhibited children, the demand to improvise with a stranger (i.e., the experimenter) a narrative about emotional conflict presents enormous affect regulation difficulties. However, even consistently inhibited children can learn strategies for affect regulation that permit them to conquer what once seemed frightening situations. Whether this occurs in a given situation often depends on the capacities of an extremely sensitive partner to get involved in an emotional apprentice experience.

Susan's story stem narratives describe several moments in an overall emotional apprenticeship experience focused on daring to engage in what otherwise might be a frightening activity. Susan apprentices chiefly with her father, who remembers having grown up and remaining painfully shy.

Method

Susan was a participant in a longitudinal study on infant predictors of inhibited and uninhibited profiles in children conducted by Kagan and Snidman and their associates (Kagan, 1994a; Kagan et al., 1989; Kagan, Snidman, & Arcus, 1993). Susan was also part of a subgroup of 24 children chosen to represent the range of inhibited/uninhibited temperament. The subgroup consisted of normally developing children and children at the extremes of inhibited/uninhibited temperament. The children and their parents were observed during lab and home visits, which included the MacArthur Story Stem Battery, free play, and other tests, interviews, and questionnaires. Thus, Susan and her family were seen in the narrative portion of the study when she was 36, 48, and 60 months old. Sessions were videotaped and then transcribed using CHILDES (see Bretherton & Oppenheim, chapter 3, this book). The transcripts were marked off into minute-long segments to portray the tempo of the interaction. The linguistic transcription was supplemented with detailed notes regarding voice tone, glance, gesture ,and location. The story stems selected illustrate the emotional apprenticeship process. The first story stem served as a warm-up and might be considered as the base line for Susan's inhibited behavior. We then selected to present the first paternal initiative that mobilized the apprenticeship process (between story stem 3 and 4). The following co-construction (story stem 4) illustrates the emotional apprenticeship in action. Story stem 8 portrays the impact of the emotional apprenticeship on Susan's behavior and marks a shift point in the story stem session.

According to the assessments of the observations at the Infant Lab, Susan remained classified as a very inhibited child throughout this period (N. Snidman, personal communication, 1998, July). However, Susan's behavior in the context of play narratives showed significant qualitative changes in this same period. While it is impossible to attribute causation, Susan and her father's interactions capture the essence of emotional apprenticeship.

Susan's Story Stems at Age 3

In response to the first request for her to continue a story stem, Susan was immobilized. She called desperately for her mother and continuously searched for a closer contact with her. Once Susan was situated close to her mother, Susan stayed in that location touching, leaning, and having close eye contact with her. From that position, Susan was attentive and engaged with the examiner, communicating with her nonverbally (e.g., shaking her head to signify no and smiling as the examiner sang "Happy Birthday"). But, increasingly, she distanced herself from the experimenter. As Kagan and his associates (1993) indicate, latency to the first spontaneous comment and the percentage of silent time are extremely sensitive indices of shyness. In the first story stem with the examiner (an unfamiliar adult), Susan responded only five times, using only one or two words. None of these replies was spontaneous. Susan was silent for almost a full minute before her first utterance.

What follows is a transcript of the first (warm-up) story stem that used the theme of Birthday, and the description of the emotional apprenticeship process as it unfolds in the subsequent story stems.

TIME	*TURN*	*UTTERANCE*
0:00	E:	We've got some people we'd like you to meet. Now this is Mary. She has blond hair like you.
	S:	Turns and calls for mom when E leans in toward her.
	E:	And this is her sister Jane. And who do you think that one will be? Guess.
	S:	Nervously fidgets and doesn't respond.
	E:	If I bring out this person does it make it easier?
1:00	S:	(softly) Mom and Dad.

E: Mom and Dad, good job. And who might that be here?

S: Turns toward Mom and leans against her leg.

E: OK. Let's say that's grandma. In our first story, its Mary's birthday. Can you put everyone around the table? We are going to celebrate Mary's birthday.

2:00 S: (To Mom) You help me.

E: I'll help you Susan. How's this. I'll put Mom here. (W/Mom toy) "Come in everyone. Let's sit around the table and celebrate Mary's birthday." Do you want to put Mary in since it's her birthday?

S: Nods no. Fidgets nervously.

E: (w/Mary doll) "Here I come. I'm coming to the table." Do you want to put Jane her sister at the table?

S: Nods no.

E: Knocks two toys down.

E: Oopsy. I knocked them over. They fall down very easily. Let's sing Happy Birthday to Mary.

3:00 S: Turns to Mom and nervously smiles to E.

E: Want to show me Mary blowing out the candles?

S: Nods yes with her head tilted on her shoulder.

E: Go ahead. Show me how Mary blows out candles. Everyone's waiting and she's going to make a wish too. Wanna show Mary blowing out candles?

S: (timidly) No.

E: I'll try it, then you could try it. (Pretends to blow out candles). OOPS she missed one. Want to go ahead and try?

S: Turns toward Mom.

M: Go ahead.

E: Go ahead. It's OK. No. Well-OK (W/Mom toy) "I'll go get a knife and cut up the cake." Cut. Cut. Cut. Can you have Dad give a little cake to everybody?

S: (No reply.)

E: Can you show me Dad handing out the cake?

S: Nervously fidgets. Puts hands between her legs and looks toward ground.

4:00 E: How about I show you once? There he gave some cake to Mary because she is the birthday girl. Now you try.

S: Turns and grabs Mom's arm.

E: It's OK. Go ahead. I'll have Dad hand out all of it. What kind of cake do you think they're having? (Pretends to eat cake) Yum, yum.

S: Chocolate (leaning on Mom)

E: Chocolate. Yeah.

	S:	Nods yes.
	E:	Do you think it has chocolate frosting, too?
	S:	Nods no.
	E:	No. What kind of frosting do you think it has?
5:00	S:	Vanilla. (Moves away from Mom and speaks louder)
	E:	Chocolate and vanilla. Sounds good to me. Yum, yum.
	S:	Claps her hands and grins.
	E:	(w/Mom toy) "I want some more." Can you show me Mom eating some more?
	S:	Nods no.
	E:	No? Do you think anybody else says anything?
	S:	Nods no.
	E:	Do you think Mom likes her cake?
	S:	With her fingers in her mouth, she nods yes.
	E:	Yeah.
6:00	S:	Nods yes again.
	E:	Should we go on to another story?
	S:	Nods yes.

As the transcript indicates, Susan is extremely reluctant to approach and interact with the examiner. The examiner, well aware of Susan's shyness, begins gradually ("We've got some people we'd like you to meet"); the examiner affiliates herself with the family ("we") and only requests that Susan "meet" the toy people as they are lifted out of a box. She tries to establish links between Susan and the doll ("She has blond hair like you"), possibly to make the figure familiar, likeable, and less frightening. But once the experimenter leans in toward Susan, Susan pulls back and seeks her mother. She refuses even to guess who might come out of the box next. As the stem proceeds, Susan eventually responds to questions with a nod or offers single-word descriptors, as when she describes a toy cake as "chocolate" or "vanilla." But throughout the first narrative stem, Susan initiates neither language nor action. The experimenter's style and script are dramatically affected; she provides a running commentary, full of small invitations to Susan. The resulting pattern, quite different from the examiner's basic script, demonstrates how mutual this system of playing together is. When Susan's play is nonexistent or fragmentary, the examiner fills the space by asking Susan a flurry of simple questions, urging her to take parts. The consequence is a scene operated wholly by the experimenter—just the opposite of what was sought.

The Apprenticeship Process: Daring to Play

When Susan's father replaced her mother, after two additional story stems, a very specific emotional apprenticeship developed. Susan's father patiently was helping Susan to regulate her fear and stretching her tolerance for public performance. Following this third stem, Susan gradually moved away from her frozen position, which was facilitated by the father's help. What follows is the father's invitation for an emotional apprenticeship dialogue that took place just before the Mom's Headache story stem (no. 4).

F: Taps Susan on her shoulder

F: Could you introduce me to Mary before you go on to the next story? Can I meet her?

S: Hesitatingly hands the doll to father, making no eye contact.

F: Sits still for several moments, caressing the doll in his hand and looking at Susan.

S: Suddenly turns to her father, makes eye contact, touches his hand, which holds the doll and smiles.

F: Pretty cool.

Even within an increasingly familiar context (at home, with her father, using dolls that she has seen in action), Susan met her father's request slowly, only gradually shifting from a stiff and withdrawn position to a position in which she turned to face her father. Her father's behavior consistently expresses ease and patience. He presents a possibility ("Could you") as compared to the earlier experimenter command "Show me and tell me what happens now." In his turn to Susan, he presupposes that they are already engaged in make believe play, when referring to the doll by name and asking to be introduced. At first he enters only vocally, speaking low and using an intonation, which approaches chant or singing. Intuitively he held the doll gently, only caressing it. This is a next step in the apprenticeship; she enters, but the figure will not be animated until *she* chooses. This contrasts sharply with the examiner's immediate treatment of the figures as "live" and under the examiner's control from the start. When Susan touches his hand holding the doll, he does not attempt to push the narrative along with any additional requests. He only certifies their shared interest ("Pretty cool"). Once she has declared her interest, he acknowledges it, but leaves her room to become the animating force. Throughout, Susan's father stays at the border of pragmatic action and play. He never directly invites her to tell a story (although he carefully presumes that it is a possibility). Susan's father takes her step by step into engaging in play. He models an episode of gradual entry without becoming overwhelmed: eye contact, low-stakes engagement with the preliminaries (i.e., exchanging the doll), and a preface about what might or could happen (i.e., "Could you introduce her to me?"). At the same time, the process is designed to draw her into being an author, not a witness. This specific fragile engagement came to a closure, setting a new level of affect regulation and easiness. Susan took the Mary doll from her father and placed it on the "stage." This prompted the examiner to present the next story stem. Susan needed additional support in order to become involved in the following story stems presented by the examiner. When the examiner presented the next story stem (Mom's Headache), Susan initially retreated from the play.

TIME	*TURN*	*UTTERANCE*
0:00	E:	(Holds up the Mom doll) "Oh Mary I have got such a headache. I just have to have it quiet, and turn off this TV. I'm going to lie down. Can you do something quiet for a while?" (w/Mary doll) "Sure Mom I'll read a book." (Mom turns off TV and lies down.)
	E:	Now, let's start the story. (Ding-dong) It's her friend Sally. Mary comes to the door and says, "Hi Sally" and Sally says, "Can I come in and play? There's this great TV show on I want to watch."
	E:	Show me and tell me what happens now.
	S:	Moves away, nods no, shrugs shoulders, rubs hands, head down, twists her body away from the scene of the play narrative.
1:00	E:	Does Mary say anything?
	S:	Plays with shoe lace, nods yes while making eye contact with the E.
	E:	Yeah. What does Mary say?
	S:	Fidgets, more body twisting
	E:	You can whisper it to me. Can you tell me what Mary says?
	E:	(whispers) No?
	E:	(W/Sally) "Oh Mary may I come inside? The show is about to start." Show me and tell me what happens now.
2:00	S:	Fidgets, looks at her hands, plays with shoelaces, rubs her palms, moves from side to side.
	E:	Does she say something to her friend Sally?
	S:	Nods no, fidgets.
	E:	No.
	F:	(Changing his voice to a higher and melodic one.) Does she just have her standing out there on her doorstep?
	S:	Nods yes, giggles, makes eye contact with father, face brightens, continues to fidget.
	F:	Forever, and ever and ever? (Voice moving to higher and higher notes) That sounds kind of silly to me.
3:00	S:	Laughs, rubs her eyes, hand stretched toward father.
	E:	Until the winter comes and then she gets snowed on. You show me what happens, Susan.
	S:	Playing with shoe, nods no.
	E:	No.
	S:	No.

Susan froze again when the examiner asked her, "What happens now?" It bids her to jump into the world of symbolic play that she refused to enter earlier. On the other hand, her father's initial comment ("Does she just have her standing out there on her doorstep?") once again hovers at the border between everyday discourse and make-believe. His is a real-world question that once again presupposes that the figure is a person and that she is standing on a doorstep, but he never demands that Susan commit herself to inventing her. Instead, he jokes with her. The joke requires shared meaning and pretense, but nothing more. Susan nods yes and giggles. In so doing, she assents to enter a semi-fictional world, accompanied by her father. He "stretches" her engagement one more notch, extending the fictional situation, suggesting how funny its trajectory could be. He exaggerates ("Forever and ever and ever?"), assuming the role of the one who dares to sound silly and giving her the right to forward or pause the incipient narrative. When Susan follows, her father escalates the humor: "That sounds pretty silly to me." With this move, he turns her nod into a move in a nearly imagined world. With these linked, but extremely gradual moves, her father stretches Susan's tolerance for playing "in public."

At this juncture, Susan and her father begin to co-construct make-believe narratives in response to the story stems. He continually maintains the connection between familiar everyday actions and the world of play, often through creating an intermediate zone of hypotheticals. These hypotheticals signal how engaged he is by the play scenario, without usurping the creative role (and responsibility) from Susan. For instance, in the story stem where a child makes his father a gift of a painting, he says, "If I were the father, I would say 'It's a great picture, let's hang the picture. Where?'" As the stems continued, Susan became more active, moved the dolls around, and made a number of short, spontaneous comments.

The crucial shift in Susan's behavior and expression took place in the Lost Keys story stem (no. 8). In this story stem Susan played forcefully, using active movements and utterances. Susan enjoys having the mother doll and the father doll knock each other down, and the Mary doll knock both of them down. Nevertheless, Susan avoided the problem presented in the lost keys story stem. At this point, the examiner probed:

TIME	*TURN*	*UTTERANCE*
0:00	E:	"What happens about the keys?" (with Mom doll.) "I still can't find my keys. You lost them. Where are my keys?"
	S:	Uses Mary doll to push others off board.
	E:	What's happening? Is she [Mary doll] jumping up and down?
	S:	Knocking foot on the floor, continuing to make the dolls march.
	E:	She's knocking them out? Does anyone do anything about the keys?
	S:	Giggles.
	E:	So no one can go anywhere because they have no keys?
1:00	F:	They are going to stand around and talk now.
	E:	Mary says "You lost your key. Oh, no, what do you think we should do about your keys?"
	E:	What do you think happens Susan?
	S:	Susan withdraws, nods no, folding the placemat she's sitting on, fidgeting.

	E:	You don't know?
	F:	What do we do when we lose something?
	E:	Does anyone go and look for them?
	S:	Takes Mary doll and marches around.
	E:	Mary goes and looks for the keys.
2:00	E:	So what do Mom and Dad do?
	S:	Mom's going to look for them.
	E:	Mom's going to go look for them.
	S:	Acts out Mom looking for the keys: she moves across the room, knocking the floor with Mom doll while moving around.
	S:	Mom's coming back now.
3:00	E:	Yea. And what happened, did she find the keys?
	S:	No. She couldn't.
	E:	Uh-oh. Dad's turn.
	S:	Uses Dad doll and marches around

Her father's interjection ("What do we do when we lose something?") triggered a shift in Susan's response; for the first time in the session, she addressed a conflict, within the terms of the make-believe frame of a co-constructed narrative. His subtle intervention is a vivid illustration of the graduated quality of an emotional apprenticeship process. Susan is the agent and author, but he will intervene to help her regulate her response to this new kind of demand. His remark ("What do we do when we lose something?") allows a sidebar exchange that is safely within the pragmatic realm of everyday experience. Whether intended or not, his remark also provides her with many more play moves (i.e., moving the different figures as if they are looking). When Susan continued the Lost Keys story stem, she initiated a series of searches for the keys. While playing out these searches, Susan became active and animated, talking as she moved around the whole room, in full command of the dolls. In this latter portion of the story stem, Susan's behavior is open and expressive. Her father's interventions and her increasing engagement made a once-threatening situation manageable and enjoyable. From this moment in the session, Susan continued to be fully engaged and animated, constructing her own narratives and verbally addressing the conflicts they presented. She no longer sought her father's contact to buffer her distress. He, in turn, did not intervene. Hence, as Susan assumed more and more of the authorship (cf. table 10.1), her father's participation decreased (table 10.2).

Interestingly, Susan's father's gentle and buffering communications may grow out of his own history. During the examiner's separate interview with the parents, when asked to whom Susan is more similar emotionally, the father answered: "I think on things that are emotions that are out there, on her peaks—I think she's more like me." Describing how his perception of Susan's difficulties is colored by his understanding of his own, he added: "I always see her at her worst. . . . I can identify more than I'd like to with how she is acting and how she is feeling."

TABLE 10.1 Number of Words Uttered by Susan for Each Story-stem Narrative at Age 3

Story stem	1	2	3	4	5	6	7	8	9	10	11	12	13	14	15
Number of words	3	0	0	18[a]	28	19	21	71	30	62	53	72	18	50	225

[a]Susan's narration here had to do not with the story-stem conflict presented to her but with her favorite game. This was then connected by the examiner to the story.

His own capacity for self-reflection and identification with Susan's emotional peaks seemed to have influenced his interventions (Fonagy, Steele, Steele, Moran, & Higgitt, 1991; Steele et al., chapter 9, this book). At the same time, these comments remind us, these interactions were also his opportunity to reimagine and transform his own history of learning how to regulate overwhelming emotions.

Susan's Story Stems at Age 5: Future Directions

One can only speculate about links between Susan's apprenticeship at age 3 and similar processes at age 5. But it is useful to ask to what extent Susan's play is different or similar. Since the story stem task was administered at age 5 in the same order as it was at age 3, we may compare Susan's behavior at both times. The following is a transcript of the Birthday Story stem (no. 1) at age 5. In contrast to her behavior during the Birthday Story stem at age 3, Susan at age 5 is very involved in the narrative: she immediately responds, she gives a spontaneous response after just 7 seconds, and she continues to be forthcoming throughout the session. Her responses are highly animated not only in ways that echo the examiner's dramatic style but also in ways that Susan invents (see italicized items).

TIME	*TURN*	*UTTERANCE*
0:00	E:	This is Mary and do you know what?
	S:	What?
	E:	This is Mary's sister, Jane.
	S:	*She has no eyes.* Giggles.
	E:	Her eyes are kind of faded aren't they?
	S:	Yeah.
	E:	And who might this be, Susan?
	S:	Her Mom and Dad.

TABLE 10.2 Number of Times the Parents Intervened in Story Stem at Age 3

Story stem	1	2	3	4	5	6	7	8	9	10	11	12	13	14	15
Mother	1	0[a]													
Father		2	13	7	1	4	2							1	

[a]The father replaced the mother after the second story stem.

E: Her Mom and Dad and who's the one with gray hair?

S: Her grandma.

E: Yes, Her grandma. And they have a dog named Barney and he's going to go away for a little while, but he'll be back soon.

S: *He could just be (hiding).*

E: He could be. Right now let's go over names again. Can you tell me their names. Mary and her sister Jane.

S: Mom, Dad, and Grandma.

E: Mom, Dad, and Grandma. Good Susan. Now you know what we are going to do?

S: *And Barney the dog.*

E: And Barney the dog. He'll be back. Do you remember last year when we told stories and I told the beginning of the story and who told the end?

S: Me.

E: You got to tell the whole rest, right. So let's try it.

0:55 S: *Mary has a cake.*

E: Do you remember this story? In the first story it's Mary's birthday. So Mom and Dad bake a special cake. Show me and tell me what happens next.

S: *Mary your cake is done.*

E: Who said, "Mary your cake is done?"

S: Her Mom.

E: OK.

S: Her sister is over and going over on her dress. Mom and Dad are over talking to grandma over here in the living room. And they are watching her sister because she came along and *stole the cake.*

E: Her sister stole the cake and hid it, Wow!

S: Yes.

E: So what else happens in this story?

S: And then Mom and Dad and Grandma come in and she says, "Hey, where's my cake?" (W/Jane) and she said, "I don't know" and she's really lying.

E: She says, I don't know and she's really lying. So what happens at the end of the birthday party?

S: (*Screaming*) Dad says, "Hey, where is the cake?"

2:00 E: Dad says, "Where is the cake?"

S: And he knew that she hid it because no one else did.

E: Ah-ha.

S: (w/Dad) "You hid it—go get it now" So she went over and got it.

E: Then she went over and got it.

S: *But she ate all of it.*

E: But she ate all of it. Wow. So what happens at the end? So Mary got to eat any of it? That's kind of a sad birthday.

At age 5, Susan behaves spontaneously: she volunteers and introduces the dolls and the story stem's subject (cake); she initiates the use of a dialogue mode ("Mary, your cake is done"); she takes risks of correcting the examiner and adding information that the examiner deleted ("And Barney the dog"); she raises "dangerous/bad" themes continuously throughout the story stem session (sister "stole the cake" and "ate it all"); and even shows at times bold behavior (screaming). It is clear that some portions of the earlier apprenticeship are now well within Susan's grasp: engagement, animation, and sustained collaborative effort with the examiner. However, other aspects of affective regulation remain less modulated, specifically, how to problem-solve in stories where distressing internal states (like issues connected to possession and competition) may have been provoked. Thus, Susan and her family's apprenticeship hopefully will have other chapters.

Conclusion

Emotional apprenticeship is suggested to affect the development of affect regulation and to allow for gradual stretching of the nonconscious self-regulation skills. It is suggested that the knowledge that emerges from emotional apprenticeship experiences is mostly of procedural nature. The example presented sheds light on several aspects of moments in what was a sustained emotional apprenticeship for an inhibited child, Susan. At 3, the effects of sensitive interchange, especially with her father, progressed and Susan's behavior grew less and less inhibited. Some of these features continued to characterize Susan's behavior throughout the rest of the session. Several of the features offered in this apprenticeship at age 3 were available 2 years later.

This suggests (though in no sense does it prove) that emotional apprenticeships do occur and can be successful. However, these examples also portray how sustained such apprenticeships must be if they are to address not just outward behaviors (i.e., engagement and animation during play) but affective structures such as reactions to distress. While this material adds to the growing evidence for the proposition that the *dynamic* process between the intra-individual and interpersonal components affect the individual's behavior (Scarr, 1992; Sameroff, 1993; Sameroff & Chandler, 1975), this is a sustained process in no way limited to the earliest years. It has been suggested that we think of emotional apprenticeship in terms of continuous change of affective self-regulation that falls into the realm of nonconscious mental activities that organize automatically functioning procedures (Emde, 1993) so that the acquisition of language and verbal skills does not overshadow the impact of the nonverbal, procedural knowledge of affect regulation. Hence, emotional apprenticeship might be considered as procedural knowledge that underlies a skill that need not be represented in consciousness in order for one to manifest the skill.

NOTE

This work has been done with the support of Jerome Kagan and Nancy Snidman, Department of Psychology, Harvard University. Our chapter is based on their concept of behavioral inhibition and their extended longitudinal studies on temperament. We are grateful to them for their inspiration in bringing this work to fruition.

REFERENCES

Beebe, B., & Jaffe, J. (1992). Mother-infant vocal dialogues predict infant attachment, temperament and cognition. *Infant Behavior and Development, 15,* ICIS. Abstracts Issue, p. 48.

Beebe, B., & Lachmann, F. M. (1994). Representation and internalization in infancy: Three principles of salience. *Psychoanalytic Psychology, 11*(2), 127–165.

Beebe, B., & Lachmann, F. M. (1998). Co-constructing inner and relational processes: Self and mutual regulation in infant research and adult treatment. *Psychoanalytic Psychology, 15,* 480–516.

Beebe, B., Lachmann, F. M., & Jaffe, J (1997). Mother-infant interaction structures and presymbolic self and object representations. *Psychoanalytic Dialogues, 7,* 133–182.

Bretherton, I., Prentiss, C., & Ridgeway, D. (1990). Family relationships as represented in a story-completion task at thirty-seven and fifty-four months of age. *New Directions for Child Development, 48,* 85–105.

Bruner, J. (1981). The social context of language acquisition. *Language and Communication, 1*(2/3), 155–178.

Chaiklin, S., & Lave, J. (1993). *Understanding practice: Perspectives on activity and context.* New York: Cambridge University Press.

Cohen, N. J., & Squire, L. R. (1980). Preserved learning and retention pattern-analyzing skill in amnesia: Dissociation of knowing how knowing that. *Science, 221,* 207–210.

Emde, R. N. (1993). Epilogue: A beginning—Research approaches and expanding horizons for psychoanalysis. *Journal of the American Psychoanalytic Association, 41*(Suppl), 411–424.

Fivush, R. (1991). The social construction of personal narratives. *Merrill-Palmer Quarterly, 37*(1), 59–81.

Fonagy, P., Steele, M., Steele, H., Moran, G., & Higgitt, A. (1991). The capacity for understanding mental states: The reflective self in parent and child and its significance for security of attachment. *Infant Mental Health Journal, 12*(3), 201–218.

Freud, S. (1961). Inhibition, symptoms and anxiety. In J. Strachey (Ed. & Trans.), *The standard edition of the complete psychological works of Sigmund Freud* (Vol. 20, pp. 75–175). London: Hogarth. (Original work published 1926)

Hudson, J. (1990). The emergence of autobiographical memory in mother-child conversation. In R. Fivush & J. Hudson (Eds.), *Knowing and remembering in young children* (pp. 166–196). Cambridge: Cambridge University Press.

Kagan, J. (1994a). *Galen's prophecy.* New York: Basic.

Kagan, J. (1994b). On the nature of emotion. In N. A. Fox (Ed.), *The development of emotion regulation: Biological and behavioral considerations* (pp. 7–24). *Monographs of the Society for Research in Child Development,* Vol. 59 (2–3), Serial No. 240.

Kagan J., Reznick, J. S., & Gibbons, J. (1989). Inhibited and uninhibited types of children. *Child Development, 60,* 838–845.

Kagan, J., Reznick, J. S., & Snidman, N. (1988). Biological bases of childhood shyness. *Science, 240,* 167–171.

Kagan, J., & Snidman, N. (1991). Temperamental factors in human development. *American Psychologist, 48,* 856–862.

Kagan, J., Snidman, N., & Arcus, D. (1993). On the temperamental categories of inhibited and uninhibited children. In K. H. Rubin & J. B. Asendorpf (Eds.), *Social withdrawal, inhibition and shyness in childhood* (pp. 19–28). Hillsdale, NJ: Lawrence Erlbaum.

Kestenberg, J. (1985). The flow of empathy and trust between mother and child. In E. J. Anthony & G. H. Pollack (Eds.), *Parental influences in health and disease* (pp. 137–163). Boston, MA: Little Brown.

Labov, W. (1972). *Language in the inner city.* Philadelphia: University of Pennsylvania Press.

Main, M. (1993). Discourse, prediction and studies in attachment: Implications for psychoanalysis. *Journal of the American Psychoanalytic Association, 41*(Suppl), 209–244.

Malatesta, C. Z. (1985). The developmental course of emotion expression in the human infant. In G. Zivin (Ed.), *Expressive development: Biological and environmental interactions* (pp. 183–220). New York: Academic Press.

McCabe, A., & Peterson, C. (1991). Getting the story: A longitudinal study of parental styles in eliciting oral personal narratives and developing narrative skill. In A. McCabe & C. Peterson (Eds.), *Developing narrative structure* (pp. 215–253). Hillsdale, NJ: Lawrence Erlbaum.

Nachmias, M., Gunnar, M., Mangelsdorf, S., & Parritz, R. H. (1996). Behavioral inhibition and stress reactivity: The moderating role of attachment security. *Child Development, 67,* 508–522.

Nelson, K. (Ed.). (1989). *Narratives from the crib.* Cambridge, MA: Harvard University Press.

Oppenheim, D., Emde, R. N., & Wamboldt, F. S. (1996). Associations between 3-year-olds' narrative co-constructions with mothers and fathers and their story completions about affective themes. *Early Development & Parenting, 5,* 149–160.

Oppenheim, D., Nir, A., Warren, S., & Emde, R. N. (1997). Emotion regulation in mother-child narrative co-construction: Associations with children's narratives and adaptation. *Developmental Psychology, 33,* 284–294.

Polanyi, L. (1985). *Telling the American story: A structural and cultural analysis of conversational storytelling.* Norwood, NJ: Ablex.

Rogoff, B. (1990). *Apprenticeship in thinking: Cognitive development in social context.* New York: Oxford University Press.

Rosenberg, D. M. (1984). *The quality and content of preschool fantasy play: Correlates in concurrent social-personality functioning and early mother-child attachment relationships.* Unpublished doctoral dissertation, University of Minnesota.

Sameroff, A. J. (1993). Models of development and developmental risk. In C. H. Zeanah, Jr. (Ed.), *Handbook of infant mental health* (pp. 3–13). New York: Guilford Press.

Sameroff, A., & Chandler, M. (1975). Early influences on development: Fact or fancy? *Merrill-Palmer Quarterly, 21,* 267–294.

Scarr, S. (1992). Developmental theories for the 1990s: Development and individual differences. *Child Development, 63,* 1–19.

Slade, A. (1987). Quality of attachment and early symbolic play. *Developmental Psychology, 23*(1), 78–85.

Stern, D. N. (1983). Early transmission of affect: Some research issues. In J. Call,

E. Galenson, & R. Tyson (Eds.), *Frontiers of infant psychiatry* (pp. 52–69). New York: Basic Books.

Stern, D. N. (1985). *The interpersonal world of the infant.* New York: Basic Books.

Stern, D. N. (1993). Why study children's narratives? *Newsletter of the World Association for Infant Mental Health, 1,* 1–3.

Stern, D. N. (1994). One way to build a clinically relevant baby. *Infant Mental Health Journal, 15,* 9–25.

Stern, D. N. (1995). *The motherhood constellation.* New York: Basic Books.

Vygotsky, L. S. (1978). *Mind in society: The development of higher psychological processes.* Cambridge, MA: Harvard University Press.

Winnicott, D. W. (1953). Transitional objects and transitional phenomena: A study of the first not-me possession. *International Journal of Psychoanalysis, 34,* 89–97.

Wolf, D. (1990). Being of several minds: Voices and versions of the self in early childhood. In D. Cicchetti & M Beeghly (Eds.), *The self in transition: Infancy to childhood* (pp. 183–212). Chicago: University of Chicago Press.

Wolf, D., & Hicks, D. (1989). The voices within narratives: The development of intertextuality in young children's stories. *Discourse Processes, 12,* 329–351.

ROBERT B. CLYMAN

11

Portrayals in Maltreated Children's Play Narratives: Representations or Emotion Regulation?

Maltreated children's perspectives of their experiences within their families may mediate their subsequent development in a number of important social domains. Individual differences in maltreated children's developing knowledge of how caregivers parent children, for example, may contribute to the variability in whether they subsequently maltreat their own children (Kaufman & Zigler, 1987). Recently, investigators have begun to use story stem narratives with young children to assess children's understanding of family relationships (Buchsbaum & Emde, 1990; Bretherton, Ridgeway, & Cassidy, 1990). In this technique, an experimenter tells the beginning of a story using a doll family and props (called the story stem) and then asks the child to "show me and tell me what happens now." The story stems typically pose interpersonal dilemmas for the children to address. A number of studies provide growing evidence that children's narrative portrayals of child and parent characters are systematically related to the children's interpersonal behavior and experiences. This suggests that children's mental representations of themselves and their parents, their memories, beliefs, and expectations about behavior, influence how they portray characters in their narratives.

However, data from narrative and related techniques with maltreated children have only been inconsistently related to maltreated children's parenting experiences or to their own behavior. These mixed results raise the possibility of important influences other than the children's mental representations of their experiences that affect how maltreated children portray child and parent characters in their stories. Another possible influence on narrative behavior that may be particularly salient for maltreated children is that they may use stories to regulate their emotions (e.g., Oppenheim & Waters, 1995). Children tell stories to explore "possible worlds" and to make sense of their experiences (Bruner, 1986, 1990; Emde, Kubicek, & Oppenheim, 1997). Children can use storytelling to imagine how they wish their world might be, or to come to terms with how it actually is. This is inherently an affective process, and it may be particularly salient for maltreated children, who must cope with harsh or neglectful parenting. Although the concept of emotion regulation has a variety of meanings (e.g., Thompson, 1994), the emotion regulation hypothesis asserts that children modify or avoid portraying specific behaviors by the characters in their narratives in order to regulate their negative emotions. For example, the emotion regulation hypothesis suggests that maltreated children would be *less* likely than nonmaltreated children to portray scenarios such as children in distress that are painful and remind them of their maltreatment. Their portrayals, therefore, would not reveal their memories, beliefs, and expectations (the representational hypothesis), but they would portray characters differently to regulate their emotions or avoid portraying events that elicit negative emotions. The representational hypothesis would predict the opposite, that they would be more likely to portray children in distress because they were maltreated.

This chapter reviews available studies and presents preliminary data regarding whether maltreated children's mental representations or their emotion regulation strategies influence their portrayals of characters in their narratives. The term "portrayal" will be used to refer to children's verbalizations and enactments of characters' behavior in their stories to highlight the distinction between their actual narrative behavior and the children's mental representations of themselves and their parents. The chapter begins by reviewing studies that delineate what is known about the influence of children's mental representations on their narrative portrayals, for both maltreated and nonmaltreated children. Then data will be presented to determine if maltreated children are more or less likely than nonmaltreated children to portray parent and child characters in accordance with their experiences, or if the data suggest they modify their portrayals to regulate their emotions. These findings will then be used to illustrate a number of issues that complicate attempts to draw inferences about both children's representations and their emotion regulation strategies from their narrative portrayals. The discussion concludes with avenues for subsequent research.

Studies of Children's Narrative Portrayals

A number of studies have demonstrated relations between children's portrayals of characters in their stories and their experiences and behavior. In our review, however, since studies using the story stem narrative technique remain limited, additional studies will be reviewed to inform our understanding of these issues.

Studies of Nonmaltreated Children

Studies in normative and high-risk samples other than maltreated children provide support for a representational hypothesis that children portray characters in their narratives in accord with their experiences. At least four studies have examined children's narrative portrayals in relation to their interpersonal behavior in normative samples. Mize and Ladd (1988) found that children who told stories where puppets acted in a friendly manner were rated by their teachers and observers as having more prosocial and less aggressive behavior. Warren, Oppenheim, and Emde (1996) found that "aggressive/destructive themes," which included aggression, personal injury, and atypical negative responses, were associated with both parent- and teacher-rated externalizing behavior in these children. Another study found that parent-reported and observed measures of moral conduct, measured when the children were both toddlers and preschoolers, were associated with moral behaviors in the children's narratives when they were preschoolers (Kochanska, Padavich, & Koenig, 1996). In a study of twins, three classes of narrative behavior were examined: conflict, affiliative, and moral behaviors. Three-year-olds' conflict behaviors positively and affiliative behaviors negatively predicted teacher-rated hostility and hyperactivity when the children were 5 years old. However, moral behaviors in the narratives were not related to the teachers' ratings of the children's behavior, and none of the three types of behaviors systematically predicted parent reports of problematic behaviors (Zahn-Waxler, Schmitz, Fulker, Robinson, & Emde, 1996). These studies used different approaches to aggregating the individual narrative portrayals into superordinate categories, which may account for some of the differences in the findings.

One study of 4- to 5-year-old children at high, moderate, and low risk for behavior problems found that risk status interacted with gender in relation to the children's narrative behaviors (Zahn-Waxler et al., 1994). For example, in the story stems that portrayed a character in distress, high-risk girls were more prosocial than the moderate-risk girls and all three groups of boys. This study also found modest relations between doll characters' prosocial and aggressive behaviors in the narratives and the child's empathic and prosocial behaviors in response to others' simulated distress in the laboratory that support the representational hypothesis (Zahn-Waxler, Cole, Welsh, & Fox, 1995).

However, some of these studies included additional behaviors in the coding systems of narrative behaviors. One study incorporated the children's responses to a question about what they themselves would do if they were presented with the situation that occurred in the story stem (Kochanska, Padavich, & Koenig, 1996). Another study coded the child subject's actions (e.g., aggression) along with the characters' actions in the stories (Warren, Oppenheim, & Emde, 1996). The implications for testing hypotheses about narrative portrayals due to these method differences are not clear.

Surprisingly few studies have examined if children's portrayals of parents in their narratives relate to the children's actual parenting experiences. One normative study found that children whose narrative portrayals of mothers were more positive and disciplinary had mothers who reported less psychological distress (Oppenheim, Emde, & Warren, 1997). Studies have also found that traumatic experiences influence children's narrative behaviors. For example, children who were directly exposed to urban riots had more aggression in their play than children who were not directly exposed to the riots (Farver & Frosch, 1996).

This supports clinical studies that have found that children traumatized by natural disasters reenact their traumatic experiences in pretend play with their peers (Bloch, Silber, & Perry, 1958; Newman, 1976; Saylor, Swenson, & Powell, 1992).

Attachment studies suggest that children's narrative portrayals are influenced by both their mental representations, in the sense of their memories, beliefs, and expectations about how they and their parents act within the attachment relationship, and by their emotion regulation strategies. At least four studies compared narrative measures of attachment in response to story stems about separations and reunions with parents to children's attachment behavior during actual separations and reunions with their primary caregivers (Cassidy, 1988; Bretherton, Ridgeway, & Cassidy, 1990; Solomon, George, & De Jong, 1995; Oppenheim, 1990, cited in Oppenheim & Waters, 1995). At least three additional studies used the Klagsbrun and Bowlby (1976) adaptation of Hansburg's Separation Anxiety Test (SAT), which elicits children's responses to a series of pictures of a family involved in separations (Main, Kaplan, & Cassidy, 1985; Slough & Greenberg, 1990; Shouldice & Stevenson-Hinde, 1992). Children's responses to both measures were related to their attachment status.

These attachment studies incorporated both how the children and parents were portrayed in the stories and features of the child's affect regulation (or dysregulation) in assigning the child to an attachment category based on his or her narrative performance (Oppenheim & Waters, 1995). Characteristics of secure children's narratives, for example, included positive portrayals such as whether parent characters responded sensitively to the children's needs, and, as features of affect regulation, whether the stories were coherent and emotionally open. Insecure children's narratives often avoided portraying the separation from the parents, or the children were described in idealized terms, both of which suggest the children modified their portrayals of characters to regulate their emotions. It is unclear in these studies whether the characterizations of the children and parents *or* the affect regulation strategies were more strongly related to the children's attachment classification. Future research could discriminate these possibilities by testing for the relevant relations, controlling for the other variable.

Studies of Maltreated Children

These findings suggest that nonattachment studies offer support that representations influence nonmaltreated children's narrative portrayals and that attachment studies suggest that both representations and emotion regulation strategies may influence nonmaltreated children's narrative portrayals. We now examine this question for maltreated children. Children who have been maltreated are an important population in which to examine these issues. They and their parents display a range of maladaptive behaviors that could be portrayed in children's narratives (Rogsoch, Cicchetti, Shields, & Toth, 1995; Knutson, 1995). However, the children have incentives to modify the portrayal of these behaviors in their narratives due to the negative emotions such portrayals may evoke, such as being reminded of their parents' neglectful or aggressive behavior.

Whereas studies of maltreated children provide evidence for the representational hypothesis, they provide even stronger evidence for the emotion regulation hypothesis. Perhaps the best evidence that maltreated children portray their experiences in their stories is derived from studies of sexually abused children. They are more likely than children who are not sexually abused to enact sexual acts with anatomically correct dolls (August & Foreman, 1989). Another set of studies also provides support for the representational hypothesis. One study elicited stories from 6- to 8-year-old children about characters' responses to another character's kind acts. The maltreated children were less likely than the nonmaltreated children to have parent or child characters reciprocate the *child* characters' acts of kindness, but were more likely to have child characters reciprocate the *adult* characters' kind acts with a kind act (Dean, Malik, Richards, & Stringer, 1986), suggesting that the maltreated children have developed an understanding that it is their role to care for their parents. Another study with preschool children found that maltreated children portrayed maternal and child figures more negatively than nonmaltreated children, using aggregates of positive and negative behaviors in the narratives (Toth, Cicchetti, Macfie, & Emde, 1997). A related study found that maltreated children were less likely to portray parents or children relieving other children's distress than nonmaltreated children (Macfie et al., 1999). Furthermore, physically abused children were more likely to portray caretaking behaviors by child figures for the parent figures than nonmaltreated children were (Macfie et al., 1999). Two other studies provide additional insights. McCrone, Egeland, Kalkoske, and Carlson (1994) found that maltreated sixth graders' stories revealed more positive "relationship expectations," but the measure incorporated both content and affect regulation features, such as narrative coherence. Abused boys were more likely than nonabused boys to describe their caregivers more negatively (Herzberger, Potts, & Dillon, 1981). However, the abused boys were residing in a group home, confounding maltreatment with service use, thus limiting the inferences that can be drawn.

Studies of maltreated children provide evidence that children alter their narrative portrayals to regulate their emotions. Alessandri (1991) found that 85% of the symbolic play themes enacted by maltreated children during playtime in a preschool reflected nurturant roles, compared to 42% of the nonmaltreated children's symbolic play themes. These studies that provided evidence for the influence of representations also reveal the children's active emotion regulation strategies. In the study by Macfie et al. (1999), maltreated children were more likely to relinquish the narrative frame and relieve the child characters' distress through their own verbalizations or actions than nonmaltreated children, even though they were less likely to portray characters relieving children's distress. One strategy children may use to regulate negative emotions they experience while telling stories is to discontinue narrating the story and become an actor themselves in the story (Scarlett & Wolf, 1979). The maltreated children may have stepped into the story to relieve their own distress as the painful story was told. In the related study, sexually abused children were more likely to portray child characters positively than nonmaltreated children were. If replicated in a larger sample, it may reflect the sexually abused children's need to reverse their own negative self-appraisals as they portray children in their stories (Toth, Cicchetti, Macfie, & Emde, 1997). Two studies of fantasy aggression on the Thematic Apperception Test (TAT) revealed contradictory findings on whether abused children were more aggressive (Reidy, 1977; Straker & Jacobson, 1981). In another study, maltreated children were more likely to be confused in their relationship with their mothers than nonmaltreated children, based on their reporting both a need for psychological proximity and felt positive emotions in their relationships with their mothers (Lynch & Cicchetti, 1991). The maltreated children reported that they felt positively toward their mothers in this study, rather than reporting negative feelings toward them, which suggests the children were regulating their emotions. Using other methods, two studies found that young maltreated children rated themselves as more competent than matched nonmaltreated children and more competent than their teachers rated them (Vondra, Barnett, & Cicchetti, 1989, 1990). Indeed, normative studies indicate that preschoolers and early school-age children overrate their own competence, demonstrating unrealistic self-perceptions until around the third grade (Ruble, 1983; Stipek, 1984). This suggests that young children, particularly young maltreated children, may describe themselves in overly positive terms. Taken together, these studies yield a mixed picture regarding how maltreated children portray and describe themselves and significant others. Some of the variability may stem from differences in which behavioral domains, such as sexual behavior or aggression, were studied. Overall, however, these studies suggest that representations and emotion regulation strategies both influence maltreated children's portrayals of child and adult characters in their narratives.

I next present preliminary data from a study on maltreated children's narratives that addresses whether maltreated children portray their mental representations or regulate their affects when telling stories. Specific narrative behaviors were selected based on my interest in examining representations and affect regulation strategies relevant for maltreated children. Because much of the prior research has focused on moral behaviors, eight moral behaviors that are particularly relevant for maltreated children were coded in the study: compliance, discipline, acknowledgment of responsibility, avoidance of responsibility, prosocial behavior, affiliative behavior, disobedience, and aggression. Four additional narrative behaviors were selected because they have particular salience to maltreated children: sexual behavior, distress, whether the parents excluded the children from their presence or the children avoided their parents ("avoidance/exclusion"), and whether the subjects described characters negatively in their stories ("negative characterizations"). Because there is evidence that some narrative behaviors, such as aggression and prosocial behavior, show gender differences (Libby & Aries, 1989; Macfie et. al., 1999), I have included gender in all of the analyses. To provide some continuity with previous studies, which vary on whether they have analyzed narrative behaviors for all characters together or for child and parent characters separately, I report the data both ways (the sum of child and parent behaviors does not always equal the total number of narrative behaviors for each category because the children occasionally introduce other types of characters into their stories, such as police officers). The story stems (the initial part of the story that the experimenter begins) were selected to address a range of common events and experiences within families that were expected to evoke the narrative behaviors that are the focus of this report. The study compared the representational hypothesis that children would enact less positive and more negative narrative behaviors with the emotion regulation hypothesis that predicts the reverse findings.

Method

Participants

The sample included 56 five-year-old children who an urban Department of Social Services had referred for services due to issues related to child maltreatment and a comparison group of 27 children who, according to the parents and the state child abuse registry, had not been maltreated. All children in the maltreatment group had been physically abused, sexually abused, or neglected, as determined by a review of state records using the Barnett, Manly, and Cicchetti (1993) system. Fifty-four male and 29 female children were seen. Twenty-nine children were African American, 12 were Hispanic, and 42 were Caucasian. Receptive language scores using the Peabody Picture Vocabulary Test (PPVT) were available for 73 of the 83 children. There were no differences between groups on age, race, or PPVT scores. All families received Aid to Families with Dependent Children.

Procedures

The story stems administered to the children included story stems from the MacArthur Story Stem Battery and some specifically designed for this study (they are described in more detail in Buchsbaum, Toth, Clyman, Cicchetti, & Emde, 1992). The story stems are brief vignettes about a family with a mother, father, and two children dolls who were the same gender as the subject. They pose dilemmas for either a child or parent character to resolve. The child subject is then asked to "show me and tell me what happens now." The examiner employs standardized prompts to assist the child in completing the story. Ten story stems were administered: Nap Story (a child is told to go to bed and then is placed in his or her room between the bed and a toy box), New Horse Story (one child pushes another child off of a toy horse), Moral Dilemma Story (child wants to get a band-aid for an injured peer but is not allowed to touch anything on the bathroom shelf), Exclusion Story (the parents ask the child to play alone so they can be by themselves), Cooking Story (the child is warned not to get too close to the stove, but the child cannot wait for dinner and reaches up and knocks over a pot of gravy, burning himself or herself), Parent Argument Story (parents argue over who lost the car keys), Grocery Store Story (mother sees the child take a candy bar), Bicycle Story (child falls off of a bicycle and hurts his or her knee),

Family Fun Story (children are asked what they would like to do that would be fun for the whole family), and Prohibition Story (children are left alone with a plate of freshly baked cookies).

The children's narratives were videotaped from behind a one-way mirror, and they were later coded from the videotapes by two raters blind to the child's maltreatment status and the study's hypotheses. Twelve types of behaviors were coded each time they occurred in a narrative, based on either the child's verbal statements or actions. The positive actions included compliance with a parental directive, discipline, acknowledgment of responsibility (e.g., "I'm sorry"), prosocial behavior (including empathic statements, helping, and sharing), and affiliative behavior (e.g., hugging, kissing). The negative actions included distress (e.g., pain, sadness, fear, or other indices of distress such as an injury), negative characterizations (e.g., "he's bad"), disobedience, aggression (including expressions of hostility and verbal and physical aggression), avoidance of responsibility (e.g., "he did it"), avoidance/exclusion (in the parent-child relationship), and sexual behavior.

Thirty-four percent of the sample was coded by both raters to assess reliability. The reliability analysis proceeded in stages. The first question was whether the two coders agreed that a classifiable action had occurred. The percent agreements (agreements/[agreements + disagreements]) on whether a classifiable action occurred were calculated for each subject. The median percent agreement per subject was 80%, with a range of 66% to 88% across subjects. Differences in judgment were conferenced by the two raters, and those events that were judged as classifiable actions were further analyzed. Second, those behaviors judged as classifiable actions were then classified into 1 of the 12 behavioral categories. The agreement on which of the 12 types of actions occurred was calculated for each subject and had a median kappa of .97, with a range of .75 to 1.0. Third, raters decided which character enacted each type of action, termed the "agent" here. The median kappa for judging the agent for each type of action was .91, with a range of .80 to .94. For example, if mother gave Dick a Band-aid, the type of action was prosocial, and the mother was coded as agent. The "agent" for distress was the character in distress, and the "agent" for negative attributions was the character who was characterized negatively. I report compliance and disobedience only when a child character engaged in these actions, and I report discipline only when it was enacted by a parent figure. All differences between coders were discussed, and the final conferenced judgments were entered into the data analyses.

Results

A preliminary analysis was conducted to compare the frequency with which maltreated and nonmaltreated children enacted the different types of coded behaviors. Maltreated children depicted 45.9 portrayals and nonmaltreated children depicted 36.8 portrayals in their 10 stories ($t = 3.13$, $p < .01$). There was no difference between female and male subjects in their number of characterizations (43.7 vs. 41.6, respectively, $p < .49$). Accordingly, all analyses of variance (ANOVAs) were conducted on the percentage of each child's actions that were classified within each category (e.g., in analyses of prosocial behavior, the dependent variable is the percentage of each child's coded actions that were prosocial). For all ANOVAs, the arcsine transformation was applied because the data for every type of action were positively skewed. Arcsine transformed percentages for each type of characterization were entered into 12 2 (maltreatment) x 2 (gender) ANOVAs. In addition, for the 73 children for whom PPVT scores were available, correlations between PPVT scores and the 12 different types of narrative portrayals ranged from .01 to .21 (all *ps* > .05).

The first question asked whether there were differences in maltreated and nonmaltreated children's narrative portrayals of 12 types of behaviors. The results for the 12 ANOVAs are presented in table 11.1. The five positive behaviors are listed first. Six of the 12 types of actions demonstrated significant main effects of one or both independent variables. In accordance with a representational hypothesis, the maltreated children portrayed less prosocial behavior, more disobedience, and more sexual behavior in their stories than their nonmaltreated counterparts. In accordance with an emotion regulation hypothesis, the maltreated children portrayed fewer characters in distress than nonmaltreated children did.

There were also significant gender effects. Girls were more likely to portray prosocial and affiliative behavior than boys. A main effect of gender on aggression was qualified by a maltreatment x gender interaction. A post-hoc Student-Newman-Keuls test indicated that maltreated boys had more aggressive actions in their narratives than did maltreated girls, nonmaltreated boys, and nonmaltreated girls.

Table 11.2 presents the untransformed percentages of the different types of portrayals when they are distinguished by whether they were enacted by child or parent characters in the narratives. Eight types of character portrayals were included in these analyses. Compliance, disobedience, and discipline were not analyzed here, as they were only coded when enacted by one character, so the data on these narrative behaviors were presented in table 11.1. Avoidance/exclusion was not further analyzed as 95% of these actions consisted of children avoiding parents. Arcsine transformed percentages for each type of action were entered into 16 2 (maltreatment) x 2 (gender) ANOVAs for each of the 16 agent-action combinations.

There was a main effect of maltreatment status on portrayals of children in distress. Maltreated children portrayed children in distress less often than did nonmaltreated children. In terms of sexual behavior, the child subjects indicated in 56% of the sexual acts that they themselves acted sexually (e.g., "I did it"), rather than one of the characters in the story. Accordingly, sexual behavior was analyzed using an additional ANOVA with the same independent variables (maltreatment and gender), and the dependent measure was the arcsine transformed percentage of actions in which the subject talked about being the agent of the sexual behavior. Maltreated children were more likely to indicate that they themselves enacted sexual behavior than did the nonmaltreated children.

TABLE 11.1 Percentage of Portrayals in Children's Narratives by Maltreatment Status and Gender

Action	Maltreated: Mean % (*SD*)			Nonmaltreated: Mean % (*SD*)				
	Total ($n = 56$)	Female ($n = 17$)	Male ($n = 39$)	Total ($n = 27$)	Female ($n = 12$)	Male ($n = 15$)	F_{group}	F_{gender}
Compliance	7.0 (5.8)	8.9 (7.9)	6.2 (4.5)	7.7 (4.1)	7.5 (3.3)	7.8 (4.7)	0.14	1.28
Discipline	16.8 (6.3)	19.6 (5.1)	15.6 (6.4)	17.8 (7.6)	17.4 (8.2)	18.1 (7.3)	0.01	1.03
Acknowledgment of responsibility	5.5 (3.2)	6.3 (3.8)	5.1 (2.8)	6.4 (3.8)	6.2 (4.4)	6.6 (3.4)	0.20	0.12
Prosocial	4.7 (4.3)	7.4 (5.0)	3.5 (3.3)	7.7 (5.2)	8.2 (4.2)	7.3 (6.0)	4.47*	5.00*
Affiliative	6.6 (3.8)	8.7 (4.2)	5.7 (3.3)	3 (5.2)	10.0 (6.2)	5.1 (2.9)	.11	16.53***
Distress	9.3 (5.2)	7.9 (4.1)	10.0 (5.5)	.6 (6.2)	12.5 (5.20)	12.6 (7.0)	7.13**	0.73
Negative attributions	1.3 (1.8)	0.9 (1.7)	1.4 (1.9)	1.3 (1.9)	0.8 (1.3)	1.6 (2.3)	0.00	1.51
Disobedience	14.7 (3.9)	15.4 (4.2)	14.4 (3.8)	12.7 (6.3)	12.1 (4.1)	13.2 (7.7)	4.81*	0.05
Aggression	18.6 (12.3)	10.6[a] (8.5)	22.1[a,b,c] (12.1)	12.8 (6.8)	11.8[b] (4.3)	13.6[c] (8.3)	0.93	7.10**[d]
Avoidance of responsibility	3.6 (3.7)	2.7 (2.5)	4.1 (4.1)	2.9 (3.5)	3.6 (3.0)	2.4 (3.8)	0.68	0.27
Avoidance/Exclusion	3.7 (2.6)	3.8 (2.4)	3.6 (2.6)	4.3 (3.0)	3.8 (2.2)	4.7 (3.6)	0.36	0.06
Sexual behavior	1.8 (2.6)	1.9 (2.3)	1.8 (2.7)	0.3 (1.0)	0.2 (0.8)	0.3 (1.2)	10.69**	0.05

*$p \leq .05$.

**$p \leq .01$.

***$p \leq .001$.

[a,b,c]Identical superscripts indicate groups that differ at the .05 level.

[d]Group x gender interaction, $F = 4.68$, $p \leq .05$.

Gender effects were also significant. Girls were more likely to portray children acting prosocially than were boys. Girls were also more likely than boys to portray affiliative behavior in children. For affiliative behavior by parents, the main effect of gender was qualified by an interaction between maltreatment and gender. A post-hoc Student-Newman-Keuls test indicated that nonmaltreated girls portrayed parents as more affiliative than did nonmaltreated boys. Boys were more likely than girls to portray children as aggressive in the narratives. There was an interaction between maltreatment and gender on the portrayal of parents as aggressive. A post-hoc Student-Newman-Keuls test indicated that maltreated boys portrayed parents as more aggressive in their narratives than did maltreated girls and nonmaltreated boys. Maltreated girls were less aggressive than nonmaltreated girls.

Study Discussion

The results suggest that the portrayals of characters in maltreated children's narratives reflect both their representations and their emotion regulation strategies. First, a number of portrayals in the narratives provided support for the representational hypothesis. The maltreated children were more likely than their nonmaltreated counterparts to portray child characters disobeying their parents in the stories and more likely to portray sexual behavior in their narratives. The maltreated children were also less likely to portray prosocial behavior in their stories, although only a trend remained for parent prosocial behaviors when parent and child behaviors were examined separately. The maltreated boys were more likely than nonmaltreated boys and maltreated girls to portray parents as aggressive. It is surprising that there were no differences between the maltreated and nonmaltreated children in the portrayal of child characters as aggressive.

The study also provides partial support for the view that maltreated children's emotion regulation strategies influence how they portray characters in their story stem narratives. Maltreated children were less likely to portray children in distress than were nonmaltreated children. Because maltreated children use less internal state language than nonmaltreated children (Beeghly & Cicchetti, 1994), I reanalyzed the data excluding behavioral expressions of distress (e.g., "she fell"), only including negative affect language (e.g., "she's sad"). No effects of maltreatment or gender were found, suggesting that a deficit in the use of internal state language did not account for these findings. The maltreated girls were less aggressive than the nonmaltreated girls, which may also indicate the effects of their emotion regulation strategies.

Although maltreated children were more likely than nonmaltreated children to portray sexual behavior in their narratives, these data are nevertheless suggestive that the children may have been regulating their emotions when they told these particular stories. The maltreated children's stories had more than 10 times as many sexual acts in which they identified themselves as the character who engaged in sexual behavior than in the nonmaltreated children's stories, even though there were no significant differences in the children's portrayals of *char-*

TABLE 11.2: Percentage of Portrayals by Agent in Maltreated and Nonmaltreated Children's Narratives by Gender

Action	Maltreated: Mean % (*SD*)			Nonmaltreated: Mean %(*SD*)				
	Total ($n = 56$)	Female ($n = 17$)	Male ($n = 39$)	Total ($n = 27$)	Female ($n = 12$)	Male ($n = 15$)	F group	G gender
Acknowledgment of responsibility								
Child agent	3.2 (2.8)	3.6 (3.3)	3.0 (2.6)	3.6 (3.6)	3.9 (4.2)	3.3 (3.0)	0.17	0.57
Parent agent	1.6 (2.0)	1.8 (2.3)	1.6 (1.8)	2.2 (2.5)	1.7 (2.4)	2.6 (2.6)	0.41	0.54
Prosocial								
Child agent	1.9 (2.2)	2.7 (2.5)	2.0 (2.0)	2.6 (3.3)	3.9 (4.2)	1.6 (2.1)	.91	7.64****
Parent agent	2.5 (3.4)	4.3 (4.6)	1.8 (2.4)	4.8 (4.8)	4.5 (3.5)	5.1 (5.7)	3.68*[a]	1.12
Affiliative								
Child agent	2.0 (2.6)	2.9 (2.9)	1.55 (2.4)	1.5 (2.5)	2.2 (2.8)	.9 (2.1)	1.3	4.6**
Parent agent	1.6 (2.0)	1.8 (1.8)	1.48 (2.1)	1.7 (3.4)	3.4 (4.5)	.3 (.9)	.16	8.6**[b]
Distress								
Child agent	8.3 (4.9)	7.6 (4.0)	8.6 (5.3)	11.6 (5.9)	11.4 (5.3)	11.7 (6.5)	5.51**	0.32
Parent agent	1.1 (2.2)	0.2 (0.6)	1.4 (2.6)	0.6 (1.2)	0.8 (1.2)	0.5 (1.3)	0.02	0.42[c]
Negative attributions								
Child agent	0.6 (1.2)	0.7 (1.3)	0.6 (1.2)	0.7 (1.7)	0.2 (0.8)	1.1 (2.2)	0.15	0.99
Parent agent	0.4 (1.1)	0.2 (0.7)	0.5 (1.2)	0.5 (1.1)	0.5 (1.1)	0.4 (1.2)	0.02	0.17

Aggression								
Child agent	14.0 (9.9)	7.7 (6.2)	16.7 (10.0)	9.3 (6.5)	7.6 (4.0)	10.6 (7.8)	1.89	7.12***
Parent agent	3.8 (4.0)	1.7 (2.5)[1,2]	4.7 (4.1)[1,3]	3.0 (2.7)	3.9 (1.7)[2]	2.3 (3.1)[3]	0.20	.01[d]
Avoidance of responsibility								
Child agent	2.7 (3.2)	1.9 (2.0)	3.0 (3.6)	1.4 (2.2)	2.2 (2.6)	0.8 (1.8)	3.06*	0.73
Parent agent	0.8 (1.6)	0.8 (1.5)	0.9 (1.7)	1.3 (2.6)	1.0 (2.1)	1.6 (2.9)	0.30	0.26
Sexual behavior								
Child agent	0.3 (1.1)	0.3 (0.8)	0.3 (1.2)	0.1 (0.3)	0.0 (0.0)	0.1 (0.4)	1.42	0.15
Parent agent	0.3 (0.9)	0.6 (1.1)	0.2 (0.8)	0.1 (0.6)	0.0 (0.0)	0.2 (0.8)	2.33	0.44[e]
Subject agent	1.1 (1.9)	1.0 (1.7)	1.1 (2.0)	0.1 (0.5)	0.2 (0.8)	0.0 (0.0)	7.95***	0.08

[a]For group x gender interaction $F = 2.783+$.
[b]For group x gender interaction $F = 5.90^{*}$.
[c]For group x gender interaction $F = 3.61+$.
[d]For group x gender interaction $F = 14.12^{***}$. Identical subscripts ([1–3]) indicate groups that differ at the .05 level.
[e]For group x gender interaction $F = 2.86+$.
$^{*}p \leq .10$.
$^{**}p \leq .05$.
$^{***}p \leq .01$.
$^{****}p \leq .001$.

acters acting sexually in the stories. The maltreated children's relinquishment of the narrative frame, often to answer the examiners' inquiries about who acted sexually when it was ambiguous, may reflect their attempt to regulate the emotions evoked in enacting the sexual behavior. They may have characterized themselves as the sexual perpetrator rather than an adult doll figure to lessen their sense of victimization and to actively master their fears. Further analyses of sexual behavior by the subtype of maltreatment were precluded as only 14 children in the sample were known to have been sexually abused. Overall, these findings need to be replicated due to the limited sample size, the multiple comparisons, and the need to duplicate these definitions of which behaviors indicate the influence of the children's representations and which behaviors indicate the influence of affect regulation strategies.

It is possible, however, that maltreated children are more likely to regulate their emotions by avoiding certain enactments in their narratives. Indeed, distressed children, whether they are distressed due to painful experiences or emotional or behavioral problems, may be more likely to regulate their affect through the use of avoidance in their narratives. Children who are emotionally healthy may have less need and be more able to explore emotional issues when telling stories than their more distressed counterparts. Further research is needed to test this hypothesis.

Overall, both groups of children showed wide variability in their portrayals of both parent and child characters, despite the group differences found. This may reflect that maltreated children are quite heterogeneous as a group. Although legal maltreatment is related to a range of inadequate parenting behaviors (Rogsoch, Cicchetti, Shields, & Toth, 1995), there is substantial variability in maltreating parents' caregiving behaviors. Similarly, maltreated children do not consistently display maladaptive behaviors (Knutson, 1995), and we may expect their portrayals of child characters to show similar variability.

The study also illustrates some of the benefits and tradeoffs of different data-analytic strategies. First, testing hypotheses about individual narrative actions (e.g., child compliance or prosocial behavior), rather than aggregating these behaviors in the analyses, has both benefits and disadvantages. The approach risks the loss of power and the problems of multiple comparisons. But closely related categories of narrative portrayals did not always show the same effects of maltreatment. For example, although maltreated children were more likely than the nonmaltreated children to portray children as disobedient, they did not characterize children as less compliant with parents' directives. Furthermore, the correlations between the individual types of character portrayals may be low, as they were in this study. Additionally, while theory may be helpful in guiding the aggregation of narrative behaviors into categories such as moral behaviors, there is limited theory to guide the aggregation of behaviors into overarching categories that are most likely to reflect either the child's mental representations or emotion regulation strategies. We have limited theory to indicate which types of narrative portrayals are most likely to be portrayed in children's stories based on the child's mental representations, and which narrative portrayals are most likely to be excluded or transformed in accord with the child's emotion regulation goals.

Second, the data also suggest the value of including gender in the analyses, as there were significant gender differences for aggression, affiliative, and prosocial behavior, as in previous studies. Another incentive to include gender in the analyses is that risk status and gender may interact in their effects on narrative behaviors. In this study, the maltreated boys portrayed parents as more aggressive than the nonmaltreated boys and the maltreated girls did. Zahn-Waxler and colleagues also found an interaction between gender and risk status (Zahn-Waxler, Cole, Richardson, Friedman, Michel, & Belouad, 1994). In response to story stems that portrayed a character in distress in that study, the high-risk girls enacted more prosocial behavior than the moderate-risk girls and all three groups of boys. Only by disaggregating the different types of narrative characterizations and including gender in the analyses can these patterns be identified and their meaning understood.

General Discussion

This section reconsiders the two influences on children's narrative portrayals that have been addressed in this chapter: children's mental representations and their emotion regulation strategies. This discussion identifies additional complexities in both constructs that need to be addressed to draw inferences about children's mental representations from their narrative portrayals.

The chapter began with the hypothesis that children develop mental representations that encode their experiences of themselves and their parents that subsequently influence the stories they tell. These might be called cognitive representations, because they encode the children's memories, beliefs, and expectations about parent-child interactions. However, children also develop moral representations. Moral representations are prescriptive. They encode how the child believes one ought to behave, or how it is morally permissible to behave. Moral representations include beliefs such as "I should help others" or "I should share my toys." Although moral representations are beliefs, they are distinguished from other beliefs by the child's attitude that people should behave in accordance with the belief. By moral representation, we mean that the child's attitude is that one ought to (or it is permissible to) behave in accordance with the proposition, not mere knowledge of the moral rules. Children may or may not behave in accordance with their moral representations.

Most of the behaviors researchers analyze in studies of children's narratives are moral behaviors, such as compliance, disobedience, and prosocial behavior. However, it is rarely clear if a child's narrative enactment reflects a cognitive or a moral representation. For example, we do not know if the disobedience that the maltreated children portrayed in their stories is indicative of their representations of how they behave (a cognitive representation) or of how they believe it is permissible for them to behave (a moral representation). The children's narrative behavior offers few clues to support this judgment. Indeed, different studies interpret the identical narrative behaviors as evidence of cognitive representations (e.g., McCrone et. al., 1994; Macfie et. al., 1999) and as evidence of moral representations (Kochanska, Padavich, & Koenig, 1996). It will be important for future research to distinguish these two constructs.

There is also additional complexity in understanding how maltreated children's emotion regulation strategies influence their narrative enactments. I have focused on one type of emotion regulation strategy so far. In this strategy, children avoid or modify their portrayals of characters, so that the resulting portrayal is inconsistent with their cognitive or moral representations. For example, the maltreated children may have avoided portraying children in distress in their stories to regulate the negative emotions that the stories evoked. But the psychoanalytic writings on which these ideas are based emphasize that children's play is based on both their wishes and fears. They suggest that play enactments can be based on fantasy rather than experiences and that children repeat events in their play to master their anxiety (Freud, 1920/1955; Waelder, 1993; Emde, 1995). The children in this study who enacted sexual behavior in their stories may have been attempting to actively regulate the complex emotions the sexual abuse memories evoked. Reenacting the traumatic events may help them to make sense of their experiences, to regulate the affects evoked in remembering or portraying those experiences, and to desensitize themselves from their impact. Although psychoanalysts have emphasized that children repeat behaviors to master their anxiety, children might reenact events that evoke any emotion, not just anxiety. This type of emotion regulation strategy, then, can result in children portraying characters in ways that are *consistent* with their cognitive and moral representations, in contrast to emotion regulation strategies that lead children to portray characters in ways that are *inconsistent* with their cognitive and moral representations. The observation that a child is portraying characters in ways that are consistent with that child's cognitive representations does not rule out the possibility that they are also doing so to regulate their emotions. Indeed, they may be doing both.

The related clinical observation that traumatized children both portray and avoid portraying their traumatic experiences in their stories has been codified in the diagnosis of posttraumatic stress disorder (*DSM IV*; American Psychiatric Association [APA], 1994). The clinical criteria include reexperiencing the trauma, including play reenactments, and avoiding cognitions and affects that are associated with the trauma, including avoiding reenacting the traumatic event in play. While it is known that children traumatized by sexual abuse (August & Foreman, 1989) and natural disasters (Bloch, Silber, & Perry, 1958; Newman, 1976; Saylor, Swenson, & Powell, 1992) reenact their traumatic experiences in their play, little is known about how physical abuse or neglect affects children's specific play reenactments.

Philosophers use a construct termed propositional attitudes that unify our understanding of all four of the influences on children's narrative behavior that have been discussed. Cognitive representations, moral representations, emotion regulation strategies that result in portrayals consistent with the child's cognitive and moral representations, and emotion regulation strategies that result in portrayals inconsistent with the child's cognitive and moral representations can all be conceptualized in terms of the child's propositional attitudes. Propositional attitudes are a type of mental representation that incorporates both a proposition, such as "Mommy helps me if I am hurt," with an attitude toward that proposition, such as the *belief* that the proposition is true. Beliefs, desires, and fears, for example, are all propositional attitudes. Propositional attitudes are central components of folk psychology theories of how the mind functions.

The constructs under discussion here incorporate both a proposition and an attitude toward that proposition. The child's verbal description or physical enactment in the narrative communicates the proposition. For example, in telling a story, a child subject may say "mommy helps her," or a child character may refuse to go to bed when told to by mother. With cognitive representations, the attitude is the child's memories or beliefs that this has occurred or the child's expectations that this will occur. For moral representations, the attitude is the child's belief that mother should help her. An alternative way to conceptualize both types of emotion regulation strategies is to think of them as "affective representations" (see chapter 1). Affective representations are propositions that enable a child to express or modulate emotions. The child's "attitude" toward the proposition is the emotion: for example, a child fears her parent's aggression.

The central dilemma in interpreting children's narrative portrayals is that the narratives typically communicate only the proposition and not the child's "attitude" toward the proposition. If a child subject portrays a child character as disobedient, we do not know if the child believes he or she is disobedient, believes it is permissible to be disobedient, or is portraying the fear the child experiences in enacting disobedience in an attempt to master that fear. The narrative reveals the proposition, but additional data are usually needed to infer the child's attitude toward the proposition.

Researchers need additional strategies to draw inferences about the type of propositional attitudes that are revealed in children's narratives. A number of research strategies may be helpful to address these issues. Consider again the question of which type of representation influences a child to portray a mother as sensitively caring for her child in the narratives. Studies can test if the child's (inconsistent) affective representations influence the narrative portrayal, in contrast to either cognitive, moral, or consistent affective representations, by comparing groups that differ in their parenting experiences, as in this chapter. But additional studies are needed to determine if narrative portrayals of positive caregiving behavior reflect the children's experiences or their sense of what is right. An independent assessment of the children's developing sense of internalized conscience, or another measure of their expectations or experience, is needed. Another possibility, for example, is that studies could examine relations between children's narrative portrayals and their parenting experiences, controlling for the children's observed moral behavior, or vice versa. Simultaneous measures of parenting and moral behavior will be needed to test if narrative portrayals differentially relate to cognitive or moral representations. And the more that the quality of parenting and the children's moral behavior covary in the sample, the more difficult it will be to test the hypothesis. Finally, additional measures of the child's emotion regulation strategies that directly measure the child's emotion expression and coping strategies while telling the narratives may be helpful in discriminating between affective representations that are consistent or inconsistent with the child's cognitive and moral representations.

In the beginning of this chapter, I observed that one incentive for examining maltreated children's representations was that it may help to explain whether they subsequently maltreat their own children. But the development of maltreating behavior, in some children, may be more closely related to their developing moral representations that such behavior is permissible than to their developing cognitive representations, their knowledge of how their parents raised them. As this example illustrates, further knowledge about cognitive and moral representations, as well as affect regulation strategies, may contribute to our understanding of a range of developmental outcomes for maltreated children.

NOTE

This research was supported by funds from the John D. and Catherine T. MacArthur Foundation Network on Early Childhood Transitions, an NIMH Institutional Postdoctoral Research Training Grant #5-P32-MH15442-14, and an NIMH Scientist Development Award for Clinicians #1K20 MH01279-01. I acknowledge helpful discussions with Dr. Robert N. Emde and Dr. David Oppenheim, and Dr. Mary Jo Coiro's contributions to the data analyses. I am very greatful to Dr. Sheree Toth and Dr. Jody Todd-Manly for their contributions to the data collection and conceptual work on the original study.

REFERENCES

Alessandri, S. M. (1991). Play and social behaviors in maltreated preschoolers. *Development and Psychopathology, 3*(2), 191–205.

American Psychiatric Association. (1994). *Diagnostic and statistical manual of mental disorders* (4th ed.). Washington, DC: American Psychiatric Association.

August, R. L., & Foreman, B. D. (1989). A comparison of sexually and nonsexually abused children's behavioral responses to anatomically correct dolls. *Child Psychiatry and Human Development, 20,* 39–47.

Barnett, D., Manly, J. T., & Cicchetti, D. (1993). Defining child maltreatment: The interface between policy and research. In D. Cicchetti & S. L. Toth (Eds.), *Child abuse, child development, and social policy* (pp. 7–73). Norwood, NJ: Ablex.

Beeghly, M., & Cicchetti, D. (1994). Child maltreatment, attachment, and the self system: Emergence of an internal state lexicon in toddlers at high social risk. *Development and Psychopathology, 6,* 5–30.

Bloch, D., Silber, E., & Perry, S. (1958). Some factors in the emotional reaction of children to disaster. *American Journal of Psychiatry, 133,* 416–422.

Bretherton, I., Ridgeway, D., & Cassidy, J. (1990). Assessing internal working model of the attachment relationship: An attachment story completion task for 3-year-olds. In M. T. Greenberg, D. Cicchetti, & E. M. Cummings (Eds.), *Attachment in the preschool years* (pp. 273–308). Chicago: University of Chicago Press.

Bruner, J. (1986). *Actual minds, possible worlds.* Cambridge, MA: Harvard University Press.

Bruner, J. (1990). Culture and human development: A new look. *Human Development, 33,* 344–355.

Buchsbaum, H. K., & Emde, R. N. (1990). Play narratives in thirty-six-month-old children: Early moral development and family relationships. *Psychoanalytic Study of the Child, 40,* 129–155.

Buchsbaum, H. K., Toth, S. L., Clyman, R. B., Cicchetti, D., & Emde, R. N. (1992). The use of a narrative story stem technique with maltreated children: Implications for theory and practice. *Development and Psychopathology, 4,* 603–625.

Cassidy, J. (1988). Child-mother attachment and the self in six-year-olds. *Child Development, 59,* 121–134.

Dean, A. L., Malik, M. M., Richards, W., & Stringer, S. A. (1986). Effects of parental maltreatment on children's conceptions of interpersonal relationships. *Developmental Psychology, 22*(5), 617–626.

Emde, R. N. (1995). Fantasy and beyond: A current developmental perspective on Freud's "Creative Writers and Daydreaming." *Monograph Series of the International Journal of Psycho-Analysis* (pp. 133–163). New Haven: Yale University Press.

Emde, R. N., Kubicek, L., & Oppenheim, D. (1997). Imaginative reality observed during early language development. *International Journal of Psycho-Analysis, 78*(1), 115–133.

Farver, J. M., & Frosch, D. L. (1996). L. A. stories: Aggression in preschoolers' spontaneous narratives after the riots of 1992. *Child Development, 67,* 19–32.

Freud, S. (1955). Beyond the pleasure principle. In J. Strachey (Ed. & Trans.), *The standard edition of the complete psychological works of Sigmund Freud* (Vol. 18, pp. 7–64). London: Hogarth Press. (Original work published 1920)

Herzberger, S., Potts, D. A., & Dillon, M. (1981). Abusive and nonabusive parental treatment from the child's perspective. *Journal of Consulting & Clinical Psychology, 49*(1), 81–90.

Kaufman, J., & Zigler, E. (1987). Do abused children become abusive parents? *American Journal of Orthopsychiatry, 57,* 186–192.

Klagsbrun, M., & Bowlby, J. (1976). Responses to separation from parents: A clinical test for young children. *British Journal of Projective Psychology, 21,* 7–21.

Knutson, J. F. (1995). Psychological characteristics of maltreated children: Putative risk factors and consequences. *Annual Review of Psychology, 46,* 401–431.

Kochanska, G., Padavich, D., & Koenig, A. (1996). Children's narratives about hypothetical moral dilemmas and objective measures of their conscience: Mutual relations and socialization antecedents. *Child Development, 67*(4), 1420–1436.

Libby, M., & Aries, E. (1989). Gender differences in preschool children's narrative fantasy. *Psychology of Women Quarterly, 13,* 293–306.

Lynch, M., & Cicchetti, D. (1991). Patterns of relatedness in maltreated and nonmaltreated children: Connections among multiple representational models. *Development and Psychopathology, 3,* 207–226.

Macfie, J., Toth, S. L., Rogosch, F. A., Robinson, J., Emde, R. N., & Cicchetti, D. (1999). Effect of maltreatment on preschoolers' narrative representations of responses to relieve distress and of role reversal. *Developmental Psychology, 35*(2), 460–465.

Main, M., Kaplan, N., & Cassidy, J. (1985). Security in infancy, childhood and adulthood: A move to the level of representation. *Monographs of the Society for Research in Child Development, 50,* 66–104.

McCrone, E. R., Egeland, B., Kalkoske, M., & Carlson, E. A. (1994). Relations between early maltreatment and mental representations of relationships assessed with projective storytelling in middle childhood. *Development and Psychopathology, 6,* 99–120.

Mize, J., & Ladd, G. W. (1988). Predicting preschoolers' peer behavior and status from their interpersonal strategies: A comparison of verbal and enactive responses to hypothetical social dilemma. *Developmental Psychology, 24*(6), 782–788.

Newman, J. (1976). Children of disaster: Clinical observations at Buffalo Creek. *American Journal of Psychiatry, 133,* 306–312.

Oppenheim, D., Emde, R. N., & Warren, S. (1997). Children's narrative representations of mothers: Their development and associations with child and mother adaptation. *Child Development, 68*(1), 127–138.

Oppenheim, D., & Waters, H. S. (1995). Narrative processes and attachment representations: Issues of development and assessment. *Monographs of the Society for Research in Child Development, 60,* 197–215.

Reidy, T. J. (1977). The aggressive characteristics of abused and neglected children. *Journal of Clinical Psychology, 33*(4), 1140–1145.

Rogsoch, F. A., Cicchetti, D., Shields, A., & Toth, S. L. (1995). Parenting dysfunction in child maltreatment. In M. H. Bornstein (Ed.), *Handbook of parenting: Vol. 4. Applied and practical considerations of parenting* (pp. 127–159). Hillsdale, NJ: Lawrence Erlbaum.

Ruble, D. N. (1983). The development of social comparison processes and their role in achievement-related self-socialization. In E. T. Higgins, D. N. Ruble, & W. W. Hartup (Eds.), *Social cognition and social development: A sociocultural perspective* (pp. 134–157). New York: Cambridge University Press.

Saylor, C., Swenson, C., & Powell, P. (1992). Hurricane Hugo blows down the broccoli: Preschoolers' post-disaster play and adjustment. *Child Psychiatry and Human Development, 22,* 139–149.

Scarlett, W. G., & Wolf, D. (1979). When it's only make-believe: The construction of a boundary between fantasy and reality in storytelling. *New Directions for Child Development, 6,* 29–40.

Shouldice, A., & Stevenson-Hinde, J. (1992). Coping with security distress: The separation anxiety test and attachment classification at 4.5 years. *Journal of Child Psychiatry, 33*(2), 331–348.

Slough, N. M., & Greenberg, M. T. (1990). Five-year-olds' representations of separation from parents: Responses from the perspective of self and other. In I. Bretherton & M. W. Watson (Eds.), *Children's perspectives on the family: Vol. 48. New Directions for Child Development* (pp. 67–84). San Francisco: Jossey-Bass.

Solomon, J., George, C., & De Jong, A. (1995). Children classified as controlling at age six: Evidence of disorganized representational strategies and aggression at home and at school. *Development and Psychopathology, 7,* 447–463.

Stipek, D. J. (1984). Sex differences in children's attributions for success and failure on math and spelling tests. *Sex Roles, 11*(11–12), 969–981.

Straker, G., & Jacobson, R. S. (1981). Aggression, emotional maladjustment, and empathy in the abused child. *Developmental Psychology, 17*(6), 762–765.

Thompson, R. A. (1994). Emotion regulation: A theme in search of definition. *Monographs of the Society for Research in Child Development, 59,* 25–52.

Toth, S. L., Cicchetti, D., Macfie, J., & Emde, R. N. (1997). Representations of self and other in the narratives of neglected, physically abused, and sexually abused preschoolers. *Development and Psychopathology, 9,* 781–796.

Vondra, J., Barnett, D., & Cicchetti, D. (1989). Perceived and actual competence among maltreated and comparison school children. *Development and Psychopathology, 1,* 237–255.

Vondra, J., Barnett, D., & Cicchetti, D. (1990). Self-concept, motivation, and competence among preschoolers from maltreating and comparison families. *Child Abuse and Neglect, 14,* 525–540.

Waelder, R. (1993). The psychoanalytic theory of play. *Psychoanalytic Quarterly,* 208–224.

Warren, S. L., Oppenheim, D., & Emde, R. N. (1996). Can emotions and themes in children's play predict behavior problems? *Journal of the American Academy of Child and Adolescent Psychiatry, 34,* 1331–1337.

Zahn-Waxler, C., Cole, P. M., Richardson, D. T., Friedman, R. J., Michel, M. K., & Belouad, F. (1994). Social problem solving in disruptive preschool children: Reactions to hypothetical situations of conflict and distress. *Merrill-Palmer Quarterly, 40*(1), 98–119.

Zahn-Waxler, C., Cole, P. M., Welsh, J. D., & Fox, N. (1995). Psychophysiological correlates of empathy and prosocial behaviors in preschool children with behavior problems. *Development and Psychopathology,* 7, 27–48.

Zahn-Waxler, C., Schmitz, S., Fulker, D., Robinson, J., & Emde, R. (1996). Behavior problems in 5-year-old monozygotic and dizygotic twins: Genetic and environmental influences, patterns of regulation, and internalization of control. *Development and Psychopathology, 8,* 103–122.

SUSAN L. WARREN

12

Narratives in Risk and Clinical Populations

The play narrative approach is useful for studying children at risk and with identified disorders. It provides a measure, obtained directly from the child, of enacted themes and representations related to interpersonal relationship experiences. The ability to examine internal representations is useful for both developmental researchers and clinicians because it is difficult for the young child to directly report views and feelings (Harter & Pike, 1984). Play narratives allow children to express their views of themselves and others in a manner that is emotionally meaningful and fun.

Narrative representations may be multidetermined but are likely influenced by children's perceptions of their life experiences. Children may convey in their narratives their views of themselves and others through their representations of the child protagonist doll and parent and sibling dolls. Children may also demonstrate through their narratives their strategies for dealing with particular challenges and their expectations for the outcome. Play narratives also provide an opportunity for the expression of wishes and fantasies and conflict resolution (Warren, Oppenheim, & Emde, 1996).

This chapter summarizes the current research on narratives in at-risk and clinical populations. Although findings are only preliminary and considerably overlap across risk areas, this summary could aid clinicians and clinical researchers. The first part of the chapter summarizes information obtained from empirical research with children at risk for disorder. Aspects of narratives pertaining to the following risk areas are reviewed: troubled parent-child relationships, low competence/self-esteem, externalizing and internalizing behavior problems, and child maltreatment. The second part of the chapter presents impressionistic information related to use of the narrative procedures with clinical populations. Areas of further inquiry and potential uses of story stem narratives (SSNs) in clinical practice are also explored.

Empirical Research in Children at Risk for Disorder

Troubled Parent-Child Relationships

Much early work with children's SSNs has centered on associations with attachment and children's internal representations of the caregiving relationship. Children with insecure attachment likely have not experienced consistent and sensitive care (Ainsworth, Blehar, Waters, & Wall, 1978) and likely have experienced difficulties in their relationships with their caregivers. Research concerning the associations between troubled parent-child relationships and narratives may provide the clinician with additional insight into a child's views of his or her relationships with parents and others. In addition, children with troubled-parent relationships are likely at risk for clinical disorders (Warren et al., 1997).

Cassidy (1988) administered six narratives concerning attachment themes to 52 low-risk, nonclinical children approximately 6 years of age. In general, children who described the doll protagonist as someone valuable and worthy, the mother as providing safety and protection, and the relationship with the mother as special and warm were classified as having a secure relationship according to the scale developed by Main and Cassidy (1988). These children also tended to end their stories positively. Children who portrayed the doll protagonist as isolated or rejected, denied difficulties, and denied the importance of the mother-child relationship generally were classified as avoidant (Group A). Children who displayed violent, hostile, negative, or bizarre behavior in the protagonist doll and a disorganized relationship with the mother were generally classified as insecure/controlling (Group D). This work suggests that children tend to portray the doll protagonist and parent-child relationships in a way that corresponds to their self-image and their own relationships.Troubled parent-child interactions in children's play narratives might relate to the child's experience of his own troubled parent-child relationship.

Based on children's play narratives, Bretherton, Prentiss, and Ridgeway (1990) and Bretherton, Ridgeway, and Cassidy (1990) were similarly able to delineate which low-risk, nonclinical three-year-old children were securely attached versus those who were not. Attachment was classified at 18 months with the Strange Situation Procedure (Ainsworth et al., 1978) and at 3 years of age with a procedure developed by Cassidy, Marvin, and the MacArthur Attachment Group (1987). Children who were securely attached addressed the story issues openly and produced benign resolutions in which the parents were depicted as caring and the child as competent. In contrast, children who were insecurely attached tended to avoid the story issue, demonstrated odd or incoherent responses, and enacted unusual or violent endings (such as abandonment or car crashes).

Bretherton, Ridgeway, and Cassidy were not able to distinguish specific types of insecure attachment (Group A vs. Group C vs. Group D or disorganized classification) with the narratives. However, they found associations with a number of other attachment and family measures including security scores derived from the Waters and Deane (1985) Attachment Q-sorts at 25 months. Increased marital satisfaction (rated with the Dyadic Adjustment Scale; Spanier, 1976) and family adaptability and cohesion (rated with the Family Adaptation and Cohesiveness Scales [FACES II]; Olson, Bell, & Portner, 1983), as rated by mothers, were also meaningfully related to attachment security in the children's narratives. These studies support the previous work, suggesting that troubled parent-child relationships in the narratives may relate to insecure attachment and children's experiences of their own troubled relationships.

In a study focusing on narrative process and cognitive variables, Waters, Rodrigues, and Ridgeway (1998) examined the stories of 24 children from Bretherton, Prentiss, and Ridgeway's (1990) original sample at 37 and 54 months of age. Stories were coded for the number of idea units (content elaboration) and for how well the stories approximated a prototypic script based on attachment theory. Typical prototypical script elements included (1) child explores away from the caregiver, (2) child wants contact or returns if necessary, (3) some difficulty or threat arises in the story, (4) the caregiver approaches or the child seeks proximity, (5) the difficulty is resolved, (6) contact with the caregiver allows the child to return to exploration. Both content elaboration and prototypic scriptedness significantly related to attachment security as measured with the E. Waters Attachment Q-sort (Waters & Deane, 1985), even after controlling for developmental (Bayley) and vocabulary scores. This research suggests that the process by which the child tells the narratives may be just as informative as the actual content matter of the stories, with children who have secure attachment relationships telling more elaborate and coherent stories than children with insecure attachment relationships (Oppenheim & Waters, 1995).

In another study, Solomon, George, and deJong (1995) administered play narratives to 69 low-risk, nonclinical 6-year-old children. They examined the parent-child relationship by coding the child's behavior in a 5-minute reunion after separation from the mother (Main & Cassidy, 1988). The parent-child relationship classification related significantly to classification of the children's play narratives. Children with secure parent-child relationships (Group B) told "confident" stories with resolution of negative events (caregiver dolls rescuing the child dolls) and child dolls showing competent behavior and pleasure with reunion. Controlling children who were punitive in relation to their parents (Group D and unclassifiable children) told "frightened" stories with uncontrolled, unresolved danger themes. Controlling children who showed caregiving in relation to their parents told "frightened," very constricted stories. Ambivalent children (Group C) told "busy" stories with much digression and attention to irrelevant detail. This research supports the earlier work and suggests that children's differential narrative responses tend to reflect differences in parent-child relationships.

In a study to validate the Manchester Child Attachment Story Task (MCAST; Green, Stanley, Smith, & Goldwyn, 2000), a play narrative procedure designed to provide preschool attachment classifications, Goldwyn et al. described the relations they found between the 53 nonclinical, low-risk 6-year-old children's narrative responses and other measures of attachment. Ratings of insecure attachment on the MCAST were significantly associated with ratings of insecure attachment for the children on the Separation Anxiety Test (Hansburg, 1972) but not with measures of child temperament. Narratives classified as showing insecure attachment could include denying the story difficulties, leaving the parent doll out of the resolution (avoidant attachment) or dispute, and anger between the child doll and caregiver doll (ambivalent attachment). In other findings, ratings of disorganized attachment on the MCAST were significantly correlated with maternal ratings of unresolved status on the Adult Attachment Interview (AAI; Main & Goldwyn, 1985–1994) and teacher reports of behavior problems in the children. Narratives classified as showing disorganized attachment could include contradictory and disoriented behaviors, direct fear of the parent doll, and freezing or stilling. This research supports some of the previous findings, showing differential linkages between specific narrative responses and attachment-related phenomena.

In a study focusing on preschoolers' characterizations of multiple family relationships during doll play, McHale, Johnson, and Sinclair (1999) asked 49 nonclinical, low-risk 4-year-old children to tell stories about happy, sad, mad, and worried families. Doll aggression was significantly related to maternal ratings of family conflict, and doll affection was significantly related to maternal ratings of family cohesion. No such associations were found between doll stories about a day at school and maternal family ratings. Thus, the relationships children display between the dolls in their narratives may correspond at times to real-life relationship experiences.

In summary, children who may have troubled parent-child relationships may tell stories that

1. portray the child doll negatively (e.g., as incompetent, isolated, rejected, hostile, or bizarre);
2. negatively portray the relationship of the parent and child dolls (e.g., disorganized, conflictual, unsupportive);
3. do not address interpersonal issues by digressing and focusing on irrelevant details;
4. avoid important story themes or are constricted in their storytelling;
5. produce incoherent, contradictory, disorganized, or chaotic stories in which danger themes are not resolved;
6. include less elaborate and less coherent stories; and
7. include less prototypical attachment themes.

Low Competence/Self-Esteem

Some of the narrative research that has focused on parent-child relationships and attachment processes has examined issues related to child competence and self-esteem. Although these developmental processes are closely related theoretically, additional influences may potentially influence self-competence and self-esteem as children develop. Low competence and low self-esteem frequently accompany psychopathology (Fleming & Offord, 1990). Thus, narrative responses that relate to low competence and low self-esteem can be useful for predicting risk and assessing these emotional processes in a clinical population.

Page (1998) examined the narratives of 66 nonclinical 4-year-old children from postdivorce families living primarily in the custody of their mothers. The families were mostly Caucasian and middle class. Narrative representations of nurturant fathers and clear family boundaries (e.g., acknowledging in the stories that the parents do not share the same household) significantly related to greater social competence of the children as measured with the Student-Teacher Relationship Scale (Pianta & Steinberg, 1991), Preschool Behavior Questionnaire (PBQ; Behar, 1977), and Preschool Competence Questionnaire (Olson, 1985). In addition, children who would have the child doll seek proximity with the mother doll when threatened were significantly more likely to show competence and less likely to show behavior problems, as measured with the PBQ. This research suggests that how the child portrays the child doll relationships with the parent dolls in the stories may significantly predict competent child doll behaviors in the preschool setting.

Verschueren, Marcoen, and Schoefs (1996) studied 95 nonclinical, low-risk 5-year-old children and found that children who portrayed positive and open interactions with a responsive mother doll and completed the play narratives with little hesitation were significantly more likely to have positive views of themselves, as measured with a puppet interview. In contrast, children who told stories in which mother-child interactions were minimal or hostile or who were reluctant to complete the story were significantly more likely to have less positive views of themselves. Significant relations were thus found again between parent-child doll behaviors in the narratives and child self-esteem.

In another study, Oppenheim (1997) administered six narratives about attachment issues to 35 low-risk, nonclinical preschool children. He found that children who demonstrated more positive child-mother interactions and who answered the question "How do you think the little boy/girl feels?" with a feeling, and a plausible reason for the feeling, were more able to explore a new preschool and were rated as having higher self-esteem by teachers on the Self-Esteem Questionnaire (Haltiwanger & Harter, 1987). Teachers also coded these children on the Beller revised scales (Sroufe, Fox, & Pancake, 1983) as less likely to seek attention passively. This work also suggests that children who demonstrate more positive mother-child interactions in the narratives are more secure and show more competent behaviors in their lives.

In summary, the findings relating children's narratives and low competence/self-esteem are quite similar to the findings concerning narratives and troubled parent-child relationships, suggesting that these groupings are interrelated. The research suggests that children with low competence/self-esteem may show in their narratives

1. less nurturant parental behaviors and positive parent-child interactions;
2. less proximity seeking with the mother doll when threatened;

3. restricted or conflicted parent-child relationships or difficulty telling the stories; and
4. difficulties discussing emotions related to the narratives.

Externalizing Behavior Problems

Four different sets of data have been examined linking aggression and emotional dysregulation in children's narratives with reported behavior problems. Zahn-Waxler et al. (1994) examined the narratives of 4- and 5-year-old children at low, moderate, and high risk for externalizing disorders. Risk for externalizing disorders was assessed by having mothers complete the Child Behavior Checklist (CBCL; Achenbach & Edelbrock, 1983) and teachers complete the Teacher Report Form (Achenbach & Edelbrock, 1986). Zahn-Waxler et al. clustered the narratives into two groups, narratives involving interpersonal conflict and narratives involving distress. In the distress narratives, children at risk for externalizing disorders showed less compliance, fewer verbal reparative responses, and more anger. Children with antisocial and oppositional behavior enacted more aggression in the stories, and children with oppositional and attention deficit symptoms demonstrated emotional dysregulation. In the interpersonal conflict narratives, children at risk for externalizing disorders showed more avoidant behaviors, more dysregulation, and more anger (especially girls). Children with attention deficit symptoms demonstrated more aggression and less compliance in the stories. Children with antisocial, oppositional, and attention deficit symptoms showed more emotional dysregulation. In both types of narratives, children with more symptoms of anxiety displayed less anger.

Warren et al. (1996) similarly found increased aggression and emotional dysregulation (as measured by distress) in the narratives of children with more behavior problems. Fifty-one low-risk, nonclinical children were studied longitudinally at ages 3, 4, and 5. Behavior problems were scored by having mothers and fathers complete the CBCL at all three ages, and teachers completed the Teacher Report Form when the children were 5 years of age. Significant moderate correlations were reported at ages 4 and 5 between (1) aggressive themes (aggression, personal injury, and atypical negative response) and externalizing behavior problems; and (2) distress and externalizing behavior problems. Correlations were not significant for the 3-year-olds. All of the results continued to be significant after controlling for language ability, temperament, and investment in performance. Thus, narratives may be most useful in the assessment of externalizing problems in children 4 years old and older.

Additional analyses, reported in chapter 5 of this book, were conducted on the 5-year-old child follow-up from the same study as Warren et al. (1996) using the Narrative Emotion Coding system (Warren, Mantz-Simmons, & Emde, 1993). Several codes from that system significantly correlated with externalizing behavior problems reported by parents and teachers. The ratings that directly code aggression (as an initial and final response) supported the results obtained in the studies already described. However, some of the codes do not directly pertain to aggression/destructive themes and may describe other types of internal representations of children with externalizing problems. For example, children with externalizing problems created danger themes more often, suggesting that they felt vulnerable. They tended to describe the monster in one story stem as a real monster, perhaps because they felt imminent danger. Children with externalizing disorders showed more preoccupation with eating, perhaps relating to a desire for oral satisfaction. They also portrayed the child characters as unable to competently solve problems and as superheroes perhaps because they believed that only superhuman qualities could help them overcome their difficulties.

Emotional incoherence, another of the narrative codes that significantly related to externalizing problems in the analyses described in chapter 5, involves resolving difficult themes suddenly and inexplicably. This may relate to difficulties with emotional regulation.The significant correlation between emotional incoherence and behavior problems suggests that children with behavior problems may be not only prone to creating aggressive themes but also unable to coherently resolve such themes. Thus, children with externalizing behavior problems may be showing problems with emotional regulation. However, the narrative code used to measure emotional regulation here may be confounded with coherence in general. With this same sample, Oppenheim, Emde, and Warren (1997) found that narrative incoherence (telling stories that do not flow smoothly in a clear and coherent manner), in contrast to emotional incoherence (sudden shifts in emotional themes), related significantly to child behavior problems.

Another analysis with the same sample of children, reported by Oppenheim, Nir, Warren, and Emde (1997), has suggested that children with externalizing problems experience their mothers as negative and as not providing positive discipline. Four- and 5-year-old children who had more positive and disciplinary representations of their mothers and fewer negative representations had fewer externalizing behavior problems. Thus, children with behavior problems may not experience positive discipline and may view their mothers as unsupportive.

In another nonclinical sample, von Klitzing, Kelsay, Emde, Robinson, and Schmitz (2000) examined the narratives of 652 twins. Aggressive themes coded from the narratives of the 5-year-old children significantly correlated with behavior problems as measured by the CBCL completed by both parents when the child was 5 and 7 years of age and the Teacher Report Form completed by the teacher when the child was 7 years of age. Lower narrative coherence was also significantly correlated with more externalizing behavior problems. When each gender was examined separately, the relations between aggressive themes and behavior problems held for girls but not boys.

In contrast, most of the findings linking aggressive play to externalizing and internalizing peer behaviors were found for boys and not for girls in a study conducted by McHale, Johnson, and Sinclair (1999) with 43 non-clinical, low-risk 4-year-old children (22 girls, 21 boys). Children told stories about happy, sad, mad, and worried families, and unstructured peer play behaviors were independently examined and rated as positive (appropriate/rule-following, and prosocial), externalizing (noncompliant and aggressive), and internalizing (withdrawn/bystanding, and sad/dysphoric/down). Observations were also made of dyadic parent-child interactions and triadic family interactions during multiple tasks. For the total sample, decreased family support/mutuality in co-parenting and decreased affective contact related to increased aggression in the doll play. For boys only, doll play aggression related to more externalizing, internalizing, and less positive peer behaviors and mediated the relation between family behaviors and peer behaviors, suggesting that internal representations may mediate the relations between life experiences and behaviors.

In summary, children with higher levels of externalizing behavior problems have shown the following features in their narratives:

1. less compliance, fewer verbal reparative responses, and more anger;
2. more aggressive themes;
3. more distress, avoidance, and emotional dysregulation;
4. more danger themes;
5. more preoccupation with eating;
6. portraying the child doll as a superhero yet unable to competently resolve problems; and
7. negative representations of the parent dolls.

Internalizing Behavior Problems and Anxiety

In one of the samples previously described (Warren et al., 1996; Oppenheim, Emde, et al., 1997; Oppenheim, Nir, et al., 1997), Warren, Emde, and Sroufe (2000) found associations between specified narrative responses and internalizing disorders in children. For these analyses, four additional narratives about threatening situations (Warren, Emde, & Oppenheim, 1993) were created and added to the original MacArthur Story Stem Battery (Bretherton, Oppenheim, et al., 1990) (see chapter 5 for a description of the new narratives and the Narrative Emotion Coding System). Fifty-one 5-year-old children's narratives were coded (Warren, Mantz–Simmons, & Emde, 1993). The codes included representing the child doll as not competent, not having the child doll go to the parent doll for help during stressful situations, having the child doll assume the parental role or responsibilities, having troubles with separation but denying negative feelings, and ending the stories negatively. The narrative aggregate significantly predicted internalizing symptoms in the children at 5 and 6 years of age, as reported by parents and teachers using the CBCL and Teacher Report Form. The five-year-old narrative responses also significantly predicted six-year-old separation anxiety and overanxious and social phobic/avoidant disorder symptoms, as reported by mothers with the Diagnostic Interview Schedule for Children.

In a different study focusing on differential and combined effects of attachment to mother and father, Verschueren and Marcoen (1999) examined the narratives of 80 nonclinical 5-year-old children in relation to kindergarten teacher ratings of child behaviors and child self-ratings of positiveness of self. Although positiveness of self was best predicted by positive child-mother attachment relations in the narratives, the child anxious/withdrawal behavior problems, as measured by teachers, was best predicted by the quality of the child-father narrative attachment representation. Thus, children who display insecure attachment relationships in their narratives, possibly showing restricted or conflicted father-child relationships, may be more likely to demonstrate anxious/withdrawn behaviors in kindergarten. This finding warrants further research.

In summary, from evidence at hand, children with higher levels of internalizing behavior problems and anxiety may show the following features in their narratives:

1. the child doll portrayed as not competent;
2. not having the child doll go to the parent doll for help during stressful situations;
3. having the child doll assume the parental role or responsibilities;
4. troubles with separation but denying associated negative feelings;
5. ending the stories negatively; and
6. restricted or conflictual father-child relationships.

Maltreated Children

A number of researchers have studied the narratives of maltreated children and have gathered very interesting results. Buchsbaum, Toth, Clyman, Cicchetti, and Emde (1992) examined the play narratives of approximately 100 maltreated 4- and 5-year-old children. The children had experienced a range of types of maltreatment, including emotional abuse, physical abuse, sexual abuse, and neglect. Most of the children were from low socioeconomic backgrounds. A comparison group of nonmaltreated children, matched for age, gender, race, and receptive language ability, was also studied. Maltreated children's narratives showed more themes involving inappropriate aggression, punitiveness, abusive language, neglect, and sexualized behaviors than did those of the controls. In the narratives of the maltreated children, few people came to the aid of an injured doll. Moreover, maltreated children tended to include more statements about the protagonist doll as bad. The implication is that maltreated children may have internal representations that involve seeing others as nonsupportive and themselves as bad.

Buchsbaum et al. (1992) have described in detail the narrative responses of two maltreated children. The themes in the narratives seemed to correspond to the children's lives based on information available to the investigators. One child, who was emotionally, physically, and perhaps sexually abused, was not overly aggressive in her play, but did represent emotional and physical abuse, and perhaps sexual abuse, in her stories. Another child, who was physically abused and was oppositional and aggressive in his life, displayed much more anger, oppositionality, and physical aggression in his stories. This child repeatedly described incidents in which the protagonist, who had been wronged or who had done something wrong, then became aggressive. The authors speculated that such themes indicated a tendency to act as a victimizer when this child felt like a victim. The implication drawn is that narratives can help a therapist working with maltreated children assess how the children have been maltreated, anticipate the transference, identify whom the child sees as supportive, and hence facilitate a process of helping the child build on supportive relationships.

In chapter 11, Clyman reports additional findings from this sample. Maltreated children showed significantly less prosocial behavior, more disobedience, more sexual behavior, and fewer characters in distress than did the nonmaltreated children. A significant interaction with gender was also present, with maltreated boys showing more aggressive actions in their narratives, particularly in terms of portraying parents as aggressive, than maltreated girls, nonmaltreated boys, and nonmaltreated girls. This research suggests that maltreated children may display signs of their abuse (such as increased sexual behavior), as well as possible consequences of the abuse (more disobedience), in their narratives. Toth, Cicchetti, Macfie, and Emde (1997) examined the narratives of 80 maltreated children and 27 children from families receiving Aid to Families with Dependent Children who had no reports of maltreatment. The narratives of the maltreated children contained more negative maternal and self-representations, and the children were more controlling with and nonresponsive to the examiner. Thus, maltreated children may not only behave differently while telling the narratives but also show negative representations in their narratives concerning their parents and themselves.

Macfie et al. (1999), examining the same sample, found that in their narratives, maltreated children depicted significantly fewer parental doll responses to relieve distress, significantly fewer child doll responses to relieve distress, and significantly more child participant responses to relieve distress than did nonmaltreated children. When types of abuse were analyzed separately, neglected children showed fewer child doll responses to relieve distress than did the nonmaltreated and abused group; the abused group depicted more participant responses to relieve distress than did the nonmaltreated children and the neglected group; and the abused group portrayed more role reversal behaviors (child doll acting like a parent toward the parent doll) than did the nonmaltreated children. Children who had been physically abused were significantly more likely to display more role reversal behaviors. In addition, post hoc analyses demonstrated that abused and neglected children depicted significantly fewer parental responses to distress than did the nonmaltreated children. This research suggests that children who have been maltreated show different behaviors to relieve distress in their narratives and indicates possible difference in the internal representations of abused and neglected children.

In another study, Toth, Cicchetti, Macfie, Rogosch, and Maughan (2000) examined the narratives of 65 preschool children recruited from daycare centers and schools (43 maltreated and 22 nonmaltreated). A narrative aggregate of moral affiliative themes including affection, affiliation, compliance, empathy/helping, nonphysical punishment/discipline, and reparation/guilt and another aggregate of conflictual themes including aggression, destruction of objects, and escalation of conflict were created. As predicted, moral affiliation themes were significantly less likely and conflictual themes were significantly more likely in the maltreated children's narratives. As expected, maltreated children were found to have significantly more behavior problems, as rated by parents and teachers using the CBCL (Achenbach, 1991a) and Teacher Report Form (Achenbach, 1991b). Moreover, conflictual narrative themes appeared to partially mediate the relation between maltreatment and behavior problems. This suggests that maltreated children may develop conflictual representations, which may contribute to externalizing behavior problems.

In summary, evidence thus far indicates that children who have experienced maltreatment may tell stories in which

1. physical or sexual abuse or neglect is a story theme;
2. the child doll is not helped by the other dolls and there are fewer child doll and parent doll behaviors to relieve distress but more participant child behaviors to relieve distress;
3. the child doll is portrayed negatively;
4. the parent dolls are portrayed negatively;
5. the child dolls are portrayed as acting like parents in relation to the parent dolls;
6. fewer moral-affiliative themes and prosocial doll behaviors appear;
7. more conflictual, aggressive, and disobedience themes appear;
8. more sexual themes appear; and
9. the children are controlling with and nonresponsive to the examiner.

Clinical Impressions Related to Disorder and Assessment

This section discusses impressions from the literature and from a clinician's personal experience administering SSNs to over one hundred 4- to 8-year-old children with and without diagnosed disorders. Children's play has been a longstanding and valuable tool in the clinical setting for understanding children's problems and views of the world and themselves (Mayes & Cohen, 1993). Yet there has been little systematic research concerning the meaning of children's play. The SSNs are a promising method for systematically obtaining information from young children about their feelings and problems and thus may help to validate clinical interpretations based on children's play. Unfortunately, there is a paucity of research linking particular narrative responses with specific types of emotional problems. The statements that follow, which link particular types of narrative responses to specific emotional problems, are impressionistic, qualitative, and preliminary: the intent is to generate further research.

Narratives in Children with Specific Types of Emotional Difficulties

Mood Disorders In clinical work our group has administered narratives to children with major depression and bipolar disorder. Children with major depression appear to demonstrate many themes of loss and end stories in a negative manner—a feature consistent with earlier suggestions (Buchsbaum et al., 1992; Warren et al., 1997). Children with bipolar disorder (in the manic phase) tell their stories very quickly and tend to be tangential. They introduce many new or surprising elements into the stories without warning. They also display euphoria and may introduce many exciting, fun story lines (going to the circus, going to an amusement park, etc.). Further research is needed to confirm that these observations are linked to particular diagnoses.

Separation Anxiety In our clinical experience, children with separation anxiety routinely show difficulty with the separation story, which involves a forced separation of the children from the parents when the parents go on the trip. Children with separation anxiety tend to avoid the separation, having the children go on the trip with the parents instead of separating. This clinical impression requires further validation.

Social Anxiety Just as narratives appear to be useful in the assessment of parent-child relationships, they may also prove valuable in the assessment of relationships with peers. Three's a Crowd, one of the stories of the MacArthur Narrative Battery (Bretherton et al., 1990), explores this possibility, forcing the child to chose between a peer and sibling and negotiate a complex interpersonal situation. Several stories from the New MacArthur Emotion Story Stems (Warren, Emde, & Oppenheim, 1993) are also helpful (Fight with Friend and New Neighborhood). In particular, New Neighborhood has been clinically useful in the assessment of peer relationships. Children with positive peer relationships tend to portray the child protagonist as easily making new friends and being readily accepted by the other children. Children with social anxiety tend to show difficulty approaching the peers. They may portray the child protagonist negatively (e.g., say she is not wearing pretty clothes) or may show the peers as rejecting. Further research is needed to confirm these impressions.

Using Narrative Procedures in Clinical Assessment

Assessment of young children is quite difficult because they are very poor reporters of symptoms and problems (Glasberg & Aboud, 1982; Harter & Pike, 1984; Schwab-Stone, Fallon, Briggs, & Crowther, 1994). Narratives may thus prove to be quite a useful assessment tool. Buchsbaum et al. (1992) describe how the same child who answered "fine" when queried about his relationship with his maltreating mother during a clinical interview elaborated on themes of maltreatment throughout his narratives. Young children may not answer direct questions or may answer them inaccurately. Narratives, on the other hand, capture a child's attention and provide a means of obtaining information about a child's life experience. Because young children find the task to be enjoyable, narratives may also foster rapport between the child and therapist (Buchsbaum et al., 1992).

In clinical work, our group has used story stem narratives extensively to understand children's views of themselves and their relationships. Children's narrative responses have suggested potential diagnoses, including separation anxiety disorder, social phobia, mania, and depression. Our group has used narratives to understand psychodynamic processes and as a tool for the assessment of potential child neglect and abuse. M. Scheeringa (personal communication, 1995) has used a similar technique with children who have experienced trauma. He provides the child with props that are appropriate to the trauma, to allow a portrayal of experience.

Story stem narratives can also be extremely useful for assessment during treatment. A child with school phobia, who was reluctant to discuss difficult issues, became disorganized when presented with a story involving a parental conflict. She exacerbated the conflict, causing it to become more aggressive. It thus became apparent that parental conflict (though initially denied by both parents) was a significant contributor to the child's difficulties. Another child focused on a child protagonist who had broken the rules, criticizing her extensively. This became a major theme in her treatment, and the child was able to make significant progress by coming to accept the imperfect child doll.

In addition to describing parent-child relationships in general, children's narratives may also delineate specific differences in close relationships. Buchsbaum et al. (1992) describe a child who seemed to show in his narratives two different internal working models of relationships in relation to mother and father. Mother was inconsistently helpful in the stories, but father consistently helped and cared for the child. Thus, Buchsbaum et al. relate that narratives can help a therapist identify which parent a child believes is supportive.

In terms of psychodynamic processes, Buchsbaum et al. (1992) describe how children's narratives can help the therapist anticipate the patient-therapist relationship. One child, who showed confusion in his narratives between intimacy and aggression and who demonstrated aggression in his narratives when feeling vulnerable, was described as likely to act out when he began to feel close to the therapist. Another child, who showed avoidance in her stories and little reliance on others, was likely to show affective distancing and denial of concerns when upset.

In clinical work, our groups has found the narratives to be quite useful for understanding psychodynamic processes. One child showed aggression in his stories (and in his life), but the aggression always seemed to follow a loss, suggesting that his aggression was linked to difficulties handling feelings of loss. Another child showed aggression whenever parents were present in the stories, suggesting that his aggression was linked to conflict in the parent-child relationships. Thus, narratives may help clinicians identify sources of conflict that lead to behavioral problems.

Our approach clinically has been to select certain narratives that appear to relate to the child's presenting problems. If we are concerned about separation anxiety, we administer a story stem about Separation/Reunion. If we are interested in the child's response to parental relationships, we use Lost Keys and Exclusion. If there is a question of abuse, we administer Spilled Gravy. If there are problems with externalizing behaviors, we utilize transgression stories such as Spilled Juice and Candy. Barney and Canceled Visit are used to access reactions to loss. Peer relationships are best assessed with New Neighborhood. Sibling relationships can be examined with Favorite Chair and Three's a Crowd. Mother-child relationships can be examined with many of the stories, but Mom's Headache has been particularly useful. Scary Dog and Monster in the Dark are employed to access general fears/anxiety and Song to examine performance anxiety. (See chapters 3 and 5 for descriptions of these stories.)

Such work is supported by analyses that show that different stories elicit different sorts of themes. Zahn-Waxler et al. (1994) found differences in the responses of 4- and 5-year-old children at risk for externalizing disorders to two types of stories those that focused on interpersonal conflict and those that focused on distress. They found that avoidant behaviors in the interpersonal conflict stories, but not in the distress stories, were associated with externalizing behavior problems. They also found that the most evocative story stems in their population concerned separation/reunion, exclusion, a parental argument, and a story in which the mother responds with outrage to the child's deceptive act.

Limitations and Directions for Future Research

Additional research is needed to validate these preliminary clinical impressions and to refine procedures for clinical use. One approach would be to select a short battery of narratives and use these with children who have a range of clinical diagnoses. Alternatively, different batteries could be created to assess for certain types of problems (e.g., maltreatment or anxiety). Once clear linkages are established between specific responses and certain diagnoses or conditions, it would be useful to refine the coding systems so that they could be utilized immediately by a clinician, without requiring videotaping and subsequent coding. Thus, extensive aggression in the stories would suggest externalizing disorders; and sexualized behaviors might suggest sexual exposure or abuse.

There are a number of limitations of the preliminary research summarized in this chapter. Most of the studies involve small, nonclinical, low-risk samples. Thus, results may not generalize. In addition, the samples are primarily Caucasian and middle class. Research is needed with diverse racial, ethnic, and cultural groups. In support of this view, Zahn-Waxler, Friedman, Cole, Mizuta, and Hiruma (1996) found that U.S. children showed more anger, aggressive behaviors, and underregulation of emotion in their narratives than Japanese children. Thus, racial, ethnic, and cultural differences may influence children's narratives and certainly require further investigation.

An additional limitation is that the analyses are primarily correlational. Longitudinal research is needed to examine causality and developmental processes. In addition, there is more need for establishing external validity including linkages to other measures of child representations, competence, child adaptations in real-life settings, and childhood disorders.

Another limitation concerns the fact that similar narrative responses seem to relate to a number of different clinical problems. For example, portraying the parent dolls negatively could relate to troubled parent-child relationships, behavior problems, and low self-esteem. Many of these types of problems could occur together. However, it seems important for future research to include measures of multiple differentiated constructs to clarify what types of narrative responses are associated with specific outcomes.

Responses to story stem narratives provide an opportunity to capture a child's representations of his world, himself, and his caretakers. They generate additional information to that gathered by observing behavior alone and are more structured than projective tests. Narrative responses can uncover information, such as parental conflict, abuse, or child suffering, and they may suggest diagnoses. Moreover, they are fun for children to complete and easy to administer. With further research, narratives may become an extremely important tool in the assessment and treatment of young children.

NOTE

This research was supported by funds from the John D. and Catherine T. MacArthur Foundation Network on Early Childhood Transitions, NIMH postdoctoral research training grants MH15442 and IF32MH10712, and NIMH Scientist Development Award for Clinicians 1K08MH01532. I gratefully acknowledge the help and support of Dr. Robert N. Emde.

REFERENCES

Achenbach, T. M. (1991a). *Manual for the Child Behavior Checklist/4–18 and 1991 Profile.* Burlington: University of Vermont, Department of Psychiatry.

Achenbach, T. M. (1991b). *Manual for the Teacher's Report Form and 1991 Profile.* Burlington: University of Vermont, Department of Psychiatry.

Achenbach, T. M., & Edelbrock, C. S. (1983). *Manual for the Child Behavior Checklist and Revised Child Behavior Profile.* Burlington: University Associates in Psychiatry.

Achenbach, T. M., & Edelbrock, C. (1986). *Manual for the Teacher's Report Form.* Burlington: University of Vermont.

Ainsworth, M. D. S., Blehar, M. C., Waters, E., & Wall, S. (1978). *Patterns of attachment: A psychological study of the strange situation.* Hillsdale, NJ: Lawrence Erlbaum.

Behar, L. B. (1977). The preschool behavior questionnaire. *Journal of Abnormal Child Psychology, 5*(3), 265–275.

Bretherton, I., Oppenheim, D., Buchsbaum, H., Emde, R., & the MacArthur Narrative Group. (1990). *The MacArthur Story Stem Battery.* Unpublished manuscript.

Bretherton, I., Prentiss, C., & Ridgeway, D. (1990). Family relationships as represented in a story-completion task at thirty-seven and fifty-four months of age. In I. Bretherton & M. W. Watson (Eds.), *Children's perspectives on the family* (pp. 85–106). San Francisco: Jossey-Bass.

Bretherton, I., Ridgeway, D., & Cassidy, J. (1990). Assessing internal working models of the attachment relationship: An attachment story completion task for 3-year-olds. In M. T. Greenberg, D. Cicchetti, & E. M. Cummings (Eds.), *Attachment in the preschool years* (pp. 273–310). Chicago: University of Chicago Press.

Buchsbaum, H. K., Toth, S. L., Clyman, R. B., Cicchetti, D., & Emde, R. N. (1992). The use of a narrative story stem technique with maltreated children: Implications for theory and practice. *Development and Psychopathology, 4,* 603–625.

Cassidy, J. (1988). Child-mother attachment and the self in six-year-olds. *Child Development, 59,* 121–134.

Cassidy, J., Marvin, R. S., in collaboration with the MacArthur Working Group on Attachment (1987). *Attachment organization in three- and four-year-olds: Coding guidelines.* Unpublished manuscript, University of Virginia.

Fleming, J. E., & Offord, D. R. (1990). Epidemiology of childhood depressive disorders:

A critical review. *Journal of the American Academy of Child and Adolescent Psychiatry, 29*(4), 571–580.

Glasberg, R., & Aboud, F. (1982). Keeping one's distance from sadness: Children's self reports of emotional experience. *Developmental Psychology, 18,* 287–293.

Goldwyn, R., Stanley, C., Smith, V., & Green, J. (2000). The Manchester Child Attachment Story Task: Relationship with parental AAI, SAT and child behaviour. *Attachment and Human Development 2*(1), 71–84.

Green, J., Stanley, C., Smith, V., & Goldwyn, R. (2000). A new method of evaluating attachment representations in young school age children: The Manchester Child Attachment Story Task. *Attachment and Human Development, 2*(1), 48–70.

Haltiwanger, J., & Harter, S. (1987). Behavioral rating scale of presented self-esteem. Unpublished manuscript, University of Denver.

Hansburg, H. G. (1972). Adolescent separation anxiety. Springfield, IL: Charles Thomas.

Harter, S., & Pike, R. (1984). The pictorial scale of perceived competence and social acceptance for young children. *Child Development, 55,* 1969–1982.

Macfie, J., Toth, S. L., Rogosch, F.A., Robinson, J., Emde, R. N., & Cicchetti, D. (1999). Effect of maltreatment on preschoolers' narrative representations of responses to relieve distress and of role reversal. *Developmental Psychology, 35*(2), 460–465.

Main, M., & Cassidy, J. (1988). Categories of response to reunion with the parent at age 6: Predictable from infant attachment classifications and stable over a 1–month period. *Developmental Psychopathology, 24*(3), 1–12.

Main, M., & Goldwyn, R. (1985–1994). *Adult Attachment Scoring and Classification System. Unpublished scoring manual.* Department of Psychology, University of California, Berkeley.

Main, M., Kaplan, N., & Cassidy, J. (1985). Security in infancy, childhood, and adulthood: A move to the level of representation. In I. Bretherton & E. Waters (Eds.), Growing points in attachment theory and research. *Monographs of the Society for Research in Child Development, 50* (1–2, Serial No. 209): 66–104.

Mayes, L. C., & Cohen, D. J. (1993). Playing and therapeutic action in child analysis. *Journal of Psychoanalysis, 74,* 1235–1244.

McHale, J. P., Johnson, D., & Sinclair, R. (1999). Family dynamics, preschoolers' family representations, and preschool peer relationships. *Early Education and Development, 10*(3), 373–401.

McHale, J. P., Neugebauer, A., Asch, A. R., & Schwartz, A. (1999). Preschoolers' characterizations of multiple family relationships during family doll play. *Journal of Clinical Child Psychology, 28*(2), 256–268.

Olson, D. H., Bell, R., & Portner, J. (1983). *FACES II (Family Adaptability and Cohesion Evaluation Scales).* Unpublished manuscript, Department of Family Social Science, University of Minnesota, St. Paul.

Olson, S. L. (1985). *The preschool competence questionnaire: Factor structure, longitudinal stability, and convergence with ratings of maladjustment.* Unpublished manuscript, University of Michigan, Ann Arbor.

Oppenheim, D. (1997). The attachment doll-play interview for preschoolers. *International Journal of Behavioral Development, 20,* 681–697.

Oppenheim, D., Emde, R. N., & Warren, S. (1997). Children's narrative representations of mothers: Their development and associations with child and mother adaptation. *Child Development, 68,* 127–138.

Oppenheim, D., Nir, A., Warren, S., & Emde, R. N. (1997). Emotion regulation in mother-child narrative co-construction: Associations with children's narratives and adaptation. *Developmental Psychology, 33*(2), 284–294.

Oppenheim, D., & Waters, H. S. (1995). Narrative processes and attachment representations: Issues of development and assessment. In E. Waters, B. Vaughn, G. Posada, & K. Kondo-Ikemura (Eds.), Caregiving, cultural, and cognitive perspectives on secure base behavior and working models: New growing points of attachment theory and research. *Monographs of the Society for Research in Child Development, 60*(2–3), 197–215.

Page, T. F. (1998). Linkages between children's narrative representations of families and social competence in child-care settings (Doctoral dissertation, University of Wisconsin-Madison, 1998) *Dissertation Abstracts International*, 59.

Pianta, R., & Steinberg, M. (1991, April). *Relationships between children and their kindergarten teachers.* Paper presented at the Society for Research in Child Development biennial meetings, Seattle.

Schwab-Stone, M., Fallon, T., Briggs, M., & Crowther, B. (1994). Reliability of diagnostic reporting for children aged 6–11 years: A test-retest study of the Diagnostic Interview Schedule for Children—Revised. *American Journal of Psychiatry, 151*, 1048–1054.

Solomon, J., George, C., & de Jong, A. (1995). Children classified as controlling at age six: Evidence of disorganized representational strategies and aggression at home and at school. *Development and Psychopathology*, 7, 447–463.

Spanier, G. B. (1976). Measuring dyadic adjustment: New scales for assessing the quality of marriage and similar dyads. *Journal of Marriage and the Family, 38*, 15–28.

Sroufe, L. A., Fox, N. E. & Pancake, V. R. (1983). Attachment and dependency in developmental perspective. *Child Development, 54*, 1615–1627.

Toth, S. L., Cicchetti, D., Macfie, J., & Emde, R. N. (1997). Representations of self and other in the narratives of neglected, physically abused, and sexually abused preschoolers. *Development and Psychopathology, 9*, 781–796.

Toth, S. L., Cicchetti, D., Macfie, J., Rogosch, F. A., & Maughan, A. (2000). Narrative representations of moral-affiliative and conflictual themes and behavioral problems in maltreated preschoolers. *Journal of Clinical Child Psychology, 29*(3), 307–318.

Verschueren, K., & Marcoen, A. (1999). Representation of self and socioemotional competence in kindergartners: Differential and combined effects of attachment to mother and to father. *Child Development, 70*(1), 183–201.

Verschueren, K., Marcoen, A., & Schoefs, V. (1996). The internal working model of the self, attachment, and competence in five-year-olds. *Child Development, 67*, 2493–2511.

von Klitzing, K., Kelsay, K., Emde, R. N., Robinson, J., & Schmitz, S. (2000). Gender-specific characteristics of 5-year-old's play narratives and associations with behavior ratings. *Journal of the American Academy of Child and Adolescent Psychiatry, 39*(8), 1017–1023.

Warren, S. L., Emde, R. N., & Oppenheim, D. (1993). *New MacArthur Emotion Story-Stems.* Unpublished manuscript.

Warren, S. L., Emde, R. N., & Sroufe, L. A. (2000). Internal representations: Predicting anxiety from children's play narratives. *Journal of the American Academy of Child and Adolescent Psychiatry, 39*(1), 100–107.

Warren, S. L., Huston, L., Egeland, B., & Sroufe, L.A. (1997). Child and adolescent anxiety disorders and early attachment. *Journal of the American Academy of Child and Adolescent Psychiatry, 36*(5), 637–644.

Warren, S. L., Mantz-Simmons, L., & Emde, R. (1993). *Narrative Emotion Coding Manual* (NEC). Unpublished manuscript.

Warren, S. L., Oppenheim, D., & Emde, R. N. (1996). Can emotions and themes in children's play predict behavior problems? *American Academy of Child and Adolescent Psychiatry, 34*(10), 1331–1337.

Waters, E., & Deane, K. E. (1985). Defining and assessing individual differences in attachment relationships: Q-Methodology and the organization of behavior in infancy and early childhood. In: I. Bretherton and E. Waters (eds.), Growing Points of Attachment: Theory and Research. *Monographs of the Society for Research in Child Development, 50*(1–2, Serial No. 209), 41–65.

Waters, H. S., Rodrigues, L. M., & Ridgeway, D. (1998). Cognitive underpinnings of narrative attachment assessment. *Journal of Experimental Psychology, 71*, 211–234.

Zahn-Waxler, C., Cole, P. M., Richardson, D. T., Friedman, R. J., Michel, M. K., & Belouad, F. (1994). Social problems solving in disruptive preschool children: reactions to hypothetical situations of conflict and distress. *Merrill-Palmer Quarterly, 40*, 98–119.

Zahn-Waxler, C., Friedman, R. J., Cole, P. M., Mizuta, I., & Hiruma, N. (1996). Japanese and United States preschool children's responses to conflict and distress. *Child Development, 67*, 2462–2477.

JILL HODGES
MIRIAM STEELE
SAUL HILLMAN
KAYE HENDERSON

13

Mental Representations and Defenses in Severely Maltreated Children: A Story Stem Battery and Rating System for Clinical Assessment and Research Applications

This chapter describes a set of narrative stems and a rating scheme devised especially for the assessment of young children when there are concerns about maltreatment.

Young children who have been maltreated present particular conundrums of clinical assessment. Parents, if abusers, are unlikely to be reliable informants about the child. Children may have recently moved because of the maltreatment to alternative caregivers who may be just beginning to get to know them. Children themselves are often in a situation of conflict or fear about revealing unhappy experiences; and where maltreatment has been long-term, distorting their development and their view of expectable family relationships, they may perceive and report their experiences or their feelings as normal. They may also lack the vocabulary or, for instance, the cognitive differentiations between affective states, which would help to give the interviewer a picture of their situation and feelings.

Story stem assessments have been a very useful clinical tool with these children, and we now use them routinely. Relatively brief, nonthreatening for the child, and allowing nonverbal as well as verbal forms of communication, they provide a "window" into important aspects of mental functioning, including the impact of abuse on the children's basic understanding of and expectations about relationships. The child's response, in his own "voice" both verbally and nonverbally, often vividly illuminates these aspects. The technique respects the children's difficult situation, offering them the chance to demonstrate how their experiences have affected them, without ever identifying or accusing anyone.

At the same time, the concern that such an assessment is mainly a projective test, requiring subjective and potentially biased interpretation, can increasingly be countered as the international body of data grows linking features of narrative completions, rated in standard and reliable ways, to particular group characteristics. Recent research using the story stem technique has already established patterns of findings relevant to young children who have suffered maltreatment. McCrone, Egeland, Kalkoske, and Carlson (1994) noted the prevalence of negative representations, particularly aggression, in the stories of maltreated children. Macfie et al. (1999) used the MacArthur Story Stem battery and ratings with maltreated preschool children who were still living with their families. Maltreated children were less likely than nonmaltreated children to show parents and children responding to relieve distress in children. The authors comment, "By and large, neglect, without abuse, was associated with relative omission of acts to relieve distress, while abuse, especially physical abuse, was characterised by anomalous acts of commission," such as role reversal, or the child stepping into the story "frame" himself to relieve distress. This reflects other work, not based on maltreated children, demonstrating that insecure-avoidant attachment is associated with low levels of concern and comforting behaviors in preschoolers (Main & George, 1985; Kestenbaum, Farber, & Sroufe, 1989) and that disorganized attachment in infancy is associated with controlling behavior, including role reversal, in 6-year-olds (Main, Kaplan, & Cassidy, 1985).

The purpose of this chapter is to expand this body of work. First, we discuss the types of information we believe children's responses contain, stressing that we do not view the resulting play narratives as reports on autobiographic incidents. Rather, we believe children's responses delineate their most basic scripts for human relationships, particularly those between young children and their caregivers. Second, we describe a set of narrative stems and a rating scheme devised especially for assessing young children when there are concerns about maltreatment.

Narratives and Realities

Children's play narratives are neither simple imitative copies of their realities nor feelings and fantasies rather than realities, as earlier researchers like Moore and Ucko (1961), who carried out some of the earliest systematic research using doll play, thought. They bear systematic relationships to the realities, without being copies.

Stern (1985) and others have discussed how from infancy the child mentally organizes reality experience to build generalized representations of expectable interactions with others, which guide expectation and understanding. Broadly speaking, we are trying to access this kind of representation using the narrative stems.

Preschoolers build event schemata, temporally organized scripts, for events that are familiar (Nelson & Gruendel, 1981, 1986); young children asked to give specific memories of a routine real-life event tend to recall event schemata or scripts, not particular autobiographical instances (e.g., Fivush, 1984). Although there have been some questions as to how far this characteristic may represent language constraints in the retelling, rather than memory organization per se (Mandler, 1980), this feature is clearly an advantage when the task is to delineate the generic representations of relationships with parents. On occasion, the child may represent particular autobiographical memories of abuse in the narrative, which may indeed be of clinical or forensic importance. In general, however, we aim to elicit generic representations and expectations of child-parent relationships, because these are, arguably, the most likely to affect later relationships and development.

Any representation of experience has its own characteristics as well as those of the "reality" it represents. Thus, when examining the play narratives of maltreated children, we are examining how the child's mental organization has responded to adverse experiences. Where parts of reality are too painful for the child, the play narrative can reveal some of the defenses employed to keep painful aspects away from awareness. These defenses make the play narrative something other than a copy of the child's experiences; it amounts more to what the child is making of those experiences. This is important in itself in terms of trying to assess vulnerability and the potential for recovery. Thus, our perspective is that the ways in which children cope with distress as represented in the narrative stems are likely to predict their response in a new family context.

Other distortions of reality perception may occur not as a result of defense but as a result of the way in which internal working models of caregivers and caregiving develop and stabilize (Bretherton, 1985). Once organized, these models tend to become automatic, operating increasingly outside conscious awareness. As new information tends to be assimilated to existing models, relative stability results, but at the cost of some distortion of perception if external conditions have altered. Such models can thus have a powerful effect on how the individual perceives and reacts to new situations and relationships. Crittenden (1988) and others have emphasized how attachment models adaptive in one situation may become maladaptive if conditions change.

It is very important that play creates an imaginary situation, that it is not bound to reality but can take counterfactual, imaginary realities into account. Because narrative assessments can represent counterfactual possibilities, the representations displayed in the narratives may reflect not particular aspects of reality but imagined possibilities, wishes, fears, or fantasy. However, if what appears in the narrative is imagined, this implies that it forms part of an internal representation. This may be important for prognosis. An abused child who nonetheless has some mental representation of what can be expected from a good-enough parent may be better able to recognize and use good-enough parenting, should it eventually come their way, than a child who has no such representation. Wolf (1990) pointed to how children's notion of self is expanded through the construction of new scenarios out of existing elements of content. The story stems provide a way of looking at children's existing forms of mental organization and at how these shape the possibilities they can imagine in responding to a new situation.

Nonverbal as Well as Verbal Channels

Narrative assessment allows the child to produce nonverbal and verbal narratives, simultaneously. In practice, these narratives are sometimes congruent and sometimes not. It is common clinical knowledge that play can give us access to memories that *could not* be recalled by verbal means alone.

There are several reasons why information available from one "channel" may not be available from the other. In summary, these concern aspects of memory organization; the particular issue of memories of trauma; and conflict or fear about speaking about some issues.

Experiences early in the child's life, before language is developed, are not part of later verbally based memory. Such "procedural" memories are relatively slow to establish, and inflexible once established; they have been referred to as "habit" learning (Reviere, 1996), and this is of course not confined to infancy. Procedural knowledge has been defined as "information that underlies a skill but need not be represented in consciousness in order for an individual to manifest the skill" (Emde & Clyman, 1997; Cohen & Squire, 1980). As an illustration, Emde, Biringen, Clyman, and Oppenheim (1991) cite young infants' skilled face-to-face turn-taking behavior with caregivers. They point out that procedural knowledge about the consistency of emotions in self and others underlies, for example, children's capacity to monitor their parents' emotional availability or unavailability.

This form of memory, containing "rules" governing behavior and interaction with the world, is not necessarily explicitly represented, and when the child develops language, these memories are generally not available to verbal recall. Instead, they form part of the way in which the child perceives and responds to experience and may be "recalled" in perceptual, affective, or physical sensorimotor form. In psychotherapy, these nonverbal procedural memories are among those experiences that cannot be "remembered," but rather appear in other forms in the patient's behavior and experiences; they get enacted, reexperienced, repeated, in relation to the therapist in the transference, or acted-out elsewhere.

In contrast, "semantic" memories generalized from repeated experience, and specific, detailed "episodic" or "autobiographical" memories of particular events, are at least potentially available verbally. Such memories have been referred to as declarative memories, in contrast to procedural memories. They may be consciously available and capable of being explicitly stated or demonstrated in recognition or recall. They may also be defensively excluded from consciousness, thus forming part of the dynamic unconscious (Freud, 1958). Freud emphasizes the importance of the verbal/nonverbal distinction, in characterizing conscious or potentially conscious material, in contrast to unconscious, by the availability of the "word-presentation" linked to the memory trace.

Thus, to represent something as ancient and complex as his or her internal working model of an attachment relationship, the child must combine these different forms of registration of experiences with the attachment figure: nonconscious, habitual, procedural knowledge; generalized semantic memories; and specific episodic memories of discrete events. Memory that operates automatically, outside conscious awareness, requires assessment by other means than conscious verbal recall or description. Abused children may give behavioral evidence of their fearful or aversive expectations of their parents, without necessarily being able, let alone willing, to recall specific events. Play narrative assessments, because they provide for a nonverbal as well as a verbal narrative, allow the display of these nonconscious expectations. Crittenden (1994) notes that if children routinely experience abuse, these abusive experiences may no longer be represented as occasion-specific episodes but instead become a part of the child's "unscrutinised, taken-for-granted understanding of the nature of relationships." In such cases, the clearest evidence of a history of abuse may be how these "taken-for-granted" expectations guide present behavior.

These observations are supported by work on trauma and memory. Individuals may show repetitive traumatic memories through unconscious behavior and interpersonal interactions that they may not connect to an original traumatic context (Terr, 1990). These characteristics emphasize the potential usefulness of the nonverbal channel in narrative assessments with this group of children. For instance, Terr (1988) holds that early *chronic* trauma (a category that would cover much child maltreatment) tends to be represented by semantic rather than specific autobiographic, and particularly verbal, memories. Maltreated children may also have experienced extreme instances of trauma, which indeed may be the precipitant for their removal from parents. However, Reviere's review (1996) notes observations that memory impairment after trauma seems to be centered on episodic (specific autobiographical) memories. These are further indications that it is worth using indirect means to investigate the registration of attachment relationships in maltreated children, means that allow their generic representations and expectations to be displayed nonverbally as well as verbally.

Assessment and Legal Proceedings

Even where memories are available, children may deliberately try to conceal aspects of their lives and family relationships, particularly in the context of maltreatment, the more so where there are ongoing or anticipated legal proceedings (Buchsbaum, Toth, Clyman, Cicchetti, & Emde, 1992). Because the narrative assessment does not demand direct recall of autobiographical memories by the child, and also allows a displaced and nonverbal narrative, a number of these difficulties are circumvented to some extent. There are no leading questions. The assessment does not ask directly about any figures in the child's life. Thus, where the child has been "silenced" or chooses to conceal maltreatment because of love for the parent, shame, or fear, the narrative assessment does not place the child in a conflict of loyalties regarding the parent. Buchsbaum et al. (1992) noted that one child who was asked about his relationship with his maltreating mother in a clinical interview replied "fine" but showed themes of maternal punitiveness, neglect, and rejection in the narrative stem assessment. Our clinical experience indicates that such discrepancies are common.

A particularly useful feature of the story stem battery as an assessment is that it gives the child a series of potential "fresh starts," setting up new situations with the possibility of a different narrative. Child-led play interviews, although they can reveal a great deal about the child, also carry a potential drawback from the point of view of brief assessment of generic representations. Once the child's own play "narrative" is under way, particular themes could become repeated or emphasized simply because the story is flowing along a particular narrative path, rather than because those themes are characteristic of the child's underlying models for relationships. In contrast, if the child is presented with a series of diverse beginnings, but the ensuing narratives repeatedly display the same themes or characteristics, this gives stronger grounds for believing that these themes reveal underlying configurations, that they tell us something about the *generic* representations that fuel play and may also shape the expectations that young children take into both established and new relationships.

The Use of Displacement

A recent review by Woolgar (1999) points out that investigations of doll play techniques conducted in the 1940s showed that for most children, using doll families that duplicated the child's own family produced more identificatory themes, but that in some children play became inhibited if the experimenter explicitly suggested these identifications. Thus, it is helpful, and probably particularly so with maltreated children, to use a standard doll family rather than trying to replicate the child's own family configuration. The story stems do not ask children directly about their experiences or their own parents but explore their representations displaced onto the play figures. Further, two of the story stems use animal figures, providing a further step of displacement from the child's own personal experience. This is especially necessary for some maltreated children who appear to experience dilemmas or conflicts portrayed with the doll figures as too "near the bone" and anxiety-provoking. As a result, children typically tolerate the assessment without great anxiety, and even initially reluctant children often enjoy the activity.

Further reasons specific to maltreated children make a greater degree of displacement helpful. Children may choose not to reveal abuse out of loyalty, fear of retaliation, or the fear of losing the parent, or out of shame because they feel that the maltreatment indicates their own badness. Even so, in some cases, specific and as yet unreported maltreatment experiences "leaked" through the narrative despite the child's wish, conscious or otherwise, to keep them out of the picture.

The Story Stem Battery and Procedure

We currently use a set of 13 stems. Five (the LP or Little Pig stems, nicknamed after one of the stems) were originally devised, with a preliminary rating scheme (Hodges, 1990), on the basis of clinical experience in the assessment of abused children. Some of these stems originated in children's own unstructured play narratives, and when used as the basis for a story stem with other children, worked well in eliciting further material. All the LP stems were designed to elicit themes concerned with the child's expectations of relationships between parents and children, including those most central to the construct of security of attachment, namely, whether the child displays an expectation that parents will know when children need protection or comfort and will respond appropriately.

At this point in the development of the assessment, we learned of the MacArthur Story Stem Battery (MSSB), which was devised for much wider research uses and has been employed primarily with nonclinical populations (Bretherton, Ridgeway, & Cassidy, 1990; Oppenheim, Emde, & Warren, 1997). We added to our five LP stems eight selected from the MSSB that were potentially useful in the investigation of maltreated children (such as Lost Keys with its representation of parents arguing) or that expanded the areas covered (for example, to more explicit investigation of some aspects of sibling and peer relationships, as in Three's a Crowd and Bathroom Shelf). As a whole, the combined assessment battery functions to examine not only the central issues of attachment and of representations of maltreatment but also such themes as giving affection and setting boundaries. It also elicits indicators of other important aspects of the child's functioning, such as the modulation of aggression, and certain defensive maneuvers. A brief summary of the entire battery of stems is provided in appendix 1, and we describe the LP stems in more detail here.

The series of stems is always administered in the same order, LP stems followed by the MSSB stems, and uses the standard MSSB doll family of child (same gender as the child being interviewed), younger sibling (same gender), mother, and father. Two of the LP stories use animal figures. Story "props" are used, but minimally. The interview is designed for use with children between the ages of four and eight and generally takes about an hour to complete.

Interviews are videotaped and the tapes transcribed, producing a verbal "script" consisting of what the child says and what the interviewer says and "stage directions" describing what the child does—that is, the nonverbal narrative.

The LP Stems and Comments on Frequently Rated Responses

As the MacArthur stems have been described in chapter 3, we describe here only the rationale for the LP stems. The protocol appears in appendix 2.

In the first stem, Crying Outside, the interviewer shows the doll family (child, same gender sibling, mother, and father) in their house (outside and inside are represented by a corner and wall). The child figure goes outside, around the back of the house, and the interviewer says, "We can't see him now, but listen!" The interviewer makes the sound of a child crying. The first question (What's happening?) is followed by "show me and tell me what happens now." We begin with this story, rather than a more neutral- to-positive "warm-up" story, in part to convey the message that the story task is concerned not only with the positive or socially expectable but any part of the affective range. Ratings centered particularly on this stem include whether the child subject can acknowledge the doll child figure's distress, whether the parents are represented as aware of the child figure's distress, and the nature of their response, if so.

The second stem, Little Pig, uses only animal figures. The use of doll figures, though offering a displacement from the actual family, can sometimes still be too realistic for children who have had very unhappy family experiences. The use of animals offers a further step of displacement. In this stem, the child helps the interviewer set out the animals in groups (adults with young, except for a lone crocodile): camels together, cows together, lions and tigers, crocodile, pigs. The use of the word "family" is avoided in relation to the animals as it can be too anxiety-provoking. Instead, the interviewer says, "The little pig lived over here, with all the other pigs—big pigs and little pigs. And one day, this little pig went for a walk." The interviewer tells how the little pig leaves the other pigs and goes on a long walk past all the other animals, a long way away, and then the pig exclaims, "Oh! I'm lost! I can't see the other pigs! I don't know how to get back!"

Like the other stem, this separation story permits ratings of adult awareness of the child and of the adults' and siblings' response. Do the pigs realize the piglet has gone? Do they go to look for him and bring him home? Are they angry with him?

By introducing other animals, some of which are potential threats and others benign to neutral (camels, cows), the stem invites the child to show expectations of the potential responses of extrafamilial adult-like figures and of peers to the little pig's dilemma. The stem elicits a wide range of responses, for instance, denial of the problem, sometimes with the little pig omnipotently flying home; the big pigs being parents who retrieve the piglet; reunion with the pigs by other means (or a young and still "egocentric" children's version in which the piglet remains where he is and all the other pigs join him); help from other animals; going to live permanently with other animals; abandonment by the other pigs when little pig does get home; and threats and dangers with or without protection.

Based on a child's spontaneous narrative, the Stamping Elephant stem also uses animals, but in combination with the doll family. The doll family is shown having a picnic outside their house; the other animals are all in the garden. The elephant comes on the scene, "and sometimes this elephant gets a bit fierce and goes *stamp, stamp, stamp*; and the children and the animals feel scared when the elephant goes stamp, stamp." This stem introduces an explicit source of fear but does not state that the elephant is actually a danger. The elephant is specifically selected as a somewhat ambiguous figure, potentially benign as well as potentially fearsome. This potential ambiguity, in a large and powerful animal, is particularly useful with maltreated children in eliciting the "bad to good shift," which is described in more detail and which appears to be a display of multiple, unintegrated, representational models of the parent. Children tend to display this in relation to the animal figures, rather than the doll figures, underlining the usefulness of the extra step of displacement, where the anxiety associated with the actual parental figures may inhibit the display of this characteristic in relation to the doll parent figures. Also important in the ratings of this stem are issues of whether and how the adult figures act to protect the children from fear or danger and the child's response to the aggression implied in the stem: whether it is denied, managed within a coherent story, or escalated, sometimes to the point where it is rated as "extreme."

The Bikes story shows the child and friend asking Mom if they can go out on their bikes. Mom says yes, but tells them to be careful. The children go really fast on their bikes and then the child falls off. This stem is designed to explore themes of reliance on self, peers, or adults, expectations of help, and acknowledgment of distress. Themes around physical injury/death, and parental responses to injury, are often important in the responses. The Picture from School story was designed specifically to give scope for the child to represent parental interactions that are positive without being protective or comforting. These would include affection, praise, and admiration. In the stem, the child makes a picture in school and thinks "this is really good, I'm going to take it home when I go home from school"; after school he or she takes the picture, goes home, and knocks at the door. It is unsurprising that maltreated children's responses often do not display positive parent-child interactions; but we were surprised, at least initially, to find that in such children the stem often elicits particularly aggressive or bizarre disorganized responses, sometimes ignoring the story theme altogether, and sometimes including the socially expected praise for the picture but without the appropriate affect. It appears that though such children wish for a positive parental reaction, or perhaps merely know the socially expectable script, their effort to represent this in the narrative is countered by a more negative or ambivalent generic representation of likely patterns of parental response, producing rage and disorganization.

The LP Rating System

We use the MacArthur rating system for a range of categories, including resolution of conflict and codes concerning the child's affective response in the task. In addition, each story completion is rated separately for 32 themes or characteristics. These rating categories are listed, with brief definitions, in appendix 3. This coding system can be roughly organized under six overarching themes; the main rating categories included in each are given in parentheses.

1. Quality of engagement (disengagement, changes constraints, premature foreclosure);
2. Disorganization (catastrophic fantasy, atypical/bizarre, bad-good shift);
3. Aggression (coherent aggression, extreme aggression, physical punishment);
4. Child representation (child seeks help, child aggresses, child endangered, child injured/dead);
5. Adult representation (adult provides help, adult rejects, adult shows affection, adult unaware of child's distress); and
6. Positive adaptation (acknowledgment of distress, domestic life, realistic mastery).

The rating manual (Hodges, Steele, Hillman, & Henderson, 1998) provides detailed criteria and benchmark examples. For every narrative, each rating category (theme) is scored on a 3-point rating from 0 (theme not present) to 2 (definite/markedly present). Raters trained on this system for research purposes achieve good levels of reliability (kappas for rating categories range from .45 to 1.00 with a mean of .78). While all stories are coded for all 32 rating categories, certain stories elicit particular themes with greater frequency. Thus, an individual child's responses are examined from two viewpoints. Ratings for a particular category across all a child's narratives can be combined to provide an indication of how strongly a particular theme emerges for this individual; and particular stories can be examined for particular codes, so that we can examine how maltreated children's responses, evoked by a particular stem, may differ from responses of nonmaltreated children. We are currently applying the same dual procedure in research into the characteristics of different groups of children, namely, currently maltreated children; recently maltreated children who are now removed from maltreating parents; and previously maltreated children who are now in adoptive families. We are also using the narrative stems to track the process of change in the internal representations of the latter, adopted group, from placement until 2 years later.

Case Example: Individual Clinical Assessment

As part of the standard clinical team assessment, a story stem interview was carried out with "William," 6 years old. William's family had been referred because of concerns about the impact of his mother's longstanding mental health difficulties on his care and emotional development. These difficulties made her often angry with her husband and children and contributed to the sometimes violent marital relationship. She had been shocked to find herself pregnant with William and had never felt close to William since he was born. William's father tended to distance himself from the family, reducing his availability as an alternative parental figure.

William's responses to two stems follow. To assist the reader, these are given as a connected account rather than in transcript style. The stem is italicized. In the child's response, direct quotations from the child are given in quotation marks, clarifications in parentheses.

> *Little pig. (The child helps the interviewer to set out the animals in groups; the lions and tigers and cubs together, the cows and calf together, the crocodile, the camels and the little camel, the pigs and little pigs all together.) This is a story about this little pig. He lived over here, with all the other pigs, big ones and little ones. And one day, he went for a long walk. He went past the cows, and past the lions and tigers, and past the crocodile, and past the camels, and he went a* long *way. (Showing little pig all alone, at diagonally opposite corner of the table from the pigs and other animals.) And then he says, "OH! I'm lost! I can't see the other pigs! I don't know how to get back!" Show me and tell me what happens now.*

William said the little pig was lost. He then ignored the pigs and used the cows. The cow was "trotting all over the place" and said hello to other animals. "The baby calf said, 'Can you see my mummy' and walked over and saw the mummy (cow) and didn't come next to her because she was angry."

Then the baby calf went toward the crocodile "and the crocodile ate her (calf's) head off; and the mother (cow) was very upset and saw and made holes with her horns in the body of the crocodile and took the baby calf and the animal doctor came and fixed her head on. And the baby cow knew she must go to her (the mother) all the time, or daddy."

Then William showed the tiger saying to the mother cow "you silly cow. You must like babies." The tiger ate the baby cow and "bit off the Mummy cow's horn and it was gone—the cow jumped on the tiger and the tiger jumped on the cow—the cow got its horns again and it killed the tiger."

Because William's narrative had not addressed the central dilemma presented in the stem, he was then prompted with a set question as to what happened with the little pig who could not see how to get back. William said, "He sniffed his way to the pigs and went under the mummy" (showing him suckling). The tiger bit all the cows and gave them to the crocodile and the crocodile came and "ate all the baby pigs—just bones—and ate the daddy pig and ate the mummy, they was just bones."

> *Picture from School.* (*Child makes picture in school and thinks "this is really good, I'm going to take it home when I go home from school"; after school he takes picture and goes home, knocks at the door.*)

William said, "Sam (the boy protagonist) showed his Mum his picture. Mum said, 'This is silly, I'm going to put it in the bin' and she ripped it up. Silly Mummy—He took his mum to the dump and he threw her—he put his father in the bin and put the lid on. The bin men threw the bin in the dump." The dad was "covered in bruises and dirty marks." William went on, "Naughty Sam—put him (Sam) in the bin and flushed him down the toilet" and described how he went down the pipes in the dirty water. Sam carried his mum and dad and put them in the fire and "quickly they got out because sometimes people run into the ball of fire very quick." "Mum carried Sam on her shoulders and buried him in the ground so Sam can just breathe soil." Sam went onto the roof of the house pretending to be Father Christmas and "poured paper all over the place and made it cold" (i.e., torn-up paper looking like snow). Sam then frightened the younger sibling in the story and gave "soil surprises" to him and the parent figures.

The complete narrative assessment, including these examples, gave the following picture, which was provided as part of the clinical assessment.

1. William's narratives did not show parents as sources of comfort or affection for a child, or as aware of children's distress when they could be expected to be. There were no stories where the mother was shown as helpful or protective. There were some indications that the child figure knew the parent should be a source of security, but was not. This seemed well expressed when William said, "The baby calf said 'Can you see my mummy' and walked over and saw the mummy and didn't come next to her because she was angry."

2. The mother was shown as extremely rejecting in Picture from School, in which praise, affection, or admiration would be expected. This is the only stem of our battery specifically designed to elicit a positive representation of the par-

ents, and often in maltreated children it elicits very negative or disorganized representations.

3. In Bikes, in which the child hurts himself while playing, severe rejection was again displayed, in that the story completion showed both parents laughing at the child's injuries instead of providing comfort.

4. William tended to avoid acknowledgment of distress or anxiety and in several stories appeared to defend against it by a shift into bizarre, "manic," and sometimes sadistic material. This denial of distress may function defensively, to avoid being overwhelmed by pain or distress; it may be the best available strategy for young children when they cannot rely on comfort from an attachment figure. This feature therefore relates to the representation of parents as not providing protection or comfort.

5. The story completions frequently showed parental figures as aggressive toward the child, as well as rejecting.

6. The child figure was also shown as aggressive toward the parents. One likely contributor to this representation of the self is retaliatory "revenge fantasies" that develop in reponse to experiences of fear and helplessness, when the usual fight or flight responses to trauma are unavailable. This is, of course, a frequent occurrence in abuse: the child is unable either to escape the situation or to fight back in reality and instead develops conscious retaliatory fantasies (Pynoos & Eth, 1985).

7. The narratives included clear examples of "catastrophic fantasy"; these are characteristically found in children who show a disorganized attachment relationship, occurring in cases where the child has been maltreated by the parent or where the parent has been the victim of unresolved abuse or trauma (Main & Hesse, 1990; Solomon & George, 1999). The parent, whom the child needs as the source of security, is also the source of danger, making an organized response impossible. The prevalence of bizarre, incongruous material may also suggest a "disorganized" attachment relationship.

8. The narratives did not contain any instances of realistic or pleasurable domestic play, which we have found in the narratives of children who have a secure attachment relationship.

In brief, the assessment indicated a child who had been unable to develop representations of parental figures as sources of security, comfort, or affection, but experienced them as frightening, rejecting or unconcerned about him and was struggling with retaliatory aggressive feelings toward them. Perhaps it should be noted that in their aggression and bizarreness, these narratives contrast very strongly with those of children who are not distressed and affected by a history of maltreatment like William.

Interestingly, the assessment provided by the narratives was subsequently strongly endorsed by a play therapist who had seen William over a longer period, beginning prior to our assessment and continuing after it. We completed our assessment independently before discussing the findings with her. This supports the view that although the technique itself can only provide a sample of the child's representations on the particular day of assessment, this "snapshot" displays independently observable and relatively enduring features of the child's mental representations. In case it should seem that William's narrative completions are a product of his experience of play therapy, we should add that similarly vivid and revealing narrative completions are given by many children who have not experienced any form of therapy.

Reassessment After Foster Placement

How enduring are these features when the child's situation alters? William was reassessed 6 months later. He had been living in a foster home for several months. We used the same battery of narrative stems, which raises the issue, discussed elsewhere in this book, of the effect of repeating stems that children may remember. The reassessment still showed worrying features, but also showed increased coherence, with less bizarre and catastrophic material; the mother was shown less often as rejecting and occasionally as caregiving in an instrumental way: for instance, in one story attending to a child's injury. This time the Little Pig response still showed disorganization and aggression, though to a less extreme degree, with no resolution of the separation dilemma. The Picture from School response was a coherent narrative, in which the mother gave the picture to the father to put up in the child's room. Comforting behavior or affection from the parent figures were still absent from the narratives throughout. While test-retest factors may have some influence here, the reassessment suggests that even after a relatively brief period in an alternative, non-maltreating, family placement, there were some positive changes, while the negative effects of the earlier experience were nonetheless still very clear.

Studies of Children Removed From Situations of Maltreatment

The case study illustrates an interesting theoretical aspect of the narrative assessment approach; it allows examination of the mental representations of family life children are left with, when *removed* from situations of severe abuse and neglect. It is these representations that mediate, at least in part, the effects of earlier abuse on later development, in that they affect how new experiences are perceived and responded to. Assessment of these representations is therefore helpful in planning for future care and in helping new caregivers to anticipate and understand children's responses.

Narrative assessments, as indicated by the example of William, also have the potential to track changes in internal representations once the child is placed in a new setting. We are exploiting both these uses in a current research study. We are examining the frequency of key themes in the narrative completions of maltreated children, comparing those recently removed from abusive families with children removed similarly but less recently, who have just been placed in permanent adoptive families. We then follow these adoptees for the next 2 years, using narrative assessments to track changes in internal representations as they settle into their adoptive families. The children are thus retested on the same battery of stems, 1 year and 2 years after the initial assessment. The advantage of using the same battery is that it permits close, qualitative delineation, across assessment points, of the evolution of shifts that can be related to the child's experiences of the new family environment, to the child's own development, and to external evaluation of the child's behavior and functioning by teachers as well as parents. The disadvantage is obviously that there may be effects resulting only from the repetition of the same stems, even after such a time interval.

We are also comparing these two maltreated groups with children who, though their families may have experienced stresses, have never been the subject of professional concern about maltreatment, have always lived with at least one of their current parent figures, and have experienced no significant separations such as prolonged hospitalization. And we are comparing the previously maltreated adopted group with nonmaltreated children adopted as infants into nonmaltreating families.

We regard such research as critical because studies of children's mental representations of attachment relationships with parents have generally been carried out in environments characterized by continuity. This applies to earlier narrative assessment of maltreated children (Buchsbaum et al., 1992; Macfie et al., 1999), as well as children in good-enough family settings. Conversely, studies of children where there has been a marked *dis*continuity between earlier and later experiences, usually because the child has been removed from adverse circumstances, have generally not attempted to assess mental representations, but looked at behavior and cognitive development. This has been true both of studies of ex-institutional children (e.g., Hodges & Tizard, 1989a, 1989b) and the individual case studies of extreme deprivation (e.g., Koluchova, 1972, 1976; Skuse, 1984). Sharp discontinuities in the caregiving environment are rare—and usually unethical to produce experimentally—so children removed from one family environment into another provide a valuable natural experiment. However, in general, only clinical reports of children in psychotherapy have explored the internal representations and their natural history in the new setting.

Narrative assessments allow a briefer form of assessment and also allow systematic comparisons between groups of children. We conclude this chapter with a few examples of ratings where preliminary results show clear differences between previously maltreated children and nonmaltreated comparison children.

Some Preliminary Findings on Differences in Representational Models Between Previously Maltreated and Nonmaltreated Children

Some of these differences are unsurprising. For instance, themes of children or of adults being injured or dead appear most frequently in maltreated children, especially those most recently removed from situations of abuse. Other and perhaps less obvious categories also show differences.

Realistic or Pleasurable Domestic Life

We rate this category where there are even slight instances such as the following: "And he sat on the settee, watching the news, and he taked Daddy and taked him to watch the news, and he taked Mummy to watch the news." "And the daddy came (back from work) and knocked on the door. Knock, knock. And Mummy opened it and gave him a kiss, and then daddy sat down and baby sat on daddy's lap."

Given the "dollhouse" nature of the materials, it might be expected that they would, rather unspecifically, invite domestic play, in a way that would not allow much distinction between individuals or groups. In fact, we find the reverse. Maltreated children, especially the recently maltreated group, show this theme rarely compared to nonmaltreated children. What is more, systematic differences are found even within the group of nonmaltreated children. We applied our LP rating system to the London Parent-Child Project narrative assessments, which used MacArthur stems but not the LP stems. In this sample of relatively advantaged first-born children, infant attachment organization had earlier been assessed in the Strange Situation, so children's narrative assessments could be compared to their attachment category at 18 months. Within this group, the overall occurrence of the "domestic play" rating was somewhat higher than in the relatively disadvantaged comparison group. However, within the London Parent-Child Project group, secure attachment in infancy was associated with occurrence of the "domestic life" theme in the narrative assessment. In other words, even within the group of nonmaltreated children, the theme is linked to security of attachment rather than to advantaged circumstances in general.

Our clinical observations of maltreated children show a further point of contrast between nonmaltreated and maltreated groups. The story most likely to elicit the "realistic or pleasurable domestic life" theme was Picture from school, described as the only stem designed specifically to elicit positive representations of parental responses. However, in maltreated children, this stem in particular tended to elicit aggressive or "bizarre/atypical" responses, sometimes accompanied by the expectable positive "script" but with flat or otherwise inappropriate affect. Clinically, our sense was that these maltreated children knew the desirable "script" (praise, admiration, etc.) but that their effort to produce the wished-for positive parental reaction was denied by a more negative or ambivalent generic representation of likely patterns of parental response—the failure of attempted idealization, as it were. This led to the "bizarre" responses and prevented the maltreated children from displaying the spontaneous positive or everyday domesticity that formed part of the repertoire of the comparison group.

Adult Unaware/Ignores: Caregiver Responsiveness

In assessing children's generic models of attachment relationships, an obviously important dimension is the responsiveness of the caregiver. One aspect rated from the narratives is how often adults are shown not even as rejecting, but simply as unaware of children's needs or distress, when they could be expected to be so. A narrative by "Charles," 7 years old, illustrates this theme.

Crying Outside
The family are all sitting in the living room. (Family shown on sofa, watching TV.) The little boy gets up and goes outside, around the back of the house—we can't see him now, but listen! (Distressed crying sounds.) What's happening?

Charles: "He's crying." *(He's crying, why is he crying?)*

Charles: "Because he can't get back into his house." *(Long pause; interviewer asks, "show me and tell me what happens now in the story.")*

Charles: Er—I forgot. *(Charles points at the mother and father dolls:)* "They're still watching telly." *(Long pause. Interviewer asks if they heard the boy crying.)*

Charles: "No—they can't hear him because they've got it too loud."

The previously maltreated children, especially the more recently maltreated group, tend to show adults as unaware of children's distress more often than nonmaltreated children do.

Nonacknowledgment of Distress: A Defensive Manuever

Parents normally provide comfort, if a child is distressed. Children who cannot rely on this comfort have to cope with distress by other means. George (1996) describes a cognitively based model of defensive process suggesting that abused children are "trying desperately to deactivate or disconnect attachment-related fears and anxieties." One such "deactivating" coping strategy is simply not acknowledging the distress. In Ainsworth's Strange Situation, infants classified as insecure-avoidant in their attachments appear more or less oblivious to their mother's leaving, which provokes obvious distress in other children. However, physiological studies of such children during the procedure show that meanwhile they are physiologically aroused and experiencing stress (Spangler & Grossman, 1993). This avoidant picture may be accentuated in maltreated children. If a child's distress is met by nonrecognition, indifference, or active rejection, rather than by comfort, the best strategy for the child may be not to know, or show, that comfort is needed. However, though this may be the best adaptation available to the child in an abusive environment, it is much less adaptive in a new and safer environment where the child's distress can evoke a more comforting response. We found that the previously maltreated children, especially the recently maltreated group, were less able to acknowledge distress in the story characters than a nonmaltreated middle-class comparison group (Steele et al., 1999).

Similarly, it is a common clinical experience that if one asks the new foster parents of maltreated children what the child does if hurt, they report that these children do not seek comfort from any particular person but seem not even to notice that they have been hurt. Such "pain agnosia" regarding physical pain is a common finding in severely rejected children who show the condition of psychosocial dwarfism (D. Skuse, personal communication). However, until a child can acknowledge feeling anxiety or distress, it may be hard to learn that others can comfort or help him, rather than reject him or laugh at his distress. Defensive processes that once served to protect against further pain may jeopardize the adequate accommodation of internal working models to a changed reality, and hence damage optimal development. Early assessment and identification of such processes may help new foster or adoptive parents in letting their children learn the emotional uses of good caregiving.

Bad/Good Shifts: Narrative Evidence of Bowlby's "Multiple Models"

A particularly interesting difference is "bad/good shifts." That is, the child shows a character initially represented as good changing into bad, or vice versa, within the same narrative and without any apparent rationale for the change. If, for instance, the narrative were to show another character persuading the bad one to change his ways, this would *not* be rated as a bad/good shift. The bad/good shift rating also excludes instances where a child "signs off" with a storyteller's conventional happy ending in the final sentence, as in "Then the ogre became their friend after all and they all lived happily ever after." An illustration follows from "Susan" (6 years 11 months), many of whose narratives were largely nonverbal like this example.

> *Stamping Elephant*
> *The family is outside in the garden having a picnic, and the animals are in the garden too. Then a big elephant comes. And sometimes the elephant gets a bit fierce and goes stamp, stamp, stamp (demonstrating elephant stamping loudly); and the people and the animals get a bit scared when he goes stamp, stamp. Show me and tell me what happens now.*
>
> In her response, Susan first escalated the possible threat shown in the stem, by representing the elephant as really dangerous and out of control. She showed it getting more and more aggressive, shoving the pigs and other figures around, and smashing the house wall; then sticking its tail into the pigs. Then, with no link or explanation, she showed the small pigs riding on the elephant's back, making singsong noises. She would not reply when encouraged to tell what was happening. Eventually the interviewer inquired whether the elephant was being a nice elephant now and the pigs were not scared of him. Susan replied "Trick." She would not elaborate. The interviewer asked, "Who is doing the trick?" and Susan replied, "Elephant." She examined the elephant's underside and again showed the pigs balancing on the elephant's back.

This child had been removed into care after prolonged, sadistic sexual abuse by her father, apparently alluded to in this narrative. Her father was subsequently discovered to have previous convictions for the sexual abuse of children. There was unambiguous medical evidence of this child's abuse. Both parents, however, denied that he had abused her. Here, the shift, the trick, appeared to be an effort to fit together conflicting mental representations of the father. Bowlby (1988) has described children with multiple models like this instead of a single coherent representation, arising from situations where the parents insist on a denied or distorted account of traumatic events the child has actually observed. These multiple models can derive from several sources. In this case, the simplest may be a mismatch between Susan's own experience of reality (her father's sadistic abuse) and her parents' verbal account of reality (he was a nice father and never abused her). Sexual abusers often deliberately create in their child victims a sense, albeit conflicted, of being specially loved or privileged by their "special" relationship with the abuser. This is another potential source of multiple models. Attachment theory would suggest, further, that the instinctive need for the parent as a source of security asserts itself powerfully even when the parent is potentially a danger. The "disorganized" response occurs when a child is simultaneously fearful of the attachment figure and in need of that figure for a sense of safety. Abused children often strive against all odds to retain a mental representation of maltreating parents as positive and protective (Boston, 1983; Cassidy & Kobak, 1988). It is not surprising, then, that although the "bad/good shift" is relatively rare, it appears more often in the narratives of children removed from their families because of maltreatment than in nonmaltreated children's narratives.

The conflicting models of reality cannot be integrated into one coherent representation. The effect of this can be compared with the perception of a Necker cube: you can see it one way out, or the other, but what you cannot do is to see both sides out at once (fig. 13.1).

The child is struggling to represent simultaneously two incompatible versions of reality. It is a task as impossible as trying to see a Necker cube both ways out at once, and may lead to a similar phenomenon of "flipping" between one perception and another. We think it is a testament to the power of narrative stems as an assessment tool that they can capture such a phenomenon.

Summary and Conclusions

In this chapter, we have illustrated the value of narrative assessments in clinical work with young maltreated children. In brief, these assessments can provide a "window" to forms of memory and experience of attachment relationships that can be difficult or impossible to access by verbal means alone. This is of importance in the study of normally developing, nonmaltreated children just as it is for maltreated ones. The technique is of great clinical value in these latter assessments, though, in that it respects the difficult situation of already vulnerable

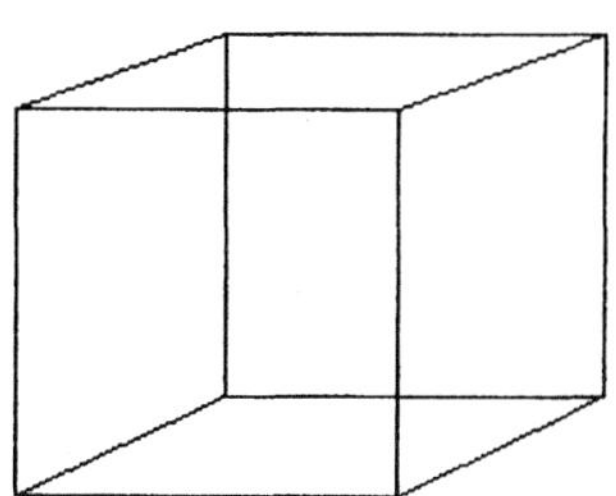

FIGURE 13.1 Necker cube

children and does not place them in further painful situations, such as conflicts of loyalty, during the assessment. Rather, it offers children a form of communication that engages them and is attuned to their own functioning. It can be uniquely helpful in these assessments, especially when the child may have experienced abuse or trauma over a long period of time, such that maltreatment experiences may be part of the unquestioned texture of the child's life.

However, the technique has a great value, beyond being a sensitive form of individual clinical assessment, in that it provides a standardized approach. This allows the development of a systematic body of research, so that normative baselines can be developed against which to compare individual children, or particular clinical groups. Thus, to give an example from our own work, we are currently examining emotionally abused children's narratives to look at how particular, independently rated forms of emotional abuse may be reflected in particular features of the child's narratives and how such children compare with nonmaltreated children and with those who have suffered other forms of abuse.

The systematic nature of the technique means that longitudinal comparisons, as well as cross-sectional ones, are possible. Thus, longitudinal changes in internal working models can be tracked, whether in normal development; in clinical work, for example, to examine effectiveness of therapeutic interventions; or in studies such as our own, in which we are examining how narratives reflect change in maltreated children's representational models, as the children adjust and develop within their adoptive families. In this study, we can relate the data from the narratives to other data, such as the adoptive parents' concurrent reports of child behavior and childrearing experience; assessments of children's self-esteem, attributions of intentionality, and cognitive functioning; and the adoptive parents' own attachment organization. Through the narratives, over time, we can examine the interactions of what the child brings to the placement, in the form of the expectations and perceptions guiding his or her behavior, and what the new parents bring to the child; and we can also look at the relationship between narrative changes and reported behavioral change in the child.

Our experience of using narrative assessment techniques, both clinically and in research, is that the research findings that are developing enhance their value as a clinical tool. Equally, their clinical sensitivity allows us as researchers to move away from too great an emphasis on adult-reported behavioral measures and to gather data reflecting children's own integration of their social, emotional, and cognitive development, given in their own voice and their own narrative form.

Appendix I

List of Story Stem Summaries

LP

1. Crying Outside (Doll family at home, child goes outside and behind house, sound of crying.)

2. Little Pig. (Little pig leaves the other pigs and goes on a long walk past all the other animals, then exclaims he is lost, can't see the other pigs, and doesn't know how to get back.)
3. Stamping Elephant. (Animals and doll family are outside the house. Elephant comes and sometimes this elephant gets a bit fierce and stamps; the children and the animals feel scared when the elephant goes stamp, stamp.)
4. Bikes. (Child and friend ask Mom if they can go out on their bikes; Mom says yes but be careful. The children go really fast on their bikes and then the child falls off.)
5. Picture from School. (Child makes picture in school and thinks "this is really good, I'm going to take it home when I go home from school"; after school he or she takes picture and goes home, knocks at the door.)

MSSB (*no. 12 modified following Fonagy et al.*)

6. Spilt Juice. (Family seated at the table drinking juice; child reaches across the table for more and spills the jug of juice over the floor.)
7. Mom's Headache. (Mom and child watching TV; Mom says she has a headache and must turn the TV off and lie down for a while, asks child to do something quietly meanwhile. Friend comes to door and wants to come in to watch TV program with child.)
8. Three's a Crowd. (Child and friend are playing ball in garden, while parents are talking to neighbors over fence. Little sibling wants to play too but friend refuses, saying he or she won't be child's friend any more if he or she lets sibling play.)
9. Burnt Hand. (Family is waiting for dinner; Mom is cooking at stove and warns child to be careful, pan is hot. Child can't wait, reaches for pan, spilling the dinner on the floor and burning hand.)
10. Lost Keys. (Child enters room to find parents angrily quarreling over who lost the keys.)
11. Bathroom Shelf. (Mother briefly goes next door to neighbor, warning children not to touch anything on the bathroom shelf while she is gone; younger sibling cuts finger and needs a band–aid.)
12. Burglar in the Dark. (Child in bed, in own room; parents on sofa. Child hears noise, lights go out, child fears it is a burglar.)
13. Exclusion Story. (Parents on sofa; father tells child they want some time alone and asks child to play in own room for a while; as child leaves, mother and father hug.)

Appendix 2

Protocol for Administering LP Stems

Story 1: Crying Outside

Characters: Child 1, Child 2, mom, dad
Props: Sofa, TV, side of house
Layout: All 4 characters sitting on sofa

Here is (Child 1) and he or she lived in a house with his or her mom and dad and little brother/sister. One day they were all sitting in their house and this little boy/girl (Child 1) went out and she went right around the back of the house; we cannot see him or her anymore but now listen (*make crying sounds*).

What's happening?

If child does say he or she is crying, acknowledge and then say, "Now, show me and tell me what happens now?"

If child does not say he or she is crying, then say, "He's crying, show me and tell me what happens now?

If nobody does anything in the story, ask, "Does anyone know he or she has gone?"

(If necessary, then ask who.)

Link to Next Story Now, in this next story, we don't need the people, but we need the animals, so help me put the people away and now let's get the animals out. (Ask child to help set out the animals in their groups.)

Story 2: Little Pig

Characters: Pigs, Cows, Lions/Tigers, Crocodile, Camels
Props: None
Layout: Animals in groups of same species.
[*Take care not to refer to "families" in administering story stem*]
In arranging animals, the animals should be in the bottom left hand of the table nearest to the child with the pig family in the corner.

Now, let me start off the story. Once there was a little pig and it lived here with all the other pigs, big ones and little ones. And the cows lived here, the lions lived here, the crocodile lived here. And the camels lived here.

One day, the little pig went for a long walk. He went a long way, past the cows, past the lions/tigers, past the crocodile, past the camels. (*Show little pig as far away as possible from all the other animals, in the top right hand corner of the table.*)

Then he said, "Oh! oh! I'm lost! I can't see the other pigs! I don't know how to get back!"

Show me and tell me what happens now.

Prompts (If little pig rejoins other pigs.) Did the other pigs say anything?

Link to Next Story Now in the next story, we have the people and the animals. (*Get the child to help set the family up having a picnic in the garden outside the house.*)

Story 3: Stamping Elephant

Characters: Elephant, all the animals, Child 1, Child 2, mom, dad
Props: Side of house
Layout: Same as for last story with family sitting on the ground (backs to the side of the house). Hold elephant out of sight as story stem begins.
The people are having a picnic in the garden and all the animals are there too. And there's a big elephant. (*Bring elephant onto table.*) The elephant sometimes gets fierce and it goes stamp, stamp, stamp (*showing elephant stamping*). The children

and the animals get a bit scared of the elephant when it is going stamp, stamp, stamp *(repeat the stamping)*.

Show me and tell me what happens now in the story.

Link to Next Story We don't need the animals now, so would you help me put them away. In the next story, we just need the people.

Story 4: Picture from School
Characters: Child 1, Child 2, mom, dad
Props: Sofa, side of house
Layout: Mom, dad, and Child 2 sitting on sofa at home
Child 1 is separate (at school).

So, here's Mom and Dad and Child 2 are at home and Child 1 is at school (*show Child 1 separate at a distance*).

And while he or she was at school he or she has made a really good picture.

And he or she thought, "This is a really good picture I've made, I like this picture. I'm going to take this home when I go home from school."

So, then school ended and he or she took his or her picture and went home, it was just round the corner, and he or she knocked at the door. (*Show child standing, knock on table for sound effect.*)

Show me and tell me what happens now.

Prompts If nothing happens,

- Does anyone say anything about his or her picture?
- What do they say/do?

If no mention of picture in child's response,

- What about his or her picture?

Story 5: Bikes
Characters: Child 1, Child 3 (same-sex friend), mom, dad, Child 2
Props: Sofa, side of house
Layout: Family at home (Examiner has Child 3 in hand)

For the story, we need Child 1's friend, what shall we call him or her?

In the next story, Child 1 is at home. There's a knock at the door. Child 1 answers it, and it's Child 1's friend (Child 3).

Child 3 says, "Let's go and play on our bikes!"

Child 1 says, "Ok, I'll go and ask my mom."

So, he or she went and asked his or her mom. (*Child 1 and Child 3 go to Mom.*)

Child 1: "Mom, can we go and play outside on our bikes?"

Mom says, "Yes, but be careful!"

We have to pretend the bikes. They went really fast on their bikes and they went "wheeeeee" (*Dramatize Child 1 and Child 3 riding fast and somewhat wildly*), but oh! (*Show Child 1 fallen on ground with friend standing next to him/her.*) What happened?

Show me and tell me what happens now.

(The MacArthur Battery stems follow on directly, using the same characters.)

Appendix 3

Little Pig Narrative Codes With Brief Definitions (From Hodges, Steele, Hillman, & Henderson, 1998)

1. *No Engagement With Story Task* The child avoids becoming engaged in a story from the start. This may be an explicit refusal or achieved by covert or indirect means.

2. *Disengagement* The child at first complies and shows some engagement with the story task, either by listening to the stem or beginning to develop a narrative, but then explicitly or covertly refuses to continue with it, and disengages from the narrative by stepping *outside* the story line so the story does not reach an end.

3. *No Closure* The child engages with the story but gets caught in an apparently endless elaboration or repetitive sequence. He or she seems unable to extricate self by some resolution either within the given story line or by bringing in other elements (such as those rated under omnipotence or altering story constraints).

4. *Premature Foreclosure* The child engages with the story and provides a resolution, but gives the interviewer the impression of wishing to get the story over as quickly as possible, avoiding any elaboration.

5. *Changing Motivational Constraints* (*Avoidance Within Narrative Frame*) The child *actively* alters the motivational constraints given by the narrative stem while continuing to address the main issue of the story. The child indicates that he or she is aware that he or she is introducing a change in what is "given."

6. *Magical/Omnipotent Responses* Responses that involve a quick magical story resolution by a wishful modification of reality or omnipotent or superhuman powers or behavior, whether required as part of the story resolution or appearing as a characteristic of the narrator or the child protagonist during the elaboration of the story.

7. *Physical Punishment* This code applies only to parents punishing children. "Routine" and relatively minor acts of punishment or discipline (e.g., a smack) are rated here. If the punishment is more severe (and may be enacted with marked affect), code as AGGRESSION.

8. *Limit Setting* This code is used if a parent or adult character sets limits, or in some way controls a child's behavior, often in response to a transgression. Acts of mild verbal punishment or discipline are incorporated under this category.

9. *Coherent Aggression* Physical or verbal aggression, excluding punishment, which seems appropriate and forms a coherent part of the narrative. These aggressive

manifestations do not appear extreme or out of proportion, allowing for a certain poetic license in the story completions, especially in the stories involving animals. Aggression does not take over the narrative to the exclusion of all else.

10. Child Shows Aggression and

11. Adult Shows Aggression Incidences of coherent and extreme aggression, if present, need to be categorized to indicate the protagonist. The categories Child Shows Aggression and Adult Shows Aggression simply record whether this aggression is shown by a child figure, an adult figure, or both.

12. Extreme Aggression Manifestations of aggression/punishment that appear excessive and extreme; or senseless, intrusive, unexpected, not of a piece with the narrative; or indicative of a violent and disorganized overall response to the story stem.

13. Catastrophic Fantasy This code also captures stories containing enormous accidents. Some examples of Extreme Aggression are also coded under this category. In addition, it includes nonaggressive disasters that are out of proportion, excessive, and out of keeping with the story stems, but that are "cold" in emotional tone.

14. Bizarre/Atypical Responses Child's narrative contains one or more incongruous features that do not appear to make sense within the story. The features are improbable and unrelated to the story, and the interviewer tends to feel a sense of bewilderment and disorganization.

15. Pleasurable/Realistic Representations of Domestic Life Representations of domestic routines and interactions, where the child's affective tone in showing these representations is positive or neutral.

16. Throwing/Being Thrown Away, Throwing/Being Thrown Out This includes instances that occur as part of a narrative, where one character throws another over the edge of the table, for example, but *also* includes cases where the child shows dolls, animals, furniture being thrown away, not necessarily integrated into the narrative.

17. Bad-to-Good Shift A character portrayed as "good" changes to "bad" (or vice versa) within the same narrative. No reason for the change is given, and there is nothing in the narrative to account for it.

18. Acknowledgment of Distress or Anxiety The child indicates acknowledgment and recognition of the emotional state of distress or anxiety of self or another story character, as presented in the stem or developed in the narrative.

19. Explicit Denial or Reversal of Perception of Distress or Anxiety This is the inverse of the previous category. It should be scored where the child *explicitly* denies or refuses to acknowledge an emotional state of distress or anxiety.

20. Realistic Active Mastery Child protagonist attempts to cope with story situation by realistic (i.e., not magical/omnipotent) active mastery. This may involve enlisting the help of others. Where the story situation involves conflict between the wishes of different individuals, realistic active mastery can involve efforts to negotiate between these, whether successfully or not.

21. Excessive Compliance Child is overly compliant. Attempts to please/placate others at the expense of acknowledging the child's own needs or wishes.

22. Child Seeks Help, Protection, or Comfort From Adult This category covers all examples where a child requests a protective, comforting, or helpful response from an adult.

23. Child Receives Help From Adult Adult is seen to provide help, comfort, or protection, whether in response to child's request or not.

24. Adult Shows Affection/Appreciation to Child The adult shows affection to the child, holds, cuddles, kisses, admires, appreciates, etc.

25. Sibs/Peers Help, Comfort, Protect Another Child The child's narrative shows a child figure providing help, comfort, or protection for another.

26. Child "Parents" or "Controls" Adult The child parents the parent figures by looking after their needs inappropriately, or bosses the parent, takes charge, and controls the parent.

27. Child Is Endangered The child's narrative shows explicit risk, threat, or danger to a child figure, from any source.

28. Child Injured/Dead and

29. Adult Injured/Dead The child makes it explicit in the narrative that a child figure/an adult figure is dead or injured. This rating is given even if a "dead" figure returns to life later in the narrative.

30. Adults Unaware Indications in the narrative that adult figures ignore the child figure and are unaware of the child figure's distress or difficulty, or do not respond when they could be expected to do so.

31. Adults Actively Rejecting The adult actively rejects the child or fails to respond to an explicit approach or appeal for help from the child (as under category 21, Child seeks help, comfort, or protection from adult).

32. Sexual Material This includes any reference to sexual behavior, or to genitals, bottoms, or breasts. It excludes kisses or cuddles given as comfort (as in no. 23), appropriate parental endearments (as in no. 24), or as greetings or goodbyes.

NOTE

We wish to acknowledge the generous support of the Sainsbury trusts (the Glasshouse Foundation and the Tedworth Charitable Trust) and the help of the many families who, together, make this research possible.

REFERENCES

Ainsworth, M., Blehar, M., Waters, E., & Wall, S. (1978). *Patterns of attachment.* Hillsdale, NJ: Lawrence Erlbaum.

Boston, M. (1983). The Tavistock Workshop: An overall view. In M. Boston & R. Szur, (Eds.), *Psychotherapy with severely deprived children,* (pp. 1–10). London: Routledge and Kegan Paul.

Bowlby, J. (1973). *Attachment and loss: Vol 2. Separation: Anxiety and anger.* London: Hogarth Press.

Bowlby, J. (1988). On knowing what you are not supposed to know and feeling what you are not supposed to feel. In *A secure base: clinical applications of attachment theory.* London: Routledge.

Bretherton, I. (1985). Attachment theory: Retrospect and prospect. In I. Bretherton & E. Waters (Eds.), *Growing points of attachment theory and research.* Child Development Monographs, 209, nos. 1–2. Chicago: University of Chicago Press.

Bretherton, I., Ridgeway, D., & Cassidy, J. (1990). Assessing internal working models of the attachment relationship: An attachment story completion task for 3-year-olds. In M. T. Greenberg, D. Cicchetti, & E. M. Cummings (Eds.), *Attachment in the preschool years* (pp. 273–310). London, University of Chicago Press.

Buchsbaum, H. K., & Emde, R. N. (1990). Play narratives in 36-month-old children: Early moral development and family relationships. *Psychoanalytic Study of the Child, 40,* 129–155.

Buchsbaum, H. K., Toth, S., Clyman, R. B., Cicchetti, D., & Emde, R. N. (1992). The use of a narrative story stem technique with maltreated children: Implications for theory and practice. *Development and Psychopathology, 4,* 603–625.

Cassidy, J., & Kobak, R. R. (1988). Avoidance and its relation to other defensive processes. In J. Belsky & T. Nezworski (Eds.), *Clinical implications of attachment* (pp. 300–323). Hillsdale, NJ: Lawrence Erlbaum.

Crittenden, P. M. (1988). Relationships at risk. In J. Belsky & T. Nezworski (Eds.), *Clinical implications of attachment* (pp. 136–174). . Hillsdale, NJ: Lawrence Erlbaum.

Cohen, N. J., & Squire, L. R. (1980). Preserved learning and retention pattern-analyzing skill in amnesia: Dissociation of knowing how knowing that. *Science, 221,* 207–210.

Emde, R. N., Biringen, Z., Clyman, R. B., & Oppenheim, D. (1991). The moral self of infancy: Affective core and procedural knowledge. *Developmental Review, 11,* 251–270.

Emde, R. N., & Clyman, R. B. (1997). "We hold these truths to be self-evident": The origins of moral motives in individual activity and shared experience. In J. D. Noshpitz (Ed.), *The handbook of child and adolescent psychiatry,* (Vol. 1, pp. 320–339). New York: John Wiley.

Fivush, R. (1984). Learning about school: The development of kindergartners' school scripts. *Child Development, 55,* 1697–1709.

Freud, S. (1958). The unconscious. In J. Strachey (Ed. & Trans), *The standard edition of the complete psychological works of Sigmund Freud* (Vol. 15, pp. 166–215). London: Hogarth. (Original work published 1915)

George, C. (1996). A representational perspective of child abuse and prevention: Internal working models of attachment and caregiving. *Child Abuse and Neglect, 20*(5), 411–424.

Hodges, J., Steele, M., Hillman, S., & Henderson, K. (1998). *Coding manual for story stem narrative responses, GOS/AFC narratives study.* Unpublished manuscript.

Hodges, J., Steele, M., Hillman, S., Henderson, K., & Neil, M. (2000). Effects of abuse on attachment representations; narrative assessments of abused children. *Journal of Child Psychotherapy, 26*(3), 433–455.

Hodges, J., & Tizard, B. (1989a). IQ and behavioural adjustment of ex-institutional adolescents. *Journal of Child Psychology and Psychiatry, 30*(1), 53–76.

Hodges, J., & Tizard, B. (1989b). Social and family relationships of ex-institutional adolescents. *Journal of Child Psychology and Psychiatry, 30*(1), 77–98.

Kestenbaum, R., Farber, E. A., & Sroufe, A. (1989). Individual differences in empathy among preschoolers: Relation to attachment history. *New Directions for Child Development, 44,* 51–64.

Koluchova, J. (1972). Severe deprivation in twins: A case study. *Journal of Child Psychology and Psychiatry, 13,* 107–114.

Koluchova, J. (1976). The further development of twins after severe and prolonged deprivation: A second report. *Journal of Child Psychology and Psychiatry, 17,* 181–188.

Macfie, J., Toth, S. L., Rogosch, F. A., Robinson, J., Emde, R. N., & Cicchetti, D. (1999) Effect of maltreatment on preschoolers narrative representations of responses to relieve distress and of role reversal. *Developmental Psychology, 35*(2), 460–465.

Main, M., & George, C. (1985). Responses of abused and disadvantaged toddlers to distress in age-mates; A study in the day-care setting. *Developmental Psychology, 21,* 407–12.

Main, M., & Hesse, E. (1990). Parents' unresolved traumatic experiences are related to infant disorganised attachment status: Is frightened and/or frightening behaviour the linking mechanism? In D. Cicchetti & M. E. Cummings (Eds.), *Attachment in the preschool years* (pp. 121–160). Chicago: University of Chicago Press.

Main, M., Kaplan, N., & Cassidy, J. (1985). Security in infancy, childhood and adulthood: A move to the level of representation. *Monographs of the Society for Research in Child Development, 50* (1–2, no. 209), 66–104.

McCrone, E., Egeland, B., Kalkoske, M., & Carlson, E. (1994). Relations between early maltreatment and mental representations of relationships assessed with projective storytelling in middle childhood. *Development and Psychopathology, 6,* 99–120.

Moore, T., & Ucko, L. E. (1961). Four to six: Constructiveness and conflict in meeting doll play problems. *Journal of Child Psychology and Psychiatry, 2,* 21–47.

Nelson, K., & Gruendel, J. (1981). Generalised event representations; basic building blocks of cognitive development. In A. Brown & M. Lamb (Eds.), *Advances in developmental psychology* (Vol. 1, pp. 131–158). Hillsdale, NJ: Lawrence Erlbaum.

Nelson, K., & Gruendel, J., (1986). Children's scripts. In K. Nelson (Ed.), *Event knowledge: Structure and function in development* (pp. 21–46). Hillsdale, NJ: Lawrence Erlbaum.

Oppenheim, D., Emde, R. N., & Warren, S. (1997). Children's narrative representations of mothers: Their development and associations with child and mother adaptation. *Child Development, 68*(1), 127–138.

Pynoos, R. S., & Eth, S. (1985). Developmental perspectives on psychic trauma in childhood. In C. R. Figley (Ed.), *Trauma and its wake: The study and treatment of post-traumatic stress disorder.* New York: Brunner/Mazel.

Reviere, S. L. (1996). *Memory of childhood trauma: A clinician's guide to the literature.* New York: Guilford Press.

Skuse, D. (1984). Extreme deprivation in early childhood—1. Diverse outcomes for three siblings from an extraordinary family. *Journal of Child Psychology and Psychiatry, 25,* 523–541.

Solomon, J., & George, C. (1999). The place of disorganisation in attachment theory. In J. Solomon & C. George (Eds.), *Attachment disorganisation* (p. 3–32). New York: Guilford Press.

Solomon, J., George, C., & De Jong, A. (1995). Children classified as controlling at age six: Evidence of disorganised representational strategies and aggression at home and at school. *Development and Psychopathology,* 7, 447–463.

Spangler, G., & Grossman, K. (1993). Biobehavioural organisation in securely and insecurely attached infants. *Child Development, 64,* 1439–1450.

Steele, M., Hodges, J., Kaniuk, J., Henderson, K., Hillman, S., & Bennett, P. (1999). The use of story stem narratives in assessing the inner world of the child: Implications for adoptive placements. In *Assessment, preparation and support: Implications from research* (pp. 19–29). London: British Agencies for Adoption and Fostering, BAAF Press..

Stern, D. N. (1985). *The interpersonal world of the infant.* New York: Basic Books.

Terr, L. (1988). What happens to early memories of trauma? A study of twenty children under age five at the time of documented traumatic events. *Journal of the American Academy of Child and Adolescent Psychiatry, 27*(1), 96–104.

Terr, L. (1990). *Too scared to cry.* New York: Basic Books.

Toth, S.L., Cicchetti, D., Macfie, J., & Emde, R. N. (1997). Representations of self and other in the narratives of neglected, physically abused, and sexually abused preschoolers. *Development and Psychopathology, 9,* 781–796.

Wolf, D. P. (1990). Being of several minds: Voices and version of the self in early childhood. In D. Cicchetti & M. Beeghly (Eds.), *The self in transition: Infancy to childhood* (pp. 183–212). Chicago: University of Chicago Press.

Woolgar, M. (1999). Projective doll play methodologies for preschool children. *Child Psychology and Psychiatry Review, 4*(3), 126–134.

CHRISTINE GERTSCH BETTENS
NICOLAS FAVEZ
DANIEL N. STERN

14

The Mother-Child Co-construction of an Event Lived by the Preschool Child: The Role of the Mother's Knowledge of "What Happened"

This chapter examines the mother's influence on the narrative skills of preschool children. It focuses on the effect of the mother's knowledge about the referent event on the accuracy of recall and the linguistic structure of the narrative. Compared to other well-investigated maternal factors that influence children's narrative constructions (such as style of interviewing), the role of the mother's information about the narrated event has not been directly studied. Yet such knowledge seems particularly relevant in light of the increased need to evaluate the value of children's testimony as witnesses or victims of abuse, and even in the more familiar context of the daily parent-child separations related to parental work or daycare practices: in both cases, the adult may have no knowledge, or only partial knowledge, of the exact content of the events narrated by the child, and not much is known about the level of the child's recall accuracy when the child is aware of the listener's degree of ignorance. More generally, the mother's knowledge or "blindness" about the narrated event may have a different impact on the process of narrative *co-construction* itself, due to unequal opportunities to contribute to the child's narrative. Considering the crucial role of co-narratives as the basis of most autobiographical memories in self-development, the clinical import of these issues is evident, and further study is required.

This study is part of a larger programmatic research project on the factors affecting the child's narratives of a lived and emotionally loaded event (for details, see Favez et al., 1994). Our concern was to explore the role played by the child's affective experience during the lived event in the narrative recounting of that event (Blaney, 1986). As a matter of fact, investigating the transformation processes affecting the narrativization of stressful experiences has recently become essential in considering the child's ability to provide legal testimony, either as witness or victim (Ceci & Bruck, 1993; Goodman et al., 1992). To solve both ecological and ethical problems related to that delicate area of investigation, several researchers have turned to medical examinations as referent events (Baker-Ward, Gordon, Ornstein, Larus, & Clubb, 1993; Ornstein, Gordon, & Larus, 1992; Saywitz, Goodman, Nicholas, & Moan, 1991). We chose instead to control more strictly the emotional burden and the temporal structure of the experience, by creating an "ad hoc" event (GEES, for Geneva Emotion Eliciting Scenario): our research strategy was based upon an 11-episode "theatrical happening" (or scenario) played by dressed up actors in our laboratory, in which the child actively participated. This *lived event* served as the referent event for the child's narrative to the mother, told immediately after the scenario (Narration Time 1) and again 2 weeks later (Narration Time 2). Half of the mothers watched the event through a one-way mirror, the other half remained "blind" to the event and were only "informed" about what happened through the child's narrative.

Mother's Knowledge and Preschool Children's Narratives

The issue of maternal influence on the child's narratives has been extensively explored, as a large part of early talk occurs within mother-child conversations. Most studies have examined conversations about past events, beginning at age 2 years: with the mother or another familiar adult, the child's narratives are more developed (i.e., include more evaluative devices, as in Miller & Sperry, 1988) and of greater duration and frequency than with siblings (Mannle, Barton, & Tomasello, 1991) or peers (Umiker-Sebeok, 1979). Initially dependent on the "scaffold" (Bruner, 1983) provided by the adult's questions, the child progressively becomes able to describe simple routines and scripts, but in a random order. From 3 years onward, the child's narratives are well organized and no longer need to be elicited; still, the adult plays an important role by filling the gaps when informed about the events mentioned by the child (Eisenberg, 1985). That last point may illustrate the major value of mother-child shared knowledge in the first stages of narrative development.

Such "conversational routines" about scripted contexts were shown to have similar relevance for conceptual (Sachs, 1983) and emotional development (Dunn, Brown, & Beardsall, 1991), as well as for the acquisition of general event memory and scripts (Shank & Abelson, 1977). Conversely, the narratives referring to specific events have been studied in relation with the development of autobiographical memory, a later memory system established approximately between 3 and 8 years of age, specifically human, and built on narrativized episodes (Nelson, 1989). As the general event memory, the autobiographical memory is considered as the product of a social construction (Nelson, 1993; Ratner, 1980), in which the mother plays a definite role by providing the child with the necessary "narrative frame."

To account for the mechanisms involved in that construction, and to understand how maternal verbal input may influence the child's ability to narrate and recall an event, most researchers refer to Vygotsky's (1978) model of adult-child "teaching" interactions: Vygotsky argued that all complex competencies are initially performed within interpersonal relationships, before becoming part of the child's intra-individual repertoire through a gradual process of internalization (we prefer the term "representation"); as the child becomes more efficient in a given task, the adult's scaffolding is less and less needed.

However, some adults appear to be less able to provide the child with convenient support. Several studies on the maternal style of narrative elicitation have revealed that the degree of elaboration characterizing the mother's discourse had qualitatively and quantitatively different outcomes for the 2½- to 3½-year-old child's narrative and memory skills, at the time (Engel, 1986, cited in Nelson, 1989; Fivush & Fromhoff, 1988), and for later development (1 year later, as in Fivush, 1991; McCabe & Peterson, 1991; Peterson & McCabe, 1992, or 2 years later, as in Reese, Haden, & Fivush, 1993). High elaborative mothers were shown to provide a great deal of narrative structure and had lengthy conversations about the past, whereas low elaborative mothers structured the child's narrative in a more repetitive way (Reese et al., 1993). Interestingly, elaborative mothers were sometimes referred to as "high information" mothers (Fivush & Fromhoff, 1988), because they simultaneously asked lots of questions and provided lots of information; in contrast, "low information" mothers asked few questions and provided less information. Another study (Tessler, 1986, cited in Nelson, 1989) focused on the maternal support during the child's encoding of the lived event (a visit to a museum at 3 years): in a free recall 1 week later, "only those objects that were discussed by mother and child together were remembered by the children. None of the questions referring to objects mentioned by mother alone, child alone, or neither one were answered correctly by any child" (Nelson, 1989, p. 142). Shared knowledge of an event appeared then to influence the recall of unique events, in addition to routine experiences.

Many recent studies have examined the manner in which the mother (or another adult) influences the child's narrative of highly salient, affectively loaded events (for a review, see Ceci & Bruck, 1993). Central issues affecting a child's testimony, such as accuracy and suggestibility, were shown to be influenced by an interviewer's emotional tone and disposition, especially in preschool children (Goodman, Rudy, Bottoms, & Aman, 1990). Though somewhat contradictory (e.g., Saywitz, Geiselman, & Bornstein, 1992), these results indicate that "positive" (e.g., warm and supportive) interviewing elicited the most accurate responses from children.

More generally, optimal affective regulation between mother and child, as opposed to over- and underregulation patterns, appears to be associated with enhanced child's abilities to focus on the affective core of a narrative (see chapter 15): optimally regulating mothers' enhanced cooperation and negotiation, pursuing shared emotions and pleasure in telling. On the other hand, overregulating mothers focused more on the conditions of the narrative and on the child's performance than on the narrative itself. Finally, underregulating mothers entirely followed the child's discourse, providing minimal support to the dialogue.

According to Pettit, Fegan, and Howie (1990), the interviewer's knowledge about the narrated event precisely affects her style of questioning and in turn the accuracy of the child's report: 3- to 5-year-old preschoolers were questioned 2 weeks after they experienced a staged event. The interviewers had either full knowledge of the event (condition 1), inaccurate information (2), or no information (3). Children's responses were most accurate in the first condition and least accurate in the inaccurate condition, as the child was influenced by the large amount of misleading questions. Interestingly, the first children questioned in the third condition were relatively accurate, but as the interviewer became progressively "informed" through the successive interviews, she asked more misleading questions and negatively influenced the children's accuracy. Another study (Goodman, Sharma, Golden, & Thomas, 1991) showed that parents were better at eliciting accurate information from their child than unfamiliar adults, even when given inaccurate information. Intimate knowledge and familiarity with the child appear then to affect a child's narrative, in addition to the available information about the narrated event.

Though the possible significance of the mother's knowledge has been pointed out by many authors (Eisenberg, 1985; Lucariello & Nelson, 1987; Sachs, 1983), the extent to which it specifically affects the child's narrative recall remains unclear. As a matter of fact, most researchers have chosen to restrict their study to experiences in which the mother had participated with the child (e.g., Reese et al., 1993) or, conversely, to settings where the child thought that the listener had not been informed about the event (Hausendorf & Quasthoff, 1992). Either option appears, however, to limit the generalization of the results, as talk about shared experiences may considerably differ from narrating a personal experience to someone who was not present (McCabe & Peterson, 1991). One possible argument is that prior knowledge of the event may induce the mother to be more informative and more elaborative, influencing the child's narrative in a more positive way: in research where the parents had to elicit from their 3-year-old child a story told by the experimenter while they were absent (Pratt, Kerig, Cowan, & Pape Cowan, 1988), the authors reported that "most of the stories produced by the children contained only a little information overall (typically, two or three items), and only a few managed to tell coherent story propositions" (p. 835). The parent's lack of knowledge appeared then to reduce the child's ability to produce a coherent narration. However, the exact amount of loss of information was difficult to evaluate in the absence of a control condition where the parent was informed about the event.

The Mother-Child Narrative Co-construction

Differences in maternal influence, and particularly the impact of maternal style over the child's narrative performance, have been viewed by many authors as indicative of co-construction between mother and child. Narrative co-construction has recently been of interest, as it may account for various developmental acquisitions: narrative skills (Reese et al., 1993), autobiographical memory (Nelson,

1993), self–development (Fivush, 1991; Wolf & Hicks, 1989), moral development (Emde, Johnson, & Easterbrooks, 1988), attachment (Bretherton, 1993; see also the other related chapters here). Similarly, both notions of narrated self (Stern, 1985) and "proto-narrative envelope" (Stern, 1993a, 1993b, 1994, 1995a, 1995b) presuppose the active presence of a "narrative other."

In the clinical field as well, the joint construction of narratives with a significant other appears to hold a "magical sway" over human development and growth. Diagnostic and psychotherapeutic practices, for example, are now commonly described as (co)-narrative processes between patient(s) and therapist(s), both in person and in system-centered approaches. In his fundamental work, Spence (1982) has challenged the question of objective or neutral data in psychoanalysis (the "historical" or "archeological truth") in favor of a sufficiently coherent "narrative truth." Similarly, supporters of constructivism in general system theory consider that meaning and understanding are socially and intersubjectively created constructions and view therapeutic conversations as privileged fields where shared meanings may emerge and be modified, in order to promote the co-creation of alternative and more adaptive narratives (Anderson & Goolishian, 1988; de Shazer, 1985; Goolishian & Anderson, 1987; O'Hanlon & Weiner-Davis, 1989; Watzlawick, 1984; White & Epston, 1990).

However, the processes underlying co-constructed narratives remain unknown, essentially because co-construction has been generally mistaken for scaffolding or tutoring mechanisms. According to Beaudichon, Verba, and Winnykamen (1988), only those exchanges based on *symmetrical* competencies and relationships, as well as on goal sharing, may be considered as co-constructed. Conversely, scaffolding and tutoring (in the Vygotskian sense) rely on *asymmetrical* skills and distinct goals (the apprentice wants to "do," the expert wants to have him "doing"). Yet, in most studies dedicated to the development of narrative skills, the Vygotskian model is identified with co-construction (e.g., Ochs, Taylor, Rudolph, & Smith, 1992; Reese et al., 1993). Furthermore, many aspects of the tutoring process itself lack investigation, such as how much time is needed for a notion to be internally represented, or to what extent a newly acquired skill may be generalized from one domain to another. Both issues appear to be connected, as the child likely first needs to establish an internal representation of her newly acquired skills before generalizing them. Recent investigations document quite extended periods of time for the internalization to proceed (6 to 12 months in Peterson & McCabe, 1992, or Fivush, 1991; over 1 year in Reese et al., 1993), but explorations of the generalization issue lead to more contradictory findings. Some narrative skills developed with the mother may generalize to a narration performed with a neutral interviewer (Peterson & McCabe, 1992), even when the interviewer purposefully interacted in a different way from the mother (Tessler, 1991, in Nelson, 1993). Yet investigations of memory abilities within narratives failed to report generalization effects to other related memory tasks in preschool children (Tessler, 1986, Nelson, 1989; Weinert, 1991).

Drawing a clear distinction between co-construction and tutoring seems relevant in light of the shared knowledge issue: relying on a common knowledge base

(Lucariello & Nelson, 1987) may be more determinant in tutorial interactions, in which the mother must precisely expand the child's knowledge by means of her own prior knowledge, than in co-narratives, where both partners jointly establish an "emergent" knowledge base. Yet recent findings document an inverse relationship: according to Eder (1988), co-narratives are strictly related to shared knowledge, as collaborative narratives simultaneously emerge from and promote the development of shared perceptions and solidarity among co-narrators. Similarly, Ochs et al. (1992), in a study about familial storytelling (5-year-olds with their parents and an older sibling), underline the role of shared knowledge for the co-constructed activity of theory building.

Goals and Hypotheses

In the aforementioned studies, the absence of control over the referent event limits both the exploration of the mother's knowledge effects and the further understanding of co-construction mechanisms. This investigation is based on a unique event that includes defined episodes designed to promote specific emotions in the child and to allow for the control of the mother's access to the child's experience. These were our goals:

1. To examine the influence of the mother's knowledge of the narrated event (we will use the term mother's "information" to avoid possible confusion with the general concept of "world knowledge") on the child's narrative, immediately after the event (Narrative Time 1 or NT1) and 2 weeks later (Narrative Time 2 or NT2). We hypothesized that children whose mother had watched the scenario (informed mothers or IMs) would produce more accurate and more highly structured narratives than children of uninformed mothers (UMs).
2. To account for this possible influence in terms of co-construction versus tutoring mechanisms. We hypothesized that the narratives in the IM group would be more co-constructed, as mother and child both know the details of the referent event (symmetrical competencies) and the global meaning of the story (goal sharing). Co-constructing a narrative should also be associated, on the mother's side, with an optimal pattern of affect regulation, whereas an asymmetrical tutorial exchange based on distinct goals should be characterized by overregulation of affect (see chapter 15). As asymmetrical (or "Vygotskian") interactions allow for the progressive representation and generalization of the taught skills by the child (Beaudichon et al., 1988), the child's immediate and delayed recall will be compared in each group, as well as the respective performance of IM and UM children on a non-narrative task, a picture-sorting task about the lived event presented after the second narrative.

Except for affect regulation, maternal contributions were considered as a mediating variable and only qualitatively explored, as our main research strategy was to examine the relationships between the child's emotional experience during the lived event and the characteristics of her narrative recounting. Some examples of qualitative descriptions will be provided in the discussion to illustrate our quantitative findings.

Method

Subjects

The subjects were 55 children (31 girls and 24 boys; mean age = 4 years, 4 months; age range: 3.6 to 5.11 years).[1] One child (a 3 years, 8 months girl) refused to participate in the scenario and three children (two girls, one boy; age range: 4.0 to 5.7 years; two from IM group, one from UM group) did not return at NT2: these four children were excluded from the final sample (N= 51, 28 girls and 23 boys). Subjects were recruited through announcements in daycare centers in Geneva and came with their mothers to our laboratory. The mothers were told that we were interested in "the way children tell stories at different ages" but received no further indication about the specific procedure. All the children came from normal middle- to upper-class French-speaking homes and were born in Geneva. They were tested for their verbal abilities using the WPPSI (Wechsler, 1972): verbal IQs were within normal range (M = 114.6, SD = 17.0). To assess the possible influence of verbal IQ on the dependent variables, two groups of children (above and below group mean) were considered, "high IQ" (N= 26; M = 128; range: 115 to 147) and "low IQ" (N = 25; M = 101; range: 70 to 112). No significant effects were found on any of the dependent variables, using one-way analyses of variance (ANOVAs). Similarly, one-way ANOVAs revealed no significant effects of child's gender on the dependent variables; yet our sample may have been too limited to test such effects, and especially interaction effects between independent variables (gender, for example, was not equally distributed across age).

Design and Procedure

On their arrival at the laboratory, the child and the mother had an informal chat with the experimenter to make them comfortable. After this warm-up period, lasting usually 20 to 30 minutes, the child was separated from the mother and participated with the experimenter in an 11-episode scenario. The mother proceeded to another room and was randomly assigned to one of two conditions: uninformed mothers (25 subjects) had no direct access to the child's experience and simply waited in the adjacent room with another experimenter. Informed mothers (26 subjects) watched the scenario through a one-way mirror.

In both conditions, the child was made aware of the location of the mother by an explicit description: UM children were told that "Mom will wait for you in the other room"; IM children were told that "Mom will be able to watch the story from behind the mirror in the other room."

Nine children (5 initially assigned as UM, 4 as IM) refused to be separated from their mother (5 girls and 4 boys; mean age: 4 years, 3 months; age range: 3 years, 10 months to 4 years, 11 months): in such cases, the mother was allowed to watch the story in the same room as the child, seated on a chair and not interfering with the scenario. These mothers were obviously informed mothers, but as both mother's physical presence in the room and child's separation anxiety could have biased the results, all analyses were performed twice, on the whole sample and without these nine subjects. All results being identical, these subjects were included in the IM group.

Immediately after the scenario, the mother entered the room where the child was and asked the child to tell her the story he or she had just experienced. The precise instructions given to the mother in both conditions were different: in the UM group, we simply asked the mother to "ask her child to tell the story," whereas in the IM group, we asked both mother and child to "tell the story together, as if it was told to a third person."[2] At the end of the session, the mother was asked not to discuss the scenario at home until the second visit.

Two weeks after that first narrative (NT1), the mother and the child went back to the laboratory to tell the story again (NT2). The instructions for NT2 were the same as for NT1. After the narrative, the child was left alone with the experimenter for a picture-sorting task: nine photographs from the scenario (all episodes except the first and the eighth) were presented in a fixed random order, and the child was asked to order "these pictures made when another child was present, from the beginning of the story to its end." During both visits, the whole procedure was videotaped and the narratives were audio-recorded.

Referent Event

To have direct access to the event narrated by the child, and to systematically explore the transformations induced by the narrative process, we chose to rely on a laboratory event in which the child actively participated, allowing for detailed observations of emotional and coping behaviors (Gertsch Bettens & Favez, 1995). For methodological and ethical reasons, this event had to be (1) identical for all children, making easier the comparison of each narration with the original event; and (2) moderately stressful, but intense enough so as to elicit a specific range of controlled emotions.

We created the GEES (Geneva Emotion Eliciting Scenario), an 11-episode scenario played by two female students (one dressed as a clown, the other as a queen), and focused on the theme of separation, a highly salient theme for 4- to 5-year-old children. The episodes were of various duration in order to create a coherent "narrativized" story (Labov, 1972), with an initial orientation phase, a complicating action phase, a high point, a resolution phase, and a coda. Each episode was built so as to evoke a specific emotion: happiness, sadness, or fear. Preliminary analyses on a pilot sample ($N = 22$, 11 girls and 11 boys) confirmed that for each episode, the emotions that the episodes were designed to evoke were observed significantly more often than unexpected emotions (Favez et al., 1994). The phases of the story and the corresponding affects follow (see also table 14.1 for more details about the specific episodes):

Orientation In episodes 1 and 2, the child discovered the clown and her Teddy bear, hidden under a blanket. The child was informed that "the robot queen" would come later and take the bear to the "Robots Kingdom" for a 6-month trip. These two episodes usually elicited moderate wariness.

Complicating Action In episodes 3, 4, and 5, the child played with the clown and the "coach" (xylophone, tumbling the bear in somersaults), until the queen suddenly arrived, dressed in black, wearing a mask and a crown, and flanked by two (small) noisy robot toys. Episodes 3 and 4 evoked happiness, whereas episode 5 clearly elicited fear.

High Point In the 6th episode, the queen solemnly left with the bear and the robots. This episode, the affective core of the story, elicited intense blended emotions (fear and sadness) and maximal scores of coping behaviors.

Resolution During episodes 7, 8, and 9, the clown cried and complained about being lonely. She was comforted by the "coach" and the child, and they sang a song together in order to "make the clown feel better." The first two episodes elicited sadness, giving way to happiness during the singing.

Coda In the last episodes (10 and 11), the clown claimed to feel better and proposed a new game (soap bubbles). She then suddenly pretended to be late for an urgent meeting and abruptly left the room. Episode 10 elicited happiness, whereas episode 11 was associated with blended emotions (happiness, sadness, or fear).

For obvious ethical reasons, the child was "coached" throughout the episodes by a referent female experimenter who accompanied the child during the whole procedure. Furthermore, the students playing the clown and the queen were instructed to shorten certain episodes, should the child become too upset.

Transcription of Protocols

The child's verbal productions were transcribed from the audio-records by a trained assistant. Three definite types of speech acts were considered: clauses (complete utterances including a subject and a predicate), phatics (short incomplete utterances, yes/no answers), and silences (pauses lasting at least 5 seconds. Furthermore, references (clauses referring specifically or generally to the scenario) were opposed to off-topic talk (clauses not referring to the scenario). A second assistant, blind to the hypotheses of the research, independently transcribed 20% of the protocols: Cohen's kappas computed for the five categories yielded reliability between K = .88 (silences) and K = .95 (off-topic talk). These categories were used for the computation of indexes (see page 278).

As stated before, maternal contributions to the narratives were not studied in a systematic or quantitative way (except by Favez, chapter 15). We used the videotapes to examine qualitative features of mothers' behavior, such as types of questions, prompts, affective tone, and so on. Examples of this exploration will be provided throughout the discussion to illustrate our findings.

Narrative Accuracy Indexes

To evaluate the fit between the referent event and the narrative, we extracted each child's specific reference to the episodes from the transcriptions. Due to the

TABLE 14.1. GEES: Description of Episodes and Corresponding Emotions

Episodes	Description	Emotion
1	The "coach" tells the child that "the story is going to start now." They hear xylophone music played from under a table covered with a blanket, and go uplift the blanket.	Fear
2	Under the table are hidden a clown and her Teddy bear: they greet the child and the "coach," and the clown explains that they are celebrating bear's departure to "Robot Kingdom": the "robot queen" will come and take the bear for a six-months-trip.	Fear
3	The clown comes out from under the table and invites the child and the "coach" to play music together on the xylophone.	Happiness
4	The clown pretends that the bear wants to be hugged and tumbled in somersaults. She invites the child to bring it back and starts tumbling the bear while laughing.	Happiness
5	The queen suddenly enters the room during the "bear game," dressed in black, wearing a mask and a crown, and flanked by two noisy robot-toys. She solemnly puts them on the floor, and announces that she has to take the bear with her.	Fear
6	The clown, "coach," and child kiss the bear and say good-bye. The queen picks-up the robots and the bear without a word and comes out of the room.	Fear/Sadness
7	The clown starts to cry, complaining to be lonely. The "coach" remains neutral.	Sadness
8	After a short moment, the "coach" invites the child to comfort the clown: she comes closer and gently rocks the clown, inviting the child to imitate her.	Sadness
9	The "coach" pretends that singing a song together will help the clown to feel better. She proposes "Le Pont d'Avignon," an old traditional French song known by all children. As all three sing and dance the song, the clown shows more and more happiness.	Happiness
10	Feeling better, the clown proposes a surprise, a game with soap bubbles. The "coach" (and the child!) happily agree.	Happiness
11	The clown suddenly checks her watch, pretending to be late for an urgent meeting, quickly waves good-bye, and runs out of the room. The child is told by the "coach" that "the story is over."	Blended

limited number of episodes and to their precise definition, the coding was easy and needed no specific instruction: independent coders reached 100% agreement. Two indexes were computed, separately for NT1 and NT2:

Number of "Produced Episodes" Any episode recalled by the child was coded as a produced episode, whether mentioned spontaneously or elicited by maternal probes.[3] The index varied from 0 (no episode produced) to 11 (all episodes produced).

Narrative Sequence Index We considered the successive pairs of references (first and second reference, second and third, and so on), and assigned two points if the pair was correctly ordered (e.g., episode 3 followed by episode 4), one point if the order was correct, but one or more episodes were missing or located elsewhere in the narrative (e.g., episode 3 followed by episode 6), and, finally, no point for an incorrect sequence (e.g., episode 3 followed by episode 1). As there can be a maximum of 10 pairs (episodes 1–2 to episodes 10–11), the narrative sequence index (hereafter referred to as NSI) had a range of 0 to 20.

To allow for comparisons, we expressed indexes of narrative accuracy in percentages of their respective maximal score (11 for produced episodes, 20 for NSI).

Linguistic Structure Indexes

In addition to the accuracy indexes accounting specifically for the narrative performance, four indexes related to more general linguistic features of the narratives were computed, separately for NT1 and NT2:

Talkativeness This measure was defined as the total number of child's speech acts (clauses, phatics, and silences).

Mean Length of Utterance (MLU) This measure (here computed in words) is regarded by many authors as the best index of structural complexity until the age of 3 (Bates, Bretherton, & Snyder, 1988). At older ages, as for adult speakers, MLU becomes dependent on situational and personal factors (Johnston & Kahmi, cited in Bates et al., 1988) and may therefore be affected by the degree of mother's information about the event.

Construction Index This measure was operationally defined as the ratio between clauses and speech acts (i.e., number of clauses divided by number of speech acts). A score of 1 corresponded to an exclusive use of complete clauses (including at least a subject and a predicate); conversely, an exclusive use of phatics (yes/no, partial answers) or silences yielded a score of 0.

On-topic Talk Index This measure was operationally defined as the ratio between references and clauses (i.e., number of references divided by number of clauses). A score of 1 indicated that the whole narrative referred to the scenario, whereas a score of 0 implied that the child never referred to the scenario. "On-topic" was preferred to "off-topic talk" (e.g., Reese et al., 1993), as the creation of a specific event decreased the probability of talking about topics not related to the referent event.

Nonnarrative Sequence Index

The same procedure used to compute the "narrative sequence index" was applied to the picture-sorting task performed after the second narrative. Two points were assigned for each pair of correctly ordered pictures, one point if the order was correct but not the sequence, and no point for an incorrect pair of episodes. As there can be a maximum of eight pairs (pictures 1–2 to pictures 8–9), the "nonnarrative sequence index" (NNSI) had a range of 0 to 16. To allow for comparisons, we expressed NNSI in percentage of its maximal score (16).

Mother's Patterns of Affect Regulation

We used the three main patterns Nicholas Favez extracted from the maternal verbal productions at NT1 ($N = 46$; 22 IM, 24 UM).[4] Independent coders achieved a reliability of K = .69 to K = .86 (Cohen's kappa). More details about the scoring are provided in chapter 15.

Overregulation ($n = 22$) These mothers strictly structured the interview, relying on self-repetitions, self-expansions, orders, requests, and factual assertives.

Optimal Regulation ($n = 13$) These mothers enhanced cooperation and negotiation, relying on other-repetitions, other-expansions, expressives, and general assertives.

Underregulation ($n = 11$) These mothers spoke less than their child, asking few questions and exerting low constraint on the child's discourse.

Results

Child's Narrative Accuracy

As indicated in table 14.2, the whole sample produced on average 62.21% of the 11 episodes (about 7) at NT1 and 52.76% (about 6) at NT2. The performance on the narrative sequence index was relatively modest, reaching only 30.29% at NT1 and 26.77% at NT2.

The effects of condition (IM vs. UM) and narration (NT1 vs. NT2) on narrative accuracy indexes were examined using separate 2 x 2 repeated measures ANOVAs, with mother's information as between-subjects factor and narrative time as within-subjects factor. Table 14.2 presents the mean narrative accuracy scores. For both indexes, a significant condition effect was found for produced episodes, $F(1, 49) = 9.45$, $p < .01$, and for narrative sequence index, $F(1, 49) = 13.39$, $p < .001$: the number of produced episodes was greater in the IM group

TABLE 14.2. Mean Indexes of Narrative Accuracy (and SDs) as a Function of Mother's Information and Narrative Time

	Narrative time 1			Narrative time 2		
Narrative accuracy	Total	Informed mother	Uninformed mother	Total	Informed mother	Uninformed mother
Produced episode[a]	62.21 (23.38)	72.03 (15.41)	52.00 (26.05)	52.76 (23.57)	59.45 (16.91)	45.82 (27.58)
Narrative sequence index[a]	30.29 (18.26)	39.23 (15.47)	21.00 (16.39)	26.77 (19.69)	32.31 (17.33)	21.00 (20.67)

Note. $N = 51$.

[a]Scores expressed in percentages of maximal score.

(72.03%, about 8, at NT1; 59.45%, about 6.5, at NT2) than in the UM group (52.00%, about 6, at NT1; 45.82%, about 5, at NT2). IM children also performed better on the narrative sequence index (39.23% vs. 21.00% at NT1; 32.31% vs. 21.00% at NT2). Narrative time only significantly affected the number of produced episodes, $F(1, 49) = 10.75, p < .01$, indicating that in both conditions, more episodes were produced at NT1. The narrative sequence index was unaffected by narrative time. For both indexes of narrative accuracy, the two-way (mother's information x narrative time) interaction was not significant.

Child's Linguistic Structure

As indicated in table 14.3, the whole sample used on average 57.77 speech acts at NT1 and 44.74 at NT2, with considerable variations ($SD = 38.48$ and 22.68, respectively, for NT1 and NT2). The MLU reached about four words in both narratives (MLU = 4.02 and 3.73, respectively, for NT1 and NT2). The construction index reached 0.90 at NT1 and 0.87 at NT2, indicating that 90% and 87%, respectively, of the speech acts were complete clauses. Finally, 73% (0.73) of the clauses were on-topic talk at NT1 and 67% (0.67) at NT2.

The linguistic structure data were analyzed in the same way the narrative accuracy data were analyzed (2 x 2 repeated measures ANOVAs). Condition was found to be significant for the construction index only, $F(1, 49) = 5.83$, $p < .05$, indicating that IM children used more complete clauses and fewer phatics and silences than UM children (0.92 vs. 0.87 and 0.89 vs. 0.84, respectively, for NT1 and NT2). More important, the two-way (condition x narrative time) interaction yielded significance for MLU, $F(1, 49) = 11.20, p < .01$: one-way ANOVAs confirmed that, compared to UM children, IM children used fewer words at NT1 (3.68 and 4.37, for IM and UM, respectively), $F(1, 49) = 4.08, p < .05$, whereas both groups had about the same MLU at NT2 (3.84 and 3.62). Accordingly, the observed main effect of narrative time on MLU, $F(1, 49) = 4.83, p < .05$, corresponded to inverse tendencies in each group, IM chil-

TABLE 14.3. Mean Indexes of Linguistic Structure (and SDs) as a Function of Mother's Information and Narrative Time

	Narrative time 1			Narrative time 2		
Linguistic structure	Total	Informed mother	Uninformed mother	Total	Informed mother	Uninformed mother
Talkativeness (speech acts)	57.77	62.46	52.88	44.74	43.67	45.67
	(38.48)	(45.61)	(29.47)	(22.68)	(13.09)	(28.80)
MLU	4.02	3.68	4.37	3.73	3.84	3.62
	(1.25)	(1.40)	(0.98)	(1.02)	(1.13)	(0.89)
Construction	0.90	0.92	0.87	0.87	0.89	0.84
	(0.07)	(0.06)	(0.07)	(0.10)	(0.08)	(0.12)
On-topic talk	0.73	0.74	0.71	0.67	0.70	0.63
	(0.19)	(0.17)	(0.22)	(0.20)	(0.13)	(0.25)

Note. $N = 51$.

dren using more words at NT2 than at NT1, whereas UM children used more words at NT1 than at NT2.

Significant narrative time effects were also found for the three other linguistic structure indexes, $F(1, 49) = 7.98$, $p < .01$ (talkativeness), $F(1, 49) = 4.42$, $p < .05$ (construction), and $F(1, 49) = 5.39$, $p < .05$ (on-topic talk), indicating that in both conditions, the children talked less, used fewer complete clauses, and referred less to the scenario at NT2. Two-way (mother's information x narrative time) interaction effects were not significant.

Child's Nonnarrative Sequence Index (NT2)

The results are presented in figure 14.1: in order to allow for comparisons of nonnarrative versus narrative accuracy, we represented NSI scores at NT1 and NT2 in addition to nonnarrative sequence index scores at NT2. As indicated in figure 14.1, NNSI for the whole sample reached 48.68% ($SD = 25.07$), a much better score than the narrative sequence index at NT1 (30.29%) and NT2 (26.77%). Sorting the nine pictures appeared then to be easier than telling the 11 episodes of the story.

The effect of the mother's information on NNSI was examined using a one-way ANOVA (fig. 14.1). A significant effect was found, $F(1, 49) = 3.88$, $p < .05$, with IM children correctly recalling 55.09% of the original sequence of pictures ($SD = 27.95$), as opposed to 41.75% in UM group ($SD = 19.82$): four IM children were in particular able to order the nine pictures, whereas UM's best performance corresponded to six pictures only (one child). Thus, the influence of the mother's information on the narrative accuracy measures appeared to extend to the picture-sorting task performed *without* the mother. In both groups, the nonnarrative sequence index was superior to NSI at NT1 and NT2.

Mother's Affect Regulation

We used a chi-square test to cross mother's information conditions (IM vs. UM) with the three patterns of mother's affect regulation at NT1 (over-, optimal, and underregulation). The results are presented in table 14.4. Among informed mothers, 14 (63.64%) were classified as overregulating, 4 (18.18%) as optimal regulating, and 4 (18.18%) as underregulating. In the UM group, eight mothers (33.33%) were classified as overregulating, nine (37.50%) as optimal regulating, and seven (29.17%) as underregulating. The mother's information x affect regulation chi-square was not significant, χ^2 $(2, N = 46) = 4.30$, $p < .15$, indicating that the mother's access to the referent event was not directly connected with the mother's affect regulation during the first narrative.

We found, however, a significant post hoc cell contribution, $z = \pm\ 2.06$, $p < .05$, indicating that significantly more *informed* mothers (63.64%) were overregulating mothers: Favez (chapter 15) describes the overregulating mother as overinvolved, following her own thread instead of adjusting to the child's narrative, and very persistent in obtaining the "right" story from the child. Such extensive focusing on the child's performance and on conversational structure

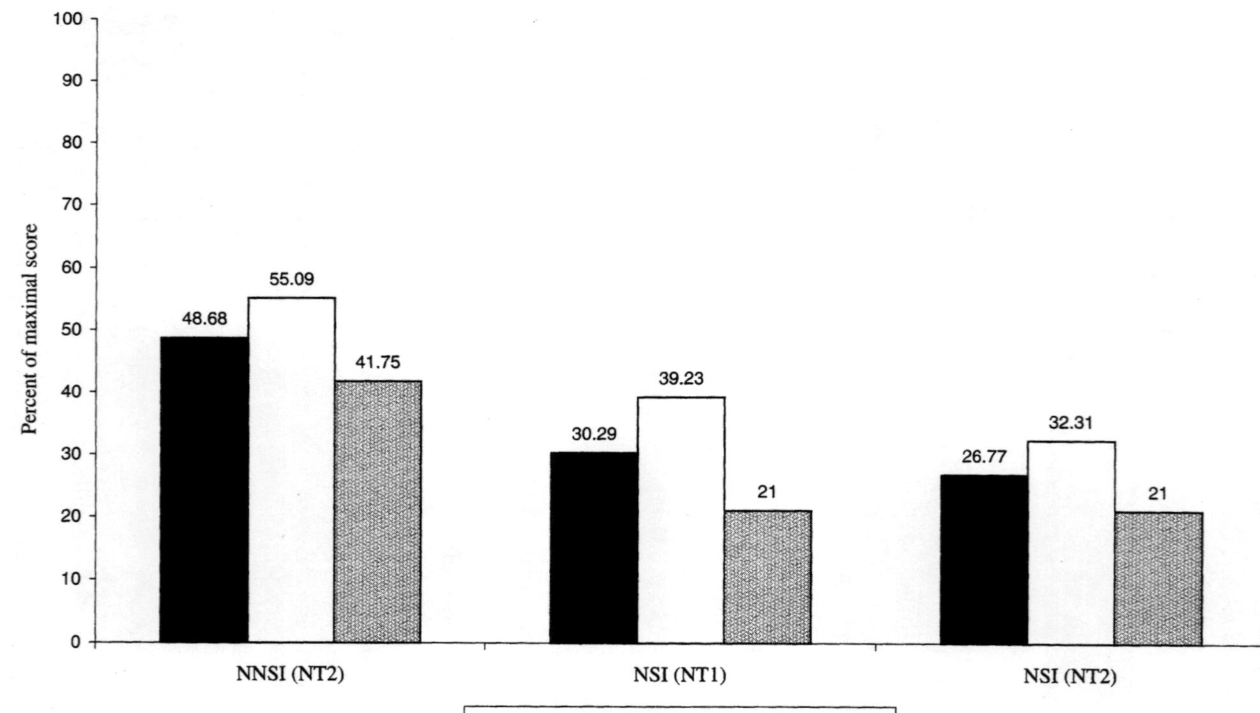

FIGURE 14.1. Effect of mother's information on non-narrative sequence index (NT2) and narrative sequence index (NT1-NT2)

TABLE 14.4. Correspondences Between Mother's Information and Mother's Patterns of Affect Regulation (NT1)

	Information		
Affect regulation	Total	Informed mother	Uninformed mother
Overregulation			
n	22	14	8
% (columns)		(63.64)	(33.33)
Optimal regulation			
n	13	4	9
% (columns)		(18.18)	(37.50)
Underregulation			
n	11	4	7
% (columns)		(18.18)	(29.17)
Total	46	22	24

Note. $(2, N = 46) = 4.30, p < .15$.

may have accounted for the IM child's better narrative accuracy and more constructed talk.

When overregulation was opposed to the two other patterns, the chi-square yielded significance, $\chi^2 (1, N = 46) = 4.29, p < .05$, indicating that most uninformed mothers were either optimal or underregulating mothers (66.67% overall). According to Favez (chapter 15), the optimal regulating mother is, as the overregulating mother, in charge of the conversational structure, but she participates to a greater extent in the elaboration of the story, completing and enriching the child's narrative; furthermore, instead of aiming at performance, she pursues shared emotions and pleasure in the act of telling. In contrast, the underregulating mother appears to be underinvolved, accepting the child's story even if incoherent and allowing the child to end the narration when he wants to. This last strategy may well have accounted for the UM child's reduced narrative accuracy and less constructed talk, but the association between the mother's lack of knowledge and the mother's ability to optimally regulate affect is puzzling and will deserve further discussion.

Though patterns of mother's affect regulation were not systematically analyzed at NT2, our qualitative descriptions revealed that informed and uninformed mothers behaved similarly in the second narrative: in both groups, the interaction was more relaxed, probably because mother and child were now familiar with the procedure and the experimenters and because they did not endure the stress induced by the scenario. Furthermore, both groups of mothers appeared to structure the second recall as a memory task, expecting that the child would tell the story by herself and focusing on what she remembered from the lived or narrated event: accordingly, informed mothers were less persistent in obtaining all details of the story, whereas uninformed mothers were able to rely on the (more or less accurate) knowledge base provided by the child's first narrative.

Discussion

This study examined the extent to which the mother's information about an event lived by the child (an 11-episode emotionally loaded scenario) affects the child's immediate recall (Narrative Time 1), delayed recall (Narrative Time 2), and nonnarrative recall (a picture-sorting task performed without the mother at NT2), as well as the process of co-narration and affect regulation. Two separate yet related questions were addressed. The first was whether the mother's information influenced the child's narrative accuracy and linguistic structure. We hypothesized that children whose mother had watched the scenario (IM) would produce more accurate and more highly structured narratives than children of uninformed mothers, at NT1 and NT2. The second question was whether such an enhanced performance corresponds to a higher degree of co-construction. We hypothesized that the narratives in the IM group would be more co-constructed and more optimally regulated, as mother and child share knowledge about the referent event. Co-construction was opposed in this assumption to tutorial (or Vygotskian) interaction, an asymmetrical exchange based on distinct goals and allowing for the progressive representation and generalization of the taught skills by the child (Beaudichon, Verba, & Winnykamen, 1988). While the issue of asymmetry was assessed by examining the relationships between mother's information and mother's pattern of affect regulation (over-, optimal, and under-regulation), representation and generalization issues were addressed by comparing the child's immediate and delayed recall and by evaluating the respective performance of IM and UM children on the picture-sorting task.

With respect to the first question, the data presented here indicate that the mother's knowledge of the referent event significantly increased the child's immediate and delayed recall accuracy but had a less clear impact on the linguistic structure: children of informed mothers produced more event-related episodes, had better sequential abilities, and their talk was more constructed, that is, included more complete clauses. At NT1, their responses were also shorter than in the UM group. Children of uninformed mothers were less accurate in their recalls and performed poorly on the narrative sequence; though their responses at NT1 were longer, they were also less elaborate, including more phatics and silences. Both groups produced narratives of equal length (in speech acts) and referred to the scenario in the same proportion.

Regarding our second question, we noted that most informed mothers were overregulating mothers, even if, overall, the mother's information was only partially related to affect regulation: contrary to our hypotheses, informed mothers appeared to establish an *asymmetrical* pattern of affect regulation, characterized by maternal overinvolvement and intensive focusing on conversational structure and child's performance. Most uninformed mothers were either optimal regulating, participating in the dialogue and aiming at shared emotions, or underregulating, namely, underinvolved and poorly structuring narrative interaction. Concerning representation issues, IM children still reached higher narrative accuracy and better linguistic construction at NT2, though qualitative descriptions revealed no differences in maternal style during second recall. Finally, IM children were also better able to generalize from narrative to nonnarrative recall, as they performed more efficiently on the picture-sorting task performed without the mother (NT2). Overall, these findings contradict our assumption of greater co-construction in the IM group and may rather indicate that informed mothers established a tutorial narrative interaction, relying on their knowledge of the story to expand the child's knowledge.

We discuss these results hereafter, emphasizing the mother's features that may have accounted for IM children's higher accuracy and more constructed talk. The second part of the discussion will be dedicated to co-construction and affect regulation. The final part relates to the possible developmental implications of our findings.

Mother's Information and Child's Recall

Produced Episodes The greater amount of event-related information recalled by IM children could indicate that informed mothers simply prompted more information to the child. As elaborative mothers have been described as "high-information" mothers (Fivush & Fromhoff, 1988), knowledge of the event could have induced a more elaborative style of maternal eliciting, promoting in turn a better child's performance. Yet Fivush (1991) observed no relationship between the amount of information provided by the 3½-year-old child and maternal style 1 year before. A more likely hypothesis is that the increased shared knowledge in the IM group egged the mother and the child on to treat the narrative situation as a scripted context, which revealed a more suitable context for temporally displaced talk and child's knowledge extension (Lucariello & Nelson, 1987). More specifically, informed dyads were able to focus to a greater extent on the events that composed the experience, because they shared knowledge about the orienting context: Peterson and McCabe (1992) noted that when mothers asked more questions about the specific events than on the orienting context, the 3-year-old child's narrative structure corresponded more strictly to the classic pattern described by Labov (1972), 6 to 12 months later. The following example illustrates how the informed mother was able to guide the "right way" for the child from the very start of the narrative, increasing the probability that the right episodes were produced:[5]

Example 1 (NT1, informed mother, girl, 4 years, 1 month):

1. M: So, what happened?
2. C: Hm
3. M: Tell me
4. C: He felt into the water and
5. M (interrupting): *No, wait honey, you're telling the wrong story. What happened when you came here into the room?*

On the other hand, uninformed mothers, who depended exclusively on the information provided by the child, probably spent more time asking questions about the orienting context (example 2) or were unable to know if the child was telling the right story (example 3):

Example 2 (NT1, uninformed mother, girl, 4 years, 2 months):

1. M: What have you seen?
2. C: A bear and a clown
3. M: *A bear, a clown and what else?*

Example 3 (NT1, uninformed mother, boy, 3 years, 8 months):

1. M: OK, then you tell me. What have you seen Pipo?
2. C: *It was . . . , hm . . . a little bit of drum playing*
3. M: Yes! and then?

Sequential Abilities IM children's increased abilities to sequence both their narrative and nonnarrative recalls may be accounted for by enhanced structuring opportunities available to the mother when informed about the event. Such mother's effects on the child's sequential abilities are largely undocumented, as these skills appear to depend predominantly on the child's cognitive skills and on the structure characterizing the event (Fivush, Kuebli, & Clubb, 1992; Mandler, 1978). Eisenberg (1985), for example, failed to observe any mother's influence on the narrative temporal structure, but she relied on a very limited and much younger sample. Yet Annunziato Dow and Johnson (1995) reveal that 2½ to 3-year-old children are sensitive to the amount of verbal information provided at the time of encoding: when the experimenter provided the most information (maximum scaffolding condition including action labels, temporal-enabling connectives, and goal statements), the children produced both more components and a better target order, as opposed to the "no information" condition (minimum scaffolding, i.e., generic verbalizations only). Though all children in our sample undoubtedly encoded some part of the event while experiencing it, our findings may indicate that only children of informed mothers benefited from a second encoding during the narrative, suggesting that when knowledge of the event is shared among narrators, storytelling becomes a "virtual" experience superimposed on the real experience. Informed mothers may have "strengthened" the child's first encoding by providing the child with the superordinate structure of the story (Nezworski, Stein, & Trabasso, 1982) or with a more efficient story schema (Poulsen, Kintsch, & Kintsch, 1979), thereby making the sequence of events either more invariant (Bauer & Mandler, 1990), more familiar (Bauer & Shore, 1987), or more logical and less arbitrary (Fivush et al., 1992). In other terms, they may have helped the child to integrate the order of the story in addition to its content and meaning (Brown, 1975). The following example illustrates how the informed mother, relying on her knowledge of the referent event, was able to help the child to tell the story in the right sequence, unlike uninformed mothers, who were more likely compelled to "pick out" elements of the content, to the best of the child's sequential abilities:

Example 4 (NT1, informed mother, girl, 4 years, 3 months):

1. M: And then, what was doing the clown?
2. C: No, but she was gone
3. M: *No honey, the clown had not left yet*

4. C: We sang "Le Pont d'Avignon"
5. M: Yes, how did you sing "Le Pont d'Avignon"?

Linguistic Structure Example 4 also illustrates child's constructed talk in the IM group, that is, the use of "subject-predicate" utterances. According to Poulsen, Kintsch, and Kintsch (1979), 4- to 6-year-olds produce more adult-like descriptive statements when relying on an ordered sequence of pictures, as opposed to a "spurious" sequence: the use of more constructed utterances by IM children may accordingly be related to their better sequential abilities. Utterances in IM group were also shorter (in words) at NT1: our qualitative analyses revealed that once "launched" on the right way, these children adopted a "discursive" style, namely, they told the story in short and precise sentences with few interruptions by the mother, except when exiting the "historical" truth (as in Example 4) and in case of very overregulating mothers. However, UM children adopted a more "dialogic" style, with less constructed talk (more phatics and silences) and longer utterances at NT1, possibly as they had to provide the mother with more information about the event (see Example 5). At NT2, both groups produced utterances of equal length, IM children being slightly less precise, and UM children being less driven to give supplementary information, as their "uninformed" mother had become informed by their first narrative.

The following example illustrates how the UM child at NT1 alternates long sentences (providing information) and phatics (adding and correcting information in response to the mother's questions). She also pauses ("...") often, as if internally reorganizing her telling:

Example 5 (NT1, uninformed mother, girl, 4 years, 7 months):
1. C: We comforted her
2. M: You, you did comfort her? . . . (waiting for answer). Yes?
3. C: *With Mary* (the "coach")
4. M: Mary did too? And how did you do?
5. C: We danced around and then she was better
6. M: Oh yes . . . So you sang, you danced around, and the bear came back
7. C: . . . no

Interestingly, Olsen-Fulero (1982) observed that discursive and dialogic styles in the preschool child's discourse were related to various maternal intentions (or agendas). Children of didactic mothers adopted a discursive style, because their mother asked few questions and appeared to instruct the child and guide his thoughts: didactic mothers "are concerned about the actual content of the conversation; it is not the process of social influence which engages them, but the process of presenting and facilitating the impact of INFORMATION" (p. 557). Informed mothers may have been more didactic, because they knew the exact nature of the "performance" to reach. On the contrary, children relying on a dialogic style in Olsen-Fulero's study had conversational mothers, specializing in questions that "allow most freedom to the child—only he knows their answers, not the mother" (p. 553). Conversational mothers were also described as more permissive, positive, and credulous, focusing less on the content of the conversation than on the fact of the conversation, in itself. Olsen-Fulero noted that they "accept the fantasized world of the child and request elaboration, rather than challenging the fit between that world and reality" (p. 562), whereas didactic mothers focus more on objective and reasonable facts. Uninformed mothers likely adopted a more conversational style, as they were unable to challenge the child's "narrative reality," although further research on the specific maternal contributions to the narratives is needed.

To summarize the discussion related to our first question, we found that IM children were more accurate in their narrative recalls and that they relied on a more "discursive" style of telling, whereas UM children were less performant and more "dialogic." On that basis, we inferred that informed mothers more extensively structured narrative interaction in a didactic manner, whereas uninformed mothers were likely to be less structuring and more conversational. We now turn to the discussion of our second assumption, namely, that informed mothers were capable of a higher degree of co-construction than uninformed mothers.

Mother's Information and Co-construction Issues

Delayed Recall Our findings on the significant decrease in the amount of episodes produced during the second recall (whole sample) are consistent with previous studies (e.g., Baker-Ward, Gordon, Ornstein, Larus, & Clubb, 1993) and may be explained in terms of forgetting some (limited) part of the original information. Yet the children may also have become "lazy," refraining from giving too much information, as the mother already knew the elements of the scenario from their first narrative. We noted that several children started the second narrative by a refusal, arguing that they had already told the story before. This hypothesis could account for the observed reductions in the linguistic measures (reduced talkativeness, less constructed and on-topic talk). Interestingly, no loss of information was observed for the narrative sequence index, indicating that sequential abilities were more resistant to loss than the number of components. This finding is consistent with former studies illustrating the significance of story schemata for the child's immediate and delayed recall abilities (Fivush & Mandler, 1985; Mandler, 1978; McClure, Mason, & Barnitz, 1979; Nezworski, Stein, & Trabasso, 1982; Poulsen et al., 1979).

Though qualitative descriptions revealed no maternal differences in the second recall, IM children's narrative performance was still enhanced at NT2: in other words, the structuring induced by the informed mother at NT1 may have become unnecessary by the second recall, as the IM child was able to rely on an efficient story schema built during the first narrative.[6] In their study on three-year-old children, Peterson and McCabe (1992) similarly observed that differences in maternal style were reduced once "the earlier scaffold has done its job" (p. 319). This finding, consistent with Vygotsky's (1978) assumption of a reduction in the adult's scaffold as the child becomes more able to perform independently, seems to confirm that knowledge of the referent event led informed mothers to establish a more tutorial interaction.

Generalization Effects Overall, sorting the pictures of the scenario remained easier than telling the story in the right order (whole sample), indicating qualitative differences between both tasks: several children were indeed able to order the nine pictures of the scenario, a performance traditionally considered beyond the seriation abilities of preoperational children (Inhelder & Piaget, 1958; Piaget, 1969). More recent studies confirm nonetheless that young children perform better on nonverbal recognition or reconstruction tasks than on narrative recalls (Brown, 1975). In our procedure, the recall may have been facilitated by the visual recognition of certain cues, as the child was allowed to manipulate the pictures.

As IM children displayed better sequential abilities than UM children on the picture-sorting task, it is unlikely that the lived sequence of episodes was simply "re-presented": the child must have relied on the story schema established with the mother, and the better this schema, the more accurately the pictures were sorted. In other words, children were able to generalize the narrative sequence discussed with the mother to a "mute" nonnarrative task (the child sorted the pictures without telling the story again) with an unfamiliar experimenter, this generalization being more applicable in the IM group. These findings contradict other studies, which failed to observe such generalization in preschool children (e.g., Tessler, 1991, in Nelson, 1993; Weinert, 1991). Nelson (1993) argued that maternal style of talking about the past may affect the way children verbalize the experience, but not the underlying memories of it. Yet our findings are consistent with Ratner's study (1980), where a significant relationship between memory demands made by mothers and memory performance on standard tasks was observed, both at 3 years and 2 years later. Our own findings confirm that the child can rely on a stable internal representation of the sequence only a few days after the experience (a much shorter delay than in preceding studies, e.g., Fivush, 1991; Peterson & McCabe, 1992; Reese et al., 1993) and that this "representation" process is facilitated by the amount of the mother's knowledge about the referent event.

Mother's Affect Regulation (Informed Mother) Our data revealed that informed mothers were mostly overregulating mothers; they emphasized conversational structure and child's performance. Like didactic mothers in Olsen-Fulero's study (1982), they devoted their energies to guide the child toward the most accurate and precise recall, relying on their knowledge base of the event in order to elicit "objective" facts from the child. Our qualitative descriptions confirmed that informed mothers were very persistent in obtaining the "right" story, behaving in a more formal manner than uninformed mothers. Hausendorf and Quasthoff (1992) similarly observed that 5-year-olds more accurately narrated a lived event in a "formal" setting (an explicitly defined "real" interview) as opposed to an "informal" setting (the child incidentally told the story to a "naive" listener while waiting for the "real" interview). Interestingly, the authors presumed that the formal setting was associated with greater adult's abilities to interact within

Vygotsky's (1962) "zone of proximal development," thereby bringing the child to a higher level of competence.

Considering that informed mothers were instructed to "tell the story together" with the child (see note 2), what factors may have compelled them to focus on the child's performance and to establish a tutorial interaction? One hypothesis relates to the child's awareness of the mother's degree of knowledge: informed mothers faced a rather uncomfortable situation, having to persuade the child to tell a story they already knew about. We actually observed, as in Hausendorf and Quasthoff's study (1992), that informed mothers often "displayed the necessary lack of knowledge for the child's story-telling to proceed" (p. 247), alleging their "ill understanding" of the story in order to "launch" child's narrative. This need for strategy may have induced informed mothers to rely on a more authoritative style (Pratt, Kerig, Cowan, & Pape Cowan, 1988). Another factor refers to the high pressure associated with informed mothers' double agenda: they were not only in charge of leading the child into telling a story (as uninformed mothers) but also had to prompt the "right" story, namely, the story designed and supposedly expected by the experimenters. The following example illustrates this point:

Example 6 (*NT1, overregulating informed mother, girl, 4 years, 3 months*):

1. M: How did you sing "Le Pont d'Avignon"?
2. C: In a round
3. M: In a round and how do you sing it? Do you know how to sing the song?
4. C: But, I feel hungry
5. M: *Yes, but honey, don't keep telling me that. For now, we finish the story . . .* (*waits for response*). *OK? You tell it right, huh?*

Obviously, chasing performance egged informed mothers on to be more demanding and accordingly less sensitive to the emotional quality of the child's recall (Mundy, Kasari, & Sigman, 1992): emotionally salient episodes were often processed in the same "cold" fashion as more ordinary episodes. We observed, for example, that informed mothers spent much time talking about Episode 4 ("tumbling the bear"), a joyful yet relatively neutral episode with respect to the story plot: a one-way ANOVA confirmed that they did so significantly more than uninformed mothers. In the next example, the high point (bear's departure and clown's cries) is only briefly evoked, as the mother continues asking more information without elaborating the child's experience at this especially salient moment of the story:

Example 7 (*NT1, overregulating informed mother, girl, 4 years, 3 months*):

1. M: Why did you sing "Le Pont d'Avignon"?
2. C: To comfort her
3. M: Ah, that's it, then she was . . . (waits for response)
4. C: Sad
5. M: That's it, why sad?

6. C: Because the clown, because the bear had left
7. M: *That's it, exactly, and you sang and danced "Le Pont d'Avignon," didn't you?*

Mother's Affect Regulation (*Uninformed Mother*) We noted that most uninformed mothers were optimal or underregulating mothers. Optimal regulating mothers were described (chapter 15) as adjusting and participating in the child's narrative while ensuring conversational structure, whereas underregulating mothers insufficiently structured the conversation, were poorly involved, and let the child organize the narrative as she wanted. Possible implications of this underregulating pattern will be discussed in the next section, as we now turn to the main features of optimal regulating uninformed mothers. Like Olsen-Fulero's (1982) conversational mothers, these mothers were more permissive and focused less on the child's performance than overregulating informed mothers. Example 5 well illustrates such optimal pattern of affect regulation: mother and child mutually complete each other, and the mother structures the narrative in a flexible way, mostly repeating and extending what the child just said; obviously, she tries to reach a coherent rather than an accurate account, taking her time before asking the next question as if internally organizing the information already available. These elements confirm that, contrary to our assumption, the narratives in the UM dyads were actually more co-constructed, at least when the mother optimally regulated affect.

Co-constructing a narrative while not sharing common knowledge of the referent event may seem paradoxical. However, mother's and child's respective contributions may have been more complementary in the UM group, as the mother provided a conversational structure in which the child inserted elements of content. IM children, though, more likely "followed" their mother, who was able to provide by herself both structure and content. Another argument in favor of a higher degree of co-construction in the UM group relates to the intense affective relationship associated with co-construction processes (Eder, 1988; Beaudichon et al., 1988). We observed that the extensive need to collaborate and negotiate in order to reach shared meaning induced a "potpourri" of positive and negative affects in most UM dyads (whether optimal or underregulating): shared pleasure when mutually adjusting, conflict when misunderstanding each other, mother's anxiety for knowledge of what the child experienced (particularly if the child refused to tell), child's happiness to detain information unavailable to the mother and to enjoy the power of intensifying suspense, child's impatience to tell the mother what happened, and so on. Conflictual exchange and shared pleasure are illustrated in the following example:

Example 8 (*NT1, optimal regulating uninformed mother, girl, 3 years, 10 months*):
1. C: She even had "bobos"
2. M: (not understanding) "Bobos"?
3. C: (angry tone) Bubbles!
4. M: Ah, bubbles!
5. C: (angry tone) But yes!

6. M: How bubbles?
7. C: (angry tone) Bubbles!
8. M: (finally understanding) She was blowing bubbles? Ah!
9. C: (interrupting) Yes, and even I did!
10. M: You blew bubbles too?
11. C: They belonged to her. They were in a plastic bag
12. M: (laughing) *The clown? The clown was in the plastic bag blowing bubbles?*
13. C: (laughing) No, the clown was sitting on the floor between both of us!
14. M: (laughing) Ahhh . . .

In this example, pursuing shared emotions obviously takes over narrative performance (the mother even "plays silly" in phrase 12, a strategy that was never observed in the IM group). Optimal regulating uninformed mothers also showed interest in the child's feelings, elaborating more extensively the emotionally loaded episodes, as in the next example:

Example 9 (*NT1, optimal regulating informed mother, girl, 3 years, 10 months*):

1. C: Then, hm . . . , it left and the clown was very sad
2. M: The bear left and the clown was very sad? Why?
3. C: Because she didn't want it to go
4. M: Ah . . . , and what happened?
5. C: Cried
6. M: *The clown cried. Was that sad? What happened?*

To summarize this second section, we found that IM children displayed better abilities to "represent" and generalize the content and sequence of the referent event and that their mother established a tutorial, formal, and rather neutral interaction. UM children were less able to represent and generalize elements of the lived event, as their mother primarily tried to obtain, in the account, coherence in default of accuracy. When the uninformed mother optimally regulated affect, the narrative interaction was largely co-constructed and elicited moments of intense affective exchange. Optimal regulating uninformed mothers also elaborated to a greater extent the emotionally salient episodes of the scenario.

Informed and Uninformed Mothers: Developmental Implications

Whether referred to as didactic (Olsen-Fulero, 1982) or "Vygotskian" (Beaudichon et al., 1988), maternal tutorial style clearly facilitate child's cognitive development. Our own findings confirm that IM children were more accurate in their narrative recalls and on the nonnarrative task, indicating a mother's knowledge influence both on sequential skills and structure of the narrative. This structuring effect may in turn enhance the child's ability to organize her "narrativized" autobiographic memory. By adding structure, meaning, and coherence to the reported event, the informed mother is likely to make the child's world more familiar, more "digestible," and ultimately more objective, more intersubjectively shared: benefiting from an easier access to historical (or archaeological) truth (Spence, 1982), the child will gain a greater sense of confidence and security about her internal and external experiences.

A child totally lacking informed partners to guide her into structuring her life would face cognitive chaos and ultimately be unable to learn and use shared symbols. Such an extreme situation is rarely encountered, except maybe in wartime, where a young child may lose at once all his "treasury" of shared knowledge about his life by losing his entire family. In ordinary life, the child more often faces intermediate situations, where parents and relatives at least partially share knowledge about her experiences, even in contemporary caregiving practices leading to frequent parent-child separations. Interestingly, several studies noted that duration of daily separations and caregiver's lack of stability increased a child's resistance, avoidance, and negative affect (Cummings, 1980; Schwartz, 1983; Belsky & Braungart, 1991). These findings, usually explained in terms of attachment mechanisms, may also be accounted for by reduced opportunities to share knowledge between parent and child. Yet it is likely that the effects of lacking an informed caregiver interact with more stable characteristics such as parental responsivity or quality of attachment (Ainsworth, 1985). Such a mutual relationship would explain why some uninformed mothers were able to optimally regulate affect during the narrative, while other uninformed mothers were under- or overregulating. The following example presents the narrative of an underregulating mother and her son:

Example 10 (*NT1, underregulating uninformed mother, boy, 3 years, 8 months*):

1. M: OK, then you tell me. What have you seen Pipo?
2. C: It was . . . hm . . . a little bit of drum playing
3. M: Yes! and then?
4. C: (rubbing his eye) *And then, there were . . . (hesitating) . . . only soap bubbles*
5. M: Soap bubbles? And they went into your eye?
6. C: Yes!
7. M: And what have you done with soap bubbles?
8. C: We blew
9. M: You blew?
10. C: Yes!
11. M: And what else?
12. C: We did nothing at all
13. M: That's all you've done? And you played with the drum?
14. C: And then we also played with the little ball over there (the "ball" holding the door open, unrelated to the story)
15. M: What have you done with the ball?
16. C: I put it in a hole, a small hole

17. M: A hole? Where was it?
18. C: In the drum
19. M: (laughing) Wow! And you made noise? How did you?
20. C: Hm, shake
21. M: Shake the drum?
22. C: Shake the drum
23. M: And what else?
24. C: Nothing!
25. M: That's it?
26. C: Yes, that's it!
27. M: OK then . . . you told it all

This mother accepts without much discussion and without further elaboration the (rather weird) story told by the child. The child obviously prefers not to tell what he went through, making only indirect allusions to some neutral elements of the scenario (the "drum," for instance, may refer to the xylophone). Regularly faced with such a loosely defined conversational frame, a child could develop an altered and incoherent sense of reality. Yet such extreme narratives were scarce in our sample, and they may still be attributed to various factors, such as a mother made shy by the experimenters, or a child skillfully refusing to tell the story. Moreover, it is likely that in our setting, as in real life, the parent's lack of knowledge (or at least partial knowledge, as the parent may still rely on her general knowledge of the child's temperament, habits, etc.) has in itself important developmental functions. First, the conversational style induced by the mother's lack of knowledge proved to provide the greatest facilitation for the child's linguistic and social abilities (Olsen-Fulero, 1982). Second, we noted that optimally regulating uninformed mothers were more apt to co-construct a joint meaning, an emergent coherence about the event narrated by the child. Polanyi (1985) similarly found that co-narration was more common in "diffuse stories" including extensive negotiation between the narrators about what actually took place and why. A consequence would be that some uninformed dyads did not aim at retrieving historical truth, but rather focused on one (among others) narrative truth (Spence, 1982). In turn, co-construction promoted affect sharing. Overall, keeping certain domains out of knowledge of her caregivers may then help the child to build a stronger emotional self: Pierrehumbert, Frascarolo, Bettschart, Plancherel, and Melhuish (1991) noted, for instance, that children reared in daycare showed greater emotional stability than home-reared children.

Real life is made from many different moments corresponding to various degrees of shared knowledge about lived experiences, with different benefits (cognitive, linguistic, social, affective) associated to each context. Accordingly, adult-child narratives are characterized by a subtle balance between knowing and not knowing (Hausendorf & Quasthoff, 1992): showing too much knowledge increases the "truth value" of the narration but may restrain the narrator's motivation to enter the telling and the amount of shared affect; yet knowing too little restricts the veracity of the recall but may enhance the co-creation of a mutually satisfying narrative truth and promote the affective bond between partners. When narrative truth constitutes the main goal of the encounter, as in therapeutic settings, such purposeful "ignorance" indeed represents a major strategy (Anderson & Goolishian, 1992; Eron & Lund, 1993): though relying on his general world knowledge and professional experience, the therapist has to abnegate his expertise to favor the patient's participation in the process of co-creation. In that sense, uninformed mothers may be compared to "involuntary" therapists, relying on a general "spare" knowledge, but ignoring the precise aspects of the child's experience. Conversely, informed mothers apparently behaved more like teachers, relying on their knowledge of "objective" facts to structure the child's narrative and reach historical truth.

Limitations of the Study and Directions for Further Research

This investigation examined the extent to which the mother's knowledge of an event lived by the preschool child affected the mother-child narrative co-construction. An 11-episode, emotionally loaded "scenario" in which the child actively participated (GEES) was created: one group of mothers (informed or IM) watched the event through a one-way mirror; the other group (uninformed) remained "blind" to the child's experience. The child told the story to the mother immediately after the event (Narrative Time 1) and 2 weeks later (Narrative Time 2) and sorted nine pictures from the scenario at NT2, without the mother. Two sets of child's measures were considered: accuracy (number of episodes recalled, narrative sequence, nonnarrative sequence) and linguistic structure (talkativeness, MLU, degree of construction, and on-topic talk). Except for patterns of affect regulation during the first narrative, the mother's contributions were only qualitatively explored. Our first assumption, namely, that the mother's information would increase the child's narrative and nonnarrative accuracy at NT1 and NT2, was confirmed. IM children also adopted a "discursive" style of telling, whereas UM children relied on a more "dialogic" style. Contrary to our second assumption of a greater co-construction in the IM group, informed mothers appeared to use their knowledge of the referent event precisely to expand the child's knowledge, thereby creating a more tutorial and less co-created pattern. This Vygotskian pattern was observed at three levels: interactional asymmetry (mother's affect regulation at NT1), representation (child's narrative accuracy at NT2), and generalization (child's nonnarrative accuracy at NT2). Most informed mothers were overregulating mothers, and they established a formal and neutral interaction aimed at performance; their children displayed better abilities to represent and generalize the content and sequence of the referent event. Some uninformed mothers were optimal regulating mothers, co-constructing narrative interaction to reach a coherent account and eliciting shared affect; other uninformed mothers were underregulating mothers, poorly structuring the child's recall. Overall, UM children were less able to represent and generalize elements of the lived event.

As the accuracy and linguistic structure measures were differently affected by the mother's knowledge of the event, it seems relevant to separate these two levels in further research. Furthermore, several limitations of this study need to be taken into account. First, quantitative analyses of the mother's linguistic contributions (e.g., types of questions, prompts, turn-taking regulation, etc.) are needed. Similarly, the affective tone (e.g., collaborative, conflictual, etc.) characterizing the conversation should be considered more systematically, in light of its possible relevance to the distinction between co-narration and tutoring. Second, further exploring the characteristics of the "separation anxiety" children is necessary, as separation anxiety could be related to interactional and emotional factors not addressed in this study. Third, though the mother's knowledge of the referent event extensively affected child's recall accuracy and structure, other factors may prove important for the transformation of the lived experience into a narrated experience, such as child's affect and coping behaviors during the lived event. Our pilot results on that matter add important elements to our findings and suggest exciting implications: we found, for instance, that children exhibiting more sadness during the scenario produced longer recalls and elaborated the high point of the story (Episode 6: bear's departure) in more details. These findings will form the subject of a further report.

Finally, it is worth further considering the exact mechanisms related to the mother's knowledge influence, as several questions remain unanswered: (1) does the informed mother really know more than the child, considering that she only watched the event and not really participated in it; (2) what factors (mother-, child-, or experimenter-related), besides knowing the ins and outs of the event, accounted for the fact that the informed mother was more eager to establish a tutorial interaction, rather than a co-construction; (3) similarly, what egged uninformed mothers on to co-construct narrative interaction when simply instructed to "ask the child to tell the story"; and (4) what elements (maternal responsivity, quality of attachment) "pushed" them into optimal or underregulation of affect?

NOTES

This research was conducted as part of a research program on Children's Narratives of Lived Emotional Events, directed by Prof. D. N. Stern, at the F.P.S.E. University of Geneva, Switzerland. It was supported by the Swiss National Science Foundation (FNRS No. 32–30804.91) and by the MacArthur Foundation (John D. and Catherine T. MacArthur Foundation Research Network on Early Childhood Transitions). We gratefully acknowledge the participation of parents and children. We also gratefully thank the research team, Marie-Christine Mühlebach-Vouilloz, Christine Waldburger, Dominique Weber, and Yves de Roten, as well as D. P. Wolf, Ed.D., R. N. Emde, M.D., and D. Oppenheim, Ph.D., for helping us to improve the manuscript. Correspondence should be addressed to Christine Gertsch, ruelle des Galeries 11, 1248 Hermance Switzerland (E–mail: gertsch@uni2a.unige.ch).

1. Due to unequal sample size (respectively, 36 and 18 subjects under and over 4 years 6 months), age affects were difficult to interpret and were therefore not included

in this chapter. Overall, though, age appeared to affect only the child's linguistic structure measures and the picture-sorting performance but not the accuracy measures.

2. In our pilot study, identical instructions ("ask your child to tell the story") were used in both conditions. We observed, however, that the informed mothers' children always resisted telling the story, arguing that their mother "already knows it." For that reason, we looked for more suitable instructions to set up the conversation. One may argue that these instructions induced the IM group to co-construct their narrative to a greater extent, but, as a matter of fact, this greater co-construction more specifically characterized the UM group. Conversely, the specific instructions given to the IM group did not prevent the informed mothers from using a more tutorial style.

3. One could argue that the coding criteria favored the informed mothers, as they may have had more opportunities to prompt specific episodes to the child. We observed nevertheless that uninformed mothers were also able to provide prompts by reconstructing the episodes from the information given by the child. Furthermore, our results on the lower frequency of complete clauses in the UM group indicate that these children more often used yes-no answers to maternal probes, whereas the IM children produced more complete clauses.

4. As in chapter 15, mothers oscillating between different strategies of affect regulation ($n = 3$, 2 informed, 1 uninformed) were excluded from the analysis. Two other informed mothers were not analyzed in chapter 15.

5. For clarity of presentation, the mother's and child's contributions are listed by turns (one turn may contain several speech acts). Silences of more than 5 seconds are indicated by "...".

6. One could argue that the better performance in the IM group resulted from greater rehearsal opportunities during the interval between the two narratives, as the informed mother disposed of the necessary elements to prompt the child with. Yet the mother was explicitly asked not to discuss the scenario, and even if she did, former studies showed that the parental preparation had no significant impact on the delayed memory abilities (Baker-Ward et al., 1993).

REFERENCES

Ainsworth, M. D. S. (1985). Patterns of infant-mother attachments: Antecedents and effects on development. *Bulletin of the New York Academy of Medicine, 61*, 771–791.

Anderson, H., & Goolishian, H. A. (1988). Human systems as linguistic systems: Preliminary and evolving ideas about the implications for clinical theory. *Family Process, 27*, 371–393.

Annunziato Dow, G., & Johnson, D. (1995). *The use of temporal connectives and goal statements to scaffold event memory in very young children.* Poster session presented at the biennial meeting of the Society for Research in Child Development, Indianapolis, IN.

Baker-Ward, L., Gordon, B. N., Ornstein, P. A., Larus, D. M., & Clubb, P. A. (1993). Young children's long-term retention of a pediatric examination. *Child Development, 64*, 1519–1533.

Bates, E., Bretherton, I., & Snyder, L. (1988). *From first words to grammar. Individual differences and dissociable mechanisms.* Cambridge: Cambridge University Press.

Bauer, P. J., & Mandler, J. M. (1990). Remembering what happened next: Very young children's recall of event sequences. In R. Fivush & J. Hudson (Eds.), *Knowing and remembering in young children* (pp. 9–29). Cambridge: Cambridge University Press.

Bauer, P. J., & Shore, C. M. (1987). Making a memorable event: Effects of familiarity and organization on young children's recall of action sequences. *Cognitive Development, 2,* 327–338.

Beaudichon, J., Verba, M., & Winnykamen, F. (1988). Interaction sociales et acquisition de connaissances chez l'enfant: une approche pluridimensionnelle. *Revue Internationale de Psychologie Sociale, 1,* 129–141.

Belsky, J., & Braungart, J. M. (1991). Are insecure-avoidant infants with extensive day-care experience less stressed by and more independent in the Strange Situation? *Child Development, 62,* 567–571.

Blaney, P. (1986). Affect and memory. *Psychological Bulletin, 99*(2), 229–246.

Bretherton, I. (1993). From dialogue to internal working models: The co-construction of self in relationships. In C. A. Nelson (Ed.), *Memory and affect in development* (Vol. 26, pp. 237–263). Papers presented at the 26th Minnesota Symposium on Child Psychology, held October 24–26, 1991. Hillsdale, NJ: Lawrence Erlbaum.

Brown, A. L. (1975). Recognition, reconstruction, and recall of narrative sequences by preoperational children. *Child Development, 46,* 156–166.

Bruner. J. (1983). *Children's talk: Learning to use language.* New York: Norton.

Buss, A. H., & Plomin, R. (1984). *Temperament: Early developing personality traits.* Hillsdale, NJ: Lawrence Erlbaum.

Ceci, S., & Bruck, M. (1993). Suggestibility of the child witness: A historical review and synthesis. *Psychological Bulletin, 113*(3), 403–439.

Cummings, E. M. (1980). Caregiver stability and day care. *Developmental Psychology, 16,* 31–37.

de Shazer, S. (1985). *Keys to solution in brief therapy.* New York: W.W. Norton.

Dunn, J., Brown, J., & Beardsall, L. (1991). Family talk about feeling states and children's later understanding of others' emotions. *Developmental Psychology, 27*(3), 448–455.

Eder, D. (1988). Building cohesion through collaborative narration. *Social Psychology Quarterly, 51*(3), 225–235.

Eisenberg, A. R. (1985). Learning to describe past experience in conversation. *Discourse Processes, 8,* 177–204.

Emde, R. N., Johnson, W. F., & Easterbrooks, M. A. (1988). The do's and dont's of early development: Psychoanalytic tradition and current research. In J. Kagan & S. Lamb (Eds.), *The emergence of morality* (pp. 227–245). Chicago: University of Chicago Press.

Eron, J. B., & Lund, J. B. (1993). How problems evolve and dissolve: Integrating narrative and strategic concepts. *Family Process, 32,* 291–309.

Favez, N., Gertsch Bettens, C., Heinze, X., Koch-Spinelli, M., Mühlebach, M.-C., Valles Almela, V., & Stern, D. N. (1994). Réalité historique et réalité narrative chez le jeune enfant: présentation d'une stratégie de recherche. *Swiss Journal of Psychology, 53*(2), 98–103.

Fivush, R. (1991). The social construction of personal narratives. *Merrill-Palmer Quarterly, 37*(1), 59–81.

Fivush, R., & Fromhoff, F. (1988). Style and structure in mother-child conversations about the past. *Discourse Processes, 11*(3), 337–355.

Fivush, R., Kuebli, J., & Clubb, P. A. (1992). The structure of events and event representations: A developmental analysis. *Child Development, 63,* 188–201.

Fivush, R., & Mandler, J. M. (1985). Developmental changes in the understanding of temporal sequence. *Child Development, 56*(6), 1437–1446.

Gertsch Bettens, C., & Favez, N. (1995). *Transforming emotional lived-experience into narrated experience in four- to five-year-old children.* Poster session presented at the biennial meeting of the Society for Research in Child Development, Indianapolis, IN.

Goodman, G. S., Pyle Taub, E., Jones, D., England, P., Port, L., Rudy, L., & Prado, L. (1992). Testifying in criminal court: Emotional effects on child sexual assault victims. *Monographs of the Society for Research in Child Development, 57*(5). Chicago: University Press.

Goodman, G. S., Rudy, L., Bottoms, B., & Aman, C. (1990). Children's concerns and memory: Issues of ecological validity in the study of children's eyewitness testimony. In R. Fivush & J. Hudson (Eds.), *Knowing and remembering in young children* (pp. 249–284). Cambridge: Cambridge University Press.

Goodman, G. S., Sharma, A., Golden, M., & Thomas, S. (1991). *The effects of mothers' and strangers' interviewing strategies on children's reporting of real-life events.* Paper presented at the biennial meeting of the Society for Research in Child Development, Seattle, WA.

Goolishian, H. A., & Anderson, H. (1987). Language systems and therapy: An evolving idea. *Psychotherapy, 24,* 529–538.

Hausendorf, H., & Quasthoff, U. M. (1992). Patterns of adult-child interaction as a mechanism of discourse acquisition. *Journal of Pragmatics, 17*(3), 241–259.

Inhelder, B., & Piaget, J. (1958). *The growth of logical thinking from childhood to adolescence.* New York: Basic Books.

Labov, W. (1972). *Language in the inner city: Study in the Black English vernacular.* Philadelphia: University of Pennsylvania Press.

Lucariello, J., & Nelson, K. (1987). Remembering and planning talk between mothers and children. *Discourse Processes, 10*(3), 219–235.

Mandler, J. M. (1978). A code in the node: The use of a story schema in retrieval. *Discourse Processes, 1,* 14–35.

Mannle, S., Barton, M., & Tomasello, M. (1991). Two-year-olds' conversations with their mothers and preschool-aged siblings. *First Language, 12,* 57–71.

McCabe, A., & Peterson, C. (1991). Getting the story: A longitudinal study of parental styles in eliciting oral personal narratives and developing narrative skill. In A. McCabe & C. Peterson (Eds.), *Developing narrative structure* (pp. 215–253). Hillsdale, NJ: Lawrence Erlbaum.

McClure, E., Mason, J., & Barnitz, J. (1979). An exploratory study of story structure and age effects on children's ability to sequence stories. *Discourse Processes, 2,* 213–249.

Miller, P. J., & Sperry, L. L. (1988). Early talk about the past: The origins of conversational stories of personal experience. *Journal of Child Language, 15*(2), 293–315.

Mundy, P., Kasari, C., & Sigman, M. (1992). Nonverbal communication, affective sharing, and intersubjectivity. *Infant Behavior and Development, 15,* 377–381.

Nelson, K. (1989). Remembering: A functional developmental perspective. In P. R. Soloman, G. R. Goethals, C. M. Kelley, & B. R. Stephens (Eds.), *Memory: Interdisciplinary Approaches* (pp. 127–150). New York & Berlin: Springer.

Nelson, K. (1993). Events, narratives, memory: What develops? In C. A. Nelson (Ed.), *Memory and affect in development* (Vol. 26, pp. 1–24). Hillsdale, NJ: Lawrence Erlbaum.

Nezworski, T., Stein, N. L., & Trabasso, T. (1982). Story structure versus content in children's recall. *Journal of Verbal Learning and Verbal Behavior, 21*(2), 196–206.

Ochs, E., Taylor, C., Rudolph, D., & Smith, R. (1992). Storytelling as a theory-building activity. *Discourse Processes, 15,* 37–72.

O'Hanlon, W. H., & Weiner-Davis, M. (1989). *In search of solutions: A new direction in psychotherapy.* New York: Norton.

Olsen-Fulero, L. (1982). Style and stability in mother conversational behaviour: A study of individual differences. *Journal of Child Language, 9*(3), 543–564.

Ornstein, P. A., Gordon, B. N., & Larus, D. M. (1992). Children's memory for a personally experienced event: Implications for testimony. *Applied Cognitive Psychology, 6,* 49–60.

Peterson, C., & McCabe, A. (1992). Parental styles of narrative elicitation: Effect on children's narrative structure and content. *First Language, 12*, 299–321.

Pettit, F., Fegan, M., & Howie, P. (1990, September). *Interviewer effects on children's testimony.* Paper presented at the International Congress on Child Abuse and Neglect, Hamburg, Germany.

Piaget, J. (1969). *The child's conception of time.* London: Routledge & Kegan Paul.

Pierrehumbert, B., Frascarolo, F., Bettschart, W., Plancherel, B., & Melhuish, E. C. (1991). A longitudinal study of infant's social-emotional development and the implications of extra-parental care. *Journal of Reproductive and Infant Psychology, 9*, 91–103.

Polanyi, L. (1985). *Telling the American story: A structural and cultural analysis of conversational storytelling.* Norwood, NJ: Ablex.

Poulsen, D., Kintsch, E., & Kintsch, W. (1979). Children's comprehension and memory for stories. *Journal of Experimental Child Psychology, 28*, 379–403.

Pratt, M. W., Kerig, P., Cowan, P. A., & Pape Cowan, C. (1988). Mothers and fathers teaching 3–year-olds: Authoritative parenting and adult scaffolding of young children's learning. *Developmental Psychology, 24*(6), 832–839.

Ratner, H. H. (1980). The role of social context in memory development. In M. Perlmutter (Ed.), *Children's memory: New directions for child development* (No 10, pp. 49–68). San Francisco: Jossey-Bass.

Reese, E., Haden, C. A., & Fivush, R. (1993). Mother-child conversations about the past: Relationships of style and memory over time. *Cognitive Development, 8*(4), 403–430.

Sachs, S. (1983). Talking about the there and then: The emergence of displaced reference in parent-child discourse. In K. E. Nelson (Ed.), *Children's language* (Vol. 4, pp. 1–28). Hillsdale, NJ: Lawrence Erlbaum.

Saywitz, K. J., Geiselman, R., & Bornstein, G. (1992). Effects of cognitive interviewing, practice, and interview style on children's recall performance. *Journal of Applied Psychology*, 77, 744–756.

Saywitz, K. J., Goodman, G. S., Nicholas, E., & Moan, S. F. (1991). Children's memories of a physical examination involving genital touch: Implications for reports of child sexual abuse. *Journal of Consulting and Clinical Psychology, 59*, 682–691.

Schwartz, P. (1983). Length of day-care attendance and attachment behavior in eighteen-month-old infants. *Child Development, 54*, 1073–1078.

Shank, R., & Abelson, R. (1977). *Scripts, plans, goals, and understanding.* Hillsdale, NJ: Lawrence Erlbaum.

Spence, D. (1982). *Narrative truth and historical truth: Meaning and interpretation in psychoanalysis.* New York: Norton.

Stern, D. N. (1985). *The interpersonal world of the infant.* New York: Basic Books.

Stern, D. N. (1993a). "L'enveloppe pré-narrative." *Journal de la Psychanalyse de l'Enfant, 14*, 13–65.

Stern, D. N. (1993b). Why study children's narratives? *Newsletter of the World Association for Infant Mental Health, 1*, 1–3.

Stern, D. N. (1994). One way to build a clinically relevant baby. *Infant Mental Health Journal, 15*(1), 9–25.

Stern, D. N. (1995a). *The motherhood constellation.* New York: Basic Books.

Stern, D. N. (1995b). Self/other differentiation in the domain of intimate socio-affective interaction: Some considerations. In P. Rochat (Ed.). *The self in infancy: Theory and research* (pp. 419–429). The Netherlands, North Holland: Elsevier Science B.V.

Umiker-Sebeok, D. J. (1979). Preschool children's intraconversational narratives. *Journal of Child Language, 6*, 91–109.

Vygotsky, L.S. (1962). *Thought and language.* Cambridge, MA: MIT Press.

Vygotsky, L. S. (1978). *Mind in society.* Cambridge, MA: Harvard University Press.
Watzlawick, P. (Ed.). (1984). *The invented reality.* New York: W.W. Norton.
Wechsler, D. (1972). *Echelle d'intelligence de Wechsler pour la période préscolaire: WPPSI.* Paris: Les Editions du Centre de Psychologie Appliquée.
Weinert, F. (1991, July). *Stability in change of memory functions in childhood.* Paper presented at the International Conference on Memory, Lancaster University. Lancaster, England.
White, M., & Epston, D. (1990). *Narrative means to therapeutic ends.* New York: Norton.
Wolf, D., & Hicks, D. (1989). The voices within narratives: The development of intertextuality in young children's stories. *Discourse Processes, 12,* 329–351.

NICOLAS FAVEZ

15

Patterns of Maternal Affect Regulation During the Co-construction of Preschoolers' Autobiographical Narratives

Affect regulation is a basic principle in human life (Emde, 1994). Several definitions of affect regulation have been offered; they share the ideas of control and transformation of the emotional experience, to heighten, maintain, or attenuate positive or negative emotions (Campos, Campos, & Barrett, 1989; Dodge, 1989; Garber & Dodge, 1991; La Greca, Siegel, Wallander, & Walker, 1992; Lazarus & Folkman, 1984; Ryan-Wenger, 1992).

Much of the literature considers early affect regulation as an epigenetic phenomenon: infants and young children learn how to regulate their emotions in the interaction with their caregiver. Different levels of mutual regulation have been described: the setting up of physiological rhythms (circadian and ultradian rhythms; Chappell & Sander, 1979; Sander, 1977), the organization of face-to-face interactions (Stern, 1977; Tronick, Als, & Adamson, 1979; Tronick, Als, & Brazelton, 1980), and the setting up of attachment relationships (Bowlby, 1969). The child interiorizes mutual regulation, which becomes part of self-regulation (Erikson, 1950; Kopp, 1989; Sander, 1962; Stern, 1985).

As Dodge and Garber have pointed out (1991), since emotion regulation is a process acquired in the interaction, there are opportunities for failure. Different patterns of affect dysregulation were made conspicuous in face-to-face interactions during the first 6 months (Stern, 1977) and in attachment interactions observed since the end of the first year (Ainsworth, Blehar, Waters, & Wall, 1978; Main & Solomon, 1986). Moreover, patterns of affect regulation between caregiver and infant are also given a central place in discussion of clinical material, wherein regulatory dysfunction is associated with disorders of caregiving relationships (Anders, 1989).

In this chapter, I would like to propose an exploratory approach of affect regulation and dysregulation operating in mother-child interactions concerning the co-construction of a narrative during preschool years. In addition to the attempt of identifying such patterns in a meaningful way, this chapter also assesses the effect of varying regulatory patterns on the narration of a lived event constructed by preschoolers. "Narrative regulation" thus becomes yet another form of affect regulation (Nelson, 1989a; Stern, 1989; chapters 1 and 2). I am thus expanding the domains of mother-child interaction in which known patterns of regulation function and may be determinant for mental health.

Affect Regulation and Dysregulation

Between the 2nd month, when visual maturation allows face-to-face interactions, and the 6th month, when the completion of visuo-manual coordination allows the child to become interested by herself[1] in objects, the child learns to regulate her level of stimulation in the face-to-face interactions with her mother[2] (cycles of engagement and disengagement) as well as the affects associated with the interaction (Brazelton, Koslowski, & Main, 1974; Stern, 1974, 1985; Tronick et al., 1979, 1980). Misadjustments in these interactions with the partner provoke reactions of disruption in the child (Murray & Trevarthen, 1985). Repetition of these misadjustments with the main partner can bring the child into clinical symptoms: for example, in the case of a parent who systematically becomes too involved in the interaction without letting the child take any initiative or giving her a chance to disengage herself. Stern (1977) and Anders (1989) describe several relational patterns that correspond to different ways of regulating the nonverbal interaction throughout infancy. We group these patterns into four wide categories, three of which are considered dysfunctional.

1. Optimal regulation: mothers offer the appropriate stimulation to the child, increasing, for example, the level of stimulation in the interaction when the child begins to lose interest or lowering it if the child is overstimulated.
2. Overregulation: mothers overstimulate the child. For instance, they interfere with the child's self-regulating acts, not respecting pauses in the visual interaction when the child turns her eyes away.
3. Underregulation: here, in contrast, mothers do not offer enough stimulation. They fail to respond to the child's stimulations or requests for stimulation, or they do so in a stereotyped manner and with impoverished affects.
4. Disorganized regulation: mothers offer stimulation to the child at inappropriate moments. They become animated when the child tends to disengage herself and they stay expressionless when engaging themselves into a social game. Another characteristic feature is the way they unpredictably move from one type of stimulation to another.

At the end of the 1st year, the establishment of the attachment relationship corresponds to a new stage in the strength of a motivational system and the expression of emotional needs (Bowlby, 1969). The child uses a variety of behaviors (search for closeness, hugs) that allow her to solicit her mother as a secure base and a source of reassurance. These behaviors organize themselves in patterns that correspond to a specific form of affect regulation based on a security-anxiety dimension and that are more or less conducive to the exploration of the surrounding world.

An experimental situation has been designed, the Strange Situation, which allows the evaluation of the child's attachment pattern by submitting her to brief separations from her mother. Again, four wide patterns of regulation can be described (Ainsworth, Blehar, Waters, & Wall, 1978; Main & Solomon, 1986). Three of them are the expression of an insecure attachment (i.e., the child fails to use her mother as a secure base when distressed).

1. Avoidant attachment: the child clearly avoids proximity and physical contact with her mother. She expresses few affects, even if she has been distressed by the separation.
2. Secure attachment: the child actively seeks proximity and contact with her mother and this is reciprocated by the mother. The affects are numerous and spontaneous: the dyad finds genuine pleasure in interacting together, and the child can express her sadness when distressed.
3. Ambivalent attachment: the child actively seeks proximity with her mother but at the same time, she is obviously resistant to contact and to interaction with her. The affects are exaggerated and negative.
4. Disorganized attachment: a disruption of the expected sequences of behavior is shown by the child. She can first seek contact with her mother and then suddenly avoid it strongly.

These patterns have been seen as different forms of mutual affect regulation situations, which test the child's capacity to cope with stress. For instance, avoidant behavior can be seen as a strategy aiming at the denial of the anxiety provoked by the situation, acting "as if nothing happened" to optimize the proximity. This behavior is in contradiction with the physiological measures proving that the child has reached a high level of stress (Grossmann & Grossmann, 1991; Main, Kaplan, & Cassidy, 1985).

The different patterns of attachment have also been described at a representational level. According to the interactional history with her mother, who can be more or less sensitive to her emotional needs, the child constructs a system of representations: the internal working model (Bowlby, 1969; Main et al., 1985). The internal working model organizes the relevant information in relation to the attachment figures, and this allows the child to build a system of expectations: an avoidant child will thus tend to avoid her mother at the time of reunion and not show attachment behavior, because she "knows" that her mother will reject or disqualify this manifestation. So the model developed by this child is one of a rejecting mother who does not pay much attention or is aversive to attachment manifestations. On the other hand, a secure child develops a model of an available, sensitive, and responsive mother. The ambivalent model is one of a mother with whom her attachment signals have to be amplified to animate the attachment relationship. Finally, the disorganized model is one of an unpredictable mother.

During the 3rd year, with the emergence of autobiographical narratives, the mother-child relationship reorganizes itself at a different level: the level of narrative interaction. A new type of regulation appears (Stern, 1989; chapters 1 and 2).

Ancient Greeks described narrative as an emotional medium: Aristotle, for example, in "Poetics" (translation of 1972, by D. W. Lucas), wrote that the function of a narrative plot (*muthos*) is an emotional discharge (*catharsis*). Closer to us, Labov (1972) has shown that autobiographical narratives of young children (ages 9 to 13) are constructed around an affective core, the high point, whose function is to communicate the affective evaluation of the events. Finally, observations have shown that narratives allow the regulation of emotions among preschool children already, be it in a monologue (Watson, 1989) or in a dialogue with family members (Dunn & Brown, 1991).

Regulatory functions of narratives are multiple. The telling of a narration is a regulation in itself of the affective state, and at the same time, can modify the stated experience (Stern, 1989). Narration, indeed, integrates the affect, cognition, and action related to an event; it brings order and differentiation according to characteristics inherent in the narrative structure: it organizes lived experience in bringing into play an actor, an action, a goal, an intention, a scene, and an instrumentality (Bruner, 1990). Moreover, the linguistic form of a narrative permits one to step back in relation to the affects and the uncertainty of the external world, by representing the world in a way that is independent from the surrounding reality (Watson, 1989). Equally important, a process of co-construction becomes possible: the child can now integrate in her own stories parts or whole stories belonging to others and thus create mutual experiences, the meaning of which is shared with her mother (Stern, 1990).

We have seen that for two earlier forms of regulation, the nonverbal social interaction in the first 6 months of life and the attachment negotiation at the end of the 1st year, the child learns to regulate her emotions in conjunction with her mother. We assume that this third level of regulation, the constructing and telling of a narrative, is also learned in the interaction. The questions to explore, then, are these: how does the mother regulate the behavior of her child in the narrative interaction? Are the patterns of regulation seen in early nonverbal interactions and in attachment interactions similar to those found in the regulation of the constructing and telling of a narration?

A partial answer to the first question can be found in the field of the "memory talk." Authors have demonstrated two types of conversational maternal styles to teach the child to speak in the past tense.

1. Some mothers involve themselves in memory narratives elaborating different aspects of the lived experience and asking the child questions that will encourage her to give information. Children of such mothers are rapidly able to construct narratives and have a tendency to speak about their past (Fivush & Fromhoff, 1988; Hudson, 1990; Nelson, 1989b, 1990).
2. Other mothers use memory talk in a pragmatic way by simply answering the child's comments. These children's aptitude to talk about the past develops much slower.

These findings can be seen in terms of affective regulation, although the mother's impact on the child's narratives has been evaluated as a function of cognitive or linguistic criteria (length of the speech, mastery of grammatical forms used when talking about the past, accuracy of the mentioned events in comparison with the real events). It can be assumed that children of mothers who correspond to the first style will have more possibilities to express affects in their speech and to discover the pleasure of talking about past events. Children of mothers who correspond to the second style will, on the other hand, consider talking as a pragmatic act and not as a shared affective experience.

One of the problems in studying emotional regulation in verbal dialogue is finding the level of adequate description of the mother's speech behavior. For this purpose, I propose an approach derived from the philosophy of language (Grice, 1975; Searle, 1969), which describes the rules guiding a conversation.

Rules of Conversation: Cooperation and Intentionality

A theoretical consideration is required at this point. To evaluate the discourse style of co-construction, we need recourse to a conceptual system that treats the basic elements of conversation. This is also absolutely necessary from a methodological point of view, since we will borrow descriptive elements from the analysis of conversation. The patterns of regulation in the discourse will be described as a two-level function-regulating conversation: cooperation and intentionality. Thus, one can describe systematically how the mother regulates affects in the narratives through her conversational behavior.

Cooperation is defined in terms of four dimensions of functioning: quantity, quality, relevancy, and manner (Grice, 1975). The quantity maxim suggests that an utterance must carry out some—but not too much—information. The quality maxim says that the contribution has to be truthful. The relevancy maxim asserts that the contribution has to be significant in the context of the conversation. The manner maxim says that the speaker must not be obscure and ambiguous. The degree of cooperation of an individual in the dialogue is defined according to how these maxims are respected.

Very early on, children perceive their adult conversational partners as cooperative, truthful, and non-deceptive. Children also prove to be cooperative. They supply their adult partner with the type of information they think is being requested (Ceci & Bruck, 1993).

These quite obvious maxims are the basic rules the child learns in order to carry out a conversation and to infer the meaning of a proposition. Although it does not necessarily threaten the course of the conversation, the maxims are often transgressed (the use of a metaphor, for example, does not respect the maxim of quality). People in interaction have to use inferences to adapt to the apparent transgression (the metaphoric use can, for example, be interpreted as the speaker's wish to emphasize an event). The "work" of the listener consists of constantly inferring the speaker's intentions. Works on children's suggestibility have shown that even the very young are able to read or decipher the intentions of adults questioning them and to adapt to these intentions, even though this might conflict with their knowledge of events. The adult's repetitive questions about the story read the day before encourage young children to change their answers, because they interpret the adult's persistence as a sign that their answer is not correct (Warren, Hulse-Trotter, & Tubbs, 1991).

The speaker's deliberate transmission of an intention is referred to as an illocutionary act. This kind of act obeys a certain number of conventions (Searle, 1969). For instance, when asking for salt during a meal, "Could you please pass the salt," the speaker is not asking whether the person is capable of doing it but she is expressing her wish to have some salt. This form is determined by a certain number of shared social rules (politeness does not allow a straightforward order), and in all likelihood the other person will act in an appropriate way without even verbally commenting on her action. Before anything, language is for Searle a "rule-governed form of behavior." Two sets of rules regulate the use of language (Searle, 1971): the regulatory rules that specify what is authorized and what is not ("Do or do not X," "One ought not utter obscenities at formal gatherings") and the constitutive rules that create or define new forms of behavior ("X counts as Y," "A checkmate is made if the king is attacked in such a way that no move will leave it unattacked"). Illocutionary acts are performed in accordance with a set of constitutive rules that compose the semantic system of a language (Searle, 1971, 1975). The two styles of mothers in memory talk—either defined by construction of a narration or by a more pragmatic discourse—can, for example, be understood as the result of different intentions in the act of communication.

Functionalist approaches of language development show how the acquisition of these rules begins even before the first words are present (Bates, Camaioni, & Volterra, 1979; Dore, 1975): a 10–month-old child pointing at an object trying to bring the adult's attention to it is performing a "proto-declarative."

Returning now to my central concern, I will describe patterns of regulation in the co-construction of a narrative as a function of those two levels, cooperation and intentionality.

Hypothesis

The first hypothesis is descriptive. I hypothesize that functionally meaningful patterns of affect regulation exist in mothers' conversational behavior with 4- and 5-year-olds in ways that are similar to those described at earlier ages. These patterns can be described, on the one hand, as a more or less well-accomplished cooperation in the narration, and on the other hand, as intentions aiming either toward construction of narratives or toward a pragmatic goal.

The second hypothesis explores the predictive validity of such patterns of maternal affect regulation. I postulate that the patterns have a measurable effect on preschoolers' telling about a lived event. Specifically, I hypothesize that an optimal regulation pattern allows the affective core of the story to be mentioned, mainly the high point, whereas a dysfunctional regulation pattern hinders such a retelling after an experienced event.

Method

Population

The population consists of 49 mother-child dyads recruited in kindergartens. All children have French as their mother tongue. Out of the 54 dyads that form our complete population (see chapter 14), 5 dyads were excluded as outliers in a preliminary analysis.[3]

This sample is composed of 21 boys and 28 girls. Most of the children's ages (45) vary from a minimum of 3 years, 6 months to a maximum of 5 years, 1 month; four children are slightly older, ages going from 5 years, 7 months to 5 years, 11 months. The population's mean age is 4 years, 5 months.

The conditions of recruitment did not allow us to control the families' socioeconomic background, but the socioeconomic status differences in Geneva are much less spread apart than in the United States and other countries. Effectively, we are dealing in Geneva with what would correspond to a middle-class, educated population in the United States.

Procedure

The procedure is explained in detail in chapter 14. Its main points will be recalled here. The child, separated from her mother, is actively involved in a standard scenario, the Geneva Emotion-Eliciting Scenario (GEES), which involves different characters: a clown and a queen of the robots, played by women experimenters, and a large teddy bear. Right after the scenario, mothers are given instructions to ask their child to talk about what just happened. We use two experimental conditions: one group of mothers watches the performance through a one-way mirror (informed mothers [IMs], $n = 25$), while another group does not see it (uninformed mothers [UMs], $n = 24$).

The central theme of the scenario is the separation of the clown from her friend the bear. The scenario is structured according to Labov's (1972) classical description of the narrative: (1) orientation (discovery of the characters), (2) complicating action (playing together), (3) high point (the separation), (4) resolution (comforting), and (5) coda (end of the story).

Coding

The dialogue between the mother and the child is transcribed verbatim and subdivided into clauses defined by the presence of a subject and a predicate.

A first macroanalytical coding of the mother's discourse is done to determine the type of cooperation present in terms of Grice's maxims (1975).[4] The quantity maxim refers in the dialogue to the principal speaker. The relevancy maxim is linked with the consistency and the thematic content that organize the dialogue. The manner maxim refers to the degree of pressure the mother exerts on the child to obtain a narration from her. This corresponds to a qualitative description.

A second coding of the mother's discourse is performed at a microanalytic level. Every utterance is coded on a grid of illocutionary acts based on Searle (1969, 1975), Dore (1979), and Demetras, Nolan Post, and Snow (1986). The different categories are described in table 15.1.

The coding of children's narratives is based on a content analysis. Each utterance is coded depending on which part of the scenario it refers to (see table 15.1). Two other categories of references have been added: a category for utterances that refer to the features of the objects and of the characters of the scenario (e.g., color of the clothes, size of the objects), and a category for all other utterances that are not directly related to the scenario (features of the experimental situation, e.g., description of the room, of the camera, or negotiation with the mother, e.g., "I don't want to tell the story"). Thus, seven categories of references are possible in the child's narrative: the five parts of the scenario and these two supplementary categories of "Objects and characters" and "Others" references.

Reliability

Two judges scored independently 20% of the transcripts. I was the first coder; the second one was an undergraduate student, blind to the hypotheses of the research. The reliabilities were computed at three levels (Cohen's kappa): (1) concerning the four categories of cooperation, the raters achieved a reliability of K = .69; (2) for the maternal illocutionary acts, their agreement was between K = .70 and K = .86; (3) for the child narrative categories, their agreement was between K = .71 and K = .78.

The absence of independence between the different levels of coding (the same two coders have operated at all levels), due to organization constraints, imposes some restrictions on the results.

TABLE 15.1. Categories of Illocutionary Acts

Illocutionary acts	
General assertives	Mentioning the presence or absence of somebody or something ("there was a clown")
Factual assertives	Mentioning the accomplishment of an action ("the clown took the bubbles")
Self-repetitions	Repeating word-to-word information already given by oneself
Other-repetitions	Repeating word-to-word information already given by someone else
Self-expansions	Clarifying what one has already said, adding information
Other-expansions	Clarifying what someone else has already said, adding information
Orders	Any imperative attempt to obtain something from the other person ("tell me the story!")
Requests	Any nonimperative attempt to obtain something from the other person ("what happened next?")
Expressives	Affective evaluation ("I was frightened")
Back channel regulators	Short statements, sounds, or words used to connect statements and to maintain listener's attention

Results

Question 1: Are There Several Maternal Patterns of Regulation?

Our group was able to classify the mothers in four groups, making use of three dimensions of cooperation (i.e., three of Grice's maxims): quantity, relevancy, and manner.

Group 1 The mother has a larger number of speaking turns; she holds the floor most of the time (quantity). The child's discourse has little impact on the mother's behavior: the mother does not use what the child says as a base but follows her own idea (relevancy). She asks a large number of questions and insists more than once to obtain the information the child does not want to or is unable to give her. The degree of constraint is high: the mother structures the interview in a very strict manner, insisting that the child talk about the story (manner). The mother's main strategy is the pursuit of performance; cooperation in this case is such that it is pushed in the direction of an overengagement. Twenty-two mothers were classified in this category.

Group 2 Here, too, the mother has more speaking turns than the child (quantity). But in this group, the child's discourse is greatly taken into account: mother follows, completes, and enriches what the child says (relevancy). She also asks a lot of questions and tries to obtain answers. The degree of constraint is once again high but this time in terms of negotiation (manner). The mother's main strategy is the pursuit of shared emotions and of pleasure in the act of telling about the story. Cooperation is optimal. Thirteen mothers were classified in this category.

Group 3 The child speaks more often than the mother (quantity). The importance given to her discourse is maximal: the mother entirely follows what she is telling her, even though she might be incoherent or even if she tells several different stories (relevancy). The mother does not ask many questions and does not insist when the child does not want to answer. The degree of constraint is low: if the child refuses to talk about the story, the mother decides to end the narration (manner). The main strategy is to let the child do what she wants. Cooperation is minimal. Eleven mothers were classified in this category.

Group 4 This group is hard to define with the terms used for the other categories. The mother in this case tends to oscillate between the different strategies without being able to choose either one, or she distinguishes herself by the use of incoherent strategies: she is very constraining in insisting that the child tells about the story, but not in questioning her or trying to obtain information. Cooperation is disorganized. Three mothers were classified in this category.

The second level of analysis concerns intentionality. The mothers' utterances were coded according to their illocutionary function. Table 15.2 describes the illocutionary acts used by mothers (because of its small size, the fourth group was withdrawn from the analysis). Whatever group they have been classified in, mothers mainly ask questions: almost 40% of their utterances are requests. Seventeen percent of the discourse consists in general assertives, but they are mostly used by mothers belonging to the second group. Repetition of the child's discourse is also found among all groups in a large proportion (about 12%) and almost 9% of back channel regulators are also present. The small number of expressives has to be emphasized: less than 2%.

To reduce the complexity of the data, a principal component analysis was conducted. As is often the case when dealing with frequencies, the data distance themselves from a normal distribution. For the purpose of analyses, data were transformed in function of $\sqrt{x}$ (Fox, 1993), so that they would better fit the assumptions of the normal distribution. A two-factor solution was extracted (Eigenvalues > 1). Table 15.3 presents the factor loadings, Eigenvalues, percent variance accounted for, and labels.

The first factor, accounting for 37.6% of the variance, is labeled conversational structure because of high positive loadings with self- and other-repetitions (.69 and .78), self- and other-expansions (.59 and .56), orders (.56), requests (.86), and back channel regulators (.72). In a descriptive way, this factor defines a communicative intentionality that aims at organizing the conversation at a formal level. This concerns the structuring of the child's and of their own discourse, as well as the request for information.

The second factor, accounting for 22.8% of the variance, is labeled text, because of high positive loadings with general and factual assertives (.68 and .77) and expressives (.82). This factor describes an intentionality toward putting into shape a narrative, where one gets involved with the factual events (events that occur during the scenario or during the narrative situation) and where affective evaluations are given.

Our group postulated that patterns of affective regulation are linked with cooperation and intentionality. To test this hypothesis, we crossed data obtained

TABLE 15.2. Mean Numbers of Mothers' Illocutionary Acts by Maternal Group

			Groups					
			1 (*n* = 22)		2 (*n* = 13)		3 (*n* = 11)	
Illocutionary acts	Population *M*	%	*M*	*SD*	*M*	*SD*	*M*	*SD*
General assertives	14.3	16.8	13.6	11.4	25.4	25.8	3.8	3.6
Factual assertives	7.4	8.7	12.5	10.8	8.3	8.3	1.5	1.9
Self-repetitions	2.4	2.9	4.0	3.4	2.5	2.2	0.8	0.9
Other-repetitions	9.7	11.5	12.6	9.1	13.1	9.4	3.5	3.1
Self-expansions	2.6	3.0	3.7	3.0	2.8	2.9	1.2	1.3
Other-expansions	5.0	5.9	5.5	3.2	6.4	3.4	3.1	2.3
Orders	3.2	3.8	5.5	5.9	4.0	5.0	0.2	1.4
Requests	31.3	36.8	40.7	20.1	38.9	28.5	14.2	9.4
Expressives	1.6	1.9	1.3	1.2	2.8	2.5	0.8	1.2
Back channel regulators	7.3	8.6	9.0	6.4	9.3	7.7	3.6	3.1

TABLE 15.3. Factors for the Mothers' Illocutionary Acts

Illocutionary acts	Factor 1	Factor 2
Requests	**0.86**	0.27
Other-repetitions	**0.78**	0.20
Back channel regulators	**0.72**	–0.17
Self-repetitions	**0.69**	0.39
Orders	**0.64**	0.35
Self-expansions	**0.59**	0.30
Other-expansions	**0.56**	0.22
Expressives	–0.03	**0.82**
Factual assertives	0.42	**0.77**
General assertives	0.41	**0.68**
Eigenvalues	4.83	1.21
% variance	37.60	22.80

Factor 1 = conversational structure; Factor 2 = text.

through the two levels of analysis. Table 15.4 indicates that the mean factorial scores in the maternal groups of cooperation are different.

To test whether these differences are significant, we conducted two separate analyses of variance with the maternal groups as between-subjects factor. Table 15.5 shows the results.

Factor 1, conversational structure, differentiates the three groups, $F(2) = 14.80$, $p < .001$. All the different groups contrast in a significant way. Mothers classified in Group 1 prove to have the strongest conversational structure. Concerning this dimension, mothers belonging to Group 2 fall between the two other groups. Mothers classified in Group 3 have the lowest conversational structure.

The second analysis shows that factor 2, text, also differentiates the groups, $F(2) = 3.14, p < .05$, but that only one contrast is significant: mothers of Group 2 have more text than mothers of Group 3. Although none of the differences is significant, mothers classified in Group 1 fall between these two other groups.

A picture and typology of the different maternal patterns emerges from these results. At the level of cooperation, Group 1 mothers are overengaged. At the level of intentionality, they are the ones with the strongest conversational structure and the least involved in the making of the text. They are thus mainly concerned with the situation and not with the narration. This pattern is overregulating.

TABLE 15.4. Means of Factorial Scores by Maternal Groups

	Groups		
Factors	1 ($n = 22$)	2 ($n = 13$)	3 ($n = 11$)
Conversational			
structure	0.59	–0.20	–0.95
text	0.11	0.44	–0.54

TABLE 15.5. ANOVA(S), Mean Differences, and Specific Contrasts between Maternal Groups for Illocutionary Factors

			Mean differences		
Factors	F	df	1 vs. 2	1 vs. 3	2 vs. 3
Conversational					
structure	14.80***	2	0.80**	1.55***	0.75*
text	3.14*	2	−0.43	0.55	0.98**

Fisher's LSD:
*$p < .05$.
**$p < .01$.
***$p > .001$.

The cooperation level of Group 2 is optimal. At the level of intentionality, these mothers maintain a certain conversational structure, and they are strongly involved with the text. Maintaining the context and producing narratives are both present. This pattern corresponds to optimal regulation.

Finally, the degree of cooperation of Group 3 mothers is minimal. At the level of intentionality, a weak conversational structure and low involvement at the level of the text are characteristic of this group. They do not offer interactional scaffolding and do not seem to be very concerned by the narrative. This pattern is underregulating.

Question 2: Do These Patterns Have an Effect on the Restitution of Affects in the Child's Narratives?

The second hypothesis of the chapter is that these patterns do influence the child's narratives and, in particular, the narration of the affective high point of the scenario. This part contains the affective load of the story and induces most of the expressions of fear and sadness in the child during the scenario (Favez et al., 1994), as well as producing special coping behaviors (Favez et al., 1995). Table 15.6 describes children's narratives for each maternal pattern and for the overall population.

The Elements of the Scenario The resolution (15.13%) and the coda (10.05%) are the most mentioned elements, followed by the complicating action elements (9.84%) and the orientation elements (6.61%). The high point (4.91%) is the least mentioned element.

The High Point When not mentioned, the high point creates a "gap" in the middle of the narration. This gap is more obviously present in the overregulating and the underregulating groups of mothers. By contrast, the resolution was emphasized in all groups.

Objects and Characters and Others References Taken as a whole, references to "objects and characters" of the scenario, as well as all "others" references, consti-

TABLE 15.6. Parts of Children Narratives: Mean Numbers by Maternal Patterns

Parts of the narratives	Population M	%	Overregulating (n = 22) M	SD	Optimal regulating (n = 13) M	SD	Underregulating (n = 11) M	SD
Orientation	3.8	6.6	4.7	4.2	4.2	2.6	2.4	2.9
Complicating action	5.7	9.8	7.5	6.4	5.0	3.7	3.9	3.6
High point	2.8	4.9	2.5	2.4	4.1	2.9	1.1	1.2
Resolution	8.7	15.1	5.7	4.3	6.5	3.6	4.9	3.5
Coda	5.8	10.0	5.7	4.2	8.5	5.6	3.7	4.8
Objects and characters	15.2	26.4	10.5	9.5	9.0	5.8	5.1	6.2
Other	15.6	27.1	25.2	29.5	22.5	22.5	9.2	8.3
Length of narratives (all parts together)	57.7		61.8	60.5	59.8	46.7	30.3	30.5

tute, in all groups, the most important part of the discourse (more than 50% for these two categories).

The Effect of the Maternal Patterns on Children's Narrations To quantitatively assess differences between groups, our group conducted a multivariate analysis of variance 4 (maternal patterns) × 7 (children's narrations) with maternal patterns as between-subjects factor and the content of the children's narrations as a within-subjects factor. Table 15.7 presents the results of this analysis.

Analyzing the contrasts confirms the fact that children of optimal-regulating mothers tend to mention more often the high point than both the children of overregulating mothers, $F = 4.5, p < .05$, and more than the children of underregulating

TABLE 15.7. MANOVA and Specific Contrasts Between Maternal Patterns for Children Narratives

Parts of the narratives	Contrasts between patterns (F) Over/optimal	Over/under	Optimal/under
Orientation	0.01	3.16	2.21
Complicating action	0.67	2.31	0.45
High point	4.51*	2.57	10.62**
Resolution	0.84	0.25	1.51
Coda	2.76	1.73	6.78*
Objects and characters	0.90	6.29*	5.60*
Other	0.73	8.09**	5.11*
Length of narratives (all parts together)	0.23	10.83***	11.41***

Between subjects: $F = 6.9$, $p < .01$, within-subjects: $F = 41.6$, $p < .001$.
*$p < .05$.
**$p < .01$.
***$p < .001$.

mothers, $F = 10.6, p < .01$. Concerning the elements of the scenario, there are no other differences apart from the coda, which is mentioned more by children of optimal-regulating mothers than by children of underregulating mothers, $F = 6.8$, $p < .05$.

Children of underregulating mothers mention "objects and characters" significantly less than children of the two other groups, and they also have less "other" references. This shows that this group has shorter narratives than the ones produced by the two other groups. This is confirmed by an analysis of the length of the narratives (the sum of all parts of the narratives), which shows that the optimal-regulating group, $F = 11.4, p < .001$, as well as the overregulating group, $F = 10.8, p < .001$, have longer narratives than the underregulating group.

Other Variables

The pattern of regulation seems to be independent from the information available to the mother about the event (having seen the scenario or not). This issue is presented and discussed in chapter 14.

Similarly, the type of maternal regulation is independent from the child's gender and age (three categories of ages: from 3.0 to 3.11, from 4.0 to 4.11, and from 5.0 to 5.11).

Discussion

The purpose of this chapter was to identify different maternal patterns of regulation of the construction of narrative and to test whether these regulatory patterns are associated with preschoolers' mentioning the emotionally charged event of a lived experience. Our group postulated that patterns of maternal affect regulation similar to those described for other aspects of mother–child relationships (e.g., nonverbal interactions and attachment) would be present in the case of interaction involving the co-construction of a narrative. This hypothesis seems to be confirmed.

Four categories of regulation emerged: overregulating mothers, optimal-regulating mothers, and underregulating mothers. Because of its small size, a fourth group was not included. The qualitative description allows us to hypothesize that this group corresponds to a disorganized pattern; a steady conversational pattern is hard to pick out. Further observations will be needed to describe this group in a more thorough way.

These different patterns correspond to distinctive conversational cooperation and communicative intentions. Overregulating mothers are overinvolved in the dialogue, and they aim to maintain the conversational structure, repeating and extending their own and their child's discourse. Their participation in elaborating the text of the narrative is small. Optimal-regulating mothers are involved both in the conversational structure and in the text of the narrative. They act on conversational structure, which allows them to maintain a certain structure and to contain the child's narrative, and they also participate in the elaboration of the text, using expressives known to play a fundamental role in the construction of narratives (Labov, 1972). Underregulating mothers are the least involved in the co-construction. They offer the least conversational structure, they let the child deal with the text of the narrative as she wishes, and they accept that the child ends her narration when she wants to. Their participation in the story is minimal.

The following examples illustrate the verbal interactions related to these three patterns of regulation. Mothers who overregulate the narration give to the interaction the tone of a negotiation about the structure of the conversation and not about the text of the narrative. This focus on the situation does not leave enough space for the child to build narration. The following example illustrates this process (girl, 4.3 years old):

C: Yes that's it we sang Avignon's bridge

M: But she went out with or without the bear?

C: Without the bear.

M: Without the bear and then?

C: And then he was crying he wanted to come with us.

M: *And then they went to get him. Who went to get that bear?*

C: The lady who was with me.

M: Would you sit up straight, please?

This example shows that the child starts by falsely saying that the queen of robots left without the bear, but later she is able to mention affects when she talks about the clown's sadness. At that moment, the mother ignores what the child said and continues asking questions (in italics). Instead of elaborating the emotion the child is telling her about, the mother goes on seeking information. She remains also careful about the child sitting up straight, though it does not seem crucial at this precise moment (last question).

Mothers who regulate the interaction in an optimal way not only maintain the structure of the conversation but get also involved with the text of the narrative. Moreover, they use a lot of expressives, which allows them to share with the child their emotional experience. The following example illustrates this process (girl, 3.10 years old):

M: Were you sad yourself when the bear left, and the clown too?

C: No.

M: *Well, myself, I was a bit sad when I saw the clown cry because the bear was leaving*

. . . and later . . .

C: Who took the bear away?

M: I don't know. You didn't see who took it? I didn't see what happened.

C: It was . . . with a mask, and a crown . . .

M: OOOOh yes! Someone went in with a mask.

C: I was afraid of her.

M: You were afraid of her?

C: Yes.

The mother offers conversational structure by asking questions. She talks about affects in a straightforward way and instead of insisting to obtain a longer answer, she mentions her own affects (in italics). Later on, she pretends she does not remember who took the bear. Instead of compelling the child in saying she should remember it, the mother puts the stress on her own pretended forgetfulness. When the child explains, the mother "remembers" suddenly the person with the mask. The two partners share in that manner a common knowledge of the same event, and the child verbalizes her own affects: the fear of the queen of robots. The mother then stresses these affects by repeating what the child has said.

Mothers who underregulate the interaction do not offer enough structure to the conversation, and they have little involvement in the elaboration of the text of the narrative. The child is thus in front of a disengaged mother (girl, 4.3 years old).

C: There was a teddy bear.

M: Oh yes.

C: But he left

M: *Oh*

C: There was a made-up clown

M: Make-up

In this example, the mother does not offer the conversational structure, and the child decides which information she will give. Even when she mentions the high point about the teddy bear, the parent does not get involved in the text of the narrative (in italics). The child then immediately talks about something different, describing one of the characters (the clown).

I have hypothesized that these patterns are differentially favorable to the narration, especially with regard to mentioning what I have defined as the high point (the affective core of the story): the bear's departure. This event, which concerns separation, is especially hard to integrate into the narration (the theme of separation is particularly meaningful for children of this age; see Bowlby, 1969). Coding the children's narratives shows that they tend to leave this element out, elaborating more what happened before or after the high point.

If one considers all the elements of the scenario (from the moment the characters are introduced to one another to the soap bubbles play at the end), one notices that the different groups differ only slightly as a function of the maternal patterns, except precisely in the case of this central affective part, the departure of the bear. Here, children of optimal-regulating mothers mention this part more than the children of the two other groups. Moreover, in all groups, the mention of the high point is reduced relatively to the other parts of the scenario. However, in the optimal-regulating group, this reduction is the least marked. It is thus worth noting that the groups differ only as a function of that part that is the most affectively loaded, which tends to show that the described patterns are effectively specifically related to the affect regulation.

On the other hand, if one considers the elements external to the scenario's action but that still have a link with the story, like the description of the characters' physical aspect, for example, one can notice that children of underregulating mothers do not produce as rich narratives as children of the two other groups. Finally, in the same way, all the utterances grouped in the category "other" are less present, suggesting that in this group the least negotiation takes place around the narration.

These descriptions of the verbal interaction between mother and child are not sufficient. Another important step would be to explain how the pattern of narrative regulation can affect the child in a lasting way and influence her self-regulation. To do this, one must examine what type of representation the child constructs from these interactions (Stern, 1995a, 1995b). Such an analysis goes beyond the scope of this chapter; however, I would like to propose a preliminary explanation by using the concept of "schemas-of-being-with" (Stern, 1994).

Recurrence of patterns of conversational regulation within the narrative interaction brings the child to create what we call a "schema-of-co-constructing-a-narration"; this schema concerns what the child knows she can or has to talk about with her mother and how she has to do it. This is of crucial importance because it indicates that her narration not only depends on what she knows of the event but also on to whom she is telling it. This schema can also determine the way she tells herself a story, that is, the way she gives sense to her experiences.

If we resume the three examples already mentioned, we can speculate that the schema constructed by the child of the overregulating mother will be one of a mother who always asks more from her and who is more interested by her performance than by what she might have felt. On the other hand, the child of the optimal-regulating mother will develop a schema of a mother who offers a steady context and at the same time is capable of sharing emotions. Finally, the child of the underregulating mother will create a schema of a mother who is not involved with her affects and who does not use the verbal interaction as a moment of exchange.

If we follow the line of thought suggesting that autobiographical narration contributes to constituting the self (Bruner, 1986; Stern, 1995a), developmental and clinical implications of these regulation patterns are obvious.

Conclusions and Future Directions for Research

In this chapter I extended the concept of patterns of affective regulation of mother-child interaction to interaction involving the co-construction of a narrative. The importance of this concept has been demonstrated in the fields of early nonverbal interactions and of attachment and appears to play an important role here too.

An exploratory approach has shown that the patterns of maternal regulation can be defined according to two conversational rules: cooperation and intentionality. This approach needs to be confirmed; the stability of these observations should first be tested, in order to see if the described patterns make sense ecologically. Their validity should then be tested, to evaluate if they correspond to the identified patterns of affect regulation. An external validation is also needed to confirm the functional consequences of presumed dysregulation.

I can also mention a methodological limitation of this study: we have a good reliability on the measures (categories of cooperation, maternal illocutionary acts, and child narratives), but there is a lack of independence of raters across the levels of measure. Therefore, we should replicate the study with different independent raters for each measure.

Several questions emerge out of this work. After having drawn a parallel between some types of regulation that have been observed in different domains, we may be asked whether these patterns are linked with certain types of interaction, that is, play, attachment, and narration, or if they correspond to mothers' global characteristics, which appear consistently throughout the different domains.

Another crucial question is how these patterns influence the child: what are the representations emerging from the narrative interaction, and what are their effects on the child's personality, as well as on self-regulation? I have suggested that a "schema-of-co-constructing-a-narration" may build on a "schema-of-being-with." The latter concept has been created by Stern (1994) to describe the child's representations at a preverbal stage; it is thus necessary to examine the specificities of these narrative representations in the experiment.

Finally, the predominance of the overregulating pattern (22 out of 49 mothers, 45%) came as a surprise; patterns of dysregulation are usually deviations from the norm and not the most frequent patterns. The situation of observation itself could offer a possible explanation: some of the children's and mothers' level of emotional arousal might not be high enough to require much affect regulation, and therefore these dyads have focused on the narrative's accuracy and structure more than on the emotions associated with it.

A way of solving this problem would be to reproduce the analysis on a larger population constituting groups in which the emotional activation was at the same level (measured for example by facial expressions) and then check the distribution of the regulation patterns for given emotional levels.

In sum, the notion of regulatory patterns found in early social interactions and attachment negotiations appears to apply equally well to the interaction involving the co-construction of a narrative. We seem to be dealing with fairly pervasive patterns of parent-infant regulation that operates across domains.

NOTES

This research was conducted as part of a research program on children's narratives of lived emotional events directed by D. N. Stern, M.D., at the FPSE, University of Geneva, Switzerland, and supported by FNRS Grant No. 32–30804.91, and the MacArthur Foundation (MacArthur Research Network on the Transition from Infancy to Early Childhood). The results presented in this chapter are part of a doctoral dissertation. Research team: Christine Gertsch Bettens, Yves de Roten, Marie-Christine Mühlebach Vouilloz, Christine Waldburger, Dominique Weber. Translation: Dominique Weber, Jeannine de Haller. I would like to thank Thierry Lecerf, psychologist at the University of Geneva, for the help given to analyze the data. Author's address: Department of Psychology, University of Fribourg, 2 rou de Faucigny, 1700 Fribourg, Switzerland. E-mail: nicolas.favez@unifr.ch.

1. Since all the narrative examples of this chapter will deal with girls, I deliberately chose to speak of the child as "she."

2. It could be the father or any other caregiver, of course. But the mother being in most cases in our society the main caregiver, I will, as a matter of convenience, go on talking of the mother for the rest of the chapter.

3. An examination of the repartition of the dyads along the two factors showed that those five cases were misclassified.

4. I do not consider the quality maxim in this chapter. In Grice's theory, the quality maxim can be expressed as follows: be truthful. It refers not only to accuracy but also to sincerity. Main (1995) considers that this maxim is violated in the Adult Attachment Interview, when the parent is using only highly positive adjectives to describe her own parents and then failed to support them. In our situation, it is impossible to evaluate whether the child is sincere, even when she is wrong according to the unfolding of the events, because we do not have any observation external to our situation that would allow the evaluation of her sincerity. We have thus decided to leave this maxim out.

REFERENCES

Ainsworth, M. D., Blehar, M. C., Waters, E., & Wall, S. (1978). *Patterns of attachment.* Hillsdale, NJ: Lawrence Erlbaum.

Anders, T. (1989). Clinical syndromes, relationship disturbances, and their assessment. In A. Sameroff & R. Emde (Eds.), *Relationship disturbances in early childhood* (pp. 125–144). New York: Basic Books.

Aristotle (1972). *Poetics* (D. W. Lucas, Trans). Oxford: Clarendon Press.

Bates, E., Camaioni, L., & Volterra, V. (1979). The acquisition of performatives prior to speech. In E. Ochs & B. Schieffelin (Eds.), *Developmental pragmatics* (pp. 111–129). New York: Academic Press.

Bowlby, J. (1969). *Attachment and loss. Vol. 1: Attachment.* New York: Basic Books.

Brazelton, T., Koslowski, B., & Main, M. (1974). The origins of reciprocity: The early mother-infant interaction. In M. Lewis & L. Rosenblum (Eds.), *The origins of behavior: The effect of the infant on its caregiver* (pp. 49–76). New York: Wiley.

Bruner, J. S. (1986). *Actual minds, possible worlds.* Cambridge, MA: Harvard University Press.

Bruner, J. S. (1990). *Acts of meaning.* Cambridge, MA: Harvard University Press.

Bruner, J. S., & Lucariello, J. (1989). Monologue as narrative recreation of the world. In K. Nelson (Ed.), *Narratives from the crib* (pp. 73–97). Cambridge, MA: Harvard University Press.

Campos, J. J., Campos, R. G., & Barrett, K. C. (1989). Emergent themes in the study of emotional development and emotion regulation. *Developmental Psychology, 25*(3), 394–402.

Ceci, S., & Bruck, M. (1993). Suggestibility of the child witness: A historical review and synthesis. *Psychological Bulletin, 113*(3), 403–439.

Chappell, P., & Sander, L. W. (1979). Mutual regulation of the neonatal-maternal interactive process: Context for the origins of communication. In M. Bullowa (Ed.), *Before speech* (pp. 89–109). Cambridge: Cambridge University Press.

Demetras, M., Nolan Post, K., & Snow, C. (1986). Feedback to first language learners: The role of repetitions and clarification questions. *Journal of Child Language, 13,* 275–292.

Dodge, K. A. (1989). Coordinating responses to aversive stimuli: Introduction to a special section on the development of emotion regulation. *Developmental Psychology, 25*(3), 339–342.

Dodge, K. A., & Garber, J. (1991). Domains of emotion regulation. In J. Garber & K. A. Dodge (Eds.), *The development of emotion regulation and dysregulation* (pp. 3–11). Cambridge: Cambridge University Press.

Dore, J. (1975). Holophrases, speech acts and language universals. *Journal of Child Language, 2,* 21–40.

Dore, J. (1979). Conversational acts and the acquisition of language. In E. Ochs & B. Schieffelin (Eds.), *Developmental pragmatics* (pp. 339–361). New York: Academic Press.

Dunn, J., & Brown, J. (1991). Relationships, talk about feelings, and the development of affect regulation in early childhood. In J. Garber & K. A. Dodge (Eds.), *The development of emotion regulation and dysregulation* (pp. 208–242). Cambridge: Cambridge University Press.

Emde, R. N. (1994). Individuality, context, and the search for meaning. *Child Development, 65,* 719–737.

Erikson, E. H. (1950). *Childhood and society.* London: Hogarth.

Favez, N., Dicker Halpérin, M., Gertsch Bettens, C., Koch-Spinelli, M., Mühlebach, M.-C., Vallès Almela, V., & Stern, D. N. (1995). Le rôle des comportements de "coping" (faire face) dans le développement des narrations chez le jeune enfant: présentation d'une grille de codage. *Les Cahiers du CERFEE, 11–12,* 103–117.

Favez, N., Gertsch Bettens, C., Heinze, X., Koch-Spinelli, M., Mühlebach, M.-C., Valles Almela, V., & Stern, D. N. (1994). Réalité historique et réalité narrative chez le jeune enfant: présentation d'une stratégie de recherche. *Revue Suisse de Psychologie, 53*(2), 98–103.

Fivush, R., & Fromhoff, F. (1988). Style and structure in mother-child conversations about the past. *Discourse Processes, 11*(3), 337–355.

Fox, J. (1993). Regression diagnostics: An introduction. In M. Lewis-Beck (Ed.), *Regression analysis* (pp. 245–334). London: Sage.

Garber, J., & Dodge, K. A. (1991). *The development of affect regulation and dysregulation.* Cambridge: Cambridge University Press.

Grice, H. P. (1975). Logic and conversation. In P. Cole & J. L. Morgan (Eds.), *Syntax and semantics* (pp. 41–58). San Diego, CA: Academic Press.

Grossmann, K., & Grossmann, K. (1991). Attachment quality as an organizer of emotional and behavioral responses in a longitudinal perspective. In C. M. Parkes, J. Stevenson-Hinde, & P. Marris (Eds.), *Attachment across the life cycle* (pp. 93–114). London: Tavistock/Routledge.

Hudson, J. (1990). The emergence of autobiographical memory in mother-child conversation. In R. Fivush & J. Hudson (Eds.), *Knowing and remembering in young children* (pp. 166–196). Cambridge: Cambridge University Press.

Kopp, C. B. (1989). Regulation of distress and negative emotions: A developmental view. *Developmental Psychology, 25*(3), 343–354.

Labov, W. (1972). *Language in the inner city.* Philadelphia: University of Pennsylvania.

LaGreca, A., Siegel, L., Wallander, J., & Walker, E. (1992). *Stress and coping in child health.* New York: Guilford Press.

Lazarus, R. S., & Folkman, S. (1984). *Stress, appraisal and coping.* New York: Springer Verlag.

Main, M. (1995). Recent studies in attachment. Overview, with selected implications for clinical work. In S. Goldberg, R. Muir, & J. Kerr (Eds.), *Attachment theory* (pp. 407–474). Hillsdale, NJ: Analytic Press.

Main, M., Kaplan, N., & Cassidy, J. (1985). Security in infancy, childhood, and adulthood: A move to the level of representation. In I. Bretherton & E. Waters (Eds.), *Growing points of attachment theory and research* (pp. 66–104). Chicago: University Press.

Main, M., & Solomon, J. (1986). Discovery of an insecure-disorganized/disoriented attachment pattern. In T. B. Brazelton & M. Yogman (Eds.), *Affective development in infancy* (pp. 95–124). Norwood, NJ: Ablex.

Murray, L., & Trevarthen, C. (1985). Emotional regulation of interactions between two-month-olds and their mothers. In T. Field & N. Fox (Eds.), *Social perception in infants* (pp. 177–197). New York: Ablex.

Nelson, K. (Ed.) (1989a). *Narratives from the crib.* Cambridge, MA: Harvard University Press.

Nelson, K. (1989b). Remembering: A functional developmental perspective. In P. Soloman, G. Goethals, C. Kelley, & B. Stephens (Eds.), *Memory: interdisciplinary approaches* (pp. 127–150). New York: Springer.

Nelson, K. (1990). Remembering, forgetting, and childhood amnesia. In R. Fivush & J. Hudson (Eds), *Knowing and remembering in young children* (pp. 301–316). Cambridge: Cambridge University Press.

Ryan-Wenger, N. (1992). A taxonomy of children's coping strategies. *American Journal of Orthopsychiatry, 62*(2), 256–263.

Sander, L. W. (1962). Issues in early mother-child interaction. *Journal of American Academy of Child Psychiatry, 1*(1), 141–166.

Sander, L. W. (1977). Regulation of exchange in the infant-caretaker system: A viewpoint on the ontogeny of "structures." In N. Freedman & S. Grand (Eds.), *Communicative structures and psychic structures* (pp. 13–34). New York: Plenum Press.

Searle, J. R. (1969). *Speech acts: An essay in the philosophy of language.* Cambridge: Cambridge University Press.

Searle, J. R. (1971). What is a speech act? In J. R. Searle (Ed.), *The philosophy of language* (39–53). Oxford: Oxford University Press.

Searle, J. R. (1975). A classification of illocutionary acts. In K. Gunderson (Ed.), *Minnesota Studies in the Philosophy of Science. Vol. 7: Language, mind and knowledge* (pp. 344–369). Minneapolis: University of Minnesota Press.

Stern, D. N. (1974). The goal and structure of mother-infant play. *Journal of Child Psychiatry, 13*(3), 402–421.

Stern, D. N. (1977). *The first relationship: Infant and mother.* London: Open Books.

Stern, D. N. (1985). *The interpersonal world of the infant.* New York: Basic Books.

Stern, D. N. (1989). The representation of relational patterns: Developmental considerations. In A. Sameroff & R. Emde (Eds.), *Relationship disturbances in early childhood* (pp. 52–69). New York: Basic Books.

Stern, D. N. (1990). *Diary of a baby.* New York: Basic Books.

Stern, D. N. (1991). *The development of children's narratives: Their correspondence to objective reality; the role of affect and adult input on their formation.* University of Geneva, Request to the Swiss National Science Foundation N°32–30804.91.

Stern, D. N. (1994). One way to build a clinically relevant baby. *Infant Mental Health Journal, 15*(1), 9–25.

Stern, D. N. (1995a). *The motherhood constellation.* New York: Basic Books.

Stern, D. N. (1995b). Self/other differentiation in the domain of intimate socio-affective interaction: Some considerations. In P. Rochat (Ed.), *The self in infancy: Theory and research* (pp. 419–429). New York: Elsevier.

Tronick, E., Als, H., & Adamson, L. (1979). Structure of early face-to-face communicative interactions. In M. Bullowa (Ed.), *Before speech. The beginning of interpersonal communication* (pp. 349–400). Cambridge: Cambridge University Press.

Tronick, E., Als, H. & Brazelton, T. (1980). Monadic phases: A structural descriptive analysis of infant-mother face to face interaction. *Merrill-Palmer Quarterly, 26* (1), 3–24.

Warren, A. R., Hulse-Trotter, K., & Tubbs, E. (1991). Inducing resistance to suggestibility in children. *Law and Human Behavior, 15*, 273–285.

Watson, R. (1989). Monologue, dialogue and regulation. In K. Nelson (Ed.), *Narratives from the crib* (pp. 263–283). Cambridge, MA: Harvard University Press.

R. LANDAU
Y. ESHEL
V. KIPNIS
M. BEN-AARON

16

Relationships and Interactions of Mothers and Metaplot with 3-Year-Old Kibbutz Children in Two Functional Contexts

Developmental regulation is carried out mainly through relationships (Emde & Sameroff, 1989). From infancy, the child participates in a network of relationships (Belsky, 1981; Maccoby & Martin, 1983; van Ijzendoorn, Sagi, & Lambermon, 1992), which, in early childhood, consist mostly of family members (father, mother, siblings). However, many children are also cared for by additional female caregivers who are not part of the family. These women replace the mother in caring for the child's basic needs for part of the day and thus may be considered as functionally equivalent to the mother. The term "multiple mothering" is sometimes used to indicate this constellation.

Within the family, mother-infant relationships have been the most extensively studied (Ainsworth, Blehar, Waters, & Wall, 1978; Bowlby, 1969/1982, 1973, 1980; Emde & Buchsbaum, 1990; Sander, 1984; Stern, 1977; Winnicott, 1965). Research on father-infant relationships appeared later and has indicated that infants are attached to their fathers but that this is not always similar to their attachment to their mothers (Fox, Kimmerly, & Schafer, 1991; Grossmann, Grossmann, Huber, & Wartner, 1981; Lamb, 1976; Lamb, Hwang, Frodi, & Frodi, 1982; Main & Weston, 1981; Sagi et al., 1985). However, the Strange Situation, a method developed to study mother-infant attachment relationships (Ainsworth et al., 1978), did not reveal which aspects of father-infant relationships are different. The relationships within each of the two dyads and their functions could be more broadly identified only when direct observations of father-infant and mother-infant interactions in various contexts were conducted in the same study (Lamb, 1976, 1977).

The research strategy used in most studies on mother-child and another female caregiver–child relationships resembles the one previously used in the study of father-infant relationships, namely, evaluating dimensions developed to study mother-infant relationships, such as attachment, compliance, or sensitivity (Ainsworth et al., 1978; Feldman & Sarnat, 1986; van Ijzendoorn et al., 1992). In addition, mother-child and caregiver-child relationships were rarely investigated simultaneously for the same child (Belsky, 1990). In studies that used the Strange Situation, infants were found to form attachments to a female caregiver who was not part of the family (Goosen & Ijzendoorn, 1990; Sagi et al., 1985), indicating that there is some equivalence of function between a caregiver and the mother. However, to better specify similarities and differences in each relationship pattern, we need observations of several functional contexts for each of the two dyads in the same study. In such a study, the different functions that each of the two relationships may have for child development can be identified. Moreover, it can help to further qualify what is unique to mother-child relationships.

Concepts used to describe the uniqueness of mother-child relationships usually refer to the shared subjective aspects of experience: to intersubjectivity that includes shared attention, intention, affect, and meaning (Sroufe & Fleeson, 1986; Stern, 1985; Travertan, 1978), to a "we" feeling (Emde, 1988; Emde & Buchsbaum, 1990), to intimacy (Emde, 1989; Maccoby, 1992) or intimate attachment (Bowlby, 1980), and to "fitting together" (Sander, 1984). In early childhood, especially during infancy, most "fitting together" is carried out by the mother. In the course of development, the child's part in the "fitting together" increases and at about 3 years the mother-child relationship becomes much more of a "goal corrected partnership" (Bowlby, 1969/1982).

Elaborating on Winnicott's insights, Sander (1984) stressed that in addition to the infant's needs for fitting together, for shared intersubjective experiences with his or her mother, there is also a need for separateness, for being alone with one's personal life. This separateness enables the child to experience his or her emotions, wishes, intentions, and interests and develop individuality. However, the need of the child is to be alone in a specific and perhaps paradoxical way: to be alone in the presence of others with whom the infant developed shared experience and meaning, security, a sense of continuity in the relationships, and some kind of intimacy. This way of being alone is distinguished from being withdrawn. According to Winnicott (1965) and Sander (1984), from the infant's side, the relationship with mother consists of an integration or harmony between two polarities: being together and being alone in the mother's presence. This constellation, according to Winnicott (1965), is characteristic of intimate relationships in children and mature people as well. Another characteristic of intimate relationships, mentioned by Erikson (1963), is commitment to concrete affiliations and partnerships. Commitment implies continuity in relationships. The continuous commitment for the overall well-being of the child, including togetherness or partnerships, is typical of mother-child relationships, whereas caregiver-child relationships are limited in time and in overall responsibility. Thus, it seems reasonable to suppose that mother-child relationships are more intimate than caregiver-child relationships, which leads us further to hypothesize that the pattern of behavior in which there is an integration between the two polarities, being together and being alone in the presence of the other, will characterize more mother-child relationships than caregiver-child relationships.

Relationships are the product of the interactional history (Hinde, 1979). Relationships are regularities in patterns of interaction or recurrent themes, over time. They cannot be viewed directly, yet they can be described (Sroufe, 1989). However, their description cannot be based only on one specific interaction or even one type of interaction, "but on the frequencies and relative frequencies of several types of interaction over a period of time" (Hinde, 1983, p. 45). Relationships are coherent wholes; they often show stability and continuity (Sroufe, 1986, 1989); thus, they can be detected at different times and in different functional contexts. Moreover, although relationships refer to a dyad, they can be captured while observing one partner "because each partner's behavior reflects expectations and feelings built up over time in the course of the relationship" (Sroufe, 1986, pp. 60–61). Thus, the study of the mother's and the caregiver's interaction behavior with the same child in different functional contexts can capture and compare mother-child and caregiver-child relationships.

The kibbutz is an ideal setting for studying similarities and differences between mother-child and caregiver-child relationships. In the kibbutz, mother and caregiver (*metapelet*) perform similar functions in caring for the child's everyday needs for part of the day, as do mothers and caregivers in the city. However, in the kibbutz, the metapelet and the parents of the child are part of the same communal community. The metapelet is assigned to her job by the community, and the overall well-being of the children is conceived to be the responsibility of the whole community. Children are conceived of as the "kibbutz' children" (Aviezer, van Ijzendoorn, Sagi, & Schuengel, 1994) or "our" children by most members of the kibbutz.

Still, mother and metapelet are expected to have different roles in caring for the child. Metaplot take a greater part in disciplining children, in promoting their cognitive abilities, and in teaching them the social norms of the kibbutz and of group life. Mothers take a greater part in fulfilling the emotional needs of children and developing their individuality and sensitivity to others (Beit-Hallahmi & Rabin, 1982; Feldman & Yirmia, 1986; Shash, 1977). In addition, the context in which mother-child and metapelet-child interactions take place is different: nursery school groups in the kibbutz consist of about six children of the same age. Mothers interact with their children at home, in a private rather than public setting, where rules of behavior are less formal, less uniform, and more flexible, and where available siblings are of different ages.

Attachment studies have yielded findings consistent with differing roles. In spite of the central role of the metaplot in the life of kibbutz children (Fox, 1977; Golan, 1961; Oppenheim, Sagi, & Lamb, 1988), more children were found to be securely attached to their mothers than to their metaplot in family-based as well as in communal sleeping arrangements (Donnell, 1991; Sagi et al., 1985; van Ijzendoorn et al., 1992). If mother-child and metapelet-child relationships differ with regard to intimacy in the kibbutz setting, it may be reasonable to suppose that this distinction characterizes mother-child and caregiver-child relationships in most other settings where the continuity of caregiver-child relationships and their commitment are much more limited.

The method used in this study is mother-child and metapelet-child co-construction of narratives. The narratives are co-constructed by mothers and metaplot with the same children during two functional contexts. In one context, a narrative on a fun day is co-constructed using a Duplo dollhouse and a doll family. This context enables active free play during narrative co-construction and is pleasant. In the second context, a narrative is co-constructed from an emotional evocative picture book, on sibling rivalry, without a text. This context is mainly verbal, more stressful, and calls for greater adult direction. The narrative method may enable us to capture aspects of "how" and "what" in the interpersonal communication between the child and his mother or metapelet (Oppenheim & Waters, 1995).

The actions and verbal communication between the participants in these co-construction tasks are divided into two broad categories: specific interactions and patterns of relationships. The patterns of relationships studied were intimacy between the child and people who care for him and task-related or "work" relationships. Intimate relationships are identified in this study by a pattern of behavior that combines the following: being attuned to and participating in the other's expressions of personal wishes and interests not directly related to the task, and indulgence in one's own wishes and interest in the presence of the other. We will consider the relationships to be more task-related or "working relationships" when the participants will hardly diverge from the task.

The research hypotheses refer to a comparison between mothers and metaplot with regard to relationship patterns and specific interactions and to a comparison between the two functional contexts.

For behaviors describing relationships we hypothesize the following:

1. Metaplot will adhere to the task more often than mothers during the two co-construction tasks.
2. Mothers and their children will diverge from the task together more often than metaplot and children.
3. Mothers more often than the metaplot will diverge from the task (by introducing their wishes and playing by themselves outside the task), although the child will be involved in the task.

For interaction variables, we hypothesize the following:

1. Mothers will relate more often than metaplot to the child's wishes, interests, and to emotional themes, whereas metaplot will relate more often than mothers to external events and to cognitive aspects.
2. Metaplot will relate more often than mothers to schedules, compliance, and order.
3. With regard to mode of regulation, metaplot will correct/change what the child did or said more often than mothers. They will initiate more interactions as well as elaborate more often on what they say to the child than mothers. Mothers will help and approve the child's behavior and will elaborate on what children said and did more often than metaplot.

4. With regard to questions and information given, metaplot will teach children and will ask them more direct questions than mothers, whereas mothers will give the child more information than metaplot.

With regard to the effects of the functional context, we hypothesize the following:

1. Mothers and metaplot will refer more often to objects, events, and actions in the external world, as well as to rules of behavior during co-constructing a narrative with the dollhouse. They will refer more often to wishes and needs as well as to emotions in co-constructing a narrative from the emotionally evocative book.
2. Mothers and metaplot will reinforce, confirm, and elaborate on the child's actions and thoughts more often during co-constructing a narrative with the dollhouse, whereas they will elaborate on their own actions and thoughts and take more initiative when co-constructing a narrative from the emotionally evocative book.
3. Mothers and metaplot will ask more direct questions aimed at teaching the child during co-constructing the narrative from the emotionally evocative book on sibling rivalry, whereas during narrative co-construction with the dollhouse, a free play task, they will ask more nondidactic and direct questions and refer more often to actions and events.

Method

Sample

This sample consisted of 15 girls and 21 boys (M = 36.9, SD = 1.59), their mothers, and metaplot. The sample included the children of eight kibbutzim whose ages ranged between 35 and 38 months in the winter and spring of one year. Children were enrolled in a junior kindergarten, where they stayed 6 days a week from 7 in the morning to 4 in the afternoon. They were cared for throughout these hours, in groups of about 6 children, by metaplot, who were responsible for their education and well-being, and spent the rest of the day and the night with their families. The total number of metaplot in the present sample was 16.

Narrative Co-construction Tasks

The interactions and the behaviors describing the relationship to be presented in this report were investigated by two coconstruction tasks devised by the MacArthur Network on the Transition from Infancy to Early Childhood (Oppenheim & Renouf, 1991).

The first task was to co-construct a story with a dollhouse and a doll family. Children were given Duplo toy pieces of furniture, house appliances, and family dolls. They and the adult were asked to use these articles for co-constructing a story together. When the mother interacted with the child, the instructions were: "We have some toys here. Please help (child's name) to compose a story on a fun day at home. Dad and Mom have a day off and they have fun together with (child's name). You can compose any story you wish. Try to help (child's name) to tell what the participants do and feel. We have about 8 minutes for this task." When the metapelet interacted with the child, she was asked to compose the story on having fun when only the metapelet and the child are in the children's house.

The second task was to co-construct a story from a picture book without a text (*One Frog Too Many* by Mercer Mayer; see Eshel, Landau, Yam, & Ben-Aaron, 1997). The adult and the child were presented with this picture booklet, which described, among other things, a sibling rivalry between an older frog and its young sibling. The instructions were: "We have here a special book from which you and (child's name) can compose a story. In the book there are pictures without a text. Would you please help (child's name) to compose the plot and the responses and feelings of the various participants. You have for this task about 8 minutes."

So that comparisons could be made between tasks and adults, the picture book was divided into two halves. Half of the children co-constructed the first part with their mother, and the other half with the metapelet. No child co-constructed the same part of the book twice. In each of the parts, the topic of sibling rivalry was clear, and a narrative about it could be constructed.

Procedure

The study was conducted in a room in a community house in the kibbutz from which the sample was drawn. The community house was not the children's house. It was a neutral public place that was familiar to the child and the adults. No other activity took place in this house at that time. Children came to this house twice: once with their mothers and once with their metaplot. The session with mother lasted about an hour and a half. During this session four mother-child co-construction tasks were conducted. The session with the metapelet lasted about 45 minutes in which the metapelet and the child co-constructed the same four tasks that the child co-constructed with the mother. At least 1 week was allowed between the two sessions.

To avoid order effects, children were divided randomly into two equal groups: one co-constructed first with the mother, and one co-constructed first with the metapelet. The sessions were videotaped, and the co-construction tasks were transcribed.

Coding of the Co-constructions

The behavior observed was divided into five aspects. One was related to relationships and four to specific interactions.

With regard to relationships, the following categories were coded: (1) the adult and the child are involved in the task assigned. In the other three options, one partner or both together diverge from the task assigned by distancing themselves physically or by relating to other subjects; such as aspects of the surrounding room or personal interests, wishes, and memories provoked by the task. The following options were coded for diversion: (2) only the child diverged, (3) only the adult diverged, and (4) both the child and the adult diverged together.

For the interaction, only the adult's behavior was coded. The four aspects of interaction coded were as follows: (1) content of interaction, (2) methods of regulating child's behavior, (3) questions and information given, and (4) mode of interaction. The categories under each of these aspects are presented in table 16.1.

The videotapes were transcribed, and the coders used the videotapes and the transcriptions simultaneously when coding the observations. The observation on child-adult behavior was divided into gesture units. A gesture unit started when the child either initiated a new behavior or began to react to the adult. It finished when this behavior was terminated or when it was changed in terms of one of the categories. A new unit was coded on every subsequent change. A gesture was scored for either verbal or non-verbal expression of the child. Two judges independently divided the observations of four children into gesture units. These observations were divided into 337 gesture units, and the inter-judge reliability for this division was .91. After achieving this agreement, interjudge reliability was examined by two judges for relationship codes as well as for the four aspects of interaction. The inter-judge reliability for the relationship codes, measured by the kappa coefficient, was .97, for the content of interaction it was .97, for methods of regulating child's behavior .80, for questions and information given .77, and for mode of interaction .84.

Four samples of 4 minutes each were analyzed for each child (i.e., the third to the sixth minutes from the onset of each of the two tasks) carried out with mother or with metapelet. On average, 248 gesture units were coded for each child.

Results

The research hypotheses were examined by multivariate analyses of variance (MANOVAs) with adult role (mother or metapelet) and experimental task (co-construction of a story based on a picture booklet or co-construction based on a

TABLE 16.1. Interaction Categories

Content of interaction	Modes of regulation or interaction
Referring to wishes, needs, and intentions	Elaborating/helping/continuing behavior
Referring to cognitive aspects	Elaborating on self-behavior or statement
Referring to emotional experience	Reinforcing/confirming behavior
Referring to specific emotions	Correcting/changing behavior
Referring to objects, events, and actions	Doubting statements or behavior
Referring to interpersonal norms	Initiating action or conversation
Referring to norms not related to people	Playing in parallel to the child
Questions and information given	
Asking teaching questions	Verbal interaction only
Asking general questions	Verbal interaction and touching the child
Asking specific questions	Verbal interaction and touching object
Giving information	Touching child without verbal interaction
Relating to actions and events	Handling objects

dollhouse) as the predictors, and the observation categories as the predicted variables. The unit of analysis was the relative frequency of each item in its respective observation category. The data are presented in table 16.2.

Behavior of Mother and Metapelet

For the relationships categories, the overall MANOVA was statistically significant, $F(3, 33) = 6.50, p < .002$. The data presented in table 16.2 are in line with hypothesis 1: Mother-child co-construction adhered to the experimental tasks ($M = .94$, $SD = .10$) less than metapelet-child co-construction ($M = .98$, $SD = .04$). This difference was statistically significant, $F(1, 35) = 11.00, p < .002$.

Hypothesis 2 was also supported by these data. Mother and child diverged simultaneously from the assignment ($M = .04$, $SD = .09$) more often than did the metapelet and the child ($M = .01$, $SD = .03$).

A further examination of these data shows that, in line with hypothesis 3, mothers felt free to diverge from the task while the child kept working on it ($M = .01$, $SD = .19$) more often than did the metaplot ($M = .002$, $SD = .01$). Both these differences were significant, $F(1, 35) = 6.01, p < .02$, and $F(1, 35) = 11.14$, $p < .002$, respectively.

The data in table 16.2 lend no support to the hypotheses concerning the interaction categories. Mothers did not relate more often to the child's wishes and interests, and the metaplot did not refer more frequently to cognitive issues. Metaplot did not relate more often than mothers to compliance and order. No significant differences were found between mothers and metaplot in correcting children, initiating contact with them, and elaborating on their responses, and mothers and metaplot did not differ in the way they used the experimental tasks for teaching the child.

Interestingly, a significant MANOVA appeared to support the tendency of mothers touching children more often than did the metaplot, $F(4, 32) = 2.76$, $p < .05$. A further examination of the data in table 16.2 indicates that this effect was accounted for mainly by one type of behavior: mothers touched the child more often while talking to him or her ($M = .03$, $SD = .06$) than did the metaplot ($M = .01$, $SD = .02$). The difference between these means was significant, $F(1, 35) = 9.05, p < .005$.

Context Differences

The MANOVA data in table 16.2 also pertain to the effect of the context on adult-child behavior. In line with the first hypothesis, adult-child contact in the content of interaction categories significantly differentiated between the two tasks, $F(6, 30) = 27.98, p < .0001$. In the more emotionally evocative narrative picture book task, the adults referred more often to wishes and needs of the child, $F(1, 35) = 25.84, p < .0001$, and to emotions raised by the narrative, $F(1. 35) = 135.83$, $p < .0001$. In the dollhouse narrative task, adults referred more frequently to actions and events, $F(1, 35) = 44.33, p < .0001$, and to rules of behavior, $F(1, 35) = 13.55, p < .001$.

TABLE 16.2. Means, Standard Deviations, and F Values for Adult Role by Co-constructional Task Analyses of Variance

	Adult role					Task				
	Mother		Metapelet			Dollhouse		Picture book		
Category	*M*	*SD*	*M*	*SD*	*F*(1,35)	*M*	*SD*	*M*	*SD*	*F*(1,35)
Relationships										
Both on task	.94	.10	.98	.04	11.00**	.96	.09	.96	.00	.01
A on task C off task	.01	.03	.00	.01	2.40	.00	.01	.01	.03	1.95
C on task A off task	.01	.02	.00	.01	11.14**	.01	.02	.01	.01	.04
Both off task	.04	.09	.01	.03	6.-1*	.03	.08	.02	.05	.22
Interactions										
Content of interaction										
Wishes, needs	.05	.04	.04	.04	1.37	.06	.05	.03	.03	25.84***
Cognition, thought	.03	.03	.04	.04	3.90	.03	.03	.04	.04	3.54
Emotions, general	.05	.05	.05	.05	.00	.05	.05	.05	.05	.34
Specific emotions	.09	.10	.08	.19	.08	.01	.03	.16	.09	135.83***
Objects, events	.77	.12	.77	.11	.14	.82	.09	.72	.12	44.33***
Interpersonal norms	.01	.02	.01	.03	1.05	.02	.03	.00	.00	13.55***
General norms	.01	.02	.01	.02	.01	.01	.03	.01.	02	.75
Modes of regulation										
Elaborates, child	.48	.15	.49	.15	.22	.54	.15	.42	.12	65.31***
Elaborates, herself	.14	.09	.14	.10	.01	.10	.08	.17	.09	52.33***
Reinforces	.14	.07	.15	.06	2.53	.16	.07	.13	.06	8.49***
Corrects	.04	.03	.04	.03	.04	.03	.03	.04	.03	2.11
Doubts	.02	.03	.02	.02	.50	.02	.03	.02	.02	2.06
Initiates	.18	.09	.16	.08	1.73	.13	.08	.21	.07	43.73***
Parallel play	.01	.02	.00	.01	4.30*	.01	.02	.00	.01	10.27**
Questions and information										
Teaching questions	.34	.11	.37	.12	3.88	.31	.11	.41	.10	39.66***
Giving information	.40	.11	.40	.11	.16	.40	.11	.40	.10	.20
General questions	.06	.05	.06	.05	.00	.05	.04	.06	.05	.79
Specific questions	.04	.05	.04	.04	.09	.06	.05	.02.	02	39.05***
Relating to actions	.15	.09	.13.	09	3.32	.17	.09	.12	.08	11.53**
Mode of interaction										
Verbal only	.63	.14	.66	.15	1.17	.64	.17	.65	.13	.11
Verbal and touch	.03	.06	.01	.02	9.05**	.01	.02	.04	.06	15.06***
Verbal and objects	.30	.13	.30	.14	.06	.29	.16	.31	.12	1.19
Touch only	.00	.01	.00	.01	.02	.00	.01	.00	.01	.45
Handling objects	.03	.05	.03	.05	.60	.05	.05	.00	.01	55.30***

A = adult, C = child.

*$p < .05$.

**$p < .01$.

***$p < .001$.

The two tasks also differentiated between methods of regulating child's behavior, $F(6, 30) = 21.89, p < .0001$. As expected, adults reinforced and confirmed the child more often in the dollhouse narrative co-construction, $F(1, 35) = 8.49$, $p < .01$, elaborated more frequently on his or her actions and words, $F(1, 35) = 65.31, p < .0001$, and referred to a greater extent to their own wishes and feelings and played with the Duplo blocks parallel to the child's play, $F(1, 35) = 10.27$, $p < .003$. Adults elaborated more often on their own actions and thoughts and were more initiating in the emotionally evocative narrative picture book task than in the dollhouse narrative task, $F(1, 35) = 52.33, p < .0001$, and $F(1, 35) = 43.73, p < .0001$, respectively.

The overall MANOVA for questions and information given was significant, $F(4, 32) = 15.22, p < .0001$. Examination of these categories indicates that the emotionally evocative narrative picture book task raised more direct questions aimed at teaching the child, $F(1, 35) = 39.66, p < .0001$, whereas the dollhouse narrative raised more often nondidactic direct questions and references to actions and events, $F(1, 35) = 39.05, p < .0001$, and $F(1, 35) = 11.53, p < .002$, respectively.

A significant effect was also found for mode of interaction category, $F(4, 32) = 17.90, p < .0001$. As hypothesized, the emotionally evocative narrative picture book task evoked a greater amount of adult-child physical contact than the pleasant story co-construction, $F(1, 35) = 15.06, p < .0004$.

In line with our hypothesis on relationships, none of the adult-child relationship categories was significantly affected by the functional context. No significant role by task interaction was found.

Discussion

Mother-child and metapelet-child interaction during the narrative co-construction tasks did not differ in number of gesture units. Most of mother-child, as well as metapelet-child, gesture units were task-related, as requested. However, as hypothesized, metapelet-child gesture units were more often task-oriented than were those of mother and child. No differences were found between mothers and metaplot in redirecting children's attention to the task when they diverged from it. However, mother and child diverged together from the task more often than metapelet and child, and mothers allowed themselves more often than metaplot to diverge from the task while the child was involved in it. These findings are in line with previous findings on differences in socialization roles of mothers and metaplot in the kibbutz (Beit-Hallahmi & Rabin, 1982; Feldman & Yirmia, 1986; Shash, 1977) and are consonant with the role assigned to them by the kibbutz ideology (Golan, 1961).

When diverging together from the task, mother and metapelet each related to the child's questions and comments about sounds, pictures in the room, and experimental equipment. Each participated in the child's associations about personal and common experience, wishes, and interests and referred to elicited emotions during task performance, indicating intersubjective sharing, fitting together, and some sense of "we" feelings (Emde, 1988; Emde & Buchsbaum, 1990; Sander, 1984; Stern, 1986).

Differences in patterns of behavior between the two dyads seem to describe two different kinds of relationships: "working" or task-oriented relationships versus intimate relationships. Metapelet-child patterns of behavior resembled a work relationship in which patterns of interaction were dominated by "job requirements." Mother-child patterns of behavior, on the other hand, were characterized by an integration between two polarities: togetherness or a "we" feeling and being with herself. A mother's expression of her interests and wishes in the presence of the child seem to describe an intimate kind of relationship (Winnicott, 1965). It may be that being in touch with one's subjective world, with personal wishes and interests, and with childhood memories as well, facilitates getting in touch with the child's subjective personal world and enables establishing intersubjectivity, and a special sense of "we," that characterizes this form of intimate parenting relationships.

Some patterns of behavior that characterize intimate parenting as well as "working" relationships were found in each of the two dyads. These findings indicate that there is some overlapping in the roles of mothers and metaplot, as was also found in attachment studies (Goossen & van Ijzendoorn, 1990; Sagi et al., 1985). However, according to Sroufe (1986), differences in relative frequency of interactions of a certain kind identify dominant types of relationships in a dyad. Moreover, when dominant relationships are consolidated, they serve as a context for interaction so that specific interactions can get a different meaning when interacting with mother and when with metapelet. The differences in dominance of each of the two relationships in the two dyads may point to the different functions that mothers and metaplot, and perhaps nonmaternal caregivers in general, have for child development. Mothers foster more often the child's subjective world and the child's individuality, whereas caregivers stress more frequently the requirements of the general, public, objective world, and especially the requirements of different tasks that the child is expected to fulfill at different developmental stages.

How can the existence of some intimate parenting patterns of behavior between a metapelet and a child be explained? Most of the metaplot had children of their own (not in the group of children with whom they work). It may be that the metaplot generalized some elements of the intimate relationships they had with their children to their relationships with children under their care. It is also possible that metaplot's continuous care for the children's basic needs creates moments of intersubjective communication that promote intimate patterns of interaction. It may be that these intimate patterns of interaction facilitate the effectiveness of the more dominant kind of relationships metaplot have with children, namely, "working" or task-oriented relationships.

No differences between mothers and metaplot were found for any of the 18 categories related to content of interaction, regulatory behavior, and question and information given. However, most of these categories distinguished between the two functional contexts, according to their task characteristics. In contrast, the functional contexts did not influence the relative frequency of the patterns of behavior that described the two kinds of relationships in each of the dyads. These findings are in line with claims of Sroufe (1986; 1989) and Hinde (1979; 1983) that relationships are based on the history of interactions and that they can be detected at different times and in different functional contexts.

Rates of touching the child differed between mothers and metaplot and in the two functional contexts: Mothers touched the children while talking more often than metaplot, and both of them touched the children more often in the stressful functional context. This kind of nonverbal communication seems to be a component of intimate relationships. It probably serves as a channel for expressing feelings of protection, especially during early childhood, as emphasized in attachment studies (Ainsworth et al., 1978; Bowlby, 1969/1982; Main, 1990).

Our findings indicate that at 3 years of age most of the interaction between the child and his caregivers during narrative co-construction is verbal. However, verbal narrative co-construction with an adult is accompanied more often by touching behavior in a dyad whose relationships are intimate and during a stressful functional context. A more detailed study on specific dimensions of self-touching and touching the partner is in progress.

NOTE

This study was supported by a grant from the John D. and Catherine T. MacArthur Foundation Network on the Early Childhood Transitions.

REFERENCES

Ainsworth, M. D. S., Blehar, M. C., Waters, E., & Walls, S. (1978). *Patterns of attachment: A psychological study of the Strange Situation.* Hillsdale, NJ: Lawrence Erlbaum.

Aviezer, O., van Ijzendoorn, M. H., Sagi, A., & Schuengel, C. (1994). "Children of the dream" revisited: 70 years of collective early child–care in Israeli kibbutzim. *Psychological Bulletin, 116*, 99–116.

Beit-Hallahmi, B., & Rabin, A. I. (1982). *Twenty years later: Kibbutz children grown up.* New York: Springer.

Belsky, J. (1981). Early human experience: A family perspective. *Developmental Psychology, 17*(1), 3–23.

Belsky, J. (1990). Parental and nonparental child care and children's socioemotional development: A decade in review. *Journal of Marriage and the Family, 52*, 885–903.

Bowlby, J. (1969/1982). *Attachment and loss: vol. 1. Attachment.* New York: Basic Books.

Bowlby, J. (1973). *Attachment and loss: vol. 2. Separation.* New-York: Basic Books.

Bowlby, J. (1980). *Attachment and loss: vol. 3. Loss.* New York: Basic Books.

Donnell, F. (1991). *The impact of family-based versus communal sleeping arrangements on the attachment relationships of kibbutz infants.* Master's thesis, University of Haifa, Israel. (Hebrew).

Emde, R. N. (1988). Development terminable and interminable: I. Innate and motivational factors from infancy. *International Journal of Psycho-Analysis, 69*, 23–42.

Emde, R. N. (1989). The infant's relationship experience: Developmental and affective aspects. In A. J. Sameroff & R. N. Emde (Eds.), *Relationship disturbances in early childhood* (pp. 33–51). New York: Basic Books.

Emde, R. N., & Buchsbaum, H. K. (1990). "Didn't you hear my mommy?" Autonomy with connectedness in moral self-emergence. In D. Cicchetti & M. Beeghly (Eds.), *Development of the self through the transition: Infancy through childhood* (pp. 35–60). Chicago: University of Chicago Press.

Emde, R. N., & Sameroff, A. J. (1989). Understanding early relationship disturbances. In A. J. Sameroff & R. N. Emde (Eds.), *Relationship disturbances in early childhood* (pp. 3–14). New York: Basic Books.

Erikson, H. E. (1963). *Childhood and society.* New York: Norton.

Eshel, Y., Landau, R., Yam, R., & Ben-Aaron, M. (1997). Availability of three-year-old kibbutz children in two functional contexts. *Infant Mental Health Journal, 18*, 231–246.

Feldman, S., & Sarnat, I. (1986). Israeli town and kibbutz toddler's compliance and adult's control attempts. *Merrill-Palmer Quarterly, 32*, 365–378.

Feldman, S., & Yirmia, N. (1986). Perception of socialization roles: A study of Israeli mothers in town and kibbutz. *International Journal of Psychology, 21*, 153–165.

Fox, N. (1977). Attachment of kibbutz infants to mother and metapelet. *Child Development, 48*, 1228–1239.

Fox, N. A., Kimmerly, N. L., & Schafer, W. D. (1991). Attachment to mother/attachment to father: A meta-analysis. *Child Development, 62*, 20–225.

Golan, S. (1961). *Communal education*, Merhavia, Israel: Sifriat Poalim. (Hebrew).

Goossens, F. A., & van Ijzendoorn, M. H. (1990). Quality of infant's attachment to professional caregivers: Relation to infant-parent attachment and daycare characteristics. *Child Development, 61*, 832–837.

Grossmann, K. E., Grossmann, K., Huber, F., & Wartner, U. (1981). German children's behavior towards their mothers at 12 months and their fathers at 18 months in Ainsworth's Strange Situation. *International Journal of Behavioral Development, 4*, 157–181.

Hinde, R. A. (1979). *Towards understanding relationships.* New York: Academic Press.

Hinde, R. A. (1983). Ethology and child development. In M. M. Haith, & J. J. Campos (Eds.), P. H. Mussen (Series Ed.), *Handbook of child psychology: Vol. 2. Infancy and developmental psychobiology* (pp. 27–93). New York: Wiley.

Lamb, M. L. (1976). The role of the father: An overview. In M. L. Lamb (Ed.), *The role of the father in child development* (pp. 1– 63). New York: Wiley.

Lamb, M. E. (1977). Father-infant and mother-infant interaction in the first year of life. *Child Development, 48*, 167–181.

Lamb, M. E., Hwang, C. P., Frodi, A., & Frodi, M. (1982). Security of mother- and father-infant attachment and its relationship to sociability with strangers in traditional and non-traditional Swedish families. *Infant Behavior and Development, 5*, 335–367.

Maccoby, E. E. (1992). The role of parents in the socialization of children: An historical overview. *Developmental Psychology, 28*, 1006–1017.

Maccoby, E. E., & Martin, J. A. (1983). Socialization in the context of the family: Parent-child interaction. In P. H. Mussen (Series Ed.) & E. M. Hetherington (Vol. Ed.), *Handbook of child psychology: Vol. 4. Socialization, personality, and social development* (4th ed., pp.1–101). New York: Wiley.

Main, M. (1990). Parental aversion to infant-initiated contact is correlated with the parent's own rejection during childhood: The effects of experience on signals of security with respect to attachment. In K. E. Barnard & T. B. Brazelton (Eds.), *Touch: The foundation of experience* (pp. 461–495). New York: International Universities Press.

Main, M., & Weston, D. R. (1981). The quality of the toddler's relationship to mother and father: Related to conflict behavior and the readiness to establish new relationships. *Child Development, 52*, 932–940.

Oppenheim, D., & Renouf, A. (1991). Rating scales for parent child co-construction of a frog story. Unpublished manual.

Oppenheim, D., Sagi, A., & Lamb, M. E. (1988). Infant-adult attachments and their relations to socioemotional development four years later. *Developmental Psychology, 24*, 427–433.

Oppenheim, D., & Waters, H. H. (1995). Narrative processes and attachment representations: Issues of development and assessment. *Monographs of the Society for Research in Child Development. 60*(1–2), Serial No. 244, 197–215.

Sagi, A., Lamb, M. E., Lewkowicz, K. S., Shohan, R., Dvir, R., & Estes, D. (1985). Security of infant-mother-father and metapelet attachment among kibbutz-reared Israeli children. In I. Bretherton & E. Walters (Eds.), Growing points in attachment theory and research. *Monographs of the Society for Research in Child Development, 50*, Serial No. 209.

Sameroff, A. J., & Emde, R. N. (1989). *Relationship disturbance in early childhood: A developmental approach.* New York: Basic Books.

Sander, L. (1984). Polarity, paradox and the organizing process in development. In L. D. Call, E. Galenson, & R. L. Tyson (Eds.), *Frontiers of infant psychiatry* (pp. 333–346). New York: Basic Books.

Shash, R. (1977). *Division of roles between parents and metaplot of kibbutz toddlers.* Master's thesis, Tel Aviv University, Israel. (Hebrew).

Sroufe, L. A. (1989). Relationships and relationship disturbances. In A. J. Sameroff & R. N. Emde (Eds.), *Relationship disturbances in early childhood* (pp. 97–124). New York: Basic Books.

Sroufe, L. A., & Fleeson, J. (1986). Attachment and the construction of relationships. In W. W. Hartup, & Z. Rubin (Eds.), *Relationships and development* (pp. 51–71). Hillsdale, NJ: Lawrence Erlbaum.

Stern, D. N. (1977). *The first relationship: Infant and mother.* Cambridge, MA: Harvard University Press.

Stern, D. N. (1985). *The interpersonal world of the Infant.* New York: Basic Books.

Trevarthan, C., & Hubely, P. (1978). Secondary intersubjectivity: Confidence, confiders and acts of meaning in the first year. In A. Lock (Ed.), *Action, gesture and symbol* (pp. 183–229). New York: Academic Press.

van Ijzendoorn, M. H., Sagi, A., &, Lambermon, M. W. E. (1992). The multiple caretaker paradox: Some data from Holland and Israel. In R. C. Pianta (Ed.), Beyond the parent: The role of other adults in children's lives. *New Directions in child development, 56* (pp. 5–24). San Francisco: Jossey-Bass.

Winnicott, D. (1965). *The maturational processes and facilitating environment.* New York: International Universities Press.

NINA KOREN-KARIE
DAVID OPPENHEIM
ZIPI HAIMOVICH
AYELET ETZION-CARASSO

17

Dialogues of 7-Year-Olds With Their Mothers About Emotional Events: Development of a Typology

Much has been learned during the last 30 years about security of attachment in infancy and its origins in sensitive and responsive caregiving relationships (Ainsworth, Blehar, Waters, & Wall, 1978; Bowlby, 1988; Cassidy & Shaver, 1999). Attention is now shifting to the concept of security during the years following infancy and the processes by which transformations take place from the infant and toddler-era secure base to the "psychological" secure base of the preschooler and school-age child. A number of questions can be asked. What are the dimensions of the parent-child relationships most related to security? What are the contexts in which these dimensions are most readily observed? Do parental sensitivity and responsiveness play the same role as they do in infancy? What is the child's role in sustaining a "psychological" secure base with the caregiver?

We see mother-child dialogues, particularly around the co-construction of narratives about emotional events, as a promising arena in which to look for answers to these questions (see Thompson, 2000; Waters & Cummings, 2000; Bretherton, 1990; Grossmann, 1999; Oppenheim & Waters, 1995, for a similar point). Specifically, we believe that one of the promising ways to assess security during childhood is by looking at the capacity of the child and caregiver to work together on building a shared narrative around personal and emotional events. We see the ability to construct a relevant, believable, coherent, and cooperative dialogue as one of the cornerstones of security in the years following early childhood (see also chapter 9). The goal of this chapter is to present a new approach to analyze such dialogues that focuses on the expression of security (or insecurity) during conversations about emotional events.

Several authors have pointed to the importance of mother-child conversations regarding autobiographical events for children's development (e.g., Fivush, 1991, 1994; Oppenheim & Waters, 1995; Reese & Fivush, 1993). A Vygotzkian framework has typically been adopted to conceptualize such conversations. From such a perspective (Vygotsky, 1978), parents are seen as aiding their children in narrative construction by working in the "zone of proximal development" (Rogoff, 1990). Children gradually assume increased responsibility and ability to construct such narratives by themselves, and children, through narratives, come to understand motives behind actions, as well as intentions of other people in relation to the self (Nelson, 1996). Thus, by studying the ways in which parents help their children to verbally organize past experience, we can better understand the ways by which children come to represent and to understand their own experience (Fivush, 1991, 1994; Liable & Thompson, 1998).

A corollary of a Vygotzkian approach is that individual differences in parental input and in parent-child conversations are important for the development of children's later capacity to construct emotion narratives independently. This hypothesis has received support in several studies (e.g., McCabe & Peterson, 1991; Hudson, 1990; Fivush, 1991; Harris, 1999; Dunn, 1993). Most of this work, however, was conducted from a cognitive or linguistic perspective, not from the perspectives of socioemotional development and attachment. This point is significant because cognitive and socioemotional analyses of parent-child dialogues may highlight different aspects of experience.

For example, past research from a cognitive perspective has identified two maternal styles during discussion of past events: elaborative and repetitive (Fivush, 1991), with children of elaborative mothers remembering more details regarding the past compared to those of repetitive mothers. An attachment perspective may be useful. Maternal styles are significant in terms of emotional attunement, the extent to which a mother supports a coherent narrative, and the extent to which a mother is sensitive and empathic to a child's emotional state. The two perspectives may reveal contrasting pictures. For example, maternal elaborative style while discussing a frightening event may promote a sense of security and coherence in a child if it is applied sensitively, empathetically, and constructively. Alternatively, it may elicit fear and even dysregulation if not applied in a sensitive way (e.g., by the parent insisting that the child elaborate about a traumatic event after the child refuses).

What are some of the critical features in dialogues that may constitute a "psychological secure base" for children? Research on this issue is sparce (e.g., see the pioneering work of Main, Kaplan, & Cassidy, 1985). In our own work (Etzion-Carasso & Oppenheim, 2000), we found that "open" and "nonopen" communication styles during reunion observations of 4.5-year-olds with their mothers were related to attachment assessments from infancy. Based on these findings, as well as the theoretical contributions of Bowlby (1982), Main, Kaplan, and Cassidy (1985), Bretherton (1990), and, more recently, Easterbrooks and Biringen (2000), we argue that a mother's ability to be emotionally available to her child when discussing a wide range of emotions is critical, as is her ability to structure and organize dialogues and enable the child to speak freely about topics the child chooses. A mother can also help by containing negative feelings, maintaining the child's involvement, and by enabling the child to complete a task with feelings of confidence and success.

In such an emotional climate, it may be possible for the child to explore a wide range of emotional experiences. Further, such a mother is likely to be seen by the child as a secure base from which to explore the "world of emotion" freely, knowing that the mother will still be emotionally available as a "safe haven" if needed. The child trusts that his mother will not let him be overwhelmed by negative memories and emotions but rather will show him adaptive and useful ways of dealing with such emotions. Therefore, the child is likely to contribute to the conversation when prompted and cooperate with the task at hand.

Description of Study

To examine these speculations, we observed mothers and their seven-year-old children during conversations about past emotional events. This chapter describes a coding system used to assess these conversations, as well as illustrations of mother-child dialogues. The coding system emerged from a follow-up investigation of 120 seven-year-old children (54 boys and 66 girls), who were first seen as infants along with their mothers (Sagi, Koren-Karie, Gini, Ziv, & Joels, 2002). The participants in this study were selected from a larger group ($N = 756$) whose attachment classifications as infants (assessed using the Strange Situation Procedure) were known. The selection of participants for follow-up was biased toward children who had insecure attachments as infants, so that of the 120 children studied at age 7, only 50 had secure attachments as infants.

Mothers and children were presented with four cards, on each of which a name of a feeling was written: happy, mad, sad, and scared (Fivush, 1991). Dyads were asked to remember an event in which the child felt each feeling and to jointly construct a story about each of the events. Conversations typically lasted between 5 and 15 minutes, and the entire interaction was transcribed verbatim.

Transcripts were classified into one of four groups, one reflecting "emotionally matched" dyads, presumably showing a "psychological secure base" and three reflecting "emotionally unmatched" dyads (labeled "exaggerating," "flat," and "inconsistent"), presumably showing a lack of a psychological secure base. The classifications were based on a preliminary step in which transcripts were rated on nine rating scales (e.g., cooperation and involvement, closure of negative feelings, adequacy of story), which assist in reaching a decision regarding the subsequent classification. Full details of the scales are available elsewhere (Koren-Karie, Haimovich, & Etzion-Carasso, 2000). Three independent coders coded 20% of the transcripts with high interrater reliability (kappa = .89).

Emotionally Matched: Task-Oriented, Engaged, and Cooperative

Emotionally matched dyads constructed a wide range of stories: Some were rich and full of details, while others were brief. Regardless of these differences, however, all stories constructed by these dyads provided a coherent picture with a clear and believable link between the requested feeling and the story. The stories of emotionally matched dyads were believable, and the child and the mother did not get carried away to extremes or to descriptions of exaggerated feelings.

Emotionally matched dyads were able to come up with four separate stories matching the four feelings. Stories did not have to be lengthy to qualify as a "story." Even a one-line story can be clear and directly related to the feeling it is intended to describe. For example, the child may tell a story about a time when he was happy because he got from his neighbor a gift that he had long wanted. This is a very short and perhaps simple story, but it is clear and matches the emotion label discussed (i.e., happy). Dyads who did not fulfill this condition (i.e., told only three stories or less or told stories not matched to the emotion label) were classified into one of the nonmatching groups.

In matching dyads, both the mother and the child were involved in constructing the stories. Frequently the mother structured the story and assisted in its development. This was reflected in directing questions, suggesting a theme for the story, or even deciding which story will be told. Thus, the mothers in these dyads were sometimes quite structuring, but they left "space" for the child and enabled him to tell the story as he remembered it or to change the story to fit the emotion label. These mothers typically supported the stories' progression at a rate that was appropriate to the child. If the child appeared to need more time to think, mothers in matching dyads did not push him to think faster. As a result, an ongoing dialogue developed between the mother and the child, with both having time and opportunity to contribute to the story, showing patience and acceptance of each other's ideas and suggestions.

Another feature characterizing matching dyads was guiding the dialogues toward points of strength and toward a positive closure of negative emotions. This strategy appeared to help the children feel in control, strong, and self-confident. In contrast, in some nonmatching dyads, mothers guided children toward very detailed and repetitive description of negative emotions and moved on (or permitted the child to move on) to a new feeling without an appropriate solution.

An important qualification should be mentioned here. It is common to associate a range of positive characteristics to secure mother-child dyads. Thus, in the context of the dialogues we observed, one might expect to see maternal behavior that is kind and warm, stories that are rich and detailed, and children that portray parental figures that are responsive, accessible, and understanding. Interestingly, few dyads from our sample fit these expectations. In general, we did not observe particularly rich and elaborate stories. On the contrary, quite a few children brought up negative themes such as harsh discipline, mother being inattentive, or feelings of jealousy and rejection. In emotionally matched dyads, however, these difficult themes were communicated openly, the story reached its completion without interruptions, and there was no hostility, ignoring, or dismissing reactions to the child's story. Thirty-four of the 120 dyads (28.3%) were classified as emotionally matched.[1]

Even though sharing many common characteristics, the emotionally matched group was quite diverse and heterogeneous. Some dyads were characterized primarily by the mutuality and fluency of their dialogues. Other dyads were concise and brief, but four emotionally matched stories were obtained with no resistance, hostility, boredom, or interruption. Other dyads were primarily characterized by mothers being challenging or demanding, sometimes even expressing dissatisfaction with the themes or richness of the child's stories. While these mothers were at times quite unpleasant, their children did not show signs of anger or frustration.

The following is an example of an emotionally matched dialogue.

M: When were you happy?

C: Uhm . . .

M: Try to think of something that makes you feel happy.

C: But you can help me too, mommy.

M: O.K., but try to think first by yourself.

C: I'm trying to think . . .

M: Do you remember the surprise birthday party? Were you happy then?

C: Yes, yes.

M: Would you like to tell about it?

C: Well, I, I didn't know that there will be a surprise party for me. It was really a surprise. So, first . . . Grandmother took me over to her house and dressed me with beautiful clothes. I didn't understand. I asked her why? Who has a birthday? And then she took me . . . Grandmother took me home and there you were all waiting for me, and we had the surprise birthday party with cakes and balloons and a lot of presents.

In this short example, one can see how this dyad worked together toward the completion of the task. The child was hesitant at the beginning and did not come up with an idea for a story. After trying to give the child an opportunity to choose her own theme and witnessing the child's difficulties, the mother perceived that her child needed some help. With no criticism or negativity, she suggested a theme for the story and directed the child to a specific event. In doing so, the mother demonstrated high levels of structuring, patience, and acceptance of her child. The child, in return, cooperated with her mother and showed high involvement in telling a rich, emotionally matched, elaborate, and coherent story.

We look at the moment in which the child experienced difficulties coming up with an example as a "juncture point." Such points typically occur when children challenge mothers. For example, they might be unresponsive (as in this example), choose to talk about an event that mother does not want to discuss, or be uncooperative. From the point of view of the mother, there is a juncture in the communicative process. Some mothers respond to such challenges with hostility, anxiety, derogation, or other negative acts, while others, even though they might be equally challenged, are capable of responding in an enabling and accepting manner. In the example just discussed, the child's unresponsiveness was the challenge that created the "juncture point," to which mother responded in a calm and directive way.

From an attachment perspective, we can see in this example how mother serves as a psychological secure base for her daughter. The open, tolerant, and organized manner of speech that she uses enabled the child to be hesitant and cautious at the beginning but become involved and cooperative toward the end. The child could presumably learn from such interactions (if they are typical) that a wide range of emotions is accepted and open to negotiation. The child was capable of using her mother as a secure base from which she could "go out" to the world of emotion and as a safe haven in which she could be soothed and comforted when needed. Interestingly, physical contact or warmth was less needed here. Rather, mother's supportive presence (Sroufe, Fox, & Pancake, 1983), at the level of dialogue and narrative construction, appeared to be key to the child's confident exploration of the world of emotions.

Emotionally Unmatched: Exaggerating, Overreacting, and Overwhelming

Dyads from this classification were characterized by stories charged with many emotional themes that were often quite negative, extreme, and dysregulated. Themes were often raised but immediately blocked, and dyads often got carried away to irrelevant topics. The stories presented were confusing, with many repetitions, extreme feelings, or vignettes that did not match the emotion discussed. These features resulted in incoherence. The lack of coherence was expressed in rapid shifts from one topic to the other or from one emotion to the other without completing the discussion of the previous topic. Consequently, sentences were often not linked to each other logically. An additional way in which lack of coherence was expressed was in excessive and irrelevant details. At times, it appeared that the mother and the child were deeply immersed in a pleasant conversation, but a closer analysis of the text indicated that the dyad was intensively busy talking about a topic that was not connected to the emotion about which they were expected to talk. Along similar lines, lack of coherence was expressed by repetitiveness. In these cases, the conversation appeared not to develop but rather to "go around in circles." For example, one mother asked her child: "How did you feel?" Child: "I was angry." Mother: "Were you angry?" Child: "Yes, I was very angry." Mother: "So how is it to feel angry?"

An additional feature of exaggerating dyads was their tendency toward extremes and overdramatization. For example, one child was telling a story about being afraid: "And I was SO frightened, yes, because it was such a HUGE snake, yes, and I was really afraid and shaking and I could hear my heart beat and my teeth knocking." Overdramatization could be exhibited with relation to positive feelings too. For instance, one mother asked: "When were you happy? So happy? Happy that you could feel your heart full of joy? Happy that you could dance in the street?" Even in the context of positive emotions, such parental guidance may make it difficult for the child to come up with a satisfying story.

Another feature of exaggerating dyads was boundary dissolution. One expression of such dissolution was when one of the partners, often the mother, talks about an event in a manner that does not question that the child experienced the event the same way she did. For example, a girl said that she was sad when her parents went abroad, but her mother had another example in mind and she guided the child to a different event: " Let's think about a time when *we* were sad.. you remember when aunt R. died? *We* were sad then and *we* lost our appetite and *our* faces were sad . . . it was as if we were wounded inside." Another example involves role imbalance. Here the child may take a disciplinary role toward the mother (for example, saying "speak loudly, they can't hear you") or the mother assumes a child-like manner of behaving (for example, arguing with her child as if they are equals).

Last, it was not unusual to find in exaggerating dyads the strong need of the child to please the mother. In these cases, children appeared to put their wishes aside and to guide their behaviors to live up to mothers' expectations. This need was expressed in sentences like: "You choose the card (on which the emotion was written), Mom, I'll talk about whatever you want." Sometimes this tendency was expressed in the mother's way of speaking. For example, one mother appeared to ask the child for proof of his love for her: "What made you happier, when we came back from our trip, or all the presents that we gave you?" Along similar lines another mother said, "You like candy and I don't give you candy, but you still love me!" Fifty-seven dyads (47.5%) were classified as emotionally unmatched/exaggerating.

While sharing the features just described, the emotionally unmatched/exaggerating classification was heterogeneous. Hostile dyads were characterized by mothers expressing anger, derogation, or teasing toward their children and children responding with direct anger. Other dyads were characterized by their overwhelming and confusing dialogues that were often repetitive and derailed to irrelevant topics.

The following brief example will clarify the main characteristics of the exaggerating classification.

M: O.K. What happened to us that was scary? What scared us most? What were we scared of? What was so scary? Let's try to think.

C: The amusement park, that we had.

M: The amusement park? You enjoyed it!

C: No, we had in the amusement park . . . It must have been very scary.

M: But you didn't feel scary then. Let's think about an experience that was scary.

C: When I was on that thing that was going round and round, it was very scary.

M: But you didn't cry, it didn't scare you. You enjoyed it, you were smiling all the time and you were waving to me "Hi Mommy!"

C: So what? It was scary that it was going up and down, up and down.

M: I want something that really really really scared us. Something like . . . ha. I know! The electricity blackout, do you remember?

C: (nodding).

M: What did you feel? What do you feel when you have a television working, you have the light and the radio working, and suddenly everything becomes dark and silent?

C: I was scared.

M: What do you feel in such situations?

C: Scared.

M: What do you feel?

C: Afraid.

M: What happened to you, in your body? What happened to your body during the darkness?

C: I was shocked.

M: What do you mean by being scared and shocked? It is as if you have seen a monster, your heart is beating. How does your heart feel when you are scared? What does your heart do when you are scared?

C: It beats.

M: How?

C: Very strong.

M: How strong? Show me!

C: Like that (Child slaps her own face several times and laughs).

In this example, we can see some of the main features of exaggerating dyads. First, there were high levels of intolerance and impatience from the mother's side. Immediately at the beginning of the interaction the mother did not accept her child's story and dismissed it as not interesting and not matched, thus disconfirming the child's contribution. In doing so, the mother appeared to convey to the child that what she felt was wrong. Rather than using this "juncture point" as an opportunity to learn something new about her child's inner world, the mother asserted that the feeling that the child was referring to was not a "true feeling." At the same time she let the child understand that she, the mother, knows what the child was feeling. Second, there were several markers of boundary dissolution. The mother dismissed her child's story and encouraged her to think about an event that "made *us* feel scared." By using the term "us," the mother referred to her child's emotional experiences in a way that indicated a belief that she and her child experience emotional events identically.

Third, the mother's way of talking created an overwhelming and intensified atmosphere. The mother built a frightening story and insisted that the child elaborate what it was like for her to feel scared. Moreover, she did not guide the child toward a resolution, but rather left her at the peak of the negative emotion. In this way, the mother failed to provide a secure base for her daughter. If such segments are representative, we can speculate that the child may learn two basic lessons. First, she learns that "I don't always know what my feelings are; there are others that know that better than I do." Second, the child learns that negative emotions cannot be resolved, and they are bound to be overwhelming, even in recollection.

We close our discussion of the exaggerating classification by noting that a minority of the dyads of this type showed frightened-frightening or bizarre themes.

We elaborate on this issue because of speculations that such maternal behaviors are the precursors of infants' disorganized attachment (Main & Hesse, 1990; see also Hesse, 1999; Lyons-Ruth, Bronfman, & Atwood, 1999). Although only a few dyads showed such behavior, we believed that the unusual, extreme, and potentially dysregulating nature of these dialogues merits notice and might be particularly relevant if high-risk samples will be investigated.

We would like to present next an example that demonstrates some frightening/frightened and bizarre features. The dialogue we present involves frightening elements from the side of the mother and control elements from the side of the child. Some elements of what George and Solomon (1996) referred to as "abdication of care" and Lyons-Ruth et al. (1999) identified as "helpless" maternal behavior were also observed.

C: I have nightmares.

M: Oh, another nightmare? Which one?

C: The one with the snake.

M: But a week ago you were petting a snake.

C: No, this one wasn't like it (like the one that came to his nightmares).

M: You want me to tell you the truth? I am also very scared.

C: Scared of what?

M: Of snakes (they both laugh). In reality, not just in nightmares. I don't have any nightmares, but I'm also scared.

C: I'm not afraid of snakes.

M: You know, I am afraid of snakes.

C: I . . . No.

M: I told you that I'm afraid.

C: (he is reaching his hand toward mother): Touch my hand. It's the snake.

M: (touching the child's hand)

C: You have touched the snake!

M: Do you remember the time we were at the zoo and you held a little snake? I ran away.

C: I remember which hand.

M: So you see, I'm also scared.

C: I remember which hand I petted the snake. I touched you with its hand!

M: No, it's not that bad. You have washed your hand. After all it's not the snake (mother is laughing).

C: And what if it was the snake?

M: Oh boy, I would go out. I guess I would be running out of the room.

C: And what if I would have done a snake doll? Like a real snake?

M: I would have run from the room (both laugh).

C: What if I threw a spider?

M: A spider? That would have been disgusting but not . . .

C: You would have run away!

M: No, no.

C: That's for sure. And what if I bring a real mouse?

M: No, I would jump immediately on the chair. And you? What about you?

C: I would have petted him.

M: Sure you would.

The most striking feature of this dialogue was the impression that the mother could not serve as a secure base for the child at both physical and psychological levels. More than that, she joined his fears and openly declared that she would have abandoned her maternal role as provider of safety in a situation in which her child was confronted with the issues that frighten him the most. As a response to that emotional "abdication of care" (George & Solomon, 1999), the child was trying to check his mother's ability to provide care. He confronted her with a list of what he saw as "dangerous" animals and asked reassurance that the mother would be able to act in a comforting way. Also striking is that throughout this interaction the mother behaved in a childish manner. Reading the transcript gives an impression of two children playing with frightening emotions and not of an interaction between a mother and a child.

Emotionally Unmatched: Flat, Uninvolved, and Using Only Emotional Labels

The main element of flat dyads was lack of dialogue and development of the stories. The mother and the child mentioned names of emotions and events that were related to emotions, but there was almost no development of the *meaning* of the emotion. Consequently, there was just the label, the title of the event: "I was sad because of the dog." The stories were often very short, and the child or the mother tended to use the same event to describe different feelings. In contrast with the emotionally matched-concise pattern described previously, in which the mother did not interrupt the child and did not block his speech, here, the mother quickly moved the child to the next topic. In that way the previously discussed emotion was shut down.

Another characteristic of the unmatched-flat dyads was their lack of involvement and interest in the task. Sometimes this indifference resulted in mother and child not providing four stories and consequently not completing the task. For example, one child claimed that he never felt sad and the mother accepted this claim, permitting the child to put the sad card away and continuing with the next card. Both mother and child did not seem to be bothered by their lack of ability to provide four different stories. Mothers in flat dyads did not try to refresh their children's memory or encourage them to develop a story. Thirteen dyads (10.8%) were classified as emotionally unmatched/flat.

Let us illustrate with an example how the characteristics of flat dyads are expressed.

M: Do you want to tell about something that made you happy?

C: No.

M: Something that made you happy?

C: I don't know.

M: When you came over here, were you sad? Or afraid? Or angry?

C: ......

M: Lets think. What is that? (mother points to the "scared" card)

C: Scared.

M: Right. Can you recall a time when you were scared?

C: I was scared of the dark.

M: From the dark? OK. Here is the angry.

C: I was angry at Daddy when he took me to the doctor.

M: So, you were very angry then?

C: Yes.

M: Yes? OK. What about sad?

C: When A. spanked me.

M: What? Today?

C: Yes.

M: OK. And when were you happy?

C: That I don't know.

M: You don't know when you were happy? O.K. So we are done with that task.

This dyad did not complete the task, for there was no story concerning a happy event. The mother did not try to coax the child to tell a story, but rather accepted his lack of memory as a given. The dialogue between the mother and the son was limited, and as a result we do not really know what, for example, did it mean for him to go to the doctor. Why did the child relate this experience to anger? There were no answers in the text, and neither mother nor child seemed to be bothered by that. It seems as if naming an event as sad or scary is the most they could do. Crittenden (1996) suggested that children whose parents are uncomfortable with negative affect learn that positive affect is acceptable, whereas negative affect is not. In flat dyads the child may learn that *all* emotions, positive and negative, are not acceptable. Such an emotional climate may convey to the child the message that he ought not to look deeper for reasons for his feelings and that "talking about emotions" only means labeling events with the right names. We speculate that such inhibition may leave the child anxious, confused, and helpless with regard to his or her own emotions and in contexts in which others express their feeling in a more open and elaborate manner.

Emotionally Unmatched: Inconsistent Dyads

This pattern characterized cases in which one of the partners was cooperative, coherent, and providing stories that match the emotional label, whereas the other partner blocked the opportunity for dialogues, derailed the conversation to irrelevant directions, or expressed high levels of hostility and anger. As a result, one could not evaluate the dyad as a whole unit that operates together. This is contrasted with the classifications already described, both emotionally matched and unmatched, in which both partners seemed to obey similar "rules" regarding their communication and ways of constructing a story together (even if in some cases, such as the emotionally unmatched dyads, the modus operandi of the dyad seemed less than optimal).

Another pattern of inconsistency was in cases in which mother and child discussed some emotions in an elaborate, rich, and coherent manner but showed great difficulty in maintaining these qualities when dealing with the other emotions. As a result, the transcript looked as if it was provided by two separate dyads. Sixteen dyads (13.3%) were classified as unmatched/inconsistent.

Discussion and Future Directions

During the last two decades, the field of attachment has been deeply involved in defining the meaning of security in adulthood. An important breakthrough was accomplished with Main's development of the Adult Attachment Interview (see Hesse, 1999) that conceptualized security in terms of coherent, open, and objective ways of talking about past attachment experiences. A productive line of research provided considerable empirical support to Main's ideas (see Hesse, 1999, for review). Clear and coherent thinking and talking was found to be related to infants' security of attachment with their mothers. We propose that conversations and dialogues around emotional topics and themes between children and parents, such as those presented in this chapter, may provide an important arena in which the coherency is acquired. In cases in which parent-child conversations are characterized by open, direct, reciprocal, and structuring communication patterns, the child is likely to develop accessibility to a wide range of emotions with less need to rely on defensive exclusion and distortion of reality (Easterbrooks & Biringen, 2000). The encoding, interpretation, and internalization of emotional events is likely to be matched, coherent, and organized. Consequently, we may expect that the child will be also able to talk about such events in a clear, open, and coherent way (Reese & Fivush, 1993; Bretherton, 1990; Crittenden, 1996). It is left for further, longitudinal research to examine whether emotionally matched dialogues in childhood are precursors for the autonomous, secure state of mind identified in the AAI while emotionally nonmatched dialogues are precursors of nonautonomous states of mind.

The dialogues observed in this study were heterogeneous in their content and style. Within that heterogeneity, however, structuring and organization of the interaction emerged as a main feature of emotionally matched dyads. It was not uncommon to identify cases in which the emotionally matched classification appeared counterintuitive. For example, the mother may have been demanding and even unpleasant in her responses to her child, or the child told stories in which the parental figures did not show sensitive and understanding behaviors. Many of the features that are expected in secure dyads, such as warmth, mutual enjoyment, closeness, and stories with positive parental representations were sometimes absent. Nonetheless, careful (and perhaps dispassionate) examination revealed that such dyads could still be working together and constructing emotionally matched stories. Moreover, children in such dyads appeared to feel confident to openly discuss events in which the mother was portrayed negatively, and mothers listened and helped their children to structure the story without being defensive and without trying to correct their evaluations. In these ways, matched dyads demonstrated how a psychological secure base is expressed in dialogue.

This chapter also presented examples in which children could not use their mothers as a basis for security. Instead, children through repeated interactions with their mothers could learn to dismiss or to distort their feelings. Main (1990) has suggested that at time of distress the secure infant has only one consideration in mind, namely, how to alert the parent for his wish for proximity. The insecure infant, in contrast, has to also consider the parent's response to his or her wishes. Main's observations of infants might also apply to the 7-year-olds we observed. Children in emotionally matched dyads appeared to trust and almost take for granted their mothers' positive assistance and therefore were able to focus on their feelings. On the other hand, children in emotionally nonmatched dyads, particularly of the exaggerated type, appeared to have difficulties trusting their mothers, perhaps because they had to keep in mind their mothers' emotional state and direct their behavior in accordance with their mothers' needs and wishes. Similar processes have been suggested by Cassidy and Berlin (1994) in their discussion of ambivalent (C-type) attachments. They argued that children are skillful in recognizing what leads to parental comfort and then attempt to "cooperate" with their parents in maintaining the desired state.

Our conceptualization of the psychological secure base also had methodological implications. One implication involves our reliance on transcripts of the dialogues rather than on coding the dialogues from videotape, a practice that might have permitted assessments of nonverbal communication as well. As we discussed, the central features of psychological security as expressed in mother-child dialogues were organization, structuring, coherence, and cooperation. These features are easily assessed from transcripts of dialogues. Moreover, it is our impression that working from transcripts not only makes such assessment possible but may even enhance the salience of critically important aspects of the dialogue. For example, in some cases mothers actively distorted, dismissed, disconfirmed, or colonized their children's contributions to the dialogue, while the tone of their voice was quite neutral or even pleasant. Or, in another example, the mother and the child happily co-constructed a story that had bizarre themes and was not matched to the emotion they were supposed to discuss. We believe that in both cases inspection of the transcript reveals more clearly the problematic nature of the communicative process and helps focus on the dimensions most critical for the formation of a psychological secure base.[2]

Up to now we have focused primarily on the mother as providing a psychological secure base for the child by appropriate guidance, elaboration, containment, and the like. Thus, our perspective focused on the child's needs and the mother's availability. However, we should not forget that the discussion of events that are emotionally charged for children can sometimes be also challenging for mothers. For example, when a child brings up a mother's trip abroad as an example for sadness, this is likely to raise feelings such as guilt in the mother. Thus, it becomes clear that mothers are not only engaged in responding appropriately to their children but also in regulating their own emotions. Nonetheless, in this study, we looked at things from the perspective of the child's emotional needs. Consequently, we focus on the extent to which the dialogue provides an opportunity for the child to explore his or her emotional world while relying on the assistance of an emotionally available mother.

In closing, we would like to suggest several issues for future research. First, the stability of the emotion dialogue classification over time requires attention. Ongoing work in our laboratory suggests that codable stories can be obtained from children as young as 4.5 years old, and it would be of great interest to learn about continuities and discontinuities in emotion dialogues as related to children's development. A longitudinal perspective on the maternal side of the relationship is also of great importance. It is quite possible that some mothers can be sensitive and responsive during a certain developmental phase, such as when the child is younger, but find it difficult to sustain their sensitivity at a later developmental phase. Such data will help us to gain more knowledge on issues of continuities and discontinuities of attachment relations.

It will also be important to see whether the ability to construct a coherent, fluent, and matched discourse at age 7 is related to the ability to describe a coherent, objective, and balanced narrative around childhood memories as adults classified autonomous in the AAI do. In addition, children are part of a broader network of relationships, and their emotional ecology is broad, providing opportunities for reconstructions of past narratives. How do children integrate diverse dialogic experiences? Is it possible that a child who is uncooperative, hostile, or uninvolved with the mother will behave differently when asked to do the same task with the father? Or will there be carryover from one dialogue to the other? Viewed from the parental perspective, a similar question arises: do parents show the same communicative style with all their children? It will not be surprising to find cases in which parents will show divergent styles with different children (Plomin, Defries, McClearn, & Rutter, 1997). Clearly there is room for empirical examination of these issues.

We began by raising a series of questions regarding the "psychological secure base" of the school-age child. This chapter highlights a context—emotion dialogues—in which security (and insecurity) are both expressed and maintained. We believe this work illustrates the promise of exploring connections between narrative approaches and attachment theory.

NOTES

The data for this study were collected as part of a longitudinal study supported by a grant from the national Institute of Child Health and Human Development (1RO HD25975–01) to Abraham Sagi and by a grant from the Israel Science Foundation (741/ 99–1) to David Oppenheim and Abraham Sagi. We would like to thank Yair Ziv, Motti Gini, and Tzabar Oz for their help with data collection.

1. The relatively low percentage of matched dyads should be interpreted in light of the selection of participants in this sample, which overrepresented insecure attachments.

2. On several cases, we compared the analyses of the transcripts with the observations of the interactions from videotape. Our consistent impression was that for the *purpose of the coding employed in this study,* the observation did not change or contradict the impression we got from the analysis of the transcript.

REFERENCES

Ainsworth, M. D. S., Blehar, M., Waters, E., & Wall, S. (1978). *Patterns of attachment: A psychological study of the strange situation.* Hillsdale, NJ: Lawrence Erlbaum.

Bowlby, J. (1982). *Attachment and loss: Vol.1. Attachment.* New York: Basic Books.

Bowlby, J. (1988). *A secure base: Parent-child attachment and healthy human development.* New York: Basic Books.

Bretherton, I. (1990). Open communication and internal working models: Their role in attachment relationships. In R. Thompson (Ed.), *Socioemotional development. Nebraska Symposium on Motivation,* Vol. 36 (pp. 57–113). Lincoln: University of Nebraska Press.

Bretherton, I. (1999). Updating the "internal working model" construct: some reflections. *Attachment and Human Development, 1,* 343–357.

Cassidy, J., & Berlin, L. (1994). The insecure/ambivalent pattern of attachment: Theory and research. *Child Development, 65,* 971–991.

Crittenden, P. M. (1996). Language and psychopathology: An attachment perspective. In J. H. Beitchman, N. J. Cohen, M. M. Konstantareas, & R. Tannock (Eds.), *Language, learning, and behavior disorders: Developmental, biological, and clinical perspectives* (pp. 59–77). Cambridge: Cambridge University Press.

Dunn, J. (1993). *Young children close relationships.* Newbury Park, CA: Sage.

Easterbrooks, M. A., & Biringen, Z. (2000). Mapping the terrain of emotional availability and attachment [special issue]. *Attachment and Human Development, 2* (2).

Etzion-Carasso, A., & Oppenheim, D. (2000). Open mother-preschooler communication: Relations with early secure attachment. *Attachment and Human Development.*

Fivush, R. (1991). Gender and emotion in mother-child conversations about the past. *Journal of Narrative and Life History, 1,* 325–341.

Fivush, R. (1994). Constructing narrative, emotion, and self in parent-child conversations about the past. In U. Neisser (Ed.), *The remembering self: Construction and accuracy in the self-narrative* (pp. 136–157). New York: Cambridge University Press.

George, C., & Solomon, J. (1996). Representational models of relationships: Links between caregiving and attachment. *Infant Mental Health Journal, 17,* 198–216.

George, C., & Solomon, J. (1999). Attachment and caregiving: The caregiving behavioral system. In J. Cassidy & P. R Shaver (Eds.), *Handbook of attachment* (pp. 649–670). New York: Guilford Press.

Grossmann, K. E. (1999). Old and new internal working models of attachment: The organization of feeling and language. *Attachment and Human Development, 1,* 253–269.

Harris, P. L. (1999). Individual differences in understanding emotion: The role of attachment status and psychological discourse. *Attachment and Human Development, 1*, 307–324.

Hesse, E. (1999). The adult attachment interview: Historical and current perspectives. In J. Cassidy & P. R. Shaver (Eds.), *Handbook of attachment* (pp. 395–433). New York: Guilford Press.

Hudson, J. A. (1990). The emergence of autobiographic memory in mother-child conversation. In R. Fivush & J. A. Hudson (Eds.), *Knowing and remembering in young children* (pp. 166–196). Cambridge: Cambridge University Press.

Koren-Karie, N., Haimovich, T., & Etzion-Carasso, A. (1999). *Coding system for mother-child dialogues about emotional events*. Unpublished manual, University of Haifa, Israel.

Liable, D., & Thompson, R. (1998). Attachment and emotional understanding in preschool children. *Developmental Psychology, 34*, 1038–1045.

Lyons-Ruth, K., Bronfman, E., & Atwood, G. (1999). A relational diathesis model of hostile-helpless states of mind: Expressions in mother-infant interactions. In J. Solomon & C. George (Eds.), *Attachment disorganization* (pp. 33–70). New York: Guilford.

Main, M. (1990). Parental aversion to infant-initiated contact is correlated with the parent's own rejection during childhood: The effects of experience on signals of security with respect to attachment. In K. Barnard & T. B. Brazelton (Eds.), *Touch* (pp. 461–495). Madison, CT: Internationals Universities Press.

Main, M., & Cassidy, J. (1988). Categories of response to reunion with the parent at age 6: Predictable from infant attachment classifications and stable over a 1-month period. *Developmental Psychology, 24*, 415–426.

Main, M., & Hesse, E. (1990). Parents' unresolved traumatic experiences are related to infant disorganized attachment status: Is frightened and/or frightening parental behavior the linking mechanism? In M. T. Greenberg, D. Cicchetti, & M. Cummings (Eds.), *Attachment in the preschool years: Theory, research and intervention* (pp. 161–182). Chicago: University Press.

Main, M., Kaplan, N., & Cassidy, J. (1985). Security in infancy, childhood, and adulthood: A move to the level of representation. In I. Bretherton & E. Waters (Eds.), Growing points in attachment theory and research. *Monographs of the Society for Research in Child Development, 50*(1–2), Serial No. 209, 66–104.

McCabe, A., & Peterson, C. (1991). Getting the story: A longitudinal study of parental styles in eliciting narratives and developing narrative skill. In A. McCabe & C. Peterson (Eds.), *Developing narrative structure* (pp. 217–253). Hillsdale, NJ: Lawrence Erlbaum.

Nelson, K. (1996). *Language in cognitive development: Emergence of mediated mind.* New York: Cambridge University Press.

Oppenheim, D., Koren-Karie, N., & Sagi, A. (2001). Mothers' empathic understanding of their preschoolers' inner world: Relations with early attachment. *International Journal of Behavioral Development, 25*, 16–26.

Oppenheim, D., & Waters, H. S. (1995). Narrative processes and attachment representations: Issues of development and assessment. In E. Waters, B. Vaughn, G. Posada, & K. Kondo-Ikermura (Eds.), Caregiving, cultural, and cognitive perspectives on secure base behavior and working models: New growing points of attachment theory and research. *Monographs of the Society for Research in Child Development, 60*, 197–215.

Plomin, R., Defries, J. C., McClearn, G. E., & Rutter, M. (1997). *Behavioral genetics: A primer* (3d ed.). New York: Freeman.

Reese, E., & Fivush, R. (1993). Parental styles of talking about the past. *Developmental Psychology, 29*, 596–606.

Rogoff, B. (1990). *Apprenticeship in thinking: Cognitive development in social context.* New York: Oxford University Press.

Sagi, A., Koren-Karie, N., Gini, M., Ziv, Y., & Joels, T. (2002). Shedding further light on the effects of various types and quality of early child care on infant-mother attachment relationship: The Israeli study of early child care. *Child Development, 73,* 1166–1186.

Sagi, A., Lamb, M. E., Lewkowicz, K. S., Shoham, R., Dvir, R., & Estes, D. (1985). Security of infant-mother, father, and metapelet attachments among kibbutz-reared Israeli infants. In I. Bretherton and E. Waters (Eds.), Growing points in attachment theory and research. *Monographs the Society for Research in Child Development, 50* (1–2, serial No. 209), 257–275.

Sroufe, L. A., Fox, N. E., & Pancake, V. R. (1983). Attachment and dependency in developmental perspective. *Child Development, 54,* 1615–1627.

Thompson, R. T. (2000). The legacy of early attachments. *Child Development, 71,* 145–152.

Vygotsky, L. S. (1978). *Mind and society.* Cambridge, MA: Harvard University Press.

Waters, E., & Cummings, E. M. (2000). A secure base from which to explore close relationships. *Child Development, 71,* 164–172.

Wechsler, D. (1989). *Manual for the Wechsler Preschool and Primary Scale of Intelligence–Revised.* New York: Psychological Corporation.

ORA AVIEZER

Affective Meaning Making Among Young Peers in Narrative Co-constructions

Narratives have been described as verbal methods for recapitulating experience (Labov & Waletzky, 1967). As such, they allow individuals to make sense of personal experiences and interpersonal exchanges by actively sharing them with others. A growing body of research suggests that narratives, even if only in rudimentary forms, are used by young children to represent their knowledge and understanding of personal experiences and general events (Hudson, Gebelt, Haviland, & Bentivega, 1992; Hudson & Shapiro, 1991; McCabe & Peterson, 1991; Miller, Potts, Fung, Hoogstra, & Minz, 1990; Snow & Dickinson, 1990). Yet the complex process of narrative construction places high demands on children's cognitive, linguistic, emotional, and interpersonal skills. Moreover, successful weaving of narratives in ordinary conversation requires participants to collaborate with each other (Polanyi, 1989). Thus, joint constructions in everyday talk offer young children a supportive context for their attempts to relate personal experiences and share their views.

Typically, young children construct their narratives as they interact with adults who may either elicit them actively or coach and guide children through joint constructions in the course of ordinary talk. However, the natural developmental process entails that children's interactions expand beyond communication with intimately familiar adults. Their acquired competence is put to use in interaction with other people who may be either less competent or less supportive partners. Consequently, collaborative constructions among young children whose competence is limited may be especially difficult to accomplish. Therefore, it is particularly interesting to document the process of construction of meanings in such peer interactions and examine whether it gets accomplished as a joint endeavor. This study explored these questions by examining co-constructions of narratives by young kibbutz children in the context of naturally occurring, spontaneous conversations.

Narrative Competence and the Role of Conversational Partners

Narrative competence of young children was studied mostly in the context of their interaction with adults. This reflects the widely accepted view that interaction with primary caregivers is necessary for young children's acquisition of linguistic skills, communicative competence, and social meanings (Bruner, 1983; Kaye, 1982; Miller & Sperry, 1987; Tomasello, 1992). Caregivers are familiar with children's cognitive and linguistic abilities, know their background experiences, and are sensitive to their focus of attention. Hence, they are able to provide the support children need to participate in conversation or engage in other social exchanges. It is not surprising, therefore, that the earliest achievements in conversational participation and narrative constructions (Corsaro, 1979; McCabe & Peterson, 1991; Ninio, 1988; Snow & Dickinson, 1990), as well as in make-believe (Haight, 1992; Lucariello, 1987; Miller & Garvey, 1984; Slade, 1987), are accomplished by children in the context of co-constructions with their caregivers.

Apparently, young children experience conversation as an occasion for sharing meaning in the context of narrative construction from the earliest phases of language acquisition (Eisenberg, 1985; Miller & Sperry, 1988; Ninio, 1988). Furthermore, in Miller and Sperry's (1988) study of early talk about the past, 2-year-old children used 5 times more evaluations in their talk with their mothers about past events than in their other speech. Given that evaluations convey one's perspective on events, this suggests that toddlers must already have an underlying awareness that the meaningfulness of their accounts derives from relating their own point of view. In addition, children's developing ability to speak about internal states and feelings (Bretherton & Beeghly, 1982; Ridgway, Waters, & Kuczaj, 1985) supports their proficient participation in processes of joint construction of meaning that venture away from perceivable present events. Caregivers, on the other hand, use dyadic interaction to guide children into the meanings and conventions of their culture, often by creating a coherent shared discourse about topics removed from immediate events. They tend to engage in supportive behaviors to promote children's active participation in this cooperative process.

Sustained dyadic interactions between caregivers and children do not, however, represent the typical experience of most children. Even in the Western middle class, where this pattern of interaction is most prevalent, it takes only the birth of a sibling (Dunn & Kendrick, 1982; Dunn & Shatz, 1989; Jones & Adamson, 1987) or enrollment in child care to change significantly the input and amount of attention they receive (Dickinson, 1991; Snow & Dickinson, 1990). Most young children, therefore, find themselves in multiparty interactive contexts or in environments that are less supportive than a close dyadic interaction with a caregiver.

Traditionally, interactions in such contexts were viewed as useless at best or harmful at worst for children's communicative development. However, recently it has been argued that to become competent adults, children need to learn to communicate effectively with all kinds of people. This includes people who are not very skilled themselves or are less sensitive to their partner's abilities and limitations, such as siblings and peers (Mannle, Barton, & Tomasello, 1991; Tomasello, Conti-Ramsden, & Ewert, 1990; Tomasello & Mannle, 1985). Therefore, peer interaction, with the imperfect support it provides, may be conducive for children's development of communicative skills. Yet we do not know whether peer interaction plays an equivalent role in children's organization of their insights about the meaning of events in their daily life.

Equal status and similar levels of knowledge and skill characterize children's peer interaction, unlike their interaction with adults. These similarities may present an obstacle to adequate communication and joint construction of meaning, as young children have to rely on each other to communicate effectively, convey ideas, and share views about the world. This becomes even more difficult when conversational topics are not embedded in the immediate circumstances and children need to negotiate and coordinate common meaning. Giffin (1984) explored this process in preschool children engaged in make-believe. She discovered that they used metacommunication to explicate a psychological frame of interaction that consists of a set of shared organizational rules that place events and behavior in context and make them comprehensible.

Lucariello (1987) argued that experience and knowledge of the world are important determinants of young children's participation in symbolic activity. She found that toddlers led their mothers in pretense episodes whose themes were derived from routine events, whereas mothers played a predominant role in construction of fantasy not based on such themes. In addition, data point to the facilitative role of familiarity on social interaction among young peers and on the development of specific relationships based on the continued presence of the partner (Doyle, Connoly, & Rivest, 1990; Howes, 1988). In a similar vein, one can argue that children's successful co-constructions with peers may also depend on the nature of their mutual world knowledge and experience in terms of both referential themes and metacommunicative behaviors.

Moreover, clear discourse about topics removed from immediately present events requires children to shift coherently between actual worlds in the immediate reality and possible worlds such as the past, the internal, the imagined, and the hypothetical. Such discourse also requires young children to use the language of "There and Then," the language that makes it possible to engage in discourse about conceivable worlds (Wolf, 2002). Thus, interweaving narratives in spontaneous conversation presents a challenge for young children. It compels them to work together at making sense of events that are located in contexts divorced from the "Here and Now." It also forces them to perform under conditions in which they cannot easily assume equal knowledge or rely on shared experience.

Only a handful of studies have examined the spontaneous constructions of narratives and the underlying processes of shared meaning in little children's natural conversations with peers. Umiker-Sebeok (1979) examined spontaneous narratives of 32 preschool children produced during free conversations at school. She found a marked increase in the frequency of narratives between ages 3 and 4. In addition, narratives by 4-year-old children were embedded in recent events and referred to familiar location and people less than narratives of 3-year-old children. By age 5, narrators placed more emphasis on certain meanings, thus trying to influence listeners' interpretation of events. At that age, listeners also participated more actively in the conversation. However, because the primary concern of her study was narrative competence, data analysis focused on the complexity of narrative construction and on the communicative process that creates it, rather than on how narratives are used in children's collaborative attempts to organize the meaning of their experiences.

Preece (1987) examined the narratives that three kindergarten children constructed in spontaneous conversations on their rides to school. She followed their conversations longitudinally between ages 5 and 7 to determine their use of narrative language and the types of narratives they produced. She found that the interactive situations contributed to the complexity of the narratives produced. The range of narrative types that she identified was richer than previously reported in the literature. About 50% of the narratives were personal anecdotes about past experiences of the narrator. An additional 20% were narratives relating events experienced by someone other than the narrator. However, only 12% of the narrative constructions in her data were collaboratively constructed. Imaginative narratives were most likely to be constructed together, whereas personal anecdotes were least likely to result from joint undertaking.

It is conceivable, therefore, that when children's knowledge and experience are constituted of elements familiar to their peers, narrative co-constructions will be easier and more frequent. Hence, mutual familiarity, stable presence, and extensively shared daily experiences may compensate for the limitations inherent in peer interaction and support co-construction of meaning through joint constructions of narratives. Such qualities of peer interaction are intrinsic to the ecology of kibbutz child rearing with its unique practices of childcare. Thus, little children who spend time together since infancy and have extensive experience with each other may be familiar with and share knowledge of a broad realm of events that underlie their constructions of meaning. This collective knowledge creates a common basis that enables them to coordinate their moves between actual worlds of interaction in the "Here and Now" and conversation about possible worlds of "There and Then."

Kibbutz Children

Kibbutz children are collectively cared for in children's houses while their parents work, and they are under the exclusive care of their parents for the rest of the day. Thus, kibbutz children are exposed to multiple caregivers very early in their life. Infants are brought to the infants' house around 3 months of age, but their mothers work only part time and are very involved in their daily care. During the 1st year of infants' life, a gradual shift in the responsibility for their care takes place. By the end of this year, caregivers assume full responsibility for infants' care and mothers resume a full-time workload. The formation of the peer group (six to eight children born within 12 months of each other) usually takes place when children, as a group, transfer to the toddlers' house in the middle of their 2nd year. It is quite common for kibbutz children to remain in the company of the same children throughout their school years (see Aviezer, van Ijzendoorn, Sagi, & Schuengel, 1994, for a detailed description and evaluation of kibbutz early childcare).

From the beginning, young kibbutz children grow in a stable context of peer interaction that includes a high degree of familiarity and shared experience. They spend many hours together in the children's house and often they play together in the afternoon hours when under their parents' care. Moreover, their interactions take place in a small community that has low mobility and a high degree of familiarity and involvement among people. Many of the people that kibbutz children interact with outside the children's house are also familiar to their peers. Therefore, stable, enduring relationships are inherent to toddlers' groups in kibbutzim, and they are characterized by an unusually high degree of familiarity and closeness. This creates a unique situation in which the degree of closeness characteristic of these children's peer relations is more typical of relations that develop between siblings.

This study focused on conversations among 32- to 42-month-old kibbutz children that took place in the children-houses' bedrooms with no adults present. It considered discourse among intimately familiar peers as a viable context for investigating the nature of joint constructions of meanings by young preschoolers. The main goals were to identify and describe co-constructions among young peers in general and joint constructions of narratives in particular. More specifically, the kind of narratives constructed by young peers were explored, as well as how joint constructions, as a social process, assist children in their attempts to understand themselves and others and the world around them.

Method

Subjects

Nine kibbutz toddlers (three boys), ages 32–42 months, who belonged to three different conversation groups, participated in this study. Each conversation group consisted of two girls and a boy who shared a bedroom in their kibbutz children's house. Children's ages and group membership are displayed in table 18.1. Although the kibbutz in which data were collected adhered to the practice of communal sleeping (see Aviezer et al., 1994, for details about that practice), only the children of groups 1 and 3 slept at night in the children's house. The children of group 2 slept at night in their parents' homes. These particular groups were selected out of five possible groups following caregivers' reports that in these bedrooms children tended to chat with each other before falling asleep at naptime.

TABLE 18.1. Children's Gender, Age, and Linguistic Ability According to Conversation Groups

	Gender	Age in months *M*	Age in months (*SD*)	MPU *M*	MPU (*SD*)	Upperbound MPU *M*	Upperbound MPU (*SD*)
Group 1							
Shirit	F	32		3.4		6.4	
Adi	M	32	32.7 (1.2)	4.6	4.1 (0.6)	9.9	8.2 (1.7)
Meital	F	34		4.4		8.4	
Group 2							
Anna	F	34		4.7		7.9	
Dor	M	36	37.3 (4.2)	5.2	4.9 (0.3)	14.9	11.9 (3.6)
Irit	F	42		4.9		12.9	
Group 3							
Yair	M	39		5.7		8.1	
Sara	F	41	40.7 (1.5)	3.4	4.6 (1.2)	10.1	10.7 (3.0)
Miri	F	42		5.8		14.0	

Data Collection

Children's caregivers placed a voice-activated micro-cassette tape-recorder in each bedroom as the children were put to bed and left it there until they fell asleep. This procedure was repeated on consecutive days until an hour of recorded conversation was available for each one of the groups. Four conversations for groups 1 and 3 and five conversations for group 2 were recorded on separate days and constitute the data set. Naptime was chosen as a context for collecting data on peer conversational interactions for two reasons. First, it is a time in which adults attempt to minimize their involvement in children's interaction. Second, toys that usually support children's interaction and play are limited during naptime to soft or small objects that children tend to keep by their beds.

Transcription of the recorded conversations followed the instructions of CHAT (Macwhinney, 1981). One of the caregivers and I (I am familiar with the children) doublechecked the accuracy of the transcription and identified the speakers. A second run of transcription added intonations, stress patterns, and pauses.

Coding

Units of Analysis Only conversational sequences that constituted a dialogue with coherent semantic relationships were considered in the analysis. By definition, co-constructions of meaning must involve the collaborative effort of at least two children. Thus, the minimal unit of analysis was a conversational sequence of at least two turns produced by different children who were concerned with the same topic. A speaker turn was defined as all utterances of a speaker bounded by the utterances of another speaker (Schley & Snow, 1992). The semantic relationships between turns in a sequence were considered in order to determine the boundaries between co-constructions. Thus, a shift in conversational topic marked a transition between units of co-construction within a conversational sequence.

Classification of Co-constructed Conversational Sequences Following Wolf (2002), co-constructed conversational sequences were classified into two different kinds: constructions that focused on the "Here and Now" and narratives. Dialogues and activities accompanied with speech that referred to occurrences in the immediately perceived reality were coded as events in the Here and Now. Conversational sequences were coded as narratives when their reference was removed in time and space from the reality of present events, and they expressed children's personal perspectives by means of evaluations, feelings, intentions, or plans. Personal perspectives, intentions, and motivations were included in this category because they emerge from the inner world of individual children, and they do not belong to the immediately perceived, shared reality of the conversation. Therefore, although personal perspectives often related to events in the Here and Now, they lend the co-constructions in which they were embedded the code of a narrative.

I classified co-constructions into narratives and constructions that focused on the Here and Now. A second coder I trained classified 20% of the conversational sequences for reliability assessment. The classifications of co-constructions were reliable (kappa = .85).

The following categories were used in classification of the data:

Events in the Here and Now This category referred to turn-sequences in word games or physical activity, imitation games, teasing, competition for attention, arguments about the immediate reality, and interaction around objects in the room.

Narrative Co-constructions This category was assigned to conversational sequences that referred to events removed from immediate circumstances by either belonging to a different time frame and space or to the private realm of fantasy, thought, and feeling. Four subtypes of narrative co-constructions were identified:

Personal anecdotes. Stories about past events experienced or observed by a single narrator or jointly constructed by a number of children.

Facts and behavioral scripts. Co-constructions that express knowledge of facts, world states, scripts, and rules.

Symbolic activity. Co-constructions that focused on various facets of children's role-play and fantasy. It included attempts to initiate a make-believe or a role-play game, negotiate scripts and roles, and enact make-believe, role-play, or fantasy in conversational sequences.

Personal perspective. This category reflected children's expression of their own perspective on events in their worlds. It included evaluation of actions or emotions expressed by others and expression of own emotions, thoughts, intentions, and motivations.

Linguistic Assessment

Children's linguistic ability was assessed with two measures: (1) MPU (mean morpheme per utterance), the Hebrew equivalent to MLU (Dromi & Berman, 1982), and (2) upperbound MPU. Upperbound MPU is based on children's longest utterances and indicates the upper limit of their linguistic ability. This measure was used because appropriate conversational participation requires an occasional use of short utterances that lower MPU scores.

Mean Morpheme per Utterance This score was computed, for each child, from the longest conversation of the group according to the instructions specified in Dromi and Berman (1982). MPU scores were reliable (kappa = .86).

Upperbound MPU This score was computed from the 10 longest utterances that each child produced in the conversation that was used for MPU computation.

Results and Discussion

Linguistic skills and conversational competence are essential elements in the proficiency of children necessary for them to engage in joint construction of meaning. Thus, before analyzing children's co-constructions, I will describe their linguistic ability and examine properties of their conversations. A presentation of types of spontaneous co-constructions that were identified in children's natural interaction with each other follows.

The Linguistic Conversational Context

Table 18.1 shows that age and linguistic ability were related, although there were within-group variations. Upperbound MPU scores suggest that most children could express themselves in reasonably long utterances and their linguistic competence allowed them to participate fluently in conversation.

Conversation length may influence the number of joint constructions produced and their complexity. Therefore, conversation and co-construction lengths were both defined in terms of number of speaker-turns. Table 18.2 summarizes the data on conversations' length and number of co-constructions per conversation, for each group. This table shows that the tendency to talk before falling asleep varied among the groups, and for each group there were sharp fluctuations from day to day. In addition, there were individual differences in children's participation within each group. Group 1 children, who were youngest, tended to have shorter conversations and to produce fewer joint constructions in each conversation.

Children's ability to maintain conversational topics over several speaking turns may contribute to the elaborateness of the process of joint construction of meaning. Mean length of co-constructions expressed in speaker turns was 9.83 (range:

TABLE 18.2. Number of Speaker Turns and Frequency of Co-constructions according to Group and Conversation

	Speaker turns		Number of co-constructions	
	M	(*SD*)	*M*	(*SD*)
Group 1				
Conversation 1	42		8	
Conversation 2	171		14	
Conversation 3	84		7	
Conversation 4	57		7	
Total	354	69.5 (74.14)	36	9.0 (2.92)
Group 2				
Conversation 1	97		12	
Conversation 2	206		22	
Conversation 3	42		7	
Conversation 4	249		39	
Conversation 5	104		14	
Total	698	139.6 (76.14)	94	18.8 (12.45)
Group 3				
Conversation 1	77		9	
Conversation 2	70		11	
Conversation 3	223		32	
Conversation 4	76		11	
Total	446	111.5 (55.75)	63	15.7 (5.64)

2–33), 7.43 (range: 2–24), and 7.08 (range: 2–17) for groups 1, 2, and 3, respectively. As indicated by the long sequences, children were able to maintain a topic over an impressively long string of speaker turns in all three conversation groups. This capability constitutes an important foundation for children's attempts to construct common shared meanings.

Data analysis shows that group 1 tended to maintain a topic over a significantly longer string of speaker turns compared to groups 2 and 3, $F(2, 192) = 3.17, p < .044$. This is surprising because group 1 children were younger and less competent. However, it is possible that such long sequences reflect more crude attempts of topic maintenance by using less sophisticated devices. Indeed, an inspection of the longest sequences produced by each group revealed marked differences between group 1 versus groups 2 and 3. Compared to the older groups, group 1 seemed to rely primarily on recursive repetitions in order to accomplish topic maintenance, which is demonstrated in example 1. This example presents an excerpt that opens a sequence of 25 speaker turns.

Example 1 (*Group 1*)
Adi: Meytal eh . . . eh . . . Ora work(*s*) with the tape recorder(*s*)?

Meytal: Yes

Adi: And who work(*s*) here with the tape recorders? (*pause 1.5 sec*) Shula also work(*s*) with the tape-recorder?

Meytal: No.

Adi: You too. (*pause 4.5 sec*) Ruti work(*s*) with the tape recorders too?

Meytal: Yes.

Adi: And also Ora?

Meytal: Yes.

Adi: And Miki?

A comparison of examples 2 (group 1) and 3 (group 2) may illustrate this point further. Both excerpts display negotiations of role assignment for symbolic role-play, and they demonstrate the use of different conversational strategies.

Example 2 (*Group 1*)
Meital: You (*are*) grandpa David

Adi: I (*am*) Itschak

Shirit: And I (*am*) mother Dorit, and . . .

Adi: And I (*am*) mother . . .

Meital: And you, and you (*are*) grandpa Itschak

Shirit: I (*am*) mother Varda

Meytal: Good. And you (*are*) mother the Varda and I (*am*) mother Dorit

Adi: Of. of her. of of. Itschak? (*pause 3.0 sec*) of grandfather? (*pause 5.0 sec*) I (*am*) Itschak. (*pause 2.5 sec*) I (*am*)

Example 3 (*Group 2*)
Irit: Why I (*am*) a baby.

Dor: Me too xxx (*unclear word, speaks in a baby voice*)

Irit: I (*did*) not grow up.

Anna: Yes.

Dor: Ee . . . I (*am*) cry(*ing*).

Irit: You (*are*) my sweetie. oy-vay-voy. em outside xxx (*unclear word*) baby.

Dor: Mommy I will say. Xxx (*unclear words*). here.

Irit: Nu, nu, nu to Dor. (*scolding*)

Examples 2 and 3 present negotiations of a similar problem, yet each group employs different negotiation strategies. In example 2 the children were introducing names of people who were familiar to all of them while repeating themselves or repeating after others. Hence, the resulting dialogue was constructed of a recurrent basic pattern that was repeated. However, in example 3, children used different devices to claim the role they wanted. They gave a reason ("I did not grow up") or acted a role (of a baby, of a mother). They could also exit the play frame and explain their acting to ensure proper understanding ("ee . . . I am crying"). This resulted in a shorter, but more elaborate construction that contained a more sophisticated discourse and shared meaning.

Types of Co-Constructions: Description and Examples

Altogether, 193 co-constructions were identified in the conversations of the three groups, and 69% of these co-constructions were narratives. Narratives were significantly more frequent than constructions that referred to events in the immediate perceivable reality ($z = 5.32$, $p < .000$), but their mean length was not different from that of Here-and-Now constructions. Table 18.3 presents types of co-constructions according to conversation group.

It is clear from table 18.3 that narratives dominated the joint constructions, but their relative prevalence was different in each group (56.6%, 71.2%, and 77.2%, for groups 1, 2, and 3, respectively). Compared with the older children of groups 2 and 3, the children of group 1 focused more on immediate events. These joint constructions of meaning referred to events set in the immediate reality of the interaction. In the next section, I describe characteristics of collaborative constructions in the here and now.

Joint Constructions of Meaning in the Here and Now

Constructions in the here and now used deictic markers, were usually formulated in the present tense, and referred to objects and events immediately available to everyone present. The contents of these constructions included games played in turns, negotiations over objects, and interpersonal exchanges that involved; instruction, competition, seeking of attention, teasing or alliances between children. Thus, these constructions involved mostly physical and verbal activities or action-like pragmatic use of language. However, it is also clear from table 18.3 that each group had its own characteristic style; physical and verbal activities constituted 56%, 32%, and 47% of the here-and-now co-constructions of groups 1, 2, and 3, respectively. Examples 4 and 5 present excerpts drawn from the conversations of groups 2 and 1, respectively, and focused on the discovery

TABLE 18.3. Frequencies of Co-Constructions Categories According to Conversation Groups

	Group 1	Group 2	Group 3
Here and now			
Physical activity	7	4	4
Word games	2	5	3
Interpersonal relations	2	10	3
Observations in Here and Now	5	9	5
Subtotal	16	28	15
Narratives			
Personal anecdotes	3	16	5
Facts/scripts	5	11	17
Symbolic activity	4	27	12
Personal perspective	8	12	14
Subtotal	20	66	48
Total	36	94	63

of the tape recorder. They demonstrate how the same event, that stirred a great deal of excitement in both groups, developed into two different constructions of meaning because of the interaction in each group.

Example 4 (*Group 2*)
Ana: Now your turn, your turn

Dor: Good, o.k.

Irit: Ah

Dor: Your turn Irit

Irit: (*unclear word*) In the bed.

Dor: Good, now! . . . be careful (*unclear word*) . . .

Ana: Now it (*is*) nothing. It move(*s*).

Irit: Your turn (*to Dor*).

Ana: Here. now be careful, now now in the bed . . .

Irit: Now I (*do*) like that? . . .

Dor: Good. now bring to me.

Example 5 (*Group 1*)
Adi: She put for me. she put by me the tape. (*pause 3.0 sec*) she p . . . she put by me the tape. (*pause 3.0 sec*) she put by me the tape (*repeated two more times*). Meytal (*laughing*) (*do*) not take (*pause 2.0 sec*) (*do*) not take from me O.K? (*pause 2.5 sec*) (*do*) not look (*pause 1.5 sec*) (*do*) not look o.k? (*do*) not look

Meytal: I (*am*) only look(*ing*).

Adi: How it turn(*s*)? Look how it turn(*s*).

Though both excerpts exemplify joint construction of meaning in the here and now, they manifest the effect of different interactive contexts. Example 4 illustrates a coordinated turn-taking as the children were handling the tape recorder, whereas example 5 reveals one child's (Adi) attempts to secure exclusive rights to the tape recorder before sharing with another child (Meytal) his excitement about the tape's activity. Thus, a similar event may be associated with different meanings in different conversation groups.

The challenge of communicating meanings becomes even greater when joint constructions are stimulated by occurrences removed from the immediate reality of the interaction. In addition to the need to be coherent in their expression, children have to be able to share with each other more abstract meanings such as thoughts, intentions, and feelings. It is interesting to learn what kind of ideas and concerns children tend to deal with by sharing them with their peers and how they do it. The next section addresses this issue by describing collaborative generation of narratives.

Joint Constructions of Narratives

Narratives were defined as joint constructions of meanings so that their reference was removed from the here and now. Nonetheless, narratives constituted a heterogeneous category not bound to a single time frame and space or to a particular content. Personal anecdotes, stories of personal experience, were most often formed in the past tense. Facts and behavioral scripts, descriptive statements about events and people in the world, had no particular tense associated with them, but they tended to be most complex. Symbolic activity, enacted in the world of make-believe and role-play, involved dialogues in which commands, requests, and negotiations were used, whereas narratives of personal perspective, reflecting speakers' viewpoints emerging from their internal realm, involved mutual questioning and clarifications.

Thus, as the children attempted to construct the meaning of diverse events, their narratives have taken up various forms and contents. Moreover, all coded narrative types were present in the conversations of all three groups (see table 18.3), but their relative frequency was significantly different, $\chi^2 = 13.64$, $df = 6$, $p < .03$. This suggests that each group had its own style manifested in the type of joint constructions that children tended to construct together as they negotiated meaningful issues.

Personal Anecdotes Most personal anecdotes found in the data (66.7%) were told in the conversations of group 2. These accounts were usually formulated in the past tense. They were introduced with a typical story opening, such as "once" (see example 6), or with an attention-getting phrase ("Do you know that . . . ?") announcing a story to tell.

Example 6 (*Group2*)
Irit: Dor, once I went wit(*h*) Adi by the water in the winter, once in the *winter* I went, one time to the sea, and I laughed *there*. (*She laughs*) . . . without *winter*, without *summer* (*4.0 seconds pause*).

Dor: To the deep water?

Ana: With her mother and father.

Dor: To the deep water?

Irit: Yes! and also with my *brother*

Dor: Irit, but you will fall on the floor and will get hurt

Ana: Also with your mother and father?

Irit: No! I, mother, and father, and Eitan! . . . me in the sand (*she laughs*).

Dor: You also dived

Irit: No!

Dor: Why?

Irit: Because. (*this is a legitimate answer in Hebrew*)

Dor: You were afraid of diving? (*2.0 seconds pause*) why you (*did*) not dived?

Irit: Because.

Dor: Do you know that it (*is*) fun to dive? do you know that it (*is*) fun to dive?

Irit: One man when he swim(*s*) in the water

Example 7 (Group 2)

Dor: Irit, do you know that I was three times in the hospital . . . ?

Irit: xxx (*unintelligible word*).

Dor: I was three times in the hospital.

Anna: Do you know what happened to me? Once somebody gave me a shot.

Irit: Somebody? I *did* to you a shot shot.

Anna: Oy-va-avoy to you! (*scolding*).

Dor: xxx (*unintelligible speech*).

Irit: It *hurt(s)* her.

Although personal anecdotes were often initiated by one child who acted as the narrator, the other children had the option to extend the story and support its elaboration or block its development and change the interaction altogether. Example 7 demonstrates the latter, as Irit used Anna's account to start a teasing interaction in the here and now rather than follow the story line. However, Irit's story in example 6 evolved into two simultaneous constructions, each created separately with one of the other two children, who queried her on different aspects of her experience. Anna was more interested in with whom Irit went to the sea, whereas Dor wanted to know whether she dived and how she felt about diving. Both children displayed high levels of attention and interest in Irit's story, and their appreciation of the story was shown in their questions. The conversational process in example 6 is surprisingly similar to adults' management of conversational storytelling (Polanyi, 1989).

Co-constructions of personal anecdotes were also created collectively when the narrator initiated the story using the first-person plural. This narration style indicated to the other children that they are invited to participate and add their perspective about the narrated event (see example 8).

Example 8 (Group 1)

Adi: . . . We saw, we saw in the tape that someone roar(*s*) in this tape. We saw

Shirit: It (*is*) you.

Adi: No! Irit.

Meytal: Not Irit.

Shirit: Irit yelled in this tape!

Meytal: No, no . . . Irit . . .

Shirit: And we laughed . . .

Meytal: . . . Irit and and Irit and Pamela.

Shirit: And we laughed. right?

Adi: And and Shi Shirit played and also Meytal laughed in the tape xxx . . .

Shirit: And we laughed. Right?

Adi: And I saw that you laughing. (*2.5*) and. and *suddenly* (*2.5*) e . . . Dor did not let Shirit to touch the the cassette of his Ora. (*3.0*).

Shirit: And xxx Irit in in this tape, and we laughed.

Examples 6, 7, and 8 present three processes of joint constructions of personal anecdotes in which a different mode of collaboration was used. In example 6, the narrator owned the information and the recipient children acknowledged it. Thus, they participated by requesting additional information in accordance to their interest in the story. In example 7, participation was accomplished by telling a new but related story. In example 8, on the other hand, everyone owned the information. Thus, it was acceptable to argue about the details as different children presented their perspective on the event. In the present corpus, co-construction of personal anecdotes has involved recipients' active participation whose mode of engagement varied according to their familiarity with the event.

Regardless of the process by which personal anecdotes were co-constructed, they raised characteristic topics. According to Polanyi (1989), stories are told to make a point, and only events that cause alterations in states of affairs bring about meaningful contrasts. By and large, the children's personal anecdotes conformed to this description. They often described states and occurrences that contrasted with some aspects of the reality and thus highlighted an unexpected aspect of the world. For instance, the children had no experience with tape recorders in the recording mode; they were familiar with tape recorders in play mode. Thus, the account in example 8 ("we saw in the tape that someone roars in the tape. We saw") reflected a response to the children's observing the silent moving of the tape's wheels as it was recording. In another personal anecdote initiated by the discovery of the micro-cassette tape recorder, Anna commented, "We have a big cassette not small," thus drawing on the meaningful contrast of cassette size. The anecdote in example 6 describes a summertime event but was told in January, when the weather is usually rainy and cold. Thus, the experience described in the anecdote contrasted with reality. However, since in each personal anecdote the story was jointly constructed rather than simply narrated by a single child, its point often shifted and focused on aspects of the event not initially introduced. Thus, in example 6, the point of the story became the feelings associated with diving, whereas in example 8, the point of the co-constructed narrative shifted to who was present in the episode that was collectively recalled and what role did every one play.

To summarize, children used joint constructions of personal anecdotes to focus on unusual and unexpected experiences. By relating such experiences, they generated a contrast, which provided the children with an opportunity for adding new dimensions to their meaning-making process.

Facts in the World and Behavioral Scripts

This category is broad and represents children's conventional knowledge of the physical, social, and human world. The joint constructions of all the groups contained evidence for interest in these aspects of world knowledge, although about half (51.5%) of the narratives that dealt with facts and behavioral scripts were constructed by group 3. Co-constructions that depicted factual knowledge were usually formulated in the simple or progressive present tense. Example 9 demonstrates a simple statement of facts, within a discussion about the classification of objects according to their function. In example 10 the factual statements about the contents of homes are used as explanation or justification for rejecting an invitation.

Example 9 (*Group 2*)
Dor: This (*is*) not! . . . food this (*is*) a simple pacifier.

Anna: Pacifier. Don't eat the pacifier

Irit: . . . The pacifier this (*is*) not food.

Dor: And the bottle?

Irit: Yes (*it is*) food.

Anna: Yes (*it is*) food.

Example 10 (*Group 3*)
Sara: Want to come to my house?

Miri: No I have air-condition. and animals.

Sara: Also me. I don't have air-condition.

Yair: I (*am*) animals?

Miri: But toys?

Sara: Yes. then you want to come?

Miri: No I have many things.

However, when the conversation focused on people's behavior and its rules, children tended to use more complex forms in their constructions. Examples 11, 12, and 13 demonstrate the use of present perfect, future tense, and conditionals, respectively.

Example 11 (*Group 3*)
Sara: For a time (*it has been a long time since*) you (*did*) not come to my house. for a time.

Miri: For a time you (*did*) not come . . .

Sara: No you for a time *you* (*did*) not come to my house. then then *tomorrow* then come *tomorrow* (*2.5*).

Example 12 (*Group 2*)
Dor: Right. I *I* (*am*) smart because I speak American. And you (*are*) not smart.

Irit: But when will be room. then I (*will*) could go to America.

Dor: But now (*there is*) *no* room there.

Irit: Why.

Dor: Because xxx (*unintelligible*) . . .

Irit: There is there! . . . will not be?

Dor: Not will never be room.

Irit: No xxx (*unintelligible*) . . .

Dor: No. no one . . . (*2.0*) when xxx lot of . . . many people run away from from run away . . . because many people go there. then you can not.

Example 13a (*Group 3*)
Sara: Rivka (*4.0 sec*) Rivka! (*2.0 sec*) Rivka! (*3.0 sec*) Rivka! (*2.0 sec*) Rivka! (*3.0 sec*) .

Miri: If you will speak five times it will not *help* that Rivka will come (*very quiet*).

Sara: Rivka! Xxx (*unintelligible*)

Miri: If you will speak every time, one more time then, then Rivka will not come.

Sara: Hagar! Rivka!

Yair: If you will speak loud, in a loud voice, Rivka will come.

Sara: You don't speak with, don't speak with me (*angry*) (*2.0 sec*) Rivka!

Example 13b (*Group 3*)
Sara: who (*is*) here? this (*is*) Ruti? (*3.0*)

Miri: She will not answer you like that.

Sara: I will *go out.* and I will see her?

Miri: Also the window xxx (*unintelligible*) . . .

Sara: Ruti? Ruti? Ruti. Ruti. Ruti. Ruti. Ruti. Ruti. Ruti. Ruti.

Yair: Tutim. say to her *Tu*ti (*4.0*)

Sara: She (*does*) not hear if I say to her Tuti. She hear(*s*) that I *will say xxx* xxx (*unintelligible*) (*laughs*)

Miri: She will hear if you will say oy? and ay. and (*there is*) nothing to do? say *oy* and ay. (*3.5*)

These examples indicate that sharing factual knowledge about aspects of the world was an important facet of the process of co-construction of meaning. Unlike personal anecdotes that contributed novel and unexpected angles of experience, factual information and scripts provided familiar and conventional aspects. This knowledge permitted children to express complex ideas and sophisticated relationships between events in the world. For instance, when group 3 discussed the absence of a caregiver, Sara commented that her father should have come (to replace the caregiver) but he forgot. Yair's response to this comment was that fathers want to sleep too (recall that this is naptime). Thus, in his attempt to make sense of reality, he was making a connection between an apparent event (Sara's father's failure to come) and a general fact in the world (father's need for sleep at naptime). Through a similar process (example 12), Dor used a factual assertion about the state of affairs in the world (many people coming to America) to justify his claim that Irit will not be able to go to America.

The use of conditionals in the children's strategic talk about getting the caregiver to respond (examples 13a and 13b) was fascinating. It showed how observant and perceptive children are and demonstrated the subtleties of the information they draw from their interactions with others. Moreover, this probably would not have been revealed in contexts other than such peer interaction, because the content of adults' behavioral instructions to children tend to be very different from the kind of coaching displayed here. This instructive role played by peer interaction is reminiscent of the function peers are thought to play for adolescents. To summarize, incorporating knowledge about facts and behavioral scripts into collaborative constructions of meaning underscores the part played by conventional ideas and information in the meaning-making process.

Symbolic Activity Each group was engaged in some symbolic activity during these conversations (range 20%–40%), even though available props and objects were rather sparse. Symbolic activity belongs to the world of make-believe and fantasy, which tends to be personal unless purposefully shared. Therefore, when carried out jointly with others, an interesting aspect of this activity is the manner in which children negotiate cooperation. Examples 14 and 15 demonstrate two instances of initiating role-play, a successful one (14) and an unsuccessful one (15).

Example 14 (*Group 2*)
Irit: watch something more, watch something Eitan!

Dor: I (am) not Eitan. (*quietly*)

Irit: Eitan!

Dor: I (*am*) not Eitan!

Irit: Anna (*is*) Eitan.

Dor: Nooo

Irit: You (*are*) Eitan. (*2.0 sec*) Eitan Dor eh . . . Eitan Eitan

Dor: What?

Irit: Eh . . . Eitan! Nu . . . Eitan my xxx (*unintelligible*).

Dor: I I have to earn.

Irit: What? what?

Dor: I have to earn

Irit: You (*are*) *Eitan!*

Dor: But I have to learn

Irit: You (*are*) Eitan that have to learn.

Example 15 (*Group 3*)
Yair: You (*are*) Yigal.

Miri: I (*am*) not Yigal

Yair: Why?

Miri: I (*am*) Miri!

Yair: You (*are*) not Miri you are Yigal . . . you (*are*) ***not*** Miri you (*are*) Yigal!

Miri: No!

Yair: xxx (*unintelligible*) Miri, this (*is*) Yigal. Yigal! (*calling*).

In both examples, the initial bid to engage in role-play was formulated as an assignment/command to play a role of a particular person, and it was rejected. However, in example 14, after some negotiations, Dor changed his mind and agreed to assume the role he was assigned, whereas Miri in example 15 refused to yield. Thus, both excerpts reveal the difficulty inherent in getting a partner to agree to cooperate in role-play. The partners not only need to share the motivation to play but also have to be familiar with the role models and their characteristics. The outcome in examples 14 and 15 may reflect different tactics of negotiations, but more likely they are due to different degrees of familiarity with the role model. Eitan is Irit's 5-year-old brother, whereas Yig'al is Yair's maternal great-uncle who never lived on the kibbutz and probably never visited the children's house. Thus, Dor was intimately familiar with Eitan and the circumstances of his life ("need to learn") and could come around his initial resistance, whereas Miri was requested to assume a role of a person that she never met and hardly knew. It is therefore possible that a broader base of shared knowledge may facilitate cooperation in symbolic activity and the processes of sharing meaning it involves.

An additional problem in jointly constructing symbolic play can occur when two or more children claim a particular role and they need to work out a compromise. This state of affairs was frequent for group 2 where there was a constant competition for the baby role in their popular mother-baby role-play. The children's solutions to this problem spanned the whole range between a constructive agreement on taking turns (see example 3) to a fierce exchange of words and stubborn arguments. To summarize, sharing the world of make-believe is not easy because partners may have different scripts in mind and they cannot take for granted that there is agreement on role assignment.

The contents of symbolic activity were mostly constituted of variations on role-play and some imaginative play with objects. When the play required role assignment as a precondition, negotiations over roles often became the central topic of the activity. See as an illustration example 2 in which the children of group 1 were pretending to assume the roles of real people in their world. The children in group 2 were quite preoccupied (70% of their make-believe constructions) with enacting themes of mother and baby (see example 3), and make-believe activity constituted 41% of their narratives. Groups 3 and 1, who were engaged less frequently in symbolic activity (25% and 20% out of their narratives, respectively), constructed episodes that involved fantasy, as they pretended to be witches or animals (see example 16), but such episodes were infrequent.

Example 16 (*Group 3*)
Miri: Who arrived? mouse? (*screams*)

Yair: No! this is an alligator

Miri: Alligator! *go* away

Yair: Go away you alligator!

Miri: I am, I am nice (*2.5 sec*)

In their co-construction of imaginative play, children also used objects, despite their dearth in the bedrooms. The process by which such play episodes were jointly constructed seems to be different from role-play episodes, as they were initiated by script enactment rather than by recruiting consent in advance. Thus, roles to be played were delineated rather than commanded. Examples 17, 18, and 19 illustrate this process:

Example 17 (*Group 1*)
Shirit: Do you have candy?

Adi: Yes. this is for Irit.

Shirit: Am! (*sound that stands for eating*)

Adi: Here look this is Irit's. I also need candies.

Meital: I will also eat candy

Shirit: Also also mother and father. my . . .

Meital: Who wants? who wants?

Adi: I want candies (*1.0 sec*)

Shirit: Take many

Meital: Good boy . . . take Adi

Example 18 (*Group 2*)
Dor: You (*do*) not have you (*do*) not have (a) microphone? Then I will give you *mine*.

Irit: Give! bring.

Dor: No. then I. then I will give you (*a*) *second. I have*?

Irit: Now I (*do*) not have. (*Do*) not have.

Dor: Here take your microphone.

Anna: I (*do*) not have xxx (*unintelligible*) . . . I (*do*) not have (*a*) *microphone*.

Dor: Mine.

Anna: Dor I . . .

Irit: This, this (*is*) *yuck!* (*2.0*) *I broke* the microphone. Yours.

Dor: So what. I have another one *red* . . .

Example 19 (*Group 3*)
Miri: . . . Yair (*do*) you know what I have? inside the box?

Yair: No. What (*do*) you have xxx (*unintelligible*)?

Miri: What?

Yair: xxx (*unintelligible*) gum.

Miri: And you.and you know what is inside the box? There (*are*) candies.

Yair: I have there gum. (*8.0*)

These excerpts resemble each other in their focus on sharing imaginary objects. There was neither a microphone in group 2's room nor sweets in the rooms of groups 1 and 3. Moreover, they involved the children's acting their role as they saw fit without anyone acting as the director and telling other children what to be or do. The interchange of group 1 was well coordinated and highly cooperative, which probably reflects extensive underlying agreement. The older two groups had to deal with implicit conflict (group 2, example 18) or disagreement (group 3, example 19) about the preferred course of the play. There is not enough data at this point to explain these differences.

To summarize, children inserted pretense and fantasy talk into their conversations and enacted a world of make-believe in shared symbolic play, despite the relative unavailability of toys and objects. The negotiations that accompanied role assignment and choice of script indicate that getting partners' agreement was by no means an easy task. Cooperation between children was either negotiated or recruited by initiating the script in action. The latter seemed to involve less conflict and disagreement, whereas the former was probably somewhat affected by familiarity with the proposed models. Most of the symbolic play found in these data involved role-play of familiar people, familiar roles (mother-baby), and some fantasy. The next section describes the nature of children's expression of their personal perspectives as they engaged in joint construction of meaning.

Personal Perspective

Children communicate their personal perspective when they share with others their preferences and desires, moods, and feelings, as well as their intended actions and an awareness of standards by which actions and their consequences are evaluated. Bringing personal perspectives into joint construction of meaning adds a unique dimension to mutual understanding. It exposes children to the internal experiences of others as well as to different outlooks on their own point of view. In this corpus, personal viewpoints were mostly applied to events in the here and now. Thus, statements of personal perspective were usually formulated in the present tense, except for plans and intentions that were often phrased in the future tense. Reference to emotions and mental states in past events were made only rarely.

Evaluations of actions in the here and now were regularly expressed as satisfaction or disappointment with oneself, as well as criticisms or occasional praise of others. Comments of dissatisfaction were more frequent than expressions of content, and they were mostly directed to others rather than to oneself. The general trend was to correct others' actions and express satisfaction with one's own performance. These responses indicate that children's viewpoint was guided by some standards for correct performance, even though these standards were not explicitly expressed. The arguments that occasionally occurred suggest that these standards were not always shared. Nevertheless, in those instances that standards were shared, they presented the children with very useful interpersonal experiences. Example 20 illustrates how sharing the experience of failing an implicit criterion, as well as efforts for improvement, turned a simple episode of activity in the here and now to a meaningful interpersonal experience of mutual assistance.

Example 20 (*Group 2*)

Ana: Now it (*is*) m-y turn, . . . (*2.0 sec*) it (*was*) not good, now it (*is*) my turn

Irit: One more time. I (*did*) not do it well Dor

Dor: Now it (*is*) my turn Irit

Ana: My turn

Irit: Now my turn

Dor: Now my turn, I (*did*) not do it well

Ana: I (*did*) not do it well also, let's do it together

Dor: O.K. (*they are laughing*)

Ana: It (*did*) not get to . . .

Dor: Again I (*did*) not do it well

Ana: Then let's do it together, o.k.?

Irit: Come . . . I will help

Mental states were mentioned many times in the course of children's conversations, whereas expressing feelings was not very frequent. The excerpt in example 21 is a fascinating illustration of the reference to mental states in a conversation about learning a foreign language.

Example 21 (*Group 2*)

Dor: Irit, speak to me *English*, or else you will not learn English, you will not *know*.

Irit: I want *like that.* I want with you

Dor: Yes, you will teach me Dutch?

Irit: What? Yes

Dor: This (*is*) Dutch?

Irit: A little bit.

Dor: You know that always you say words in Dutch. And I. Understand. I *only*. language. America. *not* language Dutch. I (*do*) not understand language Dutch.

Children expressed with relative ease their own desires and preferences and queried others about their wishes and abilities by using verbs like "want–not want," "need–not need," and "like–not like." They were also pretty proficient in describing their own and inquiring about others' "knowing and not knowing" as well as being "able or unable" to perform certain actions. The verbs used in reference to one's self and their frequency were comparable to the verbs used to refer to others' wishes. But the majority of references to others were formed as questions (84%), whereas references to self were formulated as assertions. Making such a distinction suggests an understanding of the internal nature of mental states and the need to ask in order to access them.

Children also talked about feelings, although sporadically. The emotions that were explicitly mentioned were anger, fear, and being left alone. Examples 22 and 23 illustrate the contexts in which anger and being left alone were discussed, respectively. Fear is brought up in example 6. These examples underscore the causal framework underlying the meaning of these emotions.

Example 22 (*Group 2*)

Irit: *I did* to you in the *nose*, I did to you in the nose

Dor: Than Ruti was angry with you?

Irit: No

Dor: When Beni hit me with the chair on the *head*, than Ruti was angry with him.

Irit: But she (*was*) not angry with me, because I am a *caregiver*

Example 23 (*Group 3*)
Yair: Let's see if Rivka and Ruti left, let's see. Let's see (*2.5*) I want a caregiver very much. (*4.0*) you (*do*) not Miri?

Sara: xxx (*unintelligible*) but Rivka was here.

Miri: Right, she already left. It seems that . . .

Sara: Ey, we are left alone here.

Miri: Right, it seems that . . . you (*did*) not say to her in t . . . it seems that we (*did*) not speak with her in time.

Sara: Then I wanted that she will not go, because xxx (*unintelligible*) we are left here alone. I (*do*) not like , that I (*am*) left here alone.

Miri: But you (*are*) not alone, you (*are*) with me and with Yair.

In example 22, adult's anger is directly associated to physical aggression. When Irit denies that Ruti the caregiver was angry with her, she grounds it in the world of make-believe in which she becomes the caregiver. In example 23, the antecedent events to the children's being left alone is their not talking to their caregiver in time to presumably inform her of their feelings about her leaving. When following this explanation, Sara reiterates her feeling; Miri and Yair attempt to offer her comfort by telling her that she is not alone because they are there. In example 6, Dor's questions to Irit about her fear of diving are left unanswered, and she eventually attempts to change the subject. Thus, in these three examples, we get a whole range of strategies for dealing with emotional issues: make-believe, offering comfort, and evasion.

However, explicit mention of emotion words was not the only way in which emotional meanings were co-constructed. In example 24, Miri expresses her feelings indirectly by threatening Sara. Although she does not use any words of feeling, it is clear that she is upset when the word *wolf* is uttered and she makes it clear in her threats.

Example 24 (*Group 3*)
Sara: Somebody laughed like a wolf. (*3.0*)

Miri: I will *hit you*

Sara: Not me xxx (*unintelligible*).

Miri: But I do not want that you will say wolf.

To summarize, much of these children's personal perspective was constituted of evaluation of actions against some criterion that was spelled out explicitly only seldom. However, the outcome of such evaluations had direct bearing on children's self-satisfaction. It may not be surprising that criticisms were so prevalent in these peer interactions, which often paint them in harsh colors. On the other hand, those instances in which there was mutual praise or kindness and comforting suggest that these relationships were complex and served as a context for sharing rich human experiences that enabled joint construction of meaning.

Summary

The results of this study show that spontaneous co-construction of narratives occurs among peers without any assistance from adults even before the age of three. This is remarkable because such processes require interpersonal competence as well as linguistic and cognitive skills, which have been assumed to exceed the capabilities of very young children. Furthermore, the thematic content of the co-constructed discourse in this study indicates that, from early in life, social interactions such as joint constructions among peers function in the multifaceted process of making sense of the world. The children shared with each other their past experiences and their thoughts about possibilities and probabilities, they used each other to understand the human and physical world, they experienced interpersonal negotiations around goals and needs, and they supported each other when emotionally aroused.

In addition, the findings suggest that familiarity and intimate mutual knowledge may compensate for little children's yet undeveloped linguistic and cognitive competence and support joint constructions removed from the immediate present. Familiarity has the potential of bringing information removed from the immediate present into participants' shared intersubjective reality and its meanings. Thus, the relatively high frequency of narratives in the data and their rich content indicate that young children use close interpersonal relationships with peers as a channel for understanding meanings in their world. The findings of this study underscore the important role played by the peer group even among very young children. Moreover, children's dialogues showed impressive conversational competence and a great deal of flexibility as they were able to use knowledge of behavioral scripts to discuss possibilities and personal anecdotal information to support factual assertions. In addition, while constructing together the realm of imagination and emotion, they showed unexpected interpersonal flexibility when negotiating shared meanings, even though this goal was not always successfully achieved.

Finally, the differences between the groups suggest that a different pattern of interpersonal relationships influences constructs and domains of shared meanings. Further research is needed to determine the relations between various processes of joint construction of narratives and the nature of the social relations that underlie it.

NOTE

This study was supported by the research committee of Oranim Teachers College. I think Prof. Ruth Berman for her generous support during various phases of the research. Special thanks are extended to the children, parents, and caregivers who so generously cooperated with me.

REFERENCES

Aviezer, O., van Ijzendoorn, M., Sagi, A., & Schuengel, C. (1994). "Children of the dream" revisited: 70 years of collective early child-care in Israeli kibbutzim. *Psychological Bulletin, 116,* 99–116.

Bretherton, I., Fritz, J., Zahn-Waxler, C., & Ridgeway, D (1986). Learning to talk about emotions: A functionalist perspective. *Child Development, 57,* 529–548.

Bruner, J. (1983). *Child's talk.* New York: Norton.

Camaioni, L. (1979). Child-adult and child-child conversations: An interactional approach. In E. Ochs & B. B. Schieffelin (Eds.), *Developmental pragmatics* (pp. 325–337). New York: Academic Press.

Corsaro, W. A. (1979). Sociolinguistic patterns in adult-child interaction. In E. Ochs & B. B. Schieffelin (Eds.), *Developmental pragmatics* (pp. 373–389). New York: Academic Press..

Dickinson, D. K. (1991). Teacher agenda and setting: Constraints on conversation in preschoolers. In A. McCabe & C. Peterson (Eds.), *Developing narrative structure* (pp. 255–301). Hillsdale, NJ: Lawrence Erlbaum.

Doyle, A. , Connoly, J., & Rivest, L. (1980). The effect of playmate familiarity on the social interaction of young children. *Child Development, 51,* 217–223.

Dunn, J., & Kendrick, C. (1982). The speech of two- and three-year-olds to infant siblings: "baby talk" and the context of communication. *Journal of Child Language, 9,* 579–595.

Dunn, J., & Shatz, M. (1989). Becoming a conversationalist despite (or because of) having an older sibling. *Child Development, 60,* 399–410.

Eisenberg, A. (1985). Learning to describe past experiences in conversation. *Discourse Processes, 8,* 177–204.

Giffin, H. (1984). The coordination of meaning in the creation of a shared make belief reality. In I. Bretherton (Ed.) *Symbolic play: The development of social understanding* (pp. 73–100). Orlando, FL: Academic Press..

Haight, W. (1992). The development of everyday pretend play: A longitudinal study of mothers' participation. *Merrill-Palmer Quarterly, 38,* 331–349.

Howes, C. (1988). Peer interaction of young children. *Monographs of the Society for Research in Child Development, 53* (1, Serial No. 217).

Jones, C. P., & Adamson, L. B. (1987). Language use in mother-child and mother-child-sibling interaction. *Child Development, 58,* 356–366.

Kaye, K. (1982). *The mental and social life of babies.* Chicago: University of Chicago Press.

Labov, W., & Waletzky, J. (1967). Narrative analysis: Oral versions of personal experience. In J. Helms (Ed.), *Essays on the verbal and visual arts* (pp. 12–44). Seattle: University of Washington Press.

Lucariello, J. (1987). Spinning fantasy: Themes, structures and the knowledge base. *Child Development, 58,* 434–442.

Mannle, S., Barton, M., & Tomasello, M. (1991). Two-year-olds' conversations with their mothers and preschool-aged siblings. *First Language, 12,* 57–71.

McCabe, A., & Peterson, C. (1991). Getting the story: A longitudinal study of parental styles in eliciting narratives and developing narrative skill. In A. McCabe & C. Peterson (Eds.), *Developing narrative structure* (pp. 217–254). Hillsdale, NJ: Lawrence Erlbaum.

Miller, P. J., & Garvey, C. (1984). Mother-baby role play: Its origins in social support. In I. Bretherton (Ed.), *Symbolic play: The development of social understanding* (pp. 101–130). Orlando, FL: Academic Press.

Miller, P., Potts, R., Fung, H., Hoogstra, L., & Minz, J. (1990). Narrative practices and the social construction of self in childhood. *American Ethnologist, 17*, 292–311.

Miller, P. J., & Sperry, L. (1987). The socialization of anger and aggression. *Merrill-Palmer Quarterly, 33*, 1–31.

Miller, P. J., & Sperry, L. (1988). Early talk about the past: The origins of conversational stories of personal experience. *Journal of Child Language, 15*, 293–315.

Ninio, A. (1988). The roots of narrative: Discussing recent events with very young children. *Language Sciences, 10*(1), 35–52.

Polanyi, L. (1989). *Telling the American story: A structural and cultural analysis of Conversational Storytelling.* Cambridge, MA: MIT Press.

Schley, S., & Snow, C. (1992). The conversational skills of school aged children. *Social Development, 1*(1), 18–35.

Slade, A. (1987). A longitudinal study of maternal involvement and symbolic play during the toddler period. *Child Development, 58*, 367–375.

Snow, C. E., & Dickinson, D. K. (1990). Social sources of narrative skills at home and at school. *First Language, 10*, 87–103.

Tomasello, M. (1992). The social bases of language acquisition. *Social Development, 1*, 67–87.

Tomasello, M., Conti-Ramsden, G., & Ewert, B. (1990). Young children's conversations with their mothers and fathers: Differences in breakdown and repair. *Journal of Child Language, 17*, 115–130.

Tomasello, M., & Mannle, S. (1985). Pragmatics of siblings speech to one-year-olds. *Child Development, 56*, 911–917.

Umiker-Sebeok, D. J. (1979). Preschool children's intraconversational narratives. *Journal of Child Language, 6*, 91–109.

Wolf, D. P. (1990). Being of several minds: Voices and versions of the self in early childhood. In D. Cicchetti & M. Beeghly (Eds.), *The self in transition: Infancy to childhood* (pp. 183–212). Chicago: University of Chicago Press.

Wolf, D. P. (2002). "There and then, intangible and internal": Narratives in early childhood. Unpublished manuscript.

INGE BRETHERTON, DAVID OPPENHEIM, HELEN BUCHSBAUM, AND ROBERT EMDE WITH THE COLLABORATION OF THE MACARTHUR TRANSITION NETWORK NARRATIVE GROUP(ROBERT CLYMAN, KURT FISCHER, DOREEN RIDGEWAY, BETSY RUBIN, MALCOLM WATSON, DENNIE WOLF, CAROLYN ZAHN-WAXLER)

Appendix
MacArthur Story Stem Battery

Story Stems in Order of Presentation

Warm-up: Birthday
1. Spilled Juice (attachment/authority)
2. Family Dog Lost/Reunion With Dog (attachment)
3. Mom's Headache (moral dilemma)
4. Gift to Mom or Dad (oedipal)
5. Three's a Crowd (peer conflict)
6. Hot Gravy (attachment/authority)
7. Lost Keys (family conflict)
8. Stealing Candy (moral)
9. Departure/Reunion (attachment)
10. Bathroom Shelf (moral dilemma)
11. Climbing the Rock (mastery, attachment)
12. Exclusion (oedipal)
13. The Cookie Jar (moral dilemma)

End: Family Fun

Although these story stems were developed to elicit children's narratives about specific listed themes (in parentheses in list), children often incorporate additional themes. Thus, attachment themes often occur during the moral stories and vice versa. However, researchers interested in particular topics may wish to administer only subsets of the story stems. This battery can either be used as a standard assessment or tailored to the needs of individual researchers/studies. Some researchers add stories of their own. If this is done, however, we recommend that the additional stories be carefully pilot-tested.

Stories 3, 4, 5, 6, 8, and 13 were specifically developed for this instrument by Bretherton and Lundquist with input from David Oppenheim, Helen Buchsbaum, Robert Emde and other members of the MacArthur Narrative Work Group. Story stems 1, 9, and 11 are from the Attachment Story Completion Task by Bretherton and Ridgeway. Story 7 was developed by Ridgeway for an earlier version of the

ASTC. Stories 10 and 12 are from a set of moral story stems developed by Buchsbaum and Emde. Story 2 was developed by Oppenheim. Throughout the pilot-testing of the story stems, members of the Narrative Work Group (MacArthur Research Network on Early Childhood Transitions) offered helpful suggestions on procedure and story stem content.

General Remarks

To distinguish the interviewed CHILD from the child figures in the story stems, references to the interviewed CHILD are always capitalized. The child figures in the story stems are always of the same sex as the CHILD.

In order to obtain useful data, it is necessary to present the story stems in standard form to all children. However, researchers with differing aims may want to change some details in the stories or may want to add their own stories. As authors of this instrument, we encourage such creativity and flexibility between studies, but to ensure comparability within studies, careful training of the interviewers is recommended (i.e., use of the same protagonists, the same props, the same wording across children). The story stems as described in this appendix are presented with the older sibling as the main protagonist, but some researchers have used the younger sibling as the main protagonist.

Family Figures and Props

We have used a variety of family figures, including "Duplo" dolls, "Playmobile" figures, small bears, and family figures available from educational supply companies. All seem to be similarly successful in engaging the children. However, it is absolutely necessary that the figures be able to stand up (in one study Barbie doll stands were used for this purpose). If the behavior of older and younger sibling is of interest, it is advisable to use siblings of different sizes. As regards realism, the props should not be so elaborate that the children are distracted by them. The family car, in particular, should just be a rectangular box large enough to hold all family members. Wheels can be painted on.

Prompts

There are different rules for prompts/demonstrations during the warm-up story (Birthday) and concluding story (Family Fun) from those for the 13 story stems that constitute the body of the MacArthur Story Stem Battery.

The purpose of the warm-up is to get the CHILD involved in pretense, that is, moving the figures and talking for them. It is therefore recommended that the Interviewer demonstrate talking for the family figures and performing their actions if the CHILD does not do so spontaneously. The purpose of the concluding story is to give the CHILD freedom to do what he or she wants.

By the end of the warm-up, the CHILD should have engaged in the following behaviors:

1. Talking with the Interviewer.
2. Manipulating the figures and props.
3. Talking through the characters.
4. Saying something that relates to the Birthday story.

If the CHILD does not, the rest of the performance may be so limited that it may be hard to interpret.

We strongly recommend that the interviewer establish rapport with the CHILD for 10 minutes or so before trying to engage the CHILD in the story task, usually in the presence of the mother. For very shy children this rapport-building period may have to be extended. With younger children, these story stems have sometimes been administered in the presence of the mother. With older preschoolers, they have been administered with the mother not present.

Introduction of Figures

The following abbreviations are used in the appendix to identify various story figures:

M = mother figure
F = father figure
G = grandmother figure
C1 = older brother-sister (Susan/George)
C2 = younger brother/sister (Jane/Bob)
C3 = friend
D = family dog (Barney)
I = interviewer

I: Look who we have here (bring out the family). Here's our family. This is Grandma, this is Mom, this is Dad, this is the big sister/brother and her/his name is Susan/George and this is the little sister/brother and her/his name is Jane/Bob and this is their dog and his name is Barney. (Show the figures to the CHILD as you name them.)

I: Who do we have here? (Get child to name each family member, with help if necessary.)

Warm-Up: Susan=S/George's Birthday

Story theme: Introduction, modeling of narration with family figures
Props: Table, birthday cake
Characters: All the family characters, including the dog (but not including the friends and other nonfamily characters)

I: You know what? It is Susan/George's birthday and Mom made her/him this beautiful cake (bring out cake). It's time for the party.

M: "Come on Grandma and Dad, Jane/Bob and Susan/George, it=s time to celebrate Susan/George's birthday.

I: Can you get the family ready at the table?

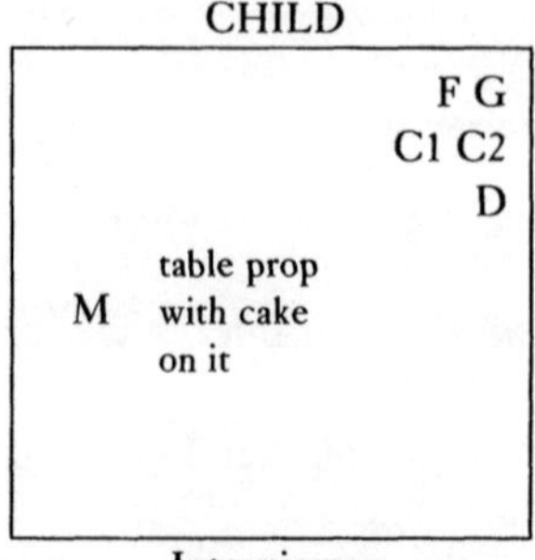

I: Show me and tell me what happens now.

Let the CHILD play with the figures or tell a story yourself if the CHILD is in need of help. Remember, however, that demonstrations or leading prompts should not be used for the 13 subsequent story stems, which should be presented in the standard fashion described for story stems 1–13.

Ideas for prompts to get the child involved:

1. Show me how they eat the cake/blow out the candles.
2. What might Susan/George say about her/his beautiful cake?
3. If the child wants to sing "happy Birthday," by all means join him/her and sing along.

1. Spilled Juice

Theme: Parental responses to accident
Props: Table, pitcher
Characters: M, F, Cl, C2

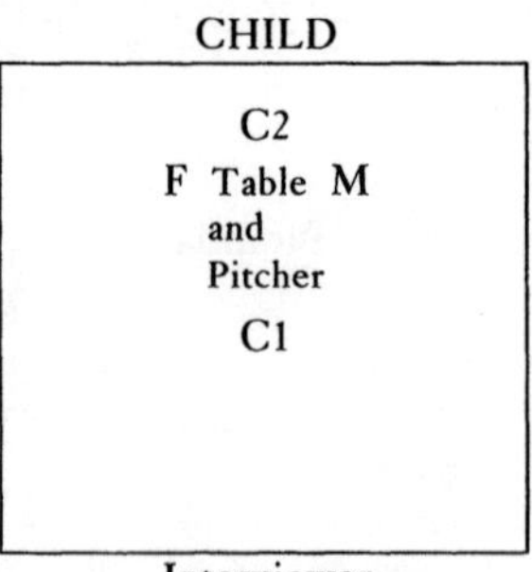

I: The family is thirsty and they are going to have some juice. Now put the family around the table so they can have some juice. (Wait until the figures are placed.)

Here's the family drinking their juice. Susan/George gets up and reaches across the table and Uh-oh! she/he spilled her/his juice all over the floor. (Make child spill the pitcher onto the floor so that it is visible to the CHILD.)

Show me and tell me what happens now.

In the following 13 story stems, only the prescribed issue prompts (that focus the child on addressing the central conflict or issue) should be used. In addition, nonleading clarification and elaboration prompts can be used. Clarification prompts are designed to encourage the CHILD to state who performed an action (e.g., when the CHILD says "He got in trouble" without specifying with whom the child got in trouble) or what the action represents (e.g., when it is not stated, and not clear from the performance, the Interviewer should ask "What are they doing?" Sometimes the child may reply "I am." In this case the Interviewer can ask: "Who in the story is doing it?"

Issue prompt: (If nothing is done about the juice)
I: What happens about Susan/George spilling the juice?

Elaboration prompt:
(If CHILD only picks up the pitcher and stops)
"Did anything else happen?"

2. The Lost Dog/Reunion With the Lost Dog

Story theme: Loss and reunion
Props: None
Characters: C1, M standing off to the side; the dog only appears in part 2 of the stem.

Part 1. Lost Dog

I: Susan/George has been thinking about playing with her/his favorite dog Barney ever since she/he woke up this morning.

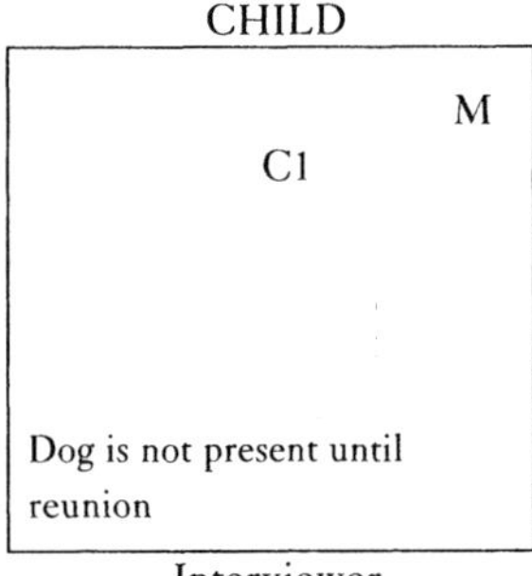

C1: "Mom, I am going out into the backyard to play with Barney."
M: "OK Susan/George."
I: So Susan/George goes out to the yard.

C1: "Oh no!! Barney's gone!" (worried voice).
I: Show me and tell me what happens now.

Note: Children frequently run to the prop box and ask for Barney. If they do, say: You will get Barney later, but now, show me what George does in the story.

Part 2. Reunion With the Lost Dog

Story theme: Reunion
Props: None
Characters: D, Cl, M

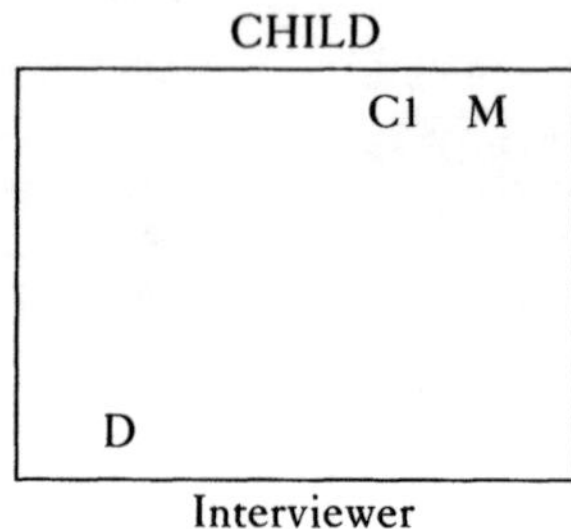

I: (Brings back Barney, places on the edge of table away from CHILD) Look who's back (in an excited tone).
Show me and tell what happens now.

Elaboration prompt: (If CHILD only reunites C1 and the dog without doing anything else)
"Do they do anything, now that Barney is back?"

3. Mom's Headache

Story theme: Dilemma about empathy with mother versus loyalty to friend
Props: Couch, television, armchair
Characters: M, C1, C3 (friend, same sex as CHILD)

I: (Set out couch, TV and chair as seen in the following—name objects as you set them up) We have a couch, a TV, and a chair.

The set-up depicted here represents the scene at the time the friend rings the doorbell (see the following).

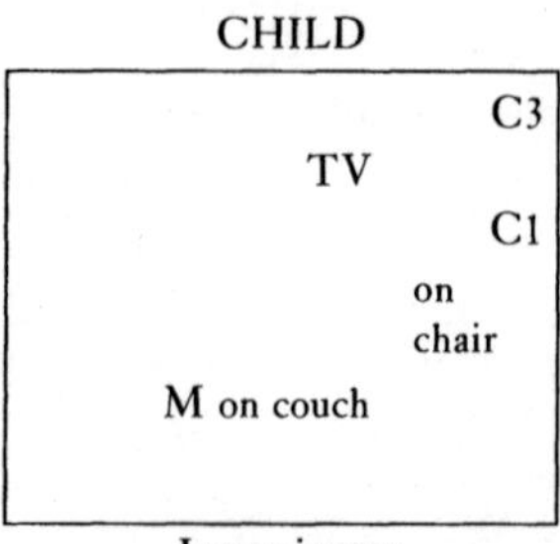

I: Mom and Susan/George are sitting and watching TV (mom turns to child).

M: "Oh Susan/George, I have such a headache! I just have to turn this TV off and lie down!" (Mom gets up and turns the TV off.)
"Susan/George, can you find something quiet to do for a while?"

C1: "Ok Mom, I'll read a book (Mom lies down on the couch and Susan/George remains in chair and reads a book).

I: ("Ding-dong" making a doorbell sound) It's Susan/George's friend, Laura/Dave.

C3: "There's this really neat show on TV, can I come in and watch with you?"

E: Show me and tell me what happens next.

Required issue prompt 1: (If Susan/George doesn't turn on the TV)
C3: "Oh come on! I know you'll really like it!"

Required issue prompt 2: (If Susan/George or friend turns on the TV)
M: "I have such a headache" (expressing mild pain)

4. Gift to Mom or Dad

Story theme: Pride/preference for one parent (Oedipal theme)
Props: None
Characters: M, F, C1

I: Susan/George worked very hard at preschool today. Do you know what he/she made? (pause) She/he made a beautiful picture.

Here's Susan/George coming home from preschool (walk Cl toward Mom and Dad).

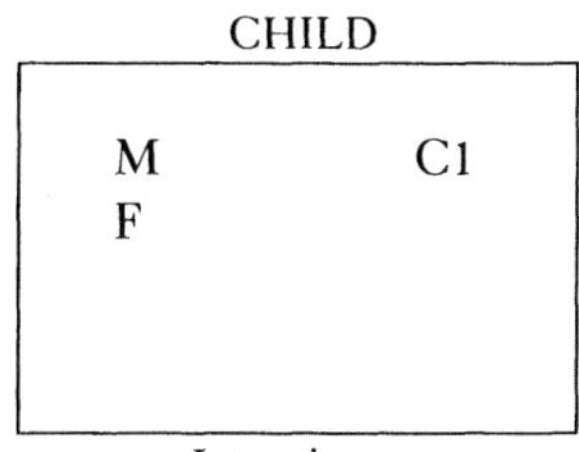

C1: "Hi, look at the picture I made at school today" (in excited tone).
Wait for a response, if none forthcoming ask:
Required issue prompt: What do mom and dad say?
Wait for a response, then continue:

I: Who does Susan/George give the picture to, Mom or Dad, Dad or Mom?

Required issue prompt 2: (If picture is given to Dad)
I: I wonder how Mom feels about Susan/George giving the picture to Dad?
(If the CHILD does not give a reason)
I: How come?

Required issue prompt 2: (If picture is given to Mom).
I: I wonder how Dad feels about Susan/George giving the picture to Mom?
(If the CHILD does not give a reason)
I: How come?

5. Three's a Crowd

Story theme: Dilemma of loyalty to friend versus empathy toward sibling
Props: Ball (alternate prop: a small wagon)
Characters: Cl, C2, C3, F, M (all same sex as CHILD)

I: Mom and Dad are talking to the neighbors and Susan/George is playing with her/his friend Laura/Dave and her/his new ball (place figures and ball as seen here).

I: Show me how they play with the ball.

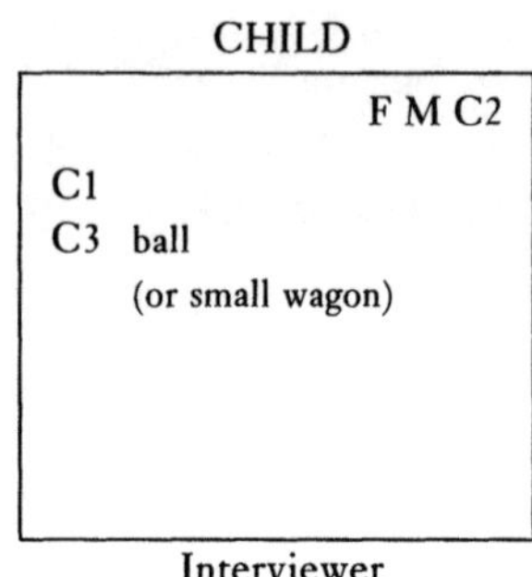

I: They're playing with Laura's/Dave's new ball.
And Jane/Bob, the little sister/brother, runs out of the house and says: "Can I play with you?"

C1: "Sure!"

C3: "No way! If you let your sister/brother play, I won't be your friend anymore!"

I: Show me and tell me what happens next.

Required issue prompt 1: (If Susan/George doesn't come to Jane's/Bob's defense)
C3: "But Susan/George, I'm your sister/brother!"

Required issue prompt 2: (If C2 [sibling] is included by C1)
C3: "But I said I don't want to play with your little sister/brother" (angrily).

6. Hot Gravy

Story theme: Disobedience/parental empathy versus authority
Props: Pan, stove
Characters: M, F, Cl, C2

I: Mom and Susan/George are at the stove. Dad and Jane/Bob are sitting at the table.

CHILD

D
Table C1
C2 M
stove

and
pan

Interviewer

M: "We're going to have a good supper but it's not ready yet. Don't get too close to the stove."

C1: "Mmmm, that looks good. I don't want to wait, I'd like some now."
(Susan/George knocks the pot of soup off the stove.)

C1: "Ow! I've burned my hand! It hurts!!"

I: Show me and tell me what happens now.

Required issue prompt 1: (If no one helps child)

I: What do they do about the hurt hand?

7. THE LOST KEYS

Story theme: Parental conflict
Props: None
Characters: M, F, Cl
Setting: Mom and Dad facing each other; child observing

I: Susan/George comes into the room and sees Mom and Dad looking at each other like this. Look at my face (show angry expression).

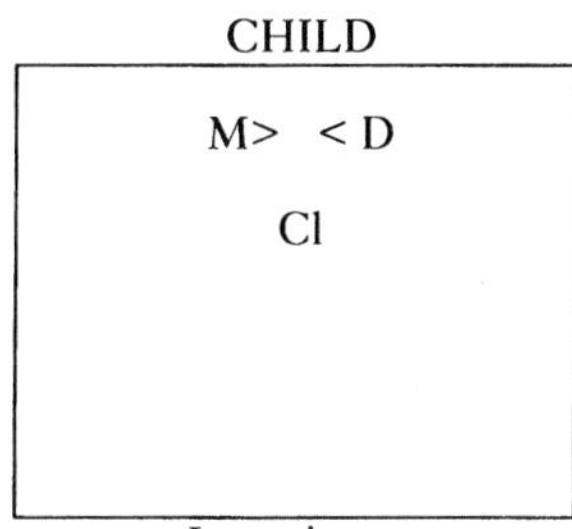

M: (Angrily) "You lost my keys!"

F: (Angrily) "I did NOT!"

M: "Yes you did, you always lose my keys!"

F: "I did not lose them this time."

I: Show me and tell me what happens now.

Issue prompt: (If child does not enact end or resolutions of conflict)

I: What's going to happen about Mom and Dad's argument?

8. STEALING CANDY

Story theme: Transgression/getting caught/shame
Props: Check-out counter
Characters: Cashier (CH), M, Cl

E: Here we have the cashier, and over here we have a shelf. You know what's on the shelf? Candy.

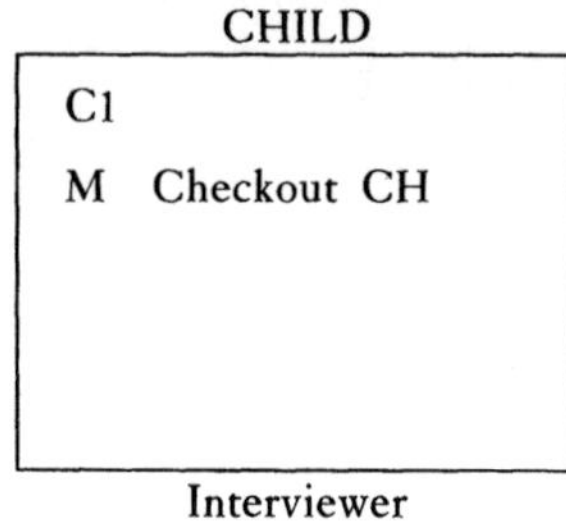

I: Here come Mom and Susan/George.

C1: "Oh candy! Can I have some?"

M: "No, you already had one today. Let's go home."

(Mom walks away. Susan/George takes a candy bar and follows Mom.)

CH: "Hey, what are you doing there?"

(Mom turns around to look.)

E: Show me and tell me what happens now.

Required issue prompt 1: (If no response to the stealing)
CH: "Hey, you took a candy bar!"

Required issue prompt 2: (If still no response to the stealing)
M: "I told you not to take candy and you did."

9. Departure Story

Story theme: Separation from parents
Props: Car
Characters: M, F, G, Cl, C2

I: Jane/Bob and Susan/George go outside to play (place figures as seen here).

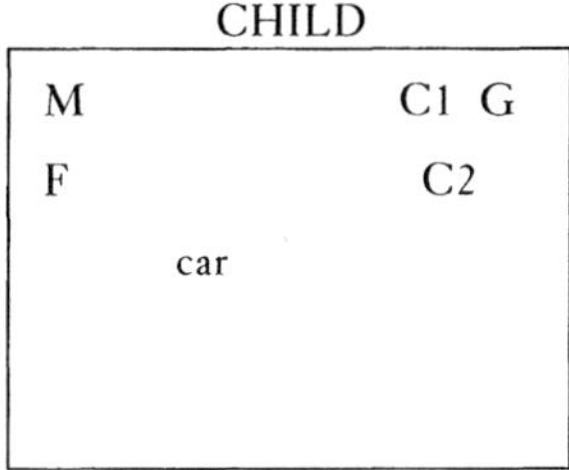

I: You know what it looks like to me? It looks like Mommy and Daddy are going on a trip. The car is parked in front of the house (bring out car).

M: "OK girls/boys, your dad and I are leaving on our trip now. See you tomorrow, Grandma will stay with you" (bring out the Grandma).

I: Show me and tell what happens now.

Important: If at all possible, let the CHILD put the figures in the car and make them drive off. Only intervene if CHILD seems unable to make the car drive off. If the CHILD puts the children in the car, say: "No, only the Mom and Dad are going." After the CHILD (or if necessary, the Interviewer) makes the car drive off, the Interviewer puts the car under the table, out of sight. If the CHILD wants to retrieve the car, the Interviewer replies: "No, they're not coming back yet."

I: And away they go! (as the car is moved under the table).

Required prompt: (If the CHILD does not spontaneously enact an activity with C1 and C2)

I: What are the children doing while the parents are gone?

9. Reunion

Story theme: Attachment
Props: Car
Characters: Cl, C2, G, M, F

Bring the car with the two parents back out from under the table, and set it on the table at a DISTANCE from the children (i.e., keep it near the Interviewer, so the CHILD has to reach for it and make it drive "home"). If the CHILD has put the children and grandmother figures in the middle of the table during the previous story, put them back close to the CHILD to create distance between the returning car and the child figures (see the following).

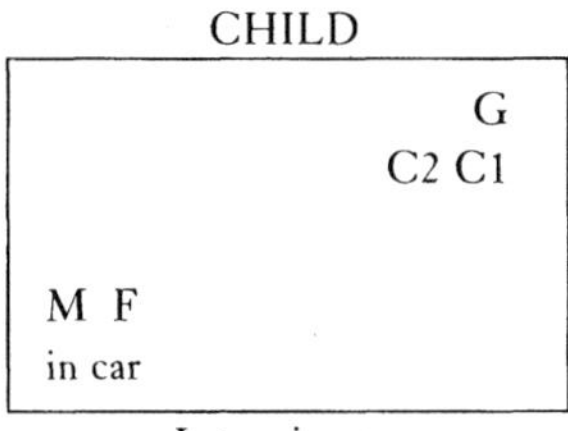

I: (In a fairly neutral voice say): It's the next day and Grandma looks out the window and she says: "Look girls/boys, I think your Mom and Dad are home from their trip. I think I can see their car."

I: (Bring out car from under the table. Do not move it toward the CHILD!) Show me and tell me what happens next.

Required issue prompt: (If CHILD does not spontaneously take the figures out of the car)

I: What do they do now that the Mom and Dad are home?

10. The Bathroom Shelf

Story theme: Dilemma of obedience to M versus empathy to sibling
Props: Bathroom shelf (in some versions there is a toilet and bathtub as well)
Characters: M, Cl, C2

Part 1. M Leaves

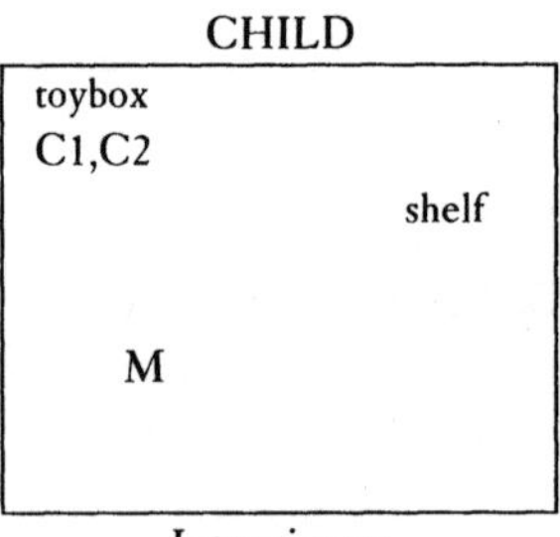

I: Let's pretend Dad has to go on an errand. Lay out bathroom shelf and say: This is the bathroom shelf, where Mom keeps the Band-aids.

The girls/boys are playing in their room and Mom comes in.

M: "Girls/boys, I have to go next door to the neighbor's to return some things, but I'll be right back. Don't touch anything on the bathroom shelf, okay?" (Put Mom under the table.)

Cl: "Okay Mom!" (Mom goes to the neighbors).

I: Jane/Bob and /Susan/George play some more (Susan/George jumps up!) .

C2: "Ow! I cut my finger, I need a band-aid!"

Cl: "But Mom said not to touch anything on the bathroom shelf."

C2: "But my finger's bleeding!"

I: Show me and tell me what happens next.

Required prompts: (If CHILD says the mother is coming back or that he/she needs the mother)

I: No, she's still at the neighbors.

Required issue prompt 1: (If C2 gets Band-aid for C1)

I: "But I thought the mom said not to touch anything on the bathroom shelf?"

Required issue prompt 2: (If C2 does not get Band-aid for C1 and C1 does care for hurt finger by self)

C2: "But my finger is bleeding."

Part 2. M Returns

I: (Brings the mother back, standing at a small distance from the children)

M: "Hi. children. I'm back."

I: Show me and tell me what happens now.

Required prompt: (If the children do not tell Mom about the hurt finger/Band-aid)
M: "What's that on your finger?"

(If the children still do not tell Mom about the hurt finger/Band-aid)
M: "Did you touch anything on the bathroom shelf?"

Note: Prior to beginning the next story, if the CHILD has not been able to respond to the dilemma with a resolution and seems anxious, say "that was a hard story." or (if one of the children took the bandaid and the mother did not "absolve" the child): "Sometimes you just have to get a bandaid, when someone's owie is bleeding." This is to reassure the CHILD.

11. Outing to the Park

Story theme: Mastery/pride
Props: Rock (a sponge, cut to look like a rock); a fairly large piece of green felt to indicate the park
Characters: M, F, C1, C2

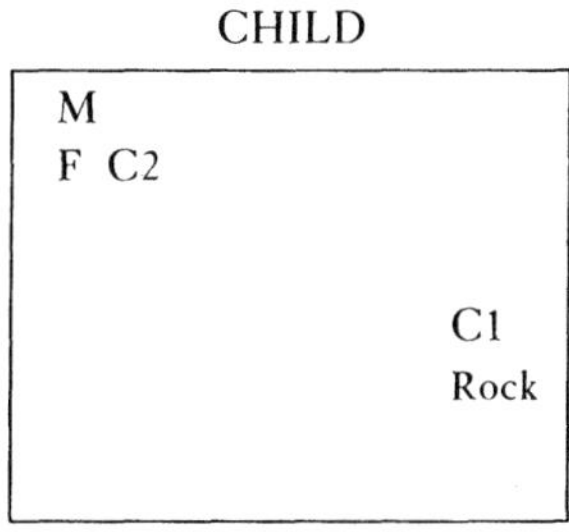

I: Today the family are going to the park together (move family closer to park, i.e., a piece of green felt).
(Walk Susan/George toward the rock.)

C1: "Oh look! See that high rock, I am going to climb right up to the very top."

M: "Oh, really? Be very careful!" (slightly alarmed voice).

I: Show me and tell me what happens now.

Note: in the Attachment Story Completion Task, this story is presented with the child telling the parents that he or she is going to climb the high rock. The child then falls off and hurts his or her knee. Whether or not the story is presented as here or as in the ASCT, it seems to elicit mastery and pain/comfort themes.

12. The Exclusion Story

Story theme: Exclusion from the parental relationship (Oedipal theme)
Props: Couch
Characters: M, F, C1

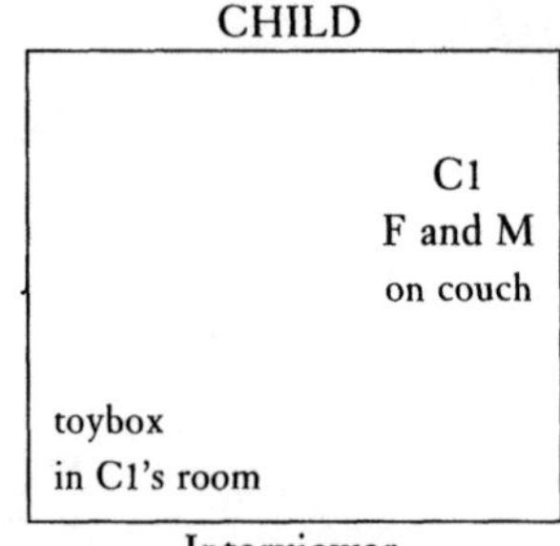

I: Mom and Dad are sitting on the couch talking.
(Note: For girls have mother ask the child to leave, and for boys have father ask the child to leave.)

M/F: "Mom/Dad and I would like some time alone. Will you go up to your room and play with your toys? Please shut your door so it's quiet."

I: (If the CHILD does not move Susan/George) "Show me how Susan/George goes to his/her room."
(After the CHILD moves Susan/George) M and F kiss. Show me and tell what happens now.

Required prompt: (If child goes to his parents have same-sex parent say)
M/F: "We asked for some time alone, didn't we?" (in mildly irritated voice).

If child complies with parents' request, complete story by having M and F say: "OK Susan/George. Thanks for letting us have some time alone."

13. The Cookie Jar

Story theme: Conflict between loyalty to parent and loyalty to sibling
Props: Table, jar
Characters: M, F, C1, C2

I: Susan/George and Jane/Bob are in the kitchen. Jane/Bob sees the cookie jar and she/he takes a cookie.

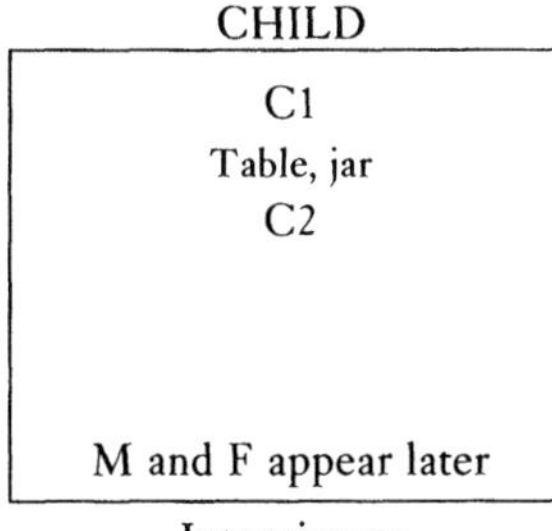

Interviewer

C1: "Mom said NO cookies!"

C2: "Please don't tell Mom and Dad about it!" (dramatic voice).

I: You know what, HERE COME MOM AND DAD!! (with emotion in voice). Show me and tell me what happens now.

Required prompt: (If nothing is said about the cookie that was taken)
M and F: "Who ate those cookies?" (emotion in voice).

14. Family Fun

This concluding story stem is designed to allow a positive, relaxed ending to the story task; it need not be presented in the same standard fashion as the other 13 story stems.

Story theme: Family fun
Props: Offer the CHILD whichever props and figures he/she would like
Characters: M, F, G, C1, C2, D

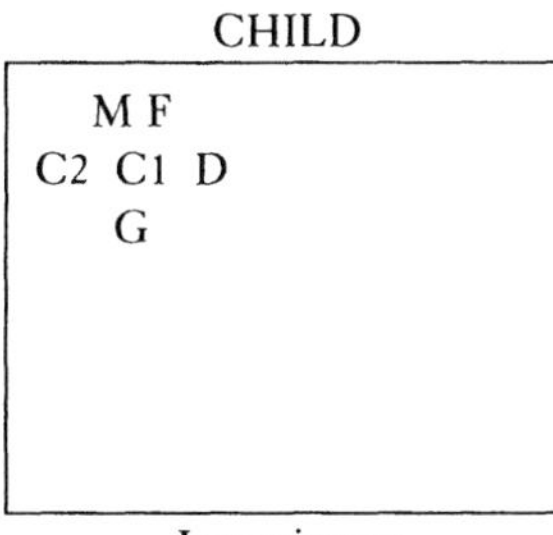

Interviewer

I: Here's the family at home

M: (Happily to father) Today is our day off, let's do something together!

F: Yeah, let's do something that would be fun for the whole family. (Mother and father turn to the children.)

M/F: Girls/boys, what would you like to do today?

I: Show me and tell what happens now.

At this point the Interviewer can become more involved, if necessary, to help the child describe a fun time together. The Interviewer can suggest activities, if the child is not able to do so, such as playing in the park or having a picnic.

This instrument was developed in 1990 as the Wisconsin version; instruction was added in 1996.This battery of story stems including attachment, family conflict, oedipal, moral, and peer themes was developed with funds from the John D. and Catherine T. MacArthur Research Network for Early Childhood Transitions. Copies of this appendix can be obtained from I. Bretherton, Waisman Center, 1500 Highland Ave., University of Wisconsin-Madison, Madison, WI 52706 or IBRETHERTON@MACC.WISC.EDU.

FOR FURTHER READING ON THE MACARTHUR STORY STEM BATTERY

Bretherton, I., Ridgeway, D., & Cassidy, J. (1990). Assessing internal working models of the attachment relationship: An attachment story completion task for 3-year-olds. In M. Greenberg, E. M. Cummings, & D. Cicchetti (Eds.), *Attachment in the preschool years* (pp. 273–308). Chicago: University of Chicago Press.

Bretherton, I., Winn, L., Page, T., MacFie, J., & Walsh, R. (1993, March). *Concordance of preschoolers' family stories with parent reports of family climate and stress.* Paper presented at the biennial meetings of the Society for Research in Child Development, New Orleans, LA.

Buchsbaum, H., & Emde, R. (1990). Play-narratives in 36-month-old children: Early moral development and family relationships. *Psychoanalytic Study of the Child, 40,* 129–155.

Oppenheim, D. (1989). *Assessing the validity of a doll play interview for measuring attachment in preschoolers.* Unpublished doctoral dissertation, University of Utah.

Oppenheim, D., & Waters, H. (1995). Narrative processes and attachment representations: Issues of development and assessment. In E. Waters, V. Vaughn, G. Posada, & K. Kondo-Ikemura (Eds.), *Caregiving, cultural and cognitive perspectives on secure-base behavior and working models: New growing points of attachment theory and research. Monographs of the Society for Research in Child Development, 60,* Serial No. 244 (2–3), 197–215.

Index